Register Now f(to You

SPRINGER PUBLISHING
CONNECT™

Your print purchase of *Theoretical Perspectives for Direct Social Work Practice, Fourth Edition,* **includes online access to the contents of your book**—increasing accessibility, portability, and searchability!

Access today at:
http://connect.springerpub.com/content/book/978-0-8261-6556-5
or scan the QR code at the right with your smartphone. Log in or register, then click "Redeem a voucher" and use the code below.

> 5CM0KV7V

Scan here for quick access.

Having trouble redeeming a voucher code?
Go to https://connect.springerpub.com/redeeming-voucher-code

If you are experiencing problems accessing the digital component of this product, please contact our customer service department at cs@springerpub.com

The online access with your print purchase is available at the publisher's discretion and may be removed at any time without notice.

Publisher's Note: New and used products purchased from third-party sellers are not guaranteed for quality, authenticity, or access to any included digital components.

SPRINGER PUBLISHING
View all our products at springerpub.com

Theoretical Perspectives for Direct Social Work Practice

Kristin W. Bolton, PhD, MSW, is an associate professor and graduate program coordinator in the School of Social Work at the University of North Carolina Wilmington. She received her PhD in social work from the University of Texas at Arlington. Dr. Bolton's research includes violence prevention, solution-focused brief therapy, and resilience across the life span.

J. Christopher Hall, PhD, LCSW, is a professor of social work at the University of North Carolina Wilmington, where he teaches graduate social work clinical practice, field, and postmodern electives. In addition to his teaching Dr. Hall has practiced for 20 years in the community assisting individuals, couples, families, and groups from a postmodern perspective.

Peter Lehmann, PhD, MSW, LCSW, is a retired professor from the University of Texas at Arlington. His primary areas of research are in solution-focused brief therapy and batterer intervention programs.

Theoretical Perspectives for Direct Social Work Practice

A Generalist-Eclectic Approach

FOURTH EDITION

Kristin W. Bolton, PhD, MSW

J. Christopher Hall, PhD, LCSW

Peter Lehmann, PhD, MSW, LCSW

EDITORS

 SPRINGER PUBLISHING

Springer Publishing Company, LLC
11 West 42nd Street, New York, NY 10036
www.springerpub.com
connect.springerpub.com/

Acquisitions Editor: Kate Dimock
Compositor: Transforma

ISBN: 978-0-8261-6555-8
ebook ISBN: 978-0-8261-6556-5
DOI: 10.1891/9780826165565

SUPPLEMENTS:
Instructor Materials:
Qualified instructors may request supplements by emailing textbook@springerpub.com

Instructor's Manual ISBN: 978-0-8261-6557-5
Instructor's PowerPoints ISBN: 978-0-8261-6559-6
Instructor's Test Bank ISBN: 978-0-8261-6558-9 (Also available on Respondus®.)

21 22 23 24 25 / 5 4 3 2 1

The author and the publisher of this Work have made every effort to use sources believed to be reliable to provide information that is accurate and compatible with the standards generally accepted at the time of publication. The author and publisher shall not be liable for any special, consequential, or exemplary damages resulting, in whole or in part, from the readers' use of, or reliance on, the information contained in this book. The publisher has no responsibility for the persistence or accuracy of URLs for external or third-party Internet websites referred to in this publication and does not guarantee that any content on such websites is, or will remain, accurate or appropriate.

Library of Congress Cataloging-in-Publication Data

Names: Bolton, Kristin W., editor.
Title: Theoretical perspectives for direct social work practice : a generalist-eclectic approach /
    Kristin W. Bolton, PhD, MSW, J. Christopher Hall, PhD, LCSW, Peter Lehmann, PhD, LCSW, editors.
Identifiers: LCCN 2021007502 (print) | LCCN 2021007503 (ebook) | ISBN 9780826165558 (paperback) |
    ISBN 9780826165565 (ebook)
Subjects: LCSH: Social service. | Human services.
Classification: LCC HV40 .T45 2022 (print) | LCC HV40 (ebook) | DDC 361.3/201--dc23
LC record available at https://lccn.loc.gov/2021007502
LC ebook record available at https://lccn.loc.gov/2021007503

Bolton: N/A
Hall: https://orcid.org/0000-0002-4767-2301
Lehmann: N/A

Contact sales@springerpub.com to receive discount rates on bulk purchases.

Publisher's Note: **New and used products purchased from third-party sellers are not guaranteed for quality, authenticity, or access to any included digital components.**

Printed in the United States of America.

Contents

Contributors

Sarah Accomazzo, PhD, MSW, is a community behavioral health services practitioner and researcher. Her practice experience includes evaluation, program improvement, administration, and consulting roles in mental health and prevention organizations and public systems throughout the California Bay Area. Her research interests include mental health assessment and service delivery in public systems and agencies serving youth and families, strengths-based practice, data-driven decision-making, and implementation and evaluation of evidence-informed interventions in real-world settings.

James Beauchemin, PhD, MSW, received his PhD from Ohio State University and MSW from the University of Vermont. Dr. Beauchemin's research interests include wellness promotion, integrated mind-body-spirit interventions, solution-focused brief therapy, and the mental health of college students.

Jeannette Bischkopf, PhD, is a professor in the faculty of social work and health at Kiel University of Applied Sciences (Germany), where she teaches psychology and counseling skills. Her research has focused on service user perspectives, mental illness and family caregivers, and the role of emotions in counseling and therapy. Her authored books in German include a self-help manual for families with a depressed family member and she is co-editor of a handbook on health social work and a book on psychiatric social work for students and practitioners.

Kristin W. Bolton, PhD, MSW, (pronouns: she/her/hers) is an associate professor and graduate program coordinator in the School of Social Work at the University of North Carolina Wilmington. She received her PhD in social work from the University of Texas at Arlington. Dr. Bolton's research includes violence prevention, solution-focused brief therapy, and resilience across the life span.

Corey Campbell, LCSW, is a PhD student at the University of Illinois, School of Social Work. He has been active in social work as a clinician since 2008. He has worked in the past in integrated care, medication-assisted treatment, and e-therapy interventions for substance use treatment. His research interests are in brief interventions for substance use and specifically motivational interviewing.

Norman H. Cobb, PhD, MSW, LCSW, is Associate Professor in the School of Social Work, University of Texas at Arlington. He received a PhD from the University of California at Berkeley and utilizes CBT interventions in his clinical practice.

Elaine P. Congress, DSW, LCSW, is a professor and associate dean at Fordham University Graduate School of Social Service. Dr. Congress has extensive practice, administrative, and academic experience with many national and international presentations on clinical practice, assessment, social work education, cultural diversity, immigrants, and social work ethics. In addition to her many journal articles and book chapters, her recent books have included *Multicultural Perspectives in Working With Families, Social Work With Immigrants and Refugees, and Teaching Social Work Values and Ethics.* Dr. Congress developed the culturagram, a family assessment tool to promote engagement, understanding, and treatment planning with families from diverse cultural backgrounds.

Shannon Cooper-Sadlo, PhD, MSW, LCSW, (pronouns: she/her/hers) is a graduate of the University of Denver MSW program, and obtained her PhD in family therapy from Saint Louis University. She is an associate clinical professor of social work at Saint Louis University. Her area of study is with women and families who have experienced incarceration and other family separation. She teaches clinical courses in both the BSSW and the MSW program. She has been in clinical practice with various populations for over 20 years and specializes in areas of couples/family therapy, substance use, co-occurring disorders, anxiety, and depression.

Jacqueline Corcoran, PhD, LCSW, is a professor at the Virginia Commonwealth University School of Social Work, where she has been on the faculty since 2000. She also served on the faculty at the University of Texas at Arlington from 1996 to 2000. Dr. Corcoran has written over 50 journal articles and 14 textbooks that are used in schools of social work throughout the United States.

Arthur Frankel, PhD, MSW, LCSW, attended the University of Michigan Ann Arbor from 1968 to 1972, after serving 2 years in the Peace Corps in India. He received his MSW, specializing in groupwork in 1970, and his PhDs in social work and psychology in 1972, with a focus on behavior therapy. In addition, Dr. Frankel has engaged in intensive post-graduate training in ego psychology and psychoanalysis, transactional analysis, and gestalt therapy. Dr. Frankel was a member of the faculty for the social work and psychology at the University of Louisville (1972–1987); social work and psychology at Rutgers University (1989–1995); social work at Yeshiva University in New York City (1995–2001); and has been a member of the faculty at the School of Social Work at the University of North Carolina Wilmington since 2001. He has many publications in a variety of areas including drugs and alcohol, behavioral techniques, and early childhood education. In addition, he has authored four books, the most recent a book on case management, in its fourth edition, and a book on psychotherapy.

Adriana Gil-Wilkerson, MSc, is a marriage and family therapist and supervisor in Houston, Texas. She began her relationship with Houston Galveston Institute (HGI) as a master level learner/intern in 2004 and has held various roles since. Adriana received her Master of Science in Psychology with a focus on Marriage and Family Therapy from Our Lady of the Lake University in 2005. She is currently a faculty member at HGI and is the Walk-In Counseling program coordinator. Adriana's research and practice are focused on providing training in collaborative practices for therapists of all backgrounds and, as a bilingual therapist, she has a passion for research about the training needs of bilingual counselors. Adriana is also a doctoral candidate at Sam Houston State University and is currently working on her dissertation.

Clay Gruber, MSW, studied social work at the University of North Carolina at Wilmington where he earned his MSW. Mr. Gruber currently works in school-based therapy, providing services for adolescents. His interests include adverse childhood experiences (ACEs), relationship therapy, and intersectionality. He is currently contributing toward research involving ACEs and their effects on sexual and gender minorities.

J. Christopher Hall, PhD, MSSW, LCSW, is a professor of social work at the University of North Carolina Wilmington where he teaches graduate social work clinical practice, field, and postmodern electives. In addition to his teaching Dr. Hall has practiced for 20 years in the community, assisting individuals, couples, families, and groups from a postmodern perspective.

Adriana Kaye, LMSW, is a doctoral student at Tulane University, emerging researcher, and scholar.

Karen S. Knox, PhD, taught social work at several universities since 1988 and was a social work practitioner for over 30 years. She is a Professor Emerita at the School of Social Work at Texas State University and retired from academia in 2018. Her areas of scholarly publications and research interests include child welfare, victim services, criminal justice, family violence, sexual abuse survivors, adolescent and adult sex offenders, and gerontology. Her clinical and direct practice experience includes working for child protective services, Austin Police Department Victim Services Division, Travis County District Attorney's Office, Travis County Juvenile Probation Adolescent Sex Offender Program, Hays and Williamson County Probation/Parole, and as a private practitioner.

Heather Lassman, PhD Candidate, MSW, is an assistant professor in the social work department at Washburn University in Topeka, Kansas. Her research focuses on exploring the factors that affect children with disabilities in the foster care system and she has presented her work at national conferences. The use of case studies, team-based learning, and critical thinking exercises are an integral part of her pedagogy.

Peter Lehmann, PhD, MSW, LCSW, is a retired professor from the University of Texas at Arlington. His primary areas of research are in solution-focused brief therapy and batterer intervention programs.

Jill Levenson, PhD, LCSW, is professor of social work at Barry University in Miami and is a SAMHSA-trained internationally recognized expert in trauma-informed care. She studies treatments and policies to prevent sexual assault, and has published over 100 articles, including projects funded by the National Institutes of Justice and the National Sexual Violence Resource Center. Her groundbreaking research on the link between childhood adversity and sexually abusive behavior has paved the way for innovations in treatment programs that now utilize a trauma-informed approach. She has also been a clinician for over 30 years, using a scientist practitioner model to inform both her research and her work with survivors, offenders, and families impacted by interpersonal violence. She has been invited to speak about trauma-informed care in clinical, correctional, and forensic settings in the United States, Canada, Australia, and New Zealand. Dr. Levenson has co-authored five books about the treatment of sexual abuse, trauma-informed care, and restorative justice.

Susan B. Levin, PhD, is the executive director of the Houston Galveston Institute (HGI). Having been with HGI for more than 25 years, she has been mentored by the creators of Collaborative Therapy, Harry Goolishian and Harlene Anderson. In addition to clinical practice, training, and administration for HGI, Sue is on the faculty of Our Lady of the Lake University's Master's psychology program, is an associate of the Taos Institute, and is a past-president of the board of directors of the Texas Association for Marriage & Family Therapy. Sue's special interests include disaster mental health, domestic violence, alternatives to traditional and medical model approaches to mental health, and supervision and consultation.

Michael A. Mancini, PhD, MSW, CDFT, (pronouns: he, his, him) is an associate professor in the School of Social Work at Saint Louis University. He received his PhD in social work from the University at Albany in 2003. His research focuses on the evaluation and implementation of integrated behavioral health services. He teaches graduate-level courses on clinical assessment, diagnosis, and treatment of behavioral health disorders. As a practitioner, he has worked as an inpatient and outpatient case manager, a program specialist for the New York State Office of Mental Health, and as a social worker and Chief of Mental Health Services at a large, maximum-security state prison.

Trevor J. Manthey, MSW, PhD, MINT Member, is engaged in researching and training interventions that help facilitate self-determination in rehabilitation settings. This interest in self-determination has led to authored publications on topics such as shared decision-making, self-directed care, motivational interviewing (MI), supported education,supported employment, and peer support. Dr. Manthey is also a member of MINT (Motivational Interviewing Network of Trainers). His work history includes over 15 years of experience in the human, social, and justice services field including both inpatient and outpatient settings.

Tina Maschi, PhD, LCSW, is a professor at the Fordham University Graduate School of Social Service and is a clinical social worker, researcher, and scholar.

Katherine Occhiuto, MSW, is a PhD candidate at the School of Social Work, Carleton University. Prior to her doctoral work, Ms. Occhiuto was a mental health Counselor and a community developer. Her dissertation focuses on the effects of systems of provision— meaning how do systems (charities, social welfare, etc.), which were set up to provide for those in need, impact users both materially and relationally.

Anka Roberto, DNP, MPH, PMHNP-BC, APRN, is an assistant professor at the University of North Carolina Wilmington. She has over 20 years of professional nursing experience in providing care to the pediatric and neonatal population. Her clinical background includes working on in-patient pediatric settings, community/public health settings, and with children and families as a psychiatric nurse practitioner. Her clinical trajectory is treating clients holistically across the life span as she works with children, adults, and families in the aftermath of trauma. Her area of research and scholarship is posttraumatic growth, spirituality, and resiliency in the aftermath of trauma. She is EMDR (Eye Movement Desensitization and Reprocessing)–trained and has authored book chapters and articles on trauma and resilience.

Albert R. Roberts, PhD, taught at several universities for over 35 years, and was a professor for 19 years in the School of Arts and Sciences at Rutgers, the State University of New Jersey, Livingston College Campus, teaching criminal justice and social work until his death in 2008. He is most well known for his research and publications in the fields of crisis intervention, family violence, and forensic social work. He was the author or editor of over 250 publications, including 38 books. Dr. Roberts was the Editor-in-Chief of two professional journals, three book series for Springer Publishing, and the *Social Worker's Desk Reference* published by Oxford University Press, which has become a standard reference in the field. Dr. Roberts received numerous awards for his teaching and scholarly publications, was a Fellow of the American Orthopsychiatric Association, and was a member of the Academy of Criminal Justice Sciences, the Council on Social Work Education, and the National Association of Social Workers.

Allison Salisbury, MSW, is a doctoral student at the University of Illinois at Urbana-Champaign, School of Social Work. Her research interests include criminal justice content in social work baccalaureate and master's programs.

Alicia M. Sellon, PhD, MSW, is an assistant professor for the School of Social Work at the University of North Carolina Wilmington. Her scholarship focuses on community resilience and identifying ways to make civic engagement and community participation more accessible to older adults, particularly those with disabilities. She has a number of publications and co-publications focusing on practice with older adults, and has presented her work at national and international conferences. She is also interested in instructional design and is currently certified in the fundamentals of team-based learning.

Valerie B. Shapiro, PhD, is an Associate Professor of Social Welfare at UC Berkeley, the Director of the Center for Prevention Research in Social Welfare, and the Co-Chair of the Coalition for the Promotion of Behavioral Health. Dr. Shapiro has been selected as a class of 2025 William T. Grant Foundation Scholar and is a recipient of the Prytanean Faculty Prize, recognized for scholarly achievement and distinguished teaching at UC Berkeley. She has worked in diverse practice settings as a licensed and certified social worker. Dr. Shapiro studies the prevention of mental, emotional, and behavioral problems in children and youth, primarily by studying the use of research evidence in prevention practice. She has made important contributions to the fields of strength-based assessment and social and emotional learning, including developing the *Devereux Student Strengths Assessment (DESSA)* in conjunction with colleagues at Aperture Education.

Doug Smith, PhD, LCSW, is associate professor of social work at the University of Illinois at Urbana-Champaign, and director of the Center for Prevention Research and Development (CPRD). Dr. Smith received his PhD in social work in 2006 from the University of Iowa. He has over 20 years of experience in substance use disorder prevention and treatment as a clinician, clinical supervisor, and researcher.

Catherine A. Simmons, PhD, LCSW, is a professor at the University of Colorado Colorado Springs and serves as both the inaugural Chair of UCCS Social Work and the Master of Social Work (MSW) Program Director. Prior to joining academia, Dr. Simmons spent 10 years as an Air Force officer leading family violence, substance abuse, and mental health programs. The author/editor of two books and over 60 professional papers, her research interests include interpersonal violence, measurement, strengths-based interventions, career trajectories, and issues pertaining to gender, trauma, and violence. She is also known for her leadership and program development expertise.

Kim Stansbury, PhD, MSW, is an associate professor and director of graduate program in the Department of Social Work at North Carolina State University (NCSU). She teaches Human Behavioral in the Social Environment: Social Justice and Social Work with Communities and Organizations in the MSW program. She is a graduate of the University of Southern Mississippi (BS, Criminal Justice and Psychology), Southern Illinois University (MSW), and the University of Kentucky (Ph.D in Gerontology). Dr. Stansbury joined the NC State faculty in 2015. She has published journal articles and book chapters on mental health, mental health literacy, gambling addiction, older adults, African American clergy, and older LGBTQ populations in journals such as the Journal of Gerontological Social Work, Aging and Mental Health, Religion and Spirituality, and Social Work and Mental Health. Currently, she is working on a project with Drs. Natalie Ames and Erica Campbell on the role of the Black church in domestic violence prevention and intervention.

Ashley Swinson, MSW, LCSW, is a Certified Therapist in EMDR (Eye Movement Desensitization and Reprocessing) and owns a group practice that specializes in trauma-informed services. Her clinical expertise includes the treatment of dually diagnosed eating disorders and trauma disorders, complex PTSD and dissociation, and secondary traumatic stress among professionals. She is a national speaker and lesson designer on the topics of provider sustainability and trauma-informed care in health and human services. She is also active in her local community providing specialty consultation for business owners and professionals seeking to enhance their clinical practice, and she holds an adjunct faculty position with the School of Social Work at the University of North Carolina at Wilmington.

Barbra Teater, PhD, MSW, is professor of social work and MSW Program Director at the College of Staten Island and is affiliated with the PhD in Social Welfare program at the Graduate Center, City University of New York. Dr. Teater's research focuses on social work theories and methods, research methods in social work, and ageism and creative approaches to social work practice with older adults. She is the author of the internationally bestselling text, *An Introduction to Applying Social Work Theories and Methods.*

Sarah Todd, MSW, EdD, is a professor at the School of Social Work, Carleton University. She teaches in the area of social work theory, social work education, and social work practice with individuals and communities. Her current research is in the area of uncertainty in clinical practice. Sarah is also a 3M Fellow for excellence in teaching.

Sandra Turner is an associate professor and former Associate Dean at Fordham University.

Amy Van de Motter, MSW, LCSW, has been a practicing social worker since 2009, earning her MSW degree from the University of North Carolina Wilmington. She is a licensed clinical social worker in North Carolina, and her clinical experience and area of interest has been adult mental health. She has provided outpatient counseling and therapy services to a wide range of clients, including individuals diagnosed with severe and persistent mental illness. Her experience also includes serving in the role of medical social worker with the geriatric population, providing education and support to clients and family caregivers, as well as supporting families and children through the process of adoption. Amy has been teaching full-time in the University of North Carolina Wilmington School of Social Work since August 2017.

Preface

The primary purpose of the fourth edition of this book continues to be to provide an overview of theories for direct social work practice and a framework for integrating the use of theory with central social work principles and values, as well as with the artistic elements of practice. It is intended primarily for graduate-level social work students and practitioners; however, we know that many undergraduate social work programs also use the book. This book has similarities to other books that provide surveys of clinical theories for social work practice; however, we think it has a number of distinctive and useful features. In brief, these features include: (a) grounding direct practice specialization firmly in the generalist perspective of social work practice; (b) documenting the trend toward, and rationale and empirical support for, eclecticism in the broad field of counseling/psychotherapy, and reviewing various approaches to eclecticism; (c) bringing order to and demystifying theories by differentiating among levels of theory, organizing direct practice theories into like groupings, and providing an overview of the central characteristics of each grouping of theories; (d) providing a critical perspective on the dominant, scientific paradigm of direct practice that centers the use of theory and technique, and putting equal emphasis on the artistic elements of practice; and (e) proposing the problem-solving model as a useful structure for facilitating the integration of the artistic and scientific elements of practice.

The contents of all of the chapters in this fourth edition have been revised and updated to reflect developments in theory, practice, and research since the second edition was published. In Part II of the book there is a new chapter on couples theory and intervention, as an additional metatheory for social work practice. In Part III, there are now chapters on trauma-informed practice, motivational interviewing, anti-oppressive theory, mindfulness-based practices, eye movement desensitization and reprocessing, and dialectical behavior therapy. In addition to the new chapters, there are new authors and coauthors for a number of the chapters that were refreshed for this addition.

The book is divided into four parts with a total of 23 chapters. The first two chapters constitute Part I of this book, which focuses on explicating our generalist-eclectic approach to direct social work practice. In Part II, high-level or meta-theories for direct practice are presented. The four chapters in this part focus on critical ecological systems theory, individual and family development theory, couples theory and intervention and strengths-based social work practice. Part III is divided into five sections and focuses on theories, models, and therapies for direct practice that are at a mid-level of abstraction. The five sections contain a total of 15 chapters on psychodynamic, cognitive behavioral, humanistic, critical, and postmodern theories. Part IV consists of a summary chapter that considers the similarities and differences among the theories, models, and therapies that are reviewed in the book and the principles and values that are integral to our generalist-eclectic approach. The issue of integrating the use of theory with the artistic elements of practice via the problem-solving model is also revisited in this final chapter, and implications for research and practice are discussed. In support of the book's content, qualified instructors can request an ancillary package consisting of PowerPoints, an Instructor's Manual, and a Sample Syllabus.

We are very appreciative to all of the contributing authors for taking time from their busy schedules and lives to write the original chapters contained herein. Their willingness to follow the structural guidelines for the chapters and the clarity of their writing made this manuscript possible. We feel privileged to have collaborated with a group of very gifted and personable professionals. Special thanks go to Kate Dimock for her support and patience. The timing of this text during a global pandemic required a great deal of planning and replanning and we whole-heartedly appreciate her help in this process.

Kristin W. Bolton
J. Christopher Hall
Peter Lehmann

Qualified instructors may obtain access to supplements by emailing textbook@springerpub.com

Abbreviations

AAP	American Academy of Pediatrics
ACE	adverse childhood experience
ACT	acceptance and commitment therapy
AIP	adaptive information processing
APA	American Psychiatric Association
BDI	Beck Depression Inventory
BERS-2	Behavioral and Emotional Rating Scale, Second Edition
BPD	borderline personality disorder
CBASP	cognitive behavioral analysis system of psychotherapy
CBT	cognitive behavioral therapy
CCP	Crisis Counseling Program
CDC	Centers for Disease Control and Prevention
CDOI	client-directed, outcome-informed
CEE	corrective emotional experience
CIT	crisis intervention team
CSWE	Council on Social Work Education
DBT	dialectical behavior therapy
DECA-P2	Devereux Early Childhood Assessment, Second Edition
DES	Dissociative Experiences Scale
DESSA	Devereux Student Strengths Assessment
EAP	employee assistance program
EBP	evidence-based practice
EC-PST	emotion-centered problem-solving therapy
EFFT	emotion-focused family therapy
EFMT	emotion-focused mindfulness therapy
EFT	emotionally focused therapy
EMDR	eye movement desensitization and reprocessing
EPAS	Educational Policy and Accreditation Standards
EST	empirically supported treatment
FIT	feedback-informed treatment
GFI	Galveston Family Institute
HGI	Houston Galveston Institute
IDT	intersectional design tool
IRT	Imago relationship therapy
MAT	monitor and acceptance theory
MBCT	mindfulness-based cognitive therapy
MBI	mindfulness-based intervention
MBSR	mindfulness-based stress reduction
MI	motivational interviewing
MINT	Motivational Interviewing Network of Trainers
MIT	multiple impact therapy
MMT	multimodal behavior therapy
MON	My Outcomes Now

MRI	Mental Research Institute
NASW	National Association of Social Workers
NC	negative cognition
NS	neutral stimulus
NT	narrative therapy
OARS	open-ended questions, affirmations, reflections, and summaries
OCD	obsessive compulsive disorder
OLLU	Our Lady of the Lake University
ORS	Outcome Response Scale
PC	positive cognition
PCOMS	Partner for Change Outcome Management System
PIE	person in environment
PST	problem-solving therapy
PTSD	posttraumatic stress disorder
RAI	rapid assessment instrument
REBT	rational emotive behavior therapy
SAMHSA	Substance Abuse and Mental Health Services Administration
SBP	strengths-based practice
SEPI	Society for the Exploration of Psychotherapy Integration
SRS	Session Rating Scale
STS	systematic treatment selection
SUD	Subjective Unit of Disturbance
tf-CBT	trauma-focused cognitive behavioral therapy
TIC	trauma-informed care
TJ	therapeutic jurisprudence
TTM	transtheoretical model
UCR	unconditioned response
UCS	unconditioned stimulus
UDHR	Universal Declaration of Human Rights
VOC	Validity of Cognition

Introduction

An Overview of and Rationale for a Generalist-Eclectic Approach to Direct Social Work Practice

Kristin W. Bolton, J. Christopher Hall, and Peter Lehmann

INTRODUCTION

The focus of this book is on theories for direct (or clinical, micro) social work practice. More specifically, the book focuses on theories for practice with individuals, although the relevance of these theories for practice with couples, families, and groups is also considered. Beyond simply offering in this book a survey of clinical theories, we promote what we call a *generalist-eclectic approach* for the use of theory in direct practice.

Including the word *generalist* in the name of our approach might seem odd because one of the generally accepted hallmarks of generalist social work practice is that it spans direct and indirect (or macro) practice methods, whereas our approach focuses only on direct practice. By using the word *generalist* to describe our approach to direct practice, we want to emphasize our belief that specialization in direct practice must be firmly grounded in the generalist perspective of social work practice. Simply put, we believe that the values, principles, generic processes, and holistic perspective that are integral to generalist social work practice are a necessary foundation for direct practice specialization. Although this might be taken for granted by some, we think that this sometimes gets lost in the rush for specialization.

One reason it is important to ensure that direct practice is grounded explicitly within the generalist perspective is because most theories that clinical social workers use have been developed outside of the profession, and aspects of such theories may not fit well with some social work principles. When this is the case, we think that modifications to these aspects of theories are necessary. For example, theories that place the social worker in the role of expert should be used in a more egalitarian, collaborative manner, and theories that have a specific and narrow conception of human problems should be broadened to include consideration of a wide range of factors (e.g., environmental and sociocultural factors need to be considered along with biological, intrapsychic, and interpersonal factors).

A second reason for embedding direct practice within the generalist perspective is that the latter can function to broaden the mandate and role of direct practitioners beyond narrow clinical confines. For instance, we think it is important that the focus of clinical social work should include helping clients to meet basic needs by providing them with or linking them to resources and services, and engaging in social advocacy for clients—and the generalist perspective reminds us of the importance of such helping strategies. In addition, social work students who are entering their concentration or specialization year will have the generalist grounding, and application of the direct practice theories will be reinforced by this knowledge.

This chapter provides an overview of our generalist-eclectic approach to direct practice. First, we review the major elements of the generalist social work perspective that are central to our generalist-eclectic approach to direct practice. Then, we provide an overview of the distinctive aspects of our generalist-eclectic approach. Finally, we discuss in some detail the issue of eclecticism, primarily with regard to the trend toward eclecticism over the last 35 years in the broad field of counseling/psychotherapy. The latter discussion includes (a) an overview of eclecticism that documents historical resistance to eclecticism, the fact of and reasons for the trend toward the eclectic use of theory and technique, and continuing resistance to eclecticism (particularly in the form of the empirically supported treatment [EST] movement); (b) a review of the four major approaches to eclecticism in the literature and some of the specific eclectic models within each of the approaches; and (c) a delineation of our approach to eclecticism.

ELEMENTS OF THE GENERALIST PERSPECTIVE THAT ARE CENTRAL TO OUR GENERALIST-ECLECTIC APPROACH

There are many characteristics that are common to the various descriptions of the generalist perspective in the literature. The major elements of generalist social work practice that we have adopted for our generalist-eclectic approach to direct social work practice have been drawn from a range of literature (Derezotes, 2000; Hepworth et al., 2013; Johnson & Yanca, 2007; Kirst-Ashman & Hull, 2009; Landon, 1995, 1999; Locke et al., 1998; Miley et al., 2013; Shatz et al., 1990; Sheafor & Horejsi, 2006; Sheafor & Landon, 1987; Timberlake et al., 2008; Tolson et al., 2003; Walsh, 2009). These elements are summarized in Table 1.1 and discussed subsequently.

A Person-in-Environment Perspective Informed by Ecological Systems Theory

"The central focus of social work traditionally seems to have been on people in their life situation complex—a simultaneous dual focus on individuals and environment" (Gordon, cited in Compton et al., 2005, p. 6). A generalist approach embraces this traditional person-in-environment perspective of social work practice. This perspective emphasizes the need to view the interdependence and mutual influence of people and their social and physical environments. Also, it recognizes the link between inherent troubles (i.e., individual problems) and public issues (i.e., social problems; Mills, 1959). The person-in-environment perspective has been one of the primary factors that has distinguished direct social work practice from the practice of other helping/counseling professions (e.g., psychology, marriage and family therapy, and psychiatry).

Ecological systems theory (see Chapter 4) is a conceptual framework for the person-in-environment perspective that "has been almost universally accepted in social work over the past

---

TABLE 1.1 ELEMENTS OF THE GENERALIST PERSPECTIVE THAT ARE CENTRAL TO OUR GENERALIST-ECLECTIC APPROACH

- A person-in-environment perspective that is informed by ecological systems theory
- An emphasis on the development of a good helping relationship that fosters empowerment
- The flexible use of a problem-solving process to provide structure and guidelines for work with clients
- A holistic, multilevel assessment that includes a focus on issues of diversity and oppression and on strengths
- The flexible and eclectic use of a wide range of theories and techniques that are selected on the basis of their relevance to each unique client situation

three decades" (Mattaini & Lowery, 2007, p. 39). This theory "recognizes an interrelatedness of human problems, life situations, and social conditions" (Shatz et al., 1990, p. 223). As explained in Chapter 2, it is a high-level or metatheory that is particularly useful for helping workers to see the big picture in terms of the reciprocal influence of people and the various systems (e.g., family, work, community) with which they interact. As such, it provides an "organizational tool for synthesizing the many perspectives that social workers apply in practice" (Miley et al., 2013, p. 27).

The Development of a Good Helping Relationship That Fosters Empowerment

Historically, social work has led the helping professions to advocate the importance of a collaborative, warm, empathic, and supportive worker–client relationship. Social workers have described this type of relationship as the "soul" (Biestek, 1957), "heart" (Perlman, 1979), and "major determinant" (Hollis, 1970) of the helping endeavor. Although clinical social work has drifted away from such an emphasis over the last few decades in favor of attention to the theoretical/technical/scientific aspects of practice (Coady, 1993a; Perlman, 1979), the generalist perspective has reemphasized the importance of the helping relationship.

Along with a reaffirmation of the importance of a good helping relationship, the generalist perspective has promoted a focus on empowerment. A number of authors of generalist textbooks (e.g., Landon, 1999; Locke et al., 1998; Miley et al., 2013; Timberlake et al., 2008) have combined a consideration of empowerment and the strengths perspective (Saleebey, 2013). For example, Miley et al. (2013) argued that "an orientation toward strengths and empowerment compels social workers to redefine their relationships to embrace the notion of collaboration and partnership" (p. 85). Gutiérrez (cited in Miley et al., 2013) noted that this involves basing the helping relationship on "collaboration, trust, and shared power; accepting the client's definition of the problem; identifying and building upon the client's strengths; actively involving the client in the change process; [and] experiencing a sense of personal power within the helping relationship" (p. 133).

Considerable research has been done that supports the development of a good helping relationship as one of the primary factors of client change (Flückiger et al., 2020; Wampold, 2017). This research has focused specifically on the common factors of counseling and will be discussed in more detail later in the chapter. Wampold and Imel (2015) maintain that the allegiance and rapport between social worker and client are the most important factors of therapeutic change, and positive client outcomes are difficult, if not impossible, without them.

The Flexible Use of a Problem-Solving Model

Since the formulation of the problem-solving model for social casework by Perlman (1957), problem-solving has been an integral part of social work practice. Most generalist approaches to social work practice include some version of the problem-solving model, and although there are various conceptualizations of the stages or phases of problem-solving, all versions include guidelines for the entire helping process, from initial engagement to termination.

Some generalist approaches, in an effort to emphasize a strengths focus versus a problem focus, have renamed the problem-solving model. For example, Locke et al. (1998) called their version of the problem-solving model a "phase model," and Miley et al. (2013) called their version "phases and processes of empowering practice" (p. 103). We agree, however, with McMillen et al. (2004) who contended that the "grudge match" within social work that pits strengths-based against problem-focused approaches represents a false and destructive dichotomy. Thus, our use of the term *problem-solving model* does not denote a deficit or pathology orientation to practice. As is generally the case within social work, we construe problem-solving as a collaborative process between workers and clients that has the ultimate goal of capacity building and empowering clients (see Chapter 3 for a more detailed discussion of problem-solving).

A Holistic, Multilevel Assessment

The person-in-environment perspective and the ecological systems theory suggest the necessity of a holistic, multilevel assessment. The term *holistic* refers to a "totality in perspective, with sensitivity to all the parts or levels that constitute the whole and to their interdependence and relatedness" (McMahon, 1996, p. 2). This represents a focus on the whole person (i.e., physical, emotional, and spiritual) in the context of their surroundings. Multi-level assessment goes hand-in-hand with a holistic focus because this means considering the entire range of factors, from micro to macro, that could be impacting a client. Thus, in conducting an assessment, the generalist-oriented direct practitioner should consider the potential influence of biophysical, intrapsychic, interpersonal/familial, environmental, and sociocultural factors. With regard to the latter class of factors, a generalist approach to direct practice assessment includes particular sensitivity to issues of diversity (e.g., gender, race, culture, class, sexual orientation, disability, age, religion) and oppression (Shatz et al., 1990). A generalist approach also demands that the assessment process includes a focus on clients' strengths, resources, and competencies.

The Flexible and Eclectic Use of a Wide Range of Theories and Techniques

The commitment to a holistic, multi-level assessment precludes a rigid adherence to narrow theories of human problems. A generalist approach should be "unencumbered by any particular practice approach into which the client(s) might be expected to fit" (Sheafor & Landon, 1987, p. 666). Theories can be useful in the assessment process if they are tentatively considered as potential explanations for clients' problems; however, theories represent preconceived ideas about human problems and can blind one to alternative explanations, including the explanations clients have about themselves and their own lives (Hall, 2012).

Just as the assessment process must avoid rigid adherence to narrow theoretical perspectives, the same is true for the intervention process: "The generalist perspective requires that the social worker be *eclectic* (i.e., draw ideas and techniques from many sources)" (Sheafor & Horejsi, 2006, p. 87). Generalists are open to using theories and techniques that seem most relevant to the understanding of the unique client situation: "Single model practitioners do a disservice to themselves and their clients by attempting to fit all clients and problems into their chosen model" (Hepworth et al., 2002, p. 17). Guidelines for selecting theories and techniques for particular types of clients and problems are reviewed later in this chapter in the discussion of approaches to eclecticism, as well as in Chapter 3.

DISTINCTIVE ASPECTS OF OUR GENERALIST-ECLECTIC APPROACH

A Differentiated Understanding and Demystification of Theory

One distinctive aspect to our approach of using theory in practice is differentiating between types and levels of theory, and classifying clinical theories in like groupings. Our approach to understanding theory differentiates between (a) high-level meta-theories (ecological systems and human development theories, the strengths perspective; see Part II, Chapters 3–6), (b) mid-level practice theories (see Part III, Chapters 7–22), and low-level models for specific populations and problems. Meta-theories provide general guidance for holistic assessment and the generation of ideas for intervention; mid-level practice theories provide more specific ideas and directions for assessment and intervention for a range of presenting concerns; and low-level models provide more specific guidelines for work with specific populations and problems.

Furthermore, in an effort to demystify the vast array of practice theories that exist, we classify these theories in like groupings (psychodynamic [Chapter 7], cognitive behavioral

[Chapters 8–12], humanistic [Chapters 13–15], critical [Chapters 16–18], and postmodern [Chapters 19–22]) and provide a brief overview of the distinguishing characteristics of each of these larger classifications of theory.

A Critical Perspective on the Use of Theory and Valuing the Artistic Elements in Practice

Perhaps the most distinctive feature of our generalist-eclectic approach is that it includes a critical perspective on the *scientific* view of practice, which contends that use of theory and technique reflects the essence and is the cornerstone of effective direct social work practice. We certainly do not deny the value of this scientific approach to practice (after all, this book focuses on the use of theory in practice), although we clearly favor an eclectic use of theory and technique over adherence to a single theory and its techniques. Still, a key element of our framework is the recognition and valuing of the *artistic* elements of practice (Coady, 1995; Goldstein, 1990; Kinsella, 2010; McCoyd & Kerson, 2013; Schön, 1983).

An artistic approach to practice, often referred to as *reflective practice* (Schön, 1983), includes the use of relationship-building skills, intuition, gut instincts, empathic listening, and inductive reasoning to collaboratively build with the client a theory that fits their unique situation and to problem-solve creatively. We believe that practice is at least as much art as science, and is based at least as much on reflection-in-action (Schön, 1983), intuition, inductive reasoning, theory building, and general interpersonal/relationship skill as on the deductive application of theoretical knowledge and technical skill. Theory and research that pertain to this issue are reviewed later in this chapter.

Use of the Problem-Solving Model to Integrate the Art and Science of Practice

One of the main difficulties with both theoretically eclectic and artistic, reflective, intuitive-inductive approaches to practice is a lack of structure and guidelines for practice. For example, workers who are theoretically eclectic are sometimes overwhelmed by the sheer number of theories from which to choose. Also, practice can lack coherence and direction when one moves back and forth between theories, and sometimes workers can become preoccupied with or distracted by multiple theoretical considerations. When this happens, the workers' understanding of and relationship with their clients can suffer.

On the other hand, workers who prefer a more artistic, humanistic approach to practice that is based on reflection, intuition, and inductive reasoning sometimes feel as if they are "flying by the seat of their pants." Their practice can similarly lack coherence and direction. This is a major reason why some practitioners prefer to adhere to a single theoretical orientation in their practice—a single theory approach provides clear structure and guidelines. The cost of adherence to a single theory is too large; however, there is no one theory that is comprehensive enough to fit for all clients, and clients should not be forced into theoretical boxes.

We believe that the problem-solving model offers a solution to the lack of structure and guidelines for practice that are commonly experienced by workers who prefer theoretically eclectic and/or reflective, intuitive-inductive approaches to practice. The general strategies for the various phases of helping (from engagement to termination) that constitute the problem-solving model provide useful and flexible structure and guidelines for both the scientific and artistic approaches to practice and enable workers to integrate these two approaches in their work. The generality and flexibility of the guidelines in each phase of the problem-solving process provide sufficient structure and direction for practice while also allowing workers to integrate theory and use reflection, intuition, and inductive reasoning. This issue is discussed briefly later in this chapter and in more depth in Chapter 2.

AN OVERVIEW OF ECLECTICISM

As is evident from the earlier discussion, eclecticism is an inherent orientation in generalist practice and is endorsed by most authors of generalist (e.g., Locke et al., 1998; Sheafor & Horejsi, 2006; Tolson et al., 2003) and direct practice (Derezotes, 2000; Hepworth et al., 2002) social work textbooks. For example, Hepworth et al. (2002) argued that "because human beings present a broad array of problems of living, no single approach or practice model is sufficiently comprehensive to adequately address them all" (p. 17). Also, "surveys of practitioners repeatedly indicated that one half to two-thirds of providers prefer using a variety of techniques that have arisen from major theoretical schools" (Lambert, 2013a, p. 8). One survey (Jensen et al., 1990) of a wide variety of mental health professionals revealed that the majority (68%) of social workers consider themselves eclectic, although this was the second lowest percentage among the four professional groups surveyed (corresponding figures for marriage and family therapists, psychologists, and psychiatrists were 72%, 70%, and 59%, respectively). Despite clear and logical arguments for eclecticism and its prevalence in practice, it is still a contentious issue in the helping professions—and we think this is particularly so in clinical social work (see the discussion in the Historical Resistance to Eclecticism section later in this chapter).

We would like to alert readers to the fact that our consideration of eclecticism in much of the rest of this chapter relies heavily on literature in clinical psychology because this is where most of the theory and research on eclecticism has been generated. Because of the reliance on literature from outside our profession, terms other than what we would normally use appear frequently (e.g., *therapist* instead of *worker*, *patient* instead of *client*, *therapy* instead of *direct practice* or *counseling*). We emphasize that we do not endorse the use of such terms and that our approach to eclecticism in direct practice is firmly rooted in social work values. Furthermore, we would like to point out that although most of the research on psychotherapy that we review has been conducted by psychologists and published in the psychology literature, this research has included direct social work practice. As Lambert (2013a) has pointed out, "in the United States, as much as 60% of the psychotherapy that is conducted is now provided by social workers" (p. 10).

Historical Resistance to Eclecticism

A historical perspective is necessary to understand the contentiousness of eclecticism. For most of this century, the helping professions have been marked by rigid adherence to narrow theories. Up until the 1960s, psychodynamic theory remained relatively unchallenged as the dominant theory in the helping professions (Lambert et al., 2004). As humanistic and behavioral theories gained increasing prominence in the 1960s, they began to challenge the dominance of psychodynamic theory, and this initiated the era of the "competing schools of psychotherapy." For the most part, the next 25 years were marked by rigid adherence to one or another of an increasing number of theoretical camps, rancorous debate about which theory was right, and extensive research focused on proving which therapeutic approach was the most effective. Although there were some efforts to bridge the differences among the numerous competing schools of therapy, eclecticism was clearly a dirty word. As Norcross (1997) has commented:

> You have all heard the classic refrains: eclectics are undisciplined subjectivists, jacks of all trades and masters of none, products of educational incompetency, muddleheaded, indiscriminate nihilists, fadmeisters, and people straddling the fence with both feet planted firmly in the air. (p. 87)

Unfortunately, such negative views of eclecticism are still prevalent within the field of counseling, particularly within clinical social work. Despite the endorsement of eclecticism by the generalist perspective, many social workers do not seem aware of or at least have not embraced the movement toward eclecticism that has been sweeping the larger field of psychotherapy. Also, despite the prevalence of eclecticism in practice, many social workers seem loath to admit this publicly because they know that eclecticism is still a dirty word in some circles. We have encountered many clinical social workers (academics and practitioners) who have disdain for eclecticism. One of the social work academics whom we approached to write a chapter for the first edition of this book, and who ascribed to a psychodynamic perspective, declined to contribute because of our endorsement of both a generalist perspective and eclecticism. Similarly, another academic who ascribed to a critical perspective declined to contribute a chapter to the current edition of this book for similar reasons. Unfortunately, such traditional negative views of eclecticism are difficult to change and they quickly filter down to students. We have had students tell us that their field instructors counsel them to never admit to an eclectic orientation in a job interview because it would count against them.

It is not surprising that adherence to one theoretical orientation is most prevalent for those who were trained in an older, more traditional theory. The Jensen et al. (1990) survey found that the most common exclusive theoretical orientation was psychodynamic. Furthermore, to bolster our contention about the traditional nature of clinical social work, this survey found that "of individuals endorsing an exclusively psychodynamic approach, 74% were either psychiatrists or social workers" (Jensen et al., 1990, p. 127; 25% of social workers and 36% of psychiatrists identified themselves as exclusively psychodynamic, whereas less than 10% of the other professional groups did so).

It should also be pointed out, however, that this phenomenon of adherence to one theoretical perspective also seems to be common for social workers who embrace more recent therapeutic approaches—for example, in the 1980s, family systems therapy (see Coady, 1993b); in the 1990s and forward, solution-focused therapy (see Stalker et al., 1999); and from the late 1990s and forward, many critical approaches to social work practice. Thus, we felt that it was important to emphasize our endorsement of eclecticism in the title of the book and to review the fact of and rationale for the trend toward eclecticism.

Documenting the Trend Toward Eclecticism in Counseling/Psychotherapy

Three decades ago, with regard to the broad field of counseling/psychotherapy, Garfield and Bergin (1986) concluded that the era of the competing schools of psychotherapy was over:

> A decisive shift in opinion has quietly occurred; and it has created an irreversible change in professional attitudes about psychotherapy and behavior change. The new view is that the long-term dominance of the major theories is over and that an eclectic position has taken precedence. (p. 7)

The trend toward eclecticism is evidenced in a number of ways. First, the precedence of eclecticism has been demonstrated by surveys. The Jensen et al. (1990) survey found that the majority of practitioners in each of the four groups of helping professionals were eclectic (68% overall). Furthermore, similar surveys have repeatedly indicated that one half to two thirds of practitioners in North America prefer some type of eclecticism (Lambert, 2013a).

Second, an international professional organization, the Society for the Exploration of Psychotherapy Integration (SEPI), which has been in existence for over 30 years, has been influential in furthering the study of eclecticism in psychotherapy. SEPI has published the *Journal of Psychotherapy Integration* since 1991, holds annual conferences, and has a website (www.sepi-web.org). We should clarify that the term *integration* is often used together with or instead of the term *eclecticism* in the literature. In brief, the difference between these approaches is that integration focuses on joining two or more theoretical approaches to arrive at a new, more comprehensive theory, while eclecticism simply draws on different theories and their techniques

(Lambert, 2013a). The difference between eclectic and integrative models is revisited in our discussion of approaches to eclecticism; however, for the most part, we use the term *eclecticism* to encompass both approaches.

Third, there has been a proliferation of literature on eclecticism. The number of journal articles focused on eclecticism continues to increase annually. This is also true for books on this topic. *Psychoanalysis and Behavior Therapy* (Wachtel, 1977), *Systems of Psychotherapy: A Transtheoretical Analysis* (Prochaska, 1979), and *Psychotherapy: An Eclectic Approach* (Garfield, 1980) are three of the first books that presented arguments for eclecticism and/or integration. Some of the more recent editions of such books include Dryden (1992), Stricker and Gold (1993), Garfield (1995), Gold (1996), Beutler and Harwood (2000), Lebow (2002), Norcross and Goldfried (2005), Stricker and Gold (2006), and Prochaska and Norcross (2014).

Reasons for the Trend Toward Eclecticism: Key Conclusions From Cumulative Research

Although various writers have argued for eclecticism (e.g., Thorne, 1950) or have promoted the integration of various theories (e.g., Dollard & Miller, 1950), in the more distant past, it is only in the last 35 years that a definite trend toward eclecticism has emerged in the broad field of counseling/psychotherapy. The trend toward eclecticism has been fueled primarily by two interrelated sets of research findings, which are discussed here.

THE EQUAL OUTCOMES/DODO BIRD PHENOMENON

The era of the competing schools of psychotherapy spawned an immense volume of research that overall has failed to demonstrate the superiority of one type of psychotherapy over another. Several recent, comprehensive reviews of research (Lambert, 2013b; Munder et al., 2019; Wampold & Imel, 2015) examined both numerous meta-analyses (a quantitative method that aggregates the findings of numerous studies in order to test hypotheses; e.g., Smith & Glass, 1977; Wampold et al., 1997) and exemplary studies (large, well-designed studies; e.g., the National Institute of Mental Health Treatment of Depression Collaborative Research Program [NIMH TDCRP; Elkin, 1994]) of the comparative outcomes of different therapy models.

These comprehensive reviews of the research have both reinforced what is commonly referred to as the *equal outcomes* or *Dodo bird effect* conclusion. That is, overall, studies have indicated that the various types of therapy (psychodynamic, cognitive-behavioral, humanistic, etc.) have roughly equal effectiveness, and therefore, in the words of the Dodo bird from *Alice in Wonderland*, "everybody has won, and all must have prizes" (Carroll, cited in Wampold et al., 1997, p. 203).

Although the equal outcomes conclusion is widely accepted, there are those who continue to question its legitimacy. Some critics (e.g., Beutler, 1991) have surmised that in the future, more sophisticated research designs may yield superior outcomes for specific therapy–client problem combinations. Others criticize various aspects of meta-analytic studies that support the equal outcomes conclusions (Wampold & Imel, 2015). Still others point out that some studies have found differences in outcome between approaches to treatment. In particular, some researchers contend that cognitive-behavioral approaches are more effective than other approaches with specific anxiety disorders (Wampold & Imel, 2015). We believe, however, that these contentions are not supported by empirical evidence to date. Lambert (2013b) has acknowledged tentative evidence that cognitive behavioral approaches may yield superior outcomes for a few specific, difficult problems (e.g., panic, phobias, and compulsions); however, he still accepts the general validity of the equal outcomes conclusion:

> [D]ifferences in outcome between various forms of therapy are not as pronounced as might have been expected …. Behavioral therapy, cognitive therapy, and eclectic

mixtures of these methods have shown marginally superior outcomes to traditional verbal therapies in several studies on specific disorders, but this is by no means the general case. (p. 205)

Wampold and Imel (2015) are even less accepting of the claims that cognitive behavioral approaches may be more effective with some specific problems. Their thorough, meticulous review of the research concluded that the equal outcomes result has held even in studies that have focused on specific treatments for depression and anxiety. These are two problems for which cognitive-behavioral treatments (CBTs) were thought to be particularly appropriate, and these are among the most common client problems for clinical social workers. Wampold and Imel (2015) concluded: "Claims that specific cognitive-behavioral therapies are more effective than bona fide comparisons are common but overblown and in need of additional testing" (p. 156). In addition, specific meta-studies comparing models of practice for PTSD, including cognitive, have shown no difference in treatment effectiveness (Wampold, 2019a).

Most recently, Frost et al. (2020) have questioned the claims of large effect trails which claim superioirity of one model of practice over another because the studies are not replicable. They have called for replication criteria and quality benchmarks to be considered before such trials are considered on their own or included in future meta-analysis.

Thus, we agree with Wampold and Imel's (2015) conclusion that "the Dodo bird conjecture has survived many tests and must be considered 'true' until such time as sufficient evidence for its rejection is produced" (p. 156). The acceptance of this conclusion does not lead directly to an argument for eclecticism; however, it does promote acceptance of the validity of alternative approaches. This, along with the recognition that "no single school can provide all theoretical and practical answers for our psychological woes … [makes it seem sensible] to cross boundaries, to venture beyond one's borders in search of nuggets that may be deposited among the hills and dales of other camps" (Lazarus, 1996, p. 59).

THE IMPORTANCE OF RELATIONSHIP AND OTHER COMMON FACTORS

The cumulative results of psychotherapy research have stimulated interest in what has come to be known as "common factors." The findings of nonsignificant outcome differences among the variety of different therapies (the equal outcomes phenomenon) led many researchers to latch on to the ideas promoted earlier by Rosenzweig (1936) and Frank (1961) that factors specific to the various therapies (i.e., distinctive theory and techniques) had less impact on outcomes than factors that were common across therapies—particularly worker–client relationship factors. Early research on the client-centered core conditions of empathy, warmth, and genuineness, and later research on the related concept of the therapeutic alliance, have established that relationship factors are the most powerful predictors of client outcome and that a good helping relationship is necessary for good outcome regardless of the approach to therapy (Flückiger et al., 2019; Horvath et al., 2011; Horvath & Symonds, 1991; Lambert & Barley, 2001; Wampold & Imel, 2015).

Cumulative research suggests that "common factors are probably much more powerful than the contribution of specific techniques…. Learning how to engage the client in a collaborative process is more central to positive outcomes than which process (theory of change) is provided" (Lambert, 2013b, p. 202). The two editions of Wampold's (2001; Wampold & Imel, 2015) book, *The Great Psychotherapy Debate*, focused on reviewing research related to the controversial question of whether therapy effectiveness is related more to common factors (e.g., therapeutic relationship) or specific factors (e.g., theory and technique). Wampold and Imel (2015) concluded that the research evidence provides overwhelming support for the importance of common versus specific factors. They found that the effects produced by common factors were much larger than the effects produced by specific factors and that "these effects make it evident that the 'common factors' are important considerations in the outcome of psychotherapy" (Wampold &

Imel, 2015, p. 256). Furthermore, they concluded that despite concerted efforts by many researchers to establish the importance of specific factors, "there is no compelling evidence that the specific ingredients of any particular psychotherapy … are critical to producing the benefits of psychotherapy" (p. 253).

Although a variety of factors that are common across therapies have been conceptualized and there is empirical support for the importance of a number of such factors (e.g., reassurance, affective experiencing/catharsis, mitigation of isolation, encouragement of facing problems/fears, encouragement of experimenting with new behaviors; Lambert, 2013b), the therapeutic relationship or alliance "is the most frequently mentioned common factor in the psychotherapy literature" (Grencavage & Norcross, 1990; Wampold, 2017) and it has been called the "quintessential integrative variable" (Wolfe & Goldfried, cited in Wampold, 2001, p. 150) in counseling. On the basis of their thorough review of psychotherapy research, Wampold and Imel (2015) conclude that the "relationship, broadly defined, is the bedrock of psychotherapy effectiveness" (p. 50). Again, although the research on common factors does not lead directly to an argument for eclecticism with regard to theory and technique, it does promote openness to crossing therapeutic boundaries. In fact, from within social work, Cameron (2014) has suggested that "eclecticism is equivalent to a common factors approach … in that common factors practitioners use strategies and skills that are found in many different practice approaches" (p. 152; see Approaches to Eclecticism section for further discussion of common factors).

SUMMARY

Although there have been longstanding and persuasive arguments for eclecticism, the trend toward eclecticism has been fueled largely by research findings—both the equal outcomes phenomenon and the importance of relationship and other common factors relative to specific (i.e., theory and technique) factors. As Lambert (2013b) has noted, the trend toward eclecticism "appears to reflect a healthy response to empirical evidence" (p. 206). This has led practitioners to "increasingly acknowledge the inadequacies of any one school and the potential value of others" (Norcross, 1997, p. 86). From within social work, having reviewed much of the same psychotherapy research that has been reviewed in this chapter, Cameron (2014) has concluded that "eclecticism, idiosyncratically shaped by the unique needs of clients as well as the person of the practitioner, is most effective" (p. 152).

Pockets of Resistance to Eclecticism

Acceptance of the research findings that have fueled the trend toward eclecticism has not been easy for many mental health practitioners. Four decades ago, Frank (as cited in Lambert & Ogles, 2004) anticipated resistance to his hypotheses about equal outcomes across therapies and the importance of common factors when he noted that "little glory derives from showing that the particular method one has mastered with so much effort may be indistinguishable from other models in its effects" (p. 175). Similarly, as Glass suggested in the foreword to Wampold's (2001) book, giving up the idea that one's cherished theory and associated techniques are no more effective than another approach to therapy and that effectiveness is due largely to factors that are common across therapies "carries a threat of narcissistic injury" (p. x).

Even more dramatically, Parloff (cited in Wampold, 2001) contended that, in some practitioners' minds, if the conclusion about the primary importance of common factors is accepted, "then the credibility of psychotherapy as a profession is automatically impugned" (p. 29). With regard to this last point, we would argue that acceptance of these research findings does not impugn the credibility of psychotherapy, but it does change the general conceptualization of psychotherapy from a primarily scientific, theoretical/technique-oriented enterprise to one that is more humanistic, artistic, and reflective. Wampold and Imel (2015) have called for such a shift toward what they call a "contextual model" of therapy, in which common factors are emphasized, to replace the current "medical model." Still, there is "tremendous resistance" (Lambert et al., 2004, p. 809) to accepting these research findings and this reconceptualization of psychotherapy/clinical practice. Most recently, the eclectic approach to practice has come under the eye of researchers who maintain that the use of routine client feedback to guide practice, which is then eclectically tailored based on this feedback, does not show better outcomes than standard care (Rise et al., 2016).

THE CHALLENGE OF THE EMPIRICALLY SUPPORTED TREATMENT MOVEMENT

The research findings on equal outcomes across different types of therapy, the importance of relationship and other common factors to outcomes, and the weak effect of specific techniques on outcomes stand in stark contrast to the rise of the EST movement in psychology that arose in the 1990s. As part of the broader movement toward evidence-based practice (EBP) in psychology (Barlow, 2000) and social work (Gambrill, 1999, 2006; Gibbs & Gambrill, 2002; Howard et al., 2003; Magill, 2006; Rubin & Parrish, 2007; Shdaimah, 2009), the EST movement was spurred by the Division of Clinical Psychology of the American Psychological Association, which created criteria for the empirical support of therapies.

It is clear that the implicit assumption of the EST movement is that specific ingredients (i.e., therapeutic techniques and their underlying theory) are the important curative factors in psychotherapy (Messer, 2001). The EST movement has pushed for using specific treatments with specific disorders and using only treatments that have been "proven" effective in randomized clinical trial research that includes a formal diagnosis of the client's problem, a specific treatment that is delivered in accordance with a treatment manual, and outcome measures related to the diagnosis. The result has been to develop a list of ESTs, the vast majority of which are cognitive behavioral in orientation. ESTs have become widely advocated by managed care, insurance companies, and government (Messer, 2001). In this regard, Wampold (2001) has lamented that "doctoral level psychologists and other psychotherapy practitioners (e.g., social workers, marriage and family therapists) are economically coerced to practice a form of therapy different from what they were trained and different from how they would prefer to practice" (p. 2).

Before moving to a critique of the EST movement, it is important to stress that it is much narrower than the EBP movement. As Gambrill (2006) has pointed out:

> Descriptions of EBP differ greatly in their breadth and attention to ethical, evidentiary, and application issues and their interrelationships ranging from the broad, systemic philosophy and related evolving process initiated by its originators ... to narrow views (using empirically supported interventions that leave out the role of clinical expertise, attention to client values and preferences, and application problems). (p. 339)

We agree with Gambrill (2006) that the EST movement represents "a narrow view of EBP ... that is antithetical to the process and philosophy of EBP as described by its originators" (p. 354). Thus, although we are concerned that the broader EBP movement has to some degree gotten aligned with the narrower views of the EST movement, our argument is with the latter movement and its narrow and rigid conceptualization of what constitutes evidence. We hope it is clear from our review of psychotherapy research that we believe practice should be informed by research—we just disagree with those within the EST movement about what the research to date tells us about practice and what research should focus upon going forward.

CRITIQUE OF THE EMPIRICALLY SUPPORTED TREATMENT MOVEMENT

Critics have pointed out that the predominance of CBTs in the EST list is due to the fact that other, more process-oriented therapies do not readily fit the research protocol requirements for manualized treatment and focus on specific symptoms with associated specific outcome measures, and that these requirements are biased toward CBTs (Messer, 2001; Wachtel, 2010; Wampold & Imel, 2015). Wachtel (2010) has argued that "there is an impressive body of evidence demonstrating the efficacy of a range of therapeutic approaches not on the 'EST' lists" (p. 268). Furthermore, in a provocative manner, he has contended that when EST advocates dismiss this body of evidence as irrelevant because the studies do not meet their very narrow research protocol requirements, "they engage in a kind of deceptive casuistry similar to that which characterized for years the tobacco companies' denial of the adverse health effects of cigarettes" (p. 269).

The use of treatment manuals is one of the research requirements of the EST movement that has received extensive criticism. Beyond the fact that many theoretical approaches are not structured enough to be manualized, Messer (2001) argued that overly close adherence to treatment manuals can stifle "artistry, flexibility, reflection, and imagination" (p. 8). This view is supported by Wampold and Imel's (2015) review of research, which found that "the evidence suggests that rigid adherence to a treatment protocol, particularly if it damages the relationship …, is detrimental" (p. 274). Duncan and Miller (2006) provide a thorough overview of research demonstrating that the manual is detrimental to client outcomes because counselor choice to follow the manual, rather than tailor practice to the client, undermines the client's voice and limits the counselor's ability to adjust to the nuances and needs of each specific client.

More generally, noting the decades of research that have confirmed the equal outcomes phenomenon and the importance of the counseling relationship, Wampold and Bhati (2004) argued that "there is compelling evidence that it makes more sense to think of elements of the relationship as being empirically supported rather than particular treatments" (p. 567). Similarly, Lambert (2013a) has pointed out, "the fact is that success of treatment appears to be largely dependent on the client and the therapist, not on the use of 'proven' empirically based treatments" (p. 8). Henry's (1998) argument against ESTs is still valid today:

> The largest chunk of outcome variance not attributable to pre-existing patient characteristics involves individual therapist differences and the emergent interpersonal relationship between patient and therapist, regardless of technique or school of therapy. This is the main thrust of three decades of empirical psychotherapy research. (p. 128)

We agree with those who contend that the focus of EST research is misplaced and that the results are misleading. We also concur with Wampold's (2001) conclusion that "designated ESTs should not be used to mandate services, reimburse service providers, or restrict or guide the training of therapists" (p. 225). With regard to the latter issue, Wampold and Imel (2015) argued that "training programs need to teach a variety of treatments—and … the optimal training programs will combine training in treatments and relationship skills" (p. 276). From within social work, reflecting on the strong empirical support for the importance of the helping relationship, Furman (2009) has argued similarly:

> Increasingly, schools of social work and social work training centers that focus on methods or technique … may not sufficiently help future social workers develop the capacity for self-reflection, which is a key to developing functional or "good enough" helping relationships. (p. 84)

As noted earlier, it should be clear from the emphasis we have placed on reviewing research that we are not against the general concept of EBP; however, we think that psychologists and social workers who align themselves with the assumptions and principles of the EST movement are barking up the wrong tree in searching for empirically supported theories and techniques. Instead, we think that funders, researchers, and practitioners should shift to more productive research foci.

One example of a more productive research focus is that of the American Psychiatric Association's (APA) task forces (Norcross, 2001, 2002; Norcross & Lambert, 2011; Norcross &

Wampold, 2011) that explored evidence-based therapy relationships. These task forces were established to counter, or at least balance, the EST movement. In fact, one of the conclusions of the second task force (Norcross & Wampold, 2011) was that "efforts to promulgate best practices or EBPs without including the relationship are seriously incomplete and potentially misleading" (p. 98). Among the general elements of the therapy relationship that the second task force concluded as "demonstrably effective" were the overall quality of the therapeutic relationship/alliance, empathy, and collecting client feedback. Other elements found to be "probably effective" were positive regard, collaboration, and goal consensus. "Promising" elements of the relationship but with insufficient research included genuineness/congruence and repairing problems in the therapy relationship (Norcross & Wampold, 2011).

Policy recommendations from this task force included educating clinicians about the benefits of evidence-based therapy relationships and advocating for the "research-substantiated benefits of a nurturing and responsive human relationship in psychotherapy" (Norcross & Wampold, 2011, p. 100). Reflecting on the research that supports the importance of the helping relationship, Lambert (2013b) said, "It should come as no surprise that helping others … can be greatly facilitated in a therapeutic relationship that is characterized by trust, understanding, acceptance, kindness, warmth, and human consideration" (p. 206).

The second APA task force on evidence-based therapy relationships also found that adapting the relationship style to specific client characteristics enhances the effectiveness of counseling (Norcross & Wampold, 2011). Among the most important client characteristics to which one should adapt one's relationship stance were client preferences, resistance (highly resistant clients benefit more from a minimally directive worker, and viceversa), culture, and religion/spirituality. As two of the first task force members concluded, research suggests that "improvement of psychotherapy may be best accomplished by learning to improve one's ability to relate to clients and tailoring that relationship to individual clients" (Lambert & Barley, 2001, p. 357).

Another example of a potentially productive focus for research is individual therapist differences. Although research has established equal outcomes across different types of therapy, it has also established that there are significant differences in effectiveness among therapists within each approach to therapy. Lambert (2013b) has noted that "some therapists appear to be unusually effective, while others may not even help the majority of patients who seek their services" (p. 206). From their review of research on this issue, Wampold and Imel (2015) concluded that the actions that differentiate more effective from less effective therapists include "warmth and acceptance, empathy, and focus on the other" (p. 211). On this issue, Lambert and Ogles (2004) have called for "research focused on the 'empirically validated psychotherapist' rather than on empirically supported treatment" (p. 169).

It is likely that differences in effectiveness among practitioners have much to do with the ability to establish good interpersonal relationships with clients, particularly difficult clients, and to use such relationships therapeutically (Asay & Lambert, 2001). Thus, promising foci for research on therapist differences include relationship and general interpersonal skills, interpersonal style, emotional well-being, and attitudes toward clients. Although we do not know how widespread it has become, Messer (2001) noted that it was encouraging that some "managed care companies are moving to a system of evaluating therapists and referring cases to the successful ones, rather than requiring the use of ESTs" (p. 9). On a related note, Lambert (2013b) has noted that "research suggests clients would be wise to pick a therapist as-a-person at least in parity with the selection of a kind of psychotherapy" (p. 206).

Postmodern scholars (Hall, 2008; Witkin, 2000, 2017) have critiqued the EST movement on several points specific to culture and power by questioning culturally dominant ideas of how problems are understood and subsequently assessed. This critique covers both research and ethics with postmodern scholars maintaining that both are constructions and are not objective. Questioning of research includes: Whose perceptions are measured about problems and outcomes? Who participated in the study design? Which populations are represented and can average conclusions be applied to specific clients? Are problems generalizable and compatible?

Is context stripped away from problems and outcomes in research? Ethical questions include: Who participates in how problems will be understood and the construction of the solution? How is normal and abnormal defined by a culture and society? Are many forms of living and being in a culture accepted? How were models of practice created and did marginalized populations have a voice in the creation and acceptance of these models? If models of practice are situated historically, do the models reflect current ideas about normality? Ultimately, postmodern scholars ask the question of the EST movement: Whose evidence and for what purpose (Witkin & Harrison, 2001)?

APPROACHES TO ECLECTICISM

Despite pockets of strong resistance such as the EST movement, the trend toward eclecticism and integration is clear in the broad field of counseling/psychotherapy and the profession of clinical psychology. As we have argued, however, despite the endorsement of eclecticism in the generalist perspective, this trend is less clear in direct social work practice. We think it is important for social workers to become familiar with the literature on eclecticism and integration in psychotherapy. Many of the ideas and principles in this literature (e.g., the valuing of multiple perspectives for understanding and intervening, the centrality of the helping relationship) are consistent with and can inform social work practice.

Four broad approaches to eclecticism are commonly identified in the literature: technical eclecticism, theoretical integration, assimilative integration, and common factors (Castonguay et al., 2003; Lampropoulos, 2001; Norcross, 2005; Stricker, 2010; see Table 1.2). A survey (Norcross et al., cited in Norcross, 2005) of psychologists who self-identified as eclectics and integrationists found that a sizable proportion of therapists (19%–28%) subscribed to each of these four approaches to eclecticism.

Each of the general approaches to eclecticism subsumes a number of more specific models of eclectic/integrative practice; however, not surprisingly, there are differences in the literature with regard to classifying some models. Although it is beyond the scope of this book to review specific eclectic/integrative models in detail, the following discussion of each of the four general approaches provides a brief discussion of some of the specific models that fall under their domain. Following this, we elaborate on the type of eclecticism we endorse for our generalist-eclectic approach.

Technical Eclecticism

Technical eclecticism, which is sometimes referred to as systematic eclecticism or prescriptive matching, "refers to the relatively atheoretical selection of clinical treatments on the basis of predicted efficacy rather than theoretical considerations" (Alford, 1995, p. 147). Thus, those who ascribe to technical eclecticism use clinical knowledge and research findings about what has worked best with clients with similar characteristics or problems to draw techniques from different therapy models, without necessarily subscribing to any of the theories (Norcross, 2005; Wampold & Imel, 2015). Lazarus (1996) differentiated this type of eclecticism from "the ragtag importation of techniques from anywhere or everywhere without a sound rationale" (p. 61). Technical eclecticism attempts to address the specificity question posed by Paul (cited in Lampropoulos, 2001): "*What* treatment, by *whom*, is most effective for *this* individual with *that* specific problem, and under *which* set of circumstances" (p. 7). Of the four types of eclecticism, this type pays the least attention to the integration of theories (Gold & Stricker, 2006).

MULTIMODAL BEHAVIOR THERAPY

Lazarus's (1981, 2005, 2006) multimodal behavior therapy (MMT) is one of the most prominent examples of technical eclecticism. MMT is based on assessment that specifies the client's

TABLE 1.2 APPROACHES TO ECLECTICISM/INTEGRATION

Broad Approaches	Examples of Therapies	General Characteristics of Approaches
Technical eclecticism	MMT (Lazarus, 1981, 2005, 2006) STS (Beutler, 1983; Beutler & Clarkin, 1990; Beutler et al., 2005, 2006)	Using techniques from different theories based on their proven effectiveness with similar client problems/characteristics, without necessarily subscribing to any of the theories
Theoretical integration	Integrative relational therapy (Wachtel, 1977, 1997; Wachtel et al., 2005) TTM (Prochaska & DiClemente, 1984, 2005; Prochaska & Norcross, 1999, 2014)	Integrating/synthesizing the strengths of two or more theories to create a more comprehensive theory to explain human problems and guide intervention
Assimilative integration	Assimilative psychodynamic psychotherapy (Gold & Stricker, 2001; Stricker, 2006; Stricker & Gold, 2005) Widening the scope of cognitive therapy (Safran, 1990a, 1990b, 1998; Safran et al., 2014)	Incorporating other theories and techniques into one's primary theoretical orientation
Common factors	Common factors/contextual meta-model (Frank & Frank, 1991; Wampold, 2001, 2019b; Wampold & Imel, 2015) Eclectic/integrative approach (Garfield, 1995, 2000) Client-directed, outcome-informed clinical work (Duncan et al., 2006; Miller et al., 2005, 2020)	Focusing on factors that are shared by all types of therapy and that are central to therapeutic effectiveness (e.g., a good helping relationship)

MMT, multimodal behavior therapy; STS, systematic treatment selection; TTM, transtheoretical model.

problem and their primary aspects, or modalities, of functioning (i.e., behavior, affect, sensation, imagery, cognition, interpersonal relationships, and drugs/biological functioning [BASIC I.D.]). Lazarus contended that different techniques should be selected to address the client's various prominent modalities and that these should be addressed sequentially according to their "firing order" (e.g., if client affect leads to behavior and then cognition, these modalities should be treated in this order). He also argued that therapy should address as many modalities as possible. MMT uses techniques from a variety of theories, including humanistic, psychodynamic, and family systems theories, but there is an emphasis on cognitive behavioral techniques (Lazarus, 2005, 2006).

SYSTEMATIC TREATMENT SELECTION

A second prominent example of technical eclecticism is Beutler's systematic treatment selection (STS) therapy (Beutler,1983; Beutler & Clarkin, 1990; Beutler & Harwood, 1995, 2000; Beutler et al., 2005, 2006). In this approach, techniques from a wide variety of theories are selected on the basis of "empirical evidence of usefulness rather than by a theory of personality or of change" (Beutler & Harwood, 1995, p. 89). STS focuses on matching treatment strategies and techniques to client characteristics (client–treatment matching) and is one of the most ambitious and thorough models of eclecticism. In this model, a thorough assessment of client variables (e.g., demographic qualities, coping style, level of distress, level of resistance, expectations of therapy, social supports, diagnosis) and a consideration of empirical evidence related to such variables lead to decisions about (a) treatment contexts (individual, group, marital, family therapy), (b) choice of therapist (e.g., based on interpersonal compatibility and demographic similarity), (c) goal of therapy (i.e., focus on symptoms or underlying themes), (d) primary level of experience to be addressed (affect, cognition, or behavior), (e) style of therapist (e.g., degree of directiveness, support, confrontation), and (f) therapeutic techniques (Beutler & Harwood, 1995).

The STS model has been researched extensively and the most promising results are related to matching treatment to the client's coping style and reactance/resistance level. With regard to coping style, it has been found that clients who externalize (e.g., blame others) do better in structured treatments such as CBT, whereas clients who internalize (e.g., blame themselves) do better in more process-oriented treatment (e.g., insight or relationship-oriented therapy). With regard to resistance, it has been found that clients who are highly resistant do better in less directive therapy (e.g., client centered), whereas clients low in resistance do better in more directive therapy (e.g., CBT; Schottenbauer et al., 2005).

Theoretical Integration

In this second category of approaches, "there is an emphasis on integrating the underlying *theories* of psychotherapy along with therapy techniques from each" (Prochaska & Norcross, 2014, p. 431). The goal is to produce a more comprehensive, overarching theoretical framework that synthesizes the strengths of individual theories. Norcross (2005) has referred to theoretical integration as "theory smushing" (p. 8). The ultimate form of theoretical integration would incorporate all of the various theories of therapy (i.e., those subsumed under psychodynamic, cognitive behavioral, humanistic/feminist, and postmodern classifications, as well as biological and family systems approaches) into a synthesized/unified whole. Leaving aside the question of whether such a lofty goal is viable or not, Stricker's (1994) conclusion that "psychotherapy integration has not succeeded in that grand attempt, … the leading current approaches usually incorporate two, or at most three, of these perspectives" (p. 6) still holds today. As Lampropoulos (2001) noted, theoretical integration is "the ideal, optimistic, but utopian view" (p. 6).

INTEGRATIVE RELATIONAL THERAPY
Wachtel's (1977, 1997; Wachtel et al., 2005) integration of psychodynamic and behavioral theories is the most commonly cited example of an integrative approach. Building on the earlier work of Dollard and Miller (1950), Wachtel et al. (2005) integrated the strengths of the social-learning model of behavioral theory with his interpersonal type of psychodynamic theory to create integrative relational therapy. This integrative theory posits that unconscious conflicts/anxieties and interpersonal interactions are mutually influencing and create vicious cycles (e.g., anxiety about dependency needs results in keeping people at arm's length, which heightens the anxiety). In this model, intervention involves integrating a psychodynamic focus on insight with a behavioral focus on action (e.g., skills training).

THE TRANSTHEORETICAL MODEL
The transtheoretical model (TTM; Prochaska & DiClemente, 1984, 2005; Prochaska & Norcross, 1999, 2014) is another influential integrative model. In the TTM, the selection of interventions, or change processes as they are called, is based on the assessment of two factors. First, consideration is given to the "stages of change" through which people progress. Thus, the worker needs to assess which of the five stages of change a client is in:

1. precontemplation (relatively unaware of problems with no intention to change),
2. contemplation (aware of a problem and considering, but not committed to, change),
3. preparation (intending and beginning to take initial steps toward change),
4. action (investment of considerable time and energy to successfully alter a problem behavior), and
5. maintenance (working to consolidate gains and prevent relapse).

Second, the "level/depth of change" required needs to be assessed. Thus, the worker and client need to mutually determine which of five problem levels to focus on:

1. symptom/situational problems,
2. maladaptive cognitions,
3. current interpersonal conflicts,
4. family/system conflicts, and
5. intrapersonal conflicts.

After an assessment of the client's stage of change and the level of change required, the TTM suggests that available empirical evidence of effectiveness be considered, as much as possible, to determine which interventions from different theoretical perspectives to use. In general, with regard to stages of change, techniques from cognitive, psychodynamic, and humanistic therapies are thought to be most useful in the precontemplation and contemplation stages, whereas "change processes traditionally associated with the existential and behavioral traditions … are most useful during the action and maintenance stages" (Prochaska & Norcross, 2014, p. 467). More specifically, when the level of change required is considered in the action stage, behavioral techniques would usually be chosen for the symptom/situational level, cognitive techniques would be employed at the level of maladaptive cognitions, and psychodynamic interventions would be used at the intrapersonal conflict level. The general principle in this model is to focus intervention initially at the symptom/situational level and then to proceed to deeper levels only if necessary.

Assimilative Integration

This approach to eclectic/integrative practice was the last of the four categories of eclecticism to be developed (Stricker, 2010), and was proposed initially by Messer (1992). This approach maintains that it is important to keep a firm grounding in one theory of therapy while incorporating ideas and techniques from other theories. Lampropoulos (2001) explained how assimilative integration can be seen as a bridge between technical eclecticism and theoretical integration:

> When techniques from different theoretical approaches are incorporated into one's main theoretical orientation, their meaning interacts with the meaning of the "host" theory, and both the imported technique and the pre-existing theory are mutually transformed and shaped into the final product, namely the new assimilative, integrative model. (p. 9)

ASSIMILATIVE PSYCHODYNAMIC PSYCHOTHERAPY

One example of assimilative integration is assimilative psychodynamic psychotherapy (Gold & Stricker, 2001; Stricker, 2006; Stricker & Gold, 2005). As its name indicates, this is clearly a psychodynamic therapy, but one that allows for the incorporation of more active/directive interventions "borrowed from cognitive, behavioral, and humanistic approaches" (Stricker, 2006). Gold and Stricker (2001) acknowledged that psychodynamic therapy "is very good at answering the 'why' and 'how did this happen' questions … but it is not as effective at answering questions such as 'so now what do I do' or 'how do I change this'" (p. 55). In this approach, there is an effort to introduce techniques from other theories in such a way that they are "experienced as part and parcel of a consistent approach rather than an arbitrary intrusion on the ongoing work" (Stricker, 2006, p. 55).

WIDENING THE SCOPE OF COGNITIVE THERAPY

Another example of this approach is Safran's (1990a, 1990b, 1998; Safran & Segal, 1990) attempt to widen the scope of cognitive therapy by incorporating aspects of psychodynamic (psychoanalytic and interpersonal) and humanistic theories. Beyond the cognitive and behavioral dimensions of human functioning, which are the sole foci of most CBTs, Safran's model also considers emotional, developmental, interpersonal, and conflictual dimensions. Techniques from other theoretical orientations are incorporated to address issues associated with these additional aspects of human experience. A more recent development by Safran et al. (2014) has been to augment CBT with alliance-focused training (AFT), which is derived from the relational model of psychodynamic theory and focuses on resolving problems or ruptures in the therapeutic alliance.

Common Factors

In this last category of approaches to eclecticism, there is an attempt to identify and utilize the "effective aspects of treatment shared by the diverse forms of psychotherapy" (Weinberger, 1993, p. 43). This approach has been influenced largely by the extensive work of Jerome Frank, particularly his classic book entitled *Persuasion and Healing* (Frank, 1961, 1973, and co-authored with his daughter, Frank & Frank, 1991). Frank's writing on common factors amounted to a meta-model of psychotherapy, rather than a specific approach to therapy. Wampold (2001; Wampold & Imel, 2015) has adopted Frank's broad common factors conceptualization of psychotherapy, calling it a contextual model of psychotherapy, and contrasting it to the medical model, which purports that theory and technique (i.e., specific factors) are the keys to therapeutic effectiveness.

As we have noted earlier, Wampold's (2001) and Wampold and Imel's (2015) thorough analysis of psychotherapy research provides compelling empirical support for the common factors/contextual model of psychotherapy. Although Wampold (2001) clearly attributed the meta-model discussed in his book to Frank, because of Wampold and Imel's (2015) further conceptual development and empirical validation of the model, we see this model as a joint product of these authors' work. We will review the common factors/contextual model of Frank and Wampold and Imel in some depth before considering more specific common factors therapy models.

COMMON FACTORS/CONTEXTUAL MODEL

Building on Rosenzweig's (1936) earlier ideas, Frank developed the demoralization hypothesis, which proposes that most of the distress suffered by clients stems from being demoralized and that "features shared by all therapies that combat demoralization account for much of their effectiveness" (Frank, 1982, p. 32). Frank (1982; Frank & Frank, 1991) suggested four factors that are shared by all forms of psychotherapy, as well as by religious and other secular types of healing, that represent means of directly or indirectly combating demoralization and that are primarily responsible for the effectiveness of any approach to healing.

First, and foremost, is an "emotionally supportive, confiding relationship with a helping person" (Frank, 1982, p. 19). If helpers can convince clients that they care and want to help, then this decreases clients' sense of alienation, increases expectations of improvement, and boosts morale.

Second is a "healing setting" that heightens the helper's prestige, thereby increasing the client's expectation of help, and provides safety. In psychotherapy, the healing setting is usually an office or clinic that carries the aura of science; in religious healing, it is usually a temple or sacred grove.

Third is a theoretical rationale or "myth" that provides a believable explanation for clients' difficulties. Frank uses the word *myth* to underscore the contention that the accuracy of the explanation is less important than its plausibility in the eyes of the client. Any explanation of their difficulties that clients can accept alleviates some distress and engenders hope for change.

Fourth is a set of therapeutic procedures or a "ritual" that involves the participation of the helper and client in activities that both believe will help the client to overcome the presenting difficulties. With regard to the fourth common factor, on the basis of empirical studies of therapy, Frank and Frank (1991) contended that therapeutic procedures will be optimally effective if they

- provide new learning experiences for clients (these enhance morale by helping clients to develop more positive views of themselves and their problems),
- arouse clients' emotions (this helps clients to tolerate and accept their emotions and allows them to confront and cope more successfully with feared issues and situations—thus strengthening self-confidence, sense of mastery, and morale), and
- provide opportunities for clients to practice what they have learned both within therapy and in their everyday lives (thus reinforcing therapeutic gains, a sense of mastery, and morale).

Lambert (2013b) and Wampold (2019b; 2001; Wampold & Imel, 2015) concurred with Frank that there is substantial empirical support for these therapeutic procedures that are common across therapies.

Although there is extensive empirical support for the first (therapeutic relationship) and fourth (common therapeutic procedures) of Frank's common factors, there is little research on the healing setting or on the theoretical rationale/myth. There is indirect support, however, for the latter factor. Frank's hypothesis about the importance of a theoretical rationale/myth that provides a believable explanation to clients of their problems is linked to "goal consensus and collaboration," which is one of the aspects of the therapeutic alliance for which there is strong empirical support (Ackerman et al., 2001; Norcross & Wampold, 2011). Clearly, in order to establish goal consensus and collaboration, clients must believe in workers' explanation for their difficulties and strategies for ameliorating problems. Frank and Frank (1991) maintained that in order to maximize the sense and quality of an alliance with clients,

> therapists should select for each patient the therapy that accords, or can be brought to accord, with the patient's personal characteristics and view of the problem. Also implied is that therapists should seek to learn as many approaches as they find congenial and convincing. Creating a good therapeutic match may involve both educating the patient about the therapist's conceptual scheme and, if necessary, modifying the scheme to take into account the concepts the patient brings to therapy. (p. xv)

Following Frank and Frank's line of argument, and based on his review of research, Wampold (2001) has suggested that therapists should choose an approach to counseling that accords with the client's worldview: "The therapist needs to realize that the client's belief in the explanation for their [sic] disorder, problem, or complaint is paramount" (p. 218).

Wampold and Imel's (2015) most recent development of the common factors/contextual model posits three pathways that explain the benefits of psychotherapy. The first pathway is what they call the "real" relationship, which is the development of an authentic, genuine, trusting, open, and honest relationship in which the client experiences the worker's empathy. The second pathway involves the creation of positive expectations about therapy. This relates to Frank's ideas about clients being demoralized and therapists needing to instill hope and boost morale. It also relates to Frank's ideas about providing an explanation for the client's problem that is plausible to them and suggesting therapeutic actions that are in keeping with the explanation. The third pathway is what they call "specific ingredients." This does not refer to the importance of specific (theory and technique) factors, but rather to the fact that all therapies, in one way or another, involve encouraging clients to engage in activities (cognitive, behavioral, and/or emotional) that promote psychological well-being or symptom reduction.

Wampold and Imel (2015) emphasize that the common factors/contextual model is primarily a relationship-based model of psychotherapy: "The intervention we discuss in this book is still mostly a human conversation—perhaps the ultimate in low technology. Something in the core of human connection and interaction has the power to heal" (p. ix).

ECLECTIC/INTEGRATIVE APPROACH

Another therapy that has been classified as a common factors model is Garfield's (1995, 2000) eclectic/integrative approach. Garfield contended that despite the many apparent differences among the various therapeutic approaches and the fact that these schools of therapy tend to emphasize the importance of their specific techniques, factors that are common across therapies account for much of their success. Garfield's (1995) model places a strong "emphasis on the therapeutic relationship and on the common factors in psychotherapy" (p. 167), while also supporting the eclectic use of interventions from different theoretical approaches. Echoing Frank, Garfield (1995) contended that "being given some explanation for one's problems by an interested expert in the role of healer, may be the important common aspect of these divergent therapies" (p. 34). Garfield (1995) rationalized the theoretical openness of his approach:

> Although the absence of a unifying and guiding theory has its drawbacks, an awareness of one's limitations and of the gaps in our current knowledge is, in the long run, a positive thing—even though it may make for uncertainties. It is better to see the situation for what it really is than to have what may be an incorrect or biased orientation. (p. 216)

Garfield's (1995) model does, however, provide some structure for practitioners by presenting general guidelines for the various stages of therapy (beginning, middle, later, and termination). This is very similar to the use of the problem-solving model in the generalist-eclectic approach. Also, Garfield's approach has elements of technical eclecticism in that therapists are advised, where possible, to choose techniques "which on the basis of empirical evidence seem to be most effective for the specific problems presented by the client" (p. 218).

CLIENT-DIRECTED, OUTCOME-INFORMED CLINICAL WORK

Another, more recent, common factors approach is the client-directed, outcome-informed (CDOI) clinical work model (Duncan et al., 2006; Hubble et al., 1999; Miller et al., 2005; Prescott et al., 2017). This model focuses on the importance of the therapeutic relationship. It emphasizes three core ingredients of the alliance: (a) shared goals for counseling, (b) consensus on the approach to counseling (means, methods, tasks), and (c) the emotional bond between worker and client. It is proposed that one key to developing a strong alliance is to adopt the client's theory of change, that is, "the client's frame of reference regarding the presenting problem, its causes, and potential remedies" (Miller et al., 2005, p. 87).

A second important key is to solicit and respond to, on an ongoing basis, client feedback regarding the therapeutic alliance. This is the "outcome-informed" element of the model. If the client voices concern about any aspect of the alliance, then "every effort should be made to accommodate the client" (p. 94). This model places very little emphasis on theory:

> The love affair with theory relegates clients to insignificant roles in bringing about change…. When therapists' models, whether integrative or not, crowd our thinking, there is little room left for clients' models—their ideas about their predicaments and what it might take to fix them—to take shape. (Duncan et al., 2006, p. 236)

Two specific branches of CDOI are that of Miller et al. (2020) Feedback-Informed Treatment (FIT), which focuses on deliberate practice; and My Outcomes Now (MON), a software version of the Partners of Change Outcome Management System (PCOMS; Sparks & Duncan, 2018). FIT is similar to CDOI in that it utilizes client feedback to tailor practice to clients but adds an additional training component for the social worker centering on the development of specific counselling skills. FIT utilizes the same measures as CDOI but uses those measures not only to tailor treatment for the client but also to provide feedback for social worker growth. MON is an online tracking program designed to make gathering client feedback easier and more manageable by agencies.

Summary

It needs to be emphasized that these four broad approaches to eclecticism are not mutually exclusive and "the distinctions may be largely semantic and conceptual, not particularly functional, in practice" (Norcross, 2005, p. 10). For example, it is unlikely that models within technical eclecticism and common factors approaches totally ignore theory, and it is quite likely that all of the approaches to eclecticism incorporate an emphasis on common factors.

We should note that there is another trend within the overall trend toward eclecticism, which is the development of eclectic/integrative therapies for specific populations and problems. Prominent examples of these include Linehan's (1993; Heard & Linehan, 2005) dialectical behavior therapy (DBT) for borderline personality disorder, McCullough's (2000, 2006) cognitive behavioral analysis system of psychotherapy (CBASP) for chronic depression, and Wolfe's (2005) integrative psychotherapy for anxiety disorders.

We do not count these eclectic/integrative therapies for specific populations and problems as a fifth classification of approaches to eclecticism because each of these more specific therapies can be subsumed under one of the four broader approaches to eclecticism. For example, DBT and CBASP can be classified as assimilative integration models because, although they integrate a number of different theories, their primary theoretical base is cognitive behavioral. Wolfe's therapy for anxiety, however, can be classified as a theoretical integration model because it blends psychodynamic and cognitive behavioral views of and treatment strategies for anxiety.

Finally, we would like to note that research on eclectic/integrative models has increased substantially over the years, although it still lags behind research on single theory approaches. In a review of research on eclectic/integrative therapies, Schottenbauer et al. (2005) concluded that there is substantial empirical support (i.e., four or more randomized controlled studies) for seven such therapies, some empirical support (i.e., one to four randomized controlled studies) for another 13, and preliminary empirical support (i.e., studies with nonrandomized control group or no control group) for another seven. In 1992, Lambert (1992) predicted:

> to the extent that eclectic therapies provide treatment that includes substantial overlap with traditional methods that have been developed and tested, they rest on a firm empirical base, and they should prove to be at least as effective as traditional school-based therapies. (p. 121)

It would seem that Lambert was right. Still, we agree with those researchers who contend that it would be more productive to focus research on exploring common factors and therapist factors that impact on outcome than continuing to focus on validating individual models of therapy, whether these are single theory or eclectic models.

RELATIONSHIP-BASED THEORETICAL ECLECTICISM: OUR APPROACH

Given our commitment to the spirit of eclecticism, as well as the obvious overlap among the various approaches to eclecticism, we believe there is value in all four approaches discussed in this chapter. Although our approach to eclecticism incorporates some aspects of all of the approaches identified in the literature, it is closest to the common factors approaches. Similar to common factors models, our approach to eclecticism embraces the prime importance of the helping relationship. We believe that a warm, genuine, trusting, empathic relationship is necessary, and sometimes sufficient, for good helping outcomes. Also, similar to the CDOI clinical work common factors model, our approach to eclecticism is critical of an overreliance on theory and values the artistic, reflective, intuitive-inductive processes of collaboratively building theories that fit the circumstances of each unique client. We agree with Cameron and Keenan (2010) who contended that a common factors model is "consistent with social work values, ethics, and practice wisdom from social work's traditions (that is, start where the client is, respect for the dignity of each person, the importance of relationships, and so forth)" (p. 64; see Cameron [2014] and Cameron & Keenan [2009, 2010, 2013] for an example of the application of the general common factors model to social work practice).

We think, however, that our approach to eclecticism does not fit neatly into the common factors category of approaches because our use of theory differs in some important ways from these approaches (see discussion later in this chapter). We think that our approach to eclecticism is distinct enough from the four approaches currently identified in the literature, and that it has enough merits, to warrant a fifth classification of eclectic practice, which we call *relationship-based theoretical eclecticism*.

Our relationship-based theoretically eclectic approach values the potential relevance of all theories and promotes the use of multiple theories and their associated techniques with individual clients. The essence of theoretical eclecticism is to consider the relevance of multiple theoretical frameworks to each client's problem situation in order to develop, collaboratively with the client, a more complex, comprehensive understanding that fits for the client and then to choose intervention strategies or techniques that fit with this in-depth understanding. As noted, however, our generalist-eclectic approach to practice does not rely solely on the use of theory to develop in-depth understanding and choose intervention strategies. The eclectic use of theory is complemented by artistic, reflective, intuitive-inductive processes, all of which are guided by the problem-solving model.

Comparison of Relationship-Based Theoretical Eclecticism to the Four Major Approaches to Eclecticism

Our approach to eclecticism is different from technical eclecticism in that it emphasizes the use of multiple theoretical perspectives, rather than focusing primarily on the techniques that are derived from theories and matching these to client characteristics or problems. It is different from theoretical integration because it does not attempt to synthesize or "smush" theories. Relationship-based theoretical eclecticism is different from assimilative integration in that it does not promote primary reliance on one theory of practice. Similar to these three approaches to eclecticism, however, our approach supports the idea of drawing techniques from a wide variety of theories, depending on their fit for particular clients. In contrast to some models in these approaches, however, our approach to matching techniques to client variables (e.g., coping style, level of resistance, stage of change) relies at least as much on worker judgment as empirical evidence.

There are two reasons why we do not favor an exclusive reliance on empirical evidence for choosing techniques. First, we agree with Stiles et al. (1995) and Wampold and Imel (2015) who contended that there is not enough empirical evidence to warrant firm decisions about such matching of techniques to client variables. Second, we do not like the mechanistic flavor of some prescriptive matching models because individual clients are too unique to rely on formulaic decisions about a certain type of intervention for a certain type of client or problem.

For these reasons, we favor what has been called *responsive matching* (Stiles et al., 1995). "Responsive matching is often done intuitively, we suspect, as practitioners draw techniques from their repertoire to fit their momentary understanding of a client's needs" (Stiles et al., 1995, p. 265). This type of matching should draw on theory and empirical findings but is more tentative and open to modification based on sensitivity to the client's response: "It is grounded in both theory and observation of the individual case" (Stiles et al., 1995, p. 265). In the same vein, Garfield (1995) has argued that:

> In the absence of research data, the therapist has to rely on his own clinical experi-ence and evaluations, or on his best clinical judgment ... and make whatever modi-fications seem to be necessary in order to facilitate positive movement in therapy. (p. 218)

Such an approach fits well with our valuing of the artistic, reflective, intuitive-inductive aspects of practice.

As mentioned, our approach to eclecticism has the most similarities with common factors approaches, particularly with regard to the emphasis placed on the worker–client relationship. Similar to all common factors approaches, and supported by a vast body of research, we empha-size the importance of a trusting, collaborative, supportive, warm, empathic helping relation-ship that is focused on instilling hope, boosting morale, and empowering the client. Other common factors that have received strong empirical support, and that we endorse, include addressing and resolving problems in the worker–client relationship (Norcross & Wampold, 2011), achieving consensus on problem formulation and goals (Ackerman et al., 2001; Norcross & Wampold, 2011), soliciting and responding supportively to client feedback (Miller et al., 2005; Norcross & Wampold, 2011), supporting emotional expression/catharsis, providing the client with mastery experiences (Lambert, 2013b), and helping clients attribute change to their own efforts (Weinberger, 1993). Also, we agree with Wampold's (2001) recommendation that, at least in parity with the emphasis placed on learning theory and technique, clinical practitioners should be trained to "appreciate and be skilled in the common ... core therapeutic skills, includ-ing empathic listening and responding, developing a working alliance, working through one's own issues, ... and learning to be self-reflective about one's work" (pp. 229–230).

Relationship-based theoretical eclecticism differs, however, from most common factors approaches in how theory is used in practice. Although Garfield's (1995) model does support the eclectic use of theory, this is largely with regard to choosing techniques and procedures for intervention. Curiously, in Garfield's (1995) book, there is virtually no discussion of using vari-ous theoretical perspectives in the assessment process to develop understanding of the client's situation, which is a central feature of our approach.

Although the common factors/contextual model of Frank and Frank (1991) and Wampold and Imel (2015) espouses the value of multiple theoretical perspectives, there are important dif-ferences between their use of theory and ours. Wampold and Imel (2015) and Frank and Frank (1991) argued that practitioners should learn as many therapy models as possible so that they can better match or modify a model to fit clients' worldview or understanding of their prob-lems. This follows from Frank's (1961; Frank & Frank, 1991) use of the word *myth* to underscore his contention that the accuracy of a theoretical rationale for the client's problem is less impor-tant than its plausibility in the eyes of the client. He argued that any explanation of their diffi-culties that clients can accept alleviates distress and engenders hope. Thus, Frank allowed for the therapist to "persuade" clients that their theoretical rationale makes sense or to modify theirr preferred theoretical understanding to fit better with the clients' understanding.

What is missing from the common factors/contextual model is the emphasis our relation-ship-based theoretical eclecticism places on an open, holistic assessment that is conducted col-laboratively with the client. In this process, the views of both worker and client are considered together with multiple theoretical perspectives in an effort to build a comprehensive and shared understanding of the client's situation. This process allows for the development of understand-ing by both worker and client that may be different from and/or more comprehensive than either of their initial understandings of the problem. A more comprehensive understanding of the problem situation can lead to formulation of strategies for intervention that have a higher likelihood for success. We agree that it is necessary to eventually arrive at an understanding of the problem that fits for the client, but we think that an open, collaborative exploration/assessment can not only expand awareness of the problem and potential solutions but can also foster the development of a strong therapeutic alliance and a sense of empowerment for the client, all of which help to overcome demoralization and instill hope.

One of the most important distinguishing features of our approach to eclecticism, which stems from its grounding in social work's generalist perspective, is that it is broader in focus and scope of intervention than most of the approaches to eclecticism that are in the clinical psychology literature. The generalist perspective of social work demands a holistic, person-in-environment focus that is sensitive to issues of diversity, oppression, and empowerment. It necessitates that direct practice be viewed broadly. Thus, as mentioned earlier, we think that the mandate and role of clinical social work include helping clients to meet basic needs by providing them with or linking them to resources and services, engaging in social advocacy, and supporting clients to engage in broader social change efforts.

Although some might view the trends in eclecticism as an incursion by psychologists into the domain of social work, we welcome this broadened understanding of eclecticism in direct practice by an allied helping profession with the hope that all helping professionals can move together in such a direction.

One potential drawback to relationship-based theoretical eclecticism, which is also shared by the common factors and technical eclecticism approaches, is that without a primary theoretical base (as in assimilative integration), or a synthesis of two or three theoretical bases (as in theoretical integration), there can be a lack of structure and guidelines for practice. In our approach, however, this is remedied by the use of social work's general problem-solving model. As explained earlier, the problem-solving model provides structure and guidelines for practice across all the phases of helping (from engagement to termination), but these are general and flexible enough to allow for an eclectic use of theory and techniques. We think that the use of the problem-solving model to guide practice in our relationship-based theoretically eclectic approach is better than using a primary theoretical base, as in assimilative integration, or using a synthesis of theories, as in theoretical integration. The latter approaches are less theoretically open and have more theoretical biases than a theoretically eclectic approach that uses a problem-solving model. Our use of the problem-solving model has parallels to Garfield's (1995) common factors approach, which provides general guidelines for what he calls "the stages of the therapeutic process" (beginning, middle, later, and termination stages).

SUMMARY

This chapter has provided an overview of our generalist-eclectic approach to direct practice. It has included a description of the elements of a generalist social work perspective that are central to our approach, a delineation of the distinctive aspects of our generalist-eclectic approach, an overview of the rationale for and trend toward eclecticism in direct practice, a review of the major approaches to eclecticism in the literature, and a discussion of relationship-based theoretical eclecticism—our particular approach to eclecticism. It was beyond the scope of this chapter to discuss many of the topics in the depth that they deserve. Readers are directed to the literature cited in our discussions for a more detailed review of topics that are of interest to them. In the next chapter, the types, levels, and classifications of theories for direct practice are discussed in an effort to demystify theory and facilitate its use in practice. In addition, a critical examination of how and the extent to which theory is used in practice is presented, and a complementary, intuitive-inductive approach that represents the art of practice is considered.

KEY REFERENCES

Only key references appear in the print edition. The full reference list appears in the digital product found on http://connect.springerpub.com/content/book/978-0-8261-6556-5/part/sec01/chapter/ch01

Ackerman, S. J., Benjamin, L. S., Beutler, L. E., Gelso, C. J., Goldfried, M. R., Hill, C., Lambert, M. J., Norcross, J. C., Orlinsky, D. E., & Rainer, J. (2001). Empirically supported therapy relationships: Conclusions and recommendations of the Division 29 Task Force. *Psychotherapy*, *38*, 495–497.

Alford, B. A. (1995). Introduction to the special issue: Psychotherapy integration and cognitive psychotherapy. *Journal of Cognitive Psychotherapy*, *9*, 147–151.

Asay, T. P., & Lambert, M. J. (2001). Therapist relational variables. In D. J. Cain & J. Seeman (Eds.), *Humanistic psychotherapies: Handbook of research and practice* (pp. 531–558). American Psychological Press.

Barlow, D. H. (2000). Evidence-based practice: A world view. *Clinical Psychology: Science and Practice*, *7*, 241–242.

Beutler, L. E. (1983). *Eclectic psychotherapy: A systematic approach*. Pergamon.

Beutler, L. E. (1991). Have all won and must all have prizes? Revisiting Luborsky et al.'s verdict. *Journal of Consulting and Clinical Psychology*, *59*, 226–232.

Beutler, L. E., & Clarkin, J. (1990). *Systematic treatment selection: Toward targeted therapeutic interventions*. Brunner Mazel.

Beutler, L. E., Consoli, A. J., & Lane, G. (2005). Systematic treatment selection and prescriptive psychotherapy. In J. C. Norcross & M. R. Goldfried (Eds.), *Handbook of psychotherapy integration* (2nd ed., pp. 121–146). Oxford University Press.

Beutler, L. E., & Harwood, T. M. (1995). Prescriptive psychotherapies. *Applied and Preventive Psychology*, *4*, 89–100.

Beutler, L. E., & Harwood, T. M. (2000). *Prescriptive psychotherapy*. Oxford University Press.

2

The Problem-Solving Model: A Framework for Integrating the Science and Art of Practice

Kristin W. Bolton and Peter Lehmann

LEARNING OBJECTIVES

- Understand the role of problem-solving in social work practice
- Understand the historical development of the problem-solving model
- Understand the different phases of a problem-solving model

INTRODUCTION

The term "problem-solving" has a slightly different meaning depending on which discipline it refers to. A cursory look suggests that there are several professions that use the term as part of their nomenclature. Curiously, a reference to social work is absent and there is no mention of it in the discussion of psychology. In spite of this, the term problem-solving has been and, in many respects, continues to be part of the social work practice literature even though as Shier (2017, p. 397) noted, "problem-solving has been little explored in relation to therapeutic intervention." Despite this, and ever since Perlman (1957) promoted a problem-solving process for social casework (i.e., direct social work practice), we believe that the problem-solving model can continue to develop into an important feature of social work practice. As summarized by McMahon (1996, p. 35), the problem-solving model has been called the general method of social work because it "may be utilized with individuals, groups, families, or communities" (McMahon, 1996, p. 35).

In this chapter, we begin by (a) making an argument via the practice of social work for the use of a problem-solving approach; (b) reviewing the early development of the problem-solving model for social work practice; (c) summarizing the recent shift in the problem-solving model including a summary of the evidence base for the use of this approach in social work practice, which we liken to an interdisciplinary social science process that will be helpful to social workers (Shier, 2017); and finally (d) discussing the phases of a problem-solving model (i.e., engagement; data collection and assessment; planning, contracting, and intervention; and evaluation and termination).

An Argument for the Use of Problem-Solving

It should go without saying that modern contemporary social work continues to have as its core values respect for the client and allowing the client to determine their own course of life. Thus, problem-solving may also be included as promoting a similar trajectory with clients. Thus, we offer a brief number of arguments for the continued attention for social work practice.

First, almost 60 years have passed since Perlman (1957) noted "a conception of human life as being in itself a problem-solving process" (p. 53). Certainly, this foreshadowed the very beginnings of generalist models of social work practice extending the use of a problem-solving process, by one name or another, to work with all levels of client systems (groups, families, organizations, and communities).

The term *problem-solving method* is meant to convey the notion that problem-solving is not a theory per se; rather, it is "a series of interactions between the client system and the practitioner, involving integration of feeling, thinking and doing, guided by a purpose and directed toward achieving an agreed-upon goal" (McMahon, 1996, p. 43). Thus, the problem-solving model is a critically important element in our generalist-eclectic approach to direct practice because its flexible structure and general guidelines for practice facilitate an eclectic use of theory and technique (the science of practice), and the use of reflective, intuitive-inductive processes (the art of practice).

Third, In the last five decades, the problem-solving model has continued to be revised and redefined, reflecting a shift in social work practice and the social sciences that is far less focused on the early psychodynamic foundations and dysfunction and more focused toward positive and healthy outcomes. Here, a more contemporary approach to problem-solving aims to reduce psychopathology by supporting new positive behaviors in a direction that maximizes one's quality of life and well-being (Nezu et al., 2013). This shift has likely come from the gradual focus on identifying the cognitive processes that maintain self-control/behavior change, along with the positive skills leading to problem-solving.

Fourth, eclectic practice does not enjoy the clear structure and explicit guidelines for practice that are afforded by following a single theory. We propose the use of a contemporary problem-solving model to help remedy the difficulties of eclectic practice. The phases of the problem-solving model (from collaborative engagement to termination) provide a flexible structure and general guidelines for practice while allowing for the eclectic application of theories and techniques.

Finally, Pierce (2012) has described the problem-solving model as pragmatic, effective, and easy to learn. He has suggested that using this approach does not take years of training and can be used efficiently in many different practice settings, often taking minimal time to implement. What at times may intuitively feel like complexity can be resolved via a straightforward manner. For example, clients may disclose life problems and not know where to start to resolve them. A problem-solving approach allows clients to break down a big problem into smaller, potentially more solvable problems, or may enable clients to brainstorm ideas for change or what could be different. Here, problem-solving through a questioning process such as probing ("How do you typically sort things out?") or reflective ("What are your best skills when it comes to managing these sorts of tough problems?") can sometimes break the impasse. We suggest that some of the general guidelines that the problem-solving process provides for assessment allow for the tentative application of multiple theoretical perspectives to help develop understanding of each unique client situation. Similarly, the general guidelines for intervention in the problem-solving model allow for the eclectic use of techniques from different theories to help clients overcome or cope more effectively with problems (we liken this to an interdisciplinary social science process that will be helpful to social workers [Shier, 2017]).

To summarize, the knowledge base of effective problem-solving of any kind might be construed as the rigorous blending of knowledge and skill with imagination and creativity. Following this line of thinking, we believe that the effectiveness of a problem-solving approach will depend upon blending the scientific (theoretical/technical) and relationship aspects of practice. Our review next considers the early development of social work's response to problem-solving, followed by changes within psychology that today continue to be applicable.

EARLY DEVELOPMENT: PERLMAN'S PROBLEM-SOLVING MODEL

The application of the problem-solving model to social work practice was first suggested by Perlman (1957) in her book *Social Casework: A Problem-Solving Process*. Perlman was influenced by Dewey's (1933) description of learning as a problem-solving process. She believed that the operations of casework are essentially those of the process of problem-solving (p. v). Perlman's problem-solving model represented an attempt to integrate or at least bridge the differences between the two dominant schools of social casework of the time. Perlman had been trained in the scientifically oriented Freudian or Diagnostic school of social casework but was attracted to many of the ideas of the humanistically oriented Functional or Rankian school of social casework. Perlman (1957) believed that the problem-solving model met the need

> for some dependable structure to provide the inner organization of the (casework) process … In no sense is such a structure a stamped out routine. It is rather an underlying guide, a pattern for action which gives general form to the caseworkers inventiveness or creativity. (p. vi)

She blended the Diagnostic school's emphasis on applying psychodynamic theory through the scientific process of study, diagnosis, and treatment, with the Functional school's emphasis on starting where the client is in the present, partializing problems into manageable pieces, and developing a genuinely supportive relationship that serves to motivate clients and free their potential for growth (Perlman, 1986). Perlman (1986) has identified the problem-solving model as an eclectic construct, with theoretical roots in psychodynamic ego psychology and selected ideas from existential, learning, and ecological systems theories.

Toward the close of her professional career, Perlman (1970) stressed that the problem-solving process does not always take place as a linear, logical progression and that in the spontaneity of action (p. 158), the steps or phases can blend together, occur out of order, and repeat in a cyclical manner. In professional helping terms, these steps/phases included: (a) identifying the problem, (b) identifying the person's subjective experience of the problem, (c) examining the causes and effects of the problem in the person's life, (d) considering the pros and cons of various courses of action, (e) choosing and enacting a course of action, and (f) assessing the effectiveness of the action.

In addition, Perlman (1970) emphasized that problem-solving is not just a cognitive, rational process and that the development of a good relationship with clients is intertwined with the problem-solving process:

> A relationship is the continuous context within which problem-solving takes place. It is, at the same time, the emerging product of mutual problem-solving efforts; and simultaneously it is the catalytic agent. (p. 151)

Perlman's conceptualization of and central ideas about the relationship places an important emphasis on collaboration and partnership between the worker and the client in all phases of the process—in Perlman's model there was more of an emphasis on the worker's primary responsibility for assessment and treatment planning (Compton & Galaway, 1999). We think these changes in emphasis are positive and they are reflected in our current conception of the problem-solving process. We understand and support the trend toward depathologizing the concerns that clients typically bring to counseling—and it should be noted that Perlman was a pioneer in this regard. Rather than deny the existence of problems and the utility of a problem-solving process, however, we prefer to promote the understanding that problems are a normal part of life. We agree with Compton and Galaway's (1994) early contention that "describing a change process as a problem-solving model is quite different from characterizing it as a problem-focus model … . the model might well be called problem-solving but strength-focused" (p. 7). The reader is referred to other social practice texts (e.g., Hepworth et al., 2002; Locke, Garrison, & Winship, 1998; O'Melia, DuBois, & Miley, 1994; Sheafor & Horejsi, 2006) that provide a more detailed but similar review of the problem-solving phases.

CURRENT DEVELOPMENT: THE CONCEPTUAL AND EMPIRICAL EXPANSION OF THE PROBLEM-SOLVING MODEL

Although the basic steps of problem-solving remain fairly constant for social work, within the last 40 years the conceptual underpinnings have evolved apart from the early writings of Perlman (Shier, 2017). Essentially, there have been at least three developments to explain problem-solving, which will be relevant to the practicing social work.

In its current state, problem-solving is seen as

> the self-directed process by which individuals attempt to identify, discover, and/or develop adaptive coping solutions for problems, both acute and chronic that they encounter in every day living. (Nezu et al., 2013, p. 8)

Here, problem-solving has long been used interchangeably with social problem-solving (D'Zurilla & Nezu, 1982) as a process that occurs for individuals in their natural environment or as has been termed the real world. Thus, adaptation to problems comes in part from functioning in the real-life social environment (i.e., the impersonal, intrapersonal, interpersonal, and broader community). The conceptual underpinnings of problem-solving has undergone some iterations and currently has established itself as a significant evidence-based practice model that continues to be useful for a generalist social work practice. In the following we summarize the three expansion phases of problem-solving as a model of practice.

Phase 1: Social Problem-Solving

In 1971, D'Zurilla and Goldfried published a first review of the theory and research related to problem-solving in the real world (later termed *social problem-solving*). This review was part of the growing change in the field of behavior modification toward a greater understanding of cognitive processes in an attempt to help develop new skills related to self-control that might also be generalized to other behavior changes.

The theory on which problem-solving therapy (PST) had been revised included three major concepts: (a) social problem-solving, (b) the problem, and (c) the solution, as summarized by D'Zurilla and Nezu (2010).

Social problem-solving was seen as dealing with all types of real-life problems, including impersonal problems (e.g., personal/intrapersonal problems [cognitive, emotional, behavioral, health], as well as interpersonal problems (e.g., interpersonal disputes, family/marital conflicts) along with problem-solving solutions. A "problem" (or problematic situation) is defined as an imbalance or discrepancy in, say, the environment or within a person between adaptive demands and the availability of effective coping responses. Any problem might be time limited or an ongoing series of challenges that include obstacles and/or roadblocks. A solution is one that achieves the problem-solving goal (e.g., changing the situation for the better, reducing negative emotions, increasing positive emotions) and that also maximizes positive consequences and minimizes negative consequences.

Based on the review herein, the authors developed a prescriptive model of problem-solving composed of problem orientation and problem-solving skills. *Problem orientation* consisted of a set of common cognitive-emotional schemas that reflected a person's beliefs, appraisals, and feeling about problems. *Problem-solving skills* referred to a number of cognitive and behavioral activities aimed at finding effective solutions or ways of coping with them. The model summarized four skills for problem-solving including defining the problem, coming up with alternative solutions, decision-making, and implementing new solutions.

A major contribution of this development was the authors' integration of the work of Lazarus (1999), which drew on a relational model of stress. Here, "stress" was seen as a person–environment relationship in which demands are appraised by the person as taxing or exceeding coping resources and threatening their well-being (Lazarus & Folkman, 1984). In this relational problem-solving model, stress was viewed as a function of the reciprocal relations among three major variables: (a) stressful life events, (b) emotional stress/well-being, and (c) problem-solving coping. Their clinical application produced a generic relational problem-solving manual (D'Zurilla & Nezu, 2007) consisting of 14 modules with the explicit goal to increase positive problem-solving and decrease negative orientation through the development of skills that could be applied to every day life. Consistent with the technical and relationship stance cited previously, there is a specific emphasis on the importance of developing a positive client–practitioner relationship and assessment process along with a host of cognitive and practical strategies to mitigate problems.

Phase 2: Social Problem-Solving and Neurodevelopment

More recently, Nezu et al. (2013) have built on the social problem-solving and relational problem-solving model and added a neurodevelopmental component. This heuristic model is seen as more expansive in nature, integrating individual problem-solving within a biopsychosocial framework. In this case, the authors focus on the relationship between psychosocial and neurobiological variables that impact stress, emotions, coping, and outcomes.

The diathesis-stress model of problem-solving is made up of three separate but interrelated systems including (a) the distal variable where the individual's early life history and experience in combination with their genotype create vulnerabilities for ongoing negative coping and problem-solving, (b) the proximal variable in which major events and daily problems interact with one another, and (c) the immediate or microanalytic variable of how both systems are mediated by various neurobiological functions (e.g., amygdala vs. cortex processing).

In system (a), one's genotype or the genetic constitution of an individual in combination with early life stress may produce certain biological vulnerabilities that will influence one's reaction or coping with stress at different points in the life cycle (e.g., adolescence, early or late adulthood) as it relates to social problem-solving. As an example, a case is made in understanding the coping of children responding to stressful life events. The authors make the point that because a child's brain is still developing, the role of social problem-solving may be limited, overtaxing coping responses with resulting sensitivity to negative biological consequences.

With respect to system (b), the authors focus on two accumulated sources of stress, major negative life events and chronic daily problems, increasing the likelihood of developing major clinical problems such as depression. This occurs through activation of one's biological systems, including the sympathoadrenal medullary (SAM) and the hypothalamic–pituitary–adrenal (HPA) axes. One outcome is the activation of the flight–fight response. The point made here is that chronic stress can result in much poorer social problem-solving and subsequent negative physical and immunological health outcomes.

System (c) moves beyond an earlier analysis of problem-solving of being a primary cognitive process (Lazarus, 1999). Here, problem-solving is seen to be mediated by a host of neurobiological processes involving brain functioning. The brain acts as a conduit for processing stress, emotional reactivity, and social problem-solving via the thalamus, amygdala, and frontal cortex. This process is described as two pathways to emotions (LeDoux, 1996): the low road that can trigger fast or automatic reactions that are not helpful to problem-solving, or the high road in which emotional processing can be analyzed, reasoned, and logically thought through with respect to solving issues.

Nezu et al. (2013) have revised the practical application of social problem-solving in Phase 1 to a shorter manualized process that relies on emotional regulation and positive thinking as a core feature of their work. Again, the work comprises and highlights the importance of a respectful therapeutic relationship that is oriented toward setting goals for the future. Skills such as open questioning and active listening with attention to detailing subjective experiences are seen as an essential

In this model, effective problem-solving and decision-making is as much an emotional as cognitive response and ultimately impacts problem-solving. Thus, for example, minimal emotional responding coupled with poor problem-solving may be moderated by how neurological systems process information. Conversely, effective problem-solving may be a function of processing both emotional responses and how one solves problems and makes decisions.

Phase 3: Emotion-Centered Problem-Solving Therapy

The last and most recent development of PST has been termed *emotion-centered problem-solving therapy (EC-PST*; Nezu & Nezu Maguth, 2019). The authors see their work as an "evolutionary process" (p. x) as to what came before. The current approach puts an emphasis on teaching individuals to understand and manage their emotional reactions to stressful events than what was included in former problem-solving protocols. EC-PST then is seen more as a psychosocial intervention within a social learning framework. Clients have a set of skills aimed at building their ability to cope effectively with a variety of life stressors. To compare the current evolution of EC-PST with their former work, two goals of Nezu and Nezu Maguth's work are summarized and include:

> "1. Successful adoption of adaptive problem-solving attitudes (e.g., optimism, enhanced self-efficacy, recognition and appreciation of the notion that problems are a normal aspect of living;
> 2. Effective implementation of certain behaviors (e.g., emotional regulation, planful problem-solving) as a means of coping with life stress and thereby attenuating the negative effects of stress on physical and mental well-being." (p. 6)

The current model carries over the diathesis stress model and neurodevelopmental perspective from Phase 2 with greater reference to brain sciences including neuroplasticity. Emphasis is also given to developing the therapeutic relationship with detail toward empathy and building hope. Clearly in this text, the authors are conveying that EC-PST is not mechanistic and rather is interactive and experiential where clients are allowed to learn, grow, and build new skills.

EC-PST consists of the following major interventions across treatment. What follows has been updated from earlier work (Nezu et al., 2013):

1. introduction, relationship development with the client and assessment/treatment planning;
2. Toolkit 1—Training in problem-solving, multitasking, and overcoming cognitive overload;
3. Toolkit 2—The Stop, Slowdown, Think, Act (SSTA) method of problem-solving under stress: overcoming emotional dysregulation and ineffective problem-solving coping;
4. Tookit 3—Healthy thinking and positive imagery: overcoming negative thinking and low motivation
5. Toolkit 4—Planful problem-solving and fostering effective problem-solving;
6. Guided practice; and
7. Future forecasting and termination.

Each of the interventions are manualized with handouts and exercises that are facilitated by the social worker/therapist. It should be noted that EC-PST also includes an integrated host of mindfulness and experiential exercises that can be used in session or for home use.

Empirical Support for the Problem-Solving Approach

In the last 40 years, the scientific and clinical application of PST has been a relatively unknown but burgeoning field to the social work profession. Since the initial publication of the model

(D'Zurilla & Goldfried, 1971), major summary reviews of empirical studies in the literature have been carried out and published in multiple formats encompassing various professional fields including social work. Although a detailed summary of the research evidence is beyond the scope of this chapter, the outcome literature remains broad featuring various clinical problems (e.g., health and behavioral health) and populations (e.g., older adults, children, adolescents, ethnic minorities, veterans, the disabled). To date, the most rigorous evaluations carried out include systematic reviews and meta-analyses. As an example, extensive systematic reviews have been done evaluating PST and depression (Nieuwsma et al., 2012; Simon et al., 2015), older adults (Kiosses & Alexopoulos, 2014), diabetes and self-management (Fitzpatrick et al., 2013), vision-impaired adults (Holloway et al., 2015), adolescent suicidal behaviors (Speckens & Hawton, 2005), and problem behaviors in school settings (Merrill et al., 2017). Likewise, a number of meta-analyses have been carried out in relation to PST and depression (Bell & D'Zurilla, 2009; Cuijpers et al., 2007, 2018), depression and anxiety disorders (Cape et al., 2010; Zhang et al., 2018), depression and the elderly (Kirkham et al., 2016), primary care settings (Linde et al., 2015), and school settings (Barnes et al., 2018). The studies listed do not include the wide ranges of clinical issues and trials published in texts using a problem-solving approach (e.g., Chang et al., 2004; McMurran & McGuire, 2005; Nezu et al., 2013).

From the host of studies cited earlier, there appears to be overwhelming evidence supporting the efficacy of PST across age groups, targeted populations, and clinical problems. These studies point to a flexibility of applications that appear to reduce problem-defined behaviors. Clearly, problem-solving as it is now seen represents an evolving model, applicable of being helpful to social workers practicing with difficult and complex issues.

THE STAGES OF PROBLEM-SOLVING FOR GENERALIST SOCIAL WORK PRACTICE

The final section of this chapter summarizes the stages of problem-solving for generalist practice. Different examples of these stages in the problem-solving process proliferate in the social work literature. Here, one can find the term "stages" identified as cycles, steps, phases, or processes with a host of numerically different methods from beginning to end. As Sheafor and Horejsi (2006) have noted, subsequent to Perlman's description of the phases of the problem-solving process, "various authors divided these phases into more discrete units, described them in more detail, and demonstrated their application in a range of helping approaches and in work with client systems of various sizes" (p. 125). We have divided the problem-solving process into four phases for the purposes of our discussion. These phases are: (a) collaborative engagement and problem definition; (b) data collection and assessment; (c) planning, contracting, and intervention; and (d) evaluation and termination. In the following, each phase is reviewed briefly with regard to general goals and strategies for achieving them. The problem-solving approach contains no assumptions about the causes of and solutions to client problems. Instead, the general guidelines of the problem-solving process provide for assessment that may allow for the tentative application to help develop understanding of each unique client situation. Similarly, the general guidelines for intervention in the problem-solving model allow for the eclectic use of techniques from different theories to help clients overcome or cope more effectively with problems.

Collaborative Engagement and Problem Definition

We agree with Perlman's (1979) contention that the social work relationship is the heart of the helping process and we believe that the engagement phase is crucial to creating the conditions from which a good helping relationship can grow. Perlman's contention along with the most recent work of Nezu and Nezu Maguth (2019) about the importance of relationship has long been supported by the literature on collaborative working relationships or therapeutic alliance. Indeed, Wampold (2001) and colleagues (e.g., Fluckiger et al., 2012, 2020; Wampold & Imel, 2015) have long argued that the quality of the alliance between client and practitioner can predict outcomes of the helping process.

We see alliance/engagement as a complex but important process that may begin prior to meeting the client for the first time. Workers will often have some information (e.g., via a referral letter or intake assessment) that allows them to do some preliminary preparation, which "involves the worker's effort to get in touch with potential feelings and concerns that the client may bring to the helping encounter" (Shulman, 1999, p. 44). If referral information is available, this may include a tentative ecological assessment of the particular problems and life circumstances of clients.

At the same time, it is important for workers to focus on themselves; that is, to become more aware of how they are feeling with regard to what they know about the client (e.g., presenting problem, cultural background, voluntary versus involuntary status). It is particularly important for workers to prepare themselves to work with clients who are involuntary and who may present as being hesitant about the helping process. Understandably, workers are often leery of dealing directly with such issues; however, if these issues are not discussed openly and worked through, engagement can remain superficial. In reflecting on to how one might engage with such clients around problem-solving, it is necessary to prepare for responding empathically and in a transparent manner without judgment versus defensively. The intent of this process prior to initial contact with clients is for workers to establish a positive internal condition that can facilitate the engagement process.

The first session with clients is important for setting the tone, the focus, and the parameters for the helping process. Wherever the first meeting may take place, it is important for the worker to attend to basic issues such as privacy and comfort. If the meeting is in the worker's agency, it is appropriate for the worker to play host and attend to social amenities. For example, a handshake with the initial introduction is usually appropriate, as is some brief social chitchat (e.g., commenting on the weather or asking clients if they had any trouble finding the agency) to "break the ice." Following this, a number of basic issues need to be attended to. Workers need to clarify their role and purpose and reach for client feedback about these issues (Shulman, 1999). Clients' problem situations need to be explored in more depth, and it is important to establish some tentative goals. Questions such as "If our work together is helpful for you, what will be different? What do you think needs to be changed in your life? or What will be important for us to work on together?" are sample questions ,setting the stage for building a helping relationship and working on what the client wants.

In attending to these engagement tasks, it is imperative that the worker's manner reflects warmth, empathy, and respect for the client. Workers need to normalize clients' problems appropriately, communicate empathy and support for their struggles. This kind of early engagement also includes attention to a client's strengths and coping abilities, reaching out for help, and desire to work on a particular goal for change. Where appropriate, engagement can be deepened by the worker's sensitive exploration of how issues of diversity (e.g., race, culture, class, gender, sexual orientation, physical capacity, age, religion/spirituality) may be related to the presenting problem or to concerns about engaging in counseling.

There is no reason to think that all of these tasks must be accomplished in a first session. We see engagement as an ongoing process that blends together with initial data collection and assessment. In fact, aspects of later phases of problem-solving are also evident in the engagement phase. For example, the provision of empathy and support is a type of intervention that can have an important impact even as early as the first session. Initial planning and contracting are evident in arriving at a tentative agreement to work together. Evaluation should be attended to with respect to eliciting client feedback about the first session, including how it fits with the client's expectations and whether they have any questions or concerns. Also, it is important to address the issue of termination in the first session with respect to the anticipated time frame for working together.

Although relationship building is an ongoing process throughout all phases of the helping process, the important foundations for this process are laid in the engagement phase but continue on throughout the entire helping process. There are a number of general strategies that can be useful in initiating a positive and therapeutic relationship. The value of social worker preparation has already been discussed as a way of developing preparatory empathy and readying oneself psychologically to be supportive and non-defensive. Another related strategy is to explore in the first session the client's thoughts, feelings, and expectations, along with their hopes about coming for counseling. As part of this exploration, it is often helpful to acknowledge and normalize the common difficulty many people have in coming for counseling and to ask about any negative preconceptions or fears about counseling that the client may have. It is also important to ask the client about any prior experience with counseling and what they did or did not like about it. The goal of such discussions is to identify any issues and show an understanding of and empathy for such issues, along with a mutual agreement about a preferred way of working together (e.g., that counseling will be a collaborative problem-solving process and/or that the client will always have the last say about what they will/will not do).

A similar process should be used on an ongoing basis to assess the quality of the helping relationship with a client and to identify and work through any problems. Research has found that problems in helping relationships are rarely identified and discussed and that, unless this happens, the relationship does not improve and the outcome is likely to be poor (Safran et al., 1990). Safran et al. (1990) developed helpful guidelines for addressing and ameliorating "ruptures" in the helping relationship. They suggested that workers should (a) continually watch for and be sensitive to signs of negative reactions from clients, (b) encourage clients to express any negative feelings and show understanding and empathy, (c) validate clients' views and experiences, and (d) take responsibility and apologize for one's contributions to the difficulties. Their research showed that when workers followed these guidelines, initially poor helping relationships could be improved dramatically (see Safran & Muran, 2000, for a more in-depth consideration of repairing relationship ruptures). In a similar vein, a key element in Miller et al.'s (2005) and others' (Hubble et al., 1999; Miller et al., 2013) outcome-informed model is to solicit and respond supportively to client feedback about the therapeutic relationship on an ongoing basis.

Data Collection, Assessment, and Generating Alternative Solutions

Data collection involves fact and information gathering with regard to issues that are most critical to the client's problem situation, and should include a focus on strengths, personal resources, and one's support network, as well as on stressors. Assessment is the culmination of data collection and involves distilling the facts that are most central to the client's worry and developing these into a succinct, coherent summary that reflects the social worker's and client's overall understanding of the problem situation. As mentioned, initial data collection often begins even before the first meeting with a client (e.g., referral information) and it is intertwined with the engagement process. In fact, as Perlman (1970) pointed out, ideally, relationship development and data collection each deepen the other. Data collection and assessment blend together and in some sense continue to evolve throughout the problem-solving process. An assessment leads to an intervention plan but carrying out the intervention plan provides new data that may build on or alter the original assessment.

Our generalist-eclectic approach to practice adheres to a person-in-environment (or ecological systems) view that emphasizes the need to consider the entire range of factors, from micro (e.g., biological and intrapsychic) to macro (e.g., environmental and sociocultural), that could impact positively or negatively on a client's circumstances. The eclectic nature of our approach also necessitates the consideration of possible multiple theoretical perspectives to help develop understanding of client's problem situations. In addition, in order to arrive at a comprehensive assessment, it is usually important to consider client history such as the genogram and their potential social network along with factors that may have impacted on the development of the situation over time. The four Ps—predisposing, precipitating, perpetuating, and protective factors (Weerasekera, 1993)—offer one useful framework for data collection and assessment that integrates the historical dimension, as well as a consideration of strengths (i.e., protective factors). The grid presented in Table 2.1 offers a conceptual framework that combines a consideration of (a) the broad person-in-environment perspective, (b) the range of theoretical perspectives covered in this book, and (c) predisposing, precipitating, perpetuating, and protective factors. Although a grid such as this could prove useful as a tool for organizing data collection, its primary utility is in providing a way of conceptualizing the range of data and perspectives that could be important to understanding any given client's problem situation.

The factors listed in Table 2.1 are only examples of the types of factors that could be considered in data collection and assessment. Obviously, the scope of information that could be relevant to any given client's problem situation is enormous. Although this may conjure the intimidating prospect of a long process of detailed, structured data collection and analysis, in practice most data collection usually flows naturally from allowing and encouraging clients to tell their stories. Aided by sensitive questions and probes that flow from the natural curiosity of the worker and their desire to be more fully understanding, clients' accounts often provide detailed information about the who, what, when, why, where, and how of their problem situations. As the worker and client collaboratively review and summarize their developing understanding of the issues, further questions usually emerge to clarify and deepen understanding.

The grid in Table 2.1 also suggests how workers might use professional knowledge to guide data collection and assessment. First, in exploring the possible predisposing, precipitating, perpetuating, and protective factors related to clients' problem situations, workers should employ a person-in-environment perspective and be cognizant of the possible influence of micro (e.g., biological) and macro (e.g., environmental and sociocultural) factors. Second, workers should also have the option of using their knowledge of various theoretical perspectives to explore the possible impact of a wide variety of factors. This is not to say that workers should explicitly check with clients about every conceivable theoretical explanation for their difficulties. Workers need to use their developing understanding of the client's story in order to ascertain whether certain lines of inquiry seem relevant. For example, if it becomes apparent that there is a clearly identifiable, recent precipitating factor for a client's difficulties and that the client had a high level of social functioning prior to this, then it would make no sense to pursue an exploration of predisposing psychodynamic factors. Thus, workers need to exercise their judgment in order to keep the data collection process focused and pertinent.

The issue of worker judgment is related to the fact that data collection and assessment are also guided by intuitive-inductive processes. As Derezotes (2000) has noted, "of all the artistic factors in social work assessment, probably the most used, yet least recognized, is intuition" (p. 24). Workers often develop intuitive hunches about various aspects of clients' problem situations as they tell their stories. If these are shared tentatively and checked out with clients, this can often lead to deeper understanding. For example, if a client is talking about an intimate relationship in glowing terms but a worker develops a sense that this is masking some underlying ambivalence about the relationship, this thought should be shared tentatively and empathically (e.g., "From how you describe your relationship, it sounds like you and your partner care very much about each other, but I am also hearing that you might have some concerns about the relationship. Is that possible?").

Furthermore, as workers hear more and more of clients stories, they often begin to put pieces together or make links in their minds. This type of inductive thinking should also be checked with clients in a tentative manner. For example, in hearing a client describe a number of different relationships, if a worker develops a sense that there may be an underlying theme of discomfort with intimacy, this idea should also be shared tentatively and empathically (e.g.,

TABLE 2.1 HOLISTIC/ECLECTIC GRID FOR DATA COLLECTION AND ASSESSMENT

	Factors Related to General Person-in-Environment Perspective				Factors Related to Theoretical Perspectives						
	Biological	Environmental	Sociocultural	Ecological Systems	Individual/Family Life Cycle	Psychodynamic	Cognitive-Behavioral	Humanistic	Critical	Postmodern	Couple/Family
Predisposing factors	Genetic vulnerability	Raised in poverty	Member of oppressed group	Social isolation	Problems in earlier stages	Early attachment problems	Poor parental role modeling	Conditions of worth imposed by parent	Capitalist, patriarchal society	Oppressive cultural story	Enmeshment in family of origin
Precipitating factors	Onset of illness	Loss of job	Experience of discrimination	Loss of social support network	Current developmental crisis	Relationship loss or problems	Classical conditioning leading to phobia	Conditions of worth imposed by adult partner	Child protection services involvement	Problem-saturated story	Separation
Perpetuating factors	Chronic mental illness	Inadequate income	Institutional racism	Social isolation	Developmental crises of other family members	Maladaptive interpersonal patterns	Irrational beliefs	Low self-esteem	Internalizing blame	Oppressive internalized view of self	Poor communication
Protective factors	Good health	Adequate income	Connected to/proud of cultural heritage	Strong social support network	Earlier developmental successes	Corrective emotional experience	Positive reinforcement from career	Unconditional positive regard from parent	Involvement in social action/social change	Small victories, unique outcomes	Good couple relationship

Source: Adapted from Weerasekera, P. (1993). Formulation: A multiperspective model. *Canadian Journal of Psychiatry, 38,* 351–358.

"Intimacy can be very uncomfortable for many people and I get the impression you may have struggled with this issue in a number of different relationships").

In the preceding example, if the worker's hypothesis about an underlying discomfort with intimacy was confirmed by the client, the worker's knowledge of psychodynamic theory (Chapter 7) might be used to explore the potential connection with early experiences of intimate relationships as undependable or unsatisfactory. In turn, this theoretically informed exploration might lead to additional theory building that might be shared in conversations with the client. The social worker may hear certain summaries that may be cognitive distortions (Chapter 8; i.e., "No one has ever really asked about my welfare"), which in turn may lead to a dialogue that could broaden narrow thinking (i.e., "What make you say that" or "Tell me about the last time anyone might have come close to showing a small interest in you").

Oftentimes, the data collection and assessment process may involve more than client verbal reports and direct observation of the client. This might include, with client consent, the gathering of information and viewpoints from family members or other professionals who know the client or referral for psychological (e.g., measures of anxiety or depression) or medical (e.g., neurological) testing. Decisions about how much information to collect from the variety of sources available should be based on the joint judgment of the worker and client as to the potential benefits and costs. There are also a number of potentially valuable tools that can be employed to facilitate data collection and assessment. Two such tools commonly used by social workers are the eco-map and the genogram. The eco-map (Hartman, 1978, 1994) depicts clients in their social environment, with attention to identifying supports and stressors (see Chapters 4 and 5). The genogram (McGoldrick & Gerson, 1985; McGoldrick et al., 1999) depicts relationships within a family over two or three generations (see Chapter 5). Another more recently developed tool is the culturagram (Congress, 1994; Congress & Kung, 2005), which helps to understand clients within their cultural context (see Chapter 5).

Although data collection and assessment processes continue to some extent throughout the problem-solving process, this phase culminates in the development of an understanding shared by the worker and client about the client's problem situation. This understanding needs to include an identification of not only the predisposing, precipitating, and perpetuating stressors (micro and macro) but also of the client's strengths and other protective factors (Weerasekera, 1993). The shared nature of this understanding is crucial and can only evolve from a truly collaborative exploration that is grounded in a relationship characterized by mutual trust, liking, and respect. Even when such a strong relationship seems to exist, it is important to check with the client that the general understanding of the problem situation fits for them. Thus, it is helpful to ask questions such as "Does this understanding of your situation fit for you?" or "Is there anything that doesn't fit for you or that I've missed?" (Barnard & Kuehl, 1995).

It is usually helpful, and usually required by agencies, that an assessment be summarized in a structured, written report. There is no definitive structure for an assessment report, but an example of a fairly comprehensive structure is provided in Table 2.2. Again, worker judgment should be used to decide how much detail should be afforded to the various issues that are included in an assessment format. The complexity of human life prevents any client assessment from being definitive and fully comprehensive. To a large degree, however, the effectiveness of the helping process depends on the quality of the assessment because it leads directly to ideas for intervention.

Planning, Contracting, and Solution Implementation

Once the worker and client arrive at a shared understanding of the client's problem situation, they need to plan and contract with each other about a course of action or intervention and then implement the plan. Again, collaboration is key in these processes. The more clients are involved in and take ownership of the plan of action, the more likely it is that they will be motivated to implement the plan. Planning and contracting involve (a) clarifying and prioritizing the

TABLE 2.2 SAMPLE FORMAT FOR AN ASSESSMENT REPORT

Identifying information (name, age, family constellation, employment, etc.)

Referral source and information

Presenting problem(s)

History of:

  Current and previous difficulties and coping

  Family of origin and individual development

  Family development

Personal functioning (strengths and difficulties):

  Physical functioning and health

  Emotional functioning

  Cognitive functioning

  Interpersonal functioning

  Spirituality

  Sociocultural factors (culture, ethnicity, class, gender, sexual orientation, etc.)

  Motivation

  Life cycle stage issues

Family functioning (strengths and difficulties):

  Functioning of various subsystems

  Communication patterns

  Affective expression and involvement

  Role performance

  Values and norms

  Spirituality

  Sociocultural factors

  Life cycle stage issues

Environmental stressors and supports (strengths and difficulties):

  Social supports

  Social stressors

  Economic situation

  Housing and transportation

  Sociocultural factors

Summary/formulation (understanding of presenting problem[s] with regard to predisposing, precipitating, perpetuating, and protective factors)

Goals and intervention plan

problems to be worked on; (b) identifying realistic goals that are concrete, specific, and achievable; (c) considering the pros and cons of various strategies for achieving goals; (d) deciding on a course of action; and (e) specifying the roles and responsibilities of the worker and client and the anticipated time lines for working together. Intervention involves carrying out the plan.

A client's need and preference, as opposed to a worker's theoretical orientation, should determine the goals and the action strategies, as well as the degree to which the plan and contract are specific and explicit. This is not to say that the worker is a silent and passive partner in such determinations. Workers have a right, and in fact a responsibility, to share their viewpoints on goals and action strategies. Ideally, decisions on these issues are consensual; however, where there are differences in opinion, workers should follow client preferences (unless of course these are illegal or involve threat of harm to self or others). As with assessment, planning and contracting should be construed as flexible and open to revision, always being mindful of client input. Clients should be asked questions such as "Do these ideas for addressing your difficulties make sense to you" and "Do you have any other ideas of how to make the changes you want?" (Barnard & Kuehl, 1995).

Planning, contracting, and implementation of solutions should be guided by the assessment. Sometimes, the determination of problems, goals, and action strategies is relatively straightforward. For example, if it has been determined that a client's most pressing problem is related to suicidal ideation, there is then an obvious need to determine risk factors for harm, whether there is a plan and if other life options are available. Most times, problems a client may bring are not easy to clarify or prioritize and solutions can seem hard to reach or a long way away. Nevertheless, the assessment provides a good place to start and the specification of problems to work on along with the potential courses of action should be guided by both deductive/eclectic theory application and intuitive-inductive processes.

The systematic treatment selection (STS) approach of Beutler et al. (2005) and the transtheoretical model (TTM) of Prochaska and DiClemente (2005), both of which were discussed in Chapter 1, offer examples of a deductive theory application approach to the process of intervention (see Chapter 1). Although empirical support has not been firmly established for any of the attempts to match client or problem characteristics with therapeutic approaches, there are a number of promising ideas with intuitive appeal in this regard. A client's natural coping style is one variable to consider in choosing a therapeutic approach. Thus, for example, the STS model suggests that clients who tend to cope by externalizing blame and punishing others are best suited to cognitive-behavioral approaches, whereas clients who tend to cope by internalizing blame and punishing themselves might best be suited to psychodynamic approaches. Another variable to consider in choosing a theory to guide intervention is the level/depth of the client problem. Thus, the TTM model contends that problems at the symptom/situational level are best suited to cognitive-behavioral approaches, whereas problems at the intrapersonal conflict level would be best suited to psychodynamic approaches.

It should be kept in mind that an eclectic use of theory might involve the sequential use and/or the simultaneous application of different theoretical perspectives. With regard to sequencing approaches, although a problem at the level of intrapersonal conflict might suggest a psychodynamic approach, a particular client may not be stable enough to tolerate painful introspection and revisiting difficult childhood issues. A cognitive-behavioral approach to building interpersonal skills and changing irrational beliefs might be a necessary step for preparing a client to do more emotional, insight-oriented work. With regard to simultaneous application of different theoretical perspectives, any combination of approaches may be appropriate to address different aspects of a client's problem situation and assist them in highlighting their inherent and environmental resources. For example, as cognitive-behavioral techniques are used to help a client become aware of irrational thoughts, solution-focused techniques are used to help the client identify exceptions to the problem and associated resources. The holistic/eclectic grid presented in Table 2.1 provides useful guidance to workers in choosing intervention approaches. This type of grid can function to remind workers of the range of theoretical perspectives to choose from, as well as of the possibilities for biological, environmental, and sociocultural intervention.

The helping process is never a straightforward application of theory and technique. Workers need to be reminded that a rigid or formula-like approach to using theory and technique in practice will take away from the collaborative process and that the quality of the relationship with the client is the best predictor of outcome. The complexity of human life precludes certainty in the helping process and necessitates that workers combine their intuition and inductive reasoning with an eclectic use of theory. Thus, throughout the intervention process, workers need to continue to listen, to provide empathy and support, to instill hope, and to use their intuition and commonsense reasoning to help clients achieve their goals. If it becomes apparent that the intervention is not achieving the desired outcome, the plan and contract, as well as the assessment, should be revisited.

Evaluation and Termination

Evaluation is an ongoing process that should begin in the early phases of helping and continue as work makes progress. Evaluation should address the process and outcome of helping: By meeting and engaging with clients are goals being met, and is what one is doing helpful and/or meaningful to the process of change? Workers need to constantly check with clients about their satisfaction with the helping process (e.g., "Are you getting what you need here?," or "How do you feel about our work together thus far?"), and they should use client feedback to make adjustments (this is often referred to as formative evaluation). For example, the work of Scott D. Miller attests to the evidence for client feedback as a form of treatment progress. Here, Miller et al's work (e.g. Duncan et al., 2009; Miller, Hubble, & Chow, 2020; Miller et al., 2015; Prescott et al., 2017) has extensively covered FIT or feedback informed treatment, which has been included in the move towards deliberate practice. Here, evaluation of outcome relates to social workers being to develop those deliberate practice skills (Ericsson et al., 2006) skills by reflecting on and assessing the effectiveness of the interventions in relation to client goals (referred to as summative evaluation).

Evaluation of outcomes may be more or less formal and comprehensive, and as with all aspects of the helping process, clients' needs and preferences should take precedence in such decisions (i.e., the outcome and session rating scales). Outcome evaluation can be as simple as client self-reports and worker judgment. On the other hand, it has become increasingly common to use more formal tools, including standardized rating scales, task achievement scaling, goal attainment scaling, outcome checklists, individualized rating scales, and client satisfaction questionnaires (see Sheafor & Horejsi, 2006, for examples). In some situations, particularly where a client's presenting problems involve risk of harm to self or others, standardized scales and reports from others in the client's social milieu can add valuable information to client self-reports and worker evaluation. Some clients, however, find the use of more formal measurement unnecessary and alienating.

As progress toward achieving client goals becomes evident, and/or as any prescribed time limitations on the helping process approach, the worker and client should begin to discuss and negotiate the end of their work together. As mentioned previously, termination should be addressed at the beginning of the helping process with regard to contracting about the time period of work together. It should also be addressed regularly throughout the helping process by way of periodic discussions about progress toward goals and time limitations (e.g., "Given that we have three sessions left in our time together, what do you see as being most useful for us to work toward?")

Client reactions toward termination vary widely. Although some clients are more than happy to leave counseling, others may be hesitant or fearful. The quality of the helping relationship and clients' previous experiences with endings may provide some indication of their probable reactions to termination. To maximize the likelihood of a positive experience with termination, it is usually helpful to (a) discuss termination well in advance, (b) anticipate and explore feelings/ambivalence (the worker's as well as the client's feelings) about termination, (c) review the process to date of the work done, (d) articulate the gains made and compliment the client for achievements, and (e) discuss potential future difficulties, roadblocks, or red flags and develop coping strategies and supports.

SUMMARY

From a review of the early social work literature with respect to problem-solving, there remains some questions regarding the role of problem-solving in the field of social work. This chapter has provided an overview for social work practitioners of the problem-solving model and its utility as it relates to direct practice. The flexible structure and the general guidelines of the problem-solving model were highlighted through the developmental and extensive evidence-based changes in problem-solving that extends beyond social work. The chapter culminated in a discussion of a four-stage problem-solving process encapsulating a series of steps from assessment to termination. This interdisciplinary process can help the profession of social work develop a deeper knowledge base for practice that might have a continuing impact on work with diverse client populations.

KEY REFERENCES

Only key references appear in the print edition. The full reference list appears in the digital product found on http://connect.springerpub.com/content/book/978-0-8261-6556-5/part/sec01/chapter/chapter02

Barnard, C. P., & Kuehl, B. P. (1995). Ongoing evaluation: In-session procedures for enhancing the working alliance and therapy effectiveness. *American Journal of Family Therapy*, 23, 161–172.

Barnes, T. N., Wang, F., & O'Brien, K. M. (2018). A meta-analytic review of social problem-solving interventions in preschool settings. *Infant and Child Development*, 27(5), e2095.

Bell, A. C., & D'Zurilla, T. J. (2009). Problem-solving therapy for depression. A meta-analysis. *Clinical Psychology Review*, 29, 348–353.

Beutler, L. E., Consoli, A. J., & Lane, G. (2005). Systematic treatment selection and prescriptive psychotherapy. In J. C. Norcross & M. R. Goldfried (Eds.), *Handbook of psychotherapy integration* (2nd ed., pp. 121–146). Oxford University Press.

Cape, J., Whittington, C., Buszewicz, M., Wallace, P., & Underwood, L. (2010). Brief psychological therapies for anxiety and depression in primary care: Meta-analysis and meta-regression. *BMC Medicine*, 8, 38.

Chang, E. C., D'Zurilla, T. L., & Sanna, L. J. (Eds.) (2004). *Social problem solving: Theory, research and training*. American Psychological Association.

Compton, B.R., & Galaway, B. (1994). *Social work processes* (5th ed.). Brooks/Cole.

Compton, B. R., & Galaway, B. (1999). *Social work processes* (6th ed.). Brooks/Cole.

Congress, E. (1994). The use of culturagrams to assess and empower culturally diverse families. *Families in Society*, 75, 531–540.

Congress, E., & Kung, W. (2005). Using the culturagram to assess and empower culturally diverse families. In E. Congress and M. Gonzalez (Eds.), *Multicultural perspectives in working with families* (2nd ed., pp. 3–21). Springer.

Metatheories for Direct Social Work Practice

Ecological Systems Theory

Barbra Teater

- define systems theory, ecological perspective, and bioecological systems theory, and explain how they have each contributed to the development of ecological systems theory;
- identify the aim of ecological systems theory;
- list and explain the five assumptions of ecological systems theory;
- describe ecomaps and explain their role in social work practice; and
- explain the role of ecological systems theory in the assessment and intervention stages of social work practice.

INTRODUCTION

Ecological systems theory is concerned with the interaction and interdependence of individuals with their surrounding systems and encourages social workers to take a holistic view by assessing how individuals affect and are affected by such physical, social, political, and cultural systems. Likewise, the profession of social work has been fundamentally concerned with how individuals, families, groups, communities, and organizations interact with their environments and are shaped by them. The global definition of social work states that social work is "underpinned by theories of social work, social sciences, humanities, and indigenous knowledges, [and] engages people and structures to address life challenges and enhance well-being" (International Federation of Social Workers, 2014). Ecological systems theory is fundamental to social work as it serves as a theoretical basis for facilitating social evolution and individual growth and development by providing a framework to assess individuals in their environment and determine the most appropriate system in which to intervene. This chapter explores the ecological systems theory by describing its origins, through systems theory, ecological theory, and bioecological systems theory; its basic assumptions; and how the theory can be applied in social work practice.

THE ORIGINS OF THE ECOLOGICAL SYSTEMS THEORY

Ecological systems theory was developed from systems theory, ecological theory, and bioecological systems theory, which examine how individuals affect and are affected by the physical, interpersonal, social, political, and cultural systems in their lives (Langer & Lietz, 2015). Systems theory, derived from Ludwig von Bertalanffy's general systems theory, focuses on the complex parts of a system and how they interact to create a functional whole. A system is defined as "a complex of elements or components directly or indirectly related in a causal network, such that each component is related to at least some others in a more or less stable way within a particular period of time" (Buckley, 1967, p. 41). Systems theory holds that the whole of a system is greater than the sum of its parts where the elements of the system do not function in isolation but, rather, interact and depend on each other to form a functional whole. The whole system is not complete without the presence and participation of each of the elements. According to von Bertalanffy, the human being is the most complex system, composed of biological, physiological, and psychological elements. Systems theory was integrated into social work practice in the 1970s, particularly through casework (Goldstein, 1973, 1977; Pincus & Minahan, 1973, 1977), where social workers could assess an individual by looking at the other systems in the client's life, and through the holistic assessment of how the systems interacted, the social worker could determine various targets of intervention and determine the most appropriate system in which to intervene. Systems theory is widely used in social work today as an assessment framework and has been instrumental in underpinning the practice of family therapy.

Ecological theory, or the ecological perspective, derives from the field of ecology that aims to explore the interactions and interdependence of organisms with their environment. Ecological theory is a form of general systems theory, yet adds a more humanistic dimension by examining how people interact in real-life time and space and the adaptive fit of the person in the environment. An ecosystem is defined as people and their life situations, which includes the extent to which they are able to function from their interactions with other systems (Siporin, 1980). As Siporin (1980) described, "ecological theory thus deals with the web of life, at the interfaces between systems and subsystems, so that it relates to open, self-organizing, self regulating, and adaptive complexes of interacting and interdependent subsystems" (p. 509). In the 1980s, two social work academics, Alex Gitterman and Carel Germain, emphasized the ecological perspective in social work practice over general systems theory, particularly to address the "non-human" language of general systems theory and to provide additional direction to social work practice beyond the use of the theory as an assessment tool. They developed the Life Model to social work practice, which aimed to assess the person:environment fit of the client and work to enhance the quality of interactions and transactions between people and their environment. The ecological perspective is used in social work to assess individuals in the context of ecological systems with which they interact, such as their family, peer group, neighborhood, community, and institutions (e.g., school and workplace), and the extent to which the transactions within their environment are helpful or unhelpful (Ohmer, 2010). Table 3.1 provides the concepts and definitions of terms used in both systems and ecological theory.

Bronfenbrenner's Bioecological Systems Theory

The work of Bronfenbrenner (1974, 1977, 1979, 1986a, 1986b, 2006) involves the application of the ecological theory to child development, which has greatly influenced social work practice. Bronfenbrenner developed an ecological framework composed of five systems or layers of the environment (microsystem, mesosystem, exosystem, macrosystem, and chronosystem) that affect a child's development. The child is viewed as an active, growing human being, and the five systems are viewed as directly and indirectly affecting the child's behavior and development. Equally, the child is able to affect the systems with which they interact; thus, the influence is bidirectional; the interaction within and between the layers are important to explore. Bronfenbrenner (1992) defined the ecology of human development as:

> the scientific study of the progressive, mutual accommodation throughout the life course between an active, growing human being and the changing properties of the immediate settings in which the developing person lives, as this process is affected by the relations between these settings, and the larger contexts in which the settings are embedded. (p. 188)

TABLE 3.1 KEY TERMS IN SYSTEMS THEORY AND ECOLOGICAL THEORY

Term	Definition
System	A set of elements that are orderly and interrelated to make a functional whole[1]
Subsystem	A subsystem is one part or element of a larger system, but the subsystem can act as a smaller system on its own (i.e., an individual is a subsystem of their family, yet the individual is a system on their own)
Open system	Open systems interact with their environment and are affected and influenced by these interactions. The open system is continually reacting and adapting to the influences from the environment. There are two dimensions to a open system: (a) open to the environment (allowing new information to enter the system) and (b) open to itself (allowing new information to circulate within the system).[2] Different systems vary in the degree to which they are open, some being more open than others
Closed system	Closed systems do not interact with their environment and are unaffected and uninfluenced by the environment. Different systems vary in the degree to which they are closed, some being more closed than others (i.e., a family may be influenced and affected by their environment, but they are resistant to change and prefer to remain stuck in their static processes)[3]
Boundaries	Each system has a boundary that distinguishes it from other systems. Boundaries may be physical or psychological.[3] The extent to which the boundaries are permeable differs by system as some systems allow information to freely enter or cross their boundary and others do not
Ecological Theory	
Person: environment fit	The actual fit between an individual's or a collective group's needs, rights, goals, and capacities and the qualities and operations of their physical and social environments within particular cultural and historical contexts. This fit could be classified as favorable, minimally adequate, or unfavorable[4]
Adaptations	Are continuous, change-oriented, cognitive, sensory-perceptual, and behavioral processes people use to sustain or raise the level of fit between themselves and their environment[4]
Life stressors	Are generated by critical life issues that people perceive as exceeding their personal and environmental resources for managing them. A stressor represents serious harm or loss and is associated with a sense of being in jeopardy[4]
Stress	Is the internal response to a life stressor and is characterized by troubled emotional or physiological states, or both[4]
Coping measures	Are special behaviors, often novel, that are devised to handle the demands posed by the life stressor. Successful coping depends on various environmental and personal resources[4]

Notes: [1]Kirst-Ashman, K. K., & Hull, G. H. (2002). *Understanding generalist practice* (3rd ed.). Brooks Cole; [2] Alexander, P. (1985). A systems theory conceptualization of incest. *Family Process, 24* (1), 79–88; [3]Preston-Shoot, M., & Agass, D. (1990). *Making sense of social work: Psychodynamics, systems and practice.* Macmillan Education; [4]Germain, C. B., & Gitterman, A. (1995). Ecological perspective. In R. L. Edward & J. G. Hopps (Eds.), *Encyclopedia of social work* (19th ed.). NASW Press.

Source: Adapted from Teater, B. (2014b). *An introduction to applying social work theories and methods* (2nd ed.). Open University Press/McGraw-Hill Education.

Thus, in order to understand human development, Bronfenbrenner believed one must have an understanding of the full environment in which the individual's growth takes place. According to Langer and Lietz (2015), "[U]nderstanding these various systems helps social workers take a holistic view of a client, offering full consideration of how people, places, and physical environment can affect a child's development" (p. 30). In 2006, Bronfenbrenner revised his theory to acknowledge and emphasize the child's own biology as a factor in influencing their environment and renamed the theory "bioecological systems theory." The five systems are described below.

Microsystem. The microsystem is the layer closest to the child and consists of relationships and interactions that the child has with their immediate surroundings, such as parents, siblings, family, peers, teachers, school, neighborhoods, or childcare environments. The interaction and influence between the child and the other elements (or systems) within this system is bidirectional and has the greatest impact on the child. For example, the child affects the attitudes, beliefs, and behaviors of the parent and the parent affects the attitudes, beliefs, and behaviors of the child. Social work practice would aim to consider the systems at this level that have the most influence on the client (Langer & Lietz, 2015) and may seek to ask such questions as: "Who (or what) are the systems in the child's life?"; "What is the quality of the relationship between the child and these systems [parents; siblings; teachers; peers; school; neighborhood; childcare]?"; and/or "To what extent do such relationships help or hinder the child's development?"

Mesosystem. The mesosystem is the layer that provides the linkage between the systems in the microsystem, which can consist of relationships and/or direct interactions that have a bidirectional influence. For example, the connection between the parents and the school, between the school and the neighborhood, or between the childcare facility and the parents' workplace. Social work practice would aim to assess the quality of relationships among the systems and the extent to which the relationships are promoting the child's growth and development, and may seek to ask such questions as: "To what extent does the interaction between two or more systems [parents; school; childcare; neighborhood; parent's workplace; church] help or hinder the child's growth and development?"; and/or "To what extent are the child's needs supported by the other systems in the child's life?"

Exosystem. The exosystem layer consists of the interaction between two or more systems that cause an indirect influence on another system. This layer consists of the larger social system that can comprise decisions, events, and contingencies in which the child has no influence (Johnson, 2008). For example, the school could receive a funding cut that causes the school to eliminate after-school programs and in turn causes the parent to be under increased financial pressure due to paying for after-school childcare. Such pressure causes the parent to feel stressed, which influences the parent's interaction with the child. Here the child is affected despite having no formal relationship with the funding agency creating the cut to after-school programs. The child's growth and development is affected by the interaction of an external system with a system in the child's microsystem. Social work practice would aim to assess the larger structures that are indirectly influencing the quality of relationships among the systems within the child's microsystem and the extent to which these interactions and influences are promoting the child's growth and development. Social workers may seek to ask such questions as: "To what extent are external structures [policies; rules; regulations] influencing the ability of systems within the child's microsystem to meet the child's needs and promote growth and development?" and/or "What needs to happen in order to overcome barriers to the systems in the child's microsystem meeting the needs of the child and promoting growth and development?"

Macrosystem. The macrosystem layer consists of the larger systems that influence a child's life, such as policies and legislation, cultural values, customs, and beliefs, entitlement services and programs, and resources. The systems within the macrosystem influence the child by infiltrating all the layers (exosystem, mesosystem, and microsystem). For example, societal views about access to healthcare will influence the ability of a parent to access affordable healthcare when their employer does not provide health insurance, and the ability of the parent to address their health concerns and needs will influence their ability to effectively function as a parent, thus influencing the extent to which the child's need are being met. Social work practice would aim to assess the societal policies, legislation, programs, resources, and cultural values, customs, and beliefs that are influencing the exo, meso, and microsystems and helping or hindering in meeting the child's needs and in promoting growth and development. Social workers may ask such questions as: "To what extent do policies, programs, and resources limit or fail to meet the needs of targeted populations?" and/or "How does the dominant cultural norms, values, and beliefs include or exclude certain populations in their quest for growth and development?"

Chronosystem. The chronosystem layer includes the dimensions of time or the events that have occurred in the child's life. Events can encompass external events, such as natural disasters, terrorist attacks, or a parent's death; and internal events, such as biological, physiological, or psychological changes within the child. The events experienced by the child will influence the way in which they respond to changes and developments in their future. For example, a child whose parents divorced when the child was 8 years old and felt a sense of abandonment when one of the parents left may have difficulties securing attachments with significant others in the future. Social work practice would aim to assess the significant external and internal events that occurred in the child's life that could influence their ability to experience positive growth and development or influence the ways in which the child responds to events in the future. Social workers may ask such questions as: "What significant external and internal events occurred in the child's life?" and "To what extent have such events influenced the ways in which the child responds to changes and development as they grow and develop?"

Each layer in Bronfenbrenner's bioecological framework is viewed as critical in the development of a child and any changes or conflicts within one layer will influence and affect the other layers. Thus, applying bioecological systems theory to social work practice involves not only assessing the child (or client system) within the client's immediate environment but also an assessment of how the other layers of the environment interact and affect each other. Although this section has discussed bioecological systems theory in relation to a child, the theory can be applied to a client system of any age. Figure 3.1 depicts how the four systems, or layers, are nested within each other and how, along with the chronosystem (or dimension of time), they influence each other.

ECOLOGICAL SYSTEMS THEORY EXPLAINED

Ecological systems theory has integrated the basic premises and frameworks from general systems theory, ecological theory, and bioecological systems theory. The aim in applying ecological systems theory is to assess all the systems in a client's life that can influence the extent to which the client can grow and develop. Based on this assessment, the social worker will determine the most appropriate system in which to intervene in order to alleviate distress and/or dysfunction in the client's life and provide avenues and opportunities for positive growth and development. In achieving this aim, clients will experience a "goodness-of-fit" between themselves and their environment, which involves an "exchange balance, or positive reciprocal complementarity, in mutual need-meeting relationships, between sub-systems, and between the ecosystem and its environment" (Siporin, 1980, p. 510). According to Ohmer (2010), goodness-of-fit or a strong person-in-environment configuration "suggests that nutritive environments provide the necessary resources, security, and support at the appropriate times in the appropriate ways, but hostile environments inhibit development and the ability to cope owing to a lack of distortion of environmental supports" (p. 3).

Applying ecological systems theory to social work practice involves examining the exchanges of individuals within their social, physical, and cultural environments (Gitterman, 2009). Social

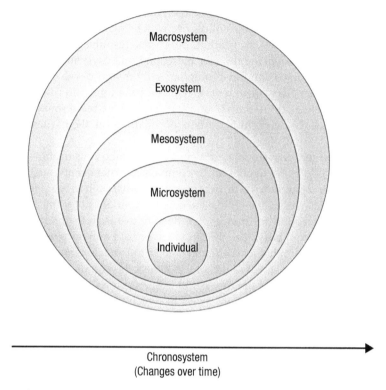

FIGURE 3.1 Bronfenbrenner's bioecological systems theory: Individual nested within systems.

environments include exchanges and interactions with friends, family, social and community networks, and the political, legal, and economic structures that shape the way in which the environment operates and orders itself. The physical environment includes the built world, such as buildings and structures, as well as the natural world, and the cultural environment includes the values, beliefs, norms, and customs that shape individuals' values, perspectives, and expectations (Teater, 2014a). Assessing the relationships, interactions, and interdependencies between the individual (family, group, and/or community) and the social, physical, and cultural environments, and intervening in one or more systems to enhance the goodness-of-fit between the client and their environment is the crux of ecological systems theory.

The relationships and interactions between the individuals and their environments are not viewed as static, but, rather, evolve over time and are influenced by historical and cultural influences. Ecological systems theory does not take a simple cause-and-effect linear approach when examining the relationship between two or more systems where A causes B; thus, the focus of intervention is on A. Rather, ecological systems theory assesses the interactions between A and B and the ways in which A's response to B influences B's response to A, as well as assesses how other environmental factors are influencing A and B's interaction and response to one another (Gitterman & Germain, 2008). In completing this type of assessment, the social worker may discover that the most appropriate system in which to intervene is neither A nor B but rather the social, physical, and/or cultural environment in which they live, which is the source of stress and strain (Teater, 2014a).

Ecological systems theory assumes individuals try to maintain a good level of fit between themselves and their environment where the environment is providing the necessary resources to meet their needs and the individuals have the necessary strengths, resources, and capacity to grow and develop (Teater, 2014a). Individuals may experience stress when the environment fails to provide the necessary resources, and there is a poor level of adaptive fit between the individual and their environment. It is often at this time that individuals voluntarily or involuntarily seek the assistance of a social worker. The social worker aims to work with the individual to assess the goodness-of-fit between the client and their environment and seeks to improve the quality of exchange between the client and their environment by either changing the client's perceptions and behaviors, or changing the response or influence from the environment on the client (Gitterman, 2009; Teater, 2014a).

Basic Assumptions of Ecological Systems Theory

There are five basic assumptions that underpin ecological systems theory (Gitterman, 2011; Gitterman & Germain, 2008; Teater, 2014b). The assumptions are listed in Table 3.2 and are described in detail in the following.

1. *The whole system is greater than the sum of its parts.* A system is composed of elements or subsystems that interact and depend on each other in order to create a functional whole. Although it may seem that the parts of the system add up to create the whole system, this is not the case as the relationships and interactions between the elements of the system increase the complexity of the system (Langer & Lietz, 2015). For example, an individual, as a system, is composed of biological, physiological, and psychological elements that interact and influence each other to create the whole individual system. A client presenting with psychological difficulties may actually be experiencing a biological problem that is influencing their psychological state. Failing to assess the source of the presenting problem could further perpetuate the problem. Another example includes a family system composed of two parents and two children. The system is not merely four people, but the system also includes the relationship between the two parents, the relationship between the siblings, and the relationship between each of the parents and each of the children. The relationship between the two parents not only feed into how the parents are as individual systems, but equally the relationship influences the way in which the parents function with their children. As Langer and Lietz (2015) state, "these dynamics are elements of the system, showing this family system is not the sum of its parts, [...] but is also defined by the patterns of behavior, rules, beliefs, and values that make them a family" (p. 38). In viewing a system, social workers should identify the different elements that comprise the system and examine the extent to which they are working together to make the functional whole. Intervening into one element of the system without fully assessing the whole system could contribute to the continuation of the presenting problem and further reduce the goodness-of-fit of the client.

TABLE 3.2 ASSUMPTIONS OF ECOLOGICAL SYSTEMS THEORY	
Assumption 1	The whole system is greater than the sum of its parts
Assumption 2	The parts of a system are interconnected and interdependent
Assumption 3	A system is either directly or indirectly affected by other systems
Assumption 4	All systems have boundaries and rules
Assumption 5	Systems strive for a goodness-of-fit with their environment

Sources: Gitterman, A., & Germain, C. B. (2008). *The life model of social work practice: Advances in theory and practice* (3rd ed.). Columbia University Press; Teater, B. (2014a). Social work practice from an ecological perspective. In C. W. LeCroy (Ed.), *Case studies in social work practice* (3rd ed., pp. 35–44). Brooks/Cole; Teater, B. (2014). *An introduction to applying social work theories and methods* (3rd ed.). Open University Press/McGraw-Hill Education.

2. *The parts of a system are interconnected and interdependent.* As indicated in Assumption 1, each system is composed of elements that work together to create a functional whole. Therefore, a change or movement in one element (or subsystem) will cause a change or movement in another element; thus, all the elements of the system are interconnected and interdependent. Langer and Lietz (2015) state, "the interactions among entities are not linear, where one entity affects the others. Instead, exchanges among systems bring about changes to one another over time" (p. 38). For example, the way in which person A approaches person B will influence how person B responds to person A. The relationship between A and B may also be influenced by the environmental factors that could influence A and B's interaction and the way in which they are responding. After identifying the elements that comprise a system, social workers should assess the ways in which the parts of the system interact and interconnect to make the whole as well as the environmental factors that could be influencing the interaction; the intervention may actually be in the external environment versus the couple, as the environmental factors are the source of stress and strain between A and B.

3. *A system is either directly or indirectly affected by other systems.* While the elements of the system create a functional whole, the functioning of a system is also influenced directly or indirectly by other systems; an individual will respond to the environment and the environment will respond to the individual. For example, a family system is directly or indirectly affected by other systems, such as the school, childcare facility, workplace, extended family, community, and society. Some of the influences can be direct, such as a workplace specifying the work hours of a parent, which impacts the amount of time the parent is able to spend with a child. Other influences can be indirect, such as a closing of a school in the community that forces another school to have over enrollment, which affects the quality of education a child receives. Social workers are tasked with assessing the client system and the elements that comprise the system as well as exploring the other systems in the client's life and the extent to which they are directly or indirectly affecting the client.

4. *All systems have boundaries and rules.* All systems have boundaries and rules that define and distinguish them from each other and separate them from their environment. The boundaries of systems can be permeable at different points, which depends on the extent to which the system is open or closed. Open systems are receptive to change and development and will allow transactions with the surrounding environment, whereas closed systems are more resistant to outside influences and would prefer to remain static. Although each system has its distinct boundary, some boundaries overlap, such as a family system, which has a parent–parent subsystem and a parent–child subsystem. The rules of the system often define the boundaries of the system and the extent to which they are permeable (open or closed), which typically creates predictability that helps the system to function efficiently. Social workers will assess the boundaries and rules of the client system and the extent to which they are open or closed to influences from their environment. The work with the client may involve strengthening or redefining the boundary of the client, changing the rules of the client system, and/or working with the client to be more or less influenced by the environment.

5. *Systems strive for a goodness-of-fit with their environment.* Systems strive to maintain an internal balance, to grow and develop in an effort to reach goals, and to have a good fit with their environment despite conflicting influences. Systems have a desire to adapt to their environment and to make the changes needed to protect them and to grow and develop. The extent to which a system can adapt to the environment is key to experiencing goodness-of-fit and in minimizing stress or dysfunction. Teater (2014b) defines good and bad levels of adaptedness:

> [A] good level of adaptedness means that individuals view themselves as full of strengths, resources and the capacity to grow and develop while also feeling as if their environment is providing the necessary resources in order to grow and develop. A poor level of adaptedness would involve individuals feeling that the

environment does not provide the necessary resources nor do they feel as if they have the strengths, resources, and capacity to grown and develop. (p. 26)

Social workers will assess the level of fit between the client system and the environment and may seek to intervene in the client system or external systems in order to alleviate distress and to promote growth and develop through a stronger goodness-of-fit.

APPLYING ECOLOGICAL SYSTEMS THEORY TO PRACTICE

These five assumptions help to guide the use of ecological systems theory in the assessment and intervention stages of social work practice. The following discusses how the ecological systems theory can be used in the assessment and intervention stages of social work practice by applying the theory to a fictitious client, Michael, who was referred to a school social worker due to "disruptive behavior" in the classroom.

Assessment

A social worker using an ecological systems theory would conduct a holistic, multisystem assessment of the client (individual, family, group, community, organization) by examining the elements that comprise the system, the other systems that directly or indirectly affect the client system, the interactions and relationships among these systems (including any boundaries and rules), and the extent to which such interactions and relationships are contributing to the goodness-of-fit between the client system and the environment. This assessment enables the social worker to widen the view of the client's presenting problem beyond the client and to examine if other systems in the client's environment are contributing to the presenting problem. Thus, the social worker may determine the best system in which to intervene is not the client but, rather, another system that is directly or indirectly affecting the client and contributing to the presenting problem.

Bronfenbrenner's bioecological framework is a useful tool to guide a social worker's assessment of the client. The social worker can position the individual as a system composed of biological, physiological, and psychological elements, and identify the other systems within the client's microsystem. The social worker can then assess the relationship and interactions between the systems within the microsystem (the mesosystem layer). The social worker will also assess for any other systems that indirectly affect the individual (those in the exosystem layer) as well as any larger systems, such as policies, legislation, cultural values and beliefs, and programs and resources that infiltrate all the other system layers and affect the individual system (macrosystem). Finally, the social worker will explore the historical influences (time dimension) that may shape the individual in how they respond to future events and situations.

An ecomap serves as a visual tool for assessing a client within the environment. An ecomap is an extension of a genogram, which was originally developed by social worker and social work academic Dr. Ann Hartman (see Hartman, 1978). A genogram is a graphic illustration of a client's family tree that uses symbols to reflect the gender of systems and subsystems as well as the relationship and connections between them; for example, a circle represents a female and a square represents a male, and a horizontal solid line that connects these two individuals indicates that the male and female are in a partnered relationship. The ecomap extends the genogram by graphically depicting an individual or client system within their environment. When working with an individual or family client system, the ecomap usually begins with a genogram of the client system and then extends into an ecomap that identifies the other external systems that influence the client system, such as social, personal, economic, and/or political systems (e.g., the use of Bronfenbrenner's five systems to position the client in relation to the other systems in the client's environment). The relevance of the ecomap to assessment in ecological systems theory is the identification of the quality of connections and influence between the client system and the external systems. The type of line and direction of arrows that connect the systems visually display the relationships and connections. These relationships and connections can be positive, nurturing, and supportive, or they can be negative or stressful, leading to distress, dysfunction, or a source of conflict. Figure 3.2 presents the basic symbols and lines used to create a genogram and ecomap. The ecomap enables the social worker and client to visually see the systems in the client's life and the extent to which the relationships and interactions with the various systems and the environment is helping or hindering the client's goodness-of-fit. The ecomap can also help to visually identify systems that provide resources and support as well as systems that are the source of tension and conflict.

Figure 3.3 illustrates an ecomap for Michael, an 8-year-old male who was referred to a school social worker due to disruptive behaviors in the classroom. In meeting with Michael and conducting a biopsychosocial assessment, the social worker constructs an ecomap to identify the systems in Michael's life and to explore any sources of tension and conflict and sources of support and resources. Some social workers may simply assess the identified problem as Michael's inability to behave and respond appropriately in the classroom, and then focus the intervention solely on Michael in an attempt to change his behavior, for example, through behavioral therapy. Yet, a social worker working from an ecological systems perspective would first conduct a holistic assessment to determine the most appropriate system in which to intervene in order to alleviate the presenting problem. An ecomap is a useful tool in conducting a holistic assessment. The social worker would first establish a relationship with Michael enabling him to feel comfortable in talking with the social worker and sharing his story. The social worker will also need to talk to other systems in Michael's life, for example his teacher and his parents, in order to collect information to complete a holistic assessment.

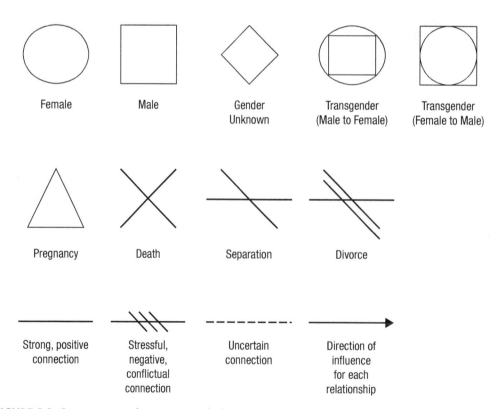

FIGURE 3.2 Genogram and ecomap symbols and key.

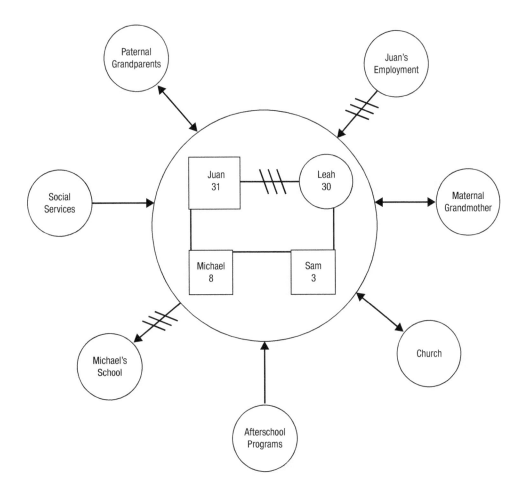

FIGURE 3.3 Example ecomap for Michael.

Michael's ecomap indicates he lives with this mother and father, Juan (31 years old) and Leah (30 years old), and his 3-year-old brother, Sam. Juan and Leah are in a stressful relationship where they are in the process of separating and making arrangements about who will leave the house, financial arrangements, and how Juan and Leah will share responsibility of the children. Michael has expressed his parents' pending separation as a source of stress and concern for him (a present life stressor). Michael indicates he is worried about what will happen to his mother if his father leaves and if he and his brother, Sam, will be able to spend time with both parents if his parents separate. Michael states he lays awake at night unable to sleep and listens to see if he can hear his parents talking to find out if they are going to separate or not. Michael says he is tired when he is in school and is often thinking about his parents and his little brother.

Juan is employed but has a stressful relationship with his employer who does not guarantee a set number of hours for Juan to work a week, thus, limiting the extent to which Juan and Leah can manage the finances; this is often a source of stress and strain between Juan and Leah. Leah is the primary caregiver of Michael and Sam, and cleans houses on the side for three families for which she receives payment "under the table." Leah's mother and Juan's parents live close by and are strong sources of support to the family, both in providing limited financial support when needed and in providing occasional childcare for Michael and Sam. Michael and his family regularly attend a church in their community. Michael is currently experiencing a stressful relationship with his school, particularly in the classroom. Michael currently does not participate in after-school programs nor does the family receive any resources from social services, yet the social worker has assessed these systems as potential sources of support for Michael and the family.

Based on the construction of the ecomap, the social worker has assessed a potential source of the stressful relationship between Michael and his school may be stemming from the stressful relationship between Juan and Leah and how this has impacted the home environment. The social worker also assesses that Juan's unpredictable employment has potentially contributed to the stressful relationship between Juan and Leah, thus indirectly affecting Michael's goodness-of-fit. In moving forward, the social worker identifies sources of support to come from the parental grandparents, the maternal grandmother, the church, after-school programs at the school, and social services. The social worker requests to meet with Juan and Leah to discuss her assessment and to provide options for interventions. Juan and Leah were both receptive to meeting with the social worker and indicated that they were open to receiving help, especially to help Michael.

As illustrated, ecomaps serve as a useful assessment tool to visually display the client system and the relationships and connections between the client system and other systems in their environment. The tool enables the social worker to identify problem areas and identify systems in which to intervene to alleviate problems, access supports and resources, and improve the goodness-of-fit between the client system and the environment.

Intervention

The holistic, multisystem assessment will illuminate to the social worker the most appropriate system in which to intervene in an attempt to enhance the functioning of the system and improve the goodness-of-fit (Langer & Lietz, 2015). The intervention may involve targeting the individual client system or targeting any of the other systems in which the client system interacts to enhance the functioning of the individual or to enhance the transaction between the client system and the environment; the goal is to improve the interaction between the client system and the environment (Langer & Lietz, 2015). As discussed, there are frameworks and tools that can be used to help with the assessment when using ecological systems theory (e.g., Bronfenbrenner's bioecological framework; ecomaps), and based on this assessment, the social worker determines which system needs the intervention. This is where the social worker would turn to the selection of a specific intervention method or selection of methods to achieve the aim of the work with the client system. For example, the social worker may use not only motivational interviewing to begin to address a behavioral change with an individual client but also advocacy to help the client access needed resources. The ecological systems theory does not specify one specific intervention that is most appropriate but, rather, encourages the social worker to select the intervention or interventions that will most effectively enhance the goodness-of-fit between the client system and the environment.

The social worker working with Michael has identified a number of interventions to alleviate the presenting problem of Michael's disruptive behaviors in the classroom and create a better goodness-of-fit for Michael. The social worker has also assessed the family to be open to change and willing to access support and resources to assist Michael as well as alleviate stress and strain between Juan and Leah. The social worker, thus, determines possible interventions to include: (a) enrolling Michael in an after-school program to engage in extracurricular activities that he enjoys, which could help to take his mind off his parents' pending separation and help to develop positive relationships with others; (b) assisting Juan and Leah in applying for financial assistance, such as Supplemental nutrition assistance program (SNAP), healthcare, and housing assistance to assist the family financially, which could reduce the stress and strain between Juan and Leah; (c) working with Juan and Leah to explore counseling or supportive services, which could be from their church or other community services, to help them work on their relationship and/or help them navigate their separation to reduce stress and conflict in their family; (d) exploring with Juan and Leah how the grandparents could assist in the transition of the family and support of Michael; (e) meeting one-on-one with Michael on a regular basis to discuss how he is coping with the transition in the family; (f) connecting Juan and/or Leah to the community job center to explore work and job skill opportunities that may lead to more secure sources of employment and income for the family; (g) advocating within the community for the availability of resources and support to low-income families, for example, free or sliding-fee scale counseling services; and/or (h) engaging in political advocacy requiring a fair living wage and access to affordable healthcare for all.

The social worker will work with Michael, and Juan and Leah to establish the goals for the work together, identify the interventions to be the focus of the work together, and continually evaluate and assess the goodness-of-fit for Michael and the family.

CONCLUSION

This chapter has explored ecological systems theory, which aims to assess clients within their environments and explore how the various systems in the environment are interacting to contribute to the presenting problems and goodness-of-fit of the clients. Social workers working from an ecological systems framework will conduct a holistic assessment that positions the client within the various systems or levels that directly or indirectly affect the client and then examine the quality of the relationship between the systems. The assessment points the social worker to the various sources of the presenting problem and highlights the system or systems that need intervention in order to strengthen the client's goodness-of-fit.

SUMMARY POINTS

- Ecological systems theory is derived from general systems theory, ecology theory, and Bronfenbrenner's bioecological systems theory.
- Ecological systems theory is concerned with the interaction and interdependence of individuals with their surrounding systems and aims for social workers to take a holistic view by assessing how individuals affect and are affected by such physical, social, political, and cultural systems.
- Ecological systems theory is based on five assumptions that examine the interaction and interdependence of systems and how the assessment of one system cannot be done in isolation, but, rather, must take into account how the systems affect and are affected by each other.
- Ecological systems theory is useful in the assessment stage of social work practice where social workers conduct a holistic assessment of the client system and the interactions and connections between the client system and the other systems in the client's environment.
- Useful assessment tools include the five layers of Bronfenbrenner's bioecological framework and ecomaps.

KEY REFERENCES

Only key references appear in the print edition. The full reference list appears in the digital product found on http://connect.springerpub.com/content/book/978-0-8261-6556-5/part/sec02/chapter/ch03

Bronfenbrenner, U., & Morris, P. A. (2006). The bioecological model of human development. In R. M. Lerner & W. Damon (Eds.), *Handbook of child psychology: Theoretical models of human development* (pp. 793–828). Wiley.

Gitterman, A., & Germain, C. B. (2008). *The life model of social work practice: Advances in theory and practice* (3rd ed.). Columbia University Press.

Langer, C. L., & Lietz, C. A. (2015). *Applying theory to generalist social work practice: A case study approach.* Wiley.

Teater, B. (2014a). Social work practice from an ecological perspective. In C. W. LeCroy (Ed.), *Case studies in social work practice* (3rd ed., pp. 35–44). Brooks/Cole.

Teater, B. (2014b). *An introduction to applying social work theories and methods* (2nd ed.). Open University Press/McGraw-Hill Education.

Teater, B. (2014). *An introduction to applying social work theories and methods* (3rd ed.). Open University Press/McGraw-Hill Education.

Individual and Family Development Theory

Elaine P. Congress

LEARNING OBJECTIVES

By the end of this chapter, you should be able to:

- discuss the individual development theory of Erikson (1994, 1997), and the family life cycle theory of Carter and McGoldrick (2004) within a continually changing social context;
- explore Kohlberg's (1981) moral stages of development and Gilligan's (1982) feminist perspective on moral development;
- discuss the development theories viewed through a cultural lens because of an increasingly culturally diverse population in the United States;
- Consider the contributions that new roles for women, social and economic trends, an increasing divorce rate, and class differences have made to the diverse forms of the family life cycle;
- review and examine family assessment tools including the ecomap (Hartman & Laird, 1983), genogram (McGoldrick et al., 2008), and culturagram (Congress, 2008), which demonstrate the excellent tools clinicans have to apply development theories to their work with individuals and families;
- discuss an intersectional design tool first introduced by Crenshaw (1989), included to help in understanding families from diverse socioeconomic classes and cultural backgrounds.

INTRODUCTION

Theories of individual and family development provide an important knowledge base for direct social work practice. These theories are particularly helpful in the data collection and assessment phase of helping because they direct the practitioner to explore the potential significance of issues that individuals and families commonly face at different stages of development. Although individual and family development theories are primarily explanatory, they often provide general ideas for intervention.

Individual and family development theories can best be studied together, as families are made up of individuals and 66% of individuals live within families (U.S. Census Bureau, 2013). This chapter focuses specifically on the individual development theory of Erikson (1994, 1997), and the family life cycle theory of Carter and McGoldrick (2004) within a changed and continually changing social context. There are also discussions of Kohlberg's (1981) moral stages of development and Gilligan's (1982) feminist perspective on moral development.

Because the United States is increasingly culturally diverse, these developmental theories are viewed through a cultural lens. Family assessment tools including the ecomap (Hartman & Laird, 1983), genogram (McGoldrick et al., 2008), and culturagram (Congress, 2008), which can help clinicians apply development theories to their work with individuals and families, are presented. Completing a culturagram on a family can help a clinician develop a better understanding of the sociocultural context of the family, which can shed light on appropriate interventions with the family (Congress & Gonzalez, 2013).

INDIVIDUAL DEVELOPMENT THEORY

The developmental theory of Erikson corresponds well with the biopsychosocial orientation of social work. Departing from Freud's psychoanalytic approach, Erikson acknowledged the importance of social variables such as the family, community, and culture in shaping the individual (Greene, 2000). His theory is an optimistic one, as he believed all individuals had the capacity to successfully master their environment. This theme is echoed in the strengths perspective in which clients are seen as having inherent capabilities for succeeding in life's activities (Saleebey, 2013). Unlike Freud, whose development stages stopped at adolescence, Erikson formulated eight life stages, starting with the infant at birth and ending with old age and death (Greene, 2017). Each life stage provided an opportunity for the individual to learn new skills for progressing to the next stage.

Using the strengths perspective as an underlying framework, each individual is seen as having the inherent capacity to successfully master the developmental challenges presented at that stage. Each stage is characterized by two contradictory extremes that produce a psychosocial crisis. Developmental crisis has been defined as an internal event that upsets the usual psychological equilibrium of the individual. Although providing a challenge, each crisis produces an opportunity for the individual to change and grow in a positive way (Roberts, 2005). These crises are normative, universal experiences, and the expectation is that individuals will be able to integrate conflicting themes and move on to the next developmental stage.

Erikson's (1994) eight stages of development, together with the ninth stage of development later formulated by Erikson (1997), provide a useful framework for understanding individual development. Information from Levinson (1978, 1996) in terms of adult development, and the feminist critique of Erikson and Levinson (Gilligan, 1982; Miller, 1991; Surrey, 1991), are also considered in the following discussion of different stages of development. It should be noted that while Gilligan's work has its legacy most notably generating a wave of new research, a renewed openness within feminism to sex differences, and the notion that abstract detachment isn't the apex of moral maturity, her research may have turned out to be more a call to arms than a work of science. Regardless, she inspired her peers to consider gender when studying individual development theory (Graham, 2012).

Trust Versus Mistrust (0–2 Years)

Occurring between birth and 2 years of age, Erikson's first stage parallels Freud's oral phase. The main issues for the infant relate to conflicts about trust and mistrust. Ideally, the infant learns about trust—the mother will be there to meet the dependent baby's needs. Early infancy provides a learning environment about trust and mistrust. If this stage is successfully mastered, the end result is hope; that is, the individual emerges with the belief that one can attain one's goal. This early developmental stage is universal throughout cultures. External social factors, however, including poverty, social dislocation, and physical and emotional neglect, can detrimentally affect the development of trust. If not successfully mastered, emotional and social detachment will be the result. An adult manifestation might be the individual who has difficulty in making a commitment to any close, interpersonal relationship. Although it is important to achieve this goal in order to move successfully onto the next stage of development, failure to achieve this goal is not irreversible. Erikson believed that teachers, clergy members, therapists, and other supportive people might help individuals revisit and resolve this psychosocial crisis in a positive way.

Autonomy Versus Shame (2–4 Years)

Erikson's second stage, which corresponds to Freud's anal stage, is described as early child-hood. Between the ages of 2 and 4, the struggle is between autonomy and shame. During this stage, children first learn to act independently without a loss of self-esteem. They struggle with overcoming a sense of shame and doubt. The positive outcome is will—that is, the promotion of autonomous behavior. A failure during this stage can lead to compulsion and guilt-ridden behavior in adults.

Initiative Versus Guilt (4–6 Years)

This third stage corresponds to Freud's genital phase. In contrast to Freud, however, Erikson focuses primarily on the social interaction rather than individual psychosexual development. Described as the play stage, children face the crisis of initiative versus guilt. Ideally, children learn to initiate and take pride in their activities; they also develop a sense of what is right and wrong. The goal for this stage is the development of purpose, in which the child learns to formulate and pursue goals (Newman & Newman, 2005). The problem is inhibition, and one sees adult manifestations of failure to pass successfully through this stage in the adult who procrastinates and avoids and is fearful of initiating any new project.

Industry Versus Inferiority (6–12 Years)

Erikson (1994) describes this period of a child's life as characterized by industry versus inferiority. At this time, the child first goes to school and learns to use knowledge and skills in a structured way. Children are interested in learning in the classroom, in the community, and from peers. However, because of external or internal factors, a child may have difficulty moving successfully through this period. There may be factors in the external environment of the community or school that detrimentally affect mastery at this level. For example, the child may live in a dangerous neighborhood and going to school may be a threatening experience. The school itself may not be a receptive environment, with a deteriorating building, lack of supplies, and an over-burdened, unresponsive teacher. The family may not provide support, which is essential in mastering this stage. For example, the mother may be overwhelmed by psychosocial-economic problems to the point that she is neglectful and abusive. Children may also have learning difficulties, such as hyperactivity, developmental disabilities, or health problems, that impede the development of competence during the latency years. Although the latency years mark a school-related separation from family for all children, these years may be especially traumatic for immigrant children. Attending school marks the entrance into an environment that is very different from the home environment. The child may be uncomfortable with English as the primary language or with the policies of American schools (Hendricks, 2005). In an earlier article (Congress & Lynn, 1994), the author presented the case example of an 8-year-old immigrant child who was extremely upset after assignment to a classroom apart from his sibling who was 11 months younger. American schools focus on the individual development of children; for that reason, even identical twins are usually placed in separate classes, if possible. Yet, this child had always been with his younger sibling, and his unhappiness caused by the school's policy of separating siblings impeded his learning and achieving mastery within the school environment.

Identity Versus Identity Confusion (12–22 Years)

The period of adolescence, between the ages of 12 and 22, is characterized by the psychosocial crisis of identity versus identity confusion (Erikson, 1994). The adolescent becomes more independent of the parents and may look more to the peer group for support and guidance. This period is often rife with struggle and conflict, both intrapsychic and interpersonal, within the family. Much attention has been given to the adolescent's attempts at separation—wanting one's own private space, extended curfew, and dress and behaviors that differ markedly from the family. This period, however, is best characterized by ambivalence. The teenager who fought so hard for an extended curfew may call home several times to see how everything is. There is a need for parents to provide structure in order to promote the establishment of identity. It should be noted that adolescence may begin prior to 12 years of age, as children often develop physically and socially at an earlier age than at the time that Erikson first developed his theory. Also, for some youth, adolescence may end prior to the late teens, as they start families of their own. For others, this adolescent phase may extend well into their 20s as they pursue graduate and postgraduate education.

Many immigrants may come from backgrounds in which the adolescence stage of development did not exist or was extremely curtailed. For families in which children married young and/or left school in early adolescence to begin working, identity formation occurs at a much younger age. There may be much conflict within families in which the parents' adolescence was limited, while their adolescent children seek the lengthy American adolescent experience of their peers.

Intimacy Versus Isolation (22–34 Years)

Erikson characterized the young adult era by the psychosocial crisis of intimacy versus isolation. Successful achievement during this period is measured by finding a love object, as well as satisfying work (Erikson, 1994). The age parameters for this stage should be viewed as very flexible. Many young adults are so involved in developing their careers during their young adult years that the development of an intimate relationship does not occur. For others, developing an intimate relationship may have occurred at a younger age. Also, in a society in which the divorce rate approaches 50%, developing a permanent love relationship in the early 20s is not a desirable goal for many young people. Although Erikson did not address the gay and lesbian population, it should be noted that the love object can be a person of the same sex. Finally, some adults choose never to find an individual person for a love relationship.

Levinson (1978) divided early adulthood into the following stages: early adult transition (17–22 years of age), entering the adult world (22–28), transition (28–33), and settling down (33–40). Important tasks included beginning careers and families. Many individuals, especially in developed countries, complete their education during the early transition years. It should be noted that the age at which individuals get married and have children has been steadily increasing (U.S. Census Bureau, 2013). The focus for many in their 20s is to complete their education and begin careers. Thus, settling down with partners and beginning families is often postponed until individuals are in their 30s. Crisis often occurs for individuals at times of transition, as for example when adolescents transit to adulthood in their late teens.

Generativity Versus Stagnation (34–60 Years)

The seventh Erikson stage occurs between 34 and 60 years and involves the psychosocial crisis of generativity versus stagnation. This period involves learning to care for others and may include having a family and/or pursuing a career. Initially, it was thought that the midlife period presented a time of crisis for men with the realization of failure to achieve previous goals, whereas for women the crisis involved children leaving the home. More recently, the midlife crisis period has been considered a myth, as both men and women tend to make positive career changes during the midlife years (Hunter & Sundel, 1989). Also, as most women now work outside the home, their role of child caretaker has declined in importance. Furthermore, one can question if this stage in truth ends at 60, as many continue to work much longer.

Levinson (1978) pointed to the crisis of transition periods during the adult middle years. He characterized this middle adulthood period as occurring between 40 and 65 years of age and divided these years into the following periods: midlife transition (40–45 years), entering middle adulthood (45–50), age 50 transition (50–55), and the culmination of middle adulthood (55–60). Middle age is often perceived as a crisis period as individuals realize career and personal limitations. There is a growing realization that they may never achieve the personal and professional goals set for themselves during the adult beginning years. This may result in major life changes, such as becoming involved with a younger woman or leaving a successful career to undertake a new simpler lifestyle. Peck (1968) has postulated four major steps that are crucial to psychological adjustment during the middle years. They are socializing rather than sexualizing human relationships, valuing wisdom rather than physical powers, emotional flexibility rather than fixation, and mental flexibility instead of rigidity.

A concern about Levinson's (1978) early research was that it focused primarily on men. Research on women (Papalia & Olds, 1995) has indicated major differences between age-linked developmental changes of men and women. Women were seen as less likely to have mentors, and more likely to have dreams that were split between relationships and achievement. Levinson (1996) studied women and concluded that women did go through predictable periods, but transitions between periods were likely to be more turbulent than for men. He noted that women who pursued traditional roles, as well as those who pursued careers, often struggled with integrating the two. Today, the dynamics of the work environment have exerted enormous pressure on working women as they need to cope with virtually two full-time jobs—one at the office and the other at home. Working women experience greater difficulty than men in balancing work and family. In order to succeed in one environment, working women are often called upon to make sacrifices in another environment as each makes different demands on them and has distinct norms to adhere to (Shobha, 2014).

Integrity Versus Despair (Age 60–Death)

Erikson (1994) described the final stage of old age as characterized by the psychosocial crisis of integrity versus despair. The psychologically healthy older person is seen as one who has come to terms with past successes and failures, one who has few regrets, and one who has accepted death. Those who do not resolve this crisis experience despair at impending death and lost opportunities. Erikson's eighth stage did not include the recent phenomenon of many older adults who now assume caretaking roles for their grandchildren. It could be argued that these grandparents may experience the generativity of an earlier stage of development. Also, as mentioned earlier, as life expectancy increases, many older people continue to work well past the age of 60.

A Ninth Stage (80 Years and Beyond)

Since Erikson's theory was last published in 1994, life expectancy has increased to 75.5 and 80.5 years for men and women, respectively (Ortman et al., 2014). The number of older people in our society is rapidly increasing and the fastest growing group of older people are the "old old" who are defined as 85 and older (AARP, 1997). To address this phenomenon, Erikson (1997) formulated a ninth stage of development for those who live into their 80s and 90s. This stage is characterized ideally by gerotranscendence. An older person achieves this stage by mastering each previous stage, as well as transcending the physical and social losses associated with old age.

Feminist Critique of Traditional Theories of Individual Human Development

Traditional theories of individual development, such as those proposed by Erikson (1994) and Levinson (1978), have been recognized as being based largely on a male, middle-class, White, Western European model. The discussion of Erikson's theory in this chapter attempted to include considerations of various types of diversity (e.g., culture, class, sexual orientation). It is also important, however, to consider the feminist critique of traditional theories of individual development.

Feminists have argued that Erikson's and Levinson's theories of human development, for the most part, ignore women's developmental experiences. Gilligan (1982) proposed that traditional theories of development represent the male experience of self-development through separation and ignore the female experience of progression toward interdependence through relationships and attachments. Similarly, Miller (1991) has pointed out that women's sense of self develops through emotional connections with and caring for others and that such experiences are ignored and undervalued by traditional theories, thus undermining the development of self-esteem for women. Surrey (1991) has explicated the self-in-relation theory of women's development, with the dual goals of "response–ability" to others and the ability to care for oneself. Feminist critiques have argued convincingly that theories of development that undervalue the importance of emotional connections are detrimental to both men and women. These critiques have made an important contribution to broadening theories of individual development so that attachment, affiliation, and relationship are valued as much as separation and self-development.

STAGES OF MORAL DEVELOPMENT

The biopsychosocial development of individuals also includes moral development. How do children learn to make decisions about right and wrong behavior? Kohlberg (1981) has postulated six stages of moral development that can be condensed into three levels. The first level includes the premoral stage (0–4 years) and the preconventional stage (4–10 years). The child follows rules, but primarily to avoid punishment by a powerful person or to satisfy one's own needs.

The second level is that of conventional/role conformity and includes a good boy/good girl orientation (stage 3) and an authority and social order maintaining orientation (stage 4). This level implies that doing right is primarily related to either the desire to meet the approval of others or be seen as a good citizen. Kohlberg believed that the second level was obtained by the majority of people.

The third level is characterized by postconventional/self-accepted moral principles and includes a contractual/legalistic orientation (stage 5) and the morality of individual principles of conscience (stage 6). At this level, individuals do what is right because it is legal and following laws is the most rational choice or because of their own moral sense of right and wrong. Kohlberg believed that one progressed through each stage sequentially and saw education as essential in promoting moral development. Gilligan (982), in her early work, took issue with Kohlberg's stages of moral development and stated that it was primarily male oriented. She questioned whether the ideal of moral development could be found only within one's self and proposed that women follow a different course of moral development. Through her research, she learned that women always considered the interpersonal and a relational perspective in making moral decisions. This reflected a different, but not an inferior, foundation for ethical decision-making.

FAMILY DEVELOPMENT THEORY

Families are made up of individuals of different ages and at different stages of development. Although early family literature focused primarily on the nuclear family in which members ranged in age from infancy to adulthood, many families now are intergenerational and may have members of all ages. In order to work effectively with individuals and families, the clinician must have an awareness of the developmental stage of each family member, as well as the stage of the family life cycle. Carter and McGoldrick (2004) have developed a family life cycle model that delineates predictable stages in family development. Similar to Erikson's model of individual development, families experience a crisis when they pass from one life cycle stage to another. If not resolved, a family's developmental crisis can lead to family conflict and breakup (Congress, 1996). The six stages of the traditional middle-class family life cycle delineated by Carter and McGoldrick (2004) are: (a) between families—the unattached young adult, (b) the joining of families through marriage—the newly married couple, (c) the family with young children, (d) the family with adolescents, (e) launching children and moving on, and (f) the family in later life.

New roles for women, social and economic trends, an increasing divorce rate, and class differences have all contributed to diverse forms of the family life cycle (Carter & McGoldrick, 2004). In the first edition of this chapter, U.S. Census Bureau data suggested that one out of two marriages ends in divorce. Current literature, however, suggests that the divorce rate is falling, especially as people are marrying later (Miller, 2014). Also, most of the divorced remarry within a few years (Congress, 1996). To address these phenomena, Carter and McGoldrick (2004) have identified family life cycle stages for divorced and remarried families. Now over 50% of all Americans are single; 30.4% of them have never been married, while 19.8% are divorced, separated, or widowed. Again, this is in sharp contrast to 40 years ago when the number of unmarried adults was 37% (Miller, 2014). Furthermore, one out of five couples chooses to remain childless, which is in sharp contrast to the 1970s when only one out of ten couples was childless (Livingston & Cohn, 2010).

While some unmarried people are in long-term lesbian and gay relationships, now many same-sex couples have opted for marriage, which is now legal in all 50 states. The number of same-sex partnerships, both married as well as living together, has increased by 80% between 2000 and 2010. Now, 25% of same-sex partnerships have children living in the household (Roberts & Stark, 2014).

While Carter and McGoldrick focused primarily on the heterosexual family life cycle, the family life cycle for lesbians and gay men has been discussed (Appleby & Anastas, 1998; Mallon, 2005). More recently, Goldberg (2010) has looked at gay and lesbian parenting from a family life cycle approach.

Although Carter and McGoldrick (2004) have developed the most comprehensive life cycle family theory, there are limitations as the focus is primarily on middle-class heterosexual families. What follows is a discussion of the stages that they have identified together with information about same-sex parents and families from different cultural and economic backgrounds. Attempts are made to acknowledge how issues of diversity limit the generalization of these stages and to relate these stages to those in individual development theory.

Stage 1: Between Families—The Unattached Young Adult

This first stage of family development usually occurs in late adolescence and early adulthood. Developmental tasks for this period have traditionally included emotional and physical separation from the family of origin, developing peer relationships, and establishing oneself in work (McGoldrick et al., 2015). It should be noted that this period may span the late part of Erikson's adolescence stage and the early part of the adult stage. Both the young adult and the parents must participate in this separation process. Ambivalence about separating may produce a family crisis. Separation involves more than physical separation. Often, young adults who do not successfully complete this process of emotional separation may have difficulties establishing their own independent family.

The age at which individuals marry for the first time is increasing; therefore, the stage of the young, unattached adult may be extended. Economic factors may contribute to young adults remaining physically and financially dependent on their parents for housing and financial support. Parents may also apply adolescent rules to young adults still living in their house, which can precipitate family crises and conflicts.

It should be noted that a lengthy stage of young unattached adulthood may be increasing for both middle-class Anglo families as well as poor, culturally diverse families. The United States has become increasingly culturally diverse, and it is estimated that by the mid-21st century the majority of people will be from backgrounds other than Western European (U.S. Census Bureau, 2010). Already one-third of U.S. citizens are immigrants or children of immigrants (U.S. Census Bureau, 2010). Many cultures continue to have an expectation that young adults remain at home until married, thus keeping offspring emotionally connected and dependent on their families. Furthermore, with adolescent single parenthood, this stage leading to marriage may not exist. Young unattached adolescents/adults may not choose to establish their own home, but rather continue to live in an intergenerational family. Although mothers and grandmothers involved in raising adolescents'/adults' children may provide needed emotional and concrete support, family conflict often occurs with regard to parental roles and power.

Serious romantic involvements during this stage pave the way for young adults to leave home and form their own families. Again, there may be family conflict when parents and adult children disagree about a future marriage partner. An increasing number of young adults choose to live together before marriage (National Health Statistics Reports, 2013). Cohabiting today does not carry the same stigma as in previous generations with about two-thirds of couples living together before marriage. At one time, marriage may have been seen as the only way for young couples to get the social support and companionship that are important for emotional health. This is not so any longer. Marriage is not necessary to reap the benefits of living together, at least when it comes to emotional health (Dush & Mernitz, 2015).

Young gay and lesbian people may experience specific challenges during this period. There may be a difficult period of "coming out to their parents" and some may even decide on a heterosexual marriage to dispel family fears about sexual orientation. Different communities in the United States may have differing acceptance of gay or lesbian youth, and there may be limited opportunities for them to meet others of the same sexual orientation.

Stage 2: The Joining of Families Through Marriage—The Newly Married Couple

The second family life cycle stage identified by Carter and McGoldrick (2004)—that of the newly married couple—is often challenging for young people. Each partner must learn that the other may have differing expectations, choices, and goals (Congress, 1996), and together the couple must learn to compromise in making both major and minor decisions. Although one might assume that this stage would be less challenging for couples who have lived together before marriage, relating to in-laws as a married couple is still apt to produce conflict (Carter & McGoldrick, 2004). The increasing rate of divorce among couples, especially in the first few years of marriage, is often the outcome of family crises and conflicts during this stage.

It should be noted that marriages occur not only among young adults but at different ages along the individual life cycle. Whereas marriage in adolescence is decreasing, an increasing number of people marry and remarry in their 30s, 40s, and 50s. Marriage also occurs among people in Erikson's eighth stage, that of old age. Although the developmental tasks around establishing an intimate relationship may be similar, other psychosocial tasks related to work issues may impact differently on newly married couples. For example, when young adults marry, they may be struggling to establish careers. When middle-aged adults with existing careers marry, however, they may be faced with the demands of finding time for their new marriage partners, relocating for one partner's career, and dealing with the familial stress of stepchildren. Older adults who marry, or remarry, may face conflict around retirement and shrinking financial resources.

Same-sex marriage is now legal in all 50 states. More and more gay and lesbian couples who have been living in long-term committed relationships of various lengths have increasingly taken advantage of this opportunity.

Stage 3: The Family With Young Children

The third family life cycle stage has been described as the "pressure cooker" phase in that the majority of divorces occur within this time period (Carter & McGoldrick, 2004). The major developmental task is faced when the couple must begin to think of themselves as a triad rather than a dyad. An infant is extremely demanding of time and attention. While the family is in this developmental phase, the child is in the first stage of individual development during which trust is so important. There are many occasions for conflict to arise during this period.

Current social trends may contribute to the stress of this period. Women are usually older and working while children are young, which produces additional stress. Also, the increase of the single-parent household often means a role overload for the primary caregiver. Furthermore, remarriages and blended families may result in the need to negotiate complicated relationships with stepparents and stepchildren (Carter & McGoldrick, 2004).

Having children of one's own often reenacts and reawakens old unresolved issues in individual members. For example, a spouse who has not been able to successfully resolve the developmental psychosocial crisis of establishing trust may be especially threatened by the birth of a baby who now receives special attention.

Another complicating factor is that in most families, children are often at different stages of individual development. For example, a multichild family may be challenged by having a new infant who is very demanding of time and attention and also a latency age child who needs help to develop peer relationships. Families may also experience a crisis in handling sibling conflict, especially of siblings of different ages with differing psychosocial needs.

Again, there may be special challenges for same-sex couples who may have to make initial parenting decisions about adoption, surrogate birth, or artificial insemination. Because same-sex couples have often been part of heterosexual marriages or relationships previously, there may be children already living with one or both parents. Although schools are now much more sensitive to different family constellations, some children may experience difficulty in explaining two father or two mother parents to both their peers and teachers.

Stage 4: The Family With Adolescents

This fourth phase has been identified as a major family crisis point (Carter & McGoldrick, 2004). While adolescents are struggling with identity and separation issues, their parents may be coping with their own issues around employment and health. Parents often have difficulty in granting adolescents any independence and may wish for a return to latency years when their children were more connected with the family. Although adolescents may seem to want more independence, there still continues to be a need for structure, and parents may alternate between being too restrictive and too lenient. Intrafamilial differences also impact on culturally diverse families during this period, as immigrant adolescents often may want to associate only with their American peers, while parents prefer the family relationship patterns they have learned in their countries of origin.

For same-sex parented families, there may be special challenges when children reach adolescence. Adolescence is the time during which young people mature physically and become aware of their own sexuality. For example, a gay male married couple struggled with how to talk to their preadolescent daughter about impending menses and finally turned to a trusted aunt for this conversation.

Stage 5: Launching Children and Moving On

Although previously referred to as the "empty nest phase," this term may not accurately reflect what actually occurs in families. First, because of economic factors, many young adults do not leave home until they are much older, and even then, they frequently return to the parental home. Second, two factors mitigate the impact of the empty nest syndrome. The majority of women with children work outside the home, and many women in midlife actively pursue new careers and higher education. This family life cycle stage may be linked to individual development issues. Parents may be struggling with midlife concerns around career changes, while their offspring are only beginning to pursue their work objectives. Difficulties may arise when parents try to enforce their unrealized career wishes on their children, as for example, when a middle-aged father who worked in a clerical social service position insisted that his son attend law school after graduating from college.

During this phase, the family changes from being a small group with one or more offspring to a dyad again. For couples who have spent most of their married years raising a family, relating as a dyad again may be challenging. Many couples, however, look forward to this phase and welcome the opportunity to be relieved of demanding child care responsibilities. Time can be spent on advancing careers, pursuing education, and travel. For these couples who were looking forward to being a dyad again, adult children who do not want to leave home or who thrust child caring responsibilities on their parents may be perceived as challenging.

Stage 6: The Family in Later Life

The final stage of the family life cycle—the family in later life—occurs when children have left home. With increasing life expectancies, this phase may span over 30 years. Although the number of older people in our population is rapidly increasing, especially as the "baby boomers" hit 60, the increase of the old (85 or older) is especially striking (Ortman et al., 2014). The transitions and tasks in later life include issues of retirement, grandparenthood, illness and dependency, and loss and death. One common challenge for individuals and couples in this period, especially for those with failing health, is the experience of role reversal with their children.

As life expectancy increases and women continue to live longer than men, the number of widowed women has and will continue to increase (Ortman et al., 2014). The majority of older people live alone in the community, not in institutional care or with their families (Ortman et al., 2014). Although elders living with families has been the pattern for many American cultural minorities, there is some evidence that this is changing. Millions of children are being raised solely by their grandparents, with numbers continuing to climb as the opioid crisis and other factors disrupt families. The American Academy of Pediatrics (AAP) found that caregivers who raise their grandchildren are able to manage as well as biological and adoptive parent caregivers (AAP, 2018).

Regardless of where they live, many culturally diverse grandmothers do not "retire" from the family in old age, but rather are called upon to serve as parents to grandchildren whose parents have died or are unable to care for their children. Does the family cease when there is one remaining member, often an elderly woman whose husband has died and whose children have developed their own families? The interest in reminiscence groups, both in nursing homes as well as in senior centers, attests to the continuing importance of family throughout the life cycle.

Loss may be an especially difficult issue for lesbian and gay families during the later years. The loss of a partner may be even more traumatic for the remaining person, because they may not be comfortable sharing with others about personal loss if they live in a homophobic community (Humphries & Quam, 1998).

IMPLICATIONS AND TOOLS FOR PRACTICE

The social worker must be cognizant of developmental theory in work with individuals and families. Making an assessment of what the current stage of development is for each individual, as well as for the total family, is particularly helpful, as there are certain needs and tasks of individuals and families at different stages.

For example, a young newly married couple in their 20s is very different from a recently divorced single-parent family with two adolescent children. In the former, each member must work on establishing a commitment to each other and the marriage; they must be able to work out issues of appropriate emotional separation from their family of origin yet realign relationships with extended families and friends to include the spouse. In the latter situation, the family must work out financial and familial relationships with the departing spouse/parent. Unless contraindicated due to issues of safety, contact with the absent spouse must be maintained and a visitation plan developed. Also, it should be noted that, according to individual development theory, adolescents are in the process of establishing their own identity apart from their parents and families. They often turn to their peers for support and guidance during this phase rather than their parents, which may cause increased conflict within a family that has already endured the crisis of separation and divorce.

Even when couples seem to be in the same family life cycle stage, there may be important differences based on their individual ages. A young couple in their 20s who are engaged to be married may be struggling with issues of separation from their family of origin, whereas a middle-aged couple engaged to be married may have to work out issues of separation and connection with previous spouses and children.

There are a number of family assessment tools that can help the practitioner identify and understand individual and family development issues. A brief overview is provided of four such tools: (a) the ecomap, (b) the genogram, (c) the culturagram, and (d) the intersectional design tool (IDT).

Ecomap

The ecomap (Hartman & Laird, 1983) is built on an ecological approach to practice and outlines the relationship of the family as a whole, and its individual members, with the outside world. It provides a snapshot of the family at a certain point in time. By looking at the ecomap, the clinician can assess the extent to which the developmental needs of the family and its individual members are being met. For example, the previously discussed newly divorced family with two adolescents should show some connection with the absent parent. If this link is missing or conflictual, family problems can be addressed in treatment. Also, the ecomap demonstrates connection with different resources in the community. It would be of concern if the ecomap illustrated that an adolescent had no connection with peers for recreational activities.

Genogram

The genogram (McGoldrick et al., 2008) is a family assessment tool that examines the intergenerational relationships within a family. The genogram maps out family constellations, relationships, and events over three generations. This tool allows the social worker to become aware of the current and past connections in the immediate family, as well as connections with extended family. The clinician is able to assess the individual and family development stages when therapeutic work begins. Also, the clinician can gain an understanding of historical issues in individual and family development.

Figure 4.1 is a genogram of the divorced family with two adolescent children that has been referred to previously. The genogram allows the clinician to examine the connection of parents and children with the extended family, as well as the absent parent. Also, it is possible to look at what was happening at key points in the family history; for example, at the time of the divorce, at the time of the children's births, and at the time of the parents' marriages. Key events such as births, separations, divorces, deaths, serious health problems, employment reversals, relocations, and other crisis events all impact individual and family development. The genogram can help to clarify when these events occurred and their impact on family development. For

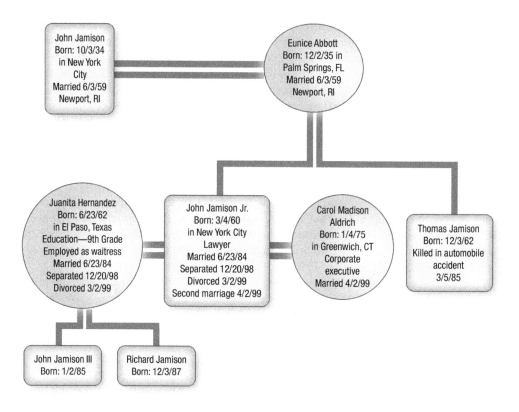

FIGURE 4.1 Genogram.

example, an examination of Figure 4.1 indicates that the Jamison/Hernandez family experienced many crises in a short period of time. John Jamison Jr. and Juanita Hernandez were divorced and shortly afterward John remarried. Also, we are aware John's new wife is in her 20s, only 10 to 12 years older than her new stepsons. The two adolescent boys live with their mother, and there is indication that both have experienced academic and behavioral problems around the time of the divorce. Although Juanita has continued as the custodial parent, the social worker would want to explore what arrangements have been made for the adolescent sons to visit their father.

In terms of important historical facts, we note that John III was born only 6 months after his parents were married, which may suggest that the couple had little time to adjust to living together as a couple before they were married. Also, there is the possibility that John Jr. and Juanita "had to get married" and that John III was not planned. The Jamison family experienced a major crisis when John III was an infant and when John Jr.'s brother was in a fatal accident. There may be pressure on the oldest male child, John Jr., and now John III, to carry on the family tradition.

Also, we note ethnic, geographic, and class differences between the Jamison and the Hernandez sides of the family. The Jamisons and the new wife, Carol Madison Aldrich, come from the Northeast, whereas Juanita was born in Texas. The Jamisons appear to be from a White, Anglo-Saxon, Protestant background, whereas Juanita is Mexican American. John Jr. has graduate education, whereas Juanita did not graduate from high school. Both sons are in the adolescent phase of development during which children strive to become more independent of their parents. Yet parental roles and values are very important in shaping adolescent and adult identities. As both parents come from such different backgrounds, the social worker would want to explore the impact this has had on the family in the past as well as the present.

Culturagram

The ecomap and genogram are useful tools in assessing the development of the family, as well as the developmental stages of its members. These tools, however, neglect the important role of culture in assessing and understanding the family. To increase understanding of the impact of culture on the family, the culturagram (Congress, 1994, 1997; Congress & Kung, 2013) has been developed and applied to work with people of color (Lum, 2003), battered women (Brownell & Congress, 1998), children (Webb, 2003), immigrants (Congress, 2004), people with health problems (Congress, 2004), and older people (Brownell, 1997). The culturagram grew out of the recognition that families are becoming increasingly culturally diverse. It is estimated that over 25% of those living in the United States are either immigrants or children of immigrants (Potocky-Tripodi, 2002). Although earlier immigrants to the United States were primarily men, recent waves of immigration have been mostly women and children (Foner, 2005). The presence of families from 125 nations in one zip code attests to the increasing diversity of our country (*National Geographic*, 1998).

Practitioners demonstrate varied degrees of cultural competence in working with individuals and families from different cultures. Schools, agencies, and governmental organizations are frequently rooted in a Western European background. Individual and family development theories were originally based on practice with traditional White American middle-class families. Cultural differences often have a major impact on individual and family development. For example, individuals and families from other cultures are often more familial and communal than their White Anglo-Saxon American counterparts. Class also may be an important factor. Middle-class families from other cultures may be more assimilated and follow Carter and McGoldrick's family development patterns more closely than poor families. The clinician must guard against judging individuals or families as pathological because they do not follow traditional individual and family development patterns. The adolescent who chooses not to separate from his parents to attend a distant college despite a full scholarship is not pathological, but perhaps is heeding a cultural norm that maintaining familial connection is more important than individual achievement. The culturally diverse family in the launching stage in which adult children choose not to move out and live independent of their parents may believe that ongoing connection with family provides essential lifetime support.

Many culturally diverse families exhibit much strength in handling the crisis of each developmental stage. Some examples of this include the single adolescent mother who struggles to receive a General Education Diploma, while working full time to support her child; the working class family in which the father, as a janitor, and mother, as a housekeeper, manage to provide for and raise a large family; and the grandmother who, despite serious health problems, cares for her grandchildren.

When attempting to understand culturally diverse families in terms of individual and family development theory, it is important to assess the family within a cultural context. Some have written about the unique characteristics of different cultures (Ho, 2004; McGoldrick et al., 1996). Considering a family only in terms of a specific culture, however, may lead to overgeneralization and stereotyping (Congress & Kung, 2013). For example, a Puerto Rican family that has lived in the United States for 40 years is very different from a Mexican family that emigrated last month, although both families are Hispanic. Also, one cannot assume even within a particular cultural group that all families are similar.

The culturagram (Figure 4.2) is a family assessment tool that represents an attempt to individualize culturally diverse families (Congress & Kung, 2013). Completing a culturagram with a family can help a practitioner develop a better understanding of the family in terms of individual and family development theory. The culturagram can be a powerful tool for better assessment, treatment planning, and intervention in work with culturally diverse families.

As is apparent in Figure 4.2, the culturagram consists of 10 major areas that are important to consider in order to understand culturally diverse families. They are: (a) reasons for

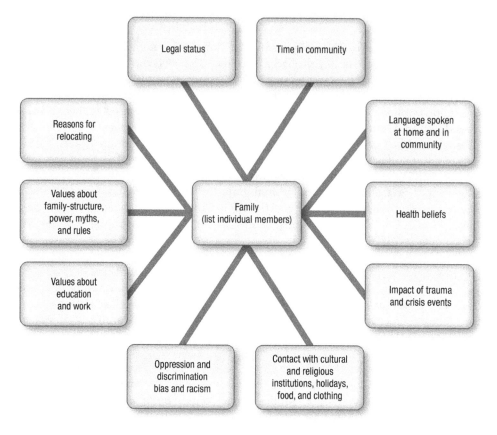

FIGURE 4.2 Culturagram.

Source: From "Using Culturagrams with Culturally Diverse Families" by Elaine Congress, pp. 969–975, Fig: 144.1 (p. 971: Culturagram–2007), in Social Workers'; Desk Reference, 2nd ed., edited by Roberts, A. & Greene, G. (2009). By permission of Oxford University Press, USA. www.oup.com

immigration; (b) length of time in the community; (c) legal status; (d) language spoken at home and in the community; (e) health beliefs; (f) impact of crisis events; (g) holidays/special events and contact with cultural/religious groups; (h) current and past discrimination, bias, and racism; (i) values about education and work; and (j) values about family, including structure, power, myths, and rules.

REASONS FOR IMMIGRATION

Reasons for immigration vary among families. Many families come because of economic opportunities in the United States, whereas others relocate because of political and religious discrimination in their country of origin. For some, it is possible to return home again, and they often travel back and forth for holidays and special occasions. Others know that they can never go home again. Economic and social differences between the country of origin and the United States can affect immigrant families. For example, in the United States, latency-aged children often attend large schools far from their communities and begin to develop peer relationships apart from their families. For culturally diverse families that come from backgrounds in which education is not easily accessible, and even young children are supposed to work and care for younger siblings, the U.S. school system, with its focus on individual academic achievement and peer relationships, may seem strange. Furthermore, immigrant children who bring a history of individual or family oppression may feel very isolated and lonely in their new environments. Individual development theory for latency-aged children, as well as family development theory for families with young children, needs to be understood in the context of immigration issues involving loss, change, and assimilation.

LENGTH OF TIME IN THE COMMUNITY

This area of the culturagram assessment provides an important context to understand culturally diverse families. Usually the family members who have arrived earlier are more assimilated than other members. Also, because of attending U.S. schools and developing peer relationships, children are often more quickly assimilated than their parents. This may lead to conflictual role reversals in which children assume a leadership role. A current phenomenon involves mothers first immigrating to the United States and then sending for their children. These circumstances can certainly impact on individual and family development. A young infant left in the care of relatives in the homeland may have difficulties in developing trust because of the lack of continuity in parenting during this crucial development period. Also, the family with young children that is disrupted when the mother emigrates may face challenges in reuniting as a family after several years' hiatus.

LEGAL STATUS

The legal status of a family may have an effect on both individual and family development. Often families consist of both documented and undocumented members. In families affected by domestic violence, often a husband with legal status may threaten his undocumented wife with reporting her undocumented status to immigration authorities. If a family is undocumented and fears deportation, individual members, as well as the family as a whole, may become secretive and socially isolated. Latency-aged children and adolescents may be discouraged from developing peer relationships because of the fears of others knowing their immigration secret.

LANGUAGE

Language is the mechanism by which families communicate with each other. Often, families may use their own native language at home but speak English when outside the home and in the community. Sometimes, children begin to prefer English as they see knowledge of this language as most helpful for survival in their newly adopted country. This may lead to conflict in families. A most literal communication problem may develop when parents speak no English, and children speak their native tongue only minimally.

HEALTH BELIEFS

Families from different cultures have varying beliefs about health, disease, and treatment (Congress, 2004; Congress & Lyons, 1992). Often, health issues impact on individual and family development, as for example when the primary wage earner with a serious illness is no longer able to work, a family member has HIV/AIDS, or a child has a chronic health condition such as asthma or diabetes. The children of immigrants may be at greater risk for certain chronic adult diseases (Santora, 2006), and the access to care and the care they receive are very important. Also, mental health problems can impact negatively on individual and family development. Families from different cultures may encounter barriers in accessing medical treatment or may prefer alternative resources for diagnosing and treating physical and mental health conditions (Congress, 2004). Many immigrants may use healthcare methods other than traditional Western European medical care involving diagnosis, pharmacology, x-rays, and surgery (Congress, 2004). The social worker who wishes to understand families must study their unique healthcare beliefs.

CRISIS EVENTS

Families can encounter developmental crises as well as "bolts from the blue" crises (Congress, 1996). As discussed previously, developmental crises may occur when a family moves from one life cycle stage to another. Life cycle stages for culturally diverse families may be quite different from those for traditional middle-class families. For example, for many culturally diverse families, the "launching children" stage may not occur at all, as single and even married children may continue to live in close proximity to the parents. If separation is forced, this developmental crisis might be especially traumatic.

Families also deal with "bolts from the blue" crises in different ways. A family's reaction to crisis events is often related to their cultural values. For example, a father's accident and subsequent inability to work may be especially traumatic for an immigrant family in which the father's providing for the family is an important family value. While rape is certainly traumatic for any family, the rape of a teenage girl may be especially traumatic for a family who values virginity before marriage. Families from different cultures who suffered a loss as a result of the 9/11 tragedy may demonstrate a variety of crisis-related symptoms (Congress & Lynn, 2005).

HOLIDAYS/SPECIAL EVENTS, CONTACT WITH CULTURAL/RELIGIOUS GROUPS

Each family has particular holidays and special events. Some events mark transitions from one developmental stage to another; for example, a christening, a bar mitzvah, a wedding, or a funeral. It is important for the social worker to learn the cultural significance of important holidays for the family, as they are indicative of what families see as major transition points in their family development. Contact with cultural and religious institutions often provides support to an immigrant family. Family members may use cultural institutions differently. For example, a father may belong to a social club, the mother may attend a church where her native language is spoken, and adolescent children may refuse to participate in either because they wish to become more Americanized. The clinician also needs to explore the role of spirituality within the immigrant family.

CURRENT AND PAST DISCRIMINATION, BIAS, AND RACISM

Many immigrants, and especially refugees, have experienced prejudice and discrimination in their countries of origin. Unfortunately, racism and discrimination do not end with immigration to the United States. Many undocumented immigrants live with the fear of being deported and separated from their families. This may be especially difficult for families whose children were born here and thus are U.S. citizens. Immigrants may be the victims of racism or discrimination because of their skin color or limited language skills.

VALUES ABOUT EDUCATION AND WORK

All families have differing values about work and education, and culture is an important influence on such values. Social workers must explore what these values are in order to understand the family. For example, employment in a high-status position may be very important to the male bread winner. Often it is especially traumatic for the immigrant family when the father cannot find any work or only work of a menial nature. Sometimes there may be a conflict in values. This occurred when an adolescent son was accepted with a full scholarship to a prestigious university 1,000 miles away from home. Although the family had always believed in the importance of education, the parents believed that the family needed to stay together and they did not want to have their only child leave home, even to pursue education.

VALUES ABOUT FAMILY

Many families from culturally diverse backgrounds may have differing views about family structure and power, based on gender and age. Often, American families are more egalitarian, with women and children having equal voices within the families. This may be very different for many families from cultures in which males were considered the most dominant, women were subservient, and children had limited voices. Also, some cultures have much respect for older people and depend on their input for decision-making, while in the United States, there is often more of a youth orientation. Because of language differences, however, often a role reversal occurs with children assuming greater power because of their greater fluency in English. In working with culturally diverse families, the clinician needs to be aware of family values that are different from those of themselves or other American families.

Intersectional Design Tool

While knowing a family's cultural background is important, knowledge of other factors are also important in understanding families. A middle-class family from Mexico whose father is in the United States on a work visa with a tech company is very different from an undocumented Mexican family supported minimally by a father making food deliveries. An intersectional approach was first introduced by Crenshaw (1989) who was concerned that knowing a person's gender was only one part of understanding a person. All people have different aspects, some of which have more power and privilege than others. Thus, Black women often faced more discrimination because of having two aspects or statuses—gender and race that had less power and privilege. This theory was expanded to include other statuses that have varying degrees of power and privilege. To help in understanding how this impacts family, the IDT (2017) was developed. Figure 4.3 includes important statuses that helps in understanding families with whom we work.

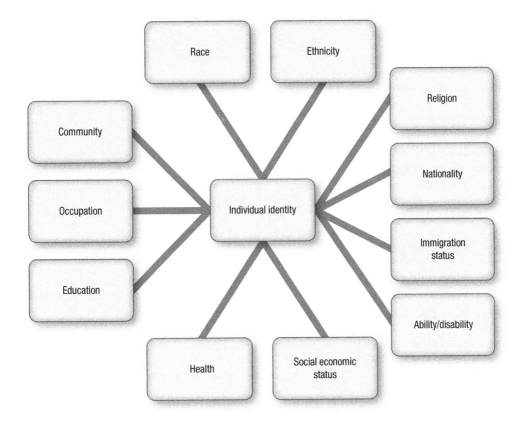

FIGURE 4.3 Intersectional design tool.

CONCLUSION

Social workers need to integrate knowledge of individual and family development theory in their work. Such knowledge can help workers identify and normalize individual and family problems. The stages of individual and family development should not, however, be applied rigidly. There is a risk of characterizing individuals or families as pathological if they do not follow the expected guidelines for the stage. Any attempt to describe "normal" development runs the risk of pathologizing those who do not fit the theoretical descriptions. It is important to recognize that theories of individual and family development have been based largely on a White, male, middle-class model. These theories must continue to be expanded to take into account various types of diversity and changing social trends.

With regard to individual development, for example, more recognition must be afforded to women's experience, and affiliation and connection need to be valued as much as separation and self-development. With regard to family development theory, the need for flexibility and multiple conceptions of normal development are necessitated by diverse types of families such as single-parent, blended, gay and lesbian, poor, and culturally diverse families. Even when changing social trends and diversity are given due recognition, individual and family development theories provide only broad guidelines in work with clients. Social workers must apply these theories in the context of the specific, unique individuals and families with whom they are working. Using the tools of the ecomap, genogram, culturagram, and an intersectional approach helps in understanding families from diverse socioeconomic classes and cultural backgrounds.

SUMMARY POINTS

- Social workers need to integrate knowledge of individual and family development theory in their work.
- Family development theory should continue to be expanded to take into account various types of diversity and changing social trends.
- There should continue to be more recognition toward a woman's experience and affiliation regarding individual development and should be valued as much as separation and self-development.
- The need for flexibility and multiple conceptions of normal development are necessary to take into account diverse families such as single parent, blended, gay and lesbian, and culturally diverse families.
- Using the tools of the ecomap, genogram, culturagram, and intersectional design helps in understanding families with diverse classes and cultural backgrounds

KEY REFERENCES

Only key references appear in the print edition. The full reference list appears in the digital product found on http://connect.springerpub.com/content/book/978-0-8261-6556-5/part/sec02/chapter/ch04

AARP. (1997). *Profile of retired persons: 1997*. Author.

American Academy of Pediatrics. (2018, November 2). Grandparents: Raising their children, they get the job done. *ScienceDaily*. Retrieved January 26, 2020 from www.sciencedaily.com/releases/2018/11/181102083452.htm

Appleby, G., & Anastas, J. (Eds.). (1998). *Not just a passing phase: Social work with gay, lesbian, and bisexual people*. Columbia University Press.

Bristowe, K., Marshall, S., & Harding, R. (2016). The bereavement experiences of lesbian, gay, bisexual and/or trans* people who have lost a partner: A systematic review, thematic synthesis and modelling of the literature. *Palliative Medicine, 30*(8), 730–744. https://doi.org/10.1177/0269216316634601

Brownell, P. (1997). The application of the culturagram in cross cultural practice with elder abuse victims. *Journal of Elder Abuse and Neglect, 9*(2), 19–33.

Brownell, P., & Congress, E. (1998). Application of the culturagram to assess and empower culturally and ethnically diverse battered women. In A. Roberts (Ed.), *Battered women and their families: Intervention and treatment strategies* (pp. 387–404). Springer.

Congress, E. (1994). The use of culturagrams to assess and empower culturally diverse families. *Families in Society, 75*, 531–540.

Congress, E. (1996). Family crisis—Life cycle and bolts from the blue: Assessment and treatment. In A. Roberts (Ed.), *Crisis intervention and brief treatment: Theory, techniques, and applications* (pp. 142–159). Nelson Hall.

Congress, E. (1997). Using the culturagram to assess and empower culturally diverse families. In E. Congress (Ed.), *Multicultural perspectives in working with families* (pp. 3–16). Springer.

Congress, E. (2004). Cultural and ethnic issues in working with culturally diverse patients and their families: Use of the culturagram to promote cultural competency in health care settings. *Social Work in Health Care, 39*, 249–262.

Couples Theory and Interventions

Clay Gruber and J. Christopher Hall

This chapter discusses some of the most common theories and interventions used with couples, as well as introduces contemporary or developing methods. Running themes of communication, differentiation, and relational growth are noted throughout.

LEARNING OBJECTIVES

By the end of this chapter, you should be able to:

- describe theoretical frameworks involving couples social work practice;
- understand the implementation of those frameworks via case studies;
- identify the similar themes and principles of different family and couples theories;
- inform social work practitioners of modern developments, interventions, and influential names in the field of couples therapy; and
- understand the context for couples therapy models outside of the typical nuclear, heterosexual, White, and middle-class couple.

HISTORY OF COUPLES COUNSELING IN SOCIAL WORK

Though literature related to couples counseling has exploded in recent years, it is not a modern invention. For decades, couples therapy existed in a realm outside of the clinical mental health field that it is associated with today. The practice of working with couples was previously reserved for priests or obstetricians-gynecologists (Gurman & Fraenkel, 2002). As the field has developed, much has changed. Couples counseling is now a major component of mental health practice, and literature surrounding the topic is ever-expanding.

Considering the ethics and value base of social work, it should not come as a surprise that social workers began to place importance on the quality of loving relationships and recognizing their impact on clients. In fact, formal couples counseling has its origins firmly rooted in the field of social work. Far before the development of the field of marriage and family therapy in the 1950s, Mary Richmond in her classic book *Social Diagnosis* (1917) emphasized interventions for the entire family, including recognition of the quality of the relationship between mother and father. Jane Addams discussed the quality of relationships in *Democracy and Social Ethics* (1902), specifically when discussing her concept of *sympathetic knowledge*. Addams believed that we come to know one another in relationships and while part of knowledge rests in the collection of facts, relational knowledge comes through the experience of truly knowing and being connected to others, and that one's well-being and quality of life are determined in part by the quality of those relationships in which one participates. In addition to creating the historical basis for couples counseling, some of the most well-known and influential couples and family counselors have been social workers including Virginia Satir, Insoo Berg, Steve de Shazer, Jay Haley, Lynn Hoffman, Froma Walsh, and Michael White.

ATTACHMENT THEORY AS RELATED TO COUPLES

Attachment theory is a developmental theory that was originally used to describe infant behavior and emotional development as a consequence of interactions with their parents or primary caregivers (Bowlby, 1969). While the theory was originally designed to describe infants, the attachment styles described by the theory affect human behavior well into adulthood. As Bowlby (1979; an early pioneer in attachment theory) stated, individuals' attachment styles follow them "from the cradle to the grave" (p. 127). In the late 1980s and early 1990s, attachment theory began to be applied in the context of adult friendships and relationships (Hazan & Shaver, 1987, 1990; Shaver et al., 1988). It became evident that the principles defining the relationship between mother and infant were also applicable to adult interpersonal relationships. As Shaver et al. (1988) state in *The Psychology of Love*, "To the extent that adolescent and adult romantic love are also attachment processes, many of the concepts and principles of attachment theory should apply to them" (p. 69).

The literature that began to extend attachment theory to adults showed that our primary attachment figure changes as we age. While our parents fill that role as infants, adolescents in high school are equally as likely to endorse peers as their primary attachment figures as their parents (Freeman & Brown, 2001). As adolescents transition into adulthood, relationship dynamics change once again as young adults begin to identify romantic partners as their primary attachment figures (Rosenthal & Kobak, 2010; Shaver & Mikulincer, 2008).

The most recent advancements in attachment theory encompass all close relationships maintained by an individual and how needs and expectations are met within those relationships. For example, one tenet of attachment theory is that humans innately seek social, physical, and emotional contact with others. People require a reliable "secure base" from which they can depart, develop, and return (Bowlby, 1988). Without that base, uncertainty manifesting as anxiety can overwhelm the individual. Conversely, the presence of a predictable base is calming and assists in emotional regulation and autonomy.

The attachment structure can best be visualized as a bungee jumper leaping from a great height. To summon the courage to jump, a jumper must have immense trust in the cord and tether. In attachment theory, the "secure base" attachment figure serves as an anchor to which a person can attach their "emotional bungee cord." They can then plunge into the depths of self-exploration, confident that they will always have a place to return to and once again find solid ground. The strength of that base is determined by a few key factors: accessibility, responsiveness, physical proximity, and emotional engagement, though these factors change over time and require less physical proximity in adulthood (Johnson, 2019). Thus, stronger and more secure bonds lead to deeper, more confident self-exploration.

Those who have strong, secure attachments have several defining traits. Secure individuals are comfortable with their need for closeness with others (Johnson, 2019). Additionally, they have positive expectations of others and are more capable of postformal thought (Sinnott et al. 2017). These traits are considered beneficial for the individual but also appear to serve as a protective factor against stress (Johnson, 2019; Mikulincer & Shaver, 2019). When attachments are not secure, individuals exhibit different behaviors to help cope with the loss or unreliability of their home base. Those behaviors act as an emotional "fight or flight" instinct. Fight or flight responses vary from person to person but fall into three main categories (Johnson, 2019). The first, called "preoccupied," prevents anxiety by persons depending heavily on others. They avoid the stress of not having a reliable base by never leaving in the first place. The second response, called "dismissive," approaches the conflict with an opposite solution. Dismissive individuals strive for self-sufficiency and view their attachment to others as a vulnerability. By distancing themselves, they navigate the conflict of unreliable bonds by avoiding attachment altogether. The third and final response is called the "disorganized" attachment style. Individuals in this style exhibit negative health outcomes such as greater emotional disturbances (Beeney et al., 2017), increased rates of borderline personality disorder (Khoury et al., 2019), developmental symptoms such as low recognition of other's emotions (Forslund et al., 2017), and even enlarged amygdalas (a part of the brain that assists in emotional regulation; Lyons-Ruth et al., 2016). This attachment style usually stems from a history of trauma and is categorized by the paradoxical view that attachment is both the source of and the solution to anxiety (Johnson, 2019).

Even if a strong bond is developed, the strength of that security is not permanent. Security can dissolve or improve, based on further interactions with the attachment figure. Security dissolution can occur when an attachment bond is damaged or is lost altogether, resulting in immense stress and occasionally traumatization (Mikulincer et al., 2003). Conversely, bonds can also strengthen. This malleability presents social workers with an opportunity to provide an intervention to help strengthen bonds, client relationships, and client well-being.

Emotionally Focused Therapy

Emotionally focused therapy (EFT) utilizes the tenets of attachment theory to create a theory-informed intervention. EFT carries with it two primary missions: processing and regulating emotion (Johnson, 2019). EFT is humanistic and experiential in nature, valuing and accepting the individual and their unique life experiences and emotions. In EFT, emotional processing is viewed as a joint effort, requiring input from each member of the couple. When conflict is viewed as an emotional clash between two individuals, co-regulation of emotions as a couple becomes an obvious source of resolution. To partake in this joint emotional exploration, each partner must feel secure in their attachment to each other.

EFT begins with emotional de-escalation and emotional observation. Most couples will present to therapy with a negative pattern of emotions and dialog, often laden with critique and withdrawal. The social work practitioner works together with the couple to identify the damage to their perception of their partner as a secure base as well patterns of negative communication that stem from those perceptions. Specific emphasis is placed on reframing the problem in the vocabulary of attachment theory. One or both members of the couple do not feel wholly secure in their base; therefore, conflict triggers attachment anxieties. Those anxieties feel like threats and fight or flight instincts kick in, often resulting in partners attacking each other with criticism or fleeing through withdrawal. This language also helps remove the problem emphasis from an individual partner and instead places the focus on the subconscious interactions between the couple.

The social work practitioner then works with the couple to promote the recognition and communication of their attachment needs. For example, when a spouse complains that their partner forgets to take out the trash, they often report the secondary emotion—that they are angry. The social work practitioner would seek to deepen that thought and find the primary emotion: often that the individual feels unheard in the relationship. Communication of their needs is then transferred away from the secondary feeling, and emphasis is instead placed on communicating their primary emotions and attachment needs.

Couples often find that this way of communicating is not necessarily difficult, but different from their typical style. The social work practitioner then encourages the couple to process the experience of exploring emotions together. The couple often finds a more emotionally vulnerable conversation is more constructive. This step not only validates the couple for allowing themselves to be vulnerable but also emphasizes a situation in which their partner was a secure base for them. Couples terminate from EFT feeling more secure in their attachment, more skilled in emotional awareness and regulation, and more accepting of each other's emotions (Zuccarini et al., 2013).

Overall, EFT has been shown to be a highly effective application of attachment theory in both couples and families (Beasley & Ager, 2019; Wiebe & Johnson, 2016). Additionally, recent research has shown that EFT is highly effective with gay and lesbian relationships (Hardtke et al., 2010) and is even being modified to focus on the specific challenges those relationships experience (Allan & Johnson, 2016).

SOUND RELATIONSHIP HOUSE THEORY

Sound relationship house theory and the Gottman model that stems from it are empirically backed, highly effective methods of approaching couple's counselling (Bradley & Gottman, 2012; Buehlman et al., 1992; Garanzini et al., 2017; Gottman & Gottman, 2008). There is a particular focus on communication (especially in the context of conflict) and building friendship within the relationship in this approach. Conflict is inevitable and sometimes perpetual in relationships (Anderson et al., 2010). It is with that principle in mind that sound house theory addresses how couples resolve conflict instead of taking on the impossible task of avoiding conflict altogether. The Gottmans, the creators of sound relationship house theory and the Gottman method (a therapeutic intervention built from their findings), describe sound relationships as a house with seven levels built upon pillars of trust and commitment. The foundation of this house is built on understanding and the creation of a positive bond between the couple so that, when conflict arises, a positive tone has already been established. The main floors of the house address conflict and the positive-to-negative sentiment balance of the relationship. The core helps couples stay mindful and constructive with their communication during times of conflict. Finally, the top layers address the long-term structure of the relationship and focus on creating a shared meaning and goals for the couple. This conceptualization of couples therapy has been found to be effective in many settings including heterosexual, gay, and lesbian marriages (Garanzini et al., 2017; Gottman et al., 2019), and couples in poverty (Bradley & Gottman, 2012).

The first level of the sound relationship house involves building love maps. The love map exercise involves partners asking their spouse a series of basic questions with the intention of building a stronger connection in the couple. Questions such as "What is your favorite tree" and "What is your partner's favorite restaurant" tend to reveal deeper emotions as the responder recalls the narrative that led to their answer. Strong friendships act as a protective factor during problem-solving that can help the couple avoid escalations and conflict.

The second level of the sound relationship house involves the sharing of fondness and admiration. This level, like the love map level, seeks to build a relationship that is founded on positive views of one another. Building such a view is easy in the start of a relationship, but couples often find that, later, it begins to take effort. Limerence, colloquially called "puppy dog love," tends to blind couples to any potential issues that may arise in a relationship. A steady supply of oxytocin warps the lens through which a partner is received, often resulting in unabashed admiration. However, on average, the limerent phase fades around 2 years into a relationship (Tennov, 1979). Therefore, a conscious effort toward maintenance of positive feelings toward the partner is required. Fondness is shown by expressing a positive regard for one's partner. Phrases such as "I'm proud of the way you dealt with that issue at work" or and "I'm impressed that you know so much about your hobbies" are typical ways one can express fondness. In addition to building a positive view of a partner in the person delivering the message, these expressions also validate the recipient, confirming their partner's continued positive regard toward them. Building the core of a relationship upon positive views of each other helps limit contempt in future times of conflict. If the foundational view of one's partner is positive, it becomes much easier to handle conflict from a positive, problem-solving perspective (Navara et al., 2016).

The third level involves turning toward instead of away from a partner's bids for connection. Bids for connection are often short, small verbal phrases from partners that carry a heavier subtext. That subtext, is often a request for an emotional connection. Take for example an individual who asks their partner to help them water the flowers. Watering the flowers is a task that, for most people, is easily accomplishable by one's self. The intent of the request was not to ask for help with a difficult task—the request was for the couple to spend time together. It is important to note that these bids are not passive-aggressive in nature. Instead, they're positive calls for the couple to strengthen their emotional connection and therefore should be embraced or, in the language of sound relationship house theory, turned toward.

Creating a positive sentiment override is the fourth level. Positive sentiment override is comparable to what is colloquially known as "benefit of the doubt." Those in positive sentiment override tend to take neutral remarks positively. Couples in negative sentiment override take comments that are rated neutral by external judges as negative (Weiss, 1980). Additionally, those who are in positive sentiment override have increased relationship stability and marital satisfaction (Buehlman et al., 1992; Fincham et al., 1995). To build a positive sentiment override, the Gottmans utilize what they call the "emotional bank account." There must be five positive interaction deposits for every negative interaction withdrawal to maintain a neutral account balance (Navarra et al., 2016). Positive interactions can be turning toward a bid for connection or expressing admiration. This concept helps explain the previous three layers of the sound house—building a strong positive balance early will help when the inevitable withdrawals occur.

The fifth layer, managing conflict, is slightly denser, consisting of two sublevels. The first sublevel is to manage how conflict is approached; specifically, the way complaints are introduced. Gentle introductions reduce negative affect escalation, a particularly harmful conflict pattern in which negativity is matched with an even higher level of negativity. The second sublevel involves creating an active and continuing dialog surrounding problems that will persist over the entire life course of the relationship. From a conflict resolution approach, voicing the concern is vital as it helps prevent pent up aggression and resentment. The removal of that resentment is particularly important when perpetual problems are involved. Creating a perpetual line of communication to address perpetual problems removes the opportunity for pent up anger to fester and negatively impact the romantic relationship (Navarra et al., 2016).

The sixth layer turns back toward addressing not only the future conflict before it occurs but also the future of the relationship and the individuals within it. The goal of this level is to honor one another's life dreams. The Gottmans postulate that many perpetual conflicts stem from individuals feeling that they are sacrificing part of their dreams (Gottman & Gottman, 2008). Exploring each other's aspirations by adopting an approach of curiosity and support helps avoid these conflicts. Couples then gain perspective into their partner's dreams that may feel violated or sacrificed in the relationship. This gained perspective provides context during arguments and reduces the likelihood of resentment toward the partner (Gottman & Gottman, 2008).

The seventh and final layer is to build a shared meaning system. The Gottmans state, "master couples intentionally build a shared story of their relationships and a sense of purpose and shared meaning in which their own individual existential struggles become merged, in part, into a system of shared meaning" (Gottman & Gottman, 2008, p. 159). Couples achieve this shared system by utilizing three key strategies: (a) creating rituals of connection that help form a reliable emotional bond (e.g., having dinner together, traditions involving birthdays or holidays); (b) supporting their partner's roles in life such as their career, family, and friends; and (c) sharing life goals with their partners. While those goals may have been formed before the genesis of the relationship, others may be formed later in the relationship (e.g., becoming a parent or traveling the world together). The shared dreams help give a relationship meaning and shared goals to work collaboratively toward.

CASE STUDY 5.1

Jack, 27, and Diane, 26, have been married for 3 years and have recently agreed to participate in therapy as their marriage is, in their words, "not what it once was." Jack and Diane are relatively affluent, both working in the tech industry where they first met 5 years ago. Diane has aspirations of getting a master's degree in computer programming. Jack supports Diane in this endeavor, and she plans on applying to a local university in the fall. Meanwhile Jack is rising through the ranks at his job and is currently in consideration for a promotion. Diane is very supportive of Jack's aspirations, citing a promotion and increased salary will help them financially when she begins her master's program. Despite these positive sentiments, the couple reports that "it's somehow the small things that cause all of our issues and it's tearing our marriage apart."

Jack and Diane came in for a series of three assessment studies—the first as a couple and the following two they attended individually. In their joint session, they were asked to give a brief story of why they were attending therapy and the history of their relationship. Jack and Diane reported that they both attended a nearby university and graduated the same year with the same degree, but never knew each other. It was only when they started working together at Tech Inc. that they began to talk. The couple said it was "love at first sight." They would go on fun, interesting dates, and explore new parts of the city together. After a year of dating, Jack proposed, and a year after that, they were married. Exploration has been a continued theme in their marriage. Without the responsibility of children, they are able to travel often. In spite of this, the couple reports that, "since getting married, the relationship has gotten more difficult." While they are more than willing to express their love for each other, the words sometimes feel hollow to the recipient. Jack and Diane "feel like roommates" and say they often engage in self-described petty arguments. Toward the end of their joint session, the couple was asked to discuss a recent conflict. They discussed an incident that has occurred frequently in their marriage—a debate as to who would take care of the dog that day. "Taking care of the dog" is defined in their relationship as refilling the food and water dish as well as taking the dog for a walk. Jack stated that the day before the session, Diane and Jack returned home from work and needed to care for their dog. John began describing the situation, saying that Diane asked him to take care of those duties, but Diane quickly interrupted saying, "I only asked because I had taken care of the dog that morning." John acknowledged her interjection as true and continued, saying he asked if they could split duties that day—he would let the dog out while Diane refilled the food and water. Diane then stated that she believed Jack was trying to get out of his share of the daily chores to which Jack sighed and responded, "she says I'm lazy." From there, things escalated, quickly devolving into an attack–defend–counter attack pattern of interaction.

During the first individual session, Diane described her family background. Her father was described as a "country boy" and a widower who was very focused on his career throughout Diane's childhood in the rural American South. More than anything, her father emphasized that his children learn financial independence and "toughness." Diane stated that the toughness and independence ingrained in her were both a benefit and a detriment to her relationship with Jack. She stated that Jack was raised to be sensitive and that they balanced each other out. However, she also stated the difference in personalities often led to conflict. Diane preferred utilitarian displays of affection like doing chores or cleaning the home, whereas Jack liked emotionally driven displays such as cuddling and physical affection. Diane stated that, while she loved Jack, she felt that his softness made him lazy.

Jack's individual session also began with a brief description of family history. He stated that his parents had a bad marriage and that he wanted to break from that pattern. His father was an aggressive alcoholic and generally apathetic of his relationship with his mother. Like Diane, Jack was also very invested in the relationship and loved his spouse but couldn't figure out why they always fought. When talking about the relationship, Jack was despondent, saying he was running out of hope for the relationship. Jack said he has become increasingly angry when they get in arguments, feeling frustrated when Diane "starts taking everything personally." He said that he had recently taken to shutting down arguments by saying "let's talk about this later" but the couple never would, fearing rehashing the argument would lead to more anger instead of resolution.

Theoretical Insight

Like many couples, Jack and Diane's relationship has strengths and weaknesses. Their "sound relationship house" has a sound foundation but is missing a few key pieces on the higher levels. Their bids for emotional connection (e.g., working together to accomplish the task of taking care of the dog) are denied, there is a negative sentiment override (neutral comments are taken personally), and their communication is marred by the four horsemen. Despite these negative aspects, they also are willing to express their love and admiration for each other, support and understand each other's lifelong goals, and have a shared meaning of their relationship (traveling the world together).

The case of Jack and Diane articulates the need for a theoretical base to practice, as the highlighted gaps in their sound relationship house inform how intervention will be performed. While Jack and Diane understand each other's world and share fondness for each other, they have a key weakness in connecting on an emotional level. The build up of denied bids for affection have left their "emotional bank account" overdrawn. Work with the couple would begin by exploring those bids, defining them in a positive light. Almost all couples make bids for connection daily without realizing it—the simple awareness of these calls for attention can be enough for clients to start turning toward their partner instead of away. Another exercise that is helpful in this section is completing Chapman's love language exercise (1992). By having a better understanding of the partner's love languages, one can more easily translate and embrace their bids for connection.

Often, simple awareness of the four horsemen can be healing for the relationship. For Jack and Diane, the social worker asked them to once again act out a recent disagreement, but this time asked them to stay mindful of their communication. Incidence of the four horsemen dropped, and whenever one would slip in, the social worker would gently intervene and help keep them on track. Because the four horsemen are typical of "me versus you" conflict, the removal of these practices allowed the conflict to transition to "us against the problem."

Jack and Diane were able to learn the tools needed to properly communicate within their relationship using the sound relationship house theory and Gottman model of intervention. Again, their goal is not to reduce or avoid conflict but to instead change the perspective of the couple toward a more positive view of each other and a problem-solving method of communication.

THE IMAGO RELATIONSHIP THERAPY MODEL

Imago relationship therapy (IRT), aligning with a strengths-based perspective, views conflict as natural and an opportunity for relational growth (Hendrix & Hannah, 2011). IRT shares many aspects of attachment theory and sound house theory in that familial interactions and positive relationship affects are emphasized. As stated by Dr. Harville Hendrix (regarded as the co-creator of imago therapy with Dr. Helen Hunt) and Dr. Mo Therese Hannah (2011) , "Since interconnectedness is the defining feature of human nature (and all nature), the *perceived loss of connection is the source of all human problems*" (emphasis in original; p. 2).

IRT postulates that all children are born whole, empathic people. As the child grows through key developmental phases, this wholeness is wounded by parenting and their environment. These wounds often result in compensatory behaviors; however, like giving analgesics to a patient with a broken arm, these behaviors often provide temporary relief without resulting in any healing. Healing must instead come through relational bonds. Where parents and society failed the child, their partner must step in as a healing agent. The partner can provide the love and attachment that was missing from the wounded child's upbringing and help repair the age-old wounds (Hendrix & Hannah, 2011; Muro et al., 2015). This healing process is viewed as a collaborative one, especially between adults in relationships and also with the Imago therapist. IRT proposes four primary principles vital for repairing those wounds and fostering healthy relationships: being present, learning to talk, replacing judgment, and infusing positive regard into the relationship.

The process of being present involves separating the consciousness of the couple, promoting a mutual understanding that the couple is composed of two unique individuals with unique experiences that have shaped them over the course of their lives. The end goal, differentiation, helps build a foundation upon which an understanding of each other's wounds can be built (Hendrix & Hannah, 2011).

The second process, in contrast to the first, emphasizes togetherness as opposed to separation. However, that togetherness is not related to the joining of people but instead to communication goals. Instead of using the differentiated self to build unique monologues that contrast against each other, individuals "learn how to talk" together. This process seeks to construct an empathetic dialog between the couple, fostering connection (Hendrix & Hannah, 2011). The dialog utilizes skills used by therapists in social work practice but translates them into lay terms that are easily understood by the average couple. The Imago dialog starts by asking the listener to mirror or reflect their partner's concern. The listener summarizes and reflects back their partner's message, ensuring clarity and conveying understanding. The listener then validates their partner, accepting the concern without judgment and ensuring that their partner feels seen. Finally, the listener provides an empathic response, reflecting upon how the concern may be affecting their partner. The empathic response validates the emotions that the topic may be invoking in the partner. With the door to emotional expression opened by the listener, the speaking partner will feel safer discussing the concern's emotional impact.

The final two stages of Imago healing closely mirror the process of building positive regard in sound relationship house theory. However, Imago splits the process into two parts. The first aspect, replacing judgment, takes the dialogical connection and removes negativity. Imago therapy does so by striving to remove judgment and negativity and replacing them with curiosity and positive regard for the partner (Hendrix & Hannah, 2011). If the relationship dialog was rated on a scale of −10 to +10, this process focuses on taking a negative score and returning it to zero.

The final process, infusing positive regard into the relationship, seeks to build upon the zero and push it toward a 10. This step focuses on building a dialog that is not simply *not negative*, but is instead *positive*. This is achieved by expressing positive feelings toward one another such as admiration, praise, and acceptance (Hendrix & Hannah, 2011).

Through these stages, acceptance and healing is fostered. Hendrix and Hannah (2011) summarized the healing process of IRT with the following:

> This rupture, in order to close, needs the combined work and determination of both partners; if they are going to grow up as individuals, they need to do so as a couple. They were wounded in relationship; their relationship, therefore, is what they need to heal. (p. 4)

CASE STUDY 5.2

David and Amy had been engaged for just under a year when they presented for couples therapy services. They were self-described high school sweethearts and had been dating for 8 years before David proposed. David worked at a local bank as a teller and Amy was a dental hygienist. While engaged, they had not begun planning a wedding. The couple stated that they "weren't in any rush" and were planning to have a long engagement of around 4 years to give them the opportunity to save for their ideal wedding. In their first session, they stated that their primary presenting issue had to do with disagreements over living arrangements.

David and Amy were living independently, each renting one-bedroom apartments in Beachtown, United States. Rent was rapidly increasing in Beachtown and living separately was becoming more and more of a financial burden on the couple and thus a larger topic of conversation. Amy wanted to move in with David once they got engaged, but David disagreed. David stated that he was raised in a strict Christian household and, even though he did not participate in the religion as an adult, it was still morally wrong for a couple to live together out of wedlock.

Amy, citing David's lack of religiosity, believed that there were ulterior motives behind David's position. Amy believed that David did not want to fully commit to marrying her, saying that living together would make it feel too "official." Engagement, she said, was not legally binding like a shared lease, so there was little physical proof of them being a couple. She expressed her belief that David was using his family's religion to keep her at arm's length. When brought up between them, these accusations typically anger David and discussions escalate into screaming matches quickly.

The social worker took note of this point and used it as a segue to explore the couple's family history. David, an only child, reported that he was raised by two U.S. Army veterans who taught him values and respect. He reported that his parents were strict and had a propensity to ground him for relatively benign wrongdoings. David recalled one night in high school when he went out with friends to see a movie. He was on his way home, barely on track to meet his curfew when he realized that he needed to stop for gas. He called his mom to tell her, but she was not receptive of David's excuse, simply stating "rules are rules." David arrived home a few minutes late to his mother waiting in the living room. She lectured him and restricted his driving privileges for 2 weeks. David looks back on this memory in a positive light stating, "I've never been late to anything again."

David was also responsible for a set list of chores such as making his bed, folding laundry, and washing the dishes after dinner. He stated that his parents used the chores to teach him discipline, pointing out flaws in his folding and cleaning until he could perform the tasks perfectly every time. The chores were performed daily apart from Sunday when the family dedicated their day to church and spending family time together. David stated again that he looked back upon his childhood positively, saying that his parent's toughness made him a better man.

The social worker thanked David for sharing and moved to Amy's history. Amy described a much less organized childhood. She was the fifth of eight children, one of only two girls. Her father was a night janitor at a local office park and her mother was a third grade teacher at her elementary school. With differing shifts, limited income, and a large family to care for, the distribution of chores became a vital part of maintaining the household. Amy was responsible for cleaning the dishes and folding the laundry but, unlike David, no one went behind her to check for imperfections. She stated that she was performing chores out of household necessity, not to learn values.

She also stated that she could not relate to David's curfew story. She had very little supervision as a child and would regularly leave home without her parents even knowing where she was going. She said her parents trusted her, but Amy said the trust wasn't always earned. During high school, Amy's older siblings started to leave the home to get jobs, leaving Amy with a growing mountain of household chores. She began to grow resentful of these chores and would occasionally act out in class, sometimes even getting in physical altercations with other students. Through it all, Amy was able to graduate high school and move to Beachtown to get a dental hygiene certificate. Now, years removed from her situation, she values the lessons her parents taught her. Like David, Amy also viewed her childhood in a positive light stating that she learned how to maintain a house and learned independence through tough life experience.

Therapeutic Perspective

The social worker, having reviewed the family histories and conflict patterns within the couple, would determine that David and Amy are a Rigid–Diffuse Couple that experienced wounding in the identity phase of their childhood.

In a time in which David was supposed to be exploring and defining his identity, he was restrained to fitting within the mold that his parents deemed ideal. Despite his parents' best intentions, it was counterproductive for David's development to impose hard and fast rules in the household. It is, after all, a stage of self-exploration and restrictions limit the child's ability to safely define their identity. In reaction to these wounds, David has become what the Imago model would refer to as a *minimizer* (Luquet & Hannah, 2014). He has strong feelings about how things should be and can be quite rigid in these beliefs. He also comes across as controlling, as the idea of controlling what is right or wrong was exemplified during his childhood. While he understands Amy's desire to move in, he believes it is wrong and has taken an adamant stance against living together before marriage. While he is no longer religious, David says that the values instilled by religion still define him and are vital to being a good person. David wants to be a good person and is quick to defend his beliefs as he views anything contrary as Amy persuading him to do something immoral.

Amy, on the other hand is what the Imago model would call a *maximizer* (Luquet & Hannah, 2014). Similar to David, she was not given the chance to define her own identity, it was defined for her. But instead of having her role set by overbearing parents, it was set by absent parents. While her parents were working, she was helping maintain the house. As a middle child thrusted into an adult role, she felt invisible in her own family. Those wounds translated to a fear of not mattering or being heard in her relationships. She, like many maximizers, is complacent at first to maintain peace; however, once she feels unheard, she can tend to blame and criticize. While she was complacent with the living arrangements at first, the feeling of invisibility has slowly crept into her relationship. Now, in an effort to be acknowledged, she is lashing out, accusing David of not being invested in the relationship.

Just as each individual was exploring their identity as a young person, they are now exploring their identity as a couple. As they seek to define their couple as an identity, the past wounds they have experienced in this phase are affecting their effectiveness to communicate. David, echoing the themes of his identity phase, is trying to impose hard and fast rules, whereas Amy is trying to feel valued in a situation where she feels invisible.

The social worker will guide the couple through the collective healing of their past wounds. The social worker started healing work with this couple by first building a sense of individuality within the couple by helping them understand their own Imago or image. The individuals reflected upon their childhood experiences, especially emphasizing how those wounds have resurfaced during their relationship. This practice improved their understanding of themselves and their wounds. This process also opened the door for better shared understanding within the relationship as understanding oneself is a necessary prerequisite to having someone understand and empathize with you.

The social worker used this as a base to then create an Imago dialog between the couple. David emphasized slowing down his reactivity and receiving messages as input, not as criticism while Amy emphasized defining her views and conveying messages that appropriately express her opinions. Once the vitriol was removed from the conversation and replaced with empathy, David began to see Amy's point and Amy began to feel empowered by her more equitable standing in the relationship.

With the newfound dialectal skills and understanding of their partner's Imago, the couple discussed the matter at home several times over the following weeks, eventually deciding to move in together once their leases expired in 6 months. After discovering the space to safely discuss the topic, they found that they spent the night together most nights and, in a way, were already living together. Moving in would help consolidate their finances and give them the opportunity to begin writing their new chapter as a married couple. While initially the problem was defined as a clash of unwavering family values, the couple was able to find a solution and growth after gaining a better understanding of their partner's childhood wounds as well as their own.

Their wounds were not instantly healed, however. While Imago theory-based intervention helped give perspective to the topic of living situations, old patterns of childhood wounds can and will quickly emerge in other situations. Continued focus on healing wounds jointly as a couple is a vital part of the success and positive growth of any couple's relationship.

OTHER INFLUENTIAL COUPLES INTERVENTIONS AND PEOPLE

Bowenian Therapy

Bowenian family systems theory is a developmental theory that applies transgenerational theory to understand the relationships and interactions that occur within families. The theory applies to intergenerational nuclear families as well as intergenerational extended families, allowing for the theory to be applied to couples as well as families (Bartle-Haring et al., 2007; Jeffries et al., 2016). Bowenian therapy is unique in that, while being applied in family's and couple's therapy settings, it is practiced with individuals as well (Bowen, 1978).

The primary focus of Bowen's theory is the multigenerational transmission of patterns of interaction. For example, Bowen held that the ways in which one generation argued, coped with stress, understood roles of husband and wife, could be passed down to the next generation and, without awareness of this transmission, the next generation could replicate those patterns. These multigenerational transmissions could be healthy but in cases where the family is in conflict, maladaptive patterns could also be transferred.

Bowen viewed anxiety as the primary cause of mental health systems (Bowen, 1978). Anxiety is not easy to contain and therefore moves through the family system, usually in triads. Those triads are a by-product of what Bowen calls triangulation. Bowen believed that when anxiety erupted between two members of the family, they would bring in a third aspect to diffuse the direct tension. This concept is seen in the light-hearted example of first dates. The beginning of many first dates is characterized by awkward small talk. Both parties are feeling anxiety, especially toward each other—and so they pull in external third parties. Conversation may begin to revolve around a mutual friend, pets, or the weather. Bringing in these external factors allows for tension to diffuse and anxiety to reduce. However, the same premise can be applied to much higher-stake contexts within families and couples. For example, a couple in conflict may excessively focus on their child's life in order to diffuse the relational tension between them. The child becomes a tool of avoidance, but this ultimately perpetuates the problem.

Like many of the theories described in this chapter, balancing togetherness and autonomy (i.e., differentiation) is a primary goal of this method. Bowen stated, "The ability to be in emotional contact with others yet still autonomous in one's own emotional functioning is the essence of the concept of differentiation" (Kerr & Bowen, 1988, p. 145). To differentiate, individuals are required to approach problems with a balance of emotions and logic. In *Family Evaluation* (1988), Kerr and Bowen describe thought processes as depending on two guidance systems: the emotional guidance system and the intellectual guidance system. Balancing those guidance systems and methodically choosing which to utilize is a key aspect of differentiation.

The other key aspect is separating oneself from others. This is not an endorsement for isolation, but more so for insulation. The previously mentioned child who is drawn into their parent's conflict will likely take on some of the anxiety the parents are trying to diffuse. By insulating oneself within the system, the child will be able to maintain their role in the family while not taking on the familial anxiety as their own.

Overall, Bowenian theory describes families as being healthily developed when each family member is autonomous and differentiated, emotional consecutiveness between members is high, and interactions are considered rewarding and healthy (Bowen, 1978).

CASE STUDY 5.3

Mark and Debbie have been married for 12 years and have two children ages 5 and 9. There is currently an open social services case on the couple for parental neglect. As a part of their services, they have been required to attend parenting/couples counseling. The social worker uses a Bowenian approach and begins to look transgenerationally at the ways in which their parenting styles may have developed.

SW: Hi, Mark and Debbie. Thanks so much for sitting down with me. As I understand it you have been asked to come to see me by social services because of some parenting challenges that you'd like to overcome and put behind you. To begin, I think it could be helpful to get some idea of how you both were raised and how you came to understand parenting; would that be okay?

Mark: Yes, that's fine. We're not too excited to be here really, we just want to be left alone. (*Debbie nods her head in agreement.*)

SW: Thanks for sharing that with me and I completely understand. Let's see if we can all work together and get you both where you'd like to be as fast as we can, okay? Mark, could we start with you? Could you tell me a little about how you were raised? Who raised you and what was that like?

Mark: Well, it was my mom and me really. My dad was around but he was a jackass! So my mom was the one who raised me. She was always real nice to me and protected me from my dad a lot. My dad wasn't really around that much. He worked night shift and slept during the day. So it was really just mom and me.

SW: Thanks for sharing that, and what was your mom like? Sounds like you all spent a lot of time together.

Mark: Yeah. She was real nice to me and we were basically friends. She would tell me things about dad and I would listen and get her calm. And she would help me out, too. If I got in trouble with dad and he told me to do something, like a punishment you know, then mom would get me out of it or tell me I didn't have to. You know, things like that.

SW: Ok, so your mom was kind of like your friend, would protect you from your dad, and you would help her out, too. Your dad was removed and not around too much and when he was around he was strict, is that about right? (*Mark's head nods in agreement.*) Okay, how about you, Debbie; what was it like growing up for you?

Debbie: My mom and dad were both hands off. Way hands off. They really didn't care about me and let me do whatever I wanted. I had no curfew, I could keep beer in the fridge at 16 (*Debbie laughs*), I don't know what they were thinking except that they weren't thinking. They told me basically that they had no time for me and I was supposed to raise myself.

SW: Thanks Debbie. That sounds like it was a little confusing for you growing up?

Debbie: I think so. I mean on the one side I could do what I wanted but on the others side I didn't feel very loved.

SW: Debbie, how do you think the way you grew up affected your parenting of your children now?

Debbie: Well, I am the opposite of my parents! I love my kids and I want to do right by them. So if they do something right I love on them, but if they get out of line then I give them work or I take something away. I have rules. I'm nothing like my parents at all.

SW: Okay, so it sounds like, Debbie, that the way you grew up did affect you in the sense that you are operating in the opposite style of your mom and dad. Mark, what is your parenting like now?

Mark: Well, Debbie and me are on two different pages with the kids. I don't want them to get into trouble or have things taken away, so she and I knock-heads with each other on some things. Like our oldest had his phone taken away and she was going to keep it for a week. He came to me crying and I gave it back after 3 days. Then Debbie gets angry at me.

SW: Okay, Mark. I'm wondering if you see a pattern between the way you were raised by your mom and how she protected you, and how you are as a parent now and the way you may be protecting and aligning with your kids against Debbie?

Mark: I can see that, yeah, that makes sense. I feel like I am right, though.

SW: Alright, Debbie and Mark. Let's set aside right and wrong for now and look at what
         we have. We could have parenting patterns that have been handed down generation-
         ally. Mark, you are operating like your mom, you are being a friend and protecting,
         while, Debbie, you are operating in the opposite way of your parents, by giving rules
         and punishments where your parents did not.

In this scenario, the social worker has explored parental transgenerational patterns with
both partners and has made these patterns clear to the couple. The child is able to join with
Mark, who treats him as a friend, in order to triangulate Debbie. With this knowledge, the
social worker then assists the clients to decide whether they would like to continue these patterns in their parenting or if they would like to change them, and if so, how they would like
them to change. The couple decided to balance with each other, and Mark agreed to not save
the children from consequences and Debbie decided to change her way of loving the children
to be less severe and worried when they made mistakes. The resulting changes assisted the
children to be less confused in the family; they felt things were fairer and clearer, and their
problematic behavior diminished.

Salvador Minuchin and Structural Therapy

Salvador Minuchin was a family therapist from Argentina who developed structural family therapy in conjunction with Braulio Montalvo, a social worker at the Philadelphia Child Guidance
Clinic (Minuchin, 1967). Structural therapy posits that there are subsystems within a family and
that these subsystems work to maintain a shifting balance within the family called homeostasis.
The subsystems are the *spousal subsystem* (romantic partner and partner), the *parental subsystem*
(parent and parent), and the *sibling subsystem* (child or children). The theory maintains that these
subsystems ideally operate independently of each other and that each member of the subsystem
plays a role in that system that is separate from the roles played in other systems. There are also
boundaries between these subsystems that can be one of three types, *clear* (ideal), *rigid* (unbend-
ing or harsh), or *diffuse* (undefined and easy to cross). In an ideal relationship, there is a boundary
between roles and subsystems, and these rolls and subsystems change over time as the members
of the system change, as well as to adapt to the environment outside the system. This change and
flexibility is known as changing homeostasis.

Problems are understood to arise when the subsystem boundaries are crossed and roles
are confused. A social worker operating from a structural approach would assess the structure
of the family to determine the balance of each subsystem paying attention to how the subsystem developed. The social worker would look specifically for how each member *accommodated*
the other's needs as well as *negotiated* their needs in the relationship. A subsystem in which one
member accommodated while another did not can lead to a relationship build on animosity.
The social worker also looks for the type of boundaries between subsystems.

Second, the social worker would explore how their families of origin may be impacting their
current relationship. For example, have the mother and father of one partner given space for
that partner to be a husband and father in addition to being a son? Have the parents let go
enough so that the client can *individuate* from the family of origin? Meaning, are they both connected to and separate from the family of origin?

Third, the social worker helps the couple renegotiate and rebalance their relationships and
roles across subsystems. The worker helps re-establish boundaries among these systems so that
the homeostasis of the system can readjust to one that is more preferable to both partners.

CASE STUDY 5.4

A couple comes in to see a social worker complaining of arguing to the point of possible separation. The social worker seeks some basic background about their relationship and current

existing stressors. The couple has been together for 20 years, have three kids who are all in college, ages 18, 22, and 23. The couple owns and operates a restaurant together and often fight over business decisions. After this discussion the social worker takes out a piece of paper and draws three circles on the paper and writes both of their names in each circle.

The social worker explains to them that the three circles represent the three relationships they have with each other. The first circle is the spousal relationship, where the two are husband and wife. The second is the parental relationship and represents mother and father, while the third is the business relationship and represents them as business partners. The social worker guides a discussion about the quality of the boundaries between these three relationships and encourages the couple to keep these relationships separate. They can do this by being consciously aware and selective about the topics of conversation they choose to have and when they choose to have them. For example, they agree that when they take time away from the house together to relax (spousal subsystem), they will not talk about the kids (parental subsystem) or work (business relationship). They agree that if one brings up a topic that is unrelated to the spousal subsystem, then they have to do something kind for the other.

The social worker guides the couple through the ways in which each of these three relationships developed and if each accommodated and negotiated the relationship in a manner that was fair to both. In those places where one feels things are unfair, the issues are discussed and renegotiated. In the parental subsystem, significant discussion was had around the kids leaving the home for college and how both of their parenting styles had to adjust to this life cycle shift. Through the social worker's use of a structural approach, the couple was able to reduce conflict through the development of better boundaries between the three relationship subsystems and by renegotiating and adjusting the roles each hold.

Esther Perel

Esther Perel, a Belgian therapist trained by Salvador Minuchin, has pushed to the forefront in the world of modern couple therapy. Perel breaks down the emotional responses that couples experience, using those emotional patterns to help build a stronger bond. Perel especially focuses on the concept of mystery as a place of growth in a relationship. Mystery, as Perel describes it, is not simply being unaware of some aspects of your partner or their past. Instead, mystery stems from the individual differentiation of each member of the couple (Perel, 2007). By being differentiated—their own person—there becomes a bridge to be crossed between them. This journey, Perel believes, is a motivator that promotes success in the long-term relationship. She postulates that humans have two natural cravings in relationships: love and desire (Perel, 2007): love being a closeness and desire being a sense of adventure to explore something new. Those aspects, on the surface, seem paradoxical. To balance this need for simultaneous closeness and separation, Perel borrows from attachment theory stating that adult intimate relationships are similar to the children who have a safe home base attachment figure (Perel, 2007). Partners satisfy their craving for desire by exploring themselves and their world while also satisfying their craving for love, knowing that they have a person to return to and be close with.

Perel also expands her ideas of love and desire into other aspects of life. In *Mating in Captivity: When Three Threatens Two* (2007), she discusses the often talked about phenomenon of a newborn stifling romance in a couple. She approaches the problem through the lens of love and desire, stating that the primary caretaker of the infant (often the mother) spends much of her day communicating, attaching, and growing with her infant. The mother then ends the day with her need for closeness—love—met without ever interacting with her partner (Perel, 2007).

Perel is also a leading voice in working with relationships that have experienced infidelity. Through the lens of desire and eroticism, Perel views the prominence of infidelity as a testament that contemporary views of monogamous marriage are not practical in practice. Perel posits that infidelity in relationships is deep betrayal, often ending in existential questions, because they defy the very definition of modern marriage—that for each person, "The One" is out there (Perel, 2019). Perel goes against the grain of much of modern relationship culture, providing a unique but valuable perspective into the topic of love and desire that helps give social work practitioners a more eclectic view of the world.

Terry Real

Terry Real, a family therapist and founder of the Relational Life Institute, is another prominent figure in contemporary couples therapy. Real views couples through a lens that features gender and power as prominent factors in both problems and solutions (Real, 2008). Real highlights that the traits associated with traditional gender roles (e.g., strong, handy, provider for men; nurturing, caring, emotional for women) clash and do not lend themselves to emotional connection (Real, 2008). Real also highlights that those traits lead towardpower dynamics in the relationship. Real believes that power imbalance in a relationship is another problematic pattern (Real, 2008). By embracing and addressing the unique experiences of each gender, Real helps clients create balance in their relationship.

COMPATABILITY WITH GENERALIST-ECLECTIC FRAMEWORK

Assessing the quality of relationships and intervening with clients to assist with the enhancement of relationship satisfaction have been mainstays of social work practice since the inception of social work (Addams, 1902; Richmond, 1917). All models of practice outlined in this chapter fit within the generalist-eclectic framework of social work practice in the sense that they explore the systemic and relational aspects of the identified client. It could be argued that depending on the approach of the social worker, some models of practice outlined here could work better than others in terms of the style of the social worker. For example, a worker more attuned to post-modern ways of working may find models of couples intervention that naturally explore client strengths and resiliencies more appealing, while those social workers who are comfortable teaching skills may find modern approaches more to their liking. In both cases, exploring client desires and outcomes in an initial assessment and then matching the model of practice to the goals of the client could increase outcomes (Prescott et al., 2017) as well as enhancing the ethics of practice by meeting clients where they are (National Association of Social Workers [NASW] Code of Ethics, 2018).

CRITIQUE OF COUPLES COUNSELING THEORIES

Strengths and Limitations

While working toward the betterment of romantic relationships seems a logical goal to increase general life satisfaction and to decrease problematic issues of clients, ongoing debate continues around the effectiveness of treatments. Generally, this debate occurs between authors who conduct or write meta-studies of individual research. Alan Carr has provided an excellent summary of couples therapy research and concludes, "the overall effectiveness of systemic therapy is now well established" (Carr, 2019, p. 492). In contrast, while agreeing that couples counseling does show effectiveness, Snyder et al. (2006) explore research findings and conclude that a "sizable percentage of couples fail to achieve significant gains from couples therapy or show significant deterioration afterward" (p. 317). No doubt this debate will continue as notions of empirical truth reign supreme in the current neoliberal academic climate in which standardization of practice has been branded as paramount.

Apart from debate about effectiveness, there is considerable current and historical discussion among couples counseling theorists, particularly those who have been described as post-modern (e.g., Insoo Berg, Michael White, Bill O'Hanlon) and those who have been described as modern (e.g., Salvador Minuchin, Murray Bowen, Jay Hayley). These practitioners generally debate the manner by which counseling should occur, whether a theory of normality should be implemented, or skills taught to clients rather than exploring client organic skills, or the stance taken by the social worker. These debates can be generally distilled down to a debate between first, second, or post-order cybernetic approaches (Hall, 2017).

CONCLUSION

Couples and families are two of the most important ways individuals find unity. However, problems and conflicts are inherent to any relationship. The theories discussed in this chapter are intended to be used to inform the interventions social work practitioners use; for without hands-on intervention, theory alone is not particularly helpful. Instead, theory is a basis and language that social workers use to understand interventions.

While it is helpful, theory should not be used rigidly. Inflexible use of these theories and practices runs the risk of pathologizing and subverting therapeutic interventions. Instead, the theories outlined in this chapter serve to provide a lens through which social workers view clients and their experiences, aligning with the generalist-eclectic framework and the NASW Code of Ethics (2018). It is also important to recognize that theories of individual and family development have been based largely on a White, male, middle-class model. While this chapter makes mention of these theories in "nontraditional" relationships, further research into the topic is still developing. All of these factors lead to one basic guideline: Social workers must respect the unique nature of every person's experience and practice accordingly.

SUMMARY POINTS

In summary, this chapter has:

- explored couples theories and practices,
- described the different methods utilized by individuals to create unity within these systems while balancing autonomy,
- described the different approaches taken by clinicians to describe healthy communication,
- described influential names and practices in contemporary family and couples work, and
- provided context for how these theories are applied outside the scope of cis- heterosexual individuals (where possible).

KEY REFERENCES

Only key references appear in the print edition. the full reference list appears in the digital product found on http://connect.springerpub.com/content/book/978-0-8261-6556-5/part/sec02/chapter/ch05

Addams, J. (1902). *Democracy and social ethics. 1902.* University of Illinois Press, 2002. Addams' most recognizable philosophical work.

Allan, R., & Johnson, S. M. (2016). Conceptual and application issues: Emotionally focused therapy with gay male couples. *Journal of Couple & Relationship Therapy, 16*(4), 286–305.

Anderson, S. R., Anderson, S. A., Palmer, K. L., Mutchler, M. S., & Baker, L. K. (2010). Defining high conflict. *The American Journal of Family Therapy, 39*(1), 11–27.

Bartle-Haring, S., Glebova, T., & Meyer, K. (2007). Premature termination in marriage and family therapy within a bowenian perspective. *The American Journal of Family Therapy, 35*(1), 53–68.

Beasley, C. C., & Ager, R. (2019). Emotionally focused couples therapy: A systematic review of its effectiveness over the past 19 years. *Journal of Evidence-Based Social Work, 16*(2), 144–159.

Beeney, J. E., Wright, A. G. C., Stepp, S. D., Hallquist, M. N., Lazarus, S. A., Beeney, J. R. S., Scott, L. N., & Pilkonis, P. A. (2017). Disorganized attachment and personality functioning in adults: A latent class analysis. *Personality Disorders: Theory, Research, and Treatment, 8*(3), 206–216.

Bowen, M. (1978). *Family therapy in clinical practice.* J. Aronson.

Bowlby, J. (1969). *Attachment and loss.* Hogarth Press.

Strengths-Based Practice: A Metatheory to Guide the Social Work Profession

Catherine A. Simmons, Valerie B. Shapiro, Sarah Accomazzo, and Trevor J. Manthey

LEARNING OBJECTIVES

By the end of this chapter, you should be able to:

- categorize strengths-based practice (SBP) as a metatheory,
- review the history of understanding and using human strengths in social work practice,
- explain the central values and theoretical constructs in SBP,
- introduce the practice tenets inherent to SBP,
- incorporate SBP into each stage of the helping process, and
- illustrate SBP constructs and tenets using a multi-level case example.

INTRODUCTION

Strengths-based practice (SBP) can be best understood as a metatheory (Simmons et al., 2017) that organizes and names the otherwise unspoken rules embedded within lower level practice theories. Underlying all theories that take an SBP approach is the charge to build upon available strengths and work with clients within a positive paradigm. More specifically, the tenets of SBP promote individual well-being and reduce social problems by building upon the strengths possessed by clients (e.g., capabilities, skills) and by the client systems in which clients interact (e.g., assets, resources). Sometimes referred to as an overarching perspective (Saleebey, 2011), a philosophy, or a framework (Blundo, 2001), SBP reflects a set of underlying values and theoretical constructs used to guide our profession. Indeed, many theories that social workers use to explain human behavior, the social environment, behavior change, and social change reflect the core tenets of SBP.

The use of SBP in the professional practice of social work in the United States can be traced back to the work of Addams (1902) and the settlement house movement. In modern practice, an aspiration for strengths-based approaches can be seen across many areas of social work practice. Yet translating an ideological emphasis on strengths-based approaches into the provision of strengths-based services has been hampered by a lack of clarity around concepts and applications (Smith et al., 2014; Staudt et al., 2001). The purpose of this chapter is to organize the components of strengths-based social work into a metatheory framework. First, SBP is briefly described including the historical evolution of the use of strengths in helping relationships. Then, the central values, theoretical constructs, and major tenets guiding social work research and practice are addressed. Finally, applications of SBP across the phases of helping are presented with a case example illustrating the way SBP may be observed in various aspects of practice.

AN OVERVIEW OF STRENGTHS-BASED PRACTICE

In the English language, the word *strength* has an array of meanings. To illustrate, the Oxford online dictionary provides a lengthy definition that includes "a good or beneficial quality or attribute of a person or thing" and "the emotional or mental qualities necessary in dealing with situations or events that are distressing or difficult" (strength, n.d.). From these nontherapeutic definitions, helping professionals have expanded and used the word to encompass a range of positive attributes and resources. Among these are individual characteristics (e.g., intellectual aptitudes, knowledge, physical abilities, skills, human capacities, talents, personal interests, unique motivations), family and community relationships (e.g., high-quality attachments to family and friends, teachers, neighbors, colleagues, community organizations), and environmental assets (e.g., safe schools, neighborhoods, and communities; access to affordable and high-quality child care, health care, and economic opportunities; social policies that promote well-being; and other material and structural resources), and also dreams, aspirations, and hopes (McCashen, 2005).

Although there are a number of ways to define *strengths*, underlying similarities are apparent. Commonalities include the idea that strengths are multifaceted, operate through individual agency, exist in unique combinations for each individual, and include positive abilities, attributes, behaviors, thoughts, and resources (Simmons & Lehmann, 2013a,b). As such, focusing on a person's strengths is not unique to a single therapeutic approach nor is it a model that attempts to explain, describe, or logically represent a particular aspect, situation, or occurrence within social work (Simmons & Lehmann, 2013a,b). Instead, focusing on strengths is an overarching way to approach the helping process. Saleebey (2006) eloquently states that SBP "provides us with a slant on the world, built of words and principles … it is a lens through which we choose to perceive and appreciate" (p. 16).

From these ideas, it is helpful to consider SBP to be a metatheory that emphasizes a person's resources, capabilities, support systems, and motivations to meet challenges and overcome adversity (Barker, 2006; Simmons & Lehmann, 2013a,b). It is important to note that focusing on a person's strengths is not about ignoring the existence of very real problems or illnesses (Saleebey, 1992, 1996a, 2001, 2006, 2008, 2011). Instead, SBP emphasizes the role of strengths, abilities, social networks, positive attributes, knowledge, skills, talents, hopes, and environmental resources to both realize life goals and reduce problems and/or symptoms, ultimately helping to improve individual and social well-being. Utilizing SBP requires attention to the existing strengths of a person, family, group, community, or an organization, and leveraging and building upon these strengths to aid in recovery, empower the client, and build resilience.

The idea of incorporating strengths into the practice of understanding and change is prevalent across a wide range of helping professions. Such concepts are interdisciplinary by nature and nothing new. Metatheories are not developed in a vacuum. Most metatheories are built upon the foundational ideas of those who came before; the past shapes interpretations of the present. While not always labeled as such, elements of SBP have been discussed in the social work literature throughout much of the profession's history.

HISTORY OF UNDERSTANDING AND USING HUMAN STRENGTHS

The modern emphasis on building strengths can be traced through multiple generations of social work professionals identifying related ideas. For example, Rapp et al. (2005) identified early references to strengths in quoting one of the founders of professional social work, Addams (1902):

> We are gradually requiring the educator that he [sic] shall free the powers of each man and connect him with the rest of life. We ask this not merely because it is the man's right to be thus connected but because we have become convinced that the social order cannot afford to get along without his special contribution. (p. 178)

The writing of Jane Addams provides an early account of the emphasis social work places on strengths. However, even before the work of Jane Addams, an emphasis on individuals having a virtuous character, doing good things, and leading fulfilling lives was prevalent. Walsh (2001) noted more than 2,000 years of practical and theoretical exploration into optimal human functioning with roots in ancient Greek and Roman philosophy, Christian and Buddhist scholarship, yoga, and Chinese medicine. For example, in *Nicomachean Ethics*, the ancient philosopher Aristotle (1998/1925/350 BCE) emphasized the importance of developing a virtuous character and a man's ability to do so. More than 1,500 years later, Thomas Aquinas (1981/1920/1265–1274) wrote extensively about virtue and man's ability to do and promote good. Ancient Chinese healers viewed health as the natural order, while their role was to increase natural resistance and resilience (Strümpfer, 2005).

More recently, the origins of modern psychology have highlighted the role that transcendent experiences may play in optimal human functioning (James, 1902/1958), the idea that basic life tendencies work toward the fulfillment of life (Bühler, 1935), and how the concepts of individuation and self-realization help people achieve their potential (Jung, 1933, 1938). Similar themes in modern psychology and studies of human behavior have been reflected in the humanistic idea of inherent potential (Bugental, 1964), Frankl's concept of self-transcendence (1967), Maslow's self-actualization (1943, 1968), Rogers's (1961) ideas about the fully functioning person, Goldiamond's (2002/1974) application of constructional behavioral analysis to social problems and therapeutic intervention, and Seligman's et al.'s positive psychology (e.g., Seligman & Csikszentmihalyi, 2014; Nickerson et al., 2004).

Within the profession of social work, the focus on strengths is evident through multiple generations of social work professionals conveying related ideas, including the importance of constructive growth experiences (e.g., Robinson, 1930; Smalley, 1971), the need to work with human capacities using client-centered casework (Towle, 1954), supporting personal growth (Hamilton, 1940) and capacity building in environments (Compton & Galaway, 1989, 1999), the role of positive reinforcement and the environment in shaping positive behavior change skills (Gambrill, 2012), a dual focus on problems and strengths (McMillen et al., 2004; Simmons & Lehmann, 2013b), a strengths and skills-building model (Corcoran, 2005), a strengths approach to case management (Rapp & Goscha, 2012), and Saleebey's (1992, 1996a, 1996b, 2001, 2006, 2008, 2011) strengths perspective. Given this impressive heritage, SBP can be conceptualized as a metatheory that unites multiple concepts, constructs, and ideas foundational to social work practice across multiple systems.

CENTRAL VALUES AND THEORETICAL CONSTRUCTS

SBP incorporates the core humanistic values of the social work profession, unites multiple mid-level theoretical constructs, and provides a unique problem-solving framework. Some of these values and constructs are derived from social work, whereas others originate from broader human philosophical or psychological domains. Standard throughout is a focus on the resources possessed by clients (e.g., capabilities, skills) and client systems (e.g., assets, resources). Among the values and constructs of SBP that are particularly salient are resilience, hope, empowerment, self-determination, client involvement, and person-in-environment (Franklin, 2015; Simmons et al., 2017).

Resilience

Defined as the capacity to bounce back or recover from stressful situations (Masten et al., 2009; Smith et al., 2008), resilience is an essential component of SBP. A large amount of evidence shows that despite histories of trauma and dysfunction, the vast majority of people who experience difficult circumstances are still able to survive and oftentimes thrive (e.g., Pollack et al., 2004; Sinclair & Wallston, 2004; Smith et al., 2008). Both risk and protective factors can help the social work professional predict the likelihood of resilience (Kim et al., 2015; Shapiro & LeBuffe, 2006). Protective factors or characteristics that reduce the impact of risk can be either internal (e.g., coping skills, optimism) or external (e.g., supportive mentors, parents, or community members and community opportunities) strengths. The extent to which the concept of resilience should shape social work practice has been the topic of recent debate, with some arguing that the use of resilience has gone too far and others suggesting that it has not gone far enough (Davis, 2014; Shapiro, 2015).

Hope

Defined as the belief that good things, rather than bad things, will happen, hope can be an important strength across time and situations (Snyder & Taylor, 2000). There are two main components of hope: (a) the belief that one has the ability to create a pathway to achieve one's goals and (b) the belief that one can then start and maintain progress toward one's goals once the pathway is created (Snyder et al., 1999). If either of these components is absent, an individual may feel pessimistic, powerless, or apathetic, and can express a lack of desire to attempt to change one's situation for the better (Snyder & Taylor, 2000). As such, hope has been identified as a very important strength (Valle et al., 2006). Therefore, it is essential to SBP that therapeutic relationships induce hope (Saleebey, 2006). When people can identify goals and see potential pathways to achieve these goals, they have a tendency to experience hope (Snyder & Taylor, 2000).

Empowerment

Defined as a means by which a person creatively uses their resources to gain or use power to achieve goals, improve and control life circumstances, and positively contribute to one's community, empowerment is discussed extensively in the social work literature (Browne, 1995; Greene & Lee, 2011; Greene et al., 2005). Indeed, paying attention to clients' strengths and helping them to recognize and use their strengths is a primary means for empowering clients (e.g., Cowger & Snively, 2002; Gutierrez et al., 1998). The goal of empowerment then becomes the identification of ways in which individuals can nurture their own well-being. Empowerment is not confined by one aspect of social work practice. As Gutierrez (1990) wrote, empowerment is "the process of increasing personal, interpersonal, or political power so that individuals, families, and communities can take action to improve their situations" (p. 202). Recently, the word *genpowerment* (Beltrán, 2014, p. 1) has been suggested as an alternative term to honor the ways in which the helper and the client can generate power together, or groups of clients and communities can generate power for themselves, to supplement the idea that the helper can actively create, enable, or give power to the client (Beltrán, 2014).

Self-Determination

Defined in a variety of ways, self-determination includes individuals' rights to make their own decisions, to actively participate in the helping process, and to lead lives of their own choosing (Weick & Pope, 1988). These conceptions "contain a belief in the capacity and right of individuals to affect the course of their lives" (Weick & Pope, 1988, p. 10). Self-determination theory posits that people endeavor to experience positive growth and that people will move toward such growth when they are in situations that support autonomy, competence, and positive relationships (Ryan & Deci, 2002). As such, the more the environment supports autonomy, competence, and relationships, the more likely people will have the capacity for positive action.

Client Involvement

Client involvement refers to the extent to which clients participate and contribute to the helping process. A primary consideration of SBP is that processes be client directed, focus on client factors, and be alliance minded. The term *client directed* was coined by Duncan et al. (1992) to refer to the importance of privileging clients' perspectives and involving them in every aspect of the intervention. A focus on client factors encompasses everything clients brings to the intervention, which includes unique strengths, ideas about what might be helpful, cultural heritage, social support, life experiences, resilience, hope, wisdom, and values. Being alliance minded highlights research which found that the most important component of the change process is the client's perception about the strength of the relationship with the helper (Wampold & Imel, 2015). Primary change factors integrate a focus on the client, the client's unique strengths, and the quality of the helping relationship. Client involvement applies across levels of practice (see Shapiro et al., 2013, for an example of client involvement at the macro level).

Person-in-Environment

One of the primary foci that strength-based approaches share is the holistic focus on the individual within their environment. SBP recognizes that people exist within and are influenced by their environment; SBP views the environment as being rich in resources (Manthey et al., 2011). The goal is often to improve the goodness-of-fit between individuals and their environments (e.g., Germain & Gitterman, 1980), with the assumption that various systems include strengths as well as problems. Strengths can be identified and nurtured in interactions between clients, between clients and other individuals, or within families, groups, organizations, communities, nations, or worldwide systems. By focusing on the strengths of the individual and the environment, the social worker can assess many aspects of social phenomena, including their inherent complexity and connectedness.

MAJOR TENETS OF STRENGTHS-BASED PRACTICE

Although ideas related to SBP have been discussed periodically throughout much of social work's history, these ideas and principles were not explicitly formalized and linked together under the term *strengths* until the late 1980s (Rapp et al., 2005). At that time, Saleebey and others articulated a set of clear principles for conducting SBP and operating from a strengths perspective (Saleebey, 1992). By design, the formalization of these principles was intended to oppose a mental health system that was overly focused on diagnosis, deficits, labeling, and problems (Saleebey, 1996a, 1996b, 2001; Weick et al., 1989). The popularity of these ideas has led to an increasing number of practitioners and programs claiming that they conduct practice using an SBP model. However, many programs and workers who lay claim to being strengths based are actually still functioning from a deficit worldview or are behaviorally problem focused despite their verbal contention (Douglas et al., 2014; Rapp & Goscha, 2006). In order to address this gap between what is sometimes claimed and what, in reality, occurs, Rapp et al. (2005) developed some additional standards by which social workers could judge whether a social work practice or intervention is strengths based. The strengths principles created by Saleebey (1992, 2006) and the strengths standards created by Rapp et al. (2005) have since been combined (Manthey et al., 2011) to include the features included in Box 6.1.

BOX 6.1 Major Tenets of Strengths-Based Practice

1. Goal-oriented interventions
2. Contains a systematic means of assessing strengths
3. Sees the environment as rich in resources, and explicit methods are used to leverage client and environmental strengths for goal attainment.
4. A helping relationship is hope inducing
5. The provision of meaningful choices is central, and individuals have the authority to choose
6. Assumes that clients are best served by collaborating with practitioners
7. Assumes that trauma, abuse, illness, and struggle may be harmful but may also be sources of challenge and opportunity
8. Assumes that the worker does not know the upper limits of individuals' capacity to grow and change

Sources: From Manthey, T., Knowles, B., Asher, D., & Wahab, S. (2011). Strengths-based practice and motivational interviewing. Advances in Social Work, 12, 126–151; Rapp, C. A., Saleebey, D., & Sullivan, W. P. (2005). The future of strengths-based social work. Advances in Social Work, 6(1), 79–90; Rapp, C. A., & Goscha, R. (2012). The strengths model: A recovery-oriented approach to mental health services (3rd ed.). Oxford University Press; Saleebey, D. (Ed.). (2006). The strengths perspective in social work practice (4th ed.). Allyn & Bacon; Saleebey, D. (Ed.). (2011). The strengths perspective in social work practice (6th ed.). Allyn & Bacon.

FROM THEORY TO PRACTICE: STRENGTHS-BASED SOCIAL WORK IN THE PHASES OF HELPING

The central values, theoretic constructs, and major tenets of SBP inform each stage of the helping process across all levels of practice: engagement, assessment, intervention, and evaluation/termination. The following explores SBP in each of the phases of helping with a focus on the expectation that all social workers "recognize, support, and build on the strengths and resiliency of all human beings" (Council on Social Work Education, 2015, p. 8).

Engagement

Social work services are shaped by the environment in which the social worker and client meet, the relationship that is experienced, and the pattern of their interactions. SBP, in the ongoing process of engagement, should draw upon the strengths of the meeting environments, build positive rapport, and create positive interpersonal dynamics to leverage change. Modifications can be made to the meeting environment to make it feel as natural as possible, so that the interaction is comfortable and the client feels dignified (Smith et al., 2014). For example, a positive environment in the context of supervised visitation services would be one that is safe and with clean, unbroken furniture; interesting toys; and developmentally appropriate activities that promote opportunities for parent–child engagement and the nurturing of their shared interests and hobbies (Haight et al., 2002). Furthermore, a well-organized environment can help a client feel calm and cared for (Appelstein, 1998).

SBP can lead to stronger collaborations between the client and the social worker. Although it is often necessary to discuss problems and pathology with clients, exclusively examining this aspect of their lives can induce shame or guilt, lead to a reluctance to disclose relevant information or to participate in the services, and obscure resources available for problem-solving. In fact, clients may discover their own strengths and resources when given an intentional opportunity to explore them, generating potential solutions and a greater confidence in their capacity to implement them. When discussing a client with a parent, child, or other involved third party, spending time considering the client's positive attributes may also facilitate positive regard and nurture positive relationships on behalf of the client (LeBuffe & Shapiro, 2008).

SBP uses more than polite language to communicate respect and invite participation. Strengths-based social workers reflect authentic warmth; listen well; affirm the client's perspective, hopes, and capacities to overcome any difficulties; and, whenever possible, share and generate power with their client. For example, it is essential that SBP includes client choice making about the way their time is spent with the social worker and the goals of service provision.

A clear advantage of SBP is that it permits engagement with a client in the absence of the acute problem or crisis that creates the context for most initial visits with a social worker. For example, school-based social workers can work with a student on the absence or relative weakness of coping or self-regulation skills, social–emotional competencies, or other desirable attributes. Thus, an intervention can be implemented to strengthen these prior to the emergence of problematic behaviors (LeBuffe & Shapiro, 2004). When done effectively, this can result in the growth of characteristics that make problems less likely to occur or at least reduced in their severity, longevity, or pervasiveness (Shapiro, Accomazzo, et al., 2017). SBP embodies a spirit of prevention.

Assessment

SBP involves collecting information about the strengths of clients and client systems to inform treatment planning and implementation. Although many strengths-based assessment approaches and instruments exist (Simmons & Lehmann, 2013b), relative to the development of the assessment approaches and instruments for risks and problems, the development of validated strengths-based assessments is lagging. Informal, nonstandardized procedures (e.g., a placeholder for strengths-based narrative information on an intake form) are valuable as an initial approach. This approach, however, does not take advantage of the research available on strengths that have been empirically demonstrated to be related to wellness promotion or recovery.

Other more formalized and standardized checklist approaches to assessing strengths are also useful (e.g., Accomazzo et al., 2017) but do not guide social workers in making a determination as to how much of a particular strength is typical or whether the strength is present in sufficient quantities to be an asset to recovery. Even if a validated strengths assessment is available, if the strengths assessed as being present are not harnessed toward meaningful goal attainment, the assessment may have been in vain. It is one thing to know what strengths are present and it is another to use them meaningfully. Therefore, some strengths-based assessment developers have used a format widely used in the assessment of pathology to produce strengths-based assessments with norms calibrated on representative national samples, making themes useful in research and as defensible in practice as their problem-based counterparts (Naglieri et al., 2013). Examples of such tools that have been examined for their respective reliability and validity, and have been made available for practitioners to use, include the Ages and Stages Questionnaire—Social Emotional (Squires et al., 2002), the Behavioral and Emotional Rating Scale, Second Edition (BERS-2; Epstein, 2004; Pre-BERS; Epstein & Synhorst, 2009), the Devereux Early Childhood Assessment, Second Edition (DECA-P2; LeBuffe & Naglieri, 2012; DECA-C; LeBuffe & Naglieri, 2003; DECA-IT; Mackrain et al., 2007), the Devereux Student Strengths Assessment (DESSA; LeBuffe et al., 2009/2014; DESSA-SSE; LeBuffe et al., 2012; DESSA-Mini; Naglieri et al., 2011/2014), the Penn Interactive Peer Play Scale (PIPPS; Fantuzzo et al., 1998), and the Resiliency Scales for Children and Adolescents (RSCA; Prince-Embury, 2008).

For example, the DESSA (LeBuffe et al., 2009) can illustrate how a standardized, norm-reference behavior rating scale can help social workers and allied professionals collect strengths-based information about the children with whom they work. The DESSA was standardized on a national sample of 2,494 children, diverse in respect to gender, class, race, and ethnicity, in kindergarten through eighth grade (LeBuffe et al., 2018). The DESSA is completed by parents, teachers, or staff at child-serving agencies, including after-school, social service, and mental health programs (Shapiro et al., 2017). The assessment is composed of 72 strengths-based items, scored on a 5-point scale depicting how often the student engaged in various positive behaviors over the past 4 weeks. The DESSA is organized into eight conceptually derived scales that provide information about social–emotional competencies. These are self-awareness, social-awareness, self-management, goal-directed behavior, relationship skills, personal responsibility, decision-making, and optimistic thinking. The total of these scales is used to obtain a social–emotional composite score.

It is important to note here that there is a trap that a well-intended social worker can fall into when using a strengths assessment. This subtle trap can occur, no matter how well developed the strengths assessment is or whether the strengths assessment is standardized and validated. The trap is to use the assessment to find which strengths are lacking and then only focus on trying to develop or fix the "lacked" strengths. In this scenario, the worker inadvertently frames the discussion by what the individual is not doing well and what strengths the individual needs to develop. In order to be strengths based, the worker must focus on what the individual is doing well, what strengths are identified as already being present, and what positive goals the individual has for their future. Strengths-based assessments are defined not only by their content but also by how they are used. An assessment is only truly strengths based, in accordance to the conceptualization we have advanced in this chapter, if it clarifies what the client is already doing well or what opportunities and resources already exist in the environment, and assists them in leveraging the strengths they already have toward reaching their own identified desires and goals.

As already mentioned, SBP in general, and strengths-based assessment in particular, do not ignore problems or pretend they do not exist. It is how the practitioner frames the conversation about problems that matters. In SBP, problems are often reframed as barriers to achieving personal goals. Instead of externally pointing out and trying to fix a problem, or immediately trying to develop a strength that is lacking, the practitioner will first help the individual identify positive goals that the individual wants to achieve (strengths of desire and hopes for the future). For example, solution-focused brief therapy suggests using a "miracle question" to focus the client and clinician on envisioning what an optimal future would look like (e.g., Berg, 1994). The practitioner will then help the individual articulate what steps the client needs to take and what barriers the individual believes need to be overcome, in order to achieve that goal. If appropriate or needed, the client can be guided by the worker toward the barriers that were identified on assessments as needing development. The key here, however, is keeping the focus on reaching the positive goals while the resolution of barriers stays secondary to the positive goal attainment focus. Keeping the focus anchored on strengths-based goals allows both the individual and the worker flexibility in moving between strengths mobilization and barrier resolution strategies, all while centering a positive goal.

The DESSA can be useful in identifying strengths as well as barriers/areas for development that could be addressed for child-identified goal attainment. For example, the DESSA may reveal that the client has a particular strength in relationship skills. This knowledge may lead the social worker and client to collaboratively build barrier resolution skills and goal attainment approaches that leverage relationships (LeBuffe et al., 2009). As part of an intake assessment, the DESSA may also reveal that the child has a very low score in self-management. The items on that scale could then serve as objectives in a service plan such as "wait for his or her turn" or "accept another choice when his or her first choice is not available." These objectives would be anchored in the child's self-identified overarching strengths-based goal, such as "I want to be able to have friends that last a long time" or "I want to get along better with my teacher." The DESSA scoring system also has features to help social workers collect and compare information from a variety of informants who may spend time with the child in different environments. When a particular strength is present across environments and according to multiple raters, it may indicate a more dependable strength than if it only occurs in one environment or with only a particular rater (Rosas et al., 2007). When selecting a strengths-based assessment approach, it is important to consider whether strengths-based assessments are appropriate across diverse racial and economic circumstances (Chain et al., 2017) and the extent to which assessments are subject to rater bias (Shapiro et al., 2016).

In moving from assessment to intervention planning, the questions a worker may consider include: "What positive desires and goals might this child have?" "How can I frame a conversation to help the child identify their goals and help the child be motivated to achieve them?" "Might the child's goals influence the child to want to address a barrier?" "What environmental and internal strengths does this child have at their disposal that potentially could be identified, affirmed, and used?" and "In what perceived failures or barriers could I search for strengths and growth opportunities?" By asking the questions in this way, the intervention is not about the worker identifying a lack of strengths to remediate but rather to identify strengths that may help the child overcome barriers and progress to their goals. It is essential in SBP that the practitioner continually revisit through affirmations and conversation the existing strengths of the client that can be used to help achieve the individual's goals. The continued exploration of client strengths means that strengths assessment and utilization is an ongoing process, not only limited to an initial assessment.

A strengths-based assessment tool like the DESSA can be used across levels of practice. In group treatment settings, it can help determine areas where clients have common goals, barriers to goal attainment, or existing strengths to leverage. The group profile tool is a color-coded matrix in which each client is a row and each DESSA scale a column. Visual inspection can quickly indicate common areas of strengths and lack of strengths. These results can then inform the selection of interventions targeting the growth of certain strengths or help social workers arrange clients into pairs with complementary strengths where social learning can occur. The DESSA-Mini (Naglieri et al., 2011), which is a brief form of the DESSA that can be completed in just 1 minute, can be used across large groups of people to determine initial eligibility or recommendation for services. Strengths-based screening practices can reveal which clients might have the fewest strengths to protect them and/or help them cope with adversity, and therefore help social workers determine which clients may benefit most from preventive interventions, behavioral health services, and/or strategic SBP interactions.

Intervention

Interventions are deliberate attempts to change the state of a person or an environment. Interventions should be well planned based on high quality and comprehensive assessment information, co-created, jointly selected, or otherwise agreed to by the client, and monitored in their implementation and for their outcomes to determine if they are achieving the desired effect. If not, interventions may merely be interference or an imposition and may be unethical with the potential to do harm. Strengths-based social work helps social workers design or select better intervention strategies by insisting that (a) engagement practices prioritize client choice making and invite the kind of participation that will lead to the most high quality information gathering; (b) assessment practices are comprehensive, including reliable and valid information about a client's strengths and resources; (c) identified strengths are strategically and actively used, not just assessed; (d) the growth of positive attributes are monitored rather than focusing on the reduction of problematic behaviors; and (e) the intervention should help people move toward healthy independence, and therefore, the termination of the relationship is discussed along the way.

Intervention planning, whenever possible, should be done in partnership with the client and/or the client's caregivers. This likely means that assessment results are shared with the client—a task much easier to do when the conversation can begin with the goals, strengths, and resources that the client already has. Similarly, the client should help determine treatment goals and could even be asked to generate a goal for the social worker's practice (Smith et al., 2014).

Clients can choose goals for the social worker from a list that has examples, such as ask good questions, model behavior, offer ideas, or give cues. In this way, the client has an opportunity to consider and inform the social worker of the kind of support from the social worker that the client might find helpful or desirable.

SBP does not contend that every possible life goal, or area for development, becomes a service goal. When individuals find even small success in their attempts to reach goals, barriers in other contexts may become less apparent and goals can be achieved indirectly. For example, a child who has improved self-esteem and self-worth because a worker and teacher have maintained a strengths focus may be less likely to act out. In addition, strengths may generalize across contexts. If a child's self-identified goal is to make more supportive friends, and the child actively works on reading subtle cues in relationships in order to improve them, other benefits might also occur such as being able to recognize social cues from a teacher in the classroom.

Progress Monitoring, Evaluation, and Termination

SBP assesses and celebrates progress, early and often. When service goals are created, a time frame for making progress toward each goal should be established. The DESSA-Mini, for example, has four alternative forms so that a client's strengths can be assessed once a month. Looking over the entire course of treatment, the DESSA-Mini has a procedure built into the instrument to indicate whether maintenance and/or reliable and meaningful growth in strengths has been achieved. When working with groups of students, tests for reliable and meaningful change can be aggregated across students to determine the typical amount of growth experienced.

It is important to revisit how and when the worker–client relationship will end. The interventions should be clear and measurable so that both the worker and the client are aware of successes and know how those successes relate to the purposeful ending of the relationship. Not all relationships will end abruptly, and some settings allow for a gradual reduction of interactions over time. Other settings that do not allow for a gradual reduction of interactions will require clear discussion of termination throughout the phases of work so that the client is prepared for the ending of the relationship. Ideally, a client will have some degree of self-determination in forming this plan.

CASE STUDY 6.1

This children's mental health case example (all names and issues are fictitious) demonstrates how a clinician practicing SBP may use the eight SBP tenets outlined in this chapter during the stages of practice described earlier.

Rebecca Marris is a social worker at the Orange Grove Community Wellness Clinic, a community mental health outpatient clinic in central California that serves children and adolescents aged 5 to 18 years and their families. The clinic recently hired a new clinical director who was passionate about implementing SBP in all aspects of the clinic's work. Yesterday, Rebecca conducted a phone intake with Mrs. Vo, grandmother of Nancy Vo, a 14-year-old Vietnamese American high school freshman at the local high school. Mrs. Vo was referred to the clinic by a school counselor.

Engagement

During the 15-minute intake phone call with Nancy's grandmother, Rebecca had two main goals: (a) to confirm that Nancy was indeed eligible for services at the county-funded clinic and (b) to get Nancy and Mrs. Vo to show up in person at the clinic for a full assessment, if Nancy was deemed eligible. Rebecca began by thanking Nancy's grandmother for calling and urging her to ask questions if she did not understand something Rebecca said. Mrs. Vo reported that

Nancy was failing four classes and last week was in a screaming match with another student that had almost led to blows. Upon request, Mrs. Vo also provided relevant contextual information. Nancy was born in the United States after her mother and grandparents emigrated from Vietnam in the late 1990s. She and her 11-year-old brother, Mark, had been living with Mrs. Vo and her husband (her maternal grandparents) for the past 5 years. Nancy was 9 years old when her grandparents obtained custody of her and her brother, when it was determined that their mother could not take care of them because of mental health issues (she meets criteria for bipolar disorder) and prolonged drug use. Nancy's mother sees the children once a week with supervised visitation. Rebecca told Mrs. Vo that Nancy was eligible for services at the clinic because, as a young person involved in the child welfare system, Nancy's mental health care at the clinic would be covered by Medi-Cal, California's Medicaid program. Rebecca then invited Nancy and her grandmother to come to the clinic the next day for an assessment. Knowing that many families never make it past the intake stage, Rebecca tried to sound welcoming and friendly. She tried to inspire hope that clinic services could actually help Nancy by mentioning that the clinic has served many 14-year-old clients who are dealing with school issues. She asked how Nancy and her grandmother would be getting to the clinic and mentioned that the clinic provides free bus tickets for clients who need them.

Assessment

Nancy and her grandmother arrived at the assessment appointment the next day. Rebecca offered them drinks and snacks, asked if they needed any reimbursement for their travel costs to the clinic, and then began the assessment process. Recently, in an attempt to become more strengths based and family centered, the clinic had adopted a new assessment form called the Child and Adolescent Needs and Strengths (CANS) assessment (Lyons, 2009). This assessment requires the clinician to document both problems and strengths instead of just recording problems and symptoms. During the 2-hour assessment, Rebecca first spoke with the grandmother and Nancy together.

Mrs. Vo reported that the family has a small income from a bakery they run out of their home, but business had slowed recently and they are behind on their mortgage payments. Though they have limited English skills, they are eager to be involved in all aspects of Nancy's and Mark's lives. Nancy, though somewhat socially isolated at school, has up until now gotten nearly straight As. Her school is ranked no. 1 in the district and her grandparents want her to enroll in the free precollege tutoring program offered after school. However, Nancy is currently failing several classes and has not been sleeping at night, which her grandmother noticed because Nancy has been falling asleep at the table while doing her homework. Her grandmother added that Nancy has mood swings now, more than ever before, and it is harder to be around her.

At the beginning of the conversation, Nancy's grandmother did most of the talking and Nancy sat with her hands crossed, looking at the floor. Rebecca asked Nancy directly what she liked to do for fun—partly as an engagement strategy and partly to begin to inquire about potential strengths. Nancy took a moment to respond, and her grandmother jumped in, saying that Nancy used to read comic books but had recently stopped. Rebecca listened politely to the grandmother, acknowledged her comment, and then redirected the conversation back to Nancy to learn more about the comic books from Nancy's perspective. It was a careful balance because Rebecca wanted to make sure that both the grandmother and Nancy felt like they were collaborators and partners in the assessment process.

At one point, Nancy's grandmother started to go into detail about the time Nancy's mom overdosed and had to be hospitalized, the incident that led to Nancy and Mark being placed with their grandparents permanently. Rebecca was not sure she needed to hear all the details in order to work effectively with Nancy in the present, and she did not want to retraumatize Nancy in any way, so she made a brief reflective statement and Mrs. Vo felt heard, but then gently changed the topic. At this point, Rebecca wanted to make sure that Nancy felt that her unique voice was valued in the assessment process. So, Rebecca asked to speak with Nancy one-on-one for a few minutes. After the grandmother left the room, Nancy seemed to relax.

During their time one-on-one, Rebecca purposely asked questions to assess both problems and strengths at both the individual and the environmental level. Rebecca started off with strengths because strengths tended to be easier to talk about for many clients and she was still building rapport with Nancy. To inquire about an individual-level strength, Rebecca asked Nancy to tell her about something she enjoyed doing. Nancy reported that she had a job as a babysitter for her next door neighbor's children and that she really liked the two kids. Rebecca used this opportunity to point out a strength, noting that it sounded like Nancy really cared about the kids and that she was a big help to her neighbor. To learn about her environment, Rebecca asked Nancy to tell her a bit about her neighborhood. Nancy responded that she liked living in her grandparents' neighborhood better than living in her mom's neighborhood because she felt safer when she was walking home from school and the streets were prettier. Rebecca noted on her assessment that the neighborhood sounded like an environmental strength for Nancy.

Rebecca then moved to sensitively asking about some potential areas in her life that Nancy wanted to be better right now and some goals she wanted to achieve in the future. Nancy immediately answered that she wanted her experience at school to be better. Rebecca said that it sounded like Nancy had been having trouble at school, and asked what it was like for her at school. Nancy responded that she hated everyone because they were so nosy. Rebecca asked Nancy to give her an example of this, and Nancy reported that everyone at school knew that her mom got arrested last week for shoplifting and that the police were keeping her in jail because she had traces of drugs in her blood test. Nancy heard several students talking about it in a class.

Rebecca had not known that Nancy's mom was back in jail, and responded with empathy and that she was sorry to hear that. Nancy said angrily that her mom had promised Nancy she would not use drugs again and now Nancy would not be able to see her for a long time. Rebecca acknowledged how upsetting it must be to have heard this. She then asked Nancy what she had been doing to cope. Nancy reported that she listened to music at night really loud on her headphones and that helped. Rebecca pointed out a strength, saying that it was great that Nancy had found something that helped. Nancy smiled a bit at this comment. Rebecca also pointed out that Nancy knew herself better than anyone else, and that Nancy would be in the best position to decide what might work for her at home and in their interactions together.

As Mrs. Vo had earlier mentioned that Nancy was not sleeping at night, an individual-level barrier, Rebecca asked Nancy to tell her about what the nighttime was like and how sleeping was for her. She purposely asked the question in a vague way so that she did not assume that sleeping was a problem for Nancy. Nancy reported that she could not fall asleep and "I just can't stop thinking." Curious to learn more about this, Rebecca asked Nancy to tell her more about what that was like. Nancy reported, "I used to be able to just get my brain to stop, but now it has so many thoughts I just can't sleep." Rebecca asked Nancy to tell her about these thoughts, and Nancy reported that they were mostly worrying about her mom. Rebecca reflected Nancy's statement and Nancy got somewhat teary eyed. Rebecca continued to use empathic reflections to ensure Nancy felt understood. Rebecca then transitioned the conversation by asking Nancy to tell her what it might be like for her if she were to be able to sleep better at night. Nancy's demeanor shifted from sorrowful to more hopeful when Nancy stated that when she doesn't sleep, she "just feels run down all the time" and that it would be "awesome" if she could get the thoughts to "turn off" at night. Nancy also said that she would have "way more energy" the next day if she could get some sleep. In order to pivot into a potential strengths-based goal rather than staying focused on a problem, Rebecca then asked Nancy to talk more about what other things getting more sleep might help Nancy to accomplish. Nancy stated that it might help her to do better at school and that it might help her not be so "cranky" with her grandma. Rebecca then reframed Nancy's statement in a positive light by saying, "[So] even though you and your grandma don't always get along you care about your grandma and want things to go well between the two of you." Nancy agreed with that statement, and Rebecca affirmed Nancy for her good intention. Rebecca then linked two other identified barriers to Nancy's strengths-based desire to have a better experience at school. Rebecca stated, "You also want to have a good experience at school and you think two of the things getting in your way are feeling like people are talking about your family negatively and not getting enough sleep."

At the end of the assessment, Rebecca thanked Nancy and her grandmother for coming in. In order to indicate her hope and optimism that clinic services could help Nancy, Rebecca told Nancy that the clinic works with many young people with similar goals and barriers and that many young people found therapy useful in helping them move toward leading a life they wanted to lead. She asked if Nancy would be interested in coming back for some therapy appointments. Nancy agreed, and so they scheduled an appointment for the following week.

After they left, Rebecca entered the assessment information into an online database and wrote up her assessment case formulation, making sure to include both problems and strengths. While Rebecca assessed that Nancy did not currently meet criteria for any mental disorders as described in the *Diagnostic and Statistical Manual of Mental Disorders, Fifth Edition* (American Psychiatric Association, 2013), she indicated in her notes that, particularly as Nancy had described some symptoms consistent with various mental disorders and given her mother's mental health history, the therapist should monitor Nancy for other symptoms that might result in her meeting criteria for other disorders in the future. Rebecca was careful to document both environmental and individual strengths. The neighborhood; the bakery; potential positive relationships with grandma, her brother Mark, her neighbor, and neighbor's children; access to free afternoon tutoring; and attendance at a highly ranked school were all identified as potential environmental strengths that could be used in planning later. Rebecca's past history with obtaining As, her love for reading, her good intentions, her responsible babysitting skills, her desire to have a good school experience, and her desire to get along with her grandma were all identified as potential individual strengths that could also be used in planning.

Planning and Intervening

Rebecca's intention was to have the planning be a collaborative effort between her and Nancy. When Nancy came back for her first therapy session, Rebecca asked Nancy if they could spend some of their time together over the next few weeks thinking about their service goals. Nancy agreed, and so Rebecca asked Nancy to tell her what she hoped to get out of the sessions and what her goals were. Nancy said that she wanted to "stop failing my classes," "stop my brain from going crazy at night," and "stop feeling so angry at everyone." They discussed this, and Rebecca purposely guided the goal setting to state the objectives in positive language that focused on constructing skills and achieving goals instead of only reducing symptoms. They tried to be very concrete in their goals, coming up with: "Make a plan for when I can't sleep at night because this will help me do my homework," and "Make a plan for when I feel angry at my teachers or classmates because this will help me pay attention in my classes and help me to enjoy school." Rebecca then asked Nancy what would help her to meet these goals. Nancy did not have any ideas, so Rebecca pointed out that Nancy had already named a coping skill—listening to music when she was having trouble falling asleep—and asked her what else would help her to feel calm and relaxed at night. She also asked about resources that currently exist in Nancy's life that she could call upon, encouraging Nancy to think about a teacher or a friend who might be able to meet with her during the lunch period to help her catch up in her classes. Together, they decided that they would check in at the end of each session to see how they both felt it had gone. They also agreed to do a slightly longer check-in every four sessions to evaluate progress toward Nancy's goals.

After their planning session, Rebecca continued to consider several different interventions to identify which would be the most effective for helping Nancy to meet her goals. She decided to use two interventions that employed many strengths-based principles and fit well with a strengths-based approach to social work practice: motivational interviewing and solution-focused therapy. Motivational interviewing was useful because it provided a framework for exploring ambivalence around change, which was the case for Nancy with regard to her academics. Solution-focused therapy was useful because it provided a concrete way to focus on exploring past coping skills and developing new coping skills. Both of these interventions focused on hopes and dreams and centered the client voice, two characteristics that are consistent with SBP. Rebecca discussed these interventions with Nancy at their next appointment, and Nancy said that they sounded good to her. Rebecca asked Nancy to please make sure to ask her any questions and to let her know if she had any feedback for her.

Monitoring Progress, Evaluation, and Termination

Rebecca always left 5 minutes at the end of each session to briefly check in to see how Nancy felt about the services. After four sessions, Nancy and Rebecca spent half of a session discussing Nancy's goals and assessing how much progress they had made toward those goals. Nancy reported that she felt like she was sleeping a bit better at night but that school was still not going well. She still felt isolated by her peers, and catching up in her classes was a true challenge. Rebecca made sure to praise Nancy for making such great progress toward one of her goals. Then Rebecca suggested that they update Nancy's goals to focus on maintaining her sleep and setting more detailed school goals. After discussion, Nancy identified two new, specific, more targeted goals for school: (a) meet with an after-school tutor two times a week for 3 weeks to prepare for an upcoming history test and (b) attend a meeting of a school club she was interested in so that she could make friends with positive people who held similar interests. Rebecca helped Nancy to phrase these objectives in language that focused on constructing new skills and obtaining larger meaningful goals instead of just reducing symptoms.

After eight sessions, they reassessed progress and rewrote goals again. During the reassessment of Nancy's academic goals, Rebecca continued to elicit from Nancy individual and environmental strengths. Rebecca accomplished this by asking Nancy again about strategies and strengths she had used in the past when Nancy had been successfully achieving good grades. Nancy was able to identify strengths she had not described before, such as ways she had structured her time (individual strengths) and also the added homework assistance Nancy received from her grandmother when needed (environmental strength). Her grandmother had not been able to help Rebecca as much recently because she was spending time in the struggling bakery. Rebecca probed to see if other people had helped Nancy along the way, and Nancy said that last year her neighbor, who sometimes let Nancy babysit, would also occasionally help Nancy with her homework. The neighbor had usually helped Nancy when Nancy's grandmother did not understand Nancy's homework due to language barriers. In addition to mining for strengths from Nancy's past, Rebecca also asked questions that helped Nancy describe how achieving good grades and having a better school experience might influence her life in the future. Nancy described that doing well in her classes might ultimately help her obtain her goal of going to college and perhaps becoming a nurse. Rebecca periodically helped Nancy revisit her future dreams in relation to school performance in order to keep the discussion anchored on positive life goals rather than the current academic struggles. Rebecca and Nancy were then able to be flexible and adjust the plan to include some of the strengths identified through Nancy's past successes. Rebecca kept revisiting Nancy's academic hopes and dreams for the future in order to keep Nancy engaged in moving forward even when it was difficult or when setbacks occurred along the way. Rebecca also asked Nancy if she wanted to continue for another four sessions as she was still working toward meeting her school goals. Nancy agreed that this would be helpful.

During one meeting, Nancy entered the room in tears because she had not scored as well as she would have liked on a test. Nancy exclaimed, "I'm a failure!" Rebecca empathetically reflected Nancy's struggle by stating, "This has got to feel horrible because you've worked so hard to catch up and to get better grades." Rebecca then reframed Nancy's perceived failure by stating, "and yet you haven't given up, you have accomplished so much already, you are a persistent person." Nancy asked Rebecca if she really thought that. Rebecca was able to honestly reply that many people have given up on obtaining good grades or even given up on school all together. Rebecca then affirmed Nancy for her tenacity and her desire to do well even when it was difficult. Rebecca reframed Nancy's sorrow as a strength by stating, "[I]n fact, your sorrow that you didn't score well on the test is an indication that you care about yourself, your life, and your future goals. Your sorrow is an indication that you don't want to give up now either."

After 12 sessions, Nancy stated that she did not have time for services anymore because she wanted to join a club that met on the day Rebecca and Nancy usually met. Rebecca mentioned that she had been thinking that Nancy had met most of her therapy goals anyway, and so this might be a good time to stop their work together. Together, they reviewed their most recent goals and agreed that Nancy had met them. Rebecca suggested that they meet one more time to celebrate Nancy's successes. At their final session, Rebecca gave Nancy positive feedback about her work in therapy and pointed out how many successes she had achieved along the way. Rebecca also expressed confidence in Nancy's capacity to navigate future trials, obtain her longer term goals, and validated Nancy's worth as a person. Nancy stated that she was going to miss Rebecca and wondered if she would ever see her again. Rebecca responded with empathy, noting that many people felt similarly when ending counseling. Rebecca assured Nancy that if she wanted, she could always call her to schedule a future appointment. Nancy said that she was glad to know it was an option and thanked Rebecca for her time.

CRITIQUES OF STRENGTHS-BASED PRACTICE

There are several common critiques of SBP. First, SBP has been critiqued as overly focused on clients' strengths to the point of ignoring clients' very real problems (McMillen et al., 2004). From this perspective, SBP, in an attempt to move away from the deficit-focused, pathological models of human suffering, has accidentally and naively turned the sole focus to what is going right while refusing to acknowledge what is going wrong. In this view, SBP is, at best, overly optimistic and, at worst, insulting to clients who turn to social workers when they are experiencing major crises in their lives. Though proponents of SBP have argued that SBP at its core does include a focus on problems as well as strengths, and dual focus models have been articulated (e.g., McMillen et al., 2004; Simmons & Lehmann, 2013a, 2013b), this remains one of the common critiques of SBP. Similarly, some have argued that a focus on strengths and resilience takes attention away from important societal injustices and leads social workers to advance individualistic solutions to structural problems (Davis, 2014). By conceptualizing and enacting a multi-level SBP, however, injustices and structural problems could also be addressed through the tenets advanced in this chapter (Shapiro, 2015).

Another critique is that SBP lacks conceptual clarity. In this line of thinking, SBP is a vaguely articulated social work value or perspective on practice without one agreed-upon definition, making it difficult to apply consistently in actual practice (Probst, 2009; Smith et al., 2014). According to this argument, SBP has only been described at a surface level, resulting in concerns about the role SBP should play in the profession of social work (if any) and how to regularly apply SBP principles in practice. For example, though the term *strength* is often used in social work practice, a strength may be defined entirely differently in every intervention stage, though definitions are rarely clarified. During the assessment stage, a strength may be viewed as an already-existing asset to be identified, while during the intervention stage, a strength could be a target characteristic to be nurtured and developed or an outcome where change over time indicates success of the intervention (Probst, 2009). In order to address this critique, this chapter has defined eight tenets of SBP, provided specific suggestions on how to implement SBP at each intervention stage, and presented a case example as an illustration of SBP.

Another critique of SBP is that there is little empirical evidence for SBP (Gray, 2011; Staudt et al., 2001). As SBP has, for the most part, been vaguely defined, it has been difficult to accurately measure the implementation and impact of SBP. Thus, it is unclear as to whether clinicians who use SBP are more effective than clinicians who do not, and whether clinicians who use SBP could actually be doing more harm than good. Probst (2009) argues that discussing whether or not SBP has any empirical evidence to support it misses the larger underlying issue that SBP is more accurately described as an "applied concept" (p. 162) that operates through specific interventions, models, and practice behaviors. Thus, actual interventions that incorporate strengths-based concepts can be defined, measured, and declared efficacious or not, but the broader concept of SBP cannot be measured and should be viewed with more realistic expectations. This perspective is more in line with the current presentation of SBP as a social work metatheory, as discussed in this chapter.

CONCLUSION

Regardless of the criticisms directed toward the strengths-based perspective, an emphasis on strengths-based approaches can be seen across all areas of social work practice. With roots dating to the inception of social work as a profession, the importance of client and client–system strengths is commonly accepted among professionals in all facets of social work practice, accrediting bodies, and schools of social work in the United States and around the world. The core tenets of SBP are reflected across many of the theories that social workers use to explain human behavior, the social environment, behavior change, and social change. As such, it is logical to argue that SBP is a metatheory that organizes and names the otherwise unspoken "rules" embedded within practice. As illustrated throughout this chapter, SBP is integral to all social work practice and, in line with the generalist practice framework, helps to promote human and social well-being (Poulin, 2005). SBP is important for micro, mezzo, and macro levels of practice (Chapin, 2011), and is central to social work competence in engagement, assessment, intervention, and evaluation across work with individuals, families, groups, organizations, and communities. Viewing SBP as a metatheory reflects the central importance of its values, assumptions, and principles for all social work practice, and this will be useful in moving the field forward.

SUMMARY POINTS

- categorizing SBP as a metatheory organizes and names the otherwise unspoken rules embedded within lower level practice theories,
- the history of understanding and using strengths in social work practice can be traced to the early origins of the social work profession and encompass a diverse range of practice theories, which all share complementary philosophies and foci,
- underlying all theories that take an SBP approach is the charge to build upon available strengths and frame social work interventions within a positive paradigm,
- the tenets of SBP promote individual well-being and reduce social problems by building upon the strengths possessed by clients (e.g., capabilities, skills) and by the client systems in which clients interact (e.g., assets, resources),
- the central values, theoretic constructs, and major tenets of SBP inform each stage of the helping process across all levels of practice,
- SBP constructs and tenets were illustrated using a multi-level case example.

KEY REFERENCES

Only key references appear in the print edition. The full reference list appears in the digital product found on http://connect.springerpub.com/content/book/978-0-8261-6556-5/part/sec02/chapter/ch06

Manthey, T., Knowles, B., Asher, D., & Wahab, S. (2011). Strengths-based practice and motivational interviewing. *Advances in Social Work, 12*, 126–151.

Rapp, C. A., & Goscha, R. (2012). *The strengths model: A recovery-oriented approach to mental health services* (3rd ed.). Oxford University Press.

Rapp, C. A., Saleebey, D., & Sullivan, W. P. (2005). The future of strengths-based social work. *Advances in Social Work, 6*(1), 79–90.

Saleebey, D. (Ed.). (2011). *The strengths perspective in social work practice* (6th ed.). Allyn & Bacon.

Shapiro, V. B. (2015). Resilience: Have we not gone far enough? A response to Larry Davis. *Social Work Research, 39*, 7–10.

Simmons, C. A., & Lehmann, P. (2013b). Strengths and psychotherapy. In C. A. Simmons & P. Lehmann (Eds.), *Tools for strengths-based assessment and evaluation* (pp. 1–17). Springer.

Theories for Direct Social Work Practice

7

The Psychodynamic Approach

Arthur Frankel

LEARNING OBJECTIVES

By the end of this chapter, you should be able to:

- understand the basic theoretical foundations of ego psychology,
- understand the intervention strategies in ego psychology,
- see how ego psychology theory and practice have influenced the current practice of clinical social work.

INTRODUCTION

There is no question that Sigmund Freud, the founder of the theory that underlies ego psychology, was a genius. In his era, there was not much in the way of psychological research: no controlled group studies, no research connecting heredity with behavior patterns, and no investigations exploring the connection between brain biochemistry and behavior. Freud used observations to develop his theory in the context of his cultural and religious milieu. Over the years, many have discounted his theory as being sexist, homophobic, and biased toward the more affluent. He did not have what is now available in research and practice experience over the last 100 years to draw upon. Given that his perceptions were coming from the culture and beliefs of his times, we must give him some latitude in understanding that he was a product of his time when he developed his theory.

Given all of these limitations, what he came up with was the first comprehensive theory to explain human behavior. In addition, he developed a concurrent theory of personality development that was integrated into the theory. For the first time in history, when one asked "why" did a person act as they did, there was a coherent answer grounded in a psychological theory. Furthermore, Freud's personality theory suggested how a person developed dysfunctional behavior patterns. Imagine the power of an assessment process that uncovered where in your childhood problems originated, leading to focusing the therapeutic interventions directly at the source of the behavioral dysfunction. To this day, there has not been another psychological approach integrating a personality theory that directly connects to the practice of psychotherapy.

Regardless of whether you like or hate the constructs of Freudian theory, it has had a profound impact since its inception. The power of the theory can be still be seen, not only in the practice of psychotherapy but also in literature, cinema, the practice of the law, and personal communications. We are aware of our "ego" and how people have "Freudian slips," and we watch how people use "denial." We are well aware of and use the terms "libido," "phallic symbols," "anal retentiveness," "sexual repression," and "defense mechanisms." The idea that there is an "unconscious" part of our minds, where there are thoughts and feelings not available to awareness, has been utilized in all art forms. You can see his influence in renowned painters such as Salvador Dali and the Surrealists; in literature, Shakespeare, James Joyce, Virginia Woolf, and Dostoevsky; and in cinema, movies made by Alfred Hitchcock and Woody Allen. Freud pioneered a therapeutic process to decipher the meaning of dreams. The concept of "not guilty by reason of insanity" was formulated from Freudian theory, which suggested the concept of "mental illness." Thus, whether we like Freudian theory or not, after almost 100 years since its introduction in 1923, it still has a pervasive influence in our lives (Kelly, 2014).

HISTORICAL DEVELOPMENT

When Freud officially introduced his theory in 1923, it was groundbreaking (Freud, 1923). It offered a comprehensive explanation of human behavior and a way to intervene to change dysfunctional behavior. The treatment process was called psychoanalysis, and utilized constructs he called the id, ego, and superego. He believed that all human behavior could be explained by unconscious motivations of sexual desires and aggressive impulses. However, these motivations were in an unconscious psychological area, the id, which was not available to our awareness (Freud, 1962). It should be understood that Freud proposed his ideas as "constructs." There is not a part of the brain that has the id, ego, or superego in it. Rather, these ideas are part of a "map" of how motivational energy is focused and how it is allowed to flow, resulting in behavior.

The model for treating people who had problems emanated from the medical model, which assumed that the patient was "sick" and needed to be "cured." This approach to dysfunctional behavior morphed into what was called "mental illness," which is a term that is all too familiar today. The treatment approach was called psychoanalysis, and called for the patient to lie on a couch or sit in a comfortable chair and talk about whatever came to mind. The therapist was supposed to be quiet, making few, if any, comments during the session, which occurred as many times a week as possible, over many months or years. The stereotype of psychoanalysis became one where the patient lay on a couch talking, with the therapist sitting out of sight behind the patient. Because Freud was a medical doctor, it became the norm that the only professionals who could practice psychoanalysis had to have an MD and then be further trained in the specialty that became known as psychiatry.

Before the 1950s, when ego psychology theory and practice started to become more prevalent, the only way a person could get psychotherapy was through a psychiatrist. The idea that one needed a specially trained medical doctor, a psychiatrist, to cure mental illness was established by Freudian proponents. As mental health treatment began to become more available with the inception of the Kennedy Mental Health Act in the 1960s, psychotherapy began being delivered by psychologists and social workers. Many of these professionals were trained in a more psychosocial model using many other therapies along with ego psychology. During these years, psychiatrists were still in charge of most mental health endeavors. However, as time went on, psychiatrists started losing their leadership mantel for psychotherapy and were left with being the medical experts in dispensing psychotropic drugs. Thus, Freudian theory affected not only how therapy was done over time but also who did it and who at the agency level was in charge of clinical services.

It became clear by the 1930s that the practice of psychoanalysis presented serious service gaps. Overall, it took too much time and was too expensive to meet the mental health needs of the population. Proponents of psychoanalysis were fervently espousing its effectiveness, mostly using case study reports. However, there was no way it could be applied to those who did not have the time or money to engage in therapy three or more times a week for months or years. In addition, by the later 1930s, psychology and social work departments were beginning to assess their role in psychotherapy. Schools of social work particularly had begun systematically training professionals to work with immigrant groups and people in poverty (Hollis, 1949).

An academic movement began to emerge particularly in psychology, and to some extent in social work, to re-think how the Freudian approach could become more "user friendly" to the masses. What they came up with was called "ego psychology." It focused on the parts of Freudian theory that were more available to human awareness, those functions of the ego and superego (Blanck & Blanck, 1974).

Models of interventions were developed that allowed patients and therapists to directly interact with each other, still following basic Freudian theoretical guidelines. Now departments of psychology and social work had a therapy training model outside of psychiatry and psychoanalysis, and were able to start producing a greater number of psychotherapists than was ever possible in medical schools. Psychologists and social workers practicing ego psychology essentially took over the psychotherapeutic marketplace, so that when mental health movement started in the 1960s, ego psychology was in its heyday (Hartmann, 1958).

As the 1960s rolled on, the practice of ego psychology began to lose its luster, beginning a slide onto the banks of the mainstream of psychotherapy (Goldstein, 2015). A number of phenomena were related to this slippage. First, starting in the 1930s, the principles of behavioral theory began extensively being researched with rats. In early 1940, B. F. Skinner (1953) started publishing books and articles that suggested that behavioral theory, grounded in literally thousands of research articles with lower animals, could be applied with the same empirical rigor on humans. Behavior theory and Freudian theory are diametrically opposed at the most basic levels. What made behavior theory so attractive, especially to academic departments of psychology, was that, unlike ego psychology, behavior theory was eminently testable, resulting in an explosion of applied behavioral research on humans. By the mid 1960s, there was almost a war going on for the hearts and minds of psychologists and social workers, with some departments of psychology and social work completely dropping ego psychology in favor of behavior therapy, whereas others stubbornly hung on to ego psychology for some years. To this day, one would be very hard pressed to find a graduate department of psychology that is not behavioral.

Social work hung on to ego psychology for a little longer. In the 1940s, social work had begun to adopt ego psychology principles into what it called social casework, with Lucille Austin (1948), Florence Hollis (1949), and Helen Perlman (1957) leading the charge. The practice of ego psychology in social work was somewhat different than in psychology. Social work practice was grounded in what became known as systems theory, which assumed that all human problems were not only based on the unique psychology of each individual but were also related to how they were affected by their community, economic status, culture, and social policy. Thus, from a social work perspective, helping a person with a problem, such as depression, required work not only on their personal coping skills but also on such issues relating to community and cultural determinants, such as their being able to support their family, access to sufficient food, work issues, discrimination, and community support systems. Social casework made a valiant attempt to integrate ego psychology into a broader systems theory treatment process (Parad & Miller, 1963).

Behaviorial therapy arriving in the mid 1960s had a similar effect on ego psychology in social work as it did in psychology, but for different reasons. In those years, empirically based practice models were not as prevalent in social work as they are now, so the attraction of using an empirically based model of psychotherapy was not as strong as it was in psychology. In addition, coming along with the advent of behaviorial therapy in the mid 1960s were a number of very attractive alternative psychotherapeutic humanist theories. With such a milieu of possibilities, ego psychology was lost in the sea of new approaches (Goldstein, 2015). It was still being taught in many schools as part of an "eclectic" approach to practice, but not as much as a central focus for clinical social work.

Along the way in the psychodynamic journey of the last 100 years, there have been other offshoots from Freudian theory, owing their roots to Freud. These include self-psychology, attachment theory, relational theory, Gestalt therapy, and transactional analysis. Each of these offshoots either augmented or reacted to basic psychoanalytic theory, attempting to be more practical in implementation, such as self-psychology, person-centered therapy, Gestalt therapy, and transactional analysis, or to focus on particular aspects of psychodynamic theory more clearly, such as attachment theory, and relational theory (Miller, 1976). For example, attachment theory focused on how children became attached to their caregivers and helped explain the etiology of reactive attachment disorder (Ainsworth, 1973). Transactional analysis took the super ego, ego, and id, and redefined them into a more user friendly parent, adult, and child (Berne, 1961). Self-psychology took more of an ego psychology slant, but focused on the importance of interpersonal relationships (Kohut, 1971). Gestalt therapy focused on the here and now in its practice methodology, minimizing the importance of personal history in the behavior change process, yet it kept many of the terms and ideas from Freudian theory (Perls, 1969). Person-centered therapy, founded by Carl Rogers, who is also viewed as the founder of the humanistic therapy movement, took ego psychology principles and reworked them. Therapists were allowed to be empathetically interactive with clients, but not allowed to offer advice. He pioneered the use of active listening, showing positive regard, unconditional acceptance and the importance of the client-therapist relationship in the therapeutic endeavor (Rogers, 1951). Today, there are still pockets of proponents for these theories, but none of them are in the mainstream of the psychotherapeutic milieu in America.

It was reported in a *New York Times* essay (Cohen, 2007) that in course descriptions in 150 major American universities, where they were looking for courses that mentioned Freudian theory, 86% of these courses were offered outside of psychology departments. This led them to conclude: "Freud is widely taught at universities, except in the psychology department." Currently, formal training in psychoanalysis or ego psychology is very hard to find except in scattered private institutes. In current agency-based practice, there is an emphasis on empirically based practice methods, such as cognitive behavior therapy, positive parenting training, and contingency management with families. Professionally licensed social workers in private practice can use any psychological theory they choose, but it is not known how many might be using ego psychology or psychoanalysis as their main approach. In any case, it is likely that some of the therapeutic techniques associated with ego psychology are still alive and well.

CENTRAL THEORETICAL CONSTRUCTS

In order to understand ego psychology, we have to start with the major constructs of Freudian theory (Bellak et al., 1973; Frankel, 1984; Goldstein, 1995). There are five basic concepts that need to be discussed: the id, ego, superego, psychic energy, and the pleasure principle. To start, imagine a three-story house with a basement, a first floor, and an attic. The floors between these three levels have many trap doors that can be opened and closed. The basement is the id, the first floor is the ego, and the superego is in the attic.

The Id

The motivation for all human behavior comes from sexual and aggressive impulses residing in the id. We are born with the id, and its sexual and aggressive drives. If you think about what impulses have been historically necessary for the survival of the human race, clearly sex and aggression are important. Sexual impulses are necessary for the procreation of the species; aggressive impulses are necessary to protect the individual, family, and community from aggressors that threaten their existence.

Freud believed that the sexual and aggressive impulses coming from the id were quite primitive. For example, the powerful urge to have sex is always there, every minute of the day. The id makes no discrimination between heterosexual or homosexual urges for sex. Therefore, a man has an equal urge to have sex with women or other men as do women have the urge to have sex with men or other woman. Left to its own devices, the id would drive you to copulate with every attractive man or woman you encountered at work, in the community, or at home.

Similarly, the aggressive urge is also very raw. When you become very frustrated or angry with someone, be it a partner, relative, friend, or stranger, the id, left untethered, would urge you to kill that person. Not just to think about killing them but actually doing it.

It is obvious that these drives have to be managed and/or contained in order for there to be any kind of civilized existence. While most people are aware of their sexual and aggressive drives, the extent of the id's strength is unconscious, not available to our awareness. Thus, civilized society made rules to rein in sexual and aggressive drives. Laws were made against rape, murder, thievery, and other behaviors societies viewed as dysfunctional. These rules that make civilization possible are going directly against what the id directs us to do. The id uses the "pleasure principle" to guide its motivational energy. It wants to increase our primitive pleasures around sexual desire, and to aggress with vengeance against people who are trying to control or attack us. There is a constant state of tension between what the id directs us to do and what civilized society is requiring of us. This tension is also felt on one hand in our need to have intimacy and on the other hand, the id's desire for raw sex and aggression in our personal relationships. The ability to therapeutically interpret which drive, sex or aggression, is behind any particular dysfunctional behavior is part of the training in this approach.

The Superego

The superego is where the rules to live by reside. It houses your attitudes, what you consider right and wrong, your judgments, your gender and sexual identity, what feelings are acceptable to you, your religious beliefs, and generally, what behaviors and thoughts you consider to be acceptable for you and others. You are not born with a superego. Everything that is in the superego is initially adopted from a parent or whoever was raising you before the age of 6 years old. In addition, we have many rules, beliefs, and attitudes that are learned from the culture and ethnicity that surrounded us as children. Many of these also end up as part of your superego, having been adopted through our early childhood experiences.

The Ego

The ego has two major functions. First, it encompasses our conscious awareness of ourselves and the world around us. We use five senses to be aware of others and our environment. We are aware of cognitive and feeling processes—what we feel, and what we think and imagine. The ego is our window to life. The ego discriminates what we believe is our current reality, separating our history from the present. This is useful so that energy can be directed in the present moment for problem-solving.

The second function of the ego is to mediate between the powerful sexual and aggressive impulses coming from the id and what our superego says about how we are supposed to live our lives. The ego's basic function is to keep us from the pain of knowing how the id wants to contradict what is acceptable to our superego rules. For example, in our superego is our gender and sexual identity. If you clearly consider yourself to be heterosexual, this means you would never consider a homosexual experience or relationship. However, the sexual drives from your id say that you are as attracted to the same sex as the opposite sex and would want to actually engage sexually with same sex partners. From a Freudian perspective, this is considered to be a fact. So if by chance you met a person of the same sex, and found yourself unconsciously attracted to them, your ego would check in with your superego to ensure that you are indeed heterosexual. Then, it would counter the energy coming from the id to keep you from consciously knowing that you have sexual feelings for this same-sex person. To actually consciously feel, any same-sex sexual attraction would violate your sense of self and cause you anxiety and pain. It is the ego's job to keep you from pain as much as possible.

Similarly, in your superego is a rule, hopefully, that you should not kill people who make you very angry, including, for example, your partners and parents. So assume that you are very angry with your mother. The unbridled id sends energy urging you to kill her. The ego, sensing this heightened motivational energy coming from the id, checks in with the superego and indeed finds a rule that you should not kill people with whom you are angry. So the ego clamps down on the id energy before you can even know that unconsciously you want to kill your mother. The ego has again done its job to keep you from knowing what you unconsciously really want to do, thus avoiding this pain of knowing.

The dynamic that the ego uses to clamp down on id energy that would violate the superego rules and attitudes is the concept of psychic energy. Psychic energy is what the ego utilizes to stop or re-channel id impulses that are liable to cause you pain. Consider now the metaphor of the three-story house with lots of trap doors in the floors between the id in the cellar, the ego on the first floor, and the superego in the attic. The id is constantly sending up sexual and aggressive impulse energy into the ego through trap doors in the floor. The ego looks up through the ceiling holes to the superego in the attic to decide what to do. If the energy coming up from the id violates superego rules and would cause pain, then the ego directs psychic energy to close and hold down that basement trap door, cutting off or dampening that unacceptable sexual or aggressive impulse. To use the gender-sexual identity example, the primitive impulse to have a same-sex encounter coming up through id's trap door would be closed by the ego's psychic energy, so you wouldn't even know you felt it.

Since there are many, many trapdoors of unacceptable sexual and aggressive impulses coming up from the id, the ego is one busy construct. It needs to constantly assess whether the id energy would cause a behavior, or even the thought of a behavior, that would violate superego rules. Then it would need to use psychic energy to clamp down on the trap doors, almost like a game of "whack-a-mole." When there is sufficient psychic energy available, the ego can play this game quite well. However, when psychic energy runs low or something happens that heightens the id's sexual or aggressive impulses, there may not be enough psychic energy to keep some of the trap doors closed. There might be seepage of id impulses, allowing for a person to have some inkling of their true unconscious desires. When this happens, anxiety, depression, anger, or an uncharacteristic sexual or aggressive behavior can result. However, the ego can replenish its supply of psychic energy. When people get enough sleep, eat well, exercise, calm themselves, meditate, or problem solve, the amount of psychic energy available to the ego can increase.

Defense Mechanisms

The ego has a variety of ways to use psychic energy to protect you from knowing and experiencing unacceptable sexual and aggressive urges from the id. These are called defense mechanisms (Frankel, 1984; Laughlin, 1979). However, they are being used unconsciously. For example, if you knew that the ego was using the defense mechanism called "repression" to deny your true unconscious wish to kill your mother, then the cat would be out of that bag, and you would feel the pain of that knowing. We can on a rational level make interpretations about what defense mechanisms are being used to protect us and others. And in fact, this is what therapists in Freudian practice do. It is also very important to understand that the application of defense mechanisms is protective, helping us avoid pain. There are many times in life that it is essential that we avoid pain to maintain our stability. Therefore, the use of defense mechanisms by the ego should be viewed in the context of their value in maintaining relationships and emotional stability. There are times when it might be helpful to strengthen a defense mechanism.

Here are some of the more common defense mechanisms:

Repression: This is one of the most primitive defense mechanisms. Feelings relating to serious aggression, and sexual attraction to parents, siblings, and children are all serious dangers if they came to the level of awareness. The same can be said of feelings violating one's gender identity. The ego cannot allow even a little seepage into awareness, so it closes that id trapdoor completely with strong and constant doses of psychic energy to completely cut off the knowing of these urges.

Denial: Denial is activated when something happens and the ego is unable to deal with the pain, such as somebody dying or the loss of a job. The ego applies sufficient psychic energy to clamp down on the related id sexual or aggressive energy. When you hear that a friend or relative suddenly died, the first response coming out your mouth is "No," an immediate use of the denial defense mechanism. In this case, denial is a fleeting response, instinctually used to avoid the pain of knowing. When used for too long, denial might put a person out of contact with reality.

Projection: This is a common and widely used defense mechanism. There are many feelings we have that our superego tells us are not acceptable. Blaming is a perfect example of this phenomenon. When you have an argument with your partner, the rules of your superego may not allow you to own your part of the problem. The way your ego can protect you from the pain of owning your own anger at yourself is to project it onto your partner—it's their fault. If your friend frustrates you and you have a superego rule that you're not supposed to show anger, then the ego can arrange to channel that id seepage into a projection. "You appear angry, and I am wondering why you might be angry with me?" It is common that when people use projection as a defense mechanism, they work hard to fulfill their projection. Thus, if you pushed hard enough, your friend would likely get frustrated and blurt out, "I am not angry with you!" And then you can say, "See, I knew you were angry with me!," thus fulfilling your projection. Another stereotypic use of projection is when a dad gets very angry with any boy who touches his daughter. His superego has strict rules about having sexual feelings about his daughter. Thus, when he views another boy touching her, the id sends up his unconscious sexual attraction for his daughter. This knowing would be very painful and unacceptable for him. Thus, his ego uses psychic energy to redistribute the id urge into a projection, where he is angry with the boyfriend.

Reaction formation: When a parent gets very angry with their child, and the child ends up giving that parent a present, this is reaction formation. The child's superego won't allow them to get angry with their parent, so the ego redirects this anger energy into doing the opposite of what the id impulses are demanding. Avoiding a feeling and doing the opposite of that feeling is characteristic of reaction formation. Another example is when something very sad happens, and the person reports being very happy.

Isolation: People use this defense mechanism to separate feelings from the tasks they are doing. For example, there is a reason that surgeons are not allowed to operate on their friends or family. It is essential that they separate, or isolate, their feelings about the patient from the surgery tasks. Similarly, it is normal to associate strong caring feelings with sex acts. People who engage in "recreational sex" have to isolate these intimate caring feelings from having sex, or they would be emotionally overwhelmed as they went from one partner to another.

Displacement: A common defense mechanism. A person gets very angry at their boss, but their superego has rules about not allowing anger at authority figures. Instead, at home, they get angry with their partner, displacing the id aggressive impulse to a safer venue. People will not realize this is what they did, and the fight with the partner will seem to be valid and independent from what happened at the office. When it is deemed by your superego as too risky to show love or hate in one setting, displacement is one way the ego can redirect these id urges to a place where is it more acceptable.

Substitution: The most stereotypic example of substitution is a rebound love affair. When the first love affair ended, there was incredible pain that the person could not adequately cope with. It is the ego's job to help us avoid pain as much as possible. Therefore, a few weeks after one affair ended, another started, substituting one love attachment for another, ending all the pain from the first. Freud would also view overeating as a substitution defense mechanism, being used to avoid, albeit momentarily, anxiety or depression.

Rationalization: When a feeling becomes too threatening to one's well-being, the ego can use rationalization to reduce the pain. Rationalization intellectualizes experiences, explaining away failures in nonemotional factual ways. "Yes, I lost my job and am having severe financial difficulties, but it happens to everyone and I'll be okay." Indeed, the rationalization might be true, and the rationalization defense mechanism could be an excellent way to cope with the situation. But if it is covering up anxiety or depression, the ego will be using a lot of psychic energy to keep this defense mechanism in place, risking depleting its psychic energy reserves.

Undoing: This defense mechanism uses superstition as a way to avoid pain. For example, the childhood rhyme, "step upon a crack and break your mother's back," is a superstitious way for a child (or adult) to avoid the knowing that their id really does want them to break their mother's back. So avoiding the cracks is a symbolic affirmation of the superego rule not to angrily aggress against one's mother. Many obsessive compulsive disorder (OCD) behaviors represent an undoing defense mechanism, as these repetitive behaviors act to avoid anxiety.

Introjection or incorporation: Accepting humiliating criticism is an example of introjection. Instead of being angry and aggressive to the person delivering the criticism, one takes it in and considers it as appropriate or being deserved. The superego cannot allow the rage connected with being humiliated, so the ego arranges the energy to be turned inward as an acceptable way to deal with the id's aggressive impulses and meet the demands of the superego.

Identification: This is one of the core defense mechanisms. We will see, according to Freud, that it is the central defense mechanism used when it becomes time to establish our gender and sexual identity. More commonly, it is the source of empathy. Feeling someone else's pain is a way of avoiding that their pain is really our pain. For example, when we empathically comfort someone who has experienced a death in their family, we are crying for them, avoiding our own fear and pain of facing our own death. The same can be said when we cry when someone we don't even know dies. There are many stories from prisons and concentration camps where people have identified with the aggressors, the ego using identification to minimize the pain associated with being a victim.

Somatization: This defense mechanism occurs when people turn unacceptable feelings resulting from the id's aggressive or sexual impulses into physical symptoms. For example, a person's superego cannot allow the rage that is coming from the id about being continuously criticized. So the ego directs this energy to the body's muscular structure, or to other organs, causing aches and pains. These symptoms are very real, and the person has no idea that it is connected to the verbal abuse they are receiving.

Conversion: Of all of the defense mechanisms, this is one of the most interesting. One behavioral manifestation of this defense mechanism is called hysterical paralysis or hysterical blindness, both of which are extremely rare. After experiencing a traumatic experience, a person will literally become paralyzed in some part of their body or go blind. For example after seeing a horrific act, a person goes blind, or after accidently hitting someone, their arm becomes paralyzed. The superego was so violated that the ego used conversion to help the person avoid the pain associated with the situation in which they were involved.

Provocative behavior: This defense mechanism is a favorite for adolescents, but all ages can imbibe. When a teenager agrees with their father to take out the garbage every day and then forgets to do it, dad usually get frustrated or provoked. We are not talking about the normal "goat-getting" behavior that is common between adolescents and their parents; the teenager knows what they are doing. When the teen forgets to take out the garbage, they are *sincerely* sorry and promises to do better. The provocative behavior defense mechanism is covering up the anger they feel toward their parents. As the pattern of forgetting emerges, the teen cannot explain how this is happening. Their superego has rules about respecting their parents and taking their responsibilities at home seriously. So the ego arranges for them to "forget" as a way to channel their rage at their parents by frustrating them.

The construct of how the id, ego, and superego work using psychic energy and defense mechanisms is really quite elegant. It explains how and why we behave as we do. Seepage of sexual or aggressive impulses from the id, when complete repression fails, can be directed in many different ways using a wide variety of defense mechanisms. We can easily identify with wanting to avoid pain. There is a clear place for where our rules and attitudes reside. We know that we are aware of our world and have problem-solving skills. Sex and aggression issues are central in everyone's life, so it does seem reasonable that they play an important role in motivation of behavior. There is so much in Freudian theory that just makes sense.

Yet, the entire model is grounded on a motivational system of unconscious sexual and aggressive impulses. This construct shows both the power of the model and its limitations. If one believes there is an unconscious part of our minds, and in it are sexual and aggressive impulses, then the theory flows from there. But since the unconscious can't be accessed, except by inference, it does not allow for much empirical validation. It's almost as if one has to *believe* it to be so. This is not a great foundation for any psychological or scientific theory and is more akin to what people do when they are involved in a religion. However, the fact that the Freudian ideas have persisted for almost 100 years is a testament to the power of this theoretical construct.

Personality Development

Freud had created a model of psychology that was groundbreaking. But he didn't stop there. He created a theory of personality development that paralleled the psychology model, and explained how patterns of behavior were learned in the context of the id, ego, and superego construct. He understood that children were influenced by family dynamics from the time they were born to when they were emancipated. The personality development model he came up with predicted adult patterns of behavior based on how children were treated by their parents. He observed nuances of child and parent behavior that were deemed important in childhood development, a remarkable achievement (Erikson, 1950, 1959; Frankel, 1984; Goldstein, 2005).

Freud hypothesized that there were five major stages of child development: oral, anal, Oedipal, latency, and adolescent stages. Each stage confronted the child with a major problem to be resolved before moving on to the next stage. When the resolutions to each stage were incompletely resolved, that left unfinished business, called residuals. These residuals predicted specific dysfunctional behavior patterns as an adult.

However, no one ever leaves childhood without unfinished residuals from each stage. Residuals at each stage are also called "fixations," as the child is stuck or fixated on the issues left unresolved. The terms "oral" and "anal fixations" are familiar to most people. No parent or caregiver is perfect. At best, adults raising children love them and do the best they can. At worst, children are neglected and/or abused. Clearly, the worst-case scenario will have the most destructive residuals and these children as adults will be seriously psychologically damaged. The age ranges for each stage are approximate, as children develop psychologically as differently as they do physically.

Oral Stage (0–2 Years)

1. *The problem to be resolved:* Instant gratification and trust. Anyone who has been around babies knows that they initially explore their world through their mouths. From the time they are born, they are instinctively sucking on a nipple for food. As they learn to crawl, anything they find immediately goes into their mouths. It is no surprise that Freud called this first developmental stage the oral stage. The psychological problem facing children in

these early years is indeed acted out through the mouth, but it is more profound than just eating. Babies follow the pleasure principle. When they are hungry, they cry and expect to be fed. When they are lonely, they expect to be held and cuddled. These are instinctual needs. For this reason, in the first few months of life, mothers or fathers usually pick up their babies whenever they cry to feed them. This is called demand feeding and meets the needs of the child. Similarly, the child is usually also picked up when they cry before and after feedings, meeting the baby's need for cuddling and contact. The psychological position of the baby is one of expecting instant gratification: "I want what I want when I want it, and you are expected to give it to me." However, at some point, the baby will be put on a feeding schedule. It then becomes clear to the baby on some instinctual level that they are not getting instant gratification of their eating and contact needs as they did before. They are not happy campers.

2. Resolution: Delayed gratification and substitution. Babies instinctively begin learning techniques that calm them between feedings—they suck on things, starting with fingers. Parents/caregivers support this process by offering pacifiers. When babies realize that adults won't be picking them up as often as they feel they deserve, they latch onto objects during these lean times, stereotypically a doll, stuffed animal, or blanket. To the extent that parents/caregivers support these substitutions, it helps the child learn there are other comforting options when they are not getting fed or held. Along with learning substitution skills, the child also needs to learn that while they are not getting fed or held on demand, it eventually will happen on a regular schedule, one that they can count on. They need to learn that they can trust their caregivers to come through for them every day—feedings happen on a reasonable schedule; contact happens frequently between feedings.

3. *Residuals:* Unfinished business from this stage will come in two ways: (a) Children who have not been able to find ways to delay gratification and substitute for the loss of instant gratification; and/or (b) children who have had experiences with caregivers where their feeding and/or contact with adults was inconsistent. In both cases they will come out of the oral stage with "oral fixations" that will follow them into adulthood. Adults with oral fixations will likely be more dependent, demanding, and have serious trust issues in relationships.

Anal Stage (2–4 Years)

1. The problem to be resolved: Control, right versus wrong, and love and hate. While this stage has been associated with toilet training, it is much more pervasive an issue for a child, occurring in many aspects of a toddler's life. Toilet training, however, is a good symbolic metaphor for this stage and certainly brings to the foreground the issues faced by the child. For the first time in the child's life, they are being asked to do something that is not natural for them. Up to this point, they naturally pooped and peed whenever they felt the need. Now, caregivers are demanding that they poop and pee in a toilet. Someone is trying to control them, control their natural functions. In addition, it is being made clear to them by their caregivers, whom they love, that there is a right and wrong way to do this. This is the first time they have been exposed so directly to a moral dilemma, clearly being told what is right and what is wrong by people who are supposed to love them. They don't want to give up their poop, and often will hold it in, becoming anal-retentive. Or, they will purposely not use the toilet but go in their pants or even on the floor to frustrate the caregiver. Subsequently, as this process unfolds, they may be faced with shame and guilt, depending on how parents/caregivers are dealing with the toilet training. And it's just not for toilet training. There are other natural functions that are being asked to control, like demands they not be aggressive to siblings and peers, to control their eating habits and their sleep times. Again, issues of shame and guilt can come up, depending on how caregivers respond to their resistance to change. Often, they are very angry at attempts by caregivers to control their lives. It's not

called the "terrible two's" for nothing. They feel confused how they can feel both love and hate at the same time for people on whom they are dependent. All of this is a lot for a little tyke to handle.

2. *Resolution:* Reciprocity, conformity, integration of love–hate for the same person, and acceptance of right–wrong polarity. Again, we can use how parents respond to toilet training as an example of how they can help children get through the anal stage. If parents try to coerce or punish children in the toilet training process, or show frustration or anger, the child will eventually learn to conform, but will also learn that conformity is associated with shame and guilt. Behind shame and guilt is the rage from the id, which may manifest itself as serious residuals in adulthood. A more supportive way to help a child accept the reality of control issues is to maintain calm, and let the child learn at their own pace. Better yet is to teach the concept of reciprocity. When someone asks you to do something you really don't want to do, it is more acceptable if there is some reciprocal transaction, that is, what's in it for me to do this for you. This type of transaction is common in life, and not only saves face but also acts to develop closer relationships. One of the major techniques that are used for toilet training is to advise caregivers to offer praise and appreciation when the child has a successful attempt. The child gives up their poop for you, and you give them praise in return. Another kind of reciprocity is to allow the child to get rewards for each successful attempt. Again, they give you their poop, and you give them something in return. In this way, they learn that there can be some benefit for conformity. Similarly, if the caregiver relationship during this time is more calm, they can integrate the fact that they both love and hate the person who is trying to control them. The more contentious the caregiver relationship during the anal stage, the more difficult it will be for the child to make this love–hate integration. Similarly, the same dynamics hold for dealing with the right–wrong dilemma. In a more calm, loving parental approach during the anal stage, children will learn that when they do something wrong it can be dealt with in a more acceptable and loving way. Doing something that is considered wrong in a contentious parent–child relationship is much more dangerous to the child's well-being.

3. *Residuals:* An adult having fixations at the anal stage would be more stubborn and self-centered. They could have some ambivalence about intimate relationships, be very sensitive to being criticized, and be more rigid in their moral and personal beliefs. They might collect things and not want to throw anything away. Some OCD may also come from residuals from the oral stage, needing to control one's environment by keeping things in order.

Oedipal Stage (5–7 Years)

1. *The problem to be resolved:* Gender and sexual identity. The Oedipal stage is the most controversial of all of Freud's developmental stages. As America and the Western world went through the eras of the Women's Liberation Movement and Gay Rights Movement, the Oedipal stage as a viable construct was left in their dust. According to Freudian theory for the Oedipal stage, girls, have "penis envy," and really want to be boys. Homosexuality was viewed as a dysfunctional residual from emanating from the Oedipal stage. Up until the early 1970s, the *Diagnostic and Statistical Manual of Mental Disorders* (DSM), published by psychiatrists, reported that homosexuality was a mental illness. Neither of these ideas sat well with the more progressive psychologists and social workers after the turbulent 1960s and 1970s.

Given the limitations of the Oedipal stage of development theory, Freud did raise important developmental issues. Regardless of whether you like Freud's view or not, there must be a time in a child's life where they begin to grapple with gender issues. It would seem reasonable that this process starts when the child is in the 5- to- 7-year-old range, but certainly children are affected much earlier as caregivers impose gender roles for behavior, clothes, and play. It is clear that when there is interference with gender identity development, it has serious lifelong consequences for children.

The Oedipal stage was where children adopted their superego, and was, as the Freudian model suggested, a crucial part of how personality and behavior were controlled. With a successful superego adoption, the child's ego would have some clear guidelines to decide where to supply psychic energy and defense mechanisms. Freud believed that between the ages of 5 and 7, children were faced with a gender identity crisis connected to their parental love attachments. With the awakening of id impulses relating to sexual and gender identity, children begin to feel some unease with their parents. Boys begin to feel that the father is threatening his relationship with his mother; that he is competing with his dad for his mother's love—his father was coming between him and his mom. Similarly, a girl feels threatened that her mother was competing with her for her dad's love—her mother was coming between her and her father.

2. *Resolution:* Identification with the same-sex parent. Freud postulated that the way out of this dilemma was for the child to identify with the superego of the same-sex parent. In that adopted superego were all of the rules and attitudes about how to live your life, including what it means to be a man or a woman. So the child was not only getting the rules for their gender identity, they were also getting the whole package of life rules and attitudes carried by their same-sex parent. This identification worked to resolve the gender identity crisis by melding the child with the same-sex parent through a shared superego. Since boys were now integrated with dad through a shared superego, they both could love the mom together, and neither would need to feel any competition for mom's love. Girl's identification with their mom's superego helped them know their gender identity as well. In the same way, melding with mom's superego meant that both of them did not need to compete for dad's love.

3. *Residuals:* From Freud's perspective, residuals from this stage were caused by inadequate identification with the same-sex parent. Boys fixated at this stage are said to have an Oedipal complex and girls an Electra complex. Obviously, if parental superegos are confused or weak, then what is adopted by their children will reflect this into adulthood. The residuals in adulthood from this stage would include gender identity confusion, with possible sexual issues resulting as well. With only partial identification with the same-sex parent, boys might enter adulthood still feeling the unconscious rage of not having successfully won the competition for the mother; girls with rage of not having successfully won the competition for the dad. This could result in difficult adult parent-child relationships, and conflictual marital and parent-child dynamics. And yes, from the original Freudian theory, homosexuality could be a residual, as well.

Latency Stage (7–12 Years)

1. *The problem to be resolved:* Integration. This time is supposed to be a latent or quiet period after a very exciting and sometimes stormy journey through the oral, anal, and Oedipal stages. Now that their gender identity has been established (hopefully), and they have faced the challenges from the oral and anal stages, whatever they have learned needs to be practiced and integrated. Their new adopted superego needs a chance to be exercised in the context of family and peer relationships; there are defense mechanisms from their new superego that need some rehearsal and old ones that need to be evaluated before being put on the road in adolescence and adulthood. The ego needs to learn how to use the available defense mechanisms to deal with all of the accumulating residuals from the oral, anal, and Oedipal stages.

2. *Resolution:* Time and space. Children need this time to develop their character, allow the more varied use of their defense mechanisms, and practice the rules and attitudes of their

adopted superego. In order to accomplish this, caregivers need to allow children the time and space to be with their peers and other adults to achieve these tasks. It should be noted that during the latency stage boys tend to play with their male peers and girls with their female peers. This allows them to cement their gender identity and all of the related superego rules. Should children not be allowed this opportunity, then this would be the cause of residuals from the latency stage.

3. *Residuals:* Adults with unfinished business from this stage might be viewed as lacking character or having an undifferentiated personality and might have asexual tendencies as well. In addition, residuals from this stage predict what we now call personality disorders.

Adolescent Stage (12–18 Years)

1. *The problem to be resolved:* Dealing with sexual and aggressive impulses and developing independence. This stage has also been called the "genital phase," as many of its issues revolve around sex. Suddenly, with no real preparation, hormones begin producing greatly heightening primal sexual and aggressive impulses. The id is in high drive, and the ego is very busy, using what psychic energy is available to deal with id impulses it had never seen before. The superego rules adopted in childhood don't seem to cover this new reality. The teen is experiencing real motivation to experiment with new sexual and aggressive drives in ways quite different than were in the superego adopted from their parents. Peer influences often become more important than parents as the teen is watching how their peers are behaving and rewriting superego rules for sex and aggression. This, of course, does not make parents happy.

2. *Resolution:* Modifying the superego to reflect the new adolescent reality; managing sexual and aggressive impulses. As the years go by in adolescence, the teen is changing many of the rules in their superego to reflect their new reality. These new rules, hopefully, will allow them to act out sexually and more assertively in a manner that adapts to community norms in a safe and legal way. Unfortunately, with the advent and availability of addictive drugs, new superego rules relating to drug and alcohol experimentation can have tragic consequences. Independence from parental influences requires the adolescent to establish new more adaptive rules based on the realities of their experience, thus preparing them for eventual emancipation from their family.

3. *Residuals:* Adults who have not successfully learned to manage sexual impulses will be more likely be promiscuous and have trouble with intimacy. In addition, the stormy aggressive feelings associated with adolescence might be maintained in adulthood, making for unstable relationships. There are those, of course, whose adolescence is relatively calm. They are able to continue using the superegos adopted from their parents with little modification. If that works for them, it will not likely be problematic.

CONCEPTION OF THERAPEUTIC INTERVENTION

The Ego Psychology Treatment Process
There are five basic components in the ego psychology treatment process: assessment, ego strengthening, insight, the transference, and the corrective emotional experience (CEE; Frankel, 1984).

Assessment
During the initial client sessions, clients are encouraged to tell their story about why they are seeking treatment. Therapists are carefully listening, observing clients' interactive behavior, looking for signs where clients have been fixated, and interpreting what defense mechanisms are likely being utilized.

Ego Strengthening

Having a strong ego is of course desirable as it increases awareness and improves problem-solving. There are four ways therapists work to strengthen client egos:

Partialization. When confronted with a task or problem so big that it is seemingly unsolvable, an ego can become paralyzed. The therapist offers to help break up the problem into small more solvable tasks, thus allowing the client's ego to put energy on a more doable problem-solving process.

Offering support. Active listening is one major support for clients as it shows them that someone who cares is hearing them. Offering praise and appreciation also is important.

Improving client self-esteem and self-image. Therapists attend to positive behavior and make sure that clients do the same. Asking clients to give themselves positive self-statements is also helpful.

Providing a safe place. Clients need to know that the therapy session is a safe place (where they can share without concern of being judged or criticized, where confidentiality will be ensured, and where session schedules will be predictable) and that the structure of each session will be generally predictable.

Insight

In ego psychology treatment, it is thought that having insight into your problems supports their resolution. Insight is a connecting phenomenon. It is helping clients make the connection between what happened to them growing up and their current problematic relationships and behaviors. It often comes as an "aha" moment. Therefore, therapists support clients in remembering their history and telling their stories.

The Transference

The transference is a projective phenomenon where clients symbolically put a parent's face onto their therapist. They act out in the session to the therapist who becomes a "stand in" for their mother or father. Developing this dynamic is an important part of what will become the curative elements in the ego psychological approach. It is assumed that client problems are related to unfinished business with parents—parents were, after all, responsible for the fixations at each developmental stage. It is also assumed that there is repressed rage, fear, hurt, and/or sadness associated with these fixations. By fostering transference in the session, the therapist and client can recreate in the moment these unfinished parental dynamics. The client can then revisit the unfinished business using the therapist as a stand in for the parent, in the safety of the therapy session. Therapists can more readily foster the development of a transference by being nondirective, which is exactly what the theory tells them to do.

The Corrective Emotional Experience

All the previous four components lead to the CEE, which is a dramatic culmination of a client's work and leads to resolving client problems. When the client, through the transference reaction, finally confronts a parent on how they contributed to their present dysfunctional behavior, it can be quite dramatic and emotional. The CEE can lead to new behavior patterns.

A case study will be instructive here.

CASE STUDY

Mike, age 34, entered therapy because he was having trouble maintaining relationships. In the past 4 years, he had five girlfriends, but none lasted more than a few months. About 9 months ago, he met a woman he really liked, and with her encouragement, he entered therapy. His work had settled around his inability to keep intimate relationships with women. He was a successful businessman, lived alone, and reported that he often felt lonely and sometimes depressed. He had been in therapy for 6 months and had been spending more and more time getting in touch with feelings about his upbringing. He had recently had the insight that his inability to be vulnerable with women was one way he kept them distant. We will pick up on his session as he is talking about this new insight:

Mike:	I'm not completely sure why people want you to be vulnerable before they will love you.
Therapist:	Has that been your experience?
Mike:	Well, my former girl friend kept saying she would do anything if she could make me cry.
Therapist:	Why don't you cry?
Mike:	I want to sometimes, and I know that if I did I would probably feel better, but I just can't.
Therapist:	Why not?
Mike:	Oh, I know the traditional reasons. My mother wanted me to be strong and kept telling me that if I let myself be weak, I'd end up like my father, who was an emotional cripple. I'm sure that's the way it happened, but it doesn't do me any good to know that.
Therapist:	If that's the reason, how do you feel about it?
Mike:	Look, God damn it! I don't know how I feel. Why do you keep asking me how I feel when I don't know? (pause) Oh, god, I'm sorry for blowing up.
Therapist:	(softly) You can be angry with me, Mike.
Mike:	(tears in eyes) No, I can't. I just can't.
Therapist:	Who are you talking to, Mike?
Mike:	(pause) To you! (another pause) No, my mother. (another pause with tears now streaming down Mike's face) Oh, Mom, why wouldn't you let me feel the way I wanted to? You spent so much time worrying that I'd turn out like Daddy that you never let me feel; you never wanted to listen to how I felt. Didn't you ever want to know me? At least I could get close to Daddy, but never to you. (Mike is really sobbing now)
Therapist:	(gives Mike some tissues—there is a 5 minute pause while Mike sobs)
Mike:	(somewhat composed now) Well, mother must be so proud of me. I turned out to be just like her.
Therapist:	Not just like her, Mike. You're letting yourself be vulnerable now in front of me. (pause) I hesitate to ask you again, but how do you feel?
Mike:	(laughing) Better now. I think I needed to get that out.

The dynamic here that supported Mike's corrective emotional experience was his transference with the therapist. Mike was able to release years of grief, tears, and sadness about how he felt about growing up with his mother. By reenacting an early scene with his mother, he was able to do something he had never done—tell her how he felt. His work began a superego rewrite allowing sadness and tears, thus freeing up psychic energy that for years repressed his feelings. The freed up psychic energy could now be used for other conflict resolution (Frankel, 1984).

COMPATIBILITY WITH THE GENERALIST APPROACH

There is one overarching theory that binds together those practitioners who follow the generalist approach, particularly as it is defined in social work—systems theory. From this perspective, it is difficult to integrate the psychodynamic approach in the context of a micro, mezzo, and macro generalist practice. Almost by definition, psychodynamic theories are focused on interpsychic variables, with some offshoots moving into intrapsychic variables. This is likely the reason that in schools of social work, the psychodynamic theories, when they are taught at all, are put into the historical perspective of clinical social work. In psychology departments, the lack of an empirical foundation for ego psychology, and its humanistic offshoots, has been a serious barrier, especially when compared to the research-grounded behavioral approach.

However, there are many skills that emanated from the psychodynamic theories that are integrated into a generalist practice. These include active listening, the importance of eliciting feelings, unconditional regard, unconditional acceptance, ego-strengthening skills (support, praise, acknowledgments, having a safe place in which to work), partialization, and the idea that our history affects our present. If you look at the work of social work and psychology professional practitioners, you will see the these Freudian "skill marks" in every session.

CRITIQUE

One of the major critiques of the Freudian constructs was how difficult it has been to develop a research model that would validate their use. Unfortunately for ego psychology, and those humanistic relatives that were spawned from Freudian concepts, both independent and dependent variables are very difficult, and often impossible to define. Interventions and outcomes, in general, lack behavioral specificity, which of course, means that the effectiveness of these theories is subject to serious question about whether they work. For example, one essential basis of psychoanalysis is the id, which cannot be identified in any observable way. Even in ego psychology, where the id is downplayed as part of its theory, it still exists as a construct that explains defense mechanisms and motivational drives. Therapist behavior is another extremely difficult independent variable to define. There may be general treatment process behaviors that ego psychology therapists use, but certainly not uniformly across practitioners. Even dependent variables are hard to define. The outcomes for clients in ego psychology practice include very general concepts, such as changes in personality, CEEs, and ego strengthening. Insight, which might be behaviorally defined, has not been shown to be necessary for behavior change. In addition, even when behavioral outcomes are clarified for clients, it is impossible to attribute these changes to therapist behavior, except in a very general sense. In ego psychology, therapist intervention techniques are too variable and not easily quantified from session to session, thus making any cause-and-effect relationships between therapist interventions and client outcomes extremely difficult, if not impossible.

CONCLUSION

From a social work perspective, ego psychology theories lack the scope to be easily integrated into the systems approach, the foundation of social work practice. Social workers tend to gravitate to those theories that can be used in the context of our broad assessment and intervention approaches. This includes looking at not only the personal psychology of a person but also the whole person and the issues that affect them from family, community, organizations, social policy, and social justice. It is not a simple task to integrate ego psychology and the other humanist approaches into micro, mezzo, and macro assessments and interventions.

It is true that vestiges of Freudian theory have lasted for 100 years. Many of Freud's ideas resonate with our experiences and make sense to us; some ego psychology techniques are still being used. However, there are many professionals practicing clinical social work or psychotherapy who believe that this is not enough to justify the continued use of either psychoanalysis or ego psychology in the mainstream of practice. Yet on the mantle place of social work and psychology history, there is an important place that cannot be ignored by anyone who values our history and how it affects our present.

SUMMARY POINTS

In summary, this chapter has:

- explored the basic theoretical foundations of ego psychology,
- described the intervention strategies associated with ego psychology, and
- described how ego psychology has influenced current practice in clinical social work.

KEY REFERENCES

Only key references appear in the print edition. The full reference list appears in the digital product found on http://connect.springerpub.com/content/book/978-0-8261-6556-5/part/sec03/part/sec031/chapter/ch07

Ainsworth, M. D. S. (1973). The development of mother-infant attachment. In B. Caldwell & H. Ricciuti (Eds.), *Review of child development research* (vol. 3, pp. 1–94). University of Chicago Press.

Austin, L. (1948). Trends in differential treatment in social casework. *Social Casework*, 29, 203–211.

Bellak, L., Hurvich, M., & Gediman, H. (1973). *Ego functions in schizophrenics, neurotics, and normal*. Wiley.

Berne, E. (1961). *Transactional analysis in psychotherapy*. Grove Press.

Blanck, G., & Blanck, R. (1974). *Ego psychology: Theory and practice*. Columbia University Press.

Cohen, P. (2007). Freud is widely taught at universities, except in the psychology department. *New York Times Ideas and Trends*, November 25, 2007.

Erikson, E. (1950). *Childhood and society*. W.W. Norton.

Erikson, E. (1959). Identity and the life cycle. *Psychological Issues*, 1, 50–100.

Frankel, A. J. (1984). *Four therapies integrated*. Prentice-Hall.

Freud, S. (1923). The ego and the id. In J. Strachey (Ed.), *The standard edition of the complete psychological work of Sigmund Freud* (vol. 19). Hogarth.

Cognitive Behavioral Theory and Treatment

Norman H. Cobb

LEARNING OBJECTIVES

By the end of this chapter, you should be able to:

- learn the five behavioral principles that account for learning or loss of behavior,
- discover the role that cognitions have in the acquisition and maintenance of behavior and emotions, and
- learn to apply the behavioral principles, cognitive restructuring, and the use of mindfulness to accept and commit to change troublesome thoughts and behaviors.

INTRODUCTION

Human behavior is fascinating. We watch people and wonder how they learned to behave or to process ideas in such unique ways. Whenever we share living accommodations with other people, we are often surprised to realize that they are different from what we are. They squeeze the toothpaste tube in the "wrong" place, they put the toilet paper on the holder in the "wrong" direction, they drop their clothes on the floor, or they meticulously hang up all their clothes all the time! We may not even realize that others are thinking similar things about us. Hopefully we will all realize that we were "trained" by different parents/caregivers and our learning histories are different. What is normal in one person's thinking may not be "normal" to someone else. Each person's experiences are unique.

The vast majority of behavior (overt behavior) is learned. Ways of thinking (cognitions or covert behaviors) are also learned. Our emotional expressions are usually very similar to those expressions that we observed from our parents, caregivers, siblings, friends, and so forth. For decades, behaviorists and cognitive theorists have described how behaviors are learned and maintained in the environment. More recently, they have merged their theories, perspectives, and treatments into cognitive behavioral therapy. This chapter describes the essence of behavioral and cognitive theories, and offers some examples about how the merger of these perspectives has created the most effective interventions for learning and treatment for good behavioral and mental health.

OVERVIEW OF COGNITIVE BEHAVIORAL THEORY

For decades, theorists from the cognitive, behavioral, and psychodynamic perspectives have competed to explain human development and guide assessment and treatments in the helping professions of social work, psychology, counseling, and so forth. For example, cognitive theorists understood depression as the influence of clients' beliefs that were negative, illogical, or self-destructive. Behavioral theorists explained depression as the result of a high rate of punishers and a low rate of reinforcers (positive stimuli) in clients' environments. Psychodynamic theorists focused on the unconscious mind that contains unresolved issues from childhood and accompanying feelings and patterns of thinking and behaving.

One of the most exciting and beneficial evolutions in counseling theory and practice over the past 30 to 40 years has been the merger of significant portions of behavioral and cognitive theory. Over the years, behavioral and cognitive therapists became increasingly aware that their clients suffered from a combination of factors—some attributable to negative or irrational beliefs, others resulting from aversive and negative environments. These therapists recognized that clients with differing levels of severity of symptoms required more of either cognitive or behavioral interventions. Additionally, behavioral and cognitive theorists came to recognize that the mechanisms of learning for behaviors and thoughts are the same. Over time, the combination of cognitive and behavioral approaches has resulted in a variety of treatment methods called cognitive behavioral therapies, which have proved to be effective with an impressive list of client problems.

HISTORICAL DEVELOPMENT

Both the behavioral and cognitive traditions have their own array of famous theorists and models. In the behavioral tradition, Pavlov (1927) demonstrated that, through association in time and space, the sound of a bell could have the effect of cuing a dog to produce a physiological reaction of salivation—classical conditioning. Skinner (1953, 1974) documented that when behavior occurs, whatever follows the behavior (positive or negative) can either increase or decrease the frequency, duration, or intensity of the behavior—operant conditioning.

Bandura (1969, 1977), a behaviorist, explored the role of cognition, and how people learn vicariously, without having to immediately experience stimulus—response conditioning such as the positive or negative consequences of behavior. He asserted that merely by watching, hearing, or reading about behavior, people capture cognitive images of behavior and, in their thoughts, replay or rehearse the behavior. Furthermore, they expect to receive reinforcement or even punishment in the future if and when they perform the behavior. Bandura's consideration of cognitive mediation in behavioral learning led to developments in social learning theory (now referred to as social cognitive theory), which reflected the developing merger of behavior theory and cognitive theory.

In the cognitive tradition, Ellis (1977) contended that irrational beliefs lead people to display dysfunctional behavior. His rational emotive therapy focuses on challenging and changing those irrational or illogical beliefs. Beck's (1967, 1976; Beck et al., 1979) research led him to believe that depression was a product of people's negative beliefs about themselves, others in their world, and the future. As a result, he developed his cognitive therapy for depression.

From the constructivist perspective (Granvold, 1999), people learn covert behavior from family, friends, the environment, and so forth, and they generate their own sense of reality. Interestingly, genetics plays a role in this process. For example, years ago, I adopted two children, 7 weeks apart, from two different mothers. Within months I realized that each child, with their own genetic predispositions, responded to the world in different ways. The first child was "laid back," more relaxed with the environment, and when hungry, the cry was soft and somewhat sweet. The second child was almost the opposite. The second child was easily aroused, and when hungry, produced a cry that I described as "a fire alarm." The difference was genetic, biological in nature, but in terms of their environment, the second child was fed first! Now as adults, the first born continues to be very calm, focused on kindness, family, and being responsible at work. The second child, as an adult, is driven to move up in the company, be successful, and be active in the world. While both of them are very nurturing to their children, each one maintains their own style of intensity and involvement.

The genetic structure sets the stage for how individuals initially interact with their world of parents, family members, teachers, friends, and so forth and the result is their own cognitive structures of reality, called cognitive schemas. Schemas consist of people's attributions, perceptions, decision-making strategies, and personal logic, and in a real sense, create people's personal senses or versions of reality.

To summarize, the historical merger of behavioral, cognitive, and genetic elements enables us to understand the various processes that shape our overt and covert behaviors, and suggests methods to potentially teach and change people's thoughts and behaviors. The following details describe the various elements for treatment of behavioral and cognitive issues.

CENTRAL THEORETICAL CONSTRUCTS

From the behavioral and the cognitive perspectives, theorists have conceptualized two types of behavior—overt behavior and covert behavior. Overt behavior is composed of observable, outward actions such as walking, speaking, and waving at people to get their attention. Covert behavior is composed of behaviors that are performed in people's thoughts or cognitions and include language, perceptions, attributions of causality, and so forth, which are fundamental to people's daily functioning. We refer to the lifelong accumulation of these cognitive behaviors and experiences as people's unique learning histories. These thoughts/covert behaviors create the personal cognitive schema, which influence individuals' decisions, behaviors, and emotions. In the final analysis, these overt and covert behaviors are learned through classical and operant principles, vicarious conditioning, and ongoing life experiences.

In the following pages, a discussion of the theoretical constructs of behavioral and cognitive theories illustrate the ways in which all human beings learn and perhaps unlearn thoughts and behaviors. While learned behaviors can also be unlearned, it should be cautioned that some learned behaviors are deeply integrated into people's habits, perceptions, and emotional reactions, and they may resist change. Still, even behaviors that are a function of biological processes (e.g., genetics, drug use, brain chemistry) may be altered or at least managed by coping strategies, cognitive restructuring, and/or learning alternative behavioral patterns. The following details the fundamental principles in each theory.

Behavioral Theory

Three general paradigms are included in the behavioral learning process: classical conditioning, operant conditioning, and social learning theory. The language of "conditioning" often gets in the way of fully understanding the factors that are involved. Historically, a great deal of the early work in behaviorism took place in Eastern Europe (Kazdin, 1978). Pavlov and other researchers primarily focused on the behavior of animals, insects, and birds to understand how behavior is acquired. Those who translated the writing of these early behaviorists struggled to select the correct words to describe the elements and mechanisms of change. For instance, did Pavlov's dog "learn" about the ringing bell or was the dog "conditioned?" Obviously, they decided that dogs and the other nonhuman research subjects must have been "conditioned." Years later, when English speakers and other Western romance language speakers applied the mechanisms to humans, they continued the theme that humans are "conditioned." Now, conditioning is the proper term, but a minor alteration helps everyone grasp the enormous impact of the principles on human beings. Instead of classical conditioning, we might think of classical learning and gain greater appreciation for how human beings learn behavior. For example, many people assume that fears of snakes and rats are innate; however, they are learned, and classical conditioning/learning describes the process. In a similar perspective to classical learning, operant conditioning can be seen as operant learning, and when we remember that an "operant" is a behavior that operates in the environment, we could reframe operant conditioning as behavioral learning.

CLASSICAL CONDITIONING/LEARNING

Pavlov (1927) was well aware of the biological connection between animals' innate ability to smell or recognize food and their response of salivation. He conceptualized this as an unconditioned cause and effect. In terms of classical language, the unconditioned stimulus (UCS) is followed by an unconditioned response (UCR; Exhibit 8.1). In essence, an innate stimulus cues or triggers an innate behavior.

Pavlov decided to ring a bell when the dog food was presented. Keep in mind that the bell was originally a neutral stimulus (NS), because bells have no innate or real meaning to dogs. Pavlov discovered, however, that after repeatedly ringing the bell when the smell of dog food was presented, the bell eventually triggered the dog to salivate. The bell became a conditioned stimulus (CS), and salivation was a learned version conditioned response (CR) of the innate salivation response (UCR; Exhibit 8.2).

When we start talking about human beings, we realize how much classical conditioning/learning affects them. For example, how does a child become inseparable from the "blankie?" Most likely, the prospective parents got a small baby blanket in anticipation of their new infant. In the beginning, a blanket has no more meaning to a child than did the new bell to Pavlov's dog. However, if the parents use the baby blanket when their baby is feeding and feels comfort from the milk, the blanket takes on a magical quality. After a few weeks of association with the milk and the feeling of comfort, blankets will most likely become a significant source of comfort to the children (CS). As a result, the parents will be surprised to find that their child will not want to be separated from the "blankie" because of the comfort that it provides. If, however, the milk causes discomfort for children (in terms of allergies, medical issues in digestion, etc.), bonding with the blanket is not likely to occur. If the blanket is paired with another stimulus such as cuddling with a parent, however, bonding is likely to develop.

In another example, human beings have a similar innate connection between a loud sound (UCS) and fear/arousal response (UCR), called the startle response. This fear response was one of the ways that early human beings survived when animals in the wilderness made loud sounds, and therefore scared them. You might be surprised to realize that we do not have an innate fear of snakes, rats, spiders, and so forth, but that classical conditioning can explain how such fears might develop. For example, a child might be walking over to pick up a snake (or rat, spider, etc.) and someone yells, "No!" or "Stop!" The yelling sound triggers the startle/fear response in the child, and they associate that uncomfortable arousal with all snakes (or rats,

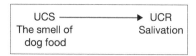

EXHIBIT 8.1 Classical conditioning: An unconditioned stimulus triggers or is followed by an unconditioned response. UCR, unconditioned response; UCS, unconditioned stimulus.

EXHIBIT 8.2 Classical conditioning: A conditioned stimulus gains the ability to trigger a very similar conditioned response. CR, conditioned response; CS, conditioned stimulus.

etc.). The fascinating part is that these children may grow up and consider their fear to be normal or natural, rather than learned.

In a related example, a child may gain a fear in a very subtle, yet classical, learning way. The child is being driven to the doctor's office to get her vaccinations for school. On the way to the doctor's office, she tells her parent that she is confused why she is going to see the doctor, because she is not sick. The mother wants to be helpful and tells her daughter that she is going to get her "shots." Well, in the mind of a 5-year-old, "shots" are delivered by guns and people on television die from being shot; therefore, the child responds with some level of arousal or fear. The parent tries to explain that the shot is actually a needle that is stuck in her arm. Now, the child is more afraid, because she has seen her grandmother's sewing needles and how much they would hurt if driven into her arm. Potentially, the situation might get even worse. The desperate parent tries to clarify and explains, "The shots are actually very sharp metal tubes that goes into your arm and allows the nurse to pump fluids into your body!" As you can imagine, the situation goes from bad to worse. The little girl may have a good start on an anxiety disorder called aichmophobia.

OPERANT CONDITIONING/LEARNING

Skinner (1953, 1974) researched operant conditioning (behavioral learning) where a behavior (classically referred to as a response—R) is followed by a stimulus (S) such that the frequency, intensity, or duration of the behavior either increases or decreases. The following behavioral principles describe the behavioral learning process.

Increasing Behavior: Both positive reinforcement and negative reinforcement increase the frequency, duration, and/or intensity of behavior. In both cases, a behavior is followed by a stimulus (S). In positive reinforcement, the stimulus is desired (Exhibit 8.3).

In negative reinforcement, a behavior (R) is followed by the termination of a negative or aversive stimulus (S–; Exhibit 8.4).

In both positive and negative reinforcement, the stimuli are vitally important. For example, in positive reinforcement, the stimuli must be of some value to the person who performed the behavior. For example, if your beloved gives you flowers and you respond with something that your beloved likes (e.g., a "thank you," a hug, or a kiss), the frequency of "flower giving" is likely to increase or at least continue, as a result of the positive reinforcement.

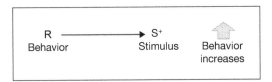

EXHIBIT 8.3 Positive reinforcement: Behavior is followed by a positive stimulus such that the frequency, intensity, or duration of behavior goes up.

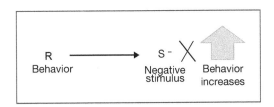

EXHIBIT 8.4 Negative reinforcement: Behavior is followed by the termination of a negative or aversive stimulus such that the frequency, intensity, or duration of behavior goes up.

Children offer great examples of the power of positive reinforcement. One boy put on his shoes, walked into the living room, and his parent clapped and said, "Wow! Look at you! You put your shoes on!" The boy got so excited that he went back into his bedroom, took off his shoes, and walked back without shoes. The parent appropriately responded with "Oh my, there you are without your shoes!" To get a second dose of positive reinforcement, he ran back into his room, put on his shoes, and walked back into the living room to receive a second dose of reinforcement!

With negative reinforcement, the behavior (R) terminates an aversive condition—a negative stimulus. For example, at night, you walk into your bedroom and you don't like the darkness; so you turn on the light. The "light-turning-on" behavior terminates the darkness (an aversive condition). After a few episodes of walking into the dark bedroom and turning on the light, you might be surprised to walk into the room in the middle of the day, and without thinking, you turn on the light. You might feel a little silly turning on the light, but in reality your "light-turning-on" behavior has been conditioned/learned and become a habit through negative reinforcement. Other examples include putting on your seatbelt to terminate the aversive dinging sound in your car or putting on sunglasses to dim the bright sunlight.

Decreasing Behavior: Punishment, response cost, and extinction decrease the frequency, intensity, or duration of behavior. As mentioned earlier, the characteristics of the stimuli that follow the behavior are all important.

In punishment, a behavior (R) is followed by a negative or an aversive stimulus (S–), such that the subsequent frequency, duration, or intensity of behavior decreases (Exhibit 8.5). To use an earlier example, your beloved gives you flowers; however, you are an ardent conservationist, and you reply, "I do not know why a responsible adult would kill a living organism to give it as some sacrificial expression of love!" As a result, I suspect this was your last gift of cut flowers.

So often when we define punishment, people think about spanking or hitting. In reality, behavior usually stops for a moment, but real learning may not take place. For example, if parents are cooking on the stove, their young children may assume that the parents are playing with the pots and pans. Children also want to play with the pans, and they typically reach for the top of the stove. Since parents want to protect their children, they may slap their children's hands away from the hot stove. At this point, children have no idea why the slap occurred, so they reach their hands back toward the stove top to play with the pans. Unfortunately, parents tend to hit the children's hands even harder, and suddenly, the children's attention turns to the pain. Most children start to cry, and many of them will say, with considerable shock, "You hit me!" At this point most children have no idea what just happened, except for the fact that their parents inflicted pain. The stopped behavior qualifies the sequence as "punishment"; however, the parents would have been smarter to pick up their children and move them to another place where a more attractive stimulus (e.g., a toy truck, special doll, TV show) offers much more attraction (reinforcing value) than the pots and pans.

Response cost is a process, mechanism, or procedure where a behavior (R) terminates a positive condition (S+), such that the subsequent frequency, duration, or intensity of behavior decreases (Exhibit 8.6).

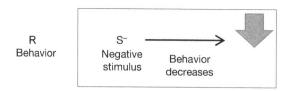

R
Behavior

S–
Negative stimulus

Behavior decreases

EXHIBIT 8.5 Punishment: Behavior is followed by a negative or aversive stimulus such that the frequency, intensity, or duration of behavior goes down.

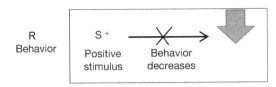

EXHIBIT 8.6 Response cost: Behavior is followed by the termination of a positive stimulus such that the frequency, intensity, or duration of behavior goes down.

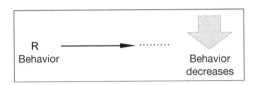

EXHIBIT 8.7 Extinction: Behavior is no longer followed by a previously reinforcing stimulus such that the frequency, intensity, or duration of behavior goes down.

For example, an adolescent recently received her driver's license, and asked to use the family car. Her parent reluctantly agreed, but since she was new to the driving role, her parent requested that she be home by 10 p.m. While she was gone with the car, she had such a wonderful time and could not imagine that her parent would mind if she was "a little late." When she returned home 2 hours after curfew, she was met by an anxious parent who said that she was now prohibited from driving the car. In operant learning terms, her lateness (R) resulted in the suspension of her driving privileges (S+). Therefore, if the frequency of her coming home late decreased, the principle of response cost occurred.

Extinction is a process, mechanism, or procedure where a behavior (R) is no longer followed by a previously reinforcing stimulus (S+), such that the subsequent frequency, duration, or intensity of behavior decreases (Exhibit 8.7).

Parent training provides a good example: Parents are trained to extinguish their children's tantrums (when they are not destructive or harmful) by ignoring the tantrum behavior. One of my favorite secretaries from the past had a son who would throw himself on the floor of the grocery store and cry if he did not get what he wanted. I instructed her to simply start reading the labels on the canned goods and act like she was paying no attention to him. On her next trip to the grocery store, her son threw himself down on the floor and started crying, and she began reading the labels. After a few minutes, he stopped crying, got up, and walked over to her, and she said, "Oh, hi!" but he threw himself back down on the floor. Fortunately, we had discussed that probability, so she went back to reading the labels on the canned goods. After the second period of crying, he stopped, she greeted him again, and much to her surprise, he was ready to continue shopping.

Timing can be everything! The early behavioral research emphasized that positive reinforcement or punishment needs to occur rather quickly after the desired or undesired behavior. For young children, the optimal time between their behavior and reinforcers or punishers was considered to be seconds or slightly longer; however, with adults, the time between behavior and the reinforcer/punisher could be considerable. For example, one partner might say to the other, "You know, that outfit you had on last night made you look fantastic!" or for the opposite, punisher effect, "It made you look fat." The time delay between behavior and response requires a cognitive process that we describe as "memory," "thought," and so forth.

From Social Learning Theory to Social Cognitive Theory

Bandura (1969, 1977, 1978, 1986) was originally a behavioral theorist, but he began to focus attention on memory and learning processes to show how people observe, hear, or read about behavior, and then perform the behavior after several days or months have passed. Bandura called this "vicarious learning" through the process of modeling. In essence, people remembered the behavior but withheld its enactment. They may have re-played the memory in their thoughts as if they were rehearsing the behavior. Later, they enacted the behavior with some expectation that they would receive a similar reinforcement (called expectancy of reinforcement).

In reality, we learn a great deal of our behavior through modeling. A 10-year-old watched another kid hold the door open for an older woman at a cafeteria. She smiled and said "Thank you." Months later, the 10-year-old took the opportunity to perform the same behavior and was delighted with the smile and "Thank you."

People often report they enact behaviors that are remarkably like those of their parents. For example, one man reported symptoms that partly resembled persistent depressive disorder (*Diagnostic and Statistical Manual of Mental Disorders, Fifth Edition* (American Psychiatric Association, 2013) a less severe, yet long-term version of major depression. When asked about his family, he described how his parents liked to stay at home, never got excited, seldom displayed emotion, never went out to eat, and did not go out with friends. The evenings were full of quiet reading, occasional TV shows, and bedtime by, what he called, "the witching hour" of 9 o'clock. Weekends were times to rest up for the coming week. He assumed that their lifestyle was normal. They modeled a life of few outside activities and few, low-key celebrations. Not surprisingly, he described himself as a "nice guy" and normal. In high school and college, he wanted to date "normal" people, which in reality meant "just like me." When he came across people who were different from his parents, he considered them to be "just a little weird." He was very attracted to a young woman that he considered to be "a little wild." She wanted to go out to eat, go dancing, and go places with friends. They dated for a while, until he found a "normal" girl who was just like him.

In another example, children learn many survival skills through modeling. For example, parents can easily demonstrate to children how to walk up to the street curb and look to the left and look to the right before crossing the street. Those same parents are often shocked to see their children look both ways and still run out in front of a car. Most parents don't realize that they also have to teach the advanced skill of looking for cars, estimating the cars' speeds, and determining if they have enough time to safely cross the street. In summary, the repeating theme is that thoughts, or covert behavior, are important to live safe, full lives.

Vicarious learning was an astragal part of Bandura's "social learning theory," but through the years, issues began to evolve due to confusion over various learning theories. To focus his perspective, Bandura (2005, 2011, 2016) switched to "social cognitive theory" to emphasize more specific elements of cognitive processing as well as well learning, memory, and so forth.

Cognitive Theory

Bandura (2018) and other cognitive theorists use the ABC model to show how cognitive theory clarifies human functioning. In this model, A is an activating event/stimulus that triggers B, a person's thoughts/beliefs (covert behaviors), and is followed by C, a behavioral or cognitive or emotional response (Exhibit 8.8). The thoughts in B are actually learned patterns of thinking and information processing (cognitive schema) that people have learned throughout their lives.

Covert behaviors are learned in a similar manner as overt behaviors. Language, beliefs, emotions, perceptions, attributions, and so forth are acquired directly through classical conditioning, operant conditioning, and/or modeling (vicarious learning). For example, children have the innate capacity to make verbal noise, but specific language skills are learned through a process of reinforcement. For instance, when infants make sounds like their caregivers' language, the caregivers say some version of, "Yea, she's talking!" Initially, infants have no idea

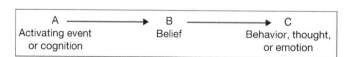

EXHIBIT 8.8 ABC model in cognitive theory.

what the sounds mean, but they love the attention (positive reinforcement); therefore, they repeat the sounds. Caregivers gradually shape children's language skills by paying more attention to sounds that resemble real words and ignoring others. As children grow, caregivers can model the words by repeating them for children and positively reinforcing the developing language skills. No one is surprised that Chinese-speaking parents end up with Chinese-speaking children, and so it goes for every language group around the world. However, this common process can be uniquely charming. This process can be duplicated for every ethnic and cultural group around the world. One of my old friends was adopted from China as an infant by parents living in East Texas. His physical characteristics look exactly like his Chinese birth mother, but when he speaks, he talks with a charming but rather disarming "Southern drawl"!

Children learn the beliefs, behaviors, emotional responses, thought patterns, attribution skills, and so forth, through the same mechanism of learning. People's thoughts (covert behaviors) can also positively reinforce their own performance of behavior. For example, a student finishes an exam and thinks, "Wow, I did it! It's finished!" Similarly, an employee thinks through a problem, develops a creative solution, and says, "I am so proud of myself." In a subtler way, if people believe that a behavior will enable them to get what they want, they may continue to undergo a punishing environment and withstand the immediate costs of that behavior. For example, people work out in the gym for hours, because they believe that it will produce better muscles or longer lives. On the other hand, victims of domestic violence may return to their abusers with the belief that perhaps they contributed to the abuse and the idea that certainly "life will be better." In a similar way, adults may continue to wear particular items of clothing despite negative comments, if they believe that they will eventually get the response that they want. In essence, beliefs, or covert behaviors, have a powerful impact on people's lives.

RATIONAL AND IRRATIONAL THOUGHTS

While we recognize that cognitions are learned, the fascinating reality is that many of those processing patterns are rational, while others are irrational. Ellis (1974, 1994; Ellis & Dryden, 2007; David et al., 2010) predicted that people will experience troublesome solutions because their thoughts are based on irrational belief systems. For example, if children are taught the irrational belief that everyone must like them, they will struggle with people who for whatever reason do not particularly care for them. In another vein, some adolescents and adults learn that love and passion are the same thing, and as a result, they may struggle with the variations of interpersonal relationships. Ellis (1994) described many common, yet irrational, thoughts. The following are a few of my personal favorites:

1. I absolutely must be competent, adequate, and achieving in all important respects or else I am an inadequate, worthless person.
2. It is awful and terrible when things are not the way I would very much like them to be.
3. Everything must be organized and, or my world is full of confusion and disarray.
4. My past history is an all-important determiner of my present behavior, and because something once strongly affected my life, it should indefinitely have a similar effect.
5. There is invariably a right, precise, and perfect solution to human problems, and it is awful if this perfect solution is not found.

Cognitive clinicians would intervene and help clients reframe their irrational beliefs with statements that are more rational. For example, "I would prefer to never make mistakes, but I know that mistakes are normal, and no one is perfect."

DYSFUNCTIONAL BELIEFS

Beck (1967, 1976; Beck et al., 1979) proposed that people typically have three negative beliefs about themselves, other people, and the future—the negative trilogy. They personally feel inadequate or faulty. For example, they may think that they are too short or too tall, certain body parts are too big or too small, or their hair is too straight or too curly. Second, they believe that other people have negative judgments about them. For example, when people hold the belief that they "don't measure up," evaluative comments from their partners, friends, bosses, and so forth may be interpreted more harshly than intended. On the other hand, people may interpret colleagues' or coworkers' compliments as fake or insincere. Finally, people can become despondent, even suicidal, because they believe that change is impossible and their lives will always be a certain way.

Beck et al. (1979) called such problematic beliefs "cognitive errors." He theorized that the negative beliefs were fundamental components of depression. He found that depressed people reported high rates of self-critical, judgmental beliefs. Some of the common cognitive errors that lead to feelings of depression include overgeneralizing (e.g., "I messed up that exam; I am not very smart!"), taking excessive responsibility (e.g., "My having a job has caused my teenager to get involved in drugs!"), and dichotomous (right/wrong) thinking (e.g., "You are either in love with me, or you are not!").

Cognitive theorists have shown how information processing affects people's judgments. For example, self-esteem (good or bad) has long been considered an important variable that influences behavior. The cognitive behavioral perspective of self-esteem is practical and treatable. Self-esteem is construed as beliefs (covert behaviors) that are the product of people's judgments about how they compare with others—either overall or with regard to specific abilities. For example, many professionals who are required to take licensing exams frequently report that they "don't do well on tests." They are making the judgment that, compared with "normal" test takers, they will do much worse on the licensing exam. As a result, they feel inferior, and unfortunately, their belief may impact their performance on the exam. As a consequence, if they do poorly on the exam, they may have "proof" that they were right, and oddly enough, if they do well on the exam, they typically attribute their success to luck.

The treatment of problematic, covert behavior such as low self-esteem requires an analysis of the components of clients' judgments. Thus, depending on people's beliefs, the intervention might focus on raising their assessment of their own testing ability based on the fact that they passed their college courses, or, on the other hand, it may focus on lowering the unrealistic assumption about other people's abilities. For example, licensing exams cover every possible area of the profession, which no one can know completely. Therefore, the realistic perspective of taking a licensing exam is to merely pass it. Also, people could be encouraged to take advantage of study aids (e.g., a licensing preparation workshop, sample multiple-choice questions) to raise their perceived level of competence.

Constructivism: Clearly, people construct their own sense of reality in numerous ways. Constructivism explains how one person may apply one set of information processing rules to one situation, while another person perceives the situation in a very different way. For example, in couples therapy, a familiar theme is presented by Granvold (2007): "Couples do not share reality, they share experiences" (p. 318). Similarly, people interweave logical judgments, illogical beliefs, and individualized wishes, and create new beliefs, new ideas, and new versions of the present or the past. As a result, people generate an endless array of hypotheses about the world; this underscores the rich diversity among individuals. The constructivist view should remind people, particularly clinical professionals, that clinical assessment is a process of discovering the specific qualities of individuals, and treatments must be individualized to clients' unique behavior and cognitions.

PHASES OF HELPING

Four phases map out a sequence for addressing clients' problems. They are engagement, assessment, intervention, and evaluation and termination.

Engagement

Cognitive behavioral therapies endorse warmth, genuineness, and empathy as core ingredients in therapeutic communication. Warmth is communicated through a combination of gestures, tone of voice, facial expressions, and so forth, that convey a caring and sociable attitude. Professional warmth gives a sense of acceptance and concern for clients, but without the trappings of a personal friendship. Genuineness refers to helpers' communications that are open, spontaneous, and not defensive, thus allowing clients to experience the genuine communicator as upfront and straightforward (Egan & Reese, 2014). Finally, empathy requires workers to consider how clients might feel about particular events, and communicate compassion and concern for the emotional impact of situations on clients.

Engagement with clients is enhanced by viewing clients' problems from the perspective of learning. Clients are empowered by the perspective that if behavior (overt or covert) is learned, it can be unlearned, or if behaviors were never learned, they can be taught. Clients are delighted to hear that they are not defective, crazy, or "bad seeds," but rather their learned behaviors are not working for them, and/or they are not getting the results they want. This perspective is underscored by workers' acceptance of clients as human beings who have concerns about problem behaviors.

Assessment

The assessment process identifies problem areas and associated behaviors that need to be increased or decreased (in frequency, duration, or intensity) and/or learned and practiced. By focusing on behavior, clients can readily answer: "What happened?" "Who did what?" and "What happened next?" Many clients are less equipped to tell us how they are feeling, and even less capable of answering "Why?" With adolescents in particular, questions about "What happened?" or "Who did what" are less threatening than "Why did you do that?" or a?" And, their classic answer to "Why?" is "I don't know."

Assessment is a stage to determine what needs to change, but it is also a process that continues throughout the relationship between workers and clients. By assessing behaviors that work and behaviors that do not work, social workers can plan fairly precise intervention methods to make changes. Also, identified behaviors allow for clear objectives by which the end product of treatment can be evaluated. Whether workers employ specific behavioral goals or single-subject design methods to track behavior change over time, identified behaviors (both overt and covert) can be used to verify treatment success or lead to strategic changes in the intervention plan.

Behavioral observation is one of the primary tools of assessment, and if properly conducted, it has high validity. Clients or observers can keep count of the frequency, duration, or intensity of behaviors. The observation serves as the baseline for future comparisons to determine change. For example, at a parent–child center, two sons were concerned about their mother's cussing, and their mother wanted them to clean up their rooms. All three agreed to the following assessment assignments: The boys would count the number of times their mother cussed in the morning and the evening. In turn, at bedtime, the mother counted the number of pieces of clothing that were left on the floor of the bedroom or bathroom. Although the task was intended to be for assessment purposes, the simple act of observing and being observed led to significant changes and agreements for future change.

Some problems, such as covert behaviors, are not as easily observed. For example, thoughts and feelings of depression are common mental health concerns. Depression, however, is a construct that takes different forms with particular clients. Internal states of anger, sadness, feelings of lethargy, and so forth are only measurable indirectly. A self-anchored rating scale from 1 to 5 allows clients to create their own scales. For example, one client was encouraged to come up with her own label for "1" to indicate unhappy feelings, and she chose "Feel like hell." For "5," she chose "Skipping down the street." The midpoint, "3," became "Just-so-so." Regardless of the label choices, the process of having clients label the points on their scale creates a sense of ownership of the scale and a subtle, yet effective, motivation to actually use the scale at home and report the results to the social worker.

Rapid assessment instruments (RAIs) enable clients to report covert behavior (Bloom et al., 2009). One of the most widely used RAIs is the Beck Depression Inventory (BDI; Beck et al., 1996). With this instrument, clients' responses to 21 questions result in a summary score that indicates their level of depression. The BDI is only one of many RAIs for depression. Corcoran and Fischer (2013) compiled a two-volume set of RAIs most commonly used by social workers, including measures for children, families, adults, and couples, that cover a wide variety of client problems.

One additional element can help clients use RAIs or self-anchored scales at home. Social workers can help clients select cues in the environment that will signal them to complete their scales. For example, a client asserted that she was angry "all the time." She was asked to keep a log of her anger and the situational contexts in the morning, afternoon, and evening. Rather than using meal times (which people sometime skip) as reminders, the client decided to tape one copy of the scale to her bathroom mirror where she brushed her hair each morning, one copy in her computer calendar at work, and another copy on her alarm clock, which she set each evening. The cues successfully reminded her to mark her scale, and later, the information helped her understand the different roles that her work, her teenage daughter, and her husband played in her emotions.

A thought record can be very helpful for clients to make the connection between their thoughts and emotions. It consists of nothing more complicated than a piece of paper with a line down the center. The left column is labeled "Thoughts," and the right column is labeled "Emotions" or "Feelings." Clients experiencing depression or grief are usually so caught up in their feelings that they have no real sense about their thoughts; therefore, the thought record is designed to help them make the connections. With one client, the thought record was placed next to the commode where the client had her morning "bathroom break" and her evening "before going to bed" moment. Another client chose to set the scale on the chair in front of the TV. Therefore, environmental cues are almost as important as clients describing the connections between thoughts and emotions.

In summary, the observations, RAIs, scales, thought records, and so forth enable clients and their social workers to pinpoint specific overt behavioral patterns and/or cognitions that, if changed, would significantly resolve their problems. Higher degrees of specificity enable more precise and, therefore, more effective methods of treatment.

Interventions

In the cognitive behavioral approach, clients are not passive recipients of a magical therapy process. Instead, they must be involved in learning about and changing behavior and cognitions. Clients are usually very responsive to being educated about the cognitive behavioral model of human functioning. Clinicians, clients, parents, and others can make reinforcers or punishers readily available in the environment and literally change how people behave and interact. In the cognitive mode, thoughts are viewed as covert behaviors that can be learned or unlearned. Information processing can be enhanced through an examination of the illogical beliefs or cognitive errors that drive actions. Since clients are seen as unique individuals, their specific, idiosyncratic beliefs, perspectives, and behaviors can be addressed in any intervention plan.

The following are brief descriptions of specific interventions that illustrate the range of cognitive behavioral treatments and their theoretical components. Most of the interventions reviewed incorporate a combination of cognitive and behavioral elements, and show that overt and covert behaviors rarely change independent of one another.

BEHAVIORAL ACTIVATION

One of the tenets of the behavioral theory of depression is that mood is dependent on the relative balance of reinforcers and punishers in people's lives. For example, people's moods are high when the levels of reinforcers (e.g., good times, happy simulating events, pleasurable activities) are high and the level of punishers is low. Depression results when punishers significantly outweigh reinforcers. The cognitive perspective takes this situation a step further and emphasizes the connection between pleasurable moments and positive thoughts. Behavioral activation is a process of helping clients recall or recognize events or activities that brought pleasure to them in the past and then motivating them to engage in those activities. The purpose is to increase the presence of positive reinforcers and, therefore, offset the level of punishers (Turner & Leach, 2012).

For example, when you ask clients what activities give them pleasure or used to give them pleasure and make them feel loved and cared for, they frequently look at you with blank expressions. A good response is to give some examples. For instance, for some people, they love to read, soak in the bathtub, go for leisurely walks, cook their favorite food, sew, and so forth. One person responded, "I used to read, but since the babies were born I have not read a word." My response was to ask what kinds of books did she like to read, and she responded, "Books where the woman was a great detective. In fact I have five or six books on the self, but I haven't read a word." Therefore, toward the end of our session, I gave her the assignment to read one chapter in one of the books. The same type of assignment would follow if she had said that she hadn't had a chance to soak in the tub, go for a walk, sew, and so forth. The goal is for her to activate an activity that has a history of making her feel loved and cared for.

CONTINGENCY MANAGEMENT TECHNIQUES

Methods that focus on altering the consequences (both positive and negative) of behavior have wide applicability. Parents can ignore irritating, yet nondestructive behaviors in their children, and give positive attention, praise, or rewards for good behavior. The lack of attention to negative behavior initiates extinction, and the positive attention to good behavior reinforces the competing behavior. For example, children can be taught to play calmly with the family dog by praising them for gently petting the dog. A key element is to remember that behavior is "functional," meaning that behavior that receives reinforcement (e.g., praise, compliments, smiles) continues or increases; however, behavior that receives no attention at all decreases in frequency, duration, or intensity.

The Premack Principle (Premack, 1965) describes how a high-probability (i.e., highly desirable) behavior is used to reinforce the performance of a lower probability behavior—a type of contingency management. Barth (1986) refers to this principle as "Grandma's Rule" and uses the example of a grandparent saying to a child, "As soon as you put your toys in the toy box, we can have a dish of ice cream." The assumption is, of course, that putting toys in a toy box is a low-frequency behavior, and eating ice cream is a high-probability behavior.

Exposure Therapies

Most fears are learned from situations in the environment but seldom from bad experiences. Many parents fear their children being licked by dogs for fear of killer bacteria. Research shows, however, that humans have significantly higher counts of bacteria in their mouths than dogs. Similarly, some people have a fear of flying, when actually, they are safer in the plane than they were on the highway driving to the airport.

A smaller number of fear responses may also be learned through operant conditioning where a person actually experiences a negative condition such as being bitten by a dog or being in an accident. For example, if you are driving through an intersection and another car runs the stop light and crashes into the side of your car, you will quickly acquire a fear or apprehension to the situation. In an interesting way, some people may develop a fear of driving, while others may focus their fear on that particular intersection or busy intersections. Another person in the same situation may focus their fears on the specific type of car involved in the wreck.

Exposure therapy may take a variety of forms, but each one involves exposure to feared objects for a certain length of time; however, with no negative consequences (no bites, no scratches, no death-inducing bacteria, etc.). The exposure to feared objects may be very gradual or all at once (called flooding).

The process of exposing clients may be real-life exposure (called "in vivo") or through imagination or virtual reality. The exposure through imagination requires therapists to verbally describe the feared object or situation. If clients begin to get too aroused, clinicians can slow down or decrease the amount of imagined exposure. In virtual reality exposure, clients can look at a video screen or wear a pair of virtual reality goggles, where computer-assisted graphics depict elements of clients' feared objects or images.

An additional step is for clinicians to help clients create hierarchies of fear-arousing situations or conditions. Although the feared object (such as snakes or airplanes) may be the same for different clients, the specific reasons or triggers for the fears are the result of the unique learning histories of individual clients.

Systematic Desensitization: In systematic desensitization (Wolpe, 1958, 1990), clients are taught to relax using breathing exercises (Madders, 1997) and deep muscle relaxation exercises (Bernstein et al., 2000; Hayes-Skelton et al., 2012; Jacobson, 1938). Next, while clients are relaxed, clinicians gradually expose clients to increasingly fearful situations according to clients' particular fear hierarchies. Clients are told that if their fear level becomes too high, they should give a signal to the clinician and the exposure will slow down or decrease in intensity.

As long as clients maintain levels of fear below their escape or panic threshold, clinicians can move on to scenarios of increased fear. The purpose is to expose clients to higher levels of fear without panic or escape, and therefore, enable them to become desensitized to feared objects or situations. The technical term for the combination of relaxation and exposure is reciprocal inhibition—relaxation inhibits the fear response.

Exposure: In comparison to systematic desensitization, other forms of exposure may or may not use relaxation, and therefore, the intervention is based on exposure without an excessive fear response. The purpose is to allow clients to experience the feared object without any actual consequences.

Clients are taught to use Subjective Units of Distress (SUDs) to describe their level of anxiety. They are asked to rank their level of fear from 1 to 10 where "1" means no fear and "10" is the highest level of fear. This process enables clients to see their level of anxiety in a more objective frame of reference.

Flooding: The technique called flooding also aims to desensitize clients to the feared object; however, rather than gradually exposing clients to a hierarchy of fears, they are given maximum exposure to their feared object. The maximum exposure takes place with clinicians talking clients through an experience confronting their particular fears.

For example, a client was afraid of elevators. The clinician walked the client down the hall to the elevators and for a few minutes described how elevators work. To add an element of humor to the anxiety-provoking environment, he discussed how some people push the elevator button more than once or even a dozen times to "make the elevators move faster." He added that the elevator will come at the same rate whether the button is pushed once or 100 times, but the end result is a somewhat superstitious belief that more pushes make it move faster.

In the next moment, the elevator doors opened and since no one was in the elevator, the clinician took the client by the arm and led the client into the elevator. The client grasped the clinician's arm with an intense grip, and as the elevator began to move, he asked the client to rate her level of anxiety from 1 to 10. Her response was a firm 9. As the elevator approached the first floor of the building, he asked her to rank her anxiety, and she replied a 7. After they exited the elevator, he congratulated her accomplishing the drop in anxiety from a 9 to a 7 and how proud he was of her. In essence, the exposure ended without any serious consequence and the two-point change in anxiety was empirical "proof" of her drop in anxiety. After three more appointments and elevator rides, her ranking dropped to a consistent and manageable 3.

Prolonged Exposure: Apart from flooding there is another form of exposure called prolonged exposure (Barlow & Brown, 1996). The length of exposure is frequently between 30 to 90 minutes. One client was afraid of being judged by other people, especially in public places. Her homework assignment was to visit the local discount store and walk from one end of the building to another and observe the reactions from other customers. She was asked to keep a record of the number of people who laughed at her and/or looked critically at her. At the end of her experience, she was amazed that almost no one gave her any attention, and those who make eye contact only smiled.

Other clients with post traumatic stress disorder (PTSD) (Foa et al., 2013) were asked to write accounts of the event or events that caused the traumatic anxiety. For example, veterans wrote their descriptions in the privacy of their own homes, which allowed them to have a prolonged exposure in private to the memories of their traumatic experiences. Later, they read their accounts to the other veterans at the Veterans Affairs hospital. In response, the clients received significant emotional support and validation from the other veterans. Later, these "new" members of the groups would then sit in on the stories of newer veterans, hear their stories, and in turn, provide them with similar levels of validation and support.

Response Prevention

A few decades ago, the treatment for compulsive behavior prescribed a gradual decrease in the frequency of compulsive actions. For example, a client with a compulsion for checking that the stove was turned off was directed to gradually decrease the number of times they checked the stove daily. More recently, research discovered that attempts at gradual response reduction may inadvertently maintain compulsive behavior (O'Hare, 2005).

Therapy now focuses on helping clients to completely stop their compulsive behavior. In "exposure with response prevention," clients and clinicians first determine the events or thoughts that trigger obsessive thoughts, and place them in a hierarchy of least to most intense. In a process similar to systematic desensitization, clients are exposed to the least intense triggers (imagined or real) and not allowed to respond with their compulsive behaviors until their level of anxiety gradually subsides. The decline in anxiety can be accelerated with relaxation, deep breathing, or reassuring comments from the clinician. The next intense trigger is presented (without allowing clients to enact their compulsive behavior) until anxiety declines, and so forth. In line with the behavioral principle of extinction, when clients no longer receive any benefit from the compulsive behavior, it declines in frequency or intensity.

Cognitive Restructuring

Beck's (1967, 1976; Beck et al., 1979) cognitive therapy is also focused on cognitive restructuring and has many similarities to Ellis's rational emotive behavior therapy (REBT). Clients' negative or destructive beliefs about themselves can be enormously troublesome. Helping clients examine their beliefs and test their validity can enable clients to replace them with more realistic or more functional thoughts. For example, in Ellis's (1994) REBT, workers' first task is to identify the irrational beliefs that are linked to clients' problems. This might involve pointing out or convincing clients that they have an "all-or-nothing" belief (e.g., "I must be perfect every time and everywhere"). Workers would then actively dispute and refute the belief by pointing out its irrational aspects. An alternative to "I must be perfect" might be "I want to be perfect every time, but sometimes I make mistakes." Also, suggest to them that they might laugh at themselves and verbalize "Oops!"

In Beck's model, however, more reliance is placed on evidence from behavioral experiments and less emphasis on philosophical challenges to cognitive assumptions. Beck used three basic questions in his approach to cognitive restructuring: "What's the evidence?" "What's another way of looking at it?" and "What are the implications of having that belief?" For example, one client believed that his father hated him. When asked for evidence, the client responded that while he was growing up, his father beat him almost every day. The worker suggested that generally fathers do not beat their kids, and asked how his father learned to do that. Calmly, the client said that his father was beaten by his father. To that the worker replied, "Oh my! Your father was an abused child!" The client was stunned, and after a few moments of absolute quiet, he suddenly shifted to compassion for his father.

Cognitive Reframing: Reframing is a specific form of restructuring. The process focuses on a client's account of a particular situation. The accounts are frequently sequential, and tend to focus on the final issue or event. For example, one client described that her husband had left her for another woman. The clinician asked how they met and what if any changes she had made in her life to meet his needs and preferences. She described how she gave up Mexican food because he hated it. She believed that no one will ever love her. At the end of the session, the clinician gave her an assignment: "Before our next appointment, I want you to get a woman friend and the two of you go out to eat Mexican food." Days later she returned, she walked into the office and said, "My friend and I ate at two Mexican food restaurants! At one I flirted with the waiter; he was half my age!" Needless to say, that session began with a very positive and hopeful attitude.

SELF-MONITORING

Self-assessment skills are useful for numerous situations and treatment interventions, because self-awareness may often lead to change. The overall purpose of self-monitoring is to help clients recognize or be more aware of their thoughts or actions (covert and overt behaviors). Journals or diaries enable clients to record their thoughts, feelings, and overt behavior. They become aware of critical self-statements, rational or irrational beliefs, and the circumstances that are associated with problematic behavior (e.g., the times when, or places where, their feelings and behavior occurred). An additional step may include suggesting to clients to think back in their history and see if their current thoughts and feelings trigger a connection to the past—a particular situation and who was involved. Frequently, a retrospective view of their learned behaviors and thoughts gives enlightening clues to their patterns of thinking and behaving.

PSYCHOEDUCATION

For many client problems (e.g., parenting, obesity, medication management), simple skills training is very effective for facilitating change. The steps generally include the following: self-monitoring the behavior to be changed, setting realistic goals, developing a plan to change behavior, teaching ways to identify antecedents for distress and developing ways to control situations, identifying consequences of behaviors, teaching self-care skills (relaxation, increase in pleasant activities, control of negative thinking or social skills), and developing an emergency plan if problems develop (Coon et al., 2003; Craighead et al., 1994; Donker et al., 2009).

For example, parent training often incorporates skills to handle tantrums, reward good behavior, and provide alternatives to physical punishment. With overeating, clients can be taught to identify places or situations where overeating is probable and develop a plan to avoid them. Setting specific meal times normalizes eating patterns and discourages late night binges. Clients can also remove foods from the house that are unhealthy and replace them with low-calorie foods. Finally, clients need to get their loved ones involved in healthy eating plans.

ANXIETY AND STRESS MANAGEMENT

Interventions to control stress and anxiety include self-talk (self-statements that are idiosyncratic to the client and produce a calming effect) and cognitive distraction where clients visualize positive and appealing scenes from their memory or imagination (Resick et al., 2008). A word of caution is necessary, however: Telling clients to relax when they are experiencing a moment of moderate to high arousal is not effective and is counterproductive. Clinicians should remember that the only things faster than arousal are cognitions. Therefore, before arousal occurs, clients need to identify phrases of self-talk, distracting thoughts, or visualizations that they can "turn on" when they experience stressful situations. For example, one client hated his boss and reported feeling constantly mad and anxious when at work. The clinician helped him select a captivating memory and visualization from his life that he could begin every morning while he started his work routine. He was encouraged to continue the visualization all day. Much to his surprise, his experience at work turned from anger and hostility to pleasant interactions with customers and peers.

We must remember that while many clients attribute panic attacks to particular environmental stressors, their personal lives are characteristically full of high levels of stress and anxiety. Learning to manage overall stress is an important part of treatment. Therefore, when people are relaxed or relatively calm, they should be taught to practice relaxation skills such as tensing and relaxing muscles (and relearning what relaxation feels like), deep breathing exercises, and positive visualizations to lower the general levels of anxiety in their lives.

SELF-TALK AND COPING STATEMENTS

Most people are familiar with the old children's book where a train struggles to reach the top of the hill by saying, "I think I can, I think I can." Adults and children can be taught self-statements that guide their behavior or encourage a sense of competence or courage. The following example is an illustration of helping a mother address her children's fear of the dark and of going to sleep. A worker at a parenting center coached a mother to go through the following bedtime routine. In the evening, right before bedtime, she and the children were to sit on the floor outside their bedroom, and she was to hold up a book and say, "This book was written by a child expert who knows everything about kids." After thumbing through the pages, she was to pretend to read and say, "Oh! Yes, the author wants me to read a special sentence, and you are supposed to repeat it after me." After the children agreed, she pretended to read and said, "Witches and ghosts (she paused for the children to repeat the words) are only real (pause) on TV and in the movies (pause). In my bed, I'm safe (pause)." Next, she said that the book directed her to repeat the phrase, but this time, the children were to whisper the sentence. She whispered, "Witches and ghosts (pause) are only real (pause) ..." and so forth. Finally, she was to instruct the children to say the words inside their heads, and she again whispered the special sentence. Finally, she told them that the expert in the book said that at any time, if they felt afraid or worried, they could say the sentence to themselves and feel safe. At the next session with the social worker, she said, "You won't believe it! It worked!"

Self-talk and coping statements can be used by everyone to benefit from self-encouragement or reassurance. Some clients who are afraid of public speaking are surprised to hear that famous public speakers are always nervous before their presentations, and they use self-statements to remember their speeches and reassure themselves. Test takers may find comfort by reassuring themselves that they are not expected to know everything, and repeat, "All I have to do is pass this test!"

Acceptance and Commitment

The evolution of cognitive behavioral interventions is considered to be in the third generation with the development of mindfulness and the acceptance and commitment perspective (Cullen, 2008; Hayes, 2004; Hayes & Strosahl, 2004; Montgomery et al., 2011; Twohig, 2012). It has laid the groundwork for clients' cognitive and decision-making role in their personal changes.

Mindfulness and Change: An earlier intervention in the area of acceptance and commitment allows a client to look at a particular event in two different aspects: the actual task verses the emotions about the event. For example a popular event is paying your bills. The first step in mindfulness is to breakdown bill paying into the actual task, almost as if it is a photograph. You are sitting at your desk. You log into the website of your bank or look over the recent paper copy of your bank statement and determine the availability of your money. Next you log in the website of the billing company (electric company, water company, etc.) or write a check. (Reminder: No emotions, no thoughts of what if, etc.) Second, you focus on your feelings of paying your bills. For example, I hate these bills, they are too high, do I have enough money, and so forth. The mindfulness process reflects that the task is clear, physical, and set, but the feelings are the function of your cognitions about money, bills, life—past, present, and future.

The actual task is set, but the cognitions are under your control. Do I want to accept these cognitions and their implications for the day, or do I want to change them. I could change the cognitions to gloom and doom ("I hate giving my money away!"), or should I change those cognitions to a celebration of my life and financial status? ("I love my electricity and my phone service, and I love being in control of my life!")

Acceptance and Commitment: Our cognitions have more impact and influence especially when they interfere with our happiness or our sense of control in our lives. Regrets about the past or fear of the future can distract us from the present moment. The intervention is not to deny our fears or regrets but to accept them and assess them within the light of who we are now, our current skills and beliefs. For example, we are different today than we were when we made mistakes in the past. Do we have to always be troubled by the past or afraid of the future? In essence, we only have control over who we are now and what we want to learn in the present.

Miller (2019) acknowledges that mindfulness and being in the present moment are difficult to grasp. He used the analogy of thinking about the taste of strawberries and who will have a better present moment experience of the taste:

> An individual who has studied the science of strawberries to the degree that he or she is considered to be the world's expert—agriculture, botany, genetics, human taste receptors that send gustatory information . . . but, has NEVER eaten a strawberry? OR

> An individual who . . . just paid close attention to all of the sensations and experiences of taking a fresh strawberry, looking at it, smelling it, placing it in his or her mouth, observing the taste and texture as he or she bites into it. (p. 2)

Mindfulness and acceptance requires a focus on the here and now, not the emotional thoughts from the past or about the future. Podina and David (2017) described an intervention for clients where the clinician suggests that their clients imagine that they are the directors of a movie, and they have control over the lead actors (who in reality are themselves). As the directors, they focus on the present—who are they now and what are they doing now. The acceptance acknowledges the past and future but focuses on a commitment to the present. In essence, we are in control of who we are now, at this given moment. For example, a client had memories of an irresponsible behavior from 10 years ago. The issue is to determine what lesson can the memory teach the client. Once the client accepts the lesson from the past, the recurrent memory no longer possesses strength and most likely fades away.

Clients must realize that they live in the present moment. All their thoughts are the product of past events, teachings, and learning. They can choose to accept or alter those thoughts to coincide with who they perceive themselves to be in the present moment. For example, one client described how she had been depressed about various events and beliefs. The clinician asked about how she was feeling in the present moment, and she replied, "No, I'm fine now." The clinician recommended that she accept who she is now, not tied to the past, and commit herself to be who she is now, and 3 minutes from now, and 3 hours from now, and tomorrow ....

APPLICATION TO COUPLES, FAMILIES, AND GROUPS

Couple Therapy

Over the span of a few years, couples too often experience extinction. In the early months of dating and being together, partners experience considerable positive reinforcement (Epstein & Baucom, 2003; Granvold, 2007). Tenderness and touch are very nurturing. They spend as much time as possible talking, sharing meals, and feeling close to each other. Many of the household tasks are shared events such as cooking, watching TV, and exercising together.

In the ensuing years, various responsibilities of child care, home chores, outside employment, and so forth become more demanding and routinized. Fewer roles are shared, and individuals assume the primary duties for various tasks. Unfortunately, the rate of compliments, words of affirmation, physical touch, and other positive interactions seem to get lost in the myriad of child, family, and work demands. After a number of years, partners feel less appreciated, and perhaps, taken for granted.

One couple commented that since the children were born, they had not been out to eat alone. They talked about how they missed the intimacy of "the early years." In reality, when the rate of positive reinforcers decline (extinction), partners become more vulnerable to outsiders who are willing to offer affirmations, compliments, touch, hugs, and other reinforcing behaviors.

Therefore, the focus on couple therapy is to increase positive reinforcements and reenergize the couple friendship, shared activities, and unconditional positive regard. With the previously mentioned couple, couple time had gotten lost in the day-to-day whirlwind of family life; therefore, their assignment was "date night." They were to hire a babysitter and go out to eat. At the restaurant, they could talk about the kids for 30 seconds, but the rest of the time, they were to talk about the food, the restaurant, and each other. As a quick footnote, with this couple, the "date night" homework assignment evolved into a weekly event and their report of date night was charming.

Epstein and Baucom (2003) reported on Stuart's (1980) "Caring Days" exercise. Each partner is instructed to make a list of behaviors (e.g., "Give me a hug," "Call me at work," "Say 'Thank you'") that, if enacted by their partner, would make them feel "loved and cared for." Certain behaviors are not permitted on the list such as expensive gifts or intense sexual behaviors. Also, they were instructed to not keep a count of behaviors or make one behavior contingent on a behavior by their partner. Each person was instructed to do as many caring (reinforcing) behaviors as they wished. At the next meeting with the clinician, the couple would discuss the assignment and determine what worked.

Couples can also be coached to recognize automatic thoughts that occur in their day-to-day interactions. Gottman's research (Gottman, 1999; Gottman & Gottman, 2015; Gottman & Silver, 2015) found that negative comments have far greater impact than positive comments. In his approach, couples are taught to recognize and eliminate caustic or contemptuous words and phrases from their interactions. Additionally, couples are encouraged to consider "positive override"—a style of attributing one's partner's aversive or negative behavior to an accidental or temporary mistake rather than to personality or character defects.

Additional communication styles help couples avoid communication errors. All couples have disagreements, but they are encouraged to recognize and avoid contemptuous terms. For example, one partner may have been upset at their partner's behavior at the Saturday night party. "I" statements help couples state their feelings and their concerns in a specific style, such as "I felt saddened when you did that thing at the Saturday party." This approach allows the first partner to "own" their feelings and communicate to the other partner. The contempt version would have been, "You were an idiot, and you always will be!"

Gottman also researched the positive effect of a couple conversation called "mirroring." The idea is based on the research finding that partners want their concerns or issues to be heard and, actually, being heard is even more validating/reinforcing than being agreed with. The mirroring begins when one partner asks, "Can we talk?" When the answer is "Yes," the partner states a concern. At various points in the statement of the concern, the other partner responds by paraphrasing the concern, and ends with the question, "Did I get that right?" If the answer is "Yes," the listener asks, "Is there more?" If the answer is "No," the listener asks, "What did I miss?" The back and forth process allows one partner to be heard, without a rebuttal, apology, or criticism from the other partner. When the first partner's concern has been fully expressed, the listener states, "Let me see if I can summarize your concern," and ends with, "Did I get that right?" After any back and forth process to clarify the summary, the listener can make a simple comment of validation such as "I know that must have made you feel …."

Other methods of cognitive behavioral theory interventions for couples can be found in Worrell (2015), Ludgate and Grubr (2018), Dattilio and Beck (2010), and Monson and Fredman (2012).

Family Treatment

In family therapy, the cognitive behavioral perspective helps family members identify their roles in the maintenance of beliefs and behavioral patterns. They are reminded that beliefs and actions continue if they are occasionally reinforced. For example, children learn to tantrum, and they use tantrums to get what they want. Parents are instructed that if the tantrum behavior is not destructive or dangerous, they should ignore the tantrum until extinction occurs.

Family members are taught that in troubled families, partners, as well as children, get more attention for negative behavior than they get for positive behavior. They are encouraged to watch for good behavior and give immediate and positive attention for the good behavior. Additionally, they are instructed to shape behavior by giving positive attention to versions of behavior that are fairly close to the fully formed behavior. Furthermore, they are encouraged, through cognitive restructuring, to develop a non-blaming attitude, where they do not take personally the difficulties of their children or their mates (Alexander & Parsons, 1982). For example, adolescents learn to avoid the axiom "It's all my parents' fault," and adults learn "I am not totally responsible for all my children's mistakes" (Ellis, 1994).

Families are taught behavioral contracting where every member of the family accepts specific roles and behaviors (Falloon, 1991, 2015). The family devises a specific plan to celebrate when everyone meets most of the terms of the contract. For example, in one family, the family determined the specific duties for each family member for each evening. The children accepted their assigned tasks, and the adolescents felt empowered when they negotiated their duties. They also planned that if 80% of the tasks were completed by Friday evening, the whole family would celebrate with "Pizza Night." If the goal was not met, the meal would be sandwiches. One parent was in charge of keeping everyone aware of their tasks and keeping a chart of their completion. During the week, the parent updated the whole family on the progress toward the 80% criterion. When Friday evening arrived, the family celebrated with pizza or accepted the consequences of not meeting the goal.

Group Treatment

The power of a single therapist is multiplied as members in group therapy participate and support each other to make changes. Individual members can model for others a willingness to accept influence from the therapist (and the therapeutic modality) and one another. They can demonstrate courage to admit past problems and take on new behaviors. Group members can also coach each other on more effective ways to think and process information more logically. They may be more effective than the group worker in questioning the beliefs and assumptions of other group members (Bieling et al., 2009; Drossel, 2008).

Group treatment models have been successful in teaching the mindfulness and acceptance and commitment approaches mentioned earlier in this chapter. The group members typically coached each other in their understanding of focusing on the present moment and evaluating past beliefs, emotions, and so forth (Kocovski et al., 2013).

Women's groups have a good history in creating and maintaining change. Women are socialized to emphasize the importance of relationships, which can translate into a willingness to accept change and experience group support. For example, one successful group work approach is for mothers who are recently divorced. The group focuses on the importance of having a structured evening routine and bedtime so that children feel a strong sense of security, and mothers have some time for themselves. The structure provides some predictability of reinforcers, such as mother's attention to each of the children, evening baths, and so forth. Schedules are developed to give the mothers some private, personal time at the end of the evening. The schedule consists of an outline of tasks with specific times so that, in succession, all the children complete their homework, take baths, and get in bed by specified times. Each child is rewarded with 5 minutes of uninterrupted time with the mother at the child's bedside. The mothers are rewarded for keeping the schedule because, when the children are in bed, they have a period of time for themselves to straighten up the house and do some type of self-care such as soak in the tub, read a book, or watch a favorite television show. The women in the group are reassured that keeping the schedule every evening might not always be possible, but regardless of what happens on any given night, they should be proud of their efforts, and they can restart the schedule for the next evening. The group setting allows the mothers to problem-solve different ways to create and carry out the schedule. As a result, mothers feel empowered and supported to be successful.

SUMMARY

The interventions reviewed represent a sampling of cognitive behavioral interventions; however, the list is not exhaustive. A wide variety of methods fit under the cognitive behavioral rubric because of their assumptions about cognitive and behavioral learning and change. The list of references at the end of this chapter contains a sampling of references to effective cognitive behavioral interventions. Readers are encouraged to scan the references and decide which ones will help them enhance their professional development.

Evaluation and Termination

Evaluation is an ongoing process in cognitive behavioral therapy. Progress toward the specific overt or covert behavioral goals, established early in treatment, is reviewed continuously. Through behavioral observation, self-anchored rating scales, RAIs, or journals, clients are largely responsible for providing the evaluative data to assess progress toward their goals. Over time, clinicians' roles may change from teachers to coaches and supporters. The clinicians may also assess progress using single-subject or single-case methods to show clients how their behaviors have changed over time. As clients become increasingly self-reliant over the course of therapy, termination is gradual. Termination becomes a time to celebrate the acquisition of new skills and to plan for ways to maintain changes following treatment. Clients are encouraged to continue to work on skills and reward themselves in meaningful ways, but they are reassured that they may return for further help if the need arises.

CASE STUDY

The following is an example of a cognitive behavioral intervention to effectively treat depression. The reader will notice different emphases on cognitive or behavioral issues in the various phases of the treatment. The combination is effective and can be tailored to the particular characteristics of various clients (Craighead et al., 1994; Dobson & Dobson, 2017; Hofmann & Asmundson, 2017; Vernon & Doyle, 2018). Mary is a young adult female who recently graduated from college. During portions of her senior year, she experienced periods of depression. She was tired and lacked interest in some of her favorite activities. Her friends could seldom get her to go out, and when she did, she had to push herself to be friendly. Some of their old jokes seemed boring or even odd. When she was at home, she preferred to stay in her room and sleep. With her roommate, she preferred to watch TV and not interact.

Step 1: Make connection between thoughts and feelings. The clinician began by helping Mary make the connection between her thoughts and her mood. He asked Mary to remember a time when one of her friends said or did something funny. During the discussion, the social worker pointed out that the memory seemed to affect her mood and made her feel happy. Similarly, she asked her to think about something that made her feel sad. She described how someone made a comment that was mean to her and how it made her feel bad about herself. Together, they concluded that critical statements or jokes at her expense really bothered her. The clinician emphasized that her thoughts about the happy memory made her appear and feel happy, and the memory of the critical remarks made her sad. The worker proposed the rationale that her thoughts determine her mood.

Step 2: Record the thoughts and the emotions. In the next step, the social worker asked Mary to self-monitor her behavior by keeping a journal of her thoughts and ideas that make her feel bad and the thoughts that make her feel good. They decided that she would place the yellow tablet on her pillow so that every night before she went to sleep, Mary would write her thoughts and emotions in her journal.

Step 3: Behavioral activation. In the next step, the worker asked Mary to list what she liked to do for fun and relaxation. The list included reading, playing with her cat, taking long baths, and going for walks. Mary stated that she had not taken the time to read or soak in the bathtub for a long time. The worker and Mary spent the next 15 minutes planning how she could find 30 minutes a day to read. Additionally, taking care of herself meant that in the next 7 days, she would take two long, hot baths.

Step 4: Establish her negative and irrational thoughts about herself. At their next meeting, Mary forgot to bring the journal, but she talked about how the experience of keeping the journal helped her become more aware of the many negative or critical thoughts about herself. Mary was surprised at how this affected her. They began to list the comments and evaluate the extent to which they were true or false. Sometimes they were able to surmise that the comments were made by people who were not very happy themselves, or perhaps the person was simply a mean person and most likely critical of everyone.

Mary mentioned how she thought that she did not look very good. The clinician used humor, directed at himself, to illustrate how parts of his own body did not match up to society's advertised image of a perfect "10." He also laughed and said that while parts of his own body were not perfect, other parts were fantastic. The humor and phrase "parts of me are fantastic" became an inside joke between them and a reassuring self-statement for Mary.

Step 5: Evaluate the credibility of her thoughts. At the next meeting, Mary brought her journal, and she and the worker used three questions to evaluate the thoughts recorded in her journal: (a) "What evidence do you have for that belief?" (b) "Is there an alternative explanation?" (c) "What are the real implications of that belief?" Together, they reframed and refocused most of Mary's worries and talked about some of Mary's assumptions about life and relationships. Some myths in Mary's thinking were exposed, and some lack of fairness in society was put in proper perspective (reframed) or even made fun of. In the end, they constructed a plan for Mary to read, take baths, and pay attention to her self-care. They devised and rehearsed a strategy where she would evaluate other people's comments, decide if they had anything of value for her, and consider attributing their comments to their own personality or biases.

Two final notes are necessary. First, the combination of therapy and medication is often necessary for clients with depression. In this particular case, the clinician believed that antidepressants were not needed to raise her mood to facilitate counseling; however, a thorough medical/psychiatric examination should always be considered. When medications are appropriate, they increase clients' ability to make use of therapeutic interventions like the one just noted.

Second, the severity of depression should determine the emphasis placed on cognitive or behavioral approaches to treatment. When clients' depression is severe, behavioral treatment methods, such as behavioral activation, are required to raise the clients' mood sufficiently before they can begin to address the cognitive aspect of treatment.

COMPATIBILITY WITH THE GENERALIST-ECLECTIC FRAMEWORK

Cognitive behavioral therapy and the generalist-eclectic framework are very compatible. Both emphasize the role of the social environment in shaping and maintaining individuals' behavior. In both approaches, clients are seen as collaborators throughout the helping process and everyone focuses on clients' strengths, concerns, and empowerment. Also, both approaches are open to incorporating a wide range of interventions from other treatment models. Some types of cognitive behavioral therapy might be more structured and prescriptive than the generalist-eclectic approach, and the artistic, intuitive aspects of practice are less emphasized. Both models have an important history in incorporating mindfulness and acceptance and commitment.

CRITIQUE OF COGNITIVE BEHAVIORAL THERAPY

Strengths

Clients are attracted to cognitive behavioral methods because of the commonsense perspective that both overt and covert behaviors are learned and can be unlearned. Typically, when clients come for treatment, they describe their problems from victim perspectives. They were victims of abusive or thoughtless parents or partners. Perhaps they are plagued by depression, fears, fate, "nerves," bad bosses, unfair practices of others, and so forth. Through the assessment process and the focus on behaviors and thoughts, clients can begin to see that all of these issues are part of their learning histories and that some of their successes and failures are attributable to previously learned behaviors and thoughts. They become aware of how past experiences have led not only to poor coping skills, helplessness, or hopelessness but also to survival and coping skills. Clients understand and appreciate the focus on learning new, more productive behaviors and ways of thinking. The cognitive behavioral model works with all ages and can be tailored to the developmental level of the client. For example, children respond best to reinforcement, non-physical punishment, and extinction, whereas adolescents and adults often learn best through instruction, modeling, and cognitive interventions.

Mindfulness helps client separate tasks from their thoughts and emotions. The refocus on the present reality of clients is a significant starting point for a commitment to the present and discarding unproductive indiscretions and embracing new perspectives of themselves.

A major strength of cognitive behavioral treatment is that a wide variety of interventions have been validated empirically for a range of client problems. The efficacy of cognitive behavioral treatments has been established in controlled research projects, and its effectiveness has been documented in numerous clinical studies (Chambless & Hollon, 1998; Chambless & Ollendick, 2001; Hollon & Beck, 2013; Jacobson & Hollon, 1996; Kalodner, 2011; Littlenfeld et al., 2003; Norcross et al., 2006).

Limitations

As mentioned earlier, the cognitive component of cognitive behavioral treatment is not appropriate for some severe problems (e.g., severe depression, psychosis, and dementia). Clients with severe problems frequently do respond, however, to behavioral interventions such as behavioral activation. Still, even though behavior is learned, some longstanding, habituated behaviors resist change. Some behaviors are considered ingrained in the personality and behavioral repertoires of individuals and are resistant to change. Similarly, some anxiety-driven behaviors are difficult to extinguish because of the perceived level of threat to the individual.

CONCLUSION

Cognitive and behavioral theories and interventions have merged, and the result is a robust theoretical perspective of human behavior and a set of powerful, empirically validated interventions that address a variety of clients' problems. In this theoretical perspective, thoughts, cognitions, feelings, moods, and actions are conceptualized as covert and overt behaviors that are learned through the processes of classical and operant conditioning or vicariously learned through modeling. When social workers hear their clients talk about vague feelings and moods, they can direct their inquiry to the beliefs that trigger and maintain them. When clients display problematic behavior, they can look for the environmental contingencies (or clients' covert behaviors) that reinforce and maintain behavior in the present.

Some cognitive behavioral interventions focus on reinforcing positive behavior or reducing negative behavior with some version of punishment, extinction, or the reinforcement of alternative, competing behavior. Other interventions focus on helping clients to evaluate the validity of their personal beliefs and to change their beliefs and internal dialogue through learned cognitive skills. Clients understand the focus on behavior and change. Treatment and the rationale make sense to them, and therefore they are more willing to cooperate. They understand how thoughts (covert behaviors) influence behavior and how overt behaviors are maintained through actual (or anticipated) reinforcement.

The increased use of mindfulness and acceptance and commitment have enabled clients to step back from old regrets or memories and choose to live their current lives in different ways. This perspective merely establishes that CBT is an involving way to view human behavior and create treatment methods that enable everyone to grow beyond our previous assumptions about our thoughts, feelings, and behavior. The continuing development and empirical validation of cognitive behavioral interventions are exciting. The future challenge lies in the necessity that trained professionals adapt cognitive behavioral interventions to fit the particular characteristics of their clients. The science embedded in the theory and interventions requires the art of caring and talented clinicians.

SUMMARY POINTS

In summary, this chapter has:

- described the five behavioral principles that account for learning or loss of behavior,
- explored the role that cognitions have in the acquisition and maintenance of behavior and emotions, and
- described the behavioral principles, cognitive restructuring, and the use of mindfulness to accept and commit to change troublesome thoughts and behaviors.

KEY REFERENCES

Only key references appear in the print edition. The full reference list appears in the digital product found on http://connect.springerpub.com/content/book/978-0-8261-6556-5/part/sec03/part/sec032/chapter/ch08

Alexander, J. F., & Parsons, B. V. (1982). *Functional family therapy*. Brooks/Cole.

Bandura, A. (1969). *Principles of behavior modification*. Holt, Rinehart & Winston.

Bandura, A. (1977). *Social learning theory*. General Learning Press.

Bandura, A. (1978). Reflections on self-efficacy. *Advances in Behavior Research and Therapy, 1*, 237–269.

Bandura, A. (1986). *Social foundations of thought and action: A social cognitive theory*. Prentice-Hall.

Bandura A. (2005). The evolution of social cognitive theory. In K. G. Smith & M. A. Hitt (Eds.) *Great Minds in Management* (pp. 9–35). Oxford University Press.

Bandura, A. (2011). Social cognitive theory. In P.A.M. van Lange, A.W. Kruglanski, & E.T. Higgins (Eds.). *Handbook of social psychological theories* (pp. 349–373). Sage.

Bandura, A. (2016). The power of observational learning through social modeling. In R. Sternberg, S. T. Fiske, & D. J. Foss (Eds.), *Scientists making a difference* (pp. 235–239). Cambridge University Press.

Bandura, A. (2018). Toward a psychology of human agency. Pathways and reflections. *Perspectives on Psychology Science, 13*, 130–136.

The Crisis Intervention Model

Karen S. Knox and Albert R. Roberts

LEARNING OBJECTIVES

After reading this chapter, the reader will be able to

- gain knowledge about both the historical development of crisis intervention theories and models, and how recent research has contributed to evidence-based practice in crisis intervention;
- understand the different levels and stages of crisis and how these may impact clients;
- identify appropriate direct practice knowledge and skills for effective crisis assessment and treatment planning;
- apply the Assessment, Crisis Intervention, and Trauma Treatment (ACT) Model and Seven-Stage Crisis Intervention Model in direct practice with clients;
- integrate crisis intervention skills within a generalist-eclectic framework when working with individuals, families, and groups; and
- critically analyze the strengths and limitations of crisis intervention.

OVERVIEW OF CRISIS INTERVENTION

Case Examples of Crisis Incidents and Reactions

CASE STUDY 9.1: SEXUAL ASSAULT

Alice was walking to her car after getting off work when she was attacked from behind. She was abducted and driven to an isolated area where her assailant raped her repeatedly over several hours before leaving her there and driving away in her car. During the attacks, the rapist held his knife against her throat and threatened to kill her if she reported him to the police. She was able to get help from a passerby after he left, and was transported to the hospital where she received medical treatment and a sexual assault examination, and the crimes were reported to law enforcement. Alice feared for her life that night and is still scared that her attacker may find her and hurt her again, since he got her home address from her driver's license when he stole her purse. The victim services crisis counselor with the police department provided crisis intervention services on the scene, while Alice was at the hospital, and during the initial criminal investigation. A week after the rape, Alice called and disclosed that she was unable to concentrate at work and is afraid of being at home alone. She was also having intrusive thoughts about the rape and terrifying nightmares. The victim services crisis counselor explained to Alice that these are typical reactions for sexual assault survivors, discussed safety plan options for her to initiate so that she could decrease her anxiety and fears at home and work, and encouraged Alice to follow up with the referral to the rape crisis center for individual and group counseling services.

CASE STUDY 9.2: SUDDEN DEATH

Jeff went to work as usual on the military base where he is a lab technician at the hospital. Later that afternoon, a gunman came onto the floor where Jeff's lab is and opened fire, killing a doctor and injuring several of his coworkers. Jeff hid in a closet while the gunman went from room to room shooting other victims. He could hear their screams and was frozen—unable to respond even though he knew others were trying to help the wounded. Even after the military police captured and arrested the gunman, he could not leave his hiding place until one of the rescuers found him. Jeff is traumatized by the fear he experienced and sounds he heard during the attack. He is feeling relief at not being hurt, but also feels guilty for not helping his friends and not trying to stop the gunman, and is ashamed that he hid while others were being shot. Jeff has not returned to work yet, and has been anxious and irritable about what to say to his friends and how his coworkers will treat him. The survivors of the critical shooting incident have been referred to the social worker at the employee assistance program (EAP). Since there are numerous employees who are in need of crisis counseling, the social worker will need to assess and plan interventions at both the individual and group levels of treatment.

CASE STUDY 9.3: NATURAL DISASTER

Ted and his family were asleep when the tornado warnings sounded and had just gotten into their bathroom for shelter when their house seemed to explode. After the tornado hit their neighborhood, Ted and his family emerged unhurt from what remained of their home to discover most of their neighborhood was gone. When their neighbors started to gather to assess the damage and try to find other survivors, Ted suffered a heart attack and his wife had to perform cardiopulmonary resuscitation on him. Emergency responders transported Ted to the nearest medical facility where he is still hospitalized. His wife and children are at the hospital waiting to hear from other family members in the area; they have no belongings, no place to stay, or transportation. Ted's wife, Amy, seems to be in shock, and the children are afraid that the tornado will come back again. The hospital social worker first attempts to find them some clean clothes and food while they are waiting to find out more from the physician about Ted's condition and medical needs. Other crisis intervention and triage services are also being set up by the community crisis management team first responders and disaster relief organizations at the hospital and disaster sites to assist survivors with basic needs services.

These case examples highlight some of the different types of crises and reactions of survivors in the aftermath of trauma. Some crisis situations are personal or family incidents, while others can be triggered by a sudden, community-wide traumatic event, such as a natural disaster, terrorist attack, or industrial accident. Survivors, family members, significant others, and witnesses of traumatic incidents usually experience a series of physiological and psychological reactions. Some common symptoms and reactions include intense fears, heightened anxiety, hypervigilance, startle reactions, intrusive thoughts, flashbacks, despair, hopelessness, irritability, terror, sleep disturbances, shock, guilt, numbness, extreme distrust of others, and shattered assumptions that they and the community where they reside are not safe. These symptoms are evidenced in the diagnosis of acute stress, and one of the goals of crisis counseling is to provide immediate interventions to help prevent or minimize these reactions from developing further into posttraumatic stress disorder (PTSD).

Understanding of Human Problems

The crisis intervention model holds that individuals will experience stressful events and crises as a natural part of life development. Using systems theory, stress is evoked when disequilibrium and anxiety occur as a result of the crisis or traumatic event, and when the individual's coping skills and resources do not adequately resolve the immediate crisis reactions and consequences. This perspective does not view the individual in crisis as pathological or mentally ill, since all human beings experience and deal with challenges presented during crises and trauma as a normal part of the human condition.

Crisis theory supports the perspective that all human beings have strengths and abilities to deal effectively with problems in living, and that crises are opportunities for individuals to utilize and build on those strengths to develop appropriate coping abilities that address the consequences of the crisis. Crisis theory espouses that the individual's motivation for change is stronger during or immediately after a crisis due to the anxiety and disequilibrium, and the individual is most receptive to helping professionals and resources to ameliorate the stressful conditions as soon as possible after the crisis. Therefore, while the social worker may need to be more directive during crisis intervention than in other treatment models, the individual is encouraged to be active and present oriented in order to gain some measure of control and stability when dealing with a crisis. Using a strengths-based approach gives survivors hope and motivation that they can meet and deal with the challenges they face as a consequence of the crisis.

Conception of Therapeutic Intervention

Persons experiencing traumatic events usually benefit from rapid assessment and crisis intervention. Crisis counseling shares many principles and strategies with brief, time-limited, task-centered, and solution-focused practice models. Crisis intervention is one of the action-oriented models that is present focused, with the target(s) for intervention being specific to the hazardous event, situation, or problem that precipitated the state of crisis. Therefore, this model focuses on problems in the here and now, and addresses past history and psychopathology only as they are relevant to any current conditions of the crisis. Crisis theory postulates that intervention is time limited to a period of 4 to 6 weeks with the goal of mobilizing needed support, resources, and the adaptive coping skills of the client to resolve or minimize the disequilibrium experienced by the precipitating event. Once the client has returned to a pre-crisis level of functioning and homeostasis, any further supportive or supplemental services are usually referred out to appropriate community agencies and service providers.

In Jeff's case example, he would receive crisis intervention and counseling services from professionals at different agencies and programs over a period of time. Crisis counselors employed in law enforcement or at the military hospital would work with him and the survivors and witnesses of the shooting incident on the scene and through the initial reporting and criminal and military investigations. Hospital emergency department social workers would provide crisis stabilization during the medical examination and treatment, and make referrals for continued hospitalization needs or discharge planning. The counselor at the EAP program would typically provide time-limited individual and group treatment, and then provide referrals for any long-term counseling services if needed. If Jeff has to testify or is involved in any court proceedings against the offender, victim-witness advocates would provide both crisis and supportive counseling services, as it is common that PTSD symptoms and traumatic memories can be triggered during this time. They would also explain the legal proceedings and protocols for survivors and witnesses, assist in trial preparation and testimony, and inform clients about other benefits such as victims compensation funds that provide financial aid for medical and counseling expenses related to the criminal offense.

While some clients stabilize and return to a level of adequate functioning within the 4- to 6-week time frame, some survivors of trauma will have longer term treatment needs. Time frames for crisis intervention vary depending on several factors, including the agency's mission and services, the client's needs and resources, and the type of crisis or trauma. Crisis intervention can be as brief as one client contact, which is typical with 24-hour suicide prevention or crisis hotlines. Some crisis situations may require several contacts over a few days of brief treatment, whereas others may provide ongoing and follow-up services for up to 10 to 12 weeks. Additional crisis intervention services may be needed in the future. An example of a one-contact case is Ted and his family, as crisis intervention services would be immediately provided to his wife and children at the hospital by the emergency department social worker for his medical emergency. However, the family is also in need of continuing medical services and basic needs services due to the tornado, and disaster relief organizations and personnel at the local and federal levels would be available for any crisis interventions and ongoing needs. This case example illustrates both the micro- and macrolevels of crisis preparedness and interagency cooperation that are necessary with large-scale crisis situations.

The immediacy and action orientation of crisis intervention require a high level of activity and skills on the part of the social worker. They also require a mutual contracting process between the client and the social worker, but the time frame for assessment and contracting must be brief by necessity. People experiencing trauma and crisis need immediate relief and assistance, and the helping process must be adapted to meet those needs as efficiently and effectively as possible. Therefore, some of the tools and techniques used in the assessment and contracting phases, such as intake forms, social history gathering, engagement of the client, and intervention planning, must be used in ways or formats that facilitate a rapid response. The assessment, contracting, and intervention stages may need to be completed and implemented on the very first client contact. Clients in an active state of crisis are more amenable to the helping process, since their usual coping strategies and resources are inadequate to deal with the crisis, and this can facilitate completion of these tasks in a brief time frame.

In the case example of Alice, the sexual assault investigation and medical needs must be assessed and intervention initiated immediately. Crisis intervention counseling would be implemented by the police social worker simultaneously during the first contact with Alice. The rape examination and police investigation could take several hours, depending on the response time by law enforcement and medical professionals. The police crisis team and hospital social worker would provide crisis intervention services until the client has stabilized and received follow-up contacts by another collateral provider of crisis services, such as a rape crisis center counselor or volunteer. Examples of interventions provided by the police crisis team and hospital social worker would include assisting with the criminal investigation, explaining medical procedures and treatments for the sexual assault, and notification of family or significant others who can provide support and resources. Other services include immediate crisis counseling and assisting with basic needs, such as providing a change of clothes, since what the survivor was wearing will be taken into evidence. Safety issues would be addressed since sexual assault victims may not feel safe at home, if the rape occurred there, or fear that the offender could return or find the person there. Safety planning, support systems, transportation after discharge, and referrals for follow-up contacts to address other immediate concerns or needs would also be provided on the first contact with Alice.

During a crisis, social workers must be knowledgeable about the appropriate strategies, resources, and other collateral services to initiate timely interventions and meet the goals of treatment. Specialized knowledge about specific types of crises, traumatic incidents, or client populations is necessary for effective intervention planning. For example, crisis intervention with victims of family violence requires education and training on the dynamics and cycle of battering and abuse, familiarity with the community agencies providing services to this client population, and knowledge about any legal options available to victims. Similarly, social workers dealing with bereavement and loss in hospice settings need to be knowledgeable about the grief process, medical terminology, specific health problems or conditions, and support services for family survivors. Due to the diversity of crisis situations and events, the basic models and skills of crisis intervention must be supplemented by continued professional education and experience with specialized client populations or types of trauma encountered in practice.

Another characteristic of crisis intervention models is the use of tasks as a primary change effort. Concrete, basic needs services such as emergency safety, medical needs, food, clothing, and shelter are the first priority in crisis intervention. Mobilizing needed resources may require more direct activity by the social worker in advocating, networking, and brokering for clients who may not have the knowledge, skills, or capacity to follow through with referrals and collateral contacts during the time of active crisis.

Of course, the emotional and psychological traumas experienced by the client and significant others are important considerations for crisis intervention. Ventilation of feelings and a complex range of emotional reactions to crises are typical; however, initially the crisis worker should focus on techniques to calm the trauma survivor and reduce any physiological and emotional responses to the crisis since research on memory consolidation and physiological reactions has found that this reduces the development of posttraumatic stress symptoms (Dyregrov & Regel, 2012; James et al., 2016; Krans et al., 2013). Skills of reflective communication, active listening, and establishing rapport are essential to this process, as are interventions that target and reduce physiological reactions, such as deep breathing, presenting a calm demeanor, using a low tone of voice, slowing down communication flow, and being mindful of body space.

HISTORICAL DEVELOPMENT

Although crisis intervention has developed into a cohesive treatment model only in the past 50 years, human beings have been dealing with crises since antiquity. In ancient Greece, the word *crisis* came from two root words—one meaning "decision" and the other meaning "turning point." Similarly, the two symbols in the Chinese language for *crisis* represent danger and opportunity. These definitions imply that crisis can be both a time for growth and impetus for change, as well as an obstacle and risk for harm and unhealthy reactions (Roberts, 2000).

Historically, family and religious systems helped people in crisis. The roots of crisis intervention developed in the 1940s and 1950s from several sources, including physicians, psychologists, psychiatrists, sociologists, social workers, and the military. Multidisciplinary teams involving these disciplines in various settings, such as public health agencies, hospitals, family counseling centers, and disaster response programs, did much of the work.

One of the pioneers in crisis intervention was Dr. Eric Lindemann, who was associated with the Harvard School of Public Health and Massachusetts General Hospital. His pioneering study on loss and bereavement with 101 survivors and family members of the victims of the Coconut Grove nightclub fire in Boston was one of the first efforts to develop a more systematic way of helping people in crisis (Lindemann, 1944). From his research, theories of the grief process and typical reactions to crisis were developed. He also concluded that the duration and severity of grief reactions appeared to be dependent on the success with which the bereaved person mourns and grieves the loss and changes, and readjusts to life without the deceased loved one (Roberts, 2005b; Yeager & Roberts, 2015a).

Other developments in psychiatry in the 1940s and 1950s contributed to the knowledge and research base of crisis intervention. From ego psychology, Erikson's (1950) stages of human development included key psychosocial crises that had to be resolved over the course of life. He postulated that crisis and major life transitions are normal in human and social development, and can help individuals develop coping skills to successfully resolve both maturational and situational crises.

Suicide prevention services were another type of community-based mental health program that developed to respond to those in crisis. Much of the pioneering work was done at the Los Angeles Suicide Prevention Center in the late 1950s and 1960s (Dublin, 1963; Farberow & Schneidman, 1961; Schneidman et al., 1970). As the suicide prevention movement developed, the Center for Studies of Suicide Prevention (now defunct) was established in 1966, and by 1972, almost 200 such programs had been established across the country (Roberts, 2005b).

The Victim Witness Assistance Act of 1982 and the Victims of Crime Act of 1984 established federal funding and state block grants for crisis intervention programs and victim advocacy services in the criminal justice system. These comprehensive programs are located at police departments, prosecutors' offices, and nonprofit agencies. Victim advocates focus on helping crime victims and family members with court-related advocacy, medical and mental health issues, and financial assistance (Roberts, 1990). States and local communities have been able to develop family violence, sexual assault, and victim services programs as a result of this federal assistance. As a result, thousands of statewide, county, and city victim service and domestic violence programs expanded to help individuals resolve particular crime-related problems and crises (Roberts, 1990, 1997).

The nature of crisis intervention changed dramatically after the Oklahoma City Federal Building bombing on April 19, 1995, and the terrorist attacks on the World Trade Center and the Pentagon on September 11, 2001. We live in an era in which sudden, unpredictable crises and traumatic events are brought into our homes by the media (Roberts, 2005b). Millions of people were affected, either directly or indirectly, by the flooding, widespread destruction of property, and evacuation of thousands of people from hurricanes Katrina and Rita in 2005, which were a wake-up call for all communities and crisis professionals to expand and coordinate interagency crisis response teams, programs, and resources.

RESEARCH AND EVALUATION

Research studies evaluating the effectiveness of crisis responses to these disasters and terrorist attacks served as guideposts for more effective macro- and microlevel crisis intervention planning (Castellano, 2003; Dass-Brailsford & Hage Thomley, 2015; Dziegielewski & Sumner, 2002; Henry, 2015; Kaul & Welzant, 2005; Underwood & Kalafat, 2002). The suddenness and severity of these national disasters and terrorist attacks that affected large numbers of people prove that it is imperative that all emergency services personnel and crisis workers be trained to respond immediately at both levels of practice.

The effectiveness of crisis intervention programs in various community-based social service, law enforcement, and mental health agencies has been another focus of research and program evaluation (Dziegielewski & Jacinto, 2015; Roberts & Everly, 2006; Vincent et al., 2015). Over the years, a proliferation of journal articles and books dealing specifically with crisis intervention models, skills, and intervention strategies for particular client groups, including youth-focused and school-based programs (Jimerson et al., 2005; Knox & Roberts, 2005, 2015; Kubiak et al., 2019), working with sexual assault and incest survivors (Edmond et al., 2004; Knox & Roberts, 2015; Schrag & Edmond, 2018), substance abuse (Substance Abuse and Mental Health Services Administration [SAMHSA], 2018; Yeager, 2002), family violence (Knox & Garcia Biggs, 2007; Paul, 2019), and crisis intervention in health and mental health settings (Couvillon et al., 2019; Ginnis et al., 2015; Kim & Kim, 2017; Registered Nurses' Association of Ontario, 2017; Wheeler et al., 2015; Yeager & Roberts, 2015a).

Research on best practices in crisis intervention provides evidence that school-based crisis intervention programs are effective in reducing symptoms of PTSD (Rolfsnes & Idsoe, 2011). Studies also report the effectiveness of crisis intervention programs for psychiatric emergencies with suicidal adolescents and other mental health crises in hospital emergency departments and for reduced rehospitalizations for persons with dementia (Dion et al., 2010; Johnson et al., 2012; Wharff et al., 2012). There is a need for more LGBTQA-specific crisis services considering that these youth are more than twice as likely to attempt suicide than their peers (Goldbach et al., 2019). Best practices for intervention with sexual harassment and assault and PTSD in military social work are also a recent focus due to the growing numbers and needs for current military members and other combat veterans from previous wars (Bell & Reardon, 2011; Yarvis, 2011).

The recent development of models for community-based crisis intervention teams (CITs) that are based on the Memphis Model aims to deal more effectively with mental health crises that involve law enforcement (Kasick & Bowling, 2015; Kubiak et al., 2017; Pelfrey & Young, 2019; Watson et al., 2017). The CIT model is multidisciplinary and includes members from law enforcement, social work, mental health, and emergency medical services to provide more comprehensive and effective crisis intervention services. The emphasis on mental health education and training for law enforcement officers, along with coordination of community resources, has shown effectiveness in changing officers' perceptions and interactions with persons experiencing mental health crises, and increasing utilization of mental health and social services resources (Kubiak et al., 2017; Pelfrey & Young, 2019).

More recent research focuses on neurobiological functions that are important treatment considerations during crisis intervention, especially to minimize or prevent the development of PTSD symptoms. Research indicates that during the 6-hour time frame post-crisis incident, interventions that disrupt the memory consolidation process can reduce flashbacks and intrusive memories of the event (James et al., 2016; Sundermann et al., 2013; Tabrizi & Jansson, 2016). Therefore, it is more beneficial to work on basic needs and use a solutions-focused approach at the beginning of crisis intervention to minimize memory consolidation, instead of focusing on the details or memories of the crisis incident that would promote memory acquisition, consolidation, and storage.

A critical process in memory consolidation is high activation of physiological, emotional, and psychological responses (Dyregrov & Regel, 2012). Crisis interventions that reduce arousal, anxiety, and fear responses, including deep breathing, low arousal communication, and other calming or stabilizing strategies, such as normalization and psychoeducation, are most useful immediately after the crisis event. Crisis survivors who are injured and need medical treatment and pain control benefit from pharmacological strategies, since using pain medication or cortisol has been found effective in reducing trauma memories and the development of PTSD symptoms (Bryant et al., 2009; Dyregrov & Regel, 2012; Holbrook et al., 2010; Yehuda & Golier, 2009). Another area of research indicates that sleep promotes the memory consolidation process, thus it is also recommended that trauma survivors not sleep during the 6-hour time frame post-crisis (Dyregrov & Regel, 2012; Wagner et al., 2006).

THEORETICAL BASE AND CENTRAL CONSTRUCTS

The major tenets of crisis intervention derived originally from psychodynamic theory, particularly ego psychology, and ecological systems theory. Central ideas borrowed from ego psychology include life developmental stages, psychosocial crises, coping skills, and defense mechanisms. From the ecological systems theory, concepts such as homeostasis, disequilibrium, and interdependence are basic principles of crisis intervention.

Cognitive behavioral models share many characteristics with the basic assumptions and techniques of crisis intervention. These are action-oriented models, with a present focus and time-limited treatment. The cognitive behavioral principle that an individual's perceptions and cognitions affect their beliefs, feelings, and behaviors in an interactive way is essential to crisis theory. The critical incident or precipitating event has to be perceived as a crisis by the client. Individuals involved in the same crisis situation may have very different perceptions, feelings, reactions, and coping skills (Datillo & Freeman, 2010; Roberts, 2005b; Yeager & Roberts, 2015a). Cognitive behavioral models that are currently being used and have been found to be effective with survivors of trauma and those with PTSD are trauma-focused cognitive behavioral treatment (CBT; Blankenship, 2017; Rubin et al., 2017), cognitive processing (Dickstein et al., 2013; Regehr et al., 2013; Suris et al., 2013), and prolonged exposure (Goodson et al., 2013; Regehr et al., 2013).

Another cognitive behavioral model that has been used in crisis intervention is eye movement desensitization and reprocessing (EMDR), which was developed in the mid-1990s by Shapiro (2017). This model is also time limited, and espouses that if trauma can produce immediate symptoms, then healing can also be accomplished in the same time frame by using this model's techniques. This approach has been widely researched and used effectively with clients who suffer from PTSD such as military combat veterans (Yarvis, 2011), natural disasters (Konut et al., 2006), and terrorism (Silver et al., 2005); sexual assault survivors (Edmond et al., 2004; Regehr et al., 2013); and other trauma victims, including children and adolescents (Farkas et al., 2010; Greyber et al., 2012; Lewey et al., 2018; Soloman et al., 2009).

The solution-focused model has been used in crisis intervention with diverse client populations and is particularly suited to managed-care policies that have institutionalized time-limited treatment in most public sector agencies, such as mental health clinics, medical or hospital settings, EAPs, and health maintenance organizations (Greene & Lee, 2015; Kondrat & Teater, 2012). Solution-focused therapy has also been recommended for survivors of sexual assault and their partners (Tambling, 2012), those suffering from substance abuse and addictions (Yeager & Gregoire, 2015), and adolescents in crisis (Hopson & Kim, 2004).

Crisis intervention theories and models have evolved to incorporate a wide variety of techniques and skills from many different theoretical approaches. This is consistent with a generalist-eclectic approach and is critical when working with diverse client populations in various crisis situations and settings. However, the basic principles and assumptions of crisis theory provide a foundation knowledge base from which more specialized strategies and techniques can be learned and developed. Two other important concepts in crisis intervention—levels of crises and stages in crisis—are discussed next.

Levels of Crises

A classification paradigm developed by Burgess and Roberts (2005; Yeager et al., 2015) for assessing emotional stress and acute crisis episodes identifies seven main levels of crises along a stress–crisis continuum. While each crisis and each individual's subjective experience of a crisis are unique, this stress–crisis continuum can be used in assessment and intervention planning to determine the level of care and most effective treatment modalities. It is important to note that the type of crisis services and the need for more intensive intervention may be necessary as the level of crisis increases along the continuum.

LEVEL 1: SOMATIC DISTRESS
This level of crisis results from biomedical causes and less severe psychiatric symptoms that cause stress and disequilibrium in the individual's life. Other situational problems, such as health/medical conditions, relationship conflicts, work-related stressors, and chemical dependency issues would be included.

LEVEL 2: TRANSITIONAL STRESS CRISIS
This involves stressful events that are an expected part of life span development. These crises are normal life tasks or activities that can be very stressful, such as premature birth, divorce, and relocation. The individual may have little or no control over the situation and is unable to cope effectively.

LEVEL 3: TRAUMATIC STRESS CRISIS
These situations are unexpected and outside the individual's locus of control. These crises can be life-threatening and overwhelming. They include combat, suicide, sexual assault, and other types of crime victimization.

LEVEL 4: FAMILY CRISIS
This relates to developmental tasks and issues associated with interpersonal and family relationships that are unresolved and harmful psychologically, emotionally, and physically to those involved. Examples of this level of crisis are child abuse, family violence, and homelessness.

LEVEL 5: SERIOUS MENTAL ILLNESS

This stems from a preexisting psychopathology, such as schizophrenia, dementia, or major depression, that can cause severe difficulties in adaptation for both the affected individual and the family support system.

LEVEL 6: PSYCHIATRIC EMERGENCIES

These are situations in which general functioning has been severely impaired, such as the acute onset of a major mental illness, a drug overdose, or suicidal attempts. The individual has a loss of personal control, and there is a threat or actual harm to self and/or others.

LEVEL 7: CATASTROPHIC CRISIS

This level involves two or more level 1 to 3 traumatic crises in combination with level 4, 5, or 6 stressors. The nature, duration, and intensity of these stressful crisis situations and events and personal losses can be extremely difficult to accept and resolve. An example of this level of crisis is losing all family members in a suicide/murder or disaster.

Stages of Crisis

The stages of crisis are similar to those of the grief process. These stages do not always follow a linear process—individuals can skip stages, get stuck in a stage, or move back and forth through successive stages. Although there are many theoretical frameworks for crisis intervention, most of them include the following four stages:

STAGE 1: OUTCRY

This stage includes the initial reactions after the crisis event(s), which are reflexive, emotional, and behavioral in nature. These reactions can vary greatly and can include panic, fainting, screaming, shock, anger, defensiveness, moaning, flat affect, crying, hysteria, and hyperventilation, depending on the situation and the individual.

STAGE 2: DENIAL OR INTRUSIVENESS

Outcry can lead to denial, which is the blocking of the impacts of the crisis through emotional numbing, dissociation, cognitive distortion, or minimizing. Outcry can also lead to intrusiveness, which includes the involuntary flooding of thoughts and feelings about the crisis event or trauma, such as flashbacks, nightmares, automatic thoughts, and preoccupation with what has happened.

STAGE 3: WORKING THROUGH

This stage is the recovery or healing process in which the thoughts, feelings, and images of the crisis are expressed, acknowledged, explored, and reprocessed through adaptive, healthy coping skills and strategies. Otherwise, the individual may experience blockage or stagnation and develop unhealthy defense mechanisms to avoid working through the impacts, issues, and emotions associated with the crisis.

STAGE 4: COMPLETION OR RESOLUTION

This final stage may take months or years to achieve, and some individuals may never complete the process. The individual's recovery leads to integration of the crisis event, reorganization of their life, and adaptation and resolution of the trauma in positive meanings of growth, change, or service to others in crisis. Many crisis survivors reach out to support and help others who suffer similar traumas through volunteer work and service organizations. For example,

Compassionate Friends offers support groups and counseling services to parents and family who have lost a child through death.

PHASES OF HELPING

The phases of helping in various models of crisis intervention are similar to each other and utilize many of the same assessment and intervention strategies (Datillo & Freeman, 2010; Everly & Lating, 2013; Greenstone & Leviton, 2011; James & Gilliland, 2017; Kanel, 2019; Roberts & Yeager, 2009). This chapter focuses on the Assessment, Crisis Intervention, and Trauma Treatment (ACT) model (Roberts, 2005a; Yeager & Roberts, 2015a) and the seven-stage crisis intervention model (Roberts, 2005a; Yeager & Roberts, 2015b).

The Assessment, Crisis Intervention, and Trauma Treatment Model

The ACT model is a conceptual, three-stage framework and intervention model that integrates various assessment and triage protocols with the primary crisis intervention strategies. The ACT model can be used with a broad range of crises and can facilitate the psychosocial/lethality assessment and helping process for effective crisis intervention across diverse types of clients and trauma situations. It is the only model that focuses explicitly on the need to assess lethality, particularly when clients present because of a life-threatening, dangerous, or violence-precipitating crisis.

The A in the ACT model refers to triage, crisis, lethality, and trauma assessment and referral to appropriate community resources. The primary goal in conducting an assessment is to gather information that can be helpful in resolving the crisis. The assessment process should provide a step-by-step method of exploring, identifying, describing, measuring, and diagnosing health and mental health concerns, environmental conditions, strengths, resilience and protective factors, lifestyle factors, and current level of functioning. Appropriate triage and trauma assessment is critical to effective crisis intervention and treatment planning.

The C in the ACT model refers to the crisis intervention treatment plan and services that are provided on the scene, through short-term treatment or by referral to other community agencies. Types of services in this phase would include immediate crisis intervention, the delivery of basic needs and disaster relief, and referral to appropriate community social services, medical facilities, and mental health agencies.

The T in the ACT model refers to the need for follow-up services and referrals to address any symptoms of PTSD and continuing traumatic stress reactions. Stress management for first responders is also addressed in this phase to deal effectively with their traumatic stress reactions and to implement recovery strategies.

Seven-Stage Crisis Intervention Model

The seven-stage crisis intervention model by Roberts (2005a; Yeager & Roberts, 2015b) describes more completely the stages of crisis intervention (see Figure 9.1). It can be used with a broad range of crises, and can facilitate the assessment and helping process for effective crisis intervention across diverse types of clients and trauma situations. This model is useful to delineate the specific tasks and strategies necessary for effective crisis intervention. The model adapts easily to the different levels of crises and to different time frames for intervention. All of these stages can be completed within one contact if necessary, and in many crisis situations, that may be all the time that is available.

Stage 1: Plan and Conduct a Crisis Assessment (Including Lethality Measures)

Assessment in this model is ongoing and critical to effective intervention at all stages, beginning with an assessment of the lethality and safety issues for the client. With depressed or

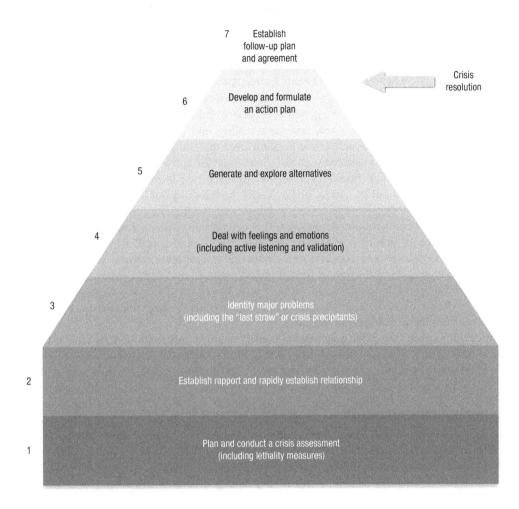

FIGURE 9.1 Seven-stage crisis intervention model.

suicidal clients, it is critical to assess the risk for attempts, plans, or means to harm oneself at the current time, as well as any previous history of suicidal ideations or attempts. With victims of rape, family violence, child abuse, or assault, it is important to assess if the client is in any current danger and to consider future safety concerns in treatment planning. In addition to determining lethality and the need for emergency intervention, it is crucial to maintain active communication with the client, either by phone or in person, while emergency procedures are being initiated (Roberts, 1998, 2005b; Yeager & Roberts, 2015b).

To plan and conduct a thorough assessment, the crisis worker also needs to evaluate the severity of the crisis, the client's current emotional state, the client's immediate psychosocial needs, and the level of the client's current coping skills and resources. In the initial contact, assessment of the client's past or pre-crisis level of functioning and coping skills is useful; however, past history should not be a focus of assessment unless related directly to the immediate traumatic event.

The goals of this stage are assessing and identifying critical areas of intervention while also recognizing the hazardous event or trauma and acknowledging what has happened. At the same time, the crisis survivor becomes aware of their state of vulnerability and initial reactions to the crisis event. It is important that the crisis worker begin to establish a relationship based on respect for and acceptance of the client, while also offering support, empathy, reassurance, and reinforcement that the client has survived and that help is available. In crisis intervention, stages 1 and 2 may occur simultaneously; however, the most important goal in stage 1 is to obtain information to determine whether the client is in imminent danger (Roberts, 2005b; Yeager & Roberts, 2015b).

STAGE 2: ESTABLISH RAPPORT AND RAPIDLY ESTABLISH A RELATIONSHIP

Stage 2 also relates to the initial contact between the crisis worker and the client, with the main tasks of establishing rapport and conveying genuine respect for and acceptance of the client. Survivors of trauma may question their own safety and vulnerability, and trust may be difficult for them to establish at this time. Therefore, active listening and empathic communication skills are essential to establishing rapport and engagement with the client. Even though the need for rapid engagement is essential, the crisis worker should try to let the client set the pace of treatment (Roberts, 2000). Many crisis victims feel out of control or powerless, and should not be coerced, confronted, or forced into action, until they have stabilized and dealt with the initial trauma reactions.

Trauma survivors may require a positive future orientation, with an understanding that they can overcome current problems and with hope that change can occur. During this stage, clients need support, positive regard, concern, and genuineness. Empathic communication skills such as minimal encouragers, reflection of thoughts and feelings, and active listening can reassure the client and help establish trust and rapport with the client. The crisis worker needs to be attentive to the tone and level of the verbal communications to help the client calm down or de-escalate from the initial trauma reactions.

The crisis worker must also pay attention to their body language and facial expressions, because trauma survivors may have been violated physically and be hypersensitive to physical space and body movements, which can frighten or startle the survivor. Facial expressions can be difficult to monitor due to their automatic nature, but this is especially important when working with disaster or trauma victims when physical damage and destruction is evident. Being observant of the survivor's physical and facial reactions can provide cues to the worker's level of engagement with the client, as well as be a gauge to the client's current emotional state. It is also important to remember that delayed reactions or flat affect is common with trauma victims, and to not assume that these types of reactions mean that the survivor is not in crisis.

STAGE 3: IDENTIFY MAJOR PROBLEMS (INCLUDING THE "LAST STRAW" OR CRISIS PRECIPITANTS)

The crisis worker should help the client prioritize the most important problems or impacts by identifying these problems in terms of how they affect the survivor's current status. Encouraging the client to talk about the precipitating event can lead to problem identification, and some clients have an overwhelming need to recall the specifics of the trauma situation. This process enables the client to figure out the sequence and context of the event, while providing information to assess and identify major problems for work.

Other crisis clients may be in denial or unable to verbalize their needs and feelings, so information may need to be obtained from collateral sources or significant others. It is essential to use a systems framework during the assessment and identification of problem stages, since crisis situations may impact at all levels of practice. Family members and significant others may be important to intervention planning in supportive roles or to ensure the client's safety. However, they may be experiencing their own reactions to the crisis situation, and this should be taken into consideration in contracting and implementing the intervention plan.

The crisis worker must ensure that the client system is not overwhelmed during this stage, and the focus should be on the most immediate and important problems needing intervention at this time. The first priority in this stage is meeting the basic needs of emotional and physical health and safety; after these have stabilized, other problems can then be addressed. In some cases, it can also be useful to identify the precipitating event or "last straw" that led the client to seek help now, and to briefly explore any previous attempts or coping strategies to deal with the problem. The focus must clearly be on the present crisis, and any exploration of past problems or issues must be done rapidly and only to aid in intervention planning (Roberts, 2005a; Yeager & Roberts, 2015b).

STAGE 4: DEAL WITH FEELINGS AND EMOTIONS (INCLUDING ACTIVE LISTENING AND VALIDATION)

Helping the client calm down and attending to physiological reactions such as hyperventilation are important activities for the crisis worker in this situation. The primary technique used by the crisis worker is active listening, which involves listening in an accepting and supportive way, in as private and safe a setting as possible. It is critical that the crisis worker demonstrates empathy and an anchored understanding of the survivor's experience, so that the client's symptoms and reactions are normalized and can be viewed as functional strategies for survival. Many victims blame themselves, and it is important to help the client accept that being a victim is not one's fault. Validation and reassurance are especially useful in this stage because survivors may be experiencing confusing and conflicting feelings.

Many clients follow the grief process when expressing and ventilating their emotions. First, survivors may be in denial about the extent of their emotional reactions and may try to avoid dealing with them in hopes that they will subside. They may be in shock and not be able to access their feelings immediately. Some clients will express anger and rage about the situation and its effects, which can be healthy as long as the client does not escalate out of control. Other clients may express their grief and sadness. The crisis worker must also be self-aware of their own emotional reactions and level of comfort in helping the client during this stage. It is important to attend to your own self-care needs to avoid burnout, emotional fatigue, and secondary traumatization effects.

STAGE 5: GENERATE AND EXPLORE ALTERNATIVES

In this stage, effective crisis workers help clients recognize and explore a variety of alternatives for restoring a pre-crisis level of functioning. Such alternatives include (a) using support systems, such as people or resources that can be helpful to the client in meeting needs and resolving problems in living as a result of the crisis; (b) developing coping skills, which are behaviors or strategies that promote adaptive responses and resolution of the crisis; and (c) increasing positive and constructive thinking patterns to reduce the client's levels of anxiety and stress.

The crisis worker can facilitate healthy coping skills by identifying client strengths and resources. Many crisis survivors feel they do not have a lot of choices, and the crisis worker needs to be familiar with both formal and informal community services to provide referrals. For example, working with a battered woman often requires relocation to a safe place for her and the children. The client may not have the personal resources or financial ability to move out of the home, and the crisis worker needs to be informed about possible alternatives, which could include a shelter program, a protective order, or other emergency housing services.

It is important to help the client generate and explore previously untried coping methods in a collaborative way, and it is equally important to examine and evaluate the potential consequences of, and the client's feelings about, those alternatives. The crisis worker may need to be more active, directive, and confrontational in this stage if the client has unrealistic expectations or inappropriate coping skills and strategies. Clients are still distressed and in disequilibrium at this stage, and professional expertise and guidance could be necessary to produce positive, realistic alternatives for the client.

STAGE 6: DEVELOP AND FORMULATE AN ACTION PLAN

The success of any intervention plan depends on the client's level of involvement, participation, and commitment. The crisis worker must help the client look at both the short-term and long-range impacts in planning intervention. The main goals are to help the client achieve an appropriate level of functioning and maintain adaptive coping skills and resources. It is important to have a manageable treatment plan that the client can follow through and be successful. Do not overwhelm the client with too many tasks or strategies, because this may set the client up for failure (Roberts, 2000).

The client must also feel a sense of ownership in the treatment plan, so that the client can increase the level of control and autonomy in their life and not become dependent on other support persons or resources. Obtaining a commitment from the client to follow through with the action plan and any referrals is an important activity for the crisis worker that can be maximized by using a mutual process in intervention planning. Ongoing assessment and evaluation are essential to determine whether the intervention plan is appropriate and effective in minimizing or resolving the client's identified problems. During this stage, the client should be processing and reintegrating the crisis impacts to achieve homeostasis and equilibrium in their life. Termination should begin when the client has achieved the goals of the action plan or has been referred for additional services through other treatment providers. Many trauma survivors may need longer term therapeutic help in working toward crisis resolution, and referrals for individual, family, or group therapy should be considered at this stage.

STAGE 7: ESTABLISH A FOLLOW-UP PLAN AND AGREEMENT

It is hoped that the sixth stage has resulted in significant changes and resolution for the client with regard to their post-crisis level of functioning and coping. This last stage should help determine whether these results have been maintained or if further work remains to be done. Typically, follow-up contacts should be done within 4 to 6 weeks after termination. It is important to remember that crisis resolution may take many months or years to achieve, and survivors should be aware that certain events, places, or dates could trigger emotional and physical reactions to the previous trauma. For example, a critical time is at the first anniversary of a crisis event, when clients may reexperience old fears, reactions, or thoughts. This is a normal part of the recovery process, and clients should be prepared to have contingency plans or supportive help through these difficult periods.

APPLICATION TO FAMILY AND GROUP WORK

The crisis intervention model is applicable to family and group crisis intervention, although there are certain considerations in relation to these levels of practice. Certain crisis situations, such as shifts in family structure and developmental changes, can affect family members differently, so the crisis worker may have to assess who in the family is experiencing crisis and who in the family will be participating in treatment. Other crisis events, such as child abuse, family violence, or criminal offenses, involve demands from community agencies that a family member change certain behaviors or ways of coping. Then there are traumatic situations that may affect all family members involved in the critical incident, such as disasters, accidents, and death.

During assessment, the family structure, dynamics, relationships, communication patterns, and support systems need to be evaluated as to potential strengths and areas in need of treatment. Assessment of how family members react to each other and to the crisis situation, including any issues of blame or guilt, is important to consider when planning interventions. How the crisis impacts on the family system as a whole and on the individuals, the amount of family cooperation, and consideration of the family's support system in terms of local community resources are also important in assessment and intervention planning. Extended family may often be involved during intervention, both at the time of active crisis and later as sources of support and resources for stabilization.

Group crisis work is used with clients experiencing similar types of trauma, such as sexual assault and child abuse survivors, individuals in community or institutional disasters, persons with chemical dependency, combat veterans, and individuals dealing with loss and bereavement. Having the support of and interaction with others who have shared similar crisis events are important benefits of group therapy. Group members can learn from each other about ways to cope and go on with their lives. As in families, group members may have different reactions, experiences, feelings, and coping skills, so intervention has to be directed at the individual level, as well as with the group as a working system. The need for individual treatment in addition to group work should be part of the assessment and action plan. Self-help and time-limited groups are also excellent resources for longer term crisis or grief work.

CRITIQUE OF CRISIS INTERVENTION

One of the strengths of crisis intervention is its effectiveness across diverse types of crises and client populations. However, although research and literature exist on specialized types of crises and clients, there is not much literature on cultural, gender, or age factors among crisis client populations (Congress, 2000; Cornelius et al., 2003; Dykeman, 2005; Stone & Conley, 2004). A meta-analysis of the federal Crisis Counseling Program (CCP) disaster mental health services for approximately 160,000 people over a 5-year period indicated that the 36 programs studied were at least at a pre-competent level of cultural competence. The programs did make efforts to reach out to diverse communities by hiring staff from different cultures, providing training in cultural competence, and engaging in ongoing cultural reassessment to improve their knowledge and services. The authors also noted that the CCPs were successful in serving racial and ethnic minority groups by recruiting indigenous community leaders as counselors and providing free mental health services in the community (Rosen et al., 2010).

More research is also needed on sexual orientation, and gender and age differences in dealing with crises, especially in the expression of emotion (Dyregrov & Regel, 2012; Goldbach et al., 2019). A study on male police officers who report traumatic exposures indicates that they adhere to traditional male gender norms and prefer not to share their memories and emotions with their peers. The authors recommend strategies that focus on strengths and provide goal-directed professional development and training for critical incident stress management (Pasciak & Kelley, 2013).

CONCLUSION

Crisis intervention is an eclectic approach that is effective across diverse types of crises, client populations, and settings. It is essential that social workers be knowledgeable and trained in basic crisis intervention skills to meet the needs of their clients. Continuing professional development through workshops, training, and professional literature on evidence-based crisis intervention models and skills is necessary for social workers and counseling professionals to provide effective and appropriate services. Further research studies on crisis intervention models and strategies are needed to develop and evaluate best practices, and program evaluations are critical for accountability and appropriate provision of crisis intervention services. This chapter has provided an overview of the principles, theoretical constructs, and basic intervention skills in crisis intervention. Crisis work can be both demanding and difficult, but its rewards can be immediate and long-lasting for both clients and social workers.

SUMMARY POINTS

- crisis intervention is grounded in an generalist-eclectic orientation and theory base and incorporates the basic principles and perspectives from systems theory, ego psychology (including life cycle/human development theory), and cognitive behavioral theories into a holistic framework for crisis intervention with diverse client populations and types of crises;

- crisis theory does not view the individual in crisis as pathological or mentally ill, since all human beings experience and deal with challenges presented during crises and trauma as a normal part of the human condition;
- crisis theory postulates that intervention is time limited to a period of 4 to 6 weeks with the goal of mobilizing needed support, resources, and the adaptive coping skills of the client to resolve or minimize the disequilibrium experienced by the precipitating event;
- crisis intervention places an emphasis on client strengths and empowerment. A strengths-based approach is inherent in the crisis intervention strategy of building on the client's own coping skills and natural support system;
- client empowerment is a natural outcome of this approach, because the focus in crisis work is to provide the support and resources for clients to resolve any negative impacts through their own growth and development and not to become dependent on others in their social environment to meet those needs;
- crisis intervention emphasizes holistic, multilevel assessment within an ecosystem perspective, and must address the biological, psychological, and environmental damage and trauma, from both a macrosystemic and an individual perspective to be effective;
- it is essential that social workers be knowledgeable and trained in basic crisis intervention skills to meet the needs of their clients. Continuing professional development on evidence-based crisis intervention models and skills is necessary for social workers and counseling professionals to provide effective and appropriate services.

KEY REFERENCES

Only key references appear in the print edition. The full reference list appears in the digital product found on http://connect.springerpub.com/content/book/978-0-8261-6556-5/part/sec03/part/sec032/chapter/ch09

Dziegielewski, S. F., & Jacinto, G. A. (2015). Designs and procedures for evaluating crisis intervention. In K. R. Yeager & A. R. Roberts (Eds.), *Crisis intervention handbook: Assessment, treatment, and research* (pp. 711–750). Oxford University Press.

Greene, G. J., & Lee, M. L. (2015). How to work with client strengths in crisis intervention: A solution-focused approach. In K. R. Yeager & A. R. Roberts (Eds.), *Crisis intervention handbook: Assessment, treatment, and research* (pp. 69–98). Oxford University Press.

James. R. K., & Gilliland, B. E. (2017). *Crisis intervention strategies*. Cengage Learning.

Kanel, K. (2019). *A guide to crisis intervention*. Cengage Learning.

Roberts, A. R., & Yeager, K. R. (2015). Lethality assessment and crisis intervention with persons presenting with suicidal ideation. In K. R. Yeager & A. R. Roberts (Eds.), *Crisis intervention handbook: Assessment, treatment, and research* (pp. 36–68). Oxford University Press.

Roberts, A. R., & Yeager, K. R. (2009). *Pocket guide to crisis intervention*. Oxford University Press.

Yeager, K. R., Burgess, A. W., & Roberts, A. R. (2015). Crisis intervention with persons diagnosed with clinical disorders on the stress-crisis continuum. In K. R. Yeager & A. R. Roberts (Eds.), *Crisis intervention handbook: Assessment, treatment, and research* (pp. 128–150). Oxford University Press.

Yeager, K. R., & Roberts, A. R. (2015). The ACT model: Assessment, crisis intervention, and trauma treatment in the aftermath of community disaster and terrorism attacks. In K. R. Yeager & A. R. Roberts (Ed.), *Crisis intervention handbook: Assessment, treatment, and research* (pp. 183–213). Oxford University Press.

Yeager, K. R., & Roberts, A. R. (2015). Bridging the past and present to the future of crisis intervention and crisis management. In K. R. Yeager & A. R. Roberts (Eds.), *Crisis intervention handbook: Assessment, treatment, and research* (pp. 3–35). Oxford University Press.

Dialectical Behavior Therapy for the Treatment of Borderline Personality Disorder

Michael A. Mancini and Shannon Cooper-Sadlo

LEARNING OBJECTIVES

By the end of this chapter, you should be able to:

1. develop an understanding of the prevalence, pathogenesis, symptomology, and course for borderline personality disorder (BPD);
2. identify the biological, psychological, and social factors that contribute to the development of BPD;
3. identify screening and assessment practices for the effective diagnosis of BPD;
4. understand the historical development, central theoretical constructs, structures, processes, evidence base, and limitations of dialectical behavior therapy (DBT); and
5. identify and effectively apply the specific practices and interventions of DBT.

INTRODUCTION

Borderline personality disorder (BPD) causes significant mental distress and impairment in psychosocial functioning (American Psychiatric Association [APA], 2013; Gunderson et al., 2018). The condition is marked by emotional dysregulation, unstable personal relationships, impulsivity, chronic anger, and identity disturbances (APA, 2013). A person with this condition often engages long-standing patterns of maladaptive coping responses that can include substance use, self-injury, suicidal behavior, aggression, and other reckless behavior. The condition is often comorbid with other psychiatric conditions including mood and anxiety disorders, eating disorders, substance abuse, posttraumatic stress disorder (PTSD), and other personality disorders (APA, 2013; Lenzenweger et al., 2007; Shea et al., 2004; Zanarini et al., 1998; Zimmerman & Mattia, 1999). While prolonged impairment in psychosocial functioning and symptom relapses are common, lasting improvement in a wide range of areas can be expected over time (Gunderson et al., 2011; Skodol et al., 2005b).

Dialectical behavior therapy (DBT; Linehan, 1993, 2015) is an intensive psychotherapy based on the cognitive behavioral model that uses individual and group sessions to help people with BPD develop adaptive coping strategies to manage symptoms and improve functioning (Linehan, 1987, 1993, 2015). DBT has been widely studied and has been found to be an effective psychotherapeutic approach to treating BPD (Cristea et al., 2017; Linehan et al., 2006; Stoffers et al., 2012).

OVERVIEW AND CLINICAL FEATURES OF BORDERLINE PERSONALITY DISORDER

There are several interrelated symptomatic clusters that comprise BPD. Sanislow et al. (2000) used factor analysis to discover three main factors that comprise BPD symptoms: (1) emotional dysregulation (e.g., anger, mood instability), (2) problems relating to other people (e.g., unstable personal relationships) and to oneself (e.g., identify disturbance and feelings of emptiness), and (3) problems managing behavior (e.g., impulsive behavior, recklessness, chronic self-harming, and suicidal behavior).

A hallmark sign of BPD is *emotional dysregulation*, which involves affective instability, chronic feelings of anger, and an intense fear of rejection and abandonment (Sanislow et al., 2000). This is the most common symptom found in 95% of BPD cases (McGlashan et al., 2005). Affective instability involves drastic fluctuations from joy to irritability and anger to intense sadness over the course of a single day. Affective instability and chronic anger have also been identified as one of the most pervasive, persistent, and stable traits of BPD (McGlashan et al., 2005).

A second clinical feature of BPD is *unstable personal relationships* with significant others, partners, caregivers, therapists, and close family members (APA, 2013). Unstable interpersonal relationships have been found in 79% of BPD cases (McGlashan et al., 2005). Persons with BPD often require a high degree of reassurance and support due to an intense fear of rejection and abandonment. Research indicates that persons with BPD may be inherently hypersensitive to negative emotional stimuli such as negative feedback or criticism, negative or ambiguous facial expressions, or perceived lack of optimal support from caregivers, friends, and significant others (Donegan et al., 2003; Korfine & Hooley, 2000). They may misinterpret mild negative critiques or ambiguous responses as rejection or abandonment resulting in anger or depression, which can lead to emotional outbursts, cruelty, aggressiveness, self-harm, suicidal behaviors, substance abuse, and sabotaging of relationships or personal goals (Lieb et al., 2004).

A third feature of the disorder is an unstable self-image or identity and a chronic sense of emptiness (Gunderson et al., 2018; Lieb et al., 2004). Chronic emptiness can lead to a pervasive sense of unfulfillment causing persons with BPD to become easily bored and restless. While searching for a sense of excitement and fulfillment, persons with BPD may engage in reckless, thoughtless, or ill-advised behaviors. While persons with BPD typically view themselves in negative terms, the lack of being moored in a stable identity can lead to drastic changes in behaviors, relationships, opinions, and points of view (APA, 2013; Gunderson et al, 2018).

A fourth common feature of the disorder that can affect up to 81% of patients is a tendency toward *impulsive and reckless behaviors* (Lieb et al., 2004; McGlashen et al., 2005). These behaviors can include engaging in physical or verbal aggression, substance abuse, unsafe sex, reckless driving, imprudent spending of money, quitting jobs, binge eating, and abruptly ending relationships, among other self-damaging behaviors. Persons with BPD have been found to have impairment in many cognitive areas of functioning including attention, memory, planning, cognitive flexibility, and problem-solving (Ruocco, 2005). These deficits may contribute to impulsive behavior seen in persons with this condition. The combination of affective instability and impulsivity inherent in BPD can make a person with the disorder highly susceptible to maladaptive coping behaviors in the face of stressful life events. For instance, persons with BPD often tend to engage in the act of "splitting" by seeing people as either all-good or all-bad (Gunderson & Links, 2008). Persons who provide optimal support are often idealized but can quickly be denigrated if support wanes. This response may be due to the fear of abandonment and/or a sense of chronic emptiness inherent in the disorder. This can invoke aggressive, angry, cruel, or manipulative responses. Persons with BPD may also withdraw and become depressed leading to engagement in self-harming or suicidal behavior (Lieb et al., 2004).

Lastly, persons with BPD engage in frequent suicidal behavior (e.g., suicidal ideation, planning/intent, attempts, and completion) as well as self-harming or non-suicidal self-injury

(NSSI) such as cutting, burning, head-banging, or punching oneself (APA, 2013; Zanarini et al., 2013). Persons with BPD are at an increased risk for suicide and complete suicide at a high rate (APA, 2013; Black et al., 2004; Gunderson et al., 2018; Lieb et al., 2004; Paris, 2002; Pompili et al., 2005). Studies indicated that as high as 75% of persons with BPD attempt suicide with approximately 10% completing suicide. Important risk factors for suicide include prior attempts, depressive symptoms, access to lethal means, alcohol and substance misuse use, hopelessness, impulsivity, and social and vocational maladaptive behaviors (APA, 2001; Black et al., 2004; Soloff & Chiappetta, 2012).

Epidemiology, Onset, and Course

At any given point in time, the prevalence of BPD in the United States is 1.6%, while the lifetime prevalence of the condition is approximately 6% (Grant et al., 2008; Lenzenweger et al., 2007). In clinical settings, BPD has been identified in 20% of psychiatric inpatients and 9 to 10% of mental health treatment outpatients (APA, 2013; Zimmerman et al., 2005). Population studies have also shown no statistical differences in prevalence rates between men and women (Grant et al., 2008; Lenzenweger et al., 2007). However, in clinical settings, women comprise 75% of BPD diagnoses (APA, 2013). This suggests that women may be more likely to seek treatment than men, or it may reflect systemic biases in diagnostic practice.

Research has indicated that persons with BPD are more likely to experience alcohol and drug use disorders (Grant et al., 2015, 2016). On average, persons with BPD have over three additional psychiatric comorbid disorders with 85% having at least one comorbid disorder (Lenzenweger et al., 2007). The most common comorbid disorders include major depressive disorder (MDD) (83%), substance use disorder (64%), PTSD (56%), eating disorders (53%), and panic disorder (48%; Shea et al., 2004; Zanarini et al., 1998; Zimmerman & Mattia, 1999).

Like most personality disorders, a diagnosis of BPD usually occurs in late adolescence and early adulthood (APA, 2013). Despite long-held assumption about the chronic nature of the condition, longitudinal studies have shown high remission rates. In one study of 175 patients, 85% met less than three diagnostic criteria for at least 12 months at 10-year follow-up (Gunderson et al., 2011). Another longitudinal study of nearly 300 patients demonstrated 10-year remission rates (defined as not meeting diagnostic criteria for at least two years) of 91% and 16-year rates to be as high as 99% (Zanarini et al., 2006, 2010, 2012). Remission was prolonged with almost 80% achieving remission for 8 years or more (Zanarini et al., 2012). Relapse rates in these studies ranged from 12% (Gunderson et al., 2011) to 34% (Zanarini et al., 2012). While improvement in many symptom domains occurred, impairment in psychosocial functioning (i.e., social relationships) was persistent over time indicating that persons with BPD experience a wide range of symptomatic improvement, yet continue to struggle with impairment in social domains (Gunderson et al., 2011; Skodol et al., 2005a).

Assessment and Diagnosis

The assessment of BPD should encompass a multidimensional approach that pays particular attention to suicidal and NSSI, violence, psychiatric symptoms, family history, substance use, childhood adverse events, and trauma. In addition to standardized instruments and client self-report, clinicians should collect information from observations, medical records, and collateral contacts in the person's social network.

Several screening and assessment forms are available for clinical use. A common and simple screening instrument with good psychometrics is the 10-item McLean Screening Instrument for BPD (Zanarini et al., 2003). The measure uses yes and no responses to 10 items that closely track diagnostic criteria for BPD. A more in-depth diagnostic interview instrument with good psychometric properties is the Revised Diagnostic Interview for Borderlines (Zanarini et al., 2002).

Section 2 of the *Diagnostic and Statistical Manual of Mental Disorders* (5th ed.; *DSM-5; APA, 2013*) lists the following diagnostic criteria for BPD (APA, 2013, pp. 663):

A pervasive pattern of instability of interpersonal relationships, self-image, and affects, and marked impulsivity, beginning in early adulthood and present in a variety of contexts as indicated by five (5) or more of the following:

1. Frantic efforts to avoid real or imagined abandonment (excluding suicidal behaviors covered in criterion 5)
2. A pattern of unstable and intense interpersonal relationships characterized by alternating between extremes of idealization and devaluation
3. Identity disturbance; markedly and persistently unstable self-image or sense of self
4. Impulsivity in at least two areas that are potentially self-damaging (e.g., spending, sex, substance abuse, reckless driving, binge eating). Excluding suicidal behaviors covered in criterion 5
5. Recurrent suicidal behavior, gestures, or threats, or self-mutilating behavior
6. Affective instability due to a marked reactivity of mood (e.g., intense episodic dysphoria, irritability, or anxiety usually lasting a few hours and only rarely more than a few days)
7. Chronic feelings of emptiness
8. Inappropriate, intense anger or difficulty controlling anger (e.g., frequent displays of temper, constant anger, recurrent physical fights)
9. Transient, stress-related paranoid ideation or severe dissociative symptoms

Differential Diagnosis

BPD shares many symptoms with other psychiatric disorders. The two disorders that are most similar to BPD are MDD and Bipolar Disorder I and II. MDD is often comorbid with BPD, and if a client meets full criteria for MDD and BPD, both conditions can and should be diagnosed. However, the negative mood symptoms and suicidality experienced across both conditions can make differential diagnosis difficult. When differentiating, it should be noted that the negative mood symptoms experienced during a major depressive episode are often more prolonged and constant throughout the day, include physical symptoms, whereas mood symptoms solely due to BPD are often triggered by external events and fluctuate throughout the day. Furthermore, the impulsive, aggressive, and interpersonal problems experienced in BPD are often not experienced in MDD (APA, 2013). Affective instability and impulsivity are commonly seen in both BPD and bipolar disorder patients. However, the mania that is experienced in Bipolar Disorder I is prolonged and constant compared to the affective instability experienced in BPD, which has a more fluctuating course that is contingent upon environmental cues (APA, 2013).

Persons with BPD have often experienced traumatic events and may experience symptoms of full or partial PTSD symptoms. While PTSD is common in persons with BPD, not all persons with BPD have PTSD, nor is PTSD necessary for a diagnosis of BPD (Zanarini et al., 1998). While the symptoms of negative cognitions and emotions such as dysphoria, shame, and guilt common in PTSD are also seen in BPD, the intrusion, hyper-vigilance, and avoidance symptoms necessary for a PTSD diagnosis are not typical of BPD. In addition, PTSD symptoms flare up due to cues or triggers in the environment, whereas symptoms of BPD are often rooted in interpersonal stressors such as rejection and criticism. Lastly, identity disturbance and the frantic efforts to avoid abandonment resulting in relational difficulties are not common in persons with PTSD (APA, 2013).

Persons with BPD and attention deficit hyperactivity disorder (ADHD) often demonstrate problems in attention and impulsivity or hyperactivity. However, persons with ADHD lack the identity disturbances, chronic suicidality, and sensitivity to abandonment seen in BPD. Persons with ADHD e also show symptoms of attention and hyperactivity issues early in the course of one's life (APA, 2013). Lastly, substance use disorders are commonly comorbid with BPD. Impulsivity, emotional lability, aggressiveness, and interpersonal problems are common across both conditions. However, many of the symptoms of substance use disorder emerge only while a person is taking substances and are often absent during remission, whereas the symptoms of BPD are persistent despite remission of substance use disorder (APA, 2013).

OVERVIEW OF DIALECTICAL BEHAVIOR THERAPY

DBT, developed by Marsha Linehan about 30 years ago, is a multifaceted, systemic model of therapy that utilizes components of cognitive behavioral therapy, behaviorism, and mindfulness (Linehan, 1987). The goal of DBT is to address emotional distress as well as the often-destructive behaviors that result from BPD. In order to address both components, DBT therapists rely on a manualized framework that incorporates skills training, collaborative problem- solving, contingency management, and mindfulness that is based in a holistic philosophy (Linehan, 1987; O'Connel, 2014). The theoretical foundation of DBT is rooted in biosocial and developmental theories to understand the complex needs of individuals who are diagnosed with BPD (Koons, 2008). In recent years, DBT has also been adapted to treat substance use disorders, eating disorders with both adult and adolescent populations, as well as PTSD with various veteran populations.

Historical Development

DBT was developed by Marsha Linehan and her colleagues at the University of Washington, Seattle, in the late 1980s and early 1990s as a response to her clinical work with chronically suicidal women who were not responding to the standard treatments of the time (Koons, 2008). Most of Linehan's patients met the criteria for BPD, due to the impulsive behavior, mood instability, and the relational distress they exhibited (Koons, 2008). These characteristics led to prematurely leaving treatment and frequent emergency hospitalizations.

Linehan theorized that the common factor that her clients experienced involved an inability to effectively regulate emotions. Linehan believed that this inability to self-regulate led clients to avoid emotions in self-destructive ways such as through substance use and self-injurious behaviors. Linehan identified this emotional dysregulation as the core of the problematic and self-destructive behaviors that are common with individuals diagnosed with BPD. Linehan argued that emotional dysregulation contributed to relational distress, impulsive and high-risk behaviors, as well as anger outbursts and cognitive impairments such as paranoia, dissociation, and in some cases, hallucinations (Koons, 2008; Linehan, 1987). DBT was developed to address the specific needs of a population that had previously not responded well to traditional treatments. Linehan's model of treatment is intended to link emotional dysregulation with specific behavioral interventions that address the unique needs of individuals diagnosed with BPD (Crowell et al., 2009). Early studies conducted by Linehan and her colleagues found that over the course of a year, clients enrolled in the DBT program engaged in less parasuicidal behaviors, continued attendance in therapy, and experienced fewer hospital admissions than the control group that received treatment as usual (TAU; O'Connell & Dowling, 2014). The 6- and 12-month follow-up evaluations reported a continued reduction in symptomatic behaviors in the DBT group compared to the TAU group (O'Connell & Dowling, 2014).

Central Theoretical Constructs

DBT is rooted in biosocial theory that explains the etiology of BPD through the lens of biological vulnerabilities exacerbated by an invalidating social environment (Koons, 2008; Linehan, 1987).

The symptoms of BPD have genetic, neurobiological, psychological (e.g., stable personality traits), and social (e.g., childhood maltreatment, trauma, early and sustained toxic stress) pathways (Gunderson et al., 2018; Skodol et al., 2002). The bio-social model of BPD positions BPD as an interaction between adverse life events such as trauma and child maltreatment, and genetic vulnerability to traits that are important to the disorder that can then lead to psychosocial problems in school, work, independent living, and personal relationships (Crowell et al., 2009; Distel et al., 2011; Gunderson et al., 2018; Linehan, 1987, 2015). Within this framework, BPD can be better considered as a combination of a disorder with a cluster of symptomatic experiences (e.g., mood and anxiety disturbance) and stable personality traits such as high antagonism, negative affectivity, and impulsivity (McGlashan et al., 2005; Skodol et al., 2005a).

Research has identified multiple neurobiological contributors to BPD. First, there is good evidence for the heritability of BPD, particularly for the personality traits of low agreeability and impulsivity (Kendler et al., 2008; Skodol et al., 2002; Torgersen et al., 2000). There is also some evidence suggesting overlap between the genes associated with impulsivity and affective instability in other major mental illness such as schizophrenia, bipolar disorder, MDD, and BPD (Witt et al., 2017). Abnormalities in the functioning and connectivity between the limbic system and prefrontal cortex may also lead to symptoms and functional impairments in learning, cognitive flexibility, memory, attention, planning, decision-making, problem-solving, impulsivity, anxiety, stress response, and emotional regulation commonly seen in persons with BPD (Ruocco, 2005).

Invalidating environments marked by the experience of childhood maltreatment in the form of physical and emotional abuse and neglect have been found to be associated with BPD (Widom et al., 2009). Linehan describes an invalidating social environment, primarily the family, in three ways: (1) an environment marked by negative, indifferent or demeaning interactions and that lacks health models of emotional expression; (2) an environment that is marked by interactions that are highly charged and emotionally toxic; and (3) a mismatch in temperament and parenting styles between a child and caregivers (Linehan, 2015). Linehan identifies three types of families that increase the probability of a child developing BPD. She describes (1) the *disorganized family*, which is characterized as neglectful or abusive; (2) the *perfect family*, which is characterized as avoidant of negative emotions; and (3) the *normal family*, in which there is a mismatch of temperament between caregivers and the child (Crowell et al., 2009; Linehan, 2015). These invalidating transactional social environments, combined with a child's biological vulnerabilities, can negatively impact a child's ability to emotionally regulate and manage behavior within a social context. Furthermore, the coping strategies developed during early emotional development are often maladaptive and become problematic in interpersonal and social functioning (Crowell et al., 2009; Koons, 2008; Linehan, 1987, 2015).

It should be noted that childhood sexual abuse, while often identified as an important contributor to BPD, has not been associated with an increased risk for BPD compared to physical abuse and neglect (Widom et al., 2009). Most people who are sexually abused do not develop BPD and many of those with BPD often have not experienced sexual abuse. However, while childhood abuse and neglect are correlated with BPD diagnoses, twin studies have found no causal link between abuse and later development of BPD traits. This research attributed the development of BPD to be more influenced by genetic vulnerabilities to pathological, emotional, and behavioral symptomologies (Bornovalova et al., 2013).

Foundations of Dialectical Behavior Therapy

DBT is a structured intervention that is based on three foundational theories: behaviorism, Zen, and dialectics. The combination of these theories addresses the consequences of the biological vulnerabilities and invalidating social environments identified as maladaptive in the Biosocial Theory. First, *behaviorism* emphasizes the importance of assessment, data collection, and analysis of the relationship between behavior and consequences. DBT utilizes similar interventions (e.g., problem-solving, skills training, contingency management, behavioral analysis, exposure, conditioning, and cognitive modification) to traditional cognitive behavioral treatment (CBT) and behavioral therapies. These interventions seek to understand how maladaptive behaviors are developed and how to replace and reinforce new, more effective behaviors (Koons, 2008; Linehan, 2015).

Second, *Zen* is an eastern philosophy based on the belief that knowledge of self is inherent in everyone. DBT has adapted this philosophy and developed the idea of the "wise mind." The wise mind is a synthesis of emotion and cognition that leads to emotion regulation and appropriate behavioral responses. To function in a state of wise mind, DBT teaches core mindfulness skills that incorporate "what skills," which are achieved through observation, description, and participation, and the "how skills." "How skills" include the acceptance of a non-judgmental stance, maintaining one-mindedness, and effectiveness (Koons, 2008; Linehan, 2015). The "what skills" allow the participant to notice and describe a situation from a non-emotional, here and now, factual place rather than from a place of emotional reactivity. The "how skills" allow the participant to accept a situation without judgment, remain focused on the here and now, as well as develop a response to the situation that effectively addresses the issue presented. This decreases emotional dysregulation and impulsivity and leads to thoughtful engagement and problem-solving. These mindfulness skills are central to DBT and are the primary way in which DBT differs from other behavioral therapies.

Third, the final tenet of DBT includes the western philosophical tradition of *dialectics* that espouses that truth is a synthesis of opposites. Dialectics understands that there is constant struggle among multiple factors and that change in one factor will cause a disruption of homeostasis and in other factors. A dialectical worldview directly challenges the dichotomous, "black and white" thinking that is common in individuals who are diagnosed with BPD. Dialectics encourages the viewpoint of "both/and" rather than an "either/or" perspective. This perspective allows for further exploration of alternative explanations and strategies for problem-solving. This is achieved when the client and the therapist can balance the concepts of acceptance and change. Acceptance is demonstrated through validation and empathy strategies, while change occurs through the implementation of behavioral interventions and skills training (Koons, 2008; Linehan, 2015).

Structure of Treatment

DBT is a highly structured treatment protocol that has several components. Each branch of the intervention provides support to the client and the therapist, and guides the course of treatment. DBT is most often delivered in outpatient settings due to the length of the treatment process. However, adaptations of DBT have been effectively deployed in hospital settings with good outcomes indicating that further study of DBT practices in inpatient settings is warranted (Bloom et al., 2012).

The first component is *individual therapy*. The role of the individual therapist is to manage and direct the treatment process. The therapist serves at the liaison to the treatment team, facilitates the development of treatment goals, and monitors progress. The therapist and the client meet once a week for one 50-minute session. During this meeting, the therapist addresses the established treatment hierarchy that has been collaboratively developed by the therapist and the client. The therapist also reinforces new behavioral skills and works to develop and maintain an effective and productive relationship with the client (Koons, 2008; Linehan, 1987, 2015).

The second component of DBT is *skills training*. This is the heart of DBT as is delivered in a group setting with other participants and two co-facilitators. The class is a two-hour session offered once a week and follows a set curricula that is broken into four modules. These modules build upon each other and always follow a set schedule of presentation. Participants are required to attend each of the modules and to successfully complete mandatory homework assignments outside of sessions. The modules are: (1) Mindfulness, (2) Distress Tolerance, (3)

Emotion Regulation, and (4) Interpersonal Effectiveness. The completion of all four modules takes approximately 10 weeks. The cycles are then repeated with the same participants two more times in order for the participants to re-learn the skills multiple times. The entire process takes approximately a year. During this time, the client also participates in weekly individual therapy sessions with the primary therapist as described in the first component (Koons, 2008; Linehan, 1987, 2015).

The third component is *therapist consultation sessions*. Due to the stressful nature of working with high acuity clients, DBT therapists and skills group facilitators meet weekly to provide support and consultation about the treatment process and the needs of participants. During this consultation time, therapists are encouraged to hold each other accountable for maintaining fidelity to the model as well as problem solve specific issues that may be occurring during treatment with an individual client or with a cohort of participants in the skills training classes. This consultation also allows for direct communication between the primary therapist and the skills facilitators in order to reduce triangulation among the team members as well as ensure that all members of the team are addressing the same treatment goals (Koons, 2008; Linehan, 1987, 2015).

The fourth component, *telephone coaching*, is an integral part of the treatment process because it allows for clients to have access to their primary therapist in the time between sessions when emotional dysregulation can lead to self-destructive behavior. Clients are informed that this is not a therapy session, rather a brief intervention to review skills and monitor safety. Clients are informed that they are to contact the therapist prior to engaging in self-injurious, suicidal, or self-destructive behavior. If they self-injure or participate in any problematic behavior, they are prohibited from contacting the therapist for 24 hours. This is to ensure that the therapist is not reinforcing negative behavior (Koons, 2008; Linehan, 1987, 2015).

Treatment Hierarchy

In DBT, the primary therapist and the client collaborate to develop an individualized, structured treatment plan based on the stage of the disorder and the identification of problematic behaviors. *Stage 1* of treatment is designed to address the most pervasive, impulsive, and dangerous behaviors. The treatment plan of stage 1 is divided into four target areas. The first target area is the behaviors that threaten life and safety. This includes homicidal or suicidal thoughts and actions, NSSI behaviors, and any other behaviors that could lead to death. The second target area is the behaviors that interfere with therapy. This includes noncompliance with treatment recommendations, nonattendance to sessions or the skills training, as well as refusal to complete assignments. The third target area focuses on the behaviors that negatively impact quality of life, such as substance abuse or disordered eating patterns. Finally, the fourth target area addresses behavioral replacement skills in which the client identifies and substitutes maladaptive coping behaviors with healthy, adaptive coping skills (Linehan, 2015).

Stage 2 of the treatment protocol occurs when there is a significant reduction in emotional and behavioral dyscontrol. While clients may continue to struggle with some emotion regulation, they are markedly less reactive and engage in less impulsive behavior. In stage 2, the primary area of focus is on acceptance. This includes acceptance of trauma, its impact on the client's life and, most importantly, of self. Therapists must not move forward with stage 2 until the client has successfully learned and deployed skills to manage the effects of trauma and emotional and behavioral dyscontrol. Otherwise, the client may be more likely to return to negative behaviors and emotion dysregulation (Linehan, 2015).

Stage 3 targets "problems in living". Once the client reaches this stage of treatment, the focus shifts from emotional and behavioral regulation to increasing skills of living. This includes managing interpersonal conflicts, applying long-term problem-solving strategies, and managing multiple stressors that are common in everyday life. This stage utilizes several strategies that are common in CBT and other behavioral treatments (Linehan, 2015).

Finally, *stage 4* focuses on building a joyful and fulfilled life. This may include seeking out new relationships, engaging in new pursuits or hobbies, or achieving lifetime goals. The development of meaningful and purposeful activities and the establishment of health social networks are the main goals of this stage. Once these elements have been successfully achieved, the client may have a renewed sense of self, as well as confidence in their abilities to problem solve and live healthy, meaningful lives. At this point, the therapist and the client can begin the therapy termination process (Linehan, 2015).

Core Strategies of Dialectical Behavior Therapy

The core strategies of DBT are based in the dialectical perspective of acceptance and change. This is achieved through a balance of problem-solving skills and validation. The *problem-solving skills* utilized in DBT are similar to those in CBT and other cognitive and behavioral interventions. To accurately develop a treatment hierarchy, the therapist conducts a behavioral assessment. From this assessment, a problem is identified as well as the likely cause(s) and barriers to resolution of the problem. Upon completion of the assessment, the specific target behaviors are identified and a strategy for solving the problem is implemented through skills training, homework, and other behavioral interventions. Contingency management, shaping, extinction and punishment, exposure-based procedures, cognitive restructuring, and consequence tracking are commonly used behavioral and cognitive strategies (Koons, 2008; Linehan, 1987, 2015).

Validation strategies are an integral part of DBT and what separates it from traditional cognitive and behavioral interventions. Validation strategies include reciprocal communication, cheerleading, and general, emotional, behavioral, cognitive, and functional validation. The focus of the validation strategies is to soothe the client, diminish self-invalidation, teach emotion observation and labeling skills, and provide opportunities for open emotional expression. The purpose of validation strategies is to enable better self-thinking and behavior management abilities and to diminish negative self-assessment. Validation strategies are utilized in both individual and group sessions. The therapist or facilitator uses purposeful validation to increase the therapeutic alliance. Effective use of validation allows a client to feel heard and acknowledged by the therapist and facilitator, which creates opportunities for problem-solving. Oftentimes, validation is a useful strategy for de-escalation of emotional reactivity, which will allow for participation in situational problem-solving (Koons, 2008; Linehan, 1987, 2015).

Empirical Support and Critique of the Dialectical Behavior Therapy Model

DBT has been found to be one of the more effective psychotherapeutic approaches to treating BPD, particularly in reducing suicidal and parasuicidal behaviors, hospitalizations, and use of emergency room services, angry outbursts, and other behaviors linked to treatment dropout (Cristea et al., 2017; Linehan et al., 2006; Stoffers et al., 2012). DBT has been adapted over the years for use with different diagnoses and populations, including older adults, substance use disorders, eating disorders, and mood disorders. The results of these adaptations have demonstrated efficacy in the reduction of problem behavior, such as binge eating or substance use (Linehan & Dexter-Mazza, 2014). DBT has also been modified to a skills-only group. This adaptation was found to decrease symptoms of mood disorders, emotional dysregulation, and symptoms of PTSD (Linehan & Dexter-Mazza, 2014).

The primary critique of DBT is the difficulty of maintaining fidelity to the model in frontline clinical work. The model requires a considerable amount of staff and resources that are not always available to agencies. Furthermore, the amount of time and training required to practice DBT is a barrier to effective implementation of the model. The challenging nature of the population combined with the intensive requirements of the model can be stressful for clinicians and supervisors. Finally, empirical studies have also identified several other approaches to treating

BPD with comparable outcomes to DBT indicating the need for further clinical trials that compare DBT with these other approaches in order to assess efficacy (Cristea et al., 2014; McMain et al., 2009).

CASE STUDY 10.1

Background information. Carrie is a 35-year-old Caucasian female referred by court order for outpatient assessment and treatment for mental illness and substance abuse. Carrie is a bright, engaging, and humorous individual. When asked what goals she would like to achieve as part of therapy, she states, "I just want to get my life somewhat stable so I can work a little and keep an apartment and not kill myself or anyone else." In the past year, she has lost two jobs and has been forced to move twice due to her aggressive behavior and substance use. For 6 months, she was homeless "surfing on my friends' couches." Currently, she has a studio apartment on the south side of the city. She is not currently employed and is living off some savings, support from parents and her small unemployment check from her last job, which will run out in two months.

During the initial intake assessment, Carrie reveals that she recently relapsed after two years of sobriety from cocaine. She began abusing substances again when she lost her job as a store clerk. When asked about the circumstances of her termination, she states, "Those people were just looking for a reason to get rid of me. They were always talking about all the things I did wrong. I got mad and told them off." After her dismissal, she tells you that she went on a cocaine and alcohol binge for several days. During this binge, she was arrested for assault. It is this incident that precipitated her referral to treatment.

When probed about the circumstances of the assault. Carrie states, "I was at a bar and I was drinking. I was in the bathroom, watching this woman next to me and she was so beautiful. She had gorgeous hair. I asked her if I could borrow her brush and she looked at me funny. She said, 'no,' and started to walk out. She pissed me off. She looked at me like I was a piece of crap. So, I grabbed her by her hair, spun her around and punched her in the face. Then all the security came in and arrested me. I think the band at the bar set me up to meet her in the bathroom because they didn't want me there."

During the assessment, Carrie discloses a childhood history of sexual and physical abuse from a neighbor and an uncle. She has also been in a number of physically and sexually abusive adult relationships. She reports that she briefly became a sex worker at the age of 25 to support her cocaine use. Carrie has numerous arrests, but this is her first possible felony charge. She reports being arrested for getting into fights, stalking a former boyfriend, and disorderly conduct. Most of these incidents occurred within the context of a relationship with a man. She has never been married and has a history of multiple relationships, many of which involve interpersonal violence. You probe further about her relationships and she reveals that her last two relationships ended because of her anger. She states, "They would say things to me or not want to come over and I would get mad. I'd curse them out and then when I wasn't mad anymore I would call them all the time. They would just stop answering the phone or they would put a restraining order on me because I would stalk them at home and at work … you know, sometimes this is just too hard. I get so lonely and when I am not in a relationship I often don't really know who I am. My former therapist said that I need to be in a relationship because I can't stand to be with myself and I think she was right. If I didn't think I would go to hell, I would probably kill myself."

During these episodes, Carrie reported that she often cuts herself with a razor or burns herself with lit cigarettes. She will also call her friends or partners and threaten to kill herself if they do not answer her calls. She has had one serious suicide attempt in which she took a handful of benzodiazepines and drank a significant amount of alcohol. She needed to have her stomach pumped at the ED and was in the hospital for several days. She denies that it was an attempt at suicide, but rather, "a mistake." She states, "If I really wanted to die I wouldn't have called my friend right after I took the pills. I was just so sad. It got blown out of proportion and I ended up in the hospital for a week."

Diagnosis

In order to determine if Carrie is an appropriate candidate for DBT, the therapist must conduct a diagnostic and pretreatment assessment. Based on the information provided, it is likely that Carrie meets the criteria for BPD. Most importantly, she exhibits a long pattern of (1) suicidal behavior and self-injury, (2) emotional dysregulation, (3) frantic efforts to avoid abandonment, (4) identity disturbance, (5) chronic feelings of emptiness, (6) substance use and other impulsive and reckless behaviors, (7) chronic anger and aggression, and (8) unstable and often violent relationships. This pattern of behavior has caused significant distress and impairment resulting in the loss of relationships, employment, and stable housing.

Treatment Approach

The following section illustrates the various stage-based treatment goals for Carrie as outlined in Linehan's DBT approach (Linehan, 2015). At the beginning of the treatment relationship, the therapist will assess for Carrie's appropriateness for DBT. Carrie must be agreeable to participating in all aspects of DBT as well as agreeing to address the behaviors that will be targeted. The therapist will provide psychoeducation regarding the Biosocial Theory of BPD and orient Carrie to the expectations of DBT. This will include a discussion of the interventions that will be utilized, including the coaching calls and skills training. Once the rules of DBT have been established and Carrie has consented to participate, Carrie and the therapist will enter into a therapeutic relationship. The therapist and Carrie will conduct a comprehensive analysis of the target behaviors and determine the appropriate level of care and interventions.

In *stage 1* of DBT, the following behaviors will be targeted: (1) life-threatening behaviors (suicidal behavior, threats of suicide, self-harming [cutting] behavior), (2) therapy-interfering behaviors (history of noncompliance with treatment providers), and (3) quality-of-life–interfering behaviors (homelessness, unemployment, substance abuse, intimate partner violence, and behavior dyscontrol with serious consequences).

Upon the successful management of *stage 1* behaviors, the underlying mental health issues and trauma can begin to be addressed in *stage 2*. For Carrie, this means that she has demonstrated the ability to utilize adaptive problem-solving and situational coping skills, resolved her employment and housing situation, and no longer engages in substance use or self-harming behaviors. In *stage 2* the therapist can move toward (1) addressing her trauma symptoms through prolonged exposure and developing grounding and other coping skills to manage trauma symptoms as they arise and (2) developing strategies to cope with severe emotional dysregulation. The focus of *stage 2* will also be to help Carrie develop acceptance of her trauma and her emotional dysregulation symptoms, and to begin to develop a sense of self and self-worth. In *stage 3*, the therapist will focus on helping Carrie develop and pursue goals, manage interpersonal distress, and develop coping skills as they apply to the development and maintenance of healthy interpersonal relationships with intimate partners, friends, family, and co-workers. Lastly, *stage 4* will focus on helping Carrie build a joyful and fulfilled life through developing healthy and meaningful pursuits.

Based on the targeted behaviors, the recommended treatment includes individual treatment, which would include a focus on tracking and challenging behaviors using diary cards and behavior chain analysis of those behaviors. It will also be necessary for Carrie to be involved in the group skills training groups. Due to the severity of Carrie's impulsive behaviors, it is likely that Carrie will need regularly scheduled coaching calls in between individual sessions and skills training sessions. Due to the number of psychosocial stressors Carrie is experiencing, it may be beneficial to also include case management services that are DBT informed. It is also important to note that during treatment, the therapist who is working with Carrie must be actively involved with the other members of the DBT consultation team. Insurance companies and agency capacity often determine treatment length. Most programs require 6 to 12 months of treatment based upon the severity of the issues presented by the client.

SUMMARY POINTS

In summary, this chapter has:

- described the prevalence, pathogenesis, symptomology, and course for BPD;
- explained the biological, psychological, and social factors that contribute to the development of BPD;
- described screening and assessment practices for the effective diagnosis of BPD;
- explored the historical development, central theoretical constructs, structures, processes, evidence base, and limitations of DBT; and
- described how to identify and effectively apply the specific practices and interventions of DBT.

KEY REFERENCES

Only key references appear in the print edition. The full reference list appears in the digital product found on http://connect.springerpub.com/content/book/978-0-8261-6556-5/part/sec03/part/sec032/chapter/ch10

American Psychiatric Association. (2013). *Diagnostic and statistical manual of mental disorders* (DSM5) (5th ed.). American Psychiatric Association.

American Psychiatric Association. (2001). Practice guideline for the treatment of patients with borderline personality disorder. *American Journal of Psychiatry, 158*, 1–52.

Black, D. W., Blum, N., & Hale, N. (2004). Suicidal behavior in borderline personality disorder: Prevalence, risk factors, prediction and prevention. *Journal of Personality Disorder, 18*(3), 226–239.

Bloom, J. M., Woodward, E. N., Susmaras, T., & Pantalone, D. W. (2012). Use of dialectical behavior therapy in inpatient treatment of borderline personality disorder: A systematic review. *Psychiatric Services, 63*(9), 881–888.

Bornovalova, M. A., Huibregtse, B. M., Hicks, B. M., Keyes, M., McGue, M., & Iacono, W. (2013). Tests of a direct effect of childhood abuse on adult borderline personality disorder traits: A longitudinal discordant twin design. *Journal of Abnormal Psychology, 122*(1), 180–194.

Cristea, I. A., Gentili, C., Cotet, C. D., Palomba, D., Barbui, C., & Cuijpers, P. (2017). Efficacy of psychotherapies for borderline personality disorder: A systematic review and meta-analysis. *JAMA Psychiatry, 74*, 319–328. https://doi.org/10.1001/jamapsychiatry.2016.4287

Crowell, S. E., Beauchaine, T. P., & Linehan, M. M. (2009). A biosocial developmental model of borderline personality disorder: Elaborating and extending Linehan's theory. *Psychological Bulletin, 135*(3), 495–510.

Distel, M. A., Middeldorp, C. M., Trull, T. J., Derom, C. A., Willemsen, G., & Boomsma, D. I. (2011). Life events and borderline personality features: The influence of gene-environment interaction and gene-environment correlation. *Psychological Medicine, 41*, 849–860. https://doi.org/10.1017/S0033291710001297

Donegan, N. H., Sanislow, C. A., Blumberg, H. P., Fulbright, R. K., Lacadie, C., Skudlarski, P., Gore, J. C., Olson, I. R., McGlashan, T. H., & Wexler, B. E. (2003). Amygdala hyper-reactivity in borderline personality disorder: Implications for emotional dysregulation. *Biological Psychiatry, 54*, 1284–1293.

Grant, B. F., Chou, S. P., Goldstein, R. B., Huang, B., Stinson, F. S., Saha, T. D., Smith, S. M., Dawson, D. A., Pulay, A. J., Pickering, R. P., & Ruan, W. J. (2008). Prevalence, correlates, disability, and comorbidity of DSM-IV borderline personality disorder: Results from the wave 2 national epidemiologic survey on alcohol and related conditions. *Journal of Clinical Psychiatry, 69*, 533–545.

11

Trauma-Informed Care for Social Workers: Theory and Practice

Jill Levenson

LEARNING OBJECTIVES

By the end of this chapter, you should be able to:

- define trauma and distinguish trauma-informed care from trauma-specific interventions,
- conceptualize client presenting problems through the lens of trauma,
- describe what it means to respond to clients and interact with them in a trauma-informed way, and
- apply ideas that translate trauma-informed principles into practice.

INTRODUCTION: DEFINING AND UNDERSTANDING TRAUMA

I once heard that the children's television host Mr. Rogers carried a quote in his wallet from a social worker. It said: "Frankly, there isn't anyone you couldn't learn to love once you've heard their story." These words bring home the essence of the social work profession: to start where the client is and to understand behavior without judging (Hepworth et al., 2016). The words take on an even more significant meaning when we recognize the prevalence of trauma in the lives of social service clients and realize that trauma symptoms often masquerade as presenting problems and undesirable behavior. In 2018, Oprah Winfrey shared a similar sentiment in an interview on the CBS show *60 Minutes*, describing how becoming trauma informed changed how she thinks about everyone in her life. Sandra Bloom (2007), who pioneered the Sanctuary Model of trauma-informed care (TIC), stressed that understanding trauma is not just about acquiring knowledge. It's about changing the way you view the world. It's about shifting the helping paradigm from "What is wrong with you?" to "What happened to you?" (Bloom, 2007).

Trauma is very common in American society, and it is therefore important for social workers to intentionally engage in trauma-informed practices (Bent-Goodley, 2018; Substance Abuse and Mental Health Services Administration [SAMHSA], 2014a). Clients are usually referred to social services at times of personal crisis, and the focus of intervention tends to be on the current presenting problem rather than on early traumatic experiences (Knight, 2015). However, current problems can intersect with the legacy of past adversities. Social workers should be aware of the ways that distant trauma can contribute to presenting problems, and how trauma-related dynamics might manifest within the helping relationship. While the terms *trauma-informed care* and *trauma-informed practice* are often used interchangeably, "*practice* is more accurately applied to clinical intervention, while *care* refers to the organizational context within which services are provided to clients" (Knight, 2018, p. 4). This chapter first describes the definitions of trauma, its prevalence, and the ways in which trauma can impact people throughout their lives. Then, the principles and components of TIC are reviewed. Finally, specific suggestions are offered for translating TIC principles into trauma-responsive social work practices. A case study illustrates the principles and practices of TIC.

WHAT IS TRAUMA?

Trauma results from a direct or witnessed experience that threatens a person's sense of physical or psychological safety (American Psychiatric Association [APA], 2013). According to SAMHSA (2014a), "[I]ndividual trauma results from an event, series of events, or set of circumstances that is experienced by an individual as physically or emotionally harmful or life-threatening and that has lasting adverse effects on the individual's functioning and mental, physical, social, emotional, or spiritual well-being" (p. 7). Trauma can take many forms, but usually involves an event that is unexpected and out of a person's control, leaving them feeling physically or psychologically threatened with a sense of helplessness and fear (Herman, 1997). Following a traumatic event, people may have difficulty sleeping, eating, or concentrating; they might have nightmares, hyperarousal to stimuli in the environment, or negative moods. These are common posttraumatic stress symptoms that can last for a short time or for years following the incident (APA, 2013).

Examples of trauma include victimization, natural disaster, illness, accident, or an unexpected event that leaves a person feeling distressed and that compromises their typical coping skills (Herman, 1997). *Acute* trauma results from a single incident, while repeated and prolonged exposure is known as *chronic* trauma (such as experiencing or witnessing domestic violence). *Complex* trauma occurs when someone is exposed to multiple traumatic events, often accumulating over time, that often include interpersonal victimization (Herman, 1997). Social workers must also be aware that oppression, discrimination, and marginalization of poor and minority groups have roots in the cultural and historical traumas associated with misuse of privilege and power; poverty and social injustice can create a vicious cycle of hopelessness, victimization, and lost potential (Pettus-Davis & Epperson, 2015).

Adverse Childhood Experiences

In 1997, the Centers for Disease Control and Prevention (CDC) began a study involving 17,000 adults to determine rates of specific types of childhood trauma in the United States. They studied 10 types of adverse childhood experiences (ACEs) and devised a scale asking about childhood abuse, neglect, and family dysfunction (Felitti et al., 1998). This groundbreaking ACE study found high reported rates of *abuse* (emotional = 11%, physical = 28%, and sexual = 21%), *neglect* (emotional = 15%; physical = 10%), and *household dysfunction*, which was defined as growing up in a home with domestic violence (13%), an absent parent (23%), substance abuse (27%), mental illness (19%), or an incarcerated (5%) member of the household. The results confirmed that child maltreatment and family dysfunction are common in American families. You can learn more about the ACE study, and download the ACE tool, at https://www.cdc.gov/violenceprevention/aces/index.html.

One's ACE score can range from 0 to 10 and reflects the number of different types of childhood traumas endorsed by the individual (Table 11.1). Higher scores indicate the accumulation of a diverse range of trauma. Multiple forms of child abuse and chaotic family life often occur simultaneously, and having experienced one type of childhood trauma significantly increases the chances of other adversities (Dong et al., 2004; Finkelhor et al., 2011). Research has clearly and consistently demonstrated the detrimental impacts of cumulative childhood trauma on behavioral, medical, and psychosocial well-being in adulthood (Anda et al., 2010; Briere & Elliot, 2003; Felitti et al., 1998; Maschi et al., 2013). As ACE scores increase, so does the risk for a

TABLE 11.1 ACE SCALE ITEMS AND PREVALENCE RATES IN THE CDC SAMPLE	
While You Were Growing Up, During Your First 18 Years of Life	**CDC**
1. Did a parent or other adult in the household often or very often swear at you, insult you, put you down, or humiliate you? Or act in any way that made you afraid that you might be physically hurt?	11%
2. Did a parent or other adult in the household often or very often push, grab, slap, or throw something at you? Or ever hit you so hard that you had marks or were injured?	28%
3. Did an adult or person at least 5 years older than you ever touch or fondle you or have you touch their body in a sexual way? Or attempt or actually have oral, anal, or vaginal intercourse with you?	21%
4. Did you often or very often feel that no one in your family loved you or thought you were important or special? Or your family didn't look out for each other, feel close to each other, or support each other?	15%
5. Did you often or very often feel that you didn't have enough to eat, had to wear dirty clothes, and had no one to protect you? Or your parents were too drunk or high to take care of you or take you to the doctor if you needed it?	10%
6. Were your parents separated or divorced, or not married to one another?	23%
7. Was your mother or stepmother often or very often pushed, grabbed, slapped, or had something thrown at her? Or sometimes often or very often kicked, bitten, hit with a fist, or hit with something hard? Or ever repeatedly hit at least a few minutes or threatened with a gun or knife?	13%
8. Did you live with anyone who was a problem drinker or alcoholic, or who used street drugs?	27%
9. Was a household member depressed or mentally ill, or did a household member attempt suicide?	19%
10. Did a household member go to prison or jail?	5%

ACE, adverse childhood experience; CDC, Centers for Disease Control and Prevention.
Source: https://www.cdc.gov/violenceprevention/childabuseandneglect/acestudy/about.html.

variety of problems later in life, including chemical dependency, suicidality, depression, cigarette smoking, physical diseases, obesity, alcoholism, intimate partner violence, sexually transmitted diseases, and unintended pregnancies (Felitti et al., 1998). The original 10 ACE items are only the tip of an iceberg; clearly there are many other childhood traumas that can impact a young life. Researchers are making efforts to expand and improve the ACE tool by studying additional early adversities such as poverty, bullying, death of family members or other losses, out-of-home placement, and exposure to community violence (Finkelhor et al., 2015).

Impact of Adverse Childhood Experiences

Growing up in a home with chronic abuse, neglect, or other sorts of family problems can introduce profound feelings of powerlessness at a young age (Bloom, 2013). ACEs are considered relational trauma, which occurs when caregivers are simultaneously *needed* and *dangerous* or *unavailable* (Steele et al., 2016). A child might feel afraid or alone, unwanted, threatened, or ignored by people on whom they are dependent, in the very place that is supposed to feel safest. In other cases, parental caretaking may be loving but inconsistent due to physical or mental illness, the stressors of poverty, or substance abuse. Over time, a traumatized child may adopt "maladaptive" coping strategies that are protective in the traumagenic environment but counterproductive in other settings. Cognitive schemas of mistrust or self-blame may become part of one's interpersonal patterns and worldview (Bloom, 2013; van der Kolk, 2006; Young et al., 2003).

The dynamics of child abuse include betrayal at the hands of a trusted person (often a care-giver), violation of hierarchical boundaries (power differentials inherent in age or role), keeping of secrets, and distortion of reality in a way that reinforces the values, beliefs, and behaviors of the abuser (Elliott et al., 2005; Harris & Fallot, 2001; Teyber & Teyber, 2017). In abusive environments, a victim's voice is denied or ignored, and the victim feels powerless to alter or leave the relationship (Harris & Fallot, 2001). Invalidation exacerbates the psychological consequences of trauma, but trauma is mitigated when clients are supported in a way that allows their traumatic stress to be expressed and processed (Whitfield, 1998).

There is a complex set of bio-psycho-social links between child trauma and its long-term consequences (Anda et al., 2010). The cumulative stress of childhood adversity increases the production of stress-related hormones associated with fight-or-flight responses, which inhibits the growth and connection of neurons in the brain (van der Kolk, 2006). These changes can contribute to impairments in self-management, attachment, and cognitive processing (Anda et al., 2006, 2010). The reciprocity between the childhood environment and neurobiology is further impacted by accumulating cascade effects: An early disadvantage in one domain impacts functioning and mastery in other developing areas (Masten & Cicchetti, 2010; Rutter et al., 2006).

For instance, changes in the brain from early trauma can affect executive functioning such as impulse control, information processing, and self-regulation. This can lead to behavioral problems in the school setting, which then compromise academic and social competence. A child's "hyperactive" behavior might make it difficult to learn, and might also elicit negative feedback from teachers and classmates. Teachers may become frustrated, impatient, and critical, or other students may not want to play with a child who cannot take turns, wait in line, or follow the rules of a game. The child may get labeled as naughty or weird. As time goes on, this may place the child at increased risk for anxiety and depression or for association with delinquent peers who provide social acceptance and a sense of belonging (Rutter et al., 2006).

Adult Trauma

Of course, interpersonal traumas that parallel ACEs can occur in adulthood too. For instance, adults can be victimized by physical or emotional abuse, domestic violence, or sexual assault. Substance addiction can be a way to self-medicate after trauma, and it can also contribute to trauma for self and for family members. Mental health problems (and related hospitalizations and/or suicidality) can have traumatic impacts on self and loved ones, as can arrest or incarceration. Finally, divorce can create much pain and loss and usually represents a traumatizing life transition. Other forms of psychological injury in adulthood include highly stressful life events, a toxic workplace, or cultural, historical, and community trauma related to poverty, marginalization, and discrimination (Kuelker, 2019; St. Vil et al., 2019). Adult traumatic experiences can also lead to neurobiological impacts and maladaptive coping.

CONCEPTUALIZING PRESENTING PROBLEMS THROUGH THE TRAUMA LENS

There is a paradigm shift that occurs when we begin to conceptualize presenting problems as symptoms of trauma. By shifting the paradigm to view client problems as survival and coping skills that developed in response to traumagenic experiences, we can begin to ask not "What's wrong with you?" but "What happened to you?" In this way, we can understand the meaning attached to those experiences, which profoundly shaped the ways clients think about themselves and others, and their expectations that the world is not a safe place. We can reframe client behaviors as a set of skills that were once adaptive in a threatening early environment but now tend to interfere with the client reaching their personal goals and establishing intimate connections with others. Like with evolution of species, adaptation behaviors evolve to help individuals adjust to the demands of the environment.

Social workers understand behavior from a person-in-environment perspective that assumes a complex intersection of bio-psycho-social factors (Kondrat, 2008). We've all engaged in the "nature versus nurture" debate about whether behavior is innate or learned. The truth is that nature intermingles with nurture; everyone is born with a temperament that may predispose them to certain characteristics, and this foundation of personality interacts reciprocally with the environment. Our relationships become a series of windows and mirrors: we learn by observing the behavior of others, and we see ourselves reflected in the ways that others treat us.

TIC emphasizes a holistic understanding of clients by thinking about problematic behaviors as rehearsed responses that once helped them cope with or adapt to a threatening environment. ACEs can disrupt neurobiological and social development, alter one's sense of self and identity, and reinforce maladaptive coping and interaction styles (Bloom, 2013; Cicchetti & Banny, 2014; van der Kolk, 2006). Developmental psychopathologists describe how we integrate past experiences into our expectations of the world (Rutter & Sroufe, 2000). In a reciprocal process, our experiences inform our expectations, and our expectations are projected onto new interactions. A pathogenic childhood environment may deprive children of relational skills that foster healthy functioning—creating a cycle of eliciting the very responses they expect and fear (Alexander, 2013).

Relational theories of social work propose that client patterns will be reenacted in the helping relationship, creating a parallel process that provides an opportunity for a corrective experience (Rasmussen & Mishna, 2018; Tosone, 2013). When our clients present for services, they may have a range of problems for which services are needed. Viewed through the lens of trauma, however, such behaviors are better conceptualized as symptoms rather than problems. Remember that early trauma induces hyperarousal, and when people grow up constantly scanning the environment for danger, they are primed to expect threats and to respond accordingly. Some people develop a sense of learned helplessness, and others take on a stance of proactive aggression. Their self-protective survival mechanisms may show up as aggressive, combative, or provocative behavior (fight response); avoidance of intimacy or tendency to self-medicate with substances, food, or compulsive behavior (flight response); or passive compliance, dependency, and difficulties setting boundaries (freeze response).

Different children in the same family can experience early life in distinctly dissimilar ways. Take, for instance, three siblings who respond to domestic violence between their parents very differently: One hides under the bed covering her ears; one tries to intervene by yelling and fighting back; and one attempts to step in and reason with the violent parent. These children are demonstrating diverse methods for dealing with distress. They grow up to interact quite differently in relationships, especially when it comes to resolving conflict and trusting others. The first tried to de-escalate her own fear by withdrawal; she becomes very passive as an adult, avoiding conflict by acquiescing to the demands of others. The second child tried to manage the intensity of their chaotic family by becoming confrontational; as an adult, his family describes him as a bully who is quick to agitation and escalation of emotions, and who has intense negative responses to any disagreement. Finally, the third child, who attempted to "make peace" and negotiate between her parents, became an attorney; the courtroom is the only place she feels in control and where she successfully uses the skills that were futile in her childhood home.

By understanding the meaning attached to traumatic events and the dynamics of early relationships, the clinician can conceptualize the role of coping strategies that were once adaptive
in the abusive childhood environment but prove to be unhealthy or harmful to self or others
across various domains of adult functioning. TIC emphasizes a holistic understanding of the
individual in the context of their collective life experiences. Maladaptive (sometimes irrational
or even abusive) attempts to cope with emotional distress are reframed as survival skills that
were programmed by painful life experiences, have been well rehearsed, and have become
ingrained. Maladaptive coping was once necessary to survive in a traumagenic environment
and sometimes interferes with the capacity to establish healthy interpersonal relationships and
boundaries. In some cases, however, it transforms into resilience.

FOCUS ON STRENGTHS AND RESILIENCE

Clearly, many children are quite resilient and thrive despite difficult circumstances. Social
workers view clients with a focus on their strengths (Saleebey, 2011). Resilience is an individual's ability to effectively adapt to stress and adversity in a healthy and integrated way over the
passage of time (Southwick et al., 2014). Resilience develops through human connections with
supportive others, internal strengths, and external resources. Research indicates that a robust
predictor of resilience for children is having at least one adult who believes in them and provides support, guidance, validation, and hope (Fraser et al., 2004; Shonkoff, 2016). In healthier
families, parents provide this for their children. In families where nurturing caregivers are
absent, children may find support through relatives, teachers, or parents of friends. It is never
too late to build and fortify resilience through collaborative and empowering relationships with
our clients. We can help them focus on their strengths, increase hope toward the future, cultivate emotional awareness, enhance effective communication, improve self-regulation, establish
support networks, and develop a flexible repertoire of coping skills.

By using a strengths-based approach, we help our clients transcend trauma and enable posttraumatic growth. In this way, we can help clients decrease problematic behavior, choose more
healthy relationships, deal with crises more effectively, and parent and protect their own children in a more nurturing and responsive manner—thereby interrupting the often intergenerational cycle of trauma and victimization (Harris & Fallot, 2001; Tedeschi et al., 2015).
Strengths-based and trauma-informed social work services help clients to engage in better reality testing and self-correction, and to face vulnerability with healthy coping, intact boundaries,
and an expanded range of problem-solving skills.

WHAT IS TRAUMA-INFORMED CARE?

TIC is a model of service delivery that incorporates evidence about the prevalence, neuroscience,
and impact of early trauma on behavior across the lifespan. Early advocates for TIC recognized
that social and psychiatric services designed to help patients could actually re-traumatize them
(Bloom, 2013; Harris et al., 2001). Health and mental health services should provide a sanctuary
from harm—a place where it is safe to be vulnerable and to heal. These TIC pioneers argued for
ensuring that important basic components are integrated into the way care is delivered. *Safety,
trust, choice, collaboration,* and *empowerment* should be consistently interwoven and applied
throughout the intake, assessment, treatment, and discharge process. Within an organization,
from the top down and the bottom up, every employee has a role to play in a trauma-informed
approach: "One does not have to be a therapist to be therapeutic" (SAMHSA, 2014a, p. 11). When
put into practice, adherence to these concepts minimizes the likelihood of re-enacting disempowering dynamics in the helping relationship. They capitalize on the opportunity to create a corrective experience for traumatized clients, generating new expectations of hope and connection.

PRINCIPLES OF TRAUMA-INFORMED CARE

Principles of TIC fit well within the environmental context and bio-psycho-social frameworks of evidence-based social work (Drisko & Grady, 2015; Knight, 2015; Kondrat, 2008; Mishna et al., 2013; Saleebey, 2011; Uehara et al., 2013). Trauma-informed social workers create service environments where emotional safety is paramount, with client-centered practices that facilitate trust, respect, choice, collaboration, hope, and shared power (Bloom, 2013; Brown et al., 2012; Fallot & Harris, 2009; Harris et al., 2001; Levenson, 2017; SAMHSA, 2014a). According to the concept of TIC put forth by SAMHSA, there are four core guiding principles to TIC, called the "Four Rs." A program, organization, or system that is trauma informed:

1. *Realizes* the widespread impact of trauma and understands potential paths for recovery;
2. *Recognizes* the signs and symptoms of trauma in clients, families, staff, and others involved with the system;
3. *Responds* by fully integrating knowledge about trauma into policies, procedures, and practices; and
4. Seeks to actively *Resist Re-traumatization* in the service delivery setting. (SAMHSA, 2014a, p. 9)

SAMHSA's trauma-informed approach adheres to these core principles rather than to a pre-scribed set of practices, interventions, or procedures (SAMHSA, 2014a). These principles generalize across diverse service delivery settings, although terminology and application may differ according to the specific problem or population. SAMHSA emphasizes the importance of helping relationships in the recovery and resilience of individuals and families impacted by trauma. Trauma-informed services are different from targeted interventions that have been tested in experimental designs; rather, they are built on a foundation of evidence from neuro-biological, psychological, and social research about the etiology and impact of trauma. They incorporate this knowledge into effective clinical practices to prioritize and enhance consumer engagement, empowerment, and collaboration (SAMHSA, 2014a).

TIC is constructed on the client's need to be respected, informed, connected, and hopeful regarding their own recovery (Bloom & Farragher, 2013; Harris et al., 2001). Many clients have encountered disdain, contempt, or judgment from others in their lives, even from helping professionals. Clients need social workers who can listen with curiosity, compassion, kindness, and respect, asking questions that give the message: "I'm genuinely interested in understanding your experience." SAMHSA's *Concept of Trauma and Guidance for a Trauma-Informed Approach* describes the six key fundamental features of TIC (SAMHSA, 2014a, pp. 11–12):

Safety: Throughout the organization, all staff and clients (whether children or adults) should feel physically and psychologically safe. The physical setting and interpersonal interactions promote a sense of safety, which clients contribute to defining. Simply recognizing the possible existence of traumatic history goes a long way in developing safe service environments. Warm and welcoming surroundings will create a sense of serenity and safe space for clients (Elliott et al., 2005). Safe relationships are consistent, predictable, and non-shaming.

Trustworthiness and transparency: Policies and practices that impact clients and staff are implemented with transparency. Within the organizational hierarchy, maintaining trust with clients, employees, and stakeholders is a prominent goal. When the client's need for safety, respect, and acceptance is recognized, an atmosphere of trust can be established (Elliott et al., 2005). Trust is earned and demonstrated over time. By eliminating ambiguity and vagueness, clients can anticipate what is expected of them and what they can expect from their service providers (Harris & Fallot, 2001).

Peer support: Peer support and mutual self-help are key vehicles for establishing hope that healing and change are possible. The term "peers" (often other trauma survivors) refers to individuals with similar experiences who become reciprocal caregivers in their own collective recovery. There is almost nothing more reassuring than sitting with others who seem to "get it." This shared humanity and connection are vital to decreasing shame and isolation. Listening to the narratives and lived experiences of consumers also helps workers understand what they need to promote recovery and healing.

Collaboration and mutuality: Importance is placed on partnering with clients and neutralizing power imbalances. Healing happens in relationships through shared power and decision-making; we facilitate self-determination and autonomy by supporting and guiding clients to explore their options and identify their best choices (National Association of Social Workers [NASW], 2018). The inherent power disparities in the worker–client relationship require constant attention. Because many ACE survivors were betrayed by those who were supposed to protect and care for them, the helping relationship is fraught with potential for re-traumatization. Clients may be motivated to please others, conform to authority, and to seek acceptance and attention; they may be inclined toward instinctive compliance and may need to be reminded that they have the right to ask questions, refuse treatment, or make requests. A truly collaborative therapeutic relationship is one in which treatment goals are discussed and agreed upon together, based on the social worker's professional knowledge along with the client's expertise about their own life history and scope of coping responses.

Empowerment, voice, and choice: Workers and agency leaders should recognize and build on strengths, fostering a belief in resilience, and in the ability of individuals, organizations, and communities to heal and thrive. Organizational leaders understand the salience of power differentials and ways in which clients, historically, have been denied voice and choice and are often recipients of coercive or oppressive treatment. Thus, collaborative decision-making and goal setting is modeled to help clients develop self-advocacy skills. Social workers facilitate recovery instead of trying to control it with paternalistic or moralistic case planning. Trauma-informed services strive to maximize clients' choices and control over their own recovery, helping them to transform from victims to survivors who direct and own their life decisions and the associated outcomes (Elliott et al., 2005). True empowerment occurs with a strength-based approach that reframes symptoms as adaptation and highlights resilience over pathology. Above all, TIC ensures that disempowering dynamics are avoided by professionals in the helping relationship.

Cultural, historical, and gender issues: Social workers should seek to avoid cultural stereotypes and be aware of implicit biases (e.g., based on race, ethnicity, sexual orientation, age, religion, gender identity, socioeconomic status). TIC appreciates the value of cultural connections. Agency values should promote policies and practices that are responsive to the diverse racial, ethnic, and cultural needs of client populations. Some racial, ethnic, and sexual minority groups have long legacies of historical trauma due to slavery, denial of civil rights, and social policies that have created enormous and unjust obstacles for them. We know that historical trauma can be transmitted intergenerationally, epigenetically, and through family dynamics. Early adversity is linked to social problems, and, though interventions for individuals are important, communities also need to invest in human capital in the interest of public good (Larkin et al., 2014).

TRAUMA-INFORMED PRACTICES: WHAT TO SAY, WHAT TO DO, AND HOW TO DO IT

Some clients seek trauma-specific therapy after a specific event that has caused difficulties coping. There are many evidence-based interventions to reduce traumatic stress symptoms and assist with developing coping strategies, such as cognitive therapies, memory reconsolidation techniques, and mindfulness strategies (Cohen et al., 2012; Najavits, 2002; Strand et al., 2013; van der Kolk, 2014). TIC, however, is a framework for understanding the nexus between current presenting problems and maladaptive survival skills that evolved due to early adversity.

TIC doesn't just treat trauma; it produces corrective encounters to change the way clients experience the world.

SAMHSA (2014a) describes the three Es of trauma: events, experience, and effects. *Events* and circumstances can be very frightening and cause psychological harm. It is the individual's *experience* of the trauma that can determine its longer term impact. In other words, people attach meaning to the things that happen to them, and this meaning can shape their view of the world, themselves, and others. For more resilient people, a terrible trauma can mean that hard things happen, but you learn you can get through it, and still perceive the world as a generally safe place. In other circumstances, someone might interpret their experience as something they deserved because they believe they are bad. These interpretations, which reflect an intersecting web of thoughts, feelings, and experiences, can lead to *effects* of trauma that vary in duration and severity for each unique individual.

TIC fosters an alliance of human connection to counteract the effects of trauma through a corrective experience that helps create a new narrative of meaning (Harris et al., 2001; Knight, 2015). Many agencies have adopted TIC initiatives and many social workers are familiar with its basic principles; it is challenging, however, to translate these ideals into real-world service delivery (Berliner & Kolko, 2016). Following are some ideas for translating TIC into action (Levenson, 2020).

Use Person-First Language

Disparaging or stigmatizing labels can become internalized into one's personal narrative and self-concept (Goffman, 1963; Maruna et al., 2004). Self-fulfilling prophecies evolve when an individual adopts assumptions made by others and then behaves in a way that is consistent with those notions (Paternoster & Iovanni, 1989). Our "looking-glass self" is formed by seeing ourselves reflected in how others treat us, and in this way, we construct our social identity (Cooley, 1902). Person-first language avoids labeling and separates the behavior from the person (Willis, 2017). The NASW code of ethics strongly values personal dignity and worth, and requires us to use respectful and non-derogatory language to describe those with whom we work (NASW, 2018). The *Publication Manual of the American Psychological Association* guides us to use neutral language that puts the person first (American Psychological Association, 2010). Words that are negative or pejorative ignore strengths-based principles and reinforce stigma. For instance, social workers should avoid labels like "offender" or "junkie," instead describing a client as someone who has engaged in criminal behavior or struggled with addiction (Robinson, 2017). Instead of saying "he's bipolar" or "she's an abuser," person-first language would state "he is a person with bipolar disorder" or "she engaged in abusive behavior."

Remember What People Need in a Crisis

Though childhood trauma is not uncommon, most clients initiate services for a recent crisis and not for past trauma (Knight, 2018). The crisis can leave a client feeling helpless and scared, reactivating posttraumatic stress. Help-seeking itself can produce feelings of vulnerability and further exacerbate hyperarousal and dysregulation (Pattyn et al., 2014). To those who grew up in abusive or neglectful homes, asking for help can seem futile or dangerous. Asking for help may activate shame, which is reinforced if clients encounter worker judgment or disdain. Thus, many clients enter our service systems with apprehension. Social service bureaucracies can be oppressive and disempowering, and many clients have encountered professionals who responded with paternalistic authoritarianism (i.e., telling clients what they should or must do). We should also be cognizant of the many ways in which our clients (especially impoverished, minority, and marginalized groups) have had limited voice and choice (SAMHSA, 2014b). In a crisis, people need to regain a sense of control and to break problems down into manageable parts so that they can explore and evaluate their alternatives. However, at times of high stress, it can be difficult to focus and problem-solve effectively. From the first point of entry into services, social workers and agency staff who exhibit a calm, warm, and welcoming demeanor provide hope that, perhaps for the first time ever, there is more to be gained than lost by relying on others for help.

Safe Relationships Are Predictable, Consistent, and Nonshaming

Helping relationships must feel safe, and safe relationships are predictable, consistent, and non-shaming. Relationship safety occurs when expectations are clear, foreseeable, and consistent, and rules are transparent and imposed impartially. However, boundaries must also be flexible enough to respond to unique circumstances without unnecessary rigidity (Najavits, 2009). Social workers are often viewed as authority figures, so it is important to demonstrate trustworthiness, dependability, and fairness. When social workers make mistakes, we should take responsibility, apologize when appropriate, and correct our actions, modeling permission for imperfection along with accountability and humility.

Safety can also be enhanced with social worker authenticity and clear relational boundaries (Covington, 2007; Tosone, 2013). Due to early relational trauma, some clients may be mistrustful and wary of professional helpers (Alexander, 2013). A lack of trust can be adaptive—skepticism protects the client from an expectation of betrayal, which is based on past experiences. What might appear at first glance to be a lack of motivation or resistance to services might actually be viewed as a useful and protective defense against feelings of vulnerability (Steele et al., 2016).

The social worker's style of interaction should be genuine and nonthreatening, warm, and positive (Rogers, 1961), allowing people to disclose information at their own pace and build trust gradually. This can be challenging when agencies require documentation of assessment reports shortly after a first intake session. Remember, though agency documentation is important, assessment is actually an ongoing process, not a one-time event. There are stages of intimacy that all relationships go through, and by respecting self-determination in this way, the worker models a process of establishing trust through active listening and responding in a truly reliable and consistent manner. In this way we build rapport, which is essential in eliciting the information that helps us make an accurate assessment. By modeling respectful boundaries, language, and collaboration, clients learn to play an interactive role in intended outcomes and to assert needs in appropriate ways (Knight, 2015). In this way, we support the cultivation of self-advocacy and self-efficacy skills. Treating everyone with compassion and respect is crucial in building trust and interpersonal safety. It is simple but not always easy.

Create Safe Spaces

Clients need physical and psychological safety in the helping environment, and these must exist from the initial point of contact (Bloom et al., 2013; Brown et al., 2012). Call centers or hotlines should be staffed with pleasant and comforting voices that calm the anxiety of reaching out for help. Conversely, robotic telephone menus and automated responses, while efficient, can seem cold and detached without personal connection. Waiting rooms should be clean and welcoming, as opposed to one that is dingy, where toys are broken or dirty, or where the furniture feels hard and institutional. A warm entry space creates a sense of serenity and sends the message: "Your comfort is important to us, and you are important." When a receptionist or practitioner smiles and greets a client by saying "We are glad you are here," a welcoming and engaging atmosphere is projected. Many of our clients' experiences have left them feeling demeaned, judged, vulnerable, or invisible. Trauma-informed environments seek to make clients feel important, valued, and respected (Elliott et al., 2005). Strategies for creating physical and psychological comfort and security offer a single message: "This is a safe environment and we won't let bad things happen here."

Ask, Don't Tell

Perhaps the most important thing we can do to empower clients is to avoid giving advice. This can be challenging, especially when clients are stuck or seem prone to repeating what we perceive to be poor choices. Social work engagement skills emphasize active listening and open-ended questions (Hepworth et al., 2016). This translates to a process by which workers listen with curiosity and compassion, sending the message: "I want to hear what you think, I want to get to know you, and I need your input!" Therapeutic engagement begins with conveying that the worker is interested in understanding the client's unique experience and perspective.

By asking questions, we collaborate with our clients to define their own goals and the means for achieving them. When we can help them view their problems as manageable and their goals as realistic, we offer hope that the self-improvements they desire are possible. When you catch yourself wanting to give advice or tell someone what to do, change it into the form of a question instead. By asking rather than telling, we honor autonomy and self-determination, which will allow the client to meaningfully prioritize their own goals and evaluate their options to figure things out for themselves (Saleebey, 2011). The worker becomes a coach, allowing the client to direct the process while collaborating with the client to model planning and decision-making skills. This fosters the empowerment that is such a critical part of TIC.

Avoid Confrontation

Confrontational methods are sometimes found in programs for addictions, interpersonal violence, or mandated services, and are ostensibly used to encourage client accountability and challenge rationalizations used to justify undesirable behavior. Recognizing and altering flawed thinking are important goals of behavioral change (Miller & Rollnick, 2002). Confrontation, however, can replicate disempowering dynamics similar to those in abusive families. When clients are challenged in ways that seem judgmental or threatening, hyperarousal can be reactivated. A defensive posture emerges, paradoxically reinforcing the client's own unhelpful ideas. Responding to clients in a negative way can stimulate shame and fear, disrupting the therapeutic alliance and preventing clients from being forthcoming (Binder & Strupp, 1997; Streeck-Fischer & van der Kolk, 2000). It is easy to underestimate how confrontation can undermine engagement. On the other hand, nonthreatening methods like motivational interviewing (Miller & Rollnick, 2002) and active listening can eliminate the need for defensiveness. This allows the clients to safely explore problems and solutions, accept feedback, and improve communication skills.

Boundaries can be fair, firm, and consistent without being punitive. In fact, people learn best from natural or logical consequences. Punitive consequences alone are usually insufficient to facilitate change. Clients need opportunities to learn how to self-correct. Most important, practitioners should help clients examine what emotional needs might be getting met through the maladaptive behavior and explore how to meet those needs in more healthy ways.

Reframe Resistance

The TIC paradigm views client problems as well-rehearsed strategies for surviving traumagenic experiences, and workers can begin by asking "What happened to you?" instead of "What's wrong with you?" (SAMHSA, 2014a). Clients' thinking about self and others is shaped by the meaning they have attached to their experiences. These perceptions are projected into expectations of others and inevitably replicated in the helping relationship (Pearlman & Courtois, 2005; Tosone, 2013). Survivors of ACEs may be predisposed to lack of trust, anxiety about being judged, avoidance of conflict, and fear of authority figures (or, alternatively, hostility and aggression, perhaps to compensate for feelings of vulnerability).

Resistance can be reframed as ambivalence, which usually reflects a simultaneous struggle between a genuine desire to change and the need to maintain what is familiar. It is difficult for anyone to give up coping strategies without knowing what will replace them, especially when they have served to protect the individual from perceived interpersonal danger. We may sometimes doubt that a client is being honest with us, or wonder why clients sabotage success if true motivation for change really exists. The social worker should expect and embrace resistance and provide an accepting environment for reflection about the pros and cons of change.

Coach De-escalation, Self-Regulation, and Relational Skills

Emotional competence and self-regulation are important pathways to self-efficacy, which is the capacity to achieve goals, accomplish tasks, and respond effectively to challenges (Bandura, 1977). Have you ever become frustrated with a client who doesn't learn from experience or repeatedly engages in self-sabotage? Growing up with adversity or family dysfunction can make it difficult to observe one's inner self and manage thoughts, emotions, and impulses. If healthy coping and self-control were not taught and modeled in the early home environment, clients don't know what they don't know. A trauma-informed worker recognizes that chronic early adversity can alter the architecture of the brain, possibly compromising executive functioning and self-regulation. Workers can coach clients to learn to self-soothe and de-escalate their emotions through grounding and mindfulness techniques.

In some psychiatric or correctional settings, the use of restraints and seclusion might be employed when a threat to self or others is present. Although maintaining safety and security is important, these methods can re-traumatize people with early histories of abuse or neglect (Frueh et al., 2005). Instead, de-escalation strategies can be used to diffuse the situation by asking questions in calming tones to assess the person's inner state, validate feelings, avoid invasion of personal space, and give people a chance to choose from an enumerated range of acceptable options. Restoring an internal locus of control can help build a flexible repertoire of coping skills to be used in various situations. In this way, we can teach skills for self-regulation and self-correction within a context of personal and environmental safety (Frueh et al., 2005).

Neutralize Power Struggles and Model Shared Power

It is important to neutralize power differentials between practitioners and clients, as there are subtle and unintended ways that power dynamics can intrude in a helping relationship. Because past relational trauma often involved betrayal by someone in a caretaking role, the potential for re-traumatization within social work practice must be carefully avoided (Pearlman et al., 2005; Tosone, 2013). Some survivors may be motivated to please others, avoid conflict, and passively comply with authority figures, creating a tendency to acquiesce to professionals. On the other hand, negative countertransference can lead practitioners to respond to challenging clients in a dogmatic, coercive, or rejecting manner (Binder & Strupp, 1997; Teyber & Teyber, 2017). "Bullying the bully" can replicate traumatic experiences in abusive families, and clients might resort to defensiveness or aggression to gain the upper hand in a power struggle. Instead, social workers can model shared power, demonstrating skills of cooperation, dialogue, perspective taking, negotiation, and compromise. By being aware of our own reactions and resisting controlling responses, we model how to respect the viewpoints of others and resolve conflict. Our therapeutic demeanor says: "I want to listen to you and understand your experience, but I have no need to win a debate or get into a power struggle with you."

Parallel Process and Use of Self

Trauma-informed practices emphasize attention to process over content so that the helping relationship becomes a model for improving relational and self-regulatory skills (Knight,

2015; Pearlman et al., 2005; Tosone, 2013). Attending to parallel process and use of self allows the social worker to respond to relational themes as they present themselves in the therapeutic encounter (Knight, 2018; Teyber & Teyber, 2017). Clients may engage therapists in replicating a parallel process that occurs in other areas of their life; similarly, we may be repeating a process that dominates the interactions in our own world of personal experience. The reciprocal nature of interpersonal communication gives social workers an abundance of ongoing opportunities to alter the interactions they have with clients in real time. Using trauma-informed practices, a social worker models boundaries and relational strategies they want the client to experience and take back to their other relationships (Bloom, 2010). This strategy requires, of course, self-awareness, self-reflection, and a willingness to engage in an authentic human relationship with our clients.

The use of self in therapy is different from self-disclosure (which usually refers to the sharing of personal information about the clinician with the client). Our code of ethics and best practices caution that personal sharing can bring with it many risks: It can take the focus off the client and onto the worker and may change the boundaries of the professional encounter in subtle ways. Use of self, however, does not require disclosure of personal information. Rather, it is a process by which the therapist explicitly or implicitly shares with the client the experience of being in a relationship together, in a way that is designed to promote perspective taking and gently alter ingrained patterns (Arnd-Caddigan & Pozzuto, 2008).

Clients' responses to workers often replicate their relational styles with others and reflect past relational trauma. Learn from your own reactions. What feelings does the client elicit in you? What does that tell you about what the client elicits in others? How can you respond differently than others to create a corrective experience? When you think about it this way, you can de-personalize it, and use your experience of being in a relationship with the client as a way to understand and help them. Clients will be able to practice new interpersonal skills within the helping relationship and then generalize them to others in their lives, enhancing their relationships and overall well-being.

CASE STUDY 11.1

Julie, a nurse who experienced early emotional neglect by her parents and was raped by a peer as a teen, developed beliefs that "others will reject, abandon, or hurt me; the world is a dangerous place; if people really knew me they would not love me." In order to self-medicate her internal pain and loneliness, she abused alcohol. She engaged in sexual activity with many men in order to manage her inner conflict about being close to others. Ambivalence about emotional intimacy led her to interact with others in ways that pushed people away, creating exactly what she expected and believed she deserved. These entrenched beliefs and interpersonal styles repeated themselves in the relationship with the social worker when the client was referred for substance abuse treatment after an arrest for drinking and driving.

She was a person for whom others were not inclined to feel much sympathy; Julie seemed to bring on her own problems and not learn from her past mistakes. The new DUI was a relapse after 3 years in recovery. In treatment, she was overtly hostile, demanding, defensive, and rejecting, sitting in group therapy sessions with her arms folded and insisting she'd been forced into treatment she did not need. She refused to talk in the group. The worker could have said: "Groups therapy is what we do here, and being in a group will help you get peer support from others. If you don't participate, I'll have to report to your parole officer that you aren't complying." Instead, he validated feelings and tried to partner with the client in seeking a solution: "I can see you are angry, and that being in a group is so uncomfortable for you," he said. "I want to know why that is. Can you try to help me understand?"

The client raised her voice: "All you need to understand is that I just had a few drinks one night after being sober for years. I'm not going to drink again." The worker empowered her to make a choice: "Would you be willing to have an individual session? After that, if you want to leave, you can." She angrily agreed and sat down with a scowl.

By validating her feelings, paraphrasing content, and asking open-ended questions, the worker helped her articulate her belief learned in childhood that her "own business is private, and people shouldn't talk with others about their problems." She readily admitted her disdain for the other group members and scoffed: "[H]ow are other addicts going to tell me what to do? They can't manage their lives either." The worker conceded the logic in this and then said: "It seems like it is hard for you to believe that others have anything to offer you. And the truth is that you are very self-sufficient. But I wonder if that feels lonely sometimes?" This led to a discussion about the need to keep people at a distance because "you can't count on anyone but yourself." She then described how the relapse occurred while watching a football game at the home of a coworker. She recognized that her drinking had always been a way of managing her social anxiety to feel less awkward around others; these feelings had been triggered while at the football party. She acknowledged the double bind that she was better able to remain sober when she isolated herself from others, but that this meant not having a support network. The worker had created a corrective experience by listening nonjudgmentally, and instead of insisting on a one-size-fits-all treatment plan of group therapy, he continued to see her individually to allow trust to build.

CONCLUSION

Carl Rogers (1961) described unconditional positive regard, as well as therapist authenticity, as foundational elements of the therapeutic encounter. When a client's basic need for safety and acceptance in the helping relationship is recognized, an atmosphere of trust can be established (Elliott et al., 2005). Trauma-informed practices model a healthy process of reliability, respect, collaboration, compassion, and genuineness. The relational elements of TIC help restore client value and self-worth through reinforcing and modeling healthy interactions.

Regardless of the problem, population, or intervention, when we listen with curiosity and kindness, we help our clients feel the power of human connections. In these important ways, social workers can avoid replicating dismissive or disempowering dynamics similar to those in troubled families. By allowing clients to participate in determining the course and process of treatment, we reinforce strengths and self-determination. By understanding each client in the context of their own life experiences and cultural background, therapists can engage clients in a collaborative process and dislodge barriers to healing. Using the helping relationship as a therapeutic tool, the collaborative partnership facilitates connection to others and thus exposure to a corrective emotional experience. This is the healing power of trauma-informed social work.

SUMMARY POINTS

- examine trauma and distinguish TIC from trauma-specific interventions,
- conceptualize client presenting problems through the lens of trauma,
- describe what it means to respond to clients and interact with them in a trauma-informed way, and
- explore ideas that translate trauma-informed principles into practice.

KEY REFERENCES

Only key references appear in the print edition. The full reference list appears in the digital product found on http://connect.springerpub.com/content/book/978-0-8261-6556-5/part/sec03/part/sec032/chapter/ch11

Bloom, S. L. (2013). *Creating sanctuary: Toward the evolution of sane societies*. Routledge.

Felitti, V. J., Anda, R. F., Nordenberg, D., Williamson, D. F., Spitz, A. M., Edwards, V., Marks, J. S. (1998). Relationship of childhood abuse and household dysfunction to many of the leading causes of death in adults: The Adverse Childhood Experiences (ACE) study. *American Journal of Preventive Medicine*, 14(4), 245–258.

Knight, C. (2015). Trauma-informed social work practice: Practice considerations and challenges. *Clinical Social Work Journal*, 43(1), 25–37.

Levenson, J. S. (2017). Trauma-informed social work practice. *Social Work*, 62(2), 105–113.

Levenson, J. S. (2020). Translating trauma-informed principles into social work practice. *Social Work*, 65(3), 288–298.

Substance Abuse and Mental Health Services Administration. (2014a). *SAMHSA's concept of trauma and guidance for a trauma-informed approach*. Substance Abuse and Mental Health Services Administration.

van der Kolk, B. (2006). Clinical implications of neuroscience research in PTSD. *Annals of the New York Academy of Sciences*, 1071(1), 277–293.

Client-Centered Theory

Amy Van de Motter

(adapted from the work of Michael Rothery and Leslie Tutty)

LEARNING OBJECTIVES

By the end of this chapter, you should be able to:

- understand the theoretical underpinnings of client-centered therapy,
- understand the central tenets of client-centered therapy, and
- apply client-centered therapy to individuals and groups.

INTRODUCTION

Developed by the psychologist Carl Rogers over a long career that ended with his death in 1987, client-centered (also referred to as nondirective and person-centered) therapy has been a major force in clinical mental health work and a counterweight to the deterministic behaviorism that Rogers rejected. Rogers has been seen by many as one of the foundational thinkers in the development of humanistic psychology, even as one of the most generally influential psychologists of the 20th century. His client-centered theory was a radical innovation for psychology; for social work, it was more a valuable refinement and reaffirmation of familiar principles, but it has nevertheless had a significant and beneficial impact on social work practice and education.

The fourth edition of the iconic *Handbook of Psychotherapy and Behavior Change* (Bergin & Garfield, 1994) is dedicated to "three distinguished pioneers who taught us how to study therapeutic change." Carl Rogers was one of the dedicatees; given his prominence at the time, it would have raised eyebrows had he been excluded. Later, however, in the sixth edition of Bergin and Garfield's handbook (Lambert, 2013), Rogers has become barely visible in the field he once dominated—in a volume of well over 800 pages, he receives seven brief citations.

If his name has faded over the past two decades, his work has never lost its significance: "Not only is the influence of Carl Rogers still keenly felt and expressed in many areas of life, but ... the future of person-centered and experiential therapies (PCE) is looking rosy. It is remarkable that in almost every area of life that he touched, Carl Rogers left a lasting impression" (Sanders, as cited in Thorne & Sanders, 2013, pp. 99–100; see also Kramer, 1995a).

In developing the client-centered model, Rogers considered that he had identified the *necessary* and *sufficient* conditions that lead to people changing. This is not a modest claim: The suggestion is that if one wants to be an effective helper, client-centered principles are something one must learn (they are necessary) and nothing else is required (they are sufficient).

The theory guiding this therapeutic method is a theory of *process*. As such, the approach is firmly aligned with the belief that we do not help our clients through an expertise with theories of personality, knowledge of family dysfunction, or a deep appreciation for critical ecological systems theory. Rather, we assist people's growth by providing a particular kind of relationship, through communications that have specific qualities.

According to client-centered theory, those essential qualities are the Rogerian *core conditions*: congruence, acceptance, and empathy. (As one would expect, terminology has varied over time and from one writer to another. Nuances that might distinguish *congruence* from *genuineness* or *authenticity* and similar semantic fine points are not important at this juncture.) When those interpersonal conditions are sufficiently available to us from our friends, loved ones, or social workers, we have what we need to grow personally, just as we grow physically when we have enough food and other necessities. Understanding exactly what those essential relational conditions are, and how we can learn to make them present in our work, was Rogers's main mission in life.

This is a deceptively simple general idea possessing considerable explanatory force. Also, it fits easily with social work's historic principles. Indeed, relationship has always been critical in social workers' eyes, identified as both the context and the means for facilitating change (Biestek, 1957; Coady, 1999; Perlman, 1957, 1979). Indeed, in a book that is rightly regarded as a classic on the topic, Biestek (1957) argued that the emphasis on relationship is so important that it serves to define us:

> This is one principal difference between social work and some of the other professions. In surgery, dentistry, and law, for example, a good interpersonal relationship is desirable for the *perfection* of the service, but it is not necessary for the *essence* of the service. The surgeon may not have a good bedside manner; the dentist may be inconsiderate of the patient's feelings; the lawyer may be cold and overly business-like. But if the surgeon operates successfully, if the dentist heals the ailing tooth, and if the lawyer wins the case, they have performed the essential service requested. Not so the caseworker. A good relationship is necessary not only for the perfection, but also for the essence, of the casework service in every setting. (p. 19)

For better and for worse, we constantly affect one another's experience, through "the rich interplay of one human mind with another" (Garrett et al., 1982, p. 4). Being thoroughly socially embedded as we are (see Chapter 4), this mutual influence is simply a fact of life, and Rogers wanted to understand how to harness its power in the service of client growth.

OVERVIEW OF THEORY

Understanding of Human Problems

Though his theory is heavily weighted toward process, Rogers did suggest a basic psychological dynamic for understanding how we become distressed. Human problems, he thought, can generally be understood as reflecting a state of incongruence. People experience pain when they perceive themselves falling significantly short of what, ideally, they wish to be. One of his interpreters explained this aspect of Rogers's theory:

> The client's self-image is contradicted by his life experience; thus ... two levels of self-being are ... constituted: one involving the .... idealized self; the other touching on and flowing from, the actual experience of self-in-process .... Determined to defend his self-concept ... the client is unable to admit into clear awareness those experiences that would interfere with his sense of self-worth. (Barton, 1980, p. 169)

Take, for example, a client who is experiencing distress associated with an addiction. From the perspective of Rogers's theory, one would determine that the client's distress is due to the incongruence between her goals of who she wants to be and what she wants to accomplish in her life, and her actions associated with her drug use. Perhaps, she has a goal of being a loving mother, but her actions do not reflect her as such, due to her all-consuming attention toward obtaining her drug of choice This incongruence causes the client to feel a range of distressing emotions, including shame, guilt, confusion, depression, and even anger. This differs from other problem conceptualization frameworks, such as the cognitive behavioral theory that posits the client's distress manifests as a result of the negative and maladaptive thoughts that she has *about* her life and her drug use. It is less about *what* is happening that is causing distress and more about the how that is *different* from the way the client wishes to be.

However, Rogers argued vehemently that beyond this it is counterproductive to approach clients with preconceptions in the form of theories of personality, or psychopathology, or anything else that might work against our openness to the uniqueness of people and their situations:

> The more I have observed therapists, and the more closely I have studied [the] research …. the more I am forced to the conclusion that … diagnostic knowledge is not essential to psychotherapy. It may even be that its defense as a necessary prelude to psychotherapy is simply a protective alternative to the admission that it is, for the most part, a colossal waste of time. (Rogers, 1957, pp. 101–102)

It is therefore fair to say that Rogers and his followers did not pursue a highly developed understanding of human problems. Instead, they worked to illuminate the interpersonal processes that represent a context within which healing naturally occurs. Taking the previous case example, the primary goal would be to create a therapeutic environment in which the client, with the support of the clinician, can explore and resolve the incongruence that exists between her drug use behaviors and her goal of being a loving mother, through self-identified motivation.

Conception of Therapeutic Intervention

Rogers believed that the conditions that enable us to develop in self-actualizing ways are universal. Good clinical social work and psychology have foundations in some of the same core elements as good parenting, good teaching, and the friendships that help us flourish. These elements, such as respect, genuineness, and caring for the individual, foster the growth and development needed for self-actualization, which from this perspective is what the clinical social worker has to offer the client. To the extent that our clients may be especially estranged from themselves, and potentially from friends and loved ones, they require us to provide those conditions in a skilled, well-attuned way, but there is nothing that distinguishes their needs from everyone else's in any formal sense.

Client-centered tenets about intervention and change have an apparent simplicity that can easily result in misunderstanding:

> Very early in my work … I discovered that simply listening to my client, very attentively, was an important way of being helpful. … Later a social worker, who had a background of Rankian training, helped me to learn that the most effective approach was to listen for the feelings. … I believe she was the one who suggested that the best response was to "reflect" these feelings back to the client—"reflect" becoming in time a word that made me cringe. But at that time, it improved my work as therapist, and I was grateful.
>
> But this tendency to focus on the therapist's responses had appalling consequences. … The whole approach came, in a few years, to be known as a technique. "Nondirective therapy," it was said, "is the technique of reflecting the client's feelings." Or an even worse caricature was simply that "in nondirective therapy you repeat the last words the client has said." (Rogers, 1980, pp. 137–139)

The process of change, in the client-centered view, is at once simple and complex. Simply put, people are naturally inclined toward growth, and given the right conditions they will come to know themselves more fully, heal old wounds, and develop greater authenticity and congruence. They will become more knowledgeable and honest, first in relation to themselves and then in relation to others.

As we have noted, the "right conditions" that facilitate such growth are relationships with particular characteristics: congruence, acceptance, and empathy. If we are honest, accepting, and understanding, our clients will benefit from their relationship with us. The apparent simplicity of this prescription belies the subtlety of the processes it describes, however—hence, Rogers's concern about being so easily misunderstood. We will have more to say about the complexity of the core conditions in the section on central theoretical constructs.

HISTORICAL DEVELOPMENT

Precursors and Original Development

Mary Richmond (1899) can be credited with early efforts to understand relationship and its critical importance: "Friendly visiting means intimate … knowledge of and sympathy with a … family's joys, sorrows, opinions, feelings. … The visitor that has this is unlikely to blunder …. [although] without it he is almost certain … to blunder seriously" (p. 180). This assertion is only marginally more cautious than Rogers's claims about necessity and sufficiency, and it represents an appreciation of the importance of empathic understanding that predates client-centered theory by a half century.

Richmond was a committed empiricist, convinced that careful case records in which services and their outcomes were documented would lead to an improved and scientific understanding of the helping process. In 1922, she wrote a short book reflecting on the essential nature of direct practice (*Social Casework*), in which she reported the results of her intensive analysis of six varied and well-documented cases.

A striking feature of Richmond's (1922) conclusions is the extent to which she attributed effectiveness of service with qualitative aspects of how workers *related* to their clients. More specifically, she identified a capacity for honesty, affectionate acceptance, and "imaginative sympathy" (p. 37) as critical factors in relationships that support change. When Rogers came to emphasize congruence, acceptance, and empathy in his own analysis of the effectiveness of psychotherapy, the language had changed but the fundamental insight had not. It is also notable that in each case, one of these conditions is paramount—Richmond's *imaginative sympathy* and Rogers's *empathy* are understood to be the dimension that encourages growth more than any other.

Since Richmond's early introduction of concepts such as *friendly visiting* and *sympathy*, social workers have striven for greater clarity in describing what it is about some relationships that makes them powerful tools for change. Different terms have been invoked in this effort to understand, such as *empathy* (Shaw, as cited in Biestek, 1957), *rapport, emotional bridging* (LeRoy, as cited in Biestek, 1957), some aspects of *transference* (Taft, as cited in Biestek, 1957; see also Garrett et al., 1982, which addresses the phenomenon without using the term), *engagement* (Smalley, 1967), and the *therapeutic alliance* (Coady, 1999).

As social work grew, it incorporated ideas from different disciplines, such as psychiatry and psychology, and our longstanding fascination with Freudian and related psychodynamic theories is a case in point—most observers see this development, in hindsight, as at least somewhat problematic. Like behaviorism in American psychology, Freud's theory was highly deterministic—it was this that caused Mary Richmond, among others, to worry about its implications for a field that had always been heavily committed to important social values.

Freudian theory also discouraged our traditional emphasis on relationship as the context and means for change:

> Although Freud paid some attention to the therapeutic relationship, he saw the development of insight and rationality, acquired through the analyst's interpretations, as the curative element in psychoanalysis. … Within psychoanalysis, of course, there has always been an interpersonal school, identified mostly with Sullivan and his followers, but until recently this school remained outside the mainstream of psychoanalytic theory. (Saari, 2002, p. 125)

One of Freud's early disciples was Otto Rank, who paid a heavy professional and personal cost for breaking with orthodox Freudian beliefs (Lieberman, 1985). In contrast to Freud's determinism, Rank ascribed critical importance to *creativity* and *will* (Menaker, 1982)—concepts that did not fit comfortably with the narrowly scientific worldview predominant at the time. Rank also insisted that the heart of helping was not in diagnoses, interpretations, and rationalistic analyses but in relationship (Menaker, 1982; Rank, 1964, 1989; Taft, 1958; see also Becker, 1973, 1975 for a more general, deep appreciation of Rank's thought).

Jessie Taft was the dean of the Philadelphia School of Social Work from 1934 to 1950. A friend of and collaborator with Rank, she wrote his biography (Taft, 1958) and translated some of his work into English, and it was she who brought him to the United States to share his ideas with American professionals. At the time, Carl Rogers was working with social workers in Philadelphia:

> From 1928 through 1939, Carl Rogers served as a therapist at the Society for Prevention of Cruelty to Children, in Rochester, New York. …. On his staff at the Rochester clinic were a number of social workers trained at the University of Pennsylvania's School of Social Work …. where Otto Rank had been lecturing since 1926. (Kramer, 1995b, p. 58)

The helping method identified with the University of Pennsylvania, the *functional* school of social work, drew heavily on Rank's ideas and made relationship a pivotal issue in its understanding of change—a sharp difference from the competing *diagnostic* school, which remained more committed to orthodox Freudianism. Early in his career, Carl Rogers was a colleague of social workers imbued with functional thinking; it is likely through their influence that he came to meet Rank:

> In June, 1936, intrigued by social workers who were telling him that *"relationship therapy"*—not "interpretive therapy"—was the emphasis of the Philadelphia School, Carl Rogers invited Otto Rank to Rochester to conduct a 3-day seminar on his new, post-Freudian practice of therapy. (Kramer, 1995b, p. 59)

This meeting was a turning point for Rogers, shaping his thinking for the rest of his life (Kramer, 1995b). Rogers, in turn, did much to clarify conceptually what the elements of a helpful relationship are and initiated a research program to measure those elements and their effects. The outcome was the client-centered school of counseling.

Otto Rank and Carl Rogers, then, are two prominent theorists whose thoughts imbue the client-centered framework. The complementarity of their ideas and values is remarkable given their differences in background. Rank was very much a product of European culture and education. Rogers, in contrast, was thoroughly American (Van Belle, 1980), the son of "a narrowly fundamentalist religious home" (Rogers, 1980, p. 27) and a graduate of universities in Wisconsin and New York.

Each man made an important mark by rebelling against his earlier training, looking for a way out of the limitations he experienced in the doctrines of the day. Rank replaced the rigid determinism of Freud's thinking with a theory that celebrated agency, the human capacity for creativity and choice (Menaker, 1982). Rogers rejected the deterministic, objective psychology that prevailed when he was starting out, offering in its place a humanistic "home-grown brand of existential philosophy" (Rogers, 1980, p. 39). In fact, calling his work "client-centered" and "nondirective" constitutes an important philosophical position on Rogers's part—a commitment to the belief that the resources for healing and growth are to be found primarily in the client, not in the theories and techniques of the helper.

Later Developments and Current Status

Few scholars have had the impact that Rogers enjoyed in his field. Since he began publishing his ideas in the early 1940s, he has stimulated an enormous response in terms of ongoing theory development and research. A perusal of influential journals such as *The Journal of Counseling Psychology* or *The Person-Centered Review* will verify that literally thousands of academic, research, and professional careers are rooted solidly in his work.

The client-centered model, as Rogers formulated it, has not gone unchallenged, and we indicate where problems arise toward the end of this chapter. However, it is remarkable, given the energy that has gone into its development, to note how the foundation Rogers laid—the concepts that are the primary focus of this chapter—remain essentially unaltered.

The effort to translate Rogers's general process conditions into operational behaviors has resulted in extensive catalogs of specific counseling skills (Ivey, 1988), and the application of these in education, industry, and other organizational domains has absorbed considerable interest and energy—as has their application cross-culturally (Sue et al., 1996).

Beyond these generalities, the scope of this chapter prevents our doing justice to the vast body of work that has grown out of client-centered theory. The extent to which derivatives of the basic model diverge from their roots varies; however, none challenges it in any fundamental way, and many pay frank homage to Rogers as the germinal thinker on whose shoulders they stand.

CENTRAL THEORETICAL CONSTRUCTS

We have noted a seeming simplicity about the basic client-centered formula for change. Drawing on Rank and other humanistic influences, Rogers came to the view that everyone has a creative capacity to make choices and is motivated to grow. These naturally present capacities and inclinations can be blocked or distorted by experience, with psychological pain as a consequence. However, in the context of a sufficiently nurturing relationship, the client will rediscover them and return to a healthy, self-actualizing path.

Congruence, acceptance (or unconditional positive regard), and empathy characterize the relational context that promotes such results. Although other ingredients have been recommended as client-centered thinking has evolved, these remain primary, and, as we have emphasized, need to be understood as complex processes.

Congruence

Congruence is interpersonal genuineness, honesty, and directness. The social worker who is self-aware, comfortable with themselves, and able to find ways to relate to clients that do not disguise who they are is relating congruently. What is meant, however, is far from simple encouragement to give free expression to whatever one thinks and feels. Congruence means that "the feelings the therapist is experiencing are available to him, available to his awareness, and he is able to live these feelings, be them, and able to communicate them if appropriate" (Rogers, 1961, p. 61; see also Rogers, 1980, p. 115).

Garrett et al.'s (1982) view of the requirements of social work interviewing is similarly demanding: "An interviewer's attention must continuously be directed in two ways: toward himself as well as toward his client" (p. 6). Both Garrett et al. and Rogers (1961), therefore, describe a disciplined effort to develop self-awareness and comfort with oneself. Further, congruence implies the ability to use that awareness in the service of the client, sharing aspects of our experience as it is *appropriate* to do so; that is, in a manner that is sensitively attuned to client needs and readiness.

This concept highlights the utmost importance of the social workers' attention to their own personal awareness, experiences, and development, as a parallel process to their work with their clients. This can be understood as a form of professional self-care; social workers seek to heighten their senses in a way that allows them to recognize and understand their own emotional and cognitive processes *in the moment* with the client, so that not only can efforts be made to prevent them from negatively impacting their wor but that they can be used strategically to enhance the relationship and the client's own growth. Take, for example, a client who experiences frequent interpersonal conflicts with others due to high demands of their time and emotional energy, and therefore has difficulty maintaining relationships. If the client pushes the social worker to be available more frequently, the social worker might set firm boundaries by sharing feelings of unease and defensiveness, thus illuminating the client's behaviors that are contributing to interpersonal conflicts. This congruence within the social worker serves as a mechanism for increased self-awareness and growth within the client, which would otherwise be missed had the social worker been less forthcoming by citing agency policy or a busy schedule for not meeting the client's demands.

Acceptance

The second condition that we provide clients in creating a context for growth is acceptance, or "unconditional positive regard," which "involves the therapist's genuine willingness for the client to be whatever feeling is going on in him at that moment … [and requires] that the therapist cares for the client in a non-possessive way … in a total rather than a conditional way …. and without reservations, without evaluations" (Rogers, 1961, p. 62). Thus, we work to establish with our clients a positive attitude about them as people unaffected by our reactions to how they feel or what they may have done. This implies the belief that we can (and must) cultivate a capacity for interpersonal generosity, based on a differentiated understanding of others as a complex mix of characteristics and potentials. Further, we can discipline ourselves so that client behaviors, characteristics, or experiences that distress us do not undermine this capacity. There is something about each client that we value with no strings attached—and we are able to communicate that effectively.

This concept can be a challenge for those who are new to the ideas and application of client-centered theory. Questions arise such as, "How can I show acceptance to a client who has assaulted their partner? How can I feel unconditional positive regard for someone who has harmed a child?" These questions are understandable and valid. The answer to them lies in the core values of the social work profession. Social workers value human beings and believe in the *inherent* dignity and worth of every individual, regardless of the acceptability of their actions. Knowing that people have the *natural* tendency toward growth allows the social worker to view each client in a light of humanity and potential, separate from the actions that might seem so egregious. Undoubtedly for some, this shift in thinking can be challenging, which only further highlights the importance of social workers' attention to their own emotions and cognitions during the therapeutic process. It is imperative that this acceptance of each client is felt and communicated genuinely. Therefore, constant self-reflection, peer supervision, and a consistent personal and professional self-care practice are critical.

Empathy

The third and preeminent element in a relational context for growth is empathy. Again, Rogers took considerable pains to be clear that he did not see empathy as achievable in a formulaic, superficial manner—the caricature being an expression of soulful concern and the words "I *know* how you feel!" Empathic understanding is never so simple:

> [Empathy] means that the therapist senses accurately the feelings and personal meanings that the client is experiencing and communicates this understanding to the client. When functioning best, the therapist is so much inside the private world of the other that he or she can clarify not only the meanings of which the client is aware but even those just below the level of awareness. This kind of sensitive, active listening is exceedingly rare in our lives, ... yet [it] is one of the most potent forces for change that I know. (Rogers, 1980, p. 116)

These definitions and elaborations remain consistent in Rogers's writing over time (compare with Rogers, 1959), and there are a number of elements in them that we would highlight. First, there is a role for intelligence, insight, training, and experience: The social worker should grasp *accurately* and *sensitively* the emotional content and meanings implied in what the client is saying.

Second, empathy as Rogers defines it is not simply understanding feelings: He is inclined to emphasize emotions, but also returns constantly to words like *experiencing* and *meaning*. Thus, the point of empathic understanding is to communicate awareness of both the emotional and narrative aspects of what the client presents. Perhaps the word *experiencing* is attractive because it addresses both feelings about events and the meanings attributed to them—aspects that are always so interdependent that the wisdom of separating them is questionable.

A third point is that empathy implies a strong psychological attunement by the worker to the experience of the client, but not a loss of boundaries. The therapist "can grasp the moment-to-moment experiencing which occurs in the inner world of the client as the client sees it and feels it, *without losing the separateness of his own identity* [italics added]" (Rogers, 1961, pp. 62–63). This is a clarification about which he was consistent:

> It means to sense the hurt or the pleasure of another as he senses it and to perceive the causes thereof as he perceives them but without ever losing the recognition that it is *as if* I were hurt or pleased and so forth. If this "as if" quality is lost then the state is one of identification. (Rogers, 1959, pp. 210–211)

Although empathy as a concept stresses engagement, clients are served best if we are fully able to step back, not only understanding their experience but also inviting new perspectives and options.

Why is empathy considered to be such a powerful precondition for growth? Rogers explains this by suggesting several benefits that accrue when we experience an empathic relationship:

1. Empathy "dissolves alienation" (Rogers, 1980, p. 151). Clients often feel alone in their problems, and an empathic relationship with a clinical social worker is a powerful antidote: "If someone else knows what I am talking about, what I mean, then to this degree I am not so strange, or alien, or set apart. I make sense to another human being" (Rogers, 1980, p. 151).
2. Empathic understanding has the effect of communicating to people that they are valued, and is therefore useful for repairing damaged self-esteem. It is Rogers's contention that empathy is not possible without caring, and the experience of being cared about encourages a sense of self-value.
3. Since empathy is nonjudgmental, "always free of any evaluative or diagnostic quality" (Rogers, 1980, p. 154), being empathically treated encourages self-acceptance. Aspects of ourselves from which we recoil are less corrosive to our self-esteem if we see that another person can hear about them without becoming threatened or angry—and may regard them as normal, even admirable, rather than as cause for shame and self-denigration.

4. When people receive empathic responses to their troubles, they are encouraged to self-explore, increasing their awareness and developing a richer experience of themselves. This is beneficial in and of itself, since a broader self-understanding exposes more options regarding how we can respond to situations. Further, when painful aspects of our experience are "fully accepted and accurately labeled in awareness" (Rogers, 1980, p. 158), we are able to respond more creatively to those issues.

PHASES OF HELPING

Four phases of helping characterize generalist social work practice: engagement, data collection and assessment, planning/contracting and intervention, and evaluation and termination. What can we suggest the contribution of client-centered theory is to facilitating this process?

Respecting *engagement*, the argument is simple. Relating honestly, respectfully, and empathically should speed the development of trust and openness. However, it may be that client-centered theory, interestingly, puts too much responsibility for such relationships on the worker. Recent research and theory emphasizes that predispositions of the client are powerful as well; however skilled we may be, we still depend on our clients to respond positively if an effective helping alliance is to be formed (Coady, 1999; Miller et al., 1997). What should a social worker do, then, if a client does not respond positively? From a client-centered perspective, the social worker might first reflect on the quality of the therapeutic skills they are using. The worker might assess whether or not they are *accurately* empathizing with the client or if they misinterpreted the client's experiences. The social worker might explore their own congruence between hertheir inner experience and their interactions with the client. The social worker might ask themselves whether they are having difficulty accepting the client unconditionally, which may be inadvertently communicated through words, actions, or body language. Ultimately, it is the responsibility of the social worker to have an open, honest conversation with the client in a way that allows for that relationship to shift toward a positive, therapeutic path.

With respect to *assessment*, it is our view that the client-centered approach offers critical process skills. However, we would also argue that social workers require more of a framework to enable decisions regarding the kinds of data that are to be collected. With an abused spouse, we are trained to explore safety issues, for example, even if these do not automatically emerge in our interview. Similarly, if we suspect child maltreatment, addictions, suicidal tendencies, a significant lack of supports and resources, or any of a host of potentially relevant matters, we are trained to invite discussion of those, and this training is a good thing. This does not deny the risk of forming premature hypotheses about what is important and ceasing to listen carefully to the client—Rogers's thinking and approach are very useful protections against this possibility. In addition, approaching new clients with openness, curiosity, empathy, and a genuine regard for them as individuals often helps the client feel safe in sharing personal details that are so vital to the assessment process.

With respect to *planning/contracting and intervention,* client-centered theory does not offer as much direction as social workers and their clients may require. The assumptions that appropriate goals and plans will emerge if clients have the opportunity to explore their experience, and that workers' congruence, acceptance, and empathy will be sufficient to enable clients to achieve their goals, are sometimes valid, but by no means always. What can be applied here is the foundational concept of allowing the client to drive the process when formulating goals. That is not to say that the social worker does not offer guidance, insight, and expertise during this phase. However, the worker must be cautious to not insert their own goals for the client in a way that overshadows what the client wants to achieve.

The client-centered model is not prescriptive with respect to the length of treatment, and the timing of termination is likely similar to what we see with other models. What the client-centered model offers regarding *termination and evaluation* is, again, its understanding of the process. In terminating, the opportunity for clients to reflect on their experience with the social worker and what it has meant to them is obviously very important, and an effective helping relationship is a context designed to encourage that. With respect to evaluation, the model suggests very good criteria for assessing the helping process, these being the core conditions, widely evaluated using the Barrett–Lennard Relationship Inventory (BLRI; Simmons et al., 1995) and clients' self-exploration. Properly speaking, these are process rather than outcome variables; outcomes independent of process have also been assessed in much recent client-centered research (Elliott et al., 2013), with measures employed that are familiar in research on other models as well. With respect to helping particular clients evaluate the success of their work, the model offers a process that facilitates that but does not suggest independent criteria for assessing the merits of goals achieved. Since it is not a domain-specific model, this is appropriate—outcomes to be evaluated will vary across people and client populations.

APPLICATION TO FAMILY AND GROUP WORK

If the basic thesis of client-centered theory is true, it should apply equally whether work is being conducted with an individual, family, group, or other social systems. It was, in fact, Rogers's (1980) position that communicational processes favoring the core conditions would make many diverse social settings more nurturing and supportive of learning and growth. He was a leader in the encounter group movement as it developed, and suggested applications of his work in educational settings, families, and organizations of various sizes and diverse purposes.

The direct evidence for the impact of client-centered methods in groups is not strong, perhaps due to significant methodological difficulties. To the extent that modeling takes place and group members learn effective communication skills that they can use in their efforts to support and help one another, it seems logical to think this would be beneficial. In family work, there is enough evidence to convince some reviewers that the core conditions do contribute significantly to positive outcomes (Gurman et al., 1986; Nichols & Schwartz, 2004; Sexton et al., 2004).

COMPATIBILITY WITH A GENERALIST-ECLECTIC FRAMEWORK

Though Rogers was suspicious about explanatory theory, the process orientation of the client-centered model invites eclecticism. Practitioners who consider themselves Rogerians freely incorporate concepts from schools of thought as diverse as behaviorism and psychodynamic theory.

Social workers who practice from a generalist-eclectic framework commonly recognize the contribution of client-centered thinking to their work. A powerful emphasis on the importance of relationship is one shared commitment; the deep respect in client-centered theory for the competency, personal power, and motivation toward health in the client is another commonality.

Rogers's insistence on the central importance of attunement to clients' experience has obvious relevance to work in situations where diversity is a factor. The process of achieving and communicating shared understanding across disparate frames of reference is considered part of all helping, so it is no surprise that this knowledge has been applied in work with diverse cultural groups (Rogers, 1980). That is not to say, however, that one can assume to reach a level of empathy that allows full understanding of a client's experience, especially when working with clients from diverse backgrounds. It would be naive to think that a Caucasian social worker could genuinely understand an African American client's experience with systemic racism in the United States in a way that allows the social worker to truly *feel* and *experience* this reality. Therefore, it should be the goal of the social worker to empathize with the emotion and the distress that result from the experience, rather than the experience itself, and to be congruent and genuine in acknowledging the cultural and experiential differences.

For similar reasons, the theory prescribes a process that will be helpful in work with people who are different from the social worker in terms of age or gender. However, it does not offer knowledge of general themes associated with gender or the life cycle—or a systematic understanding of social systems. Familiarity with such knowledge is important to generalist-eclectic workers and will need to be acquired from sources other than the client-centered literature if holistic assessments and effective use of life-cycle theories are to be achieved.

CRITIQUE: THE STRENGTHS AND LIMITATIONS OF THE MODEL

Today, several decades after Rogers began publishing and researching his work, there is no reason to question its profound impact on social work and other helping professions. The critical significance of relationship to the helping enterprise is now widely accepted as proven. Further, there is little dispute about the relevance to helping of the core conditions; while there are ongoing discussions about how they might best be defined and measured, there is a rather impressive consensus as to their basic credibility and importance.

There are, however, qualifications to suggest in relation to this theory. In part, these derive from Rogers's insistence that the core conditions are all there is, that they are the *necessary* and *sufficient* conditions for positive change. The latter part of this claim may evoke skepticism, especially among scholars and clinicians who employ other practice models, as this suggests those are unnecessary in clinical work. A more moderate approach might recognize and appreciate the importance and effectiveness of the client-centered model in building the therapeutic relationship, which is a foundational necessity within the use of any practice model (Miller et al., 1997).

Like all of us, Rogers brought to his work certain professional and cultural assumptions. He grew up imbued with the values of American pragmatism and the Protestant belief in individual salvation. This history sets a context within which he developed an approach to helping, which stresses (sometimes to the exclusion of all else) the need to assist clients in discovering the personal strengths and resources they possess so that they can apply them effectively in their lives. In his later years, Rogers worked for the development of better social conditions and more humane communities. However, it is still true that his theory could encourage an emphasis on the person of the client, a lack of attention to deprivations or sources of oppression in clients' environments, and how these elements contribute to the cognitive dissonance and distress of the client.

What this suggests, as in relation to formerly discussed aspects of this framework, is the universal importance of the social workers' awareness of both their own and their client's cultural contexts. Social workers and other clinicians are not immune from participating in discriminatory and oppressive actions when working with clients from diverse backgrounds, albeit generally committed unknowingly or with good intentions. In order to avoid perpetuating the very oppression that many clients experience, social workers first need to understand the attitudes, social structures, and stigma of society that exist, including those that impact the social worker's own belief systems (Lago, 2011). Despite best efforts to mitigate the power dynamic that naturally exists in a client–therapist relationship, the reality is that it is often felt strongly, especially by clients who have been disempowered and marginalized by society and its social structures.

It is therefore the responsibility of the social worker to recognize and acknowledge this dynamic, especially as it relates to the very core elements stressed in client-centered practice. Necessary considerations need to be made, such as whether the client's distress is better accounted for by internal incongruence or by external societal factors (or a combination of both). Also, especially when a clinician comes from the dominant culture and has not personally experienced oppression, they will consider how best to sensitively express accurate empathy, without undermining the client's unique experience of discrimination, as is done with every unique experience the client brings to treatment. To ignore those societal forces and focus attention solely on the person not only falls short of addressing the presenting issues but perpetuates oppression (Lago, 2011).

Working as they do with very difficult situations, social workers will easily recognize that a client who is hungry, or is being brutalized by an abusive parent or partner, will not necessarily have as a priority the need to explore the meanings of those experiences. Relief or protection from extremely damaging circumstances can come with concrete interventions rather than an intense helping relationship—and it may be that this is all that is required. Even when a helping relationship and the opportunity to self-explore are useful in important ways (as they must be in most cases), they will often not be *sufficient*.

Another general concern to be raised is that the client-centered model can be utopian, and this entails risks. This is not a necessary outcome of absorbing the theory, but a possible one to be guarded against—one that can be a more general problem with the humanistic approaches overall. If the goal of intervention is to help clients achieve congruence, or complete harmony within themselves, the goal is an ideal that is never fully reached. If the helper's responsibility is to strive for complete attunement with the experience of another, it is a foregone conclusion that we will always fall short.

We are likely to be more comfortable, honest, and competent in our work if we remember that our interventions are intended to ameliorate problems and achieve modest objectives. Self-actualization, personal congruence, authenticity, and other forms of salvation are not disparaged as goals, but they are lifelong pursuits and require guidance and supports different from what social workers normally offer.

Given an adequate degree of realistic modesty, there are compelling reasons for social workers to learn and continually practice the approach to relating that Rogers and his colleagues have described for us. This, however, is not all we need to know.

CASE STUDY 12.1

Regina is a 56-year-old, single, African American transgender woman living in an urban, low-income neighborhood. She received a diagnosis of schizoaffective disorder, depressive type, in her early 20s, which is currently managed with psychotropic medications and community-based supports via clinical mental health counseling and case management, provided by a licensed clinical social worker. Her symptoms generally manifest as persecutory delusions that cause significant distress, primarily around the theme that people in her neighborhood are spying on her and have planted cameras in her home and microphones in her body, and that as a result of what they see and hear are constantly planning to harm her. These symptoms are often followed by or accompany symptoms of depression, including low mood, anhedonia, distractibility, hypersomnia, and low self-esteem. In the absence of psychosis, Regina has some insight into her symptoms, recognizing the discrepancy between her thoughts and reality; however, that does not diminish the distress she experiences as a result of these symptoms.

The following transcript reflects a typical session between Regina and her clinical social worker, during which Regina's thought process and content are lucid and reality oriented. She is experiencing significant depressive symptoms, which triggered the following session, held in her home.

Regina:	*I can't talk right now. I'm just too depressed and I don't feel like it.*
Social Worker:	*Wow, you feel really low right now. This must be a tough day for you.*
Regina:	*It is. I feel so stupid because I yelled at [her neighbor] again for watching me take a shower. He wasn't, but I really thought he was this time. And that everyone was going to laugh at me, and call me names, and beat me up.*

Social Worker:	*You were having some really stressful thoughts the other day. That must've been really scary. It also sounds like you wish you had reacted differently.*
Regina:	*Yeah but I can't help it. When I think these things are happening, I just get so embarrassed and scared, and then the only thing I can do is yell or fight back. But then I get in trouble.* (Regina lives in a group home that employs consequences for disturbances with house members or neighbors.)
Social Worker:	*Well it sounds to me like you acted in a way that a lot of people would when they are afraid. It's understandable that you'd want to protect yourself from getting hurt, and that it's scary to not feel safe in your own home.*
Regina:	*It is. But then, like right now, I know that I probably am safe, and so I feel stupid and embarrassed for yelling and threatening him again.*
Social Worker:	*So while it makes sense that you felt afraid, and maybe a lot of other people would have reacted the same way, it's not the way you want to react in these situations.*
Regina:	*Right. I'm a nice person, and I have never hurt anyone. I don't want people to be scared of me, but I think they are. Everyone thinks I'm a freak, and then they see me hollering and screaming, and just think I'm even weirder.*
Social Worker:	*I heard you say that everyone thinks you're a freak and that you're weird. Can I share with you what my experience has been since getting to know you?*
Regina:	*I guess.*
Social Worker:	*I see you as a woman who has had a lot of tough things thrown at her in life, and who is working really hard to have the kind of life she wants to have, which anybody would. We live in a world that isn't always very understanding of people's differences, and that can feel really scary and sad.*
Regina:	*You're damn right. People see what they want to see, even though, if they really got to know me, I'd be their best friend and always have their backs. Because that's how I am, you know? I'd have anyone's back if they needed me.*
Social Worker:	*And you're frustrated that, when you react the way you did the other day, people don't get to see the real you.*
Regina:	*Exactly. I act like such a fool.*
Social Worker:	*And then what makes matters worse, because you do care so much about other people, you really beat yourself up about the way you react. So no wonder you feel so down today and like not getting out of the house.*
Social Worker:	*So tell me more about this "real you." What do you want people to see?*
Regina:	*That I'm kind, that I'm funny … I can be real silly, you know* (smiling). *That I'm loyal … and that I'm not crazy* (looking down). *But my whole life people told me I'm crazy, even my family. First it was because I was hyper, you know, always running around the house. Then it was because I didn't like to wear the clothes they bought me and wanted to be called a different name. Then it was because I had to go to the mental hospital. And all of that is true too, but they forgot about the other stuff. I'm still who I used to be.*
Social Worker:	*You have so many different things that make up who you are, and it feels like people only pay attention to some of them. And now you want to find a way to help them see the other things.*
Regina:	*Right. People would love the real me if they knew me. And maybe I wouldn't act so stupid.*
Social Worker:	*So being yourself, really* **feeling** *like you're being true to who you really are, would help you feel better, and maybe not so down. I'm also wondering, do you think it's okay to have bad days? To have days where you don't do* everything *exactly as you would like to? Does that make you a bad person or like you're not yourself anymore?*
Regina:	*Oh no, I know I ain't perfect* (chuckling)! *I know I'm always going to have times that I get worried people are spying on me, and you know that really stresses me*

> *out. I know that won't go away forever. But I just want to still be me even if I feel stressed out … or at least to feel like me when it's over. And I don't feel like me layin' in this bed.*

Social Worker: *It seems like what you want for your life is pretty reasonable, Regina. Something most people would want, and I bet something we can work on together.*

Regina: Well I sure hope so.

The session then progressed to a more problem-solving focus, examining times when Regina was able to act in a way she felt was congruent with her true self and exploring ways she could increase the instances of those times, both during and after episodes of psychosis and mood disturbance. Much of the work with Regina continues to be centered around building coping skills and learning to manage her symptoms, mitigating the impact of her psychosis on her mood, her safety, and her daily life.

Reading through the transcript, one can see where the core concepts of client-centered theory are applied. The social worker is using the concept of congruence, both congruence of the social worker and congruence within Regina, as a way of creating a climate of safety and trust within the session. The social worker takes an opportunity to share with Regina an honest impression of her, which is done not only to offer reassurance in a moment of low self-esteem but more importantly to share the social worker's internal experience with the client. This serves as a means of fostering trust in the relationship, as well as to encourage an alternate view of self. The social worker also uses reflections to highlight the incongruence between Regina's wishes for herself and her life and her actions. This is not done as a means of shaming or scolding, rather it is to reflect the social worker's understanding of Regina's internal experience, empathizing with her personal struggles. Simply focusing on the behaviors themselves would run the risk of creating a punitive or emotionally detached tone.

Acceptance is also observed throughout the transcript, through the social worker's neutral stance as Regina discusses intimate details about her life. They have an established working relationship, one in which Regina felt safe to discuss her experiences as a transgender woman, including how difficult it had been for her as a child. In previous conversations, she had also discussed the unique dynamic of being an African American transgender woman, living in a predominantly African American neighborhood. She felt particularly ostracized and persecuted by her own community, which one can imagine adds an additional layer of emotional distress. The social worker's acceptance of Regina for who she is, and how she wants to portray herself, allows her to more freely and openly explore and understand her own experience, which she has historically had to stifle in order to fit in and, ultimately, survive.

Empathy is also an observable concept highlighted in the transcript. When Regina continues to talk in self-deprecating language, the social worker empathizes with the fear, anxiety, shame, and sadness that fuel the behaviors she regrets. The social worker normalizes Regina's reactions without condoning them, validating her attempts to feel safe in her home and in her neighborhood. This is done in balance with returning to a focus on Regina's desired reality, so as not to get stuck in inadvertent reinforcement of her actual behaviors, a delicate and important nuance. It would also be important to empathize with the actual distressing reality that Regina is faced with, being an African American transgender woman, who is diagnosed with a mental illness, in American society. While the detailed content of her delusions do not reflect reality, her fear, insecurity, and feelings of marginalization certainly do. Empathizing with the impact of discrimination on Regina's physical and emotional well-being further fosters the therapeutic environment and demonstrates the social worker's attempt to understand, appreciate, and respect the unique difficulties Regina has had to face, and that undoubtedly contribute to her current distress.

A clinician who is oriented to a different theoretical framework might see other directions the work with Regina could take. For example, a cognitive behavioral therapist might choose to more thoroughly explore the thought processes that occur, both during episodes of psychosis and in the aftermath when Regina is feeling particularly ashamed and depressed, that fuel her anxiety, depression, and actions. That therapist might also help Regina process through the experiences that led to her belief that she is a "freak," "weird," or "stupid." Work would likely target those experiences and thought processes with the goal of establishing more helpful and adaptive ways of thinking about her experiences and the events that happen every day, so she can begin to behave in a way that aligns with her personal goals. Similarly, a trauma specialist might choose to focus on identifying and healing from traumatic events in Regina's past that continue to plague her current experiences, potentially using somatic work, mindfulness, and coping skills. Regardless of the theoretical orientation, an awareness of the potential for trauma to have occurred in Regina's life is paramount to not only creating a trusting, therapeutic environment, but also to ensuring ethically sound and safe treatment.

CONCLUSION

The relationship that social workers offer their clients has always been considered the *sine qua non* of our helping enterprise, to the extent that we may treat it overly reverentially (cf. Perlman, 1979). If we can accept a more modest position, recognizing that not all clients need a profound experience in relation to us and that in many other cases this may not be enough, then that is progress (however disillusioning).

Modifications of the Rogerian point of view will likely be a matter of continuing to recognize its contribution and importance while adding caveats and qualifications. The relationship conditions offered by the social worker *do* help create a context for change. So too, however, do other factors (Coady, 1999; Duncan et al., 1992; Miller et al., 1997). These include the social worker's techniques, "extratherapeutic" or environmental factors, and predispositions on the part of the client. Continuing to capitalize on the legacy Rogers left us will (somewhat ironically) be a matter of building a more differentiated appreciation of our clients' needs and circumstances, and a refined ability to tailor the relationship we offer to those realities. Perhaps, though it reintroduces the need for analytical thinking about clients, something that Rogers distrusted, it is a direction more congruent with his basic agenda than may seem, on the surface, to be the case.

Interest in extending Rogers's premises continues in our professional literature. For example, the question of how such Rogerian concepts as acceptance and empathy are connected to compassion (an obvious social work concern) is attracting interest (Berlin, 2005; Nussbaum, 2001; Rothery, 1999). In psychodynamic psychology, attachment theory and self-psychology have come to ascribe basic importance to attunement and empathy as necessary experiences for human flourishing—a significant change from its traditional priorities (Saari, 2002).

As we have turned to qualitative research methods as alternatives to positivistic science, we have had to consider how disciplined communication can address such matters as subjective (and intersubjective) experience. Phenomenological researchers are especially involved in questions about the "rich interplay of one human mind with another" (Garrett et al., 1982, p. 4) and with the interpretive aspect of our efforts to understand each other well (see Kögler, 1996, for an assessment of developments in this large and complex field)—these are matters on which Rogers and his followers have much to say.

With spirituality emerging as an issue that clinicians need to address more effectively (especially in an increasingly culturally diverse world), it is noted that relationality is discussed in theology with the same interest it receives from secular helpers. In this regard, we note that Rogers seems to have seen spiritual implications in his work, and to have pursued them in discussions with prominent religious thinkers such as Martin Buber, Rollo May, and Paul Tillich (Anderson & Cissna, 1997; Kirschenbaum & Henderson, 1989). Again, scholars who are engaged with the most current issues affecting social work practice and its future can continue to look back to the work of Rogers (and Richmond, among many others) for important insights.

Increasingly, Rogers's central concerns appear in contexts far beyond clinical psychology. A further interesting example is how aspects of critical social theory have shown an interest in how our ability to communicate well interacts with our responsibilities as citizens (Habermas, 1984). Also, there is a necessary moral dimension in how we treat one another, and the importance of congruence, acceptance, and empathy to the ethical demands of everyday life is highly relevant (Bly, 1996). At a more abstract level, social work's commitment to the values of social justice promotes a concern with the politics of recognition (see Fraser, 1996; McLaughlin, 2006); far from being a simple clinical technique, empathic relating is seen to be the vehicle for necessary human rights to recognition and validation.

Such extensions of his work would not likely surprise Rogers himself, since he never thought the importance of his core conditions was restricted to their use in professional helping relationships. Rather, he was clear that since his concern was for the quality of our relating, his work has implications that extend to all aspects of human life. On this point as on many others, history may well be proving him correct.

SUMMARY POINTS

- explored the theoretical underpinnings of client-centered therapy,
- explained the central tenets of client-centered therapy, and
- described the application of client-centered therapy to individuals and groups.

KEY REFERENCES

Only key references appear in the print edition. The full reference list appears in the digital product found on http://connect.springerpub.com/content/book/978-0-8261-6556-5/part/sec03/part/sec033/chapter/ch12

Anderson, R., & Cissna, K. N. (1997). *The Martin Buber—Carl Rogers dialogue: A new transcript with commentary*. State University of New York Press.
Barton, A. (1980). *Three worlds of therapy: An existential-phenomenological study of the therapies of Freud, Jung, and Rogers*. National Press Books.
Becker, E. (1973). *The denial of death*. Free Press.
Becker, E. (1975). *Escape from evil*. Free Press.
Bergin, A. E., & Garfield, J. L. (Eds.). (1994). *Handbook of psychotherapy and behavior change* (4th ed.). Wiley.
Berlin, S. (2005). The value of acceptance in social work direct practice: A historical and contemporary view. *Social Service Review, 79*, 482–510.
Biestek, F. (1957). *The casework relationship*. Loyola University Press.
Bly, C. (1996). *Changing the bully who rules the world: Reading and thinking about ethics*. Milkweed.
Coady, N. (1999). The helping relationship. In F. Turner (Ed.), *Social work practice: A Canadian perspective* (pp. 58–72). Prentice-Hall Allyn and Bacon Canada.

Emotion-Focused Therapy

Jeannette Bischkopf

By the end of this chapter, you should be able to:

- understand the theoretical underpinnings of emotion-focused therapy,
- understand the central tenets of emotion-focused therapy, and
- apply emotion-focused therapy to individuals and groups.

INTRODUCTION

Successful social work practice deeply relies on the social worker's emotional intelligence. "The emotionally charged nature of all social work encounters require practitioners to reflect on how the work impacts on them and to draw on the understanding which reflection affords to inform their practice." Social workers need to be aware of their own and their clients' emotions and to be able to use them effectively in their practice.

Understanding emotion is important for building a working relationship with the client and for making the most of a given encounter with service users. Client involvement has become a central part of practice; client participation in decision-making, for example, is key to successful outcomes and legally required in Codes of Practice. Interestingly, given the importance of the working relationship with clients, it has been discussed and studied far less in theoretical concepts in the social work literature and there are very few concepts as to how to build a professional relationship and work with it. From psychotherapy and counseling meta-analyses we know that relationship factors account for most of the change within the professional encounter and that the techniques used by the social worker do not account for more than the expectations clients have. The same pattern could be shown for all stages in casework practice in social work, where the success of assessment and intervention relied on the awareness and management of emotions. Emotional literacy and empathy skills, however, are needed to form professional relationships.

Social work practice often deals with clients in very difficult life situations, which involve powerful emotions such as shame, depression, and hopelessness. Moreover, social workers have to be able to tolerate and work with uncertainty, both with their clients and within themselves. As Ruch et al. (2010) state, "The bread and butter of social work is emotionally charged" (p. 17).

Emotional intelligence is important not only for an effective social work practice but also for social workers themselves and their own health and well-being. Compassion fatigue, vicarious trauma, and secondary traumatic stress have been described as specific risk factors for practitioners, and burnout and impaired emotional health are major health problems among social workers. One of the major symptoms of burnout is emotional exhaustion, described as emotional numbness and the inability to relate to the client in a person-to-person way. Building a working relationship with the client, however, lies at the heart of social work practice in almost all fields of direct practice, however short the client contact may be. Emotional health, therefore, is as important for social workers as it is for their clients.

In summary, a number of aspects of social work require an emotional literacy that social workers need to develop not only through everyday practice and experience but also through systematic analysis and training in how to best understand and work with emotions. Social workers need "permission, but also consideration of developing a language of emotion" (Ingram, 2013, p. 1001) and as Ingram further suggests: "It may be that social work can draw from literature relating to counselling and psychotherapy to support developments in this area" (p. 1001). Emotion-focused therapy offers a theoretically grounded and empirically tested framework for working with emotions in counseling and psychotherapy. It has been developed, practiced, and evaluated over the past 30 years within a variety of client groups and settings (Greenberg, 2014). Emotion-focused therapy can be understood as "the practice of therapy informed by an understanding of the role of emotion in psychotherapeutic change" (Greenberg, 2011, p. 3). The main goal is strengthening the self by helping the client to attend to their emotional experience and to create new meanings that will eventually alter their being in the world. Thus, the emotionally intelligent social worker (Howe, 2008) facilitates and directly works with the client's emotional processes. Emotion-focused therapy is an integrative approach that builds on various influences from both neuroscience and humanistic traditions within psychotherapy and counseling.

OVERVIEW OF EMOTION-FOCUSED THERAPY

Understanding of Human Problems

According to the humanistic and experiential perspective, people have all the resources to understand and solve their problems. They are biologically wired to move forward, grow, and make sense of their experiences. People have a tendency to self-actualize; through this self-actualization, a healthy person becomes free from inner tension, becomes aware of their emotions and reactions, and makes better choices in life.

Human problems are viewed to have "biological, emotional, cognitive, motivational, behavioral, physiological, social, and cultural sources" (Greenberg, 2014, p. 18). Emotions, however, are understood as the key processes that orient people in the world and help them evaluate whether a current situation meets their needs or not. Accordingly, "changing emotions is seen as central to the origins and treatment of human problems" (Greenberg, 2014, p. 18).

Our ability to feel has survival value for us as a species but also for us individually. Emotions are our resources to understand our personal lives; they connect our past and future and show us what we are drawn to and why. Our gut feeling is shaped by our past experiences as we see patterns and draw conclusions on an emotional level much faster than our thought and problem-solving processes can ensure. Emotional reactions thus can be understood as an economic and fast way to understand a situation. The complexity of human interaction is reduced to a decision about whether the situation in question is potentially threatening or rewarding. Therefore, even when people are not very good at distinguishing their emotional reactions, they can still say whether something felt good or bad. Asking them what exactly they felt, they may not be able to label their emotions beyond what is called valence—good or bad. Thus, we understand our emotions as our primary system that has survival value.

Moreover, emotions can only be understood in context. Feeling and display rules are culturally shaped, and meaning-making processes are deeply embedded in a person's life history and are culturally framed. In order to make informed choices and develop a systematic professional way of working with our clients, we need to integrate feeling and thinking in a way that is termed "reflective practice." People often misunderstand the process of reflection as a process of thinking about their emotional reactions and making sense of them with regard to their personal histories as well as situational factors. Thinking about emotion, however, is limited as these two processes often do not go hand in hand. We may have emotions we do not understand intellectually, or we try to talk ourselves out of an emotional state, for instance by convincing ourselves that there is no need to be afraid and worried. In most cases, the worry and anxiety will not simply disappear when we debate whether or not they are rational. Emotions do follow their own logic and thinking about them often does not alter them. What we can think about and change are our reactions to our emotions, the way we show them to others or suppress them. Thus, by thinking about our emotional reactions, we may only tap into these cultural undercurrents of emotional feeling and display rules. We also know from research in social psychology that situational factors define what emotions we feel much more than our personality traits and personal past. Thus, understanding emotions as key to human problems as well as a route to overcome them fits very well into a person-in-environment perspective in social work. Emotions, by definition, integrate biology and culture (Edwards, 1999).

From an emotion-focused perspective, we distinguish two problems clients can have related to emotional processes. One possibility is that clients can be overwhelmed by their emotions so that they cannot use the information embedded in the process, which is called an underregulated process. If emotions become too overwhelming, for example, clients can enter dissociative states in which they no longer have access to their emotions. Clients with a diagnosis of borderline personality disorder, for example, experience states of inner tension and stress that may become so overwhelming that they try to stop these states by hurting themselves. Learning to distinguish and regulate emotions, therefore, is an important goal when working with these clients. Another example of underregulated processes can be seen in violent youth—here, often emotions of anger are so overwhelming that people become aggressive. Interestingly, when working with these people, it often becomes clear that they have difficulties distinguishing social cues and experience provoking or threatening social signs in their environment more often than others. Here, the underlying pattern has to be understood and changed so that people learn to better distinguish social cues and nonverbal signs as threatening or neutral. Again, it becomes clear that working on an emotional level in order to understand clients' emotional reactions integrates inner resources and interpersonal social factors.

On the other hand, clients can be emotionally distant such that they feel too little emotion and cannot make sense of their emotions. For example, clients sometimes develop psychosomatic symptoms like headaches and feel pain in their bodies rather than their emotional pain. This process is called an overregulated process. Overregulation often occurs when clients do not give themselves permission to feel or label their feelings as silly and inappropriate. For example, many depressed clients have difficulties experiencing anger and view anger as potentially threatening their social bonds and relationships. In some cases, they may have experienced a violent home and do not have a social role model of expressing anger in a nonviolent way—experiencing anger then is often viewed as potentially harmful to others and suppressed.

Recent clinical research has shown that problems in emotion regulation are a key element in understanding how people develop symptoms and clinical disorders (e.g., depression and anxiety). Healthy functioning involves a rich emotional life as well as "being flexible" (Bonanno et al., 2004), which involves people having the ability to express as well as suppress emotions. Greenberg (2014) lists four major difficulties in emotional processing: (a) lack of awareness, (b) maladaptive emotional responses, (c) emotion dysregulation, and (d) problems in emotion/narrative construction and existential meaning. Emotion-focused therapy is designed to help people find a productive distance from their emotional experiences in order to make sense of them, use them, and be guided by them through a self-actualizing process toward better health, healthier relationships, and better decisions in life.

Conception of Therapeutic Intervention

According to the humanistic tradition, emotion-focused therapy views people as experts of their personal lives and the choices they make. Clients are seen as "active self-healers" (Bohart, 2006), making use of therapy and counseling in their own individual way. Developing, regaining, and strengthening a person's agency, thus, is a key element and therapeutic task in emotion-focused therapy. In Gendlin's (1984) tradition of "giving therapy away," the therapist in emotion-focused therapy is seen as an emotion coach, helping clients access productive emotional processes that will eventually help them deal with and overcome their problems within their own time. "EFT [Emotion-focused therapy] proposes that emotions themselves have an innately adaptive potential that if activated can help clients reclaim unwanted experience, change problematic emotional states, and change interactions" (Greenberg, 2014, p. 17).

In their article "The Essence of Process-Experiential/Emotion-Focused Therapy," Elliott and Greenberg (2007) list five central features of this approach: "neo-humanistic values, process-experiential emotion theory, person-centered but process-guiding relational stance, therapist exploratory response style, and marker-guided task strategy" (p. 241). In emotion-focused therapy, a person-centered, empathic, professional relationship is the basis for therapeutic work on emotion. According to Greenberg (2014), these are the two treatment principles: the relationship and direct therapeutic work on client emotional processes.

Empathy, positive regard, and congruence, as originally described by Rogers (1957), are key elements in building the helping relationship in emotion-focused therapy. Empathy is understood as the therapist's ability to understand the client's emotions and needs, as well as "a process of coconstructing symbols for experience" (Bohart & Greenberg, 1997, p. 6). Empathy thus develops moment by moment in the actual therapist–client interaction.

Positive regard is expressed through praising of the client—regardless of the client's life circumstances, behavior, or choices—simply for who they are. It involves a positive and optimistic outlook on the client's life and possibilities, and is closely related to humanistic values. It involves accepting personal choice and freedom and a basic trust in the client's self-actualizing tendency, resilience, and ability to develop and grow.

Congruence, on the other hand, is related to the therapist's or counselor's own integrity and maturity, and is the basis for a dialogical person-to-person encounter. More recently, this aspect has been developed further to integrate mindfulness approaches in order for the therapist to become more fully aware of the moment-to-moment process and more present in the actual moment (Greenberg & Geller, 2011). The therapist's mindfulness and presence are positively related to the client's improvement in interpersonal difficulties (Ryan et al., 2012) so that "therapist dispositional mindfulness may be an important pre-treatment variable in psychotherapy outcome" (p. 289). The two aspects of mindfulness—"act with awareness" and "accept without judgment"—proved most important for this outcome.

Mindfulness can help the therapist to develop and use their own congruence; however, it has also become a specific tradition in psychotherapy on its own accord. Gaynor (2019), for example, developed emotion-focused mindfulness therapy (EFMT), introducing mindfulness-based interventions into the therapy protocol. There is, however, an interesting distinction between the concept of mindfulness and awareness of emotion. Awareness is reached by staying with a feeling, whereas mindfulness is understood and reached by letting it pass without changing or judging it. Most exercises in mindfulness, above all meditation, try to help people focus on the current moment without judgment and letting it pass into the next moment. Awareness exercises—most of which have been developed in the tradition of gestalt therapy—help people stay and heighten a specific emotional reaction in order to fully experience and thereby understand it. For example, if a client talks about an event and unknowingly punches the armrest of their chair, their awareness may be guided toward that movement and they may be asked to focus on it and do it some more and observe their emotional reaction while doing it. The bodily movement has already carried the underlying emotion—for example, anger;

however, the client may not have been aware of this emotion. By helping the client focus on their bodily movements accompanying the conversation, the therapist may help the client to become aware of it. Awareness thus is linked to having an insight, which always integrates feeling and thinking, whereas mindfulness at its best lets go off thinking and is pure being in the moment—moment by moment.

In addition to these core conditions—positive regard and congruence, and an empathic attunement–the emotion-focused therapist has to ensure collaboration on the goals and tasks of therapy. The goal is task completion, empowerment, and integration of emotional processes that will eventually lead to more self-acceptance and a more resilient self. This goal is reached by working together on specific processing tasks that the therapist suggests to the client. Therefore, the therapist assesses the client process and listens for process markers. A process marker can be the client's voice (too distant from an experiencing voice, e.g., a lecturing voice), specific words that show a self-critical process (e.g., "I am a failure"), a specific posture that shows a collapsed helpless and hopeless self, or direct emotional expression like anger or hurt.

Emotion-focused therapy integrates various forms of working with emotion into a coherent frame. Five empirically based principles of working with emotion have been found: focusing, accepting, and allowing emotions (awareness); working with under- and overregulated emotional processes (regulation); facilitating emotional expression over suppression (expression); changing emotion by emotion (transformation); and symbolizing and reflecting emotion (reflection; Greenberg & Pascual-Leone, 2006). More recently, working with client narrative processes to promote and integrate emotional change (Angus & Greenberg, 2011) and forms of corrective emotional experiences (Castonguay & Hill, 2012) have been added as general strategies of working with emotion.

Specific strategies for working with emotions are related to in-session markers of client processes that are differentiated by the therapist. These strategies will be described more fully using a case example. In summary, emotion-focused therapy uses a process-guided approach with a special focus on microprocesses as they unfold in the session.

HISTORICAL DEVELOPMENT

Precursors

Emotion-focused therapy is based on a humanistic understanding of problems and interventions. As it applies to a person-centered way of relating to clients, its origins can be traced back to Carl Rogers's (1957) work on defining a helping relationship.

Later, Laura Rice (1974), a student of Rogers, added the "evocative function of the therapist" to client-centered therapy. Her studies of the therapy process moment-by-moment revealed that therapist interventions could deepen clients' emotional processing. Rice especially studied client vocal quality and how it shifted from external to internal when the client focused inward. Thereby, the first process measures for studying the client's change process were developed and tested (Watson & Wiseman, 2010). The focus then naturally shifted to the therapist and client–therapist interaction, asking how the client process could be best facilitated by therapist actions. At that time, Les Greenberg became a student of Laura Rice, and their idea was to develop a map of the exact steps clients go through in order for a change process to be successful.

Greenberg also worked closely with developmental psychologist Juan Pascual-Leone, who had studied with Piaget. Together they developed the model of a dialectical-constructivist understanding of the change process and an understanding and analysis of tasks that the client solves in session. A task refers to a specific cognitive emotional process (e.g., self-soothing), differentiating and integrating inner voices, solving decisional conflicts, or mourning a loss. As the main therapeutic focus was following and leading the client through the stages of emotional processes, the therapy was first (and sometimes still is) called process-experiential psychotherapy.

Greenberg et al. (1993) published a manual that focused on therapists' actions of facilitating emotional change processes moment by moment. As more and more studies revealed that the core change process was related to changing core emotional schemes, the therapy was renamed emotion-focused therapy. Moreover, an increasing number of results from affective neuroscience provided a rationale for directly working with emotion and supported the notion that emotional change lies at the heart of all human functioning, such as thought processes, motivation, and action.

The therapy sometimes is also known as process-experiential emotion-focused therapy (PE-EFT). Reconciling inner voices in conflict had been developed out of working with the couples system where real-life conflicts were acted out between two people. Developing emotion-focused therapy, therefore, was also influenced by systemic thinking and an existentialist understanding of human beings and their being in the world. As experiencing and affect are given priority over intellect and thinking, influences of gestalt therapy (Perls, 1969; Shorkey & Uebel, 2008) and the use of imagination played a crucial part in developing emotion-focused therapy. In fact, the two-chair technique and a dialogical gestalt therapy (Jacobs & Hycner, 2010) still have some similarities in how the client process is understood and utilized.

Later Developments and Current Status

Extensive work with various client populations and problems led to the development of specific approaches for specific clients. At first, emotion-focused therapy was developed and applied to clients with depressive symptoms. Two large research projects at York University in Toronto, Canada, provided the background and funding for developing emotion-focused therapy for depression (Greenberg & Watson, 2006). Specific tasks, like differentiating and integrating critical voices, were developed and evaluated in the course of these projects.

In 2010, Sandra Paivio and Antonio Pascual-Leone published the manual for emotion-focused therapy for complex trauma. It grew out of 20 years of experience working with survivors of child abuse in which a modified version of chair work was developed and widely empirically tested. This technique is called imaginal confrontation and lies at the heart of emotion-focused therapy for complex trauma. In short, in an imaginal confrontation, the client is guided through a dialogue with the imagined perpetrator in an empty chair. By guiding the client through the process in a stepwise procedure, the trauma can be integrated and healed.

Emotion-focused therapy has been developing and growing rapidly in various directions; one is further differentiation of the approach for specific client groups. Eating disorders have been successfully treated using a modified approach called emotion-focused family therapy (EFFT; Dolhanty & Greenberg, 2009). Furthermore, specific tasks for anxiety disorders have been developed, for example, enhancing clients' ability to self-soothe (Elliott, 2013). Watson and Greenberg (2017) have recently compiled a handbook for working with clients with generalized anxiety disorder in an emotion-focused way. Integrating emotion-focused therapy with cognitive behavioral therapy has been successful for clients with anxiety disorders in a randomized controlled trial (Newman et al., 2011). In a similar way, a modified form of using chair work for clients with a diagnosis of borderline personality disorder has been proposed to meet the needs of this client group (Pos & Greenberg, 2012). Finally, emotion-focused couples therapy has been further developed (Greenberg & Goldman, 2008) to directly work with power relations within a couple's system in addition to their attachment needs. Another form of couples therapy had been developed earlier by Sue Johnson, which stressed the importance of attachment as the basis for a healthy and long-lasting relationship (Johnson, 2002). Greenberg and Woldarsky-Meneses (2019) offer insight into the specific processes of forgiving and letting go in emotion-focused therapy regarding individuals and couples. Finally, Greenberg and Goldman (2018) edited a clinical handbook of emotion-focused therapy that can be seen as the most recent source of the modifications and the evidence of working successfully with various client groups.

To date, there are very few examples of emotion-focused therapy for children and youth. A form of EFFT has been developed to work successfully with children and youth with eating disorders and their families (Dolhanty & Greenberg, 2009; Robinson et al., 2013). The EFFT model has now been outlined in a clinical manual by Lafrance et al. (2019).

Therapists, however, do not only need specific skills for clients with specific problems and needs but also more general skills for working with emotion in the session. One major skill for therapists to learn and practice is their own mindfulness and presence (Greenberg & Geller, 2011). By developing mindfulness, therapists and counselors not only enhance their practice and effectiveness with service users, they also maintain and enhance their own well-being.

As emotion is understood as the key component in client change, in the future all therapeutic approaches should integrate knowledge of emotional change processes and therapists' and counselors' skills in how to best facilitate them. Greenberg (2011) states:

> The term *emotion-focused therapy* will, I believe, be used in the future, in its integrative sense, to characterize all therapies that are emotion-focused, be they psychodynamic, cognitive-behavioral, systemic, or humanistic. … What will distinguish and differentiate an approach as emotion-focused will be its emphasis on the importance of affect in human functioning and on the experience of emotion in sessions. (pp. 141–142)

Past and Current Connections to Social Work

Social work practice can be understood as emotion work that continuously needs supervision and reflection. Not surprisingly, working with the self has been an area of training of social workers as reflective practice is central in social work practice (Ruch, 2005). Self-knowledge and self-awareness are crucial in working effectively with service users. However, "it is probably more common than we might imagine for social workers and others to feel unable to really see other's pain and distress" (Ward, 2010, p. 50). Understanding emotions and being aware of them, therefore, has been introduced as the concept of the "emotionally intelligent social worker" (Howe, 2008).

Moreover, understanding the discipline according to its current definition as "a practice-based profession and an academic discipline that promotes social change and development, social cohesion, and the empowerment and liberation of people" (https://www.ifsw.org/what-is-social-work/global-definition-of-social-work/), both social work practice and emotion-focused work are based on humanistic values and ethics. In fact, emotion-focused therapy fully acknowledges peoples' choices and their ability to grow and develop. The goal of emotion-focused therapy can be seen as empowering and liberating people from inner voices that undermine a person's resilience and their capacity to grow. As the therapeutic relationship is key for a person's empowerment and change process, emotion-focused therapy can be well understood and integrated into the current turn to "relationship-based social work" (Ruch et al., 2010). This implies an understanding of service users not as rational but as relational beings. "Reconceptualising the practitioner means acknowledging their emotional responses and the emotional impact of practice on them" (Ruch et al., 2010, p. 27).

CENTRAL THEORETICAL CONSTRUCTS

Emotion-focused therapy has been described as "a treatment that is neohumanistic, process oriented, and emotion focused" (Greenberg, 2011, p. 13). Accordingly, the central theoretical constructs are neohumanistic concepts, such as the understanding of the self, self-actualization, and experiencing theory (Greenberg & Van Balen, 1998). The process orientation is grounded in dialectical constructivism, and the focusing of emotions is based on emotion theory and affective neuroscience. Moreover, emotion-focused therapy draws upon clinical research, focusing, and attachment theory. It can thus be seen as an integrative approach. As Elliott (2012) states:

> In an era of increasing demands for brief, effective treatments and criticism of humanistic/experiential psychotherapies (HEPs) for lack of theory and empirical support, Emotionally-Focused Therapy appears to offer a viable development of the humanistic and person-centred traditions, while at the same time appealing to therapists from other traditions. (p. 108)

Within the humanistic tradition, experiencing theory posits that people have an ongoing inner process of experiencing that they can attend to at any moment.

Thus, the process orientation of emotion-focused therapy relies on this moment-to-moment process of experiencing. Therapist relational conditions of accurate empathy, unconditional positive regard, and genuineness are seen as the core constructs within the therapeutic relationship that help clients to attend to their inner processes of experiencing. The self-actualizing tendency posits that this inner process of experiencing is geared toward self-actualization. Experience is continuously symbolized within the self. However, people are not aware of all their experiences in a given moment, leading to incongruence between the self and experience. This incongruence is experienced as inner tension within the person.

According to the humanistic tradition, people will be able to reduce their incongruence by becoming increasingly aware of their experiencing process and attending to their inner processes with a nonjudgmental, curious, and open attitude. They internalize the relationship characterized by accurate empathy, unconditional positive regard, and genuineness experienced in the therapist–client relationship so that they themselves can be more open toward their experiences, symbolize, and integrate them.

> It is not any one configuration within the client's Self which is important but the whole constellation of configurations and the dynamics which define their interrelationships. It is this dynamic integration which will result in an overall picture that reflects the person's Self. (Mearns & Thorne, 2000, p. 114)

The "fully functioning person," according to Rogers (1961), will be able to flexibly experience feelings in the moment and use them to make better decisions that are more in accordance with their inner life. Thus, incongruence is the core process of a person's pathology and will be reduced mainly by integrating formerly not symbolized aspects of the person's individual experiencing process. The most important therapeutic tool is the therapeutic relationship and the client's process of self-exploration, symbolizing, and meaning-making.

In emotion-focused therapy, these humanistic constructs have been described in terms of emotional processes and dialectical constructivist ideas. Dialectical constructivist theory posits that experiencing and meaning-making are in dialectic tension. "One therefore continually creates as well as discovers who one is" (Greenberg & van Balen, 1998, p. 39). Experience is organized and activated in emotion schemes, which basically operate in two different ways. New experience is either continuously integrated in existing schemes by a process of assimilation, or if new experience cannot be integrated, a new scheme emerges as the result of a process of accommodation. These processes have been described by developmental psychologist Jean Piaget (1952) and applied by Greenberg and neo-Piagetian Juan Pascual-Leone (1995, 2001, 2006) to understand emotional schemes and processes.

> When, for example, the components of a conflict are activated in therapy, the two opposing processes interact, and a new, higher level structure may be spontaneously synthesized. … This new structure captures within itself the pattern of co-activation

of the previously opposing schemes, as well as newly formulates material, thus forming a higher level structural totality. (Greenberg & Pascual-Leone, 1995, p. 180)

Thus, focusing emotion in therapy helps integrate experience into existing emotion schemes or create new, more adaptive, and healthier emotion schemes. For example, in the treatment of depression, a helplessness and hopelessness scheme coactivated with a process of anger will eventually result in the depressed person's empowerment. In this way, anger undoes hopelessness, leading to a healthier and more resilient configuration within the self (Greenberg & Watson, 2006). The change process is also facilitated by positive emotions that clients feel in their relationship with their helpers.

Emotion-focused therapy stresses that people solve cognitive-affective tasks in therapy; as a result, healthier emotion schemes emerge. The client–therapist relationship is the most important tool in therapy. Additionally, chair work has been introduced to directly activate emotion schemes and work with clients' core maladaptive emotion schemes that continuously lead to specific symptoms. For example, a depressed client may experience depressive hopelessness that stems from the client's core scheme of shame and guilt. Critical inner processes constantly activate the inner shame that is experienced as depression. In emotion-focused therapy, these maladaptive processes are activated and worked with, mainly by coactivating and synthesizing opposing processes in a guided intervention like two-chair work.

PHASES OF HELPING

The phases of helping in emotion-focused therapy are empathic attunement, as a way of engagement with the client; focus on emotion, which corresponds to data collection and assessment; activation of maladaptive emotion scheme and reflection and work with client narrative, as ways of intervention; and finally, termination of therapy.

As the therapeutic relationship is given priority over technical aspects of accessing and transforming emotion, establishing a good relationship with the client who can act as a secure base for further emotion work is essential. Although establishing a relationship is central for the beginning of therapy and the first sessions, the therapy process will often demand work on the relationship, for example, in an alliance rupture where the relationship is the focus rather than the background for other emotion work. As emotion-focused therapy is process oriented, the phases of therapy are not linear and aspects of building a relationship, assessing emotion, focusing on emotion, and ending a specific task in therapy are circular and can become the focus at any time in therapy.

Still, there is a structure that therapy can be expected to follow in a general sense and it is useful to briefly summarize this before introducing the main phases of helping in more detail. In the first five sessions of a short-term emotion-focused therapy of about 16 sessions, as the therapeutic relationship develops, therapist and client begin to focus on emotion, heighten emotional awareness, and try to understand the core emotion scheme that lies at the heart of the client's problems. Once the core scheme has been activated, usually in the middle of therapy, by, for example, repeatedly using different chair dialogs, new emotional experience will be used within the session to change the core scheme. The therapist follows the client process and makes suggestions for processing emotion further. For example, the therapist may help the client to confront a critical part of themselves with a two-chair dialog or to become angry with an abusive partner or parent in an empty chair, if there are signs indicating that these are the relevant processes. The therapist, thus, is an "emotion coach" (Greenberg, 2002), following as well as leading the client in their individual emotional process.

Experiencing new emotion is naturally followed by the client reflecting on their experience. The basic therapeutic process within a typical session in emotion-focused therapy can be described as alternating between the client's experiencing facilitated by chair work and reflecting on their emotional experiences. Ideally, individual sessions as well as the entire therapy process intensify the depth of experiencing in the middle section and move to lower experiencing and more narrative elements of meaning making toward the end. At the end of therapy, a new client narrative emerges. In successful therapies, the client views themselves as more resilient and empowered. The previous maladaptive core emotion scheme is transformed and replaced by a new one that reorganizes the person and their being in the world in a new way. A new narrative of their life emerges.

Engagement: Empathic Attunement

First, an empathic therapist–client relationship is established as it is the basis for the client and therapist to focus on emotion. In emotion-focused therapy theory, relationship and task principles have been described (Elliott et al., 2004). Clients need to feel safe and understood within the therapist–client relationship before deeper work on emotion schemes can be initiated. Here, the focus on emotion and empathic attunement blend together imperceptibly. Right from the beginning of therapy, the therapist pays attention to where the affect is most salient in the narrative the client presents. An emotion-focused therapist thus attends to emotion signals from the very beginning of therapy. Emotion signals can refer to facial expressions, emotion words, pauses, voice quality, or expression of emotions such as trembling of hands or tears. A focused voice is a signal of the client attending to an inner process and focusing inward. From the beginning of the therapeutic encounter, therapists assess how easily this can be achieved or whether the client narrative is very distant and factual.

Data Collection and Assessment: Focus on Emotion

Emotion-focused therapy case formulation centers around the core maladaptive emotion scheme, which has to be activated and understood (Goldman & Greenberg, 2014; Watson, 2010). Often the story and symptoms the client presents with are secondary to the core process. For example, a student presented with acute anxiety and on a behavioral level procrastinated and found himself in a difficult situation where he was confronted with the possibility of being expelled from his studies. On a deeper emotional level, his anxiety was driven by shame and insecurity about having chosen the wrong career and thus represents the result of a self-critical process. In emotion-focused therapy, the therapist wants to address and change the determinants of maladaptive emotions, cognitions, and behavior.

Emotion-focused therapy is a transdiagnostic treatment; a formal diagnosis of a given psychopathology is no indication for applying this approach. Rather, the client's ability to focus on emotion is important to use the therapy effectively.

Assessing emotion types and regulation strategies is essential for applying the emotion-focused therapy protocol. Emotion types can be differentiated according to their usefulness within the course of therapy; for example, as productive emotional processing if they further the process or unproductive emotional processing if they leave the person feeling stuck or overwhelmed. In order to use the information an emotion conveys, emotions cannot be experienced in an overwhelming manner, nor in a too distant manner. A working distance to one's own emotional experiencing is needed that varies from person to person.

The therapist has to judge continuously how the client experiences emotion—whether the emotion is overwhelming, meaning the emotion is undercontrolled, or whether the emotion is too distant and overcontrolled, which means that it is not felt in the moment and used. Both types of processing should be worked with for clients to achieve a working distance that enables them to feel, express, label, understand, and use their emotions. Accordingly, some clients need help with their emotional processing abilities to control their emotions when they are overwhelming, whereas others need help to enhance their emotional experiencing if they overcontrol emotional experiences or avoid and fear their feelings. Emotion-focused therapy has been compared to training in emotional intelligence. Greenberg (2002) states:

Emotional intelligence thus involves the ability to identify emotions in one's own physical states and in others and the ability to accurately express emotions and the needs related to these emotions, as well as being able to discriminate expressions in others. (pp. 58–59)

Before emotion schemes can be focused on by applying various forms of chair work in the session, the client has to develop emotion regulation strategies. Assessing clients' capacities to regulate their emotions is an essential part of the process diagnosis in emotion-focused therapy. For some clients, developing emotion regulation strategies requires another therapy that they need to complete before they can enter emotion-focused therapy. Clients with borderline personality disorder, for example, first have to learn emotion regulation strategies in dialectical behavioral therapy before they can directly work with their emotions in emotion-focused therapy. For clients with a diagnosis of generalized anxiety disorder, cognitive behavioral therapy can be integrated with emotion-focused therapy. Cognitive behavioral therapy can be used to address and manage client anxiety in the beginning part of the session before more emotion and relationship work can be used in the second part of the session (Newman et al., 2011).

Intervention: Activate Maladaptive Emotion Scheme and Work With Client Narrative

Before emotional tasks can be focused on in emotion-focused therapy, the therapist has to build an alliance with the client and get an agreement from them about focusing on emotion and working with emotion in this way. This is based on Bordin's understanding of the alliance, which encompasses a positive affective bond between client and therapist, as well as consensus about the goals of therapy and the means by which these goals can be reached (Bordin, as cited in Horvath & Bedi [2002]). Goal consensus and task collaboration are as important as the affective bond between client and therapist.

A task in emotion-focused therapy is a specific cognitive-affective process required by the client in order for them to go forward in therapy. For example, if the client experiences an emotion and does not know why, the task is to understand this emotion through a process of self-exploration that is facilitated by the therapist through a technique of empathic evocative unfolding. The therapist not only follows the client in their narrative and experiencing but also deepens the processing, for example, by using metaphors. An unclear felt sense can become clear when the right metaphor or word is found; sometimes this can be suggested by the therapist. In this task, the therapist helps the client focus and explore emotions by using specific empathic responses.

Another task is a self-critical process in which two sides within the client are in opposition. Here, the client needs to fully express both parts and their underlying needs in order to integrate them into a new emotion scheme. The therapist facilitates this process by suggesting a two-chair dialog once the two parts have become clear. As each part has its own emotions, typical sequences of emotions have been found that help the client complete this task. For example, secondary emotions of helplessness will first occur when the critical part attacks and criticizes the self in the experiencing chair and clients often first agree with the critic. Emotionally, the self will either collapse or fight back. Letting the emotions emerge naturally rather than pulling for them is important and requires specific therapist training and experience.

In successful therapies, eventually the self is empowered, and the client can acknowledge and express their needs and will start negotiating needs with the critical part of the self. An integration of both needs and parts will occur rather than the critical part fully withdrawing. Often there is worry or anxiety that drives the critical part, which has to be acknowledged and worked with.

In emotion-focused therapy, the therapist constantly makes diagnoses of the moment-to-moment process and emotional processing suggestions for the client. The therapist has to follow the client process empathically, while guiding the client toward tasks and task completion. Greenberg (2002) states: "The coach is like a guide who knows paths through the emotional terrain and the client the explorer who sets the goals, decides on the pace, and is in control of the expedition" (p. 80). The therapist has to listen for markers of client processes, recognize tasks, and make appropriate emotional processing suggestions. Marker-guided interventions are therefore at the core of emotion-focused therapy. A map of up to 10 process markers has been developed and defined to date (Elliott, 2012). Specific marker-guided interventions are embedded in the general strategies of working with emotions in therapy and in the relationship and task principles of emotion-focused therapy (Bischkopf, 2013).

Termination

As the client is seen as the "active client" (Bohart, 2006) in charge of their own process, termination is understood as a process initiated by the client. However, the therapist has to make clear from the beginning of therapy that the therapeutic relationship is temporary and will eventually come to an end.

Preparing the client for ending is an important subtask in emotion-focused therapy, and a few sessions should be reserved for ending work and addressing issues the client feels are important to work on before therapy ends. Ending therapy may be accompanied by feelings of sadness or anxiety about the future for some clients, and by feelings of pride, hope, and optimism by others. Comparing how the client entered therapy to how they leave it is a helpful intervention, especially for anxious clients. Leaving time for evaluating the therapeutic process and good moments in therapy, as well as in the client's life outside therapy, is an important step in the process of termination. Following the dialogical principle, it may also be relevant for the therapist to disclose their own experience of therapy and their own genuine reaction to ending.

APPLICATION TO FAMILY AND GROUP WORK

An EFFT model has now been outlined in a clinical manual by Lafrance et al. (2019). On the website for EFFT, the approach is described as being able to "afford families a significant role in their loved one's recovery from an eating disorder, and to empower parents and caregivers with specific skills to be effective in this role" (emotionfocusedfamilytherapy.org). Strategies of emotion coaching and relationship repair are applied using the emotion-focused therapy model. Studies and case descriptions show very promising results (emotionfocusedfamilytherapy.org). Applications of emotion-focused therapy to family and group work have been successful in systematic pilot studies, and EFFT for eating disorders (Robinson et al., 2013) has been developed and is currently being applied and researched. EFFT may be especially powerful for social workers as they are often confronted with families in crises and need of support. Adding emotion-focused perspectives to a more behavioral approach can help them to be more effective, and thanks to these new publications, rich resources are available in order to broaden clinical skills. Moreover, EFFT offers a new framework for understanding individual and family problems and possible new ways of supporting them.

To date, there are only three studies systematically addressing the application of emotion-focused therapy to group work (Pascual-Leone et al., 2011; Robinson et al., 2014; Wnuk et al., 2014). Pascual-Leone et al. (2011) reported positive outcomes for a group of incarcerated men with a history of intimate partner violence. Wnuk et al. (2014) showed a decrease in the frequency of binge episodes, improvements in mood, and improvements in emotion regulation and self-efficacy in 12 women with binge-eating disorders after a 16-week emotion-focused therapy group program. Robinson et al. (2014) collected in a pilot study pre- and postgroup data for individuals suffering from anxiety and depression. Postgroup and follow-up scores in the Difficulties in Emotion Regulation Scale (DERS) were significantly lower than pregroup scores. Although it was a very small sample of only six participants, these results are promising as emotion regulation difficulties are seen in many clinical theories as relevant for developing symptoms and psychopathology.

Participants in the last study also reported what the authors referred to as "vicarious emotional processing and learning while observing others doing chair work" (Robinson et al., 2014, p. 271). One participant, for example, said: "What that person was saying, that's when I realized, I had those feelings. And it made me go even further into myself" (Robinson et al., 2014, p. 271). Participants also reported using newly found self-soothing strategies, which are especially important for clients overcoming anxiety and depression.

As stated, EFMT developed by Gaynor (2019) is offered in a group format of eight to 12 group sessions and a one-day retreat. The groups consist of approximately eight participants, and monthly group meetings are offered to continue after the actual group has ended. Integrating mindfulness and emotion-focused strategies seems a potentially promising new way for developing group treatments—building on the evidence for mindfulness-based approaches in overcoming stress, depression, and anxiety often offered in a group format (Bohlmeijer et al., 2010).

COMPATIBILITY WITH THE GENERALIST-ECLECTIC FRAMEWORK

Emotion-focused therapy is an integrative approach that stresses the role of the therapeutic relationship and the importance of common factors in achieving therapeutic change. It therefore fits very well into a generalist-eclectic framework.

Approaches for working with emotion can be differentiated in being experiential, coping oriented, or insight oriented. Emotion-focused therapy works directly with the process of experiencing. In contrast, cognitive behavioral approaches focus more on coping with emotions by teaching skills for managing them. In anger management programs, for example, clients learn to better control their anger and express it in a socially acceptable way (Greenberg & Bischkopf, 2007). Insight-oriented approaches to working with emotions focus on the underlying symbolic meaning and help clients understand why they feel a certain way in a given situation and how that informs them about who they are or have become. Which way of working with emotion is most effective depends on the client and the client's problem. A generalist-eclectic framework allows the therapist to choose the best way of helping the client without having to follow a predefined protocol. Emotions, by definition, integrate biological, cultural, situational, and idiosyncratic aspects of the person in their environment and thus need to be understood, addressed, and worked with in an integrative manner.

CRITIQUE OF THEORY

Strengths

Because of its wide range of outcome studies, emotion-focused therapy, as a short-term therapy of 16 to 20 sessions, is listed as one of the empirically supported treatments for depression by the American Psychological Association (/www.div12.org/PsychologicalTreatments/treatments/depression_emotion.html). It is also listed in a disorder-specific review of therapies in the category of level II evidence, indicating that in the research review including all studies published between 2004 and January 2010, there was at least one randomized control trial study that showed the effectiveness of emotion-focused therapy (Australian Psychological Society, 2010). In another recent meta-analysis of depression treatments, the authors came to the conclusion that "experiential therapy might be possibly efficacious with respect to both acute response and subsequent prevention" (Hollon & Ponniah, 2010, p. 916). Thus, the potential of emotion-focused therapy for depression treatment and prevention is recognized (Cooper et al., 2010; Greenberg & Goldman, 2018).

Emotion-focused therapy is also an evidence-based treatment for trauma therapy of men and women, which is a novelty as most trauma studies mostly refer to women (Paivio & Pascual-Leone, 2010). The application of emotion-focused therapy to other client groups, especially clients with eating disorders, has yielded promising results in pilot studies (Robinson et al., 2013, 2014).

Most of those aspects of therapy that are especially relevant for change in the client's view are addressed in emotion-focused therapy. Looking back at 20 years of research on the client experience, Elliott (2008) states that the most important development is research that documents the client as an active change agent. Concepts like "the client as self-healer" (Bohart, 2004) and "self-agency" (Rennie, 2001) have been discussed and empirically studied using a variety of data collection and data analysis procedures. By asking former clients what they regard as a good outcome in psychotherapy, Binder et al. (2010) found four areas of change: better self-understanding and insight, self-acceptance, reduction of symptomatic distress/changes in behavioral patterns, and establishment of new ways of relating. Finally, various categorizations of client-perceived helpful aspects of therapy have been proposed. A meta-analysis based on seven studies examined the client-perceived impact of helpful events and found nine core categories: (a) awareness/insight/self-understanding, (b) behavioral change/problem solution, (c) empowerment, (d) relief, (e) exploring feelings/emotional experiencing, (f) feeling understood, (g) client involvement, (h) reassurance/support/safety, and (i) personal contact (Timulak, 2007).

In summary, the strength of emotion-focused therapy lies in its integrative nature and empirical validation. Its theory is based on neuroaffective evidence of the role of emotion in memory and thinking and how our identity is built. Moreover, its theory is based on evidence from psychotherapy process and outcome research that highlights emotional processes as an important common factor for therapeutic change. The marker-guided interventions are accessible for training, research, and supervision. Emotion-focused therapy theory is continuously being developed bottom-up and tested in practice.

Limitations

One limitation to the model is that there is little reference to existing concepts of emotional intelligence or other related concepts that might have the potential to inform emotion-focused practice. Although the client is seen as an active self-healer, the question remains as to who actually defines the emotional process, as most processing models are developed from an observer's perspective.

Another limitation is that emotion-focused therapy is not suited to all clients. The ability to process emotion, which is a requirement for emotion-focused therapy, can be severely damaged due to specific mental disorders or being in an acute crisis. In acute psychosis or with suicidal ideation, for example, clients are not able to make use of their emotions as they are unable to feel and differentiate them. Clients with a diagnosis of social phobia, for example, have specific biases in their emotion recognition, which have been summarized as "rejection sensitivity." These clients perceive more interactional cues for rejection—for example. in peoples' facial expression when they interact with them—compared with healthy controls (Rosenbach & Renneberg, 2011). Moreover, clients have to have at least average intelligence to use two-chair dialog and alternate between various perspectives and aspects within themselves.

With regard to the emotional processing models that guide the interventions in emotion-focused therapy, there is no evidence to date that these are culturally or gender sensitive (Levant & Silverstein, 2006). Furthermore, the processing models can be criticized, because they "portray the client as a collection of processes that are operated on and changed by therapist interventions" (Bohart, 2004, p. 105):

> Theoretically, from the "client as active self-healer" perspective, therapists' empathic responses do not "operate on" clients' experiencing levels or depth of processing independent of clients' active agency and investment. Therapists' empathy responses all by themselves do not promote clients' self-exploration. Instead, it is clients who operate on therapists' empathy responses to create these effects. (Bohart, 2004, p. 106)

For these reasons, there has been a longstanding debate whether emotion-focused therapy should still be part of the humanistic tradition.

CASE STUDY 13.1

Kate came to the psychosocial counseling service at the university where she had begun her studies. Her presenting problem was severe speech anxiety and procrastination. She had to give a presentation in one of her classes and felt paralyzed and unable to prepare for it. She was so worried about failing that she could not concentrate and reported feeling depressed and angry with herself. She had a number of somatic complaints such as sleeplessness, neck and back pain, and eating problems. She was on an antidepressant, a sleeping pill, and an anxiolytic as needed. Because of her anxieties, she was socially withdrawn and, as she had just moved to a new neighborhood, she did not have many friends. Kate was looking for help regarding her studies as she still procrastinated and felt depressed.

Kate presented with a state that in emotion-focused therapy is called "global distress," where people experience a range of unpleasant emotions such as anger, stress, feelings of depression, and anxiety, and these emotions can either be directed at themselves or others. These emotions are often overwhelming. Kate, for example, would feel unable to do anything; she would sit for hours and go over fears and worries of what might happen. Eventually, she blamed herself for being a failure and for also letting down her parents, who financed her and her studies.

The first step for her was to become aware of her self-critical voice, which constantly blamed her and put her down. The self-critical process can be understood as the core process that triggers feelings of depression and anxiety. Therefore, it was important to heighten her awareness of this process as the generator of her depression and to strengthen her agency to change that process. In a chair dialog, she confronted herself with all the demands that she felt she should, ought, and must do to be a good student. It became clear that these demands she put on herself created a pressure on her that she would feel as a heavy weight, at which point she made a connection to her neck and back pain and her depressed mood. As the chair dialog brought out the underlying primary feelings behind her fear of failure—mainly a shame-based self-structure—she also made connections to where the shame would come from in her life and why it was difficult for her to feel lovable and worthy. She depended so much on constant positive feedback and success that the possibility of negative feedback or failure created pressure in her and made her unable to learn or fulfill any of the demands she put on herself. She also questioned her choices easily.

One of the most important emotional tasks for Kate was to develop the ability to self-soothe. Once she learned to self-soothe through positive images from her past and strong positive figures in her life, for example, an aunt whom she felt close to, her symptoms became less severe. She could connect to her inner representation of her aunt and recall an image of her and what she had said, and this would help her when she felt anxious and soothe her and give her hope. Kate learned to use these images when she felt overwhelmed by negative emotions. It was also important for her to experience the shame in the session in order to change it and let more resilient parts of herself become more visible and felt.

Finally, in the self-critical dialog, it became clear that some of the demands had a history that she traced back to unfinished business with her mother. She was the second daughter of a mother who had immigrated and wanted her daughters to have the success she could never find herself. Without being directly pushed, she had accepted unknowingly the emotional pressure from her family. Some of the criticism she generated in herself actually was support to help her make the best of a given situation and not let chances go by. Healing some of the unspoken in the internal dialogue as well as the imagined dialogue with the imagined mother helped her overcome her feelings of anxiety and depression, and she depended less on medication to control her emotions. For Kate, ccepting herself was also a journey of accepting her family's background and history. Thus, emotional processing can also be understood in a systemic way.

Joy (2015) provides two case examples from the perspective of a social worker working in the context of the medical model in a hospital. Working in an emotion-focused manner here meant struggling with at least two roles—the role of the social worker resolving financial issues of the client and the role of an emotion-focused counselor, helping the client to understand and alleviate her emotional distress. Joy argues that even when the importance of emotion work is acknowledged, the frame that is set by a psychopathological medical model may make it more difficult to focus on emotion. Especially when working with clients with multiple losses, as is often the case in clients with a history of substance abuse, there is a need to acknowledge the pain and emotional distress that is associated with the loss of friends, family, or your own goals, perspectives, and dreams in life. Understanding and allowing the pain through empathic responses and time for listening will help clients to reconnect to their stronger parts within themselves, which may then lead to more self-confidence and empower clients to fight their symptoms and destructive behaviors. Connecting with the client and establishing the common goal between client and helper of an independent healthier life for the client can only be reached together and might only make sense for the client once a decision to change has been made. Marsha Linehan speaks of a decision for a new way with no self-harm and suicide attempts as a more general question that clients have to answer in order to keep focused on learning new skills and to remain hopeful that a new life is possible. Linehan is influenced by a Buddhist tradition as is a new approach merging meditation and mindfulness with emotion-focused therapy. Gaynor (2019) provides a case example using EFMT in a group format. In the case presented by Gaynor (2019), identifying and working with secondary anger and harsh self-criticism was essential in helping overcome depression and general anxiety disorder. These are interesting case examples that show how social work can integrate an emotion-focused approach and thereby be more effective in helping clients overcome their problems.

CONCLUSION

Emotion-focused therapy provides a framework for coaching clients to accept, regulate, and transform their emotions. This is relevant for many social work contexts, in counseling as well as other encounters with service users. Emotion-focused therapy guides the clients' self-actualizing process by structured interventions that focus on emotions and create new emotion schemes. The integrative nature of emotions fits into social work's person-in-environment view on mental health. Emotion-focused therapy theory and practice can help us develop emotional intelligence and competencies in our clients as well as ourselves. Being a reflexive practitioner entails therapeutic presence in the moment as well as a competent use of self in therapy and counseling. More research on emotion-focused therapy for specific groups of service users and various areas of social work practice is needed.

SUMMARY POINTS

- explored the theoretical underpinnings of emotion-focused therapy,
- explained the central tenets of emotion-focused therapy, and
- described the application of emotion-focused therapy to individuals and groups.

KEY REFERENCES

Only key references appear in the print edition. The full reference list appears in the digital product found on http://connect.springerpub.com/content/book/978-0-8261-6556-5/part/sec03/part/sec033/chapter/ch13

Angus, L. E., & Greenberg, L. S. (2011). *Working with narrative in emotion-focused therapy: Changing stories, healing lives*. American Psychological Association.

Australian Psychological Society (Ed.). (2010). *Evidence-based psychological interventions: A literature review* (3rd ed.). Australian Psychological Society.

Binder, P.-E., Holgersen, H., & Nielsen, G. (2010). What is "good outcome" in psychotherapy? A qualitative exploration of former patients' view. *Psychotherapy Research, 20*, 285–294.

Bischkopf, J. (2013). *Emotionsfokussierte Therapie. Grundlagen, Praxis, Wirksamkeit*. Göttingen u.a.: Hogrefe.

Bohart, A. (2004). How do clients make empathy work? *Person-Centered & Experiential Psychotherapies, 3*(2), 102–116.

Bohart, A. (2006). The active client. In J. C. Norcross, L. E. Beutler, & R. F. Levant (Eds.), *Evidence-based practices in mental health. Debate and dialogue on the fundamental questions* (pp. 218–226). American Psychological Association.

Bohart A. C., & Greenberg L. S. (1997). Empathy and psychotherapy: An introductory overview. In A. C. Bohart & L. S. Greenberg (Eds.), *Empathy reconsidered: New directions in psychotherapy* (pp. 3–31). American Psychological Association.

Bohlmeijer, E., Prenger, R., Taal, R. E. & Cuijpers, E. (2010). The effects of mindfulness-based stress reduction therapy on mental health of adults with a chronic medical disease: A meta-analysis. *Journal of Psychosomatic Research, 68*, 539–544.

Bonanno, G. A., Papa, A., Lalande, K., Westphal, M., & Coifman, K. (2004). The importance of being flexible: The ability to both enhance and suppress emotional expression predicts long-term adjustment. *Psychological Science, 15*(7), 482–487.

Castonguay, L. G., & Hill, C. E. (Eds.). (2012). *Transformation in psychotherapy: Corrective experiences across cognitive behavioral, humanistic, and psychodynamic approaches*. American Psychological Association.

14

Motivational Interviewing

Allison Salisbury, Doug Smith, and Corey Campbell

LEARNING OBJECTIVES

By the end of this chapter, you should be able to:

- describe the historical underpinnings generating the motivational interviewing (MI) style,
- examine theories underlying MI principles,
- integrate core elements embodying the "MI spirit" into the four processes of MI,
- utilize MI-adherent micro-skills in a variety of situations,
- integrate MI into the generalist-eclectic approach, and
- evaluate the strengths and limitations of MI.

For many individuals, the status quo is comfortable and the prospect of behavior change sets up a process where they weigh options before acting. Individuals are sometimes unsure about change. On the one hand, they may not mind their current situation or they aren't facing severe consequences, but on the other hand, they may experience a dull, nagging feeling that change would be beneficial. When you have a client experiencing ambivalence about change, regardless of behavior, MI is an appropriate approach to incorporate into your generalist-eclectic practice.

INTRODUCTION: OVERVIEW OF MOTIVATIONAL INTERVIEWING

Motivational interviewing (MI) is a communicative approach to encouragr clients who are resistant or ambivalent to make a behavior change. When applied correctly, skilled clinicians establish a collaborative, client-centered partnership before tackling their client's self-identified target behavior. You may employ a variety of techniques to establish this collaboration, including listening to their narrative, empathizing with their story, and sharing responsibility for behavior change. A successful interpersonal relationship results in a brief yet effective approach to stimulate the natural change process. A skilled clinician trained in MI guides clients through ambivalence utilizing the therapeutic relationship grounded in the "MI spirit," which involves overarching principles about the "feel" of the intervention. We will discuss these in greater detail later in the chapter. In addition to the "MI spirit," we will discuss micro-skills, including techniques that help the client feel listened to and that evoke motivation to change.

To enhance your understanding of MI, we first review the historical development and theoretical constructs of the therapeutic relationship and behavior change. As we discuss the key components of the approach, we provide an array of case scenarios. We offer two hypothetical responses to each case scenario. The first example exhibits a non-MI adherent scenario, which is not recommended for MI clinicians because they risk increasing client resistance and fracturing of collaborative relationships. The second example exhibits an MI-adherent scenario. The clinician in these examples acts according to MI values and skill sets, which we note as presented. Finally, we summarize all topics discussed in each section, apply MI to the generalist-eclectic framework, and provide a full case example for you to practice your skills.

HISTORICAL DEVELOPMENT

MI applied social psychology theories about cognitive dissonance (Festinger, 1962) and self-perception (Bem, 1972) within a client-centered framework. Departing from prior models that viewed individuals with addictions as people in denial with flawed personalities, MI instead promoted strategies respecting the autonomy of clients to make decisions and using empathy instead of confrontation. It has evolved since its initial development in 1983 (Miller, 1983), as evidenced by tens of thousands of studies and the publication of three editions of the main MI sourcebook (Miller & Rollnick, 1991, 2002, 2012).

Moyers (2004) provides an excellent accounting of the early history of MI. What is striking is how the model developed from intense clinical observation of how clients responded to certain clinician behaviors. In social work, we would say this is the ultimate example of doing practice-informed research (Council on Social Work Education, 2015). That is, clinical observations drove hypotheses about what was happening in MI, which were later tested formally in research settings. For example, Miller and his associates likely observed that confronting clients resulted in their doubling-down on being "resistant," but (highly learnable) empathy statements prompted clients' contemplation of change. This emphasis on observation never waned, forming the basis for subsequent research and model revisions.

Early emphasis focused on mastering principles such as rolling with resistance, expressing empathy, developing discrepancy, and supporting client self-efficacy. The third edition of the MI sourcebook eliminated the principles of developing discrepancy and rolling with resistance (Miller & Rollnick, 2012). Part of this was due to people conflating MI with completing a pros and cons list, a decisional balance activity. Evidence suggested that pros and cons lists, which sometimes give equal weight to reasons for and against change, reinforce client ambivalence (Miller & Rollnick, 2009). Thus, MI focuses more on eliciting change talk (formerly called client self-motivational statements), which is defined in the following.

As MI gained in popularity, there existed increasing emphasis on using MI solely for the welfare of the client. Thus, Miller and Rollnick (2012) added the concepts of compassion and equipoise as elements of MI practice. Compassion is specifically defined as keeping the client's interests central, without using MI to get clients to do something they don't want to do, such as selling them something, including unwanted social work services. Instead, social workers implement strategies in MI designed to reduce ambivalence only when doing so benefits the client and balance this against client autonomy. Increasingly, ethical discussions define the inappropriate use of resolving ambivalence. Social workers should not sway clients to get divorces or donate organs, decisions for which the best course of action for the client appears hazy at best. In such situations, pros and cons lists may be appropriate, and the clinician may assume equipoise, defined as not actively shaping the client's language in one direction (see the discussion following on eliciting and reinforcing change talk).

Another problem with MI's growing success involves safeguarding practice and training standards. Research shows that many individuals claim to be using MI but in reality use approaches straying dramatically from key quality indicators. To that end, many research studies focused on what types of training lead to competent practice of MI, perhaps more than for any other therapeutic approach. Additionally, there exists a very large network of MI trainers dedicated to promoting best practices in training, called the Motivational Interviewing Network of Trainers (MINT; n.d.). Members must demonstrate competency in delivering the model, and there are efforts within MINT to develop practitioner and trainer certifications. Currently, standardized measures of both practitioner and trainer competencies exist (Moyers et al., 2014; Smith et al., 2017). For now, social workers should refrain from telling clients that they received certification in MI. If rigorously trained, however, it is acceptable to tell clients about the training process. The highest level of rigor involves didactic training and practice, followed by competent MI trainers reviewing samples of one's clinical work (e.g., audio tapes) using established quality assurance standards.

Rollnick emphasized addressing ambivalence, and eventually the "MI spirit" was the target for attaining excellence in the approach (Moyers, 2004). MI offers a generalist perspective to social work practice because of its versatility in a variety of settings, including alcohol and other drug problems, healthcare, mandated treatment, consultations, fitness and weight loss, and schools.

CENTRAL THEORETICAL CONSTRUCTS

MI borrows concepts from social psychological theories of motivation, cognitive dissonance, attribution, and self-efficacy (Miller, 1983). This section reviews the theoretical view on client ambivalence and resistance, as well as the three theories related to motivation.

Conceptualization of Ambivalence and Resistance

Theoretically, MI assumes that ambivalence about change is a natural part of behavior change decisions. Although MI remains neutral on whether people pass through the stages of change sequentially, it shares common ground with the transtheoretical model (TTM) of change in recognizing ambivalence as a key factor in change (Prochaska & DiClemente, 1983; Prochaska et al., 1992). This contrasts with models that view reluctance to change as "denial," "resistance," or "lack of insight." When applied to the addictions realm, the goal isn't for the client to admit their addiction or to abstain from drinking; rather, the goal is to allow clients to make their own decisions (Moyers, 2014).

Motivation is construed as an interpersonal process. Consider the fact that one synonym of resist is "counter." Thus, a client cannot resist in the absence of an opposing force. Thus, the goal of MI is for social workers to not provide an opposing force. Research clearly demonstrates that clients become "resistant" when therapists use confrontation, persuasion, or other punitive tactics. In other words, saying that resistance is interpersonal means that social workers have a modicum of control over how resistant their clients are, and replacing counterproductive behaviors may result in a smoother interaction. In lay terms, it's on us social workers to not create resistant clients.

This is also to say that resistance doesn't live inside the client. Consider the phrase "They are resistant to change." In theory, MI does not view resistance as a personal attribute or trait. The implication of this view is that instead of telling clients they are in denial, haven't "bottomed-out," or are "unmotivated," social workers practicing MI validate and try to resolve their ambivalence. Social workers communicate this in many ways, through the "MI spirit," reflective listening, and strategic use of skills to elicit a client's own motivation for change. We discuss these techniques in subsequent sections.

Counter-arguing against unsolicited advice comprises a natural reaction for ambivalent individuals. Let's do a thought experiment. Take a minute to think about a discussion you had with a friend or family member who urged you to do something. Did you find yourself reacting to them with a statement that started with "Yeah that may work, but…"? Whatever follows the "but" is the natural product of ambivalence, not necessarily denial. Thus, social workers should expect mixed feelings toward change and perhaps some counter-argument from clients. In MI, we call such counter-arguments sustain talk, and we take measures to try to not meet it forcefully, but rather steer the conversation elsewhere.

Resistance is conceptualized slightly differently in MI. Whereas ambivalence pertains to the decision-making process, resistance involves the therapeutic relationship. Resistant behaviors in MI may include challenging the social worker's credentials or experience, as well as not talking or talking about something off-topic to avoid doing therapeutic work. Social workers should not quickly judge these as indications of resistance. Sometimes, these indications represent feelings associated with coercion about a problem for which they have not yet decided to change. For example, individuals mandated to parenting classes sometimes present as resentful because they feel threatened and perceive professionals as judging their parenting as inadequate. Such an individual may challenge a social worker out of fear and ambivalence about change rather than a predisposition to being difficult or resistant. In MI, social workers would convey empathy about such fear and ambivalence.

Related Theories

CLIENT-CENTERED THERAPY

Client-centered therapy suggests the interpersonal conditions for behavior change consist of three pillars: genuineness, unconditional positive regard, and empathy (Rogers, 1957, 1974). Genuineness requires inner and outer congruence, or authenticity, with your client. In MI, you can model genuineness to enhance trust and subsequently the likelihood of clients sharing their story. Unconditional positive regard considers the therapist as accepting without judgment. Rather than evaluating and giving approval to your client on whether change occurs and about the decisions they make, you validate their experiences and support their goals. Empathy offers the opportunity for a clinician to portray meaning of their client's experiences. A skilled clinician utilizes empathy in MI to consciously raise underlying substantive motives for client behaviors. These pillars are essential to the "feel" of MI, or the "MI spirit," which is further discussed in a subsequent section.

COGNITIVE DISSONANCE

The theory of cognitive dissonance suggests that people feel uncomfortable when they sense a discrepancy between their values and current behavior (Festinger, 1962). Thus, when applied to ambivalence about change, it seems logical to generate discussion about the benefits of change and the consequences of persisting in some negative behavior. For example, if your client presents a sedentary lifestyle, they may share with you the plentiful concerns from their peers and family on their enhanced risk for poor cardiovascular health. If you confront your client's enhanced risk for medical issues such as a heart attack, they may resist your genuine concerns and project feelings of discomfort, guilt, and shame. On the contrary, if you use strategies that elicit client speech about the benefits of change, it may help resolve this dissonance. That is, clients hear themselves talking about change, and behavior change may result as a solution to resolving internal tensions.

SELF-PERCEPTION THEORY

Self-perception theory (Bem, 1972) suggests that the more we talk about our values and beliefs, the more we form values surrounding such beliefs. In other words, there is something about articulating or talking out loud about something that can reinforce a belief. In MI, this influences the concept of training social workers to elicit and reinforce change talk, as well as any client speech that indicates a desire, ability, reason, or need for change. We discuss this reinforcement of change talk in a subsequent section. Additionally, clients may also express statements about their commitment to change, intentions to change (i.e., activation), and steps toward change on which they recently ventured. So, per self-perception theory, when clients talk about change, it reinforces their beliefs about the desirability of change.

COMPONENTS OF MOTIVATIONAL INTERVIEWING

The eternal "chicken or the egg" argument in MI is determining how it works. When considering this question, MI is divided into three main component areas: the "MI spirit," highlighting the relational component; counseling strategies or "micro-skills" common to many therapies; and the specific, intentional use of these micro-skills to elicit and reinforce change talk (i.e., the technical component). Since the dawn of MI, debate has emerged over which components are sentinel to client change. We continue to debate exactly how MI works at this level. Is one component superior to the other, or do the components work in concert for the best results? In this section, we focus on the relational component, defining these concepts and providing case examples of the MI-adherent and MI non-adherent social worker statements. In subsequent sections, we introduce the micro-skills and the technical component of MI (i.e., change talk).

The Relational Component of the Motivational Interviewing Spirit

The relational component of MI states that the "MI spirit," the overall "feel" of the approach, will be associated with client behavior change (Arkowitz et al., 2008; Miller & Rose, 2009). Let's examine the four components embodying this spirit: partnership, acceptance, compassion, and evocation.

PARTNERSHIP

Without a collaborative partnership involving input from both the clinician and client, there is no MI. Just like in other humanistic approaches, you treat clients as the experts in their own lives, coming to you for guidance in resolving their ambivalence. If they remain stuck on deciding whether to change, they aren't looking for your advice on *how* to change. Rather, they seek resolution behind the *why* to the change (Moyers, 2014). Thus, a common MI faux pas is offering unsolicited suggestions prior to querying, and often amplifying, client intentions to change.

Let's look at an example of detachment and an example of partnership (Exhibit 14.1). In this situation, you are working with an individual who was recently sentenced to 30 months of probation for their third conviction for driving under the influence.

MI in criminal justice settings is complex. Not only is there ambivalence about participating in mandated treatment, there is additional ambivalence in engaging in criminalized behaviors (Ginsburg et al., 2002). Although the United States' criminal justice system is notorious for punitive measures, you do not need to follow the status quo of coldness, coercion, and confrontation. In your role, you may create a case plan to address your client's risk factors for engaging in a subsequent criminalized behavior, but that doesn't mean you discount what your client considers important. In the first example, you immediately appear authoritarian, distant, and unapproachable by fixating on time wasting instead of possible ambivalence. In contrast, in the

EXHIBIT 14.1 Example of Detachment and Partnership

Example 1: Detachment	*Example 2: Partnership*
Client: I don't want to be here, I was mandated to treatment as part of my probation (*resistance*).	Client: I don't want to be here, I was mandated to treatment as part of my probation (*resistance*).
Clinician: Well, you have to be here, so let's not waste our time (*expert stance*). Why are you here today (*open-ended question*)?	Clinician: I understand why it may be difficult to be here (*sympathy*), and knowing that, what you would you like to spend time on today (*autonomy, open-ended question*)? I'd like this to be helpful to you (*partnership*).

second example, you build on the partnership by communicating your investment while eliciting theirs. You additionally empathize with your client and offer autonomy for the client to focus on their priorities, which we discuss next.

ACCEPTANCE

Accepting your client includes displaying absolute worth, affirmation, accurate empathy, and autonomy (Miller & Rollnick, 2012). As we previously mentioned, these characteristics derive from Rogers's client-centered therapy. In the previous examples, you displayed empathy by expressing the difficulty of your client's situation and understanding their frustration. Empathy is similar to sympathy, but the former takes it a step further by incorporating non-verbal cues into the meaning of your client's messages and feelings. Let's use the previous example to further examine empathy. Whereas sympathy communicates feeling sorry for your client's situation, empathy demonstrates one's ability to see the other's perspective. Although the previous situations took different directions, you know your client chose attending their first session with you despite disagreeing with the court mandate. Let's examine how to capitalize your recognition of their frustrations (Exhibit 14.2).

In the first example, you attempt to empathize with your client, but you misinterpreted their feelings by reflecting their personal anger at you, which wasn't present. The reflection missed the mark. It is alright if you are not always accurate, especially as you start out. You will learn over time how to detect meaning from your client's messages and incorporate non-verbal cues. Instead, you can look at the second example for accurate empathy. In this example, you detect their fear of failure and of facing adverse consequences. You highlight their "on thin ice" metaphor and continue with it, examining their fear of messing up, "falling" if they make one mistake with their probation conditions or treatment requirements. Your client notices you picking up on how they're feeling, and they continue the rapport building by sharing their resolution to attempt to follow their court-ordered conditions by attending your session.

Although you may not understand your client's behaviors, you should respect and attempt to understand their situation. Even if you don't agree with your client, an empathic clinician

EXHIBIT 14.2 Examples of Empathy

Example 1: Inaccurate Empathy	*Example 2: Accurate Empathy*
Client: I am just trying to avoid prison … I barely kept my job because I spent time in jail since I couldn't afford bail. I'm already on thin ice, and it doesn't help that I have to take time off work every week to come to treatment that I don't want to be at.	Client: I am just trying to avoid prison … I barely kept my job because I spent time in jail since I couldn't afford bail. I'm already on thin ice, and it doesn't help that I have to take time off work every week to come to treatment that I don't want to be at.
Clinician: You seem angry with the court and upset with me because I'm making you be here. You want to get this over with so you can get back to work and the rest of your life (*simple reflection*).	Clinician: You are disappointed of the situation you're in and scared of getting worse consequences, including losing your job and going to prison (*empathy*). You're exhausted because you feel like one misstep and … BAM! You could fall through the ice at any moment (*complex reflection*).
Client: I'm not upset with you, and I know it's my fault so I can't be angry with the court for doing what they have to do … I do want to get this over with and move on, but my sentence is 30 months, which is a long time.	Client: You're right, I feel that I can't make any mistakes, not even little ones. It's a huge step, and I'm trying to please everyone. I came here, so that's a start.

EXHIBIT 14.3 Encouraging Autonomy

Example 1: Coercion	*Example 2: Autonomy Enhancement*
Client: I am here today because I received a court order for 30 hours of substance use disorder treatment, but I don't have a problem with alcohol!	Client: I am here today because I received a court order for 30 hours of substance abuse treatment. I don't have a problem with alcohol!
Clinician: In my experience, if it walks like a duck and quacks like a duck, it's probably a duck (*expert stance*). Don't you think a DUI means you have a problem (*confrontation*)? You must follow the conditions of the court if you don't want to face further consequences, and that includes attending treatment. I'm your ally though, and I want to see you do well (*expressing support*).	Clinician: Although the court is requiring this treatment to successfully complete your probationary sentence, ultimately, it is your decision to attend and participate (*autonomy*). How do you feel about what the court is asking you to do (*partnership, open-ended question*)?
Client: I know that, but I don't have a problem with using alcohol, I messed up	Client: I feel that I shouldn't have to do this (*sustain talk*), but the other alternative is prison, which I want to avoid at all costs (*change talk*). I messed up, and I have to face the consequences.
Clinician: You were caught driving under the influence, and that seems to be the problem (*confrontation*).	Clinician: You are upset with this situation, yet you want to do something about it to avoid prison. You are here today, so you decided to avoid prison by attending treatment (*reflection focusing on change talk*).

understands and communicates their verbal and nonverbal feelings. It is essential to establish rapport and build trust for your client to feel comfortable in opening up, sharing their experiences, and examining their ambivalence. Wording matters.

Instilling a sense of client autonomy in decision-making is another way to accept your client's experiences (Exhibit 14.3). You demonstrate autonomy by reflecting your client's values and respecting their choices. We will use the previous example to illustrate autonomy. You know your client is sentenced to probation, which requires mandated alcohol treatment, and you know your client feels they do not have a say in attending this treatment. Let's examine how to encourage autonomy in this situation.

You may recognize that the first example destructs the collaborative relationship. Your client already knows the conditions of their probation. They repeated themselves because they didn't feel heard, and they further explained their situation with a sense of hopelessness. You selected their problem for them, which eliminated the client-centered relational aspect of MI. In contrast, in the second example, you recognize your client's court-ordered mandate, but you also recognize your client's choice in fulfilling that requirement. Your client does not have to complete treatment, and it is not your decision to make. You recognize their control in the decision and its consequences, positive and negative. In addition, you empathize with your client by recognizing their emotional reaction and establishing rapport, allowing them to explain their goals for attaining their choice behaviors.

COMPASSION

Miller and Rollnick (2012) recently emphasized compassion as a critical aspect of the "MI spirit." The concept seems synonymous with the idea of communicating non-possessive warmth and overlaps greatly with the concept of enhancing client autonomy. That is, some individuals came to MI thinking that it could motivate or "get" their clients to change. Yet, that mindset runs contrary to the "MI spirit" of preserving client self-direction. One misconception of MI is that it is a set of "tricks" you can use to get your clients to change. This is particularly relevant to strategies involving eliciting and reinforcing change talk, which are described in subsequent sections.

EVOCATION

In MI, evocation suggests eliciting your client's strongest reasons to change to increase the likelihood of change occurring (Moyers, 2014). As we mentioned earlier, most clients have some inherent motivation to change their target behavior. As a skilled clinician, you call out this motivation through the use of micro-counseling skills designed to elicit client change talk, which is discussed in greater detail in a subsequent section.

Summary of the Relational Component

The "MI spirit," or the relational component of MI, aligns well with social work core values, especially integrity (partnership), dignity and worth of the person (acceptance and compassion), and importance of human relationships (National Association of Social Workers, 2017). Once you and your client establish a collaborative partnership, accept your client's autonomy, present accurate empathy, illustrate compassion, and evoke change, you are ready to utilize MI-consistent techniques that promote change talk. In the next section, we tackle the four processes of MI and incorporate the micro-skills and technical components encompassing MI.

PHASES OF HELPING

Miller and Rollnick (2012) established four processes of MI: engaging, focusing, evoking, and planning. In this section, we present the micro-counseling skills and evocative strategies in the context of these four processes.

Engaging

If your client is not engaged, there is no platform to explore motivation and therefore no change. With an engaged client, it is easier to pinpoint their targeted goals for behavior change and elicit motivation to enact the change. Keep in mind the relational components we just discussed as you engage with your client.

Micro-skills such as open-ended questions, affirmations, reflections, and summaries (OARS) facilitate client engagement (Miller & Rollnick, 1991). Clinicians using MI strategically implement these skills to convey empathy and generate change talk. We review each skill independently. Note that there is a time and a place for each of these skills. Thus, rather than using them in a sequential, rigid manner, work toward flexibly rotating among them when appropriate.

The "O" in the OARS skill set stands for open-ended questions, which allow your client to freely share their story. Unlike close-ended questions, which typically are answered with "yes" or "no," you can pull information from an open-ended question to elicit change talk that continues the conversation. If you ask close-ended questions, you may end up stuck in a "question-answer trap," where you are unable to move the conversation forward. In addition, close-ended questions may remind a person of an interview because they are providing you information. Let's examine an example comparing close-ended and open-ended questions with a client considering leaving their family and caregiving role to pursue an employment opportunity (Exhibit 14.4).

In the first example, two close-ended questions yielded no new information about your client's needs or motivation. You are stuck in the question–answer loop, and you must ask a third

EXHIBIT 14.4 Close-Ended Versus Open-Ended Comparisons

Example 1 (Question/Answer Trap):	Example 2 (Open-Ended Questions):
Client: "I don't know whether I should apply for this job (*ambivalence*). I am worried about leaving my family."	Client: I don't know whether I should apply for this job (*ambivalence*). I am worried about leaving my family."
Clinician: "Do you think it will be hard for your family to adjust to you leaving, should you get this job (*close-ended question*)?"	Clinician: "What are your thoughts about applying for this job (*open-ended question*)?"
Client: "Yes."	Client: "I would be excited to take this job because it is in a city that I have always dreamed of visiting (*change talk*). However, I am worried that, if I leave, my parents won't be able to take care of themselves and my younger siblings (*sustain talk*). I visit my parents a few times a week to babysit while they are at work. If I leave, they would have to find a babysitter, which isn't affordable at the moment."
Clinician: "Do you think you would earn the job if you apply for it (*close-ended question*)?"	
Client: "I think so."	

EXHIBIT 14.5 Supporting Statement Versus Affirmation

Example 1: General Support	Example 2: Affirmation
Client: "I want to be there for my family (*ambivalence*), but I think I would earn the job if I applied for it (*change talk*)."	Client: "I want to be there for my family (*ambivalence*), but I think I would earn the job if I applied for it (*change talk*)."
Clinician: "That is great to hear (*partnership*)."	Clinician: "You have great pride in caring for your family. Your compassion can translate well into the position you are considering to applying for (*affirmation*)."

question to elicit a response that continues the conversation. How inefficient! In the second example, you strategically ask one question, and you discover that your client is an instrumental caretaker in their family. However, this may lead to sustain talk because replies to questions may go anywhere. By asking about the job, you are posing a neutral question. You may have considered asking how the client feels about leaving their family, but this may lead to sustain talk. Other strategic questions include: "Could you tell me more?" "What are your thoughts on this?" "How has this been a problem for you?" and "What have you tried that works?"

The "A" in the OARS skill set stands for affirmations, which help build a positive relationship with clients and can interrupt monotonous interactions. You may validate a personal attribute or behavior to express positive regard and empathy. However, you must be cautious to only use the same affirmation once, because subsequent times could reduce the effect of the affirmation. Let's continue the story line from the previous examples. This time, we compare a supportive statement to an affirmation (Exhibit 14.5).

In the first example, you tell your client that it is great to hear they feel capable of earning the job they are considering. You can say this because it is positive and promotes a collaborative partnership, but it may be too general because you are not focusing on the client's strengths. Notice the level of detail in the second example. Current thinking in the MI community is that

EXHIBIT 14.6 Comparing Questions and Reflections

Example 1: Open-Ended Question	*Example 2: Simple Reflection*
Client: "I feel determined to improve my life. I feel that this job could get me out of this funk I have been feeling for so long (*change talk*)."	Client: "I feel determined to improve my life. I feel that this job could get me out of this funk I have been feeling for so long (*change talk*)."
Clinician: "Can you explain this funk that you are talking about (*question*)?"	Clinician: Getting this job will help your mood and self-esteem (*reflection*)."

short, cheerleading-type affirmations, such as the first example, are less effective for building positive relationships or nudging toward resolved ambivalence.

The "R" in the OARS skill set stands for reflecting back your client's statements. Reflections are the preferred skill in MI (Moyers et al., 2014). Instead of asking questions, you can read your client's verbal and nonverbal cues to guess how they feel. In the previous example, you realized that your client was feeling uncomfortable about making a decision that will impact their family. To express empathy, respond to resistance or sustain talk, and promote change talk, you can use a few types of reflections.

One type of reflection is a simple reflection, which allows you to repeat what your client has said in your own words. This allows you to check your understanding, and if you are incorrect, the opportunity for your client to correct you. Let's continue the above conversations to compare questions and reflections (Exhibit 14.6).

In the first example, you ask for information about the "funk," so it is not actually a reflection. Reflections are statements, not questions. The question serves to clarify an emotional state, so is less adroit at resolving ambivalence. This is not to say you should avoid asking questions; however, in the second example, by rephrasing your client's statement and highlighting the change talk component, you move toward resolving ambivalence about taking a job (i.e., target behavior).

Another type of reflection is a complex reflection, which takes a deeper guess at client meaning, provides stronger emphasis on what clients said (i.e., amplification), or steers the conversation to new places. This type of reflection is the most difficult to accomplish because you want to be bold but also to be accurate. Let's take a look at our examples, comparing an inaccurate to an accurate reflection (Exhibit 14.7).

EXHIBIT 14.7 Inaccurate Versus Accurate Reflections

Example 1: Inaccurate Reflection	*Example 2: Complex Reflection*
Client: "I feel like I've done nothing with my life. All I have known is being with my family, putting my dream to visit this city on hold so I can watch my siblings grow up."	Client: "I feel like I've done nothing with my life. All I have known is being with my family, putting my dream to visit this city on hold so I can watch my siblings grow up."
Clinician: "You seem angry with your parents for pressuring you to stay in town."	Clinician: "Balancing your conflicting roles as caretaker and worker will become more difficult if you apply for this job and leave town, but on the other hand you know this is the only way to achieve your professional goals (*double-sided complex reflection*)".
Client: "I don't feel angry or pressured. My family is fully supportive of me. I just worry that they will struggle without the extra support, from being there physically and emotionally to providing extra income (*ambivalence*)."	Client: "This is the only way to achieve my professional goals (*change talk*). Family will always be there.

EXHIBIT 14.8 Summarizing

Example 1:	Example 2:
Clinician: "You're experiencing this funk that may be solved by accepting this job. However, you're worried too much about your family and you need to decide what to do (*double-sided reflection*)."	Clinician: "You've shared how important two areas of your life are conflicting: your family life and your professional life. You are dedicated to both and you are concerned whether your family will be fine if you leave. On the other hand, you could break through your funk, live in an exciting city, and grow professionally (*double-sided reflection*). You also said your family will support you if you apply for this job. This is a tough choice for you (*empathy*), and you have to make it for yourself (*autonomy*). Which way are your leaning (*open-ended question*)?"

In the first example, you misread your client's intentions. It is acceptable to be incorrect, and it is expected to happen at times. Your client will correct you, and you guess again. In this example, your client feels inadequate and does not want to miss the opportunity to reach their potential. In contrast, in the second example, you recognize your client's dilemma, with a double-sided complex reflection, which reflects both sides of ambivalence. You typically see a double-sided reflection in this format: "On the one hand, … and on the other hand …." You may also see metaphors used to help clients relate to their feelings, as seen in the "thin ice" example in the "Relational Component" section. When you use a double-sided reflection, you want to start with the ambivalence and end with the potential change (i.e., change talk). This prompts the recency effect, which encourages your client to continue discussing the change and move past their resistance.

The "S" in the OARS skill set involves summarizing your client's story, topic, or session. You want to select the important parts of your conversation with your client and use a reflection that captures the gist of your client's ambivalence and feelings to change. Summaries are appropriate as you transition to a new theme or topic or as you end your session. Let's look at these examples and summarize where your client stands with applying for the job (Exhibit 14.8).

In the first example, you are focusing against your client applying for the job, reducing their willingness to discuss a plan to pursue the option they idealize. In MI, we refer to this as reinforcing sustain talk (i.e., client speech about staying the same). In the second example, you state the ambivalence but selectively focus on change talk. However, this is balanced with empathy and autonomy-preserving statements, so it does not come on too thick. Social workers refrain from using high-pressure tactics to help clients with decisions about change. If your client responds positively, you can take this consolidated list of reasons to apply for the job before you transition into planning this change.

Let's review the OARS skills that we learned. First, we discussed how to strategically ask open-ended questions to elicit information. Next, we affirmed our client by sharing a positive quality that can facilitate your client's ability to change, should they choose to apply for the job? Then, we reflected on your client's reasons to apply for the job. Finally, we summarized the conversation and set up the conversation to discuss the application process. We reviewed examples that were inconsistent (*Example 1*) and consistent (*Example 2*) with these skills to demonstrate how to guide your client to resolve their ambivalence in an MI-consistent manner

Focusing

When your client is engaged in the session, you can turn to focusing on the targeted behavior. It is imperative that you establish the therapeutic relationship before discussing your client's target behavior; otherwise, you risk resistance to discussing this behavior. Focusing dictates that you and your client negotiate on a shared goal. You may think there is a clear focus, but your client may disagree, and you don't know what they want until you discuss and clarify their goals. For example, your client may wish to reduce but not stop their substance use, but you believe they should attend treatment and stop their substance use. Discrepancy exists between these goals, but you may combine your client's plans and your expertise to identify a shared, realistic goal.

There are a few techniques you can employ to focus on this shared goal. One technique is setting an agenda that involves the change process (Miller & Rollnick, 2012). Change brings up many emotions, positive and negative, and you want your client to be in the best position to handle these changes. Your client may feel angry or upset with reducing their substance use because this activity is a key part of their social circle. They may feel embarrassed attending treatment because they need to inform their boss when they miss work, or they don't want their family knowing about treatment but don't want them to worry about coming home an hour later twice a week. Your client may also feel excited about the change, hoping to improve their familial relationships and work productivity. Their expectations may vary, from having no concerns that they will not have any issues along the way to having concerns that every step will result in a mounting set of obstacles. You want to optimize on MI-consistent behaviors, including reflections and affirmations, when exploring these emotions.

Another technique often used in MI is providing personalized normative feedback, which highlights a discrepancy between your client's behavior and their peer's typical behaviors. Additionally, screening results that have suggested cutoffs for problems may be used. The goal of providing personalized normative feedback or cutoff-based information is to gently raise awareness about potential problems. When such information is used, it is often called motivational enhancement therapy (MET) or screening, brief intervention, and referral to treatment (SBIRT), which are both derivatives of MI. For example, when conducting a substance use screening with your client that indicates risky or problematic substance use, you want to check with your client before discussing potential changes. You can review the screening by first asking permission, an MI-adherent behavior, before comparing them to their peers or expressing concern. Asking permission further engages your client by allowing them to select whether or not to receive information (i.e., collaboration and autonomy). When discussing the screening findings, you want to link your client's behaviors with the consequences they face and how change reduces the risk for experiencing these consequences. One such example involves your client sharing that they miss work the day after binge drinking because their biting hangover causes migraines. Their substance use screen indicates that they binge drink at a rate three times higher than the national average. You can utilize this information, with your client's permission, to suggest that reducing their binge drinking to a comparable rate of their peer's may reduce incidences of work absence. This activity provides rapid focus, so is often used in medical settings when time is short.

As you and your client focus on your shared goal, you want to keep in mind that you should guide, not direct or follow. Directing results in diminishing the client's expertise and plans, and following results in reducing your expert input on resources and techniques for achieving the goal. Now that you and your client share a focused goal, we continue with the next process: evoking your client's inherent motivation to change their target behavior.

Evoking

The third process involves evoking your client's motivation to change their target behavior. This step requires skillful navigation of the technical component—cultivating change talk and softening sustain talk—in conjunction with the relational component. We will explore the technical component of MIg and offer techniques to optimize your "MI spirit."

CHANGE TALK

The technical component of MI comprises specific clinician behaviors intended to evoke and reinforce client change language. When a clinician uses MI-adherent skills—including open-ended questions, simple and complex reflections, and affirmations—their client is more likely to use change language (Arkowitz et al., 2008; Miller & Rose, 2009), and when your client voices change talk, you see a higher probability of behavior change (Magill et al., 2014, 2018). Essentially, you as a clinician are key for prompting and continuing your client's change talk and facilitating change behavior. Let's examine two key factors: cultivating change talk and softening sustain talk.

The first factor we will consider is change talk, which refers to "spontaneously occurring speech from the client that favors a desired change" (Moyers, 2014, p. 358). Formerly called client self-motivational statements, clinicians cultivate change talk because of data implicating its role in actual behavior change.

The second factor we will consider is sustain talk, which refers to client speech about avoiding change. Some sustain talk is unavoidable, and clinicians focus on softening it when they hear it. That is, completely ignoring sustain talk is indicative of low empathy, or not communicating an understanding of your client's views. So, the clinician's dilemma is how to communicate understanding while simultaneously inching toward client speech about change. A tall task! Double-sided reflections are good for simultaneous communication of empathy while also pivoting toward change talk. In short, softening sustain talk is a skill used in conjunction with cultivating change talk to shift the conversation away from status quo language to focus on change language (Moyers et al., 2014).

MICRO-SKILLS RELATED TO CHANGE TALK

One way to cultivate change talk as you move to mobilizing change talk and a change plan is the readiness ruler. The readiness ruler highlights the importance, confidence, and readiness to change. Variations of the readiness ruler exist such as: On a scale of 1 to 10 … (1) "… how important is this change," (2) "… how confident are you in this change?," and (3) "… how ready are you for this change?." If your client answers with a number greater than 1, there is a motivation to change. To hone in on change talk, ask your client why they selected their number over a lower number. Again, do not feel compelled to ask all three of these questions in a single session. It may not be appropriate. Use these questions when you identify the need to discuss either importance, client confidence, or readiness. For example, it makes little sense to use a readiness ruler to ask about the importance of change after extensive discussion of this topic. Timing and flexible use of these skills are key.

TYPES OF CHANGE TALK

In order to recognize what counts as change talk, consider the acronym "DARN CAT." "DARN" stands for the desire, ability, reasons, and need for change. "CAT" stands for commitment, activation, and taking steps. In this section, we focus on preparatory change talk, or the "DARN" part of the acronym, and in the next section, we cover how to mobilize change talk or the "CAT" part of the acronym. This is because "DARN" typically appears first in sessions when you are focusing on a target behavior. Thus, it is sometimes referred to as preparatory change talk. Desire statements indicate your client's wishes to change their target behavior (e.g., I wish I could eat better). Ability statements are about your client's confidence about implementing changing (e.g., I think I can do this if I get some support). Sometimes, clients recognize the importance of change but have low confidence. Reasons are often about the benefits for changing or the consequences of not changing (e.g., my clothes would smell better and I'm tired of being unemployed and having no purpose). Need statements are often a bit more emphatic, compared to reasons or importance statements. A client expressing the words "ought," "should," "have to," or "must" is probably talking about the need to change. Clinicians should train their ears to hear client speech about change, for the purpose of strategically reflecting it back to promote change.

PLANNING

Once your client expresses sufficient indication that change is needed, clinicians begin negotiating a change plan. Here, it is common to hear commitment language, or the "CAT" part of the acronym: commitment, activation, and taking steps. Commitment refers to client statements expressing their willingness to execute change (e.g., I am willing to work on this). Basically, listen for statements outlining intention, promise, and planning for change. Activation statements are a bit tricky but have to do with taking specific steps in the future (e.g., I will set a quit date of August 5). Your client may express the date and time, location, and action they plan to make in the impending future. Taking steps is change talk about actions already taken in the recent past (e.g., I went to all my required meetings this week). As clients share the steps they take, it is important to affirm their change to preserve motivation and influence further substantial change.

In addition to planning for change action, it is imperative to plan for follow-up to remind your clients of their commitment to change, and if change did not occur, to refocus. It is alright if your client changes their mind, something unexpected comes up, or they decide to not change the target behavior in the planned way. Refocusing allows you and your client to clarify the target behavior, reevaluate preparatory change talk, and modify action steps that align with the target behavior change. You should develop short- and long-term goals, encouraging your client to look forward into the future should the behavior change occur. If your client needs further guidance or you are not the best fit for meeting their goals, you can give what is called a "warm handoff" to another clinician. You can do this by introducing your client to the new clinician or offering to be present while your client makes the call to schedule an appointment with the new clinician. By connecting your client with a clinician best suited to help them achieve their goals, you are promoting the success of your client's target behavior change.

ASSESSING YOUR ADHERENCE TO MOTIVATIONAL INTERVIEWING

To measure the degree of success that clinicians are utilizing the relational and technical components, we use two assessment tools. First, the Motivational Interviewing Treatment Integrity Scale 4.1 (MITI 4.1; Moyers et al., 2014, 2016) is a structured measure that codifies two components: global scores and behavior counts. The four global scores are rated on a 1 to 5 scale:; they are partnership, empathy, cultivating change talk, and softening sustain talk. Three is the default score, with 5 meaning that you missed no opportunity to execute and embody the score and 1 meaning that there was no effort in attending to or practicing the score. The behavior counts, on the other hand, are recorded as the number of times each particular skill is used. The skills counted include questions, simple reflections, complex reflections, affirmations, collaborative statements, emphasizing autonomy, giving information, persuasion, persuasion with permission, and confrontation. Emphasizing, seeking, and affirming are MI adherent, and persuasion and confrontation are MI non-adherent. To achieve a "fair" score, you want to obtain a 4 for the relational component (partnership and empathy), 3 for the technical component (cultivating change and softening sustain talk), a 40:60 percent ratio of complex-to-simple reflections, and a 1:1 reflection-to-question ratio. To achieve a "good" score, you want to obtain a 5 for the relational component, 4 for the technical component, a 50:50 percent ratio of complex-to-simple reflections, and a 2:1 reflection-to-question ratio (Moyers et al., 2014). As you begin practicing with MI, we encourage you to aim for a "fair" score and progressively aiming for a "good" score.

To achieve MI adherence, you want to avoid two problematic, non-adherent behaviors: confrontation and persuasion. Confrontation is telling someone that they have a problem. This is the opposite of collaboration and autonomy and often indicates the "righting reflex," which you may enact by advising or using the expert approach to order a solution. Your client will resist confrontation because they feel they do not have a say in the target behavior and change plan. Similarly, persuasion involves convincing someone to do something to change a behavior. It may be well intended, but it comes across as an expert-learner role rather than a collaborator. Persuasion does not help your client overcome ambivalence; it instead encourages your client to take an external, passive role in their behavior change. You want your client to possess internal motivation to change, and you can achieve this by refraining from confrontation and persuasion and instead employing reflections, genuine interest, skillful questions, and evoking change talk.

COMPATIBILITY WITH THE GENERAL-ECLECTIC APPROACH

Training in MI is compatible with both generalist and specialized perspectives in social work education. First, because the fundamental skills are often learned in generalist social work courses, there is substantial overlap of training in MI and most generalist practice courses. Second, MI dovetails nicely with the core social work values and ethics, as well as student competencies defined by the Council on Social Work Education (CSWE). Thus, training in MI illustrates abstract concepts such as self-determination and the dignity and worth of the individual. As nearly all therapeutic models stress the role of empathy in clinical work, training in MI gives a concrete platform for developing student competencies in this area. Finally, CSWE (2015) specifies both engagement and use of empirically supported treatments as critical competencies for social work students.

MI makes specific use of micro-counseling skills that are driven by a specific and empirically supported model of behavior change. Thus, it can be used in specialized practice classes where students are expected to understand practice models and be able to anecdotally respond to case scenarios. Students trained in some generalist courses prior to receiving specialty training in MI often voice concerns about "putting words in their clients' mouths" when learning about complex reflections. Additionally, they have been taught to check on the accuracy of their reflections (e.g., "You feel furious about this. Do I have this right?") However, in MI, there is great emphasis on dropping such checking questions that appear after reflections because they are thought to inhibit conversation. Instead, you can incorporate a variety of theories, including unconditional positive regard, cognitive dissonance, and self-perception, into your practice.

CASE STUDY 14.1

You recently completed a course on MI and you are entering your field placement at your local health center. Your supervisor is a licensed clinical social worker and provides individual mental health therapy. You prepare to meet with your first client. You learn they scheduled this appointment because their adult children believe they are drinking too much, and it is causing strain among family members. They do not see their drinking as problematic; they drink a few beers every night to "wind down" after a long workday and help them fall asleep. They describe how they recently lost their father to an overdose and believe their children are concerned about them, despite their consistent pattern for 20 years. They don't think they have a problem, but they don't want to worry their family. You note their ambivalence and reflect on their story.

They are unsure how to best solve this problem. They are engaged, and your next step is to guide them through their change talk. Review this case study and take note of MI-adherent and MI-inconsistent behaviors.

You: So, if I hear you correctly, you really care about your kids and you don't want to be the cause of more stress in their lives (*complex reflection, raising values to reinforce change talk*).

Client: Yeah, I just don't know what to do, I don't want them to worry, but I don't think I have a problem. I just have a couple of beers every night to relax after work.

You: So, for you, your kids are so important that you would do anything to keep them from stressing out (*amplified reflection*).

Client: Yeah, I would do anything for my kids, and especially my grandkids.

You: So, on one hand you are hesitant to give up your best relaxation method, and on the other hand your family's concerns are hitting home to you in some regard (*double-sided complex reflection*).

Client: Well, they are worried that my drinking is too much, but I've been drinking like this for quite a long time, I think they are stressing more because my dad recently died of an overdose. I think this is their reason on why I should cut down.

You: I'm sorry to hear that. You really feel like you're in a pickle. You're grieving your father, and now you have this stress of your family harping on you about your drinking (*empathy, complex reflection*). Yet, you came today and are expressing some willingness to explore your families concerns about your drinking (*cultivating change talk*). So, where do you think you should go from here regarding your drinking, based on what would be useful to you (*open-ended questions, focusing on collaboration and autonomy*)?

CRITIQUE

Strengths

MI is practical when a person is ambivalent about change. You will frequently see patients in primary healthcare, substance use, and mandated treatment settings. Thus, in addition to providing a platform for learning foundation practice skills, MI—when done well—can be useful when working with clients who typically get labeled as "resistant" or "in denial."

Limitations

The greatest limitation of MI is that it is not always a stand-alone intervention (Miller & Rollnick, 2009). It is a practical model for use when change is warranted and ambivalence is present. MI is not practical for cognitive or social changes. Evoking requires change efforts in a particular direction, and you must be careful not to let this influence you too much, causing you to stray from your client's agenda. Thus, striking a balance between evoking change talk and your client's desires is always a point of controversy.

CONCLUSION

MI is a communication style that elicits your client's inherent self-motivation to change their target behavior. It can easily be blended with other interventions at points in the clinical process when client ambivalence emerges. MI includes two components: the relational component, outlining key values that enhance rapport with your client; and the technical component, inherent in the evoking phase of guiding your client through their ambivalence. Within the framework of the "MI spirit," certain micro-counseling skills are used, depending on the stage of the relationship, which is referred to in MI as the four processes: engaging, focusing, evoking, and planning. MI is useful in both generalist and specialist training settings in social work.

SUMMARY POINTS

- Conceptualize the historical underpinnings of ambivalence and resistance formulating the MI model,
- critically examine how the MI model incorporates the client-centered, cognitive dissonance, and self-perception theoretical frameworks,
- illustrate the knowledge, values, and skills embodying the components of the "MI spirit": partnership, acceptance, compassion, and evocation,
- cultivate change talk and soften sustain talk as you engage with your client in the four processes of MI: engaging, focusing, evoking, and planning, and
- integrate MI-adherent micro-skills and techniques as you practice social work from a generalist-eclectic perspective.

KEY REFERENCES

Only key references appear in the print edition. The full reference list appears in the digital product found on http://connect.springerpub.com/content/book/978-0-8261-6556-5/part/sec03/part/sec033/chapter/ch14

Miller, W. R. (1983). Motivational interviewing with problem drinkers. *Behavioural and Cognitive Psychotherapy*, *11*(2), 147–172. https://doi.org/10.1017/S0141347300006583.

Miller, W. R. & Rollnick, S. (2009). Ten things that motivational interviewing is not. *Behavioural and Cognitive Psychotherapy*, *37*(2), 129–140. https://doi.org/10.1017/S1352465809005128.

Miller, W. R. & Rollnick, S. (2012). *Motivational interviewing: Helping people change* (3rd ed.). Guilford Press.

Miller, W. R., & Rose, G. S. (2009). Toward a theory of motivational interviewing. *American Psychologist*, *64*, 527–537.

Moyers, T. B. (2004). History and happenstance: How motivational interviewing got its start. *Journal of Cognitive Psychotherapy*, *18*(4), 291–298.

Moyers, T. B. (2014). The relationship in motivational interviewing. *Psychotherapy*, *51*, 358–363.

15

Feminist Theories

Sarah Todd and Katherine Occhiuto

LEARNING OBJECTIVES

By the end of this chapter, you should be able to:

- highlight how feminist movements and theories shape social work practice,
- articulate key approaches in feminist practice,
- discuss the application of feminist theories in social work practice, and
- demonstrate connections between feminist theories and the generalist-eclectic approach.

INTRODUCTION

Feminism is defined by bell hooks (2015, p. 26) as "a struggle to end sexist oppression." She goes on to explain that feminism is "necessarily a struggle to eradicate the ideology of domination that permeates Western culture on various levels, as well as a commitment to reorganizing society so that the self-development of people can take precedence over imperialism, economic expansion, and material desires."

Feminist social work is rooted within feminist thought and strives to create a more egalitarian society (Dominelli, 2002), one in which the "so-called 'feminine' values and ways of thinking are valued as much as so-called 'masculine' ones" (Chaplin, 1989, p. 2). It is informed by feminist politics that challenge power relations that marginalize, exploit, oppress, and discriminate against people. Feminists aim to remain cognizant of the ways in which people occupy multiple and often contradictory social locations of both oppressed and oppressor, and experiences that are part of dominant society and are alternatively marginalized (Herlihy & McCollum, 2007).

Feminist social work is more of an orientation to counseling than a specific set of techniques or a singular approach (Waterhouse, 1993). Laura Brown (1994, pp. 5–6) states that "feminist therapists can be identified by how we understand what we do—the political and cultural meaning of our work—rather than by the actions we take in a therapy session." Feminism is a political worldview and a theory that a counselor brings to the counseling process and can be used as an overarching framework for whatever skills or techniques they employ. Using this flexibility, feminist social workers incorporate a range of skills that meet the unique needs of their clients and the counseling context.

Feminist social workers pay particular attention to micro and macro power inequalities and the ways in which they shape the counseling process and people's lives. They also perceive social transformation as having a key role in healing (Ross, 2010). For feminists, counseling cannot be a substitute for collective action and is instead considered to be part of a healing path toward such action. So, while feminist counseling may be carried out in a one-to-one context, there is always attention paid to facilitating a collective response to individual problems. One key aspect of feminist social work is helping women to feel that their individual problems are shared social problems.

Although feminist social work is often focused on working with women and children, a significant amount of research has been published on how much this approach can offer a wide range of clients, including men (Chester & Bretherton, 2001; Zalmanowitz et al., 2013). At the core of feminist social work is a commitment to working with clients, so that "they can achieve their greatest possible potential as individuals and as members of a world society" (Evans et al., 2011, p. ix). This includes an analysis of all social hierarchies, including racism, classism, heterosexism, and ableism. Feminist approaches to social work have been found to be helpful in working with men who have been violent in their interpersonal relationships (Zalmanowitz et al., 2013), with men who are overwhelmed with society's demands for achievement and performance (Levant, 2001), and with men who are participating in family and couples counseling (Dienhart & Myers Avis, 1991; Silverstein & Goodrich, 2001). In addition, feminist social work has increasingly put feminist theorizing about racism, classism, and ableism into action (Campbell & Gaga, 2012; Jackson, 2012; Lewin, 2012) so as to help people heal from the individual and collective trauma of these oppressive relations, and to engage in challenging and changing them.

OVERVIEW OF FEMINIST THEORY

Understanding of Human Problems

Feminist social workers locate individual and collective problems within their political contexts (Brown, 2018), and within the specific and intimate spheres of peoples' lives (Magnet & Diamond, 2010). As Evans et al. (2011, p. 22) explain, a central feature of feminist therapy is "its recognition of the connection between the internal, psychological world and the external, social world in the range of human problems." Feminists understand interlocking systems of racism, sexism, heterosexism, ableism, and classism as significantly shaping individual and collective experiences, and as leading to marginalization, exploitation, oppression, discrimination, and trauma.

Feminist social workers argue that the best people to understand the impacts of both individual and collective problems are those directly impacted by them—meaning that the greatest source of knowledge to understand a person is that person themselves (Brown, 2018). Ahmed (2017, p. 22) explains feminism as "how we survive the consequences of what we come up against by offering new ways of understanding what we come up against." With this in mind, our roles as feminist social workers are to explore with people how their problems are linked to, or shaped by, the political, local, and social contexts that they live within, and to then contribute to movements for social and political change.

While feminist social workers recognize that the roots of many issues people experience are social, and not personal, this is not used to absolve people of their individual choices and responsibilities. Such individual factors are accounted for and are understood within their environmental contexts (Evans et al., 2011). Feminist social workers also believe that the problems and symptoms that arise for many clients are often strategies for coping with oppressive and/ or difficult circumstances. Behaviors might have been useful for survival in the past but can be less helpful and even detrimental in the present. At other times, these symptoms or behaviors are strategies that people who are experiencing oppressive contexts use to communicate the contradictory and constraining nature of the environment in which they live (Enns, 2004). So, for example, women who are living in abusive relationships may behave in ways that are understood as maladaptive, but upon closer examination, one can often learn that women are exhibiting behaviors that are necessary for surviving in such a situation. Symptoms may also reflect strategies that others have taught women and that are considered appropriate, but that do not fit within the changing and multiple roles that women are asked to perform. In this context, familiar strategies may start to contribute to distress (Enns, 2004).

Conception of Therapeutic Intervention

Brown describes feminist therapy as "the practice of therapy informed by feminist political philosophies and analysis, grounded in multicultural feminist scholarship on the psychology of women and gender, which leads both therapist and client toward strategies and solutions advancing feminist resistance, transformation and social change in daily personal life, and in relationships with the social, emotional, and political environments" (Brown, 1994, pp. 21–22). Within this context, the client is understood as possessing great strengths, and the therapist is an active listener, a critical thinker, a collaborator, a co-learner, and a resource for different therapeutic approaches that could be helpful. Feminist social workers view peoples' struggles as deeply connected to the societies in which they live, and view therapy as a helpful strategy for unlearning problematic norms, and as an approach to develop a critically reflective consciousness and new strategies to improve well-being. Feminist therapists work with clients to make counseling as empowering and comfortable as they can, constantly questioning and reflecting on how the process can be better for those it is meant to serve—for example, moving from the office to an electronic platform (Brown, 2018, p. 32).

Feminist therapy, unlike many other therapeutic approaches, does not have its own set of behavioral treatment goals (Ross, 2010). Instead, it is centered around two overarching goals: (a) empowering clients and (b) critical consciousness raising; these goals are integrated throughout all the therapeutic work (Ross, 2010). The therapeutic intervention is a collaborative one, and one in which terms like "client" are problematized due to issues of power, though also recognized as encompassing the dynamics of the relationship within most contemporary settings. Feminist social workers take time to understand the reality of their clients' lives and to focus on the skills and strengths clients exhibit when trying to navigate difficult circumstances. The focus is on contextualizing those skills and working together to develop different or new approaches to manage the context. At the same time, clients and social workers explicitly recognize the contradictions and lack of choices that exist for many women, and when possible, work to change that context.

Feminist social workers integrate a variety of different approaches within their clinical work including mindfulness, motivational interviewing, narrative therapy, and cognitive behavioral therapy (Roddy, 2013; Wright et al., 2011; Zalmanowitz et al., 2013). Feminist counselors are not tied to any one approach, often drawing on different elements as deemed helpful. Further, many social workers who work within environments that specialize in certain therapeutic approaches integrate the values and principles of feminist theories within their practice. Whatever specific interventions a social worker uses, feminist counseling involves a commitment to valuing women's experiences, a focus on client goals, a dedication to ensuring the counseling process is transparent enough that clients can provide informed consent to participate, and one in which presenting problems are connected to the society and culture they are shaped by (Bricker-Jenkins et al., 1991; Dominelli, 2002; Evans et al., 2011; Magnet & Diamond, 2010).

HISTORICAL DEVELOPMENT: FEMINIST THEORIES AND SOCIAL WORK CONNECTIONS

Feminist theories have a long history, dating back to the 11th century when women, who were living in convents, reflected upon and wrote about their experiences within a religious framework (Walters, 2005), and the 15th century when Indigenous women collectively worked to resist colonization (Smith, 2011). The women's movement of the 1960s grew out of the civil rights struggle in which women of color were raising important questions about equality (Costigan, 2004). The 1960s and 1970s were also a period marked by a significant surge in feminist writing and consciousness-raising groups (Costigan, 2004). Over the centuries, the feminist movement has evolved into its current form, which continues to evolve.

Some feminist theorizing, particularly from feminists in Europe, builds upon Marxism and socialism to theorize the multiple economic and institutional oppressions shaping the lives of women. The main focus of these feminist philosophies is on changing social relationships and institutions (Jones-Smith, 2012). Other forms of feminist theory are more liberal in nature and focus on helping individual women to challenge gender inequality in society. Liberal feminist thought focuses on individual empowerment, dignity, and equality in terms of redistributing opportunities between men and women (Adamson et al., 1988; Jones-Smith, 2012).

Radical feminists deviate quite significantly from liberal feminists as they view women as having unique capacities, specifically reproductive capacity, which they understand as the basis upon which male privilege is established and as the root of male control of women's bodies. Radical feminists believe that there are meaningful differences between men and women and argue for, among other things, the creation of non-hierarchical cooperative societies based on what are perceived as female values of life-giving and nurturance (Adamson et al., 1988).

Multicultural and antiracist feminist theories focus on feminist theorizing in the context of racial and cultural diversity (Brown, 1994; Collins, 1990; hooks, 2000, 2015; Wane, 2013), some troubling the category of "women" as representing the interests of mostly White women and as failing to account for how the gendered experiences of racialized women cannot be neatly separated from intersecting relations of racism, classism, ableism, as well as other oppressive relations (Wane, 2013).

Finally, there has been a constructivist or postmodern turn in feminist theorizing that has pushed feminists to challenge their essentializing tendencies (Flax, 1990). Poststructuralism offers feminism a theory of the relationship among language, subjectivity, social organization, and power so that feminists can understand, among other things, "[W]hy women tolerate social relations which subordinate their interests to those of men and the mechanisms whereby women and men adopt particular discursive positions as representative of their interests" (Weedon, 1997, p. 12).

While informed by this theorizing, feminist counseling has largely developed and flourished outside of the university, and is situated in the feminist movement (Waterhouse, 1993). The consciousness-raising community groups of the 1960s and 1970s were not counseling groups per se, but did provide an opportunity for women to come together and challenge the ways in which therapeutics counseling practices were leaving them feeling isolated and blamed. Feminists raised concerns about the continuing omission of women from the knowledge base of psychology, the ways in which many women's reports of suffering were frequently disregarded by mental health professionals, and how women were often blamed for their experiences of sexual and physical violence. In addition, feminists argued against the overmedication of women and, in later years, the neglect of the multiple sources of oppression shaping women's lives (Worell & Remer, 2003).

During the 1960s and 1970s, many feminists also established a wide range of women-centered organizations to respond to women's experiences with issues such as domestic violence, immigration, and sexual assault. Feminist counseling, in attending to gender and power, was part of a grassroots movement focused on redressing the inherent sexism and individualization in much of psychology (Chester & Bretherton, 2001; Ross, 2010). While feminist social workers in these organizations were critical of mainstream psychology and the ways in which it perpetuated gender stereotypes, they did not deny the value of evidence-based interventions and drew on this in their practice (Brown, 1994). However, there were also tensions in this work: While focusing on the problems of men not accounting for their privilege, the White women who dominated this work also often failed to account for their own privilege (Evans et al. 2011, p. 9). This resulted in an iteration of feminism defined by White women that did not grasp how gender was not always the most salient feature of marginalization, exploitation, oppression, and/or discrimination in many women's lives (hooks, 2000; Evans et al., 2011, p. 10).

The historical and theoretical evolution of feminist theories has had a diverse and significant impact on social work. One significant influence is that feminist theories have offered social work a theoretical base upon which to understand women's pathologization as socially constructed, and as, at times, the outcome of White masculine ways of being and knowing being situated as the norm against which all other ways of being and knowing are measured. The effects of this normalization are varied, as Gremillion (2004) notes, while women are pathologized more often than men; men, particularly men of color, are criminalized more often than women. Constructivist feminist approaches have helped make sense of these disparities by challenging social workers to understand gender as resulting from complex contextual and institutional arrangements that structure our experiences and identities. This understanding has also opened up the possibility for the profession to develop interventions based on the belief that gender is fluid and often contradictory (Ross, 2010).

In challenging and reworking many of the harms of psychology, feminist counselors have also sought to retrieve components of psychology that can be helpful to women. In 1974, Juliet Mitchell published a book, *Psychoanalysis and Feminism: A Radical Reassessment of Freudian Psychoanalysis*, in which she argued that many of the critiques of Freud were actually misreadings of his work. She argued that, in fact, Freud has a lot to offer feminist counselors in attempting to understand why, despite that women often have a clear cognitive understanding of their situations, they are often stuck in unconscious patterns that seem to go against their self-interest. Today, feminists are increasingly interested in psychoanalysis as it offers a "universal theory of the *psychic* construction of gender identity based on repression" (Weedon, 1997, p. 42). Feminist therapy continues to concern "itself with the invisible and sometimes nonconscious ways in which patriarchy has become embedded in everyone's daily life—in our identities, our manners of emotional expression, and our experiences of personal power and powerlessness—to our detriment" (Brown, 1994, p. 17). Feminist social workers continue to apply their critical consciousness to more established ways of knowing, always questioning what they can draw on to work effectively with women and what remains problematic. Over the decades of the movement, these decisions have evolved and shifted from radical disengagement to periods of reengagement with the promises and potential such approaches can offer (Rasmussen & Salhani, 2010).

More recently, concerns that social work establishes more culturally appropriate healing methods are finally being realized, as racialized and Indigenous women have tirelessly pushed for the feminist agenda to focus on the interests of all women, and not just those of mostly White women. As a result, there has been diversification of feminist theory, including Black feminism, Chicana feminism, Indigenous feminism, and Trans feminism. Within these branches of feminism, women have found a variety of ways to theorize their experiences and bodies. These scholarships have exposed the limitations of earlier feminist theorizing by more concretely recognizing the realities of intersecting oppressive relations that shape the lives of many women. Through such movements, feminist social work practice has incorporated intersectionality as a core theoretical concept (Adams et al., 2016).

As hooks explains (2015, p. xv), the "feminist movement has created profound positive changes in the lives of girls and boys, women, and men, living in our society, in a political system of imperialist, white supremist, capitalist patriarchy. And even though trashing feminism has become commonplace, the reality remains: Everyone has benefited from the cultural revolutions put in place by the contemporary feminist movement. It has changed how we see work, how we work, and how we love." A challenge for feminist movements will be how to create a feminist movement of the future that can fully embrace the multiple understandings of women (Ross, 2010) while coming together around a common desire for a more equitable and socially just world (hooks, 2000).

As the movement has shifted to be more inclusive and respond to contemporary concerns, social work counseling has also shifted to respond to contemporary commitments to evidence-based practice. Clinical research has shown that feminist approaches to social work are some of the profession's most effective approaches to practice (Gorey et al., 1998). We have seen a significant move in the profession to be self-reflective and to understand practice as embedded in our own biases and the social political context in which we work. In addition, feminist models of inquiry have been widely adopted in social work as offering research methods that are congruent with the profession's values and ethics (Davis, 1986; Rubin & Babbie, 2009).

CENTRAL THEORETICAL CONSTRUCTS IN FEMINIST PRACTICE

While additional theoretical constructs are present within feminist social work, the primary constructs within therapeutic relationships include patriarchy and power, intersectionality, valuing women's experiences and stories, the personal as political as the foundation for social change, and transformation, self-actualization, and empowerment as key aspects of personal change.

Patriarchy and Power

Feminist social work first focused on patriarchy as a set of power relations in which the interests of women are subordinated to those of men. These relations continue to underpin the institutions and social practices of our society, as evidenced by women being paid less on the dollar than men (and even less if their lives are also shaped by relations of racism and ableism), the feminization of poverty, and sexual violence rates (Canadian Women's Foundation, 2018; Dominelli, 2002; Weedon, 1997).

With time, feminist theorizing of power has extended beyond patriarchal analysis to carefully attend to the ways that power shapes the process, meaning making and content of counseling. With this understanding, feminist counselors strive to create transparent, egalitarian, and consensual relationships in the counseling relationship, and in clients' lives (Herlihy & McCollum, 2007; Remer et al., 2001). While working to reduce power differentials between themselves and clients, feminist counselors are upfront about how power relations shape the therapeutic relationship (Brown, 2018). By unpacking relations of power within the counseling relationship, feminist counselors help create opportunities to examine how power shapes other areas of clients' lives (White, 2006). It also encourages feminist counselors to engage in constant self-reflection on how relations of power distort the relationship between counselor and client (Collins, 2010). Feminist counselors are also quite attentive to how the roles of counselor and client are also imbued with power and that this impacts the therapeutic relationship, distorting our common humanity. As a result, feminist counselors often use a number of strategies to create more equitable and collaborative working relationships. These strategies include cultivating clients' belief in their own life expertise and the belief that they do have the ability to resolve the challenges that they are facing. When this is done effectively, the counselor is less of an expert and more of a guide. The counseling relationship then becomes more collaborative and transparent.

Intersectionality

As Moradi and Grzanka (2017, p. 501) note, the concept of intersectionality "is rooted in the work of Black feminists and women of color activists and scholars, many of whom also identified as lesbian or queer." For many of these women, patriarchal power was not the only or even the most significant power relation impacting their lives. Intersectionality challenges singular notions of power and identity, highlighting that all women are not the same and that their experiences differ depending on overlapping or "intersecting categories of discrimination" including racism, sexism, heterosexism, ableism, classism, Islamophobia, and anti-Semitism

(Carastathis, 2014, p. 305; Crenshaw, 1989). While taking into account intersecting social locations, intersectionality also requires feminist counselors attend to relations of privilege and disempowerment that stem from each of these intersecting factors (Brown, 2018, p. 91). In addition, intersectional feminism also challenges feminists to transform the structures and systems that perpetuate a wide variety of forms of marginalization, exploitation, oppression, and discrimination (Moradi & Grzanka, 2017).

Valuing of Women's Experiences and Stories

Feminist theories prioritize the unique experiences of women as the starting place for understanding; recognizing that how women understand and talk about their lives and the world around them is grounded within their social positioning and identities (Leavy & Harris, 2019; Letherby, 2003; Wane, 2013). This is true for the counselor too, and feminist counselors are required to reflect on how their own socially constructed understandings of the world impact how they approach their work with each client (Ross, 2010).

THERE IS A PRODUCTIVE TENSION IN FEMINIST SOCIAL WORK IN WHICH FEMINISTS STRIVE TO HONOR AND BELIEVE WOMEN'S EXPERIENCES AS THEIR TRUTHS

This disrupts a history in which mental health services have often been quick to pathologize women. At the same time, the deconstructive nature of many feminist theories requires those using this theory to question, unpack, and often reframe experience within a broader social context. Individuals' experiences are recognized as representing personal truths, but are also understood as needing to be questioned and reframed through additional viewpoints and with additional information. The delicate work of a feminist social worker is to validate clients while also working with them to understand how their experiences, and perceptions of that experience, are shaped by the individual context in which they live and by broader social relations. Feminist social workers work with clients to reframe their experience while communicating respect and validation. They do so by asking questions to invite the client to reconsider, or at least question, how they are making sense of their experiences.

The Personal as Political as the Foundation for Social Change

The notion of the personal as political situates feminist theories as a structural theory in which individual problems are understood as being centrally shaped by the ways in which social institutions and social practices are organized. Feminist social workers work with clients, supporting them to see and describe their own reality—recognizing this as a necessary step in self-discovery and self-actualization (hooks, 2015). At the same time, feminist theories use the concepts of marginalization, exploitation, oppression, and discrimination to understand and demonstrate how groups of people are disadvantaged through the unequal relations of society. This results in feminists having a strong commitment to individual transformation and social change. Thus, the feminist counseling process is a delicate balance between fostering individuals' agency and ability to shape their lives and the lives of others, while also attending to the conditions of people's lives outside of their own agency, particularly systems of marginalization, exploitation, oppression, and discrimination.

Feminist social workers are also concerned with the social and political meanings of both pain and healing, and how these shared understandings shape an individual's experience. This process of meaning making has as its goal "the creation of feminist consciousness and a movement toward feminist action" (Brown, 1994, p. 17). Throughout the therapeutic relationship, feminist social workers are expected to be monitoring their own political biases and privileges (including their own versions of feminism, equity, and empowerment, which may differ from clients), empowering members of marginalized groups, and to be actively working toward movements of social change (Jones-Smith, 2012). These movements toward social change look to disrupt the problematic systems people live within and seek "collective solutions to individual problems" (Dominelli, 2002, p. 163). As hooks (2015) explains, we have all been complicit with oppressive systems, and feminism involves a conscious break within this problematic system—that is, a rejection of mom guilt, a rejection of prescribed sexuality, and/or a rejection of prescribed definitions of beauty. In these ways, the personal practice of feminist counseling is understood as political.

Transformation, Self-Actualization, and Empowerment as Key Aspects of Personal Change

Feminist theories articulate transformation as integrating individual and social changes, which are dependent upon one another. This individual change is sometimes referred to as self-actualization (Maass, 2002; McCarthy, 2013; hooks, 1993). hooks (1993, as cited by McCarthy, 2013, p. 55) explains self-actualization as "a process of knowing yourself, grounding yourself in all aspects, however especially in spiritual, mental and physical parts of the self." As when people are grounded within their own spiritual, mental, and physical self, they are often in healthy/ier relationships with themselves and can then have healthier relationships with others.

The empowerment that feminist therapy speaks of is "that of liberation from internalized forms of oppression so as to become powerful in confronting external obstacles" (Brown, 2018, p. 38). As a result, feminist practice moves back and forth between focusing on what people can do to bring about a change in their own lives, the importance of linking with community groups (for both individual healing and in solidarity), and in encouraging participation in social movements for change. Feminist social workers help clients so that they can feel less alone and can gain a greater sense of control over their lives while also feeling a sense of collective power with others.

PHASES OF HELPING

Engagement

In the engagement phase of helping, feminist social workers work to create a nonexploitative, mutual, caring, and respectful relationship (Evans et al., 2011). This is a phase in which social workers often discuss the values that will underpin the therapeutic work and give the client a sense of what the counseling process will look like. The feminist social worker is clear about their roles and the boundaries within that role, while also investing their emotional energy in connecting relationally with clients. This can look different depending on context, and different levels of self-disclosure may be shared when deemed helpful for the client. This relational work can be useful in reducing power differentials, and in fostering a space where clients feel valued and heard.

During the engagement phase, the roles of the social worker and client often need clarification because feminist social work situates the counselor more like a guide than an expert. This is countercultural to what many are used to and can be confusing when clients expect to be prescribed answers. It also requires that clients be active partners in the counseling process. Engaging in this type of relationship is understood as important for clients to gain a greater respect for themselves and their abilities, and to gain greater personal autonomy as they work toward self-actualization. When engaging clients, feminist social workers are seeking cooperation and use consensus building to develop a common aim for how the counselor and client will work together (Costigan, 2004). A key element of this process is ensuring that clients are fully informed about the counseling process and what it can and cannot offer. The engagement process is thus largely concerned with demystifying counseling and ensuring that the auton-omy of the client is respected (Ross, 2010). This is another strategy feminist social workers use to reduce how power is distributed between the counselor and the client.

Chaplin (1989) suggests that it is important for clients to feel nurtured; to facilitate this nur-turance, feminist social workers must work to develop an atmosphere of safety, trust, and respect. This is often communicated in small, but meaningful, ways such as asking women if they mind if the counselor takes notes and clearly explaining the purpose of the notes (Chaplin, 1989). The valuing of nurturance and emotions is seen as an important strategy for revaluing women-centered skills and for creating an atmosphere in which the therapeutic alliance allows important work to happen.

A lot of the focus of feminist social work is on the nature of the dialog that is developed in the relationship. In particular, attention is paid to ensuring that clients are fully engaged in the dialog and that they are given the opportunity to explore their experiences from their own perspective, and to use these conversations as an opportunity to create goals for the therapeutic work (Dewhurst & Nielsen, 2010). In feminist social work, the engagement phase also includes discus-sions about practical issues such as payment, timing of meetings, agency policies and procedures, and boundaries; these are clearly laid out so that the norms of the counseling process can be established and understood, which is helpful in developing rapport (Chaplin, 1989; Enns, 2004).

Assessment

A feminist assessment of a client involves a collaborative process of gathering information about a client's personal and social experiences and then integrating those into a feminist analy-sis of the context in which the client is living. Feminist social workers are often cautious about using diagnostic labels as they tend to locate problems within the client and distract counselors from the social factors that shape individual difficulties (Brown, 2018; Jones-Smith, 2012). At the same time, feminist counselors recognize that these labels can be necessary to access resources and can create a shared sense of experience and identity.

A feminist approach to assessment is organized around prioritizing what is necessary to promote social change and assessing the environmental contexts of women's lives so that women can experience a sense of empowerment. Often symptoms are reframed as ways of cop-ing with the oppressive environments or reflecting socialization and representing society's need to label and pathologize deviance from socialized norms and expectations. Feminist social workers seek to identify patterns in how clients' think and behave so that the themes that underpin clients' lives are more visible. Identifying oppositional thinking and internal hierar-chies and enhancing integrated ways of viewing oneself and the world are strategies often used by feminist counselors so as to help people live their lives more fully (Evans et al., 2011).

Planning and Intervening

In feminist social work, planning is done in collaboration with the client. Clients and counselors work together to establish what goals they will focus on and what the client hopes to get out of the therapeutic work (Chaplin, 1989). The goals of the client are prioritized, and the feminist counselor may provide suggestions for goals based on the information that has been shared. This phase of the counseling often involves finding a balance between helping people to heighten their awareness of how their behaviors are shaped by their environment, while also respecting that they might not see their situation in this way.

Interventions may include consciousness raising in which clients examine how oppression and socialization contribute to their personal distress and dysfunction (Jones-Smith, 2012), and strategies to analyze power and privilege. For example, Corinne a 21-year-old woman who attends college for nursing is struggling with her body image. She has gained weight since moving out of her parents' home for school. She is drained by the effort of negotiating between the pressures of school and her two part-time retail positions. Corinne finds the pressure to get "dressed-up" to go out on the weekends almost debilitating. Initially, she started just staying in for the evenings, but over the past few weeks, she has been finding it increasingly difficult to do anything in social settings. This has led to less time with her friends and some loneliness. A feminist social worker may work with Corinne to connect her body image issues to larger societal pressures about how women should look and dress (and socialize) and may then connect those to critical media literacy (Kellner & Share, 2007). Corinne may also be taught new coping skills and strategies to increase her self-esteem and self-love. The hope is that through teaching such analysis, clients will be able to deconstruct their own experiences in the future and then view things differently, improving their mental health. The goal of this work is that clients may then work collectively toward creating a more inclusive, equitable and just society through, for example, participating in body positivity campaigns.

Critical consciousness raising and analyzing power are two strategies feminist counselors use to highlight how systems may not be working in clients' best interests and may place undue care burdens on women (hooks, 2015). The role of the social worker is to support clients to learn new skills and strategies and to honor the skills and ways of knowing that clients already possess (Evans et al., 2011).

Feminist counseling often involves power analysis in which clients are helped to understand how unequal access to power and resources can influence personal realities. This helps clients to understand power differences in society. At times, interventions such as power analysis also use strategies such as bibliotherapy where counselors use nonfiction books, counseling textbooks, self-help books, educational videos, films, and even novels to facilitate a client's learning and reflection (Jones-Smith, 2012). Such an approach increases knowledge, and its collaborative format can work to decrease the power differentials between the client and the counselor.

Feminist social workers can be present or past focused. Often it is helpful to explore clients' past to see where certain ways of thinking or behaving were established and to explore whether and when they have been helpful or not. In looking into the past, clients and counselors can gain greater understanding into how our patterns of thinking and behaving are learned and can be unlearned (Chaplin, 1989).

A range of other interventions are used in feminist social work. For example, assertiveness training may be integrated to counter gendered learnings around what it means to be "female," or emotional literacy may be taught to boys and men to counter gendered learning about what it means to be "male." At other times, people are supported to be more accepting of aspects of themselves (Chaplin, 1989); for example, embracing naturally curly hair. Finally, feminist social workers may use social activism in their practice, encouraging or partnering with clients in advocacy. This might include attending or organizing a protest, volunteering at a community organization, or engaging in letter writing campaigns (Jones-Smith, 2012).

The overarching goals of feminist social work include empowerment, valuing and affirming diversity, striving for change rather than adjustment, equality, social change, and self-nurturance (Enns, 2004). They also encompass goals that are set by the client. Both counseling and individual goals are reflected upon throughout the therapeutic relationship, and during the termination and evaluation phase.

Termination and Evaluation

Most of the work of feminist social workers in the termination phase is focused on normalizing terminations as a part of day-to-day life and enhancing clients' skills to embrace endings. Feminist social workers prepare clients in advance of endings and when possible make collaborative decisions about how the ending will look (Singh & Hays, 2008). Termination often includes reflecting on the work that has been done and highlighting the strengths, growth, and changes that a client has brought to the counseling process, as well as highlighting the transferability of these within other areas of their life.

In feminist social work, termination can occur for many reasons. Ideally, terminations happen when the client's and therapist's goals have been achieved. In many contemporary short-term contexts, termination occurs when the predetermined number of sessions has concluded. As in the rest of life, there are many situations in which endings are untidy and incomplete due to a range of circumstances. These experiences can trigger anxieties about past endings and can be an opportunity to reconfigure endings as a natural phase in relationships, a rite of passage, and something to celebrate even when difficult.

In most feminist social work, evaluation is reflective in nature, and involves clients being invited to reflect on how they felt about the counseling process and how effective it was for them (Singh & Hays, 2008). In addition to this reflective evaluation, feminist social workers are increasingly evaluating their practice using research methods that are congruent with evidence-based practice (Gorey et al., 2002). Feminist social workers often seek feedback about how they can better meet the needs of clients—recognizing the need to constantly stretch and evolve within their work. This may be done through a variety of formats including dialog or an online or hardcopy survey. At all times, counselors must recognize that such feedback can be positively skewed because of the nature of the relationship and different power dynamics at play. In working to create a comfortable, inclusive, and empowering environment, feminist counselors seek feedback from clients on the nature of the therapeutic relationship not only at termination but throughout the entire process.

APPLICATION TO FAMILY AND GROUP WORK

Family Work

One of the most significant contributions that feminist theories have made to family work has been to level a critique of family therapy in terms of the implications of gender invisibility, the absence of lesbian families, sexism, and mother blaming (Luepnitz, 1997; Silverstein, 2003; Walters et al., 1988). These critiques have, in turn, resulted in the refinement of a particularly feminist approach to family counseling. Feminist theory has also challenged family therapy to develop practices that honor and are effective with lesbian couples (Halstead, 2003), and to integrate a feminist framework into research and practice with racialized and ethnically diverse families (Pinderhughes, 1986). In addition, feminist family therapists pay attention to power dynamics in heterosexual families, particularly as they relate to the gender differences in self-esteem and in terms of the respect given to partners; the manner in which contributions are valued and whether or how work sharing occurs between heterosexual partners; gendered expectations of children within families; and the apparent consensus and acceptance of gender inequality in heterosexual families (Goodrich, 2003). With respect to heterosexual two-parent families, feminist counselors are often concerned that while women are often not totally powerless in these marriages, they do not have equal or more power than their husbands (Goodrich, 2003). Feminist social workers often focus their efforts on building more egalitarian marital partnerships through practices of consciousness raising and empowerment (Nichols, 2013).

With lesbian families, feminist social workers and researchers have brought attention to the fact that in lesbian relationships, there are often concerns that overlap with those of heterosexual families, but there can also be unique issues raised in counseling that address concerns about the validity of same-sex families in a heterosexist world, questions about having children, negotiating family traditions, and negotiating any religious or spiritual beliefs (Halstead, 2003).

Another area in which feminist family therapists have made significant contributions is in terms of theorizing mothering and the ways in which mothering situates women in an often-contradictory space where their responsibilities are simultaneously impossible but also quite rewarding. For several decades, feminist writers have also contributed a great deal of knowledge about how the work of mothering varies by race and class and how these dynamics are largely ignored by society and family therapy (Collins, 1990; O'Reilly, 2010). Feminist family counselors use therapy to address the position of women in contemporary cultures and the ways in which families often reproduce this positioning even if there is no man physically present (Goodrich, 2003). Feminist family therapists often work with families to gain a language to describe how racism, ableism, heterosexism, and classism are affecting the course of the family (Silverstein & Goodrich, 2003). Thus, the core critiques and analyses of feminism have transformed the focus and practice of family counseling.

Group Work

Group work has always been a popular way for women to share their experiences and to raise their consciousness while also receiving support. Consciousness-raising groups of the past eventually evolved into self-help groups (Evans et al., 2011), places where people with similar experiences come together. For many feminist social workers, group settings are better places to deal with the political and societal elements that are often raised in individual counseling (Berwald & Houstra, 2002). Feminist group work is increasingly focused on specific issues such as body image, disabilities, abusive relationships, eating disorders, incest, and sexual abuse (Enns, 2004). Research has provided empirical evidence that women-only groups are often more effective than mixed gender groups because women show more positive growth in women-only groups (Martin & Shananhan, 1983). Other studies speak to how the atmosphere and dynamics of the group can be impacted when men are, for example, present among a group of women (Forsyth, 2018). Involvement in groups can decrease peoples' social isolation and can be a place for clients to practice skills and consider political action. Feminist groups are designed to facilitate individual, group, and social change through problem-solving dialogs such as consciousness raising, through fostering healthy boundaries and relationships, and through supporting self-actualization (Bricker-Jenkins et al., 1991; Maass, 2002).

COMPATIBILITY WITH THE GENERALIST-ECLECTIC FRAMEWORK

Feminist approaches to social work fit well within a generalist-eclectic framework because feminist counseling is more of a general orientation to counseling that works well when supplemented by more specific approaches to intervention. Feminist social workers tend to use a wide range of theories depending upon the client with whom they are working, the presenting problem, and the clinical setting.

Attention to Holistic Assessment and Use of Systems and Life Cycle Theories

Feminist theorists have long argued that holistic assessments require attention to the inner life of the client, their intimate sphere, and society as a whole. Thus, feminist assessments are well aligned with social work's notions of assessment. Feminist psychologists have also theorized extensively on the life cycle of women, which is central to feminist counseling (Enns, 2004). Any assessment that is completed by a feminist counselor considers where women are in their lives and how that life space is shaped by broader society.

Emphasis on Therapeutic Relationship and Fit With Strengths Perspective

A key component of feminist social work is to reduce power differentials between the client and the social worker, and to foster rapport. This is well matched to the generalist-eclectic approach and its prioritization of a good helping relationship that fosters empowerment.

Another component of feminist social work is a focus on clients' strengths (Evans et al., 2011). Feminist counseling emerged primarily as a result of mainstream therapeutic interventions not attending to the strengths of women and marginalized persons, particularly their ability to negotiate and resist oppressive social relations. Feminist theories of counseling are fundamentally strengths based.

Attention to Issues of Diversity and Empowerment

Social justice and attention to diversity are central to feminist counseling. At the core of this approach to counseling is the belief that changing society and the inequality faced by women; racialized persons; members of lesbian, gay, bisexual, transgender, queer, questioning, intersex, pansexual, two-spirit, and asexual (LGBTQQIP2SA) communities; and persons living with disabilities will, in turn, improve people's mental health. Feminist social workers believe that society marginalizes, exploits, oppresses, and discriminates against those who do not fit easily into the mainstream norm (Brown, 1994). In turn, empowerment is a consistent theme in feminist therapy. One key goal of this approach is to work with clients to help them gain control over their lives and bodies (Magnet & Diamond, 2010).

CRITIQUES OF FEMINIST THEORIES

Strengths of Feminist Theories

The strength of feminist theories rests in their ability to integrate the personal with the political change and to attend simultaneously to individual and social change. In addition, feminist theories have a well-articulated series of practices to equalize power in the counseling relationship. Both of these aspects of feminist counseling are congruent with social work values. The fact that feminist theory is also able to incorporate a wide range of approaches to counseling results in an approach to counseling that can be adapted to the context, the counselor, and the client. Another strength of feminist counseling is its commitment to self-reflection and to challenge expert identities and knowledge. This provides the opportunity for significant practitioner and client growth.

Limitations of Feminist Theories

Feminist approaches to social work have faced a number of criticisms. First, it is an approach that has tended to not keep up with demands for evidence-based practice. Until recently, it was often difficult to find studies that examined the effectiveness of feminist approaches to counseling. This has been gradually changing, and there are now an increasing number of studies that evaluate the effectiveness of feminist approaches in relation to other approaches to social work practice (Gorey et al., 1998; Mullen & Shuluk, 2010; Upadhyay et al., 2010).

Some critics of feminist theories remain concerned that feminist social workers impose their political agendas on clients without respecting the latter's perspective. This has been raised as a particular concern in working with women whose cultural, ethnic, or religious standpoints may conflict with Western feminist politics. This misconception has been difficult to challenge, despite feminists' active work in this area. It will require developing alliances with women from a broad range of communities in order to ensure that feminist theories are continually informed by and responsive to women in diverse social, spiritual, and economic contexts. Other critiques include the concern that in prioritizing contextual and political interpretations of clients' presenting problems, feminist counselors sometimes fail to allow opportunities for clients to take personal responsibility to act in the face of an unfair world.

Another limitation of feminist counseling is that it is not as clearly defined as many other approaches to counseling, so reaching consensus on the scope and definitions of feminist practice is often a challenge (Herlihy & McCollum, 2007). This is both a strength and a weakness of the approach as the theory's breadth creates opportunities for eclecticism that has the potential to enrich therapeutic practice.

People Most Suited to Feminist Practice

Feminist approaches to counseling are most suited to people who are dealing with issues that are shaped by oppressive relations and who might benefit from a structural analysis of their problems. It is also most suited for people who are open to, or whose value systems are already congruent with, the values espoused by feminist theories. Feminist approaches to counseling have been found to be very effective when working in the area of biculturalism, intimate violence, stigmatized health issues, self-esteem, and trauma (Nishimura, 2004; Singh & Hays, 2008; Tzou et al., 2012; Upadhyay et al., 2010).

CASE STUDY 15.1

Karin comes into counseling because she is struggling with an unplanned pregnancy. In telling her story, she states how she was "irresponsible" in terms of not taking her birth control pill regularly enough and that she feels "selfish" for wanting to terminate her pregnancy. Her reason for terminating the pregnancy is that she is a first-year university student. She lives on very little money and her partner is also a university student with few economic resources. She wants to complete university before starting a family. In addition, her family is quite religious and would be very upset to find out that she is pregnant and would see it as a sign of her sinfulness. This could threaten their economic and emotional support, which she feels is vital for her life. Karin is unsure what to do about the pregnancy. She is pro-choice but feels ashamed of making such a decision. She does not feel that raising the child or giving birth and giving the baby up for adoption are realistic choices given her situation, but she feels that they are morally better decisions. Karin has not felt that she can discuss her situation with many people. Her partner has stated that he is not ready to be a dad, but that he will try to support her with whatever decision she makes. Karin has not told any other friends or family about her situation.

   A feminist counselor would begin work with Karin by outlining what she can expect from the counseling relationship. The counselor would discuss that she cannot make a decision for Karin but can instead guide Karin to reflect on her situation, values, and beliefs, and help make her decision-making process clearer (Baker, 1995). A feminist counselor would spend a significant amount of time listening to Karin's story so as to understand the context of her story. In this situation, a feminist counselor would work to ensure that Karin has access to all the necessary information to make an informed decision. A feminist counselor is likely to contextualize Karin's story within social debates about abortion and a social political context in which there is no universal access to affordable childcare in Canada and rising tuition rates that make student poverty an increasing reality. In this way, a counselor works to ensure that Karin's personal story is explicitly linked to the social political context. This might provide an opportunity for Karin's consciousness to be raised and the possibility for her to reframe her guilt and shame. The counselor might also engage Karin in completing a gender analysis and power analysis of her situation so that relations of patriarchy around this issue could be more visible. In addition, a feminist counselor might work with Karin to encourage more self-compassion regarding managing her birth control while also reframing the discussion so as to include her partner's shared responsibility to prevent pregnancy. The feminist counselor would also validate Karin and her ability to consider this situation carefully and her care in weighing up the implications of terminating a pregnancy or having a child at this point in her life.

An exploration of Karin's spiritual beliefs may be relevant to her experience, as might some discussion about what Karin thinks about adoption, abortion, and raising a child. A counselor would not only discuss each option but also how Karin might cope longer term with any decision she makes. A feminist counselor would also be concerned with ensuring that Karin has a community to support her after she makes a decision and would suggest services, online support groups, or face-to-face groups if Karin does not feel that she can access an informal network of support. A counselor would also talk about how the experience of negotiating an unplanned pregnancy is a situation faced by many women and that Karin is not alone.

In summary, in this case, a feminist counselor would work to develop a therapeutic rapport with Karin where she feels heard and validated, work to build on Karin's strengths, would link her personal problems to the social political context, and would attempt to connect Karin to other women in similar circumstances.

CONCLUSION

Feminist theory offers social work an important critique of many other approaches to counseling, arguing that we must interrogate supposedly neutral approaches so as to uncover their implicit and explicit messaging to clients. Feminist theory has also challenged the profession of social work and provided specific techniques to balance attention to the individual with the examination of the influence of the social and political. In this way, feminist theory and social work are closely aligned, and research in each area enriches both fields. Feminist theory reminds social workers of our ongoing commitment to facilitate individual change while simultaneously working for social transformation. Feminist social work continues to evolve, innovating with new ways to intervene and ensuring the practice is relevant to multiple client groups. Feminist theory is not without its criticisms; social workers using this theory have to be careful to balance the fine line between consciousness raising and imposing a political agenda. This requires that feminist social workers commit to an ongoing practice of self-reflection. Also, the broad parameters of this approach can create confusion. However, feminist approaches to counseling remain central to social work practice and in combination with other approaches have been found to be very effective (Gorey et al., 1998; Mullen & Shuluk, 2010).

SUMMARY POINTS

- Feminist theories have evolved and diversified,
- feminist social work is an orientation to practice rather than a specific set of techniques or a singular approach (Waterhouse, 1993),
- feminist approaches to social work fit well within a generalist-eclectic framework because feminist counseling is more of a general orientation to counseling that works well when supplemented by more specific approaches to intervention,
- feminist counseling is centered around two overarching goals: (a) empowering clients and (b) critical consciousness raising; these therapeutic goals are integrated throughout all the therapeutic work (Ross, 2010),
- feminist theories remind social workers of our ongoing commitment to facilitate individual change while simultaneously working for social transformation,
- feminist theories are not without their critics; social workers using this theory must be careful to balance the fine line between consciousness raising and imposing a political agenda, which requires that feminist social workers commit to an ongoing practice of self-reflection, and
- feminist approaches to counseling remain central to social work practice and in combination with other approaches have been found to be very effective (Gorey et al., 1998; Mullen & Shuluk, 2010).

KEY REFERENCES

Only key references appear in the print edition. The full reference list appears in the digital product found on http://connect.springerpub.com/content/book/978-0-8261-6556-5/part/sec03/part/sec034/chapter/ch15

Brown, L. (2018). *Feminist therapy* (2nd ed.). American Psychological Association.

Evans, K., Kincade, E. A., & Seem, S. R. (2011). *Introduction to feminist therapy: Strategies for social and individual change*. Sage.

hooks, b. (2015). *Feminist theory: From margin to center*. Routledge.

Jagire, J., Wane, N., & Murad, J. (2013). *Ruptures: Anti-colonial and anti-racist feminist theorizing*. Sense.

Ross, L. (2010). *Feminist counseling: Theory, issues and practice*. Women's Press.

Empowerment Theory

Tina Maschi, Sandra Turner, and Adriana Kaye
(adapted from the work of Jean East)

LEARNING OBJECTIVES

By the end of this chapter, you should be able to:

- illustrate how empowerment theory and practices advance human rights and social, economic, and environmental justice;
- provide an overview of the history, values, and central concepts of empowerment theory and its close alliance with human rights, justice, and feminist theory;
- articulate how empowerment theory is used in practice during engagement, assessment, intervention, and evaluation; and
- demonstrate how empowerment theory can be applied in the field.

INTRODUCTION

The most recent Educational Policy and Accreditation Standards (EPAS) by the Council on Social Work Education (CSWE; 2015) underscores that social workers should engage in human rights and justice practice. Additionally, it recognizes that every person, regardless of their personal characteristics or societal position, has fundamental human rights; that is, everyone has a right to "freedom, safety, privacy, an adequate standard of living, health care, and education." The competency also underscores the knowledge (e.g., theory), values (e.g., ethics, attitudes and beliefs) and skills (e.g., multilevel practice strategies) that social work students are expected to understand and demonstrate. This includes that social workers not only understand the interconnections between oppression and human rights violations but also know how to apply theories of human needs, justice, and multilevel practice strategies to best ensure justice, equality, and human rights. Social workers are expected to apply their understanding of social, economic, and environmental justice to advance human rights by engaging in practices at the individual and other system levels (CSWE, 2015). Students are also asked to demonstrate in practice their knowledge of the competencies. The EPAS intervention competency includes skills such as client advocacy, case management, and group facilitation. Empowerment theory and practices are poised to do just that.

In fact, empowerment is at the heart of social work practice. It is well positioned in the preamble of the National Association of Social Workers (NASW) Code of Ethics, which states: "The primary mission of the social work profession is to enhance human well-being and help meet the basic human needs of all people, with particular attention to the needs and empowerment of people who are vulnerable, oppressed, and living in poverty" (NASW, 2017, p. 1). In this statement, empowerment can be understood as a fundamental goal that social workers pursue when the theory of empowerment is put into practice.

Additionally, empowerment is also underscored as social workers have ethical responsibilities to respect and promote clients' rights to self-determination, pursuit of life purpose, and goals, for example. Social workers generally serve individuals and groups that vary by race/ethnicity, gender identity, sexual orientation, immigration, criminal justice history, physical or mental abilities, and age. Access to power, privileges, services, and justice is often influenced by individuals' social identities or social locations (e.g., being a Caucasian abled-bodied heterosexual male compared to being an African American lesbian with a physical and mental disability female). Therefore, at the broader societal level, social workers also have an ethical responsibility to increase choice and opportunities for community, collective, and political empowerment, especially among vulnerable individuals and groups.

Interestingly, while empowerment practice is almost synonymous with social work practice, its meaning and application remain somewhat elusive and a matter of debate. In fact, interpretations of empowerment differ on whether empowerment is a philosophy, theory, or practice model (Gutierrez & Lewis, 1999; Presser & Sen, 2000). In addition, there is no consensus among scholars on a single, all-encompassing definition or conceptualization of empowerment (Speer & Peterson, 2000). Despite these differences, empowerment has continued to capture the altruistic imagination of social workers. Empowerment as a theory for direct social work practice at individual, group, community, and political levels is a staple in many social work texts that promote a generalist model of social work (Allen-Meares & Garvin, 2000; Miley et al., 2011; Robbins et al., 2012).

Therefore, it is important in any discussion of empowerment to address the many "faces" of empowerment since as a concept it varies in meaning and is defined and operationalized in varied ways (Cattaneo & Chapman, 2010). For example, empowerment is described as a **perspective or philosophy** guided by principles of social justice, such as inclusivity, equality, and an understanding of oppression. This description is closely related to empowerment as an ideal condition, a process, and a way of acting in carrying out social work roles. Common processes that social workers engage in when applying an empowerment perspective include sharing power, consciousness raising, and partnership. In contrast, as an **intervention model**, social workers engage in empowerment practices at multiple levels, such as the intrapersonal, interpersonal, and community levels to influence personal and system changes, often simultaneously. Lastly, as an **outcome**, empowerment is operationalized as an increase in power in intrapersonal, interpersonal, and community realms. At the intrapersonal level with individuals, this outcome often includes an increase in perceived competency and self-efficacy, or the ability to experience competence in one's life (Carr, 2003; Bandura, 1982). Increased self-efficacy, viewed as increased power, then translates into an increased ability to influence events in one's life, interpersonally in one's relationships and in the sociopolitical sphere. At the community or societal level, self-efficacy is linked to collective efficacy.

Many scholars have proposed definitions of empowerment; four are outlined in the following for their potential relevance to direct practice:

- "A process by which individuals, groups, and communities develop the capacity to act on their own behalf and gain a sense of power in their personal, interpersonal, and environmental interactions." (Gutierrez et al., 1998; Reichert, 2006)
- "A process through which people become strong enough to participate within, share in the control of, and influence events and institutions affecting their lives [and that, in part], empowerment necessitates that people gain particular skills, knowledge, and sufficient power to influence their lives and the lives of those they care about." (Torre, 1985, p. 18).
- "Empowerment is a phenomenological development of a certain state of mind (e.g., feeling powerful, competent, worthy of esteem), and to the modification of structural conditions in order to reallocate power [...] and refers to both the subjective experience and the objective reality." (Swift & Levin, 1987, p. 72)

- "[Empowerment is] an intentional, ongoing process centered in the local community, involving mutual respect, critical reflection, caring, and group participation, through which people lacking in an equal share of valued resources gain greater access to and control over those resources." (Cornell Empowerment Group, 1989, p. 2; Mullaly & West, 2017)

These four definitions refer to the process that influences an outcome. For example, a common outcome would be an increased internal and external sense of self and/or collective empowerment among individuals, groups, and/or communities. There also is a psychological and emotional component to empowerment. For example, individuals may experience a positive shift in their internal thoughts and emotions that they then can use to reframe their external relationships with others and their environment. The individual, group, or collective that participates in this process is perceived as becoming stronger or more empowered and more able to influence their inner and outer worlds. They do so by engaging in practice, such as critical reflection and psychological transformation, group and community participation, capacity building, and knowledge and skill attainment. Empowerment social work is much like the feminist approach that operates within a human rights and social justice framework with the goal of building a more compassionate world. The work is both clinical and community oriented (Lee, 2001).

OVERVIEW OF EMPOWERMENT THEORY

Understanding of Human Problems

Empowerment theory understands human problems in the context of a social, political, and economic environment. These individual and social structural levels are stratified, in which those with power and privilege have an advantage over those groups that are oppressed (e.g., racial/ethnic minorities, women, persons living in poverty, disability or immigration status, and/or sexual orientation). These oppressed individuals and groups tend to have a subjective experience of powerlessness until their consciousness is raised and they start to feel worthy to pursue the advantages that society has to offer (Lee, 1994; Maschi et al., 2011; Robbins et al., 2012). This understanding suggests dualistic oppressive thought processes, in which people who are the "other," who are different than the dominant group, are unworthy and undeserving of dignity, equality, and access to rights and justice. Therefore, these implicit and explicit biases fuel intergenerational, historical trauma, oppression, and social structural inequities. Consequently, systems within this type of society respond to humans in need with overt or covert oppressive tactics, such as microaggressions, and emotional, physical, and structural violence and neglect. For example, health disparities are most common among racial/ethnic minorities compared to the White majority (Mullaly & West, 2017). Empowerment theory addresses the individual in the social environment by situating human problems in a person-in-environment (PIE) perspective, "self and the social mirror" as a reflection of this interaction (Kondrat, 2013; Maschi et al., 2016). PIE perspective also proposes that successful interventions to human problems and solutions occur at the intrapersonal, interpersonal, community, and policy levels concurrently and/or sequentially. In assessing the problem, it is important to visualize the observable state of disempowerment of an individual, group, or community, as well as their ultimate, pure, and unabashed state of personal and collective empowerment, which can be a state of freedom, growth, and joy.

A Broad Perspective of the "Therapeutic" Intervention

Social workers have developed empowerment practice interventions and models with attention to vulnerable groups (Gutierrez & Lewis, 1999). The concept of therapeutic jurisprudence (TJ) clarifies the differing system levels ranging from clinical (individual, family, and group), community, and policy interventions, in which a therapeutic intervention can be designed and implemented. TJ refers to laws and policies as a social force (or agent), which may or may not give rise to unintended consequences, that may be either beneficial (therapeutic) or harmful (anti-therapeutic). Similarly, at the clinical level, the social worker may use therapeutic interventions to interrupt or change the narratives related to self-limiting beliefs (e.g., self-blame that might diminish a client's sense of well-being). The social worker then can help the client to positively reframe their negative self-perceptions to self-acceptance, self-love, and a sense of personal power and well-being. An empowerment intervention with individuals is based on the premise that intrapersonal work, that is, work on internal emotional and psychological health, will include therapeutic interventions that also promote collective experiences and social change. A policy-level empowerment intervention or social policy reform addresses the psychological and holistic well-being at the structural level. The development or amendment of a policy may help to prevent any adverse effects for marginalized groups. For example, universal healthcare is an empowerment-based policy reform that promotes equality and well-being for everyone (Kantarjia, 2019).

Historical Evolution of Empowerment Theory

The heart and soul of empowerment can be traced to Brazilian educator Paulo Freire, who developed the pedagogy of the oppressed to empower his marginalized students (Freire, 1973, 1998). For this reason, Freire is often credited with articulating the concept of empowerment as he developed his innovative theory and philosophy of education. Freire was passionate about the humanity of oppressed people. He believed it was necessary to enter their world, empathize, and identify with them in order to better understand their needs (Hipolito-Delgado & Lee, 2007). Freire was the first one who worked with empowerment theory to examine the influence of the role of race, ethnicity, culture, and class (Poorman, 2003).

In general, empowerment concepts seek to increase the personal, interpersonal, and political power of oppressed and marginalized people so that they can join as communities and take action to improve their lives (Freire, 1973; Gutierrez, 1990). Freire believed that most of the curriculum taught in schools was irrelevant to marginalized people as it did not address the social and cultural barriers of discrimination that they faced, which are the reality of their lives. He argues for situating education in the lived experience of the students (Freire, 1973). His concept of conscientization or critical consciousness is especially important to the process of personal empowerment because it signifies an awareness of oppression in our society and all the social and political implications for oppression and discrimination (Gutierrez, 1990; Freire, 1998; Hipolito-Delgado & Lee, 2007).

As noted, when applied to social work, there has been some debate as to whether to consider empowerment theory as a process or a practice model (Carr, 2003; Carroll, 1994; Gutierrez & Lewis, 1999; Presser & Sen, 2000). Based on a review of the social work literature, there seems to be general consensus that it is a process that begins by recognizing the needs of the oppressed (e.g., Simon, 1994). Beginning with the seminal work of Barbara Solomon (1976), the social work literature on empowerment theory and practice proliferated in the 1980s and 1990s. Growing out of the social movements and the War on Poverty programs, empowerment became a new way to describe and think about social work processes and social work relationships. It also created a bridge between micro and macro practice that fits ideologically with the values and mission of the profession.

Social work was not the only profession to embrace empowerment; community psychology, psychiatry, and public health also took up the study of empowerment models of intervention (Perkins & Zimmerman, 1995; Speer, 2000; Varkey et al., 2010). The self-help movement also embraced the ideas of empowerment; many client population groups joined what Simon (1994) called the "empowerment movement" (p. 29). Expanding upon the work of empowerment theorists in the 1980s and 1990s, the empowerment as a concept for social work has evolved from a philosophical level or pure theory to also include practice frameworks and methods.

Practice interventions have been developed that address both personal and structural dimensions of powerlessness and are accomplished through multilevel interventions.

Since the turn of the century, the writing and literature on the practice of empowerment has slowed in the United States but has grown internationally (McFadden, 2010). While scholars still refer to empowerment as an outcome of an intervention, with the increased significance placed on evidence-based practice, empowerment has been following suit. However, Simon (1990) noted that "empowerment, as concept with multiple and diverse historical referents, is a term that confuses even as it inspires" (p. 27). Although empowerment is noted as a contested concept, there has been much advancement in using quantitative and qualitative measures to unpack how people and communities perceive and live their personal and collective empowerment (Cyril et al., 2015; Van Dop et al., 2016).

Recent literature has integrated empowerment theory with other practice theories, such as the feminist theory. For example, Turner and Maschi (2014) state that feminist and empowerment theories are closely allied frameworks that can be integrated to address the individual to sociopolitical levels of social work assessment and intervention. In another article, Maschi et al. (2012) also argue that incorporating feminist and empowerment approaches better prepare social workers with the knowledge, values, and skills to promote human rights and social justice that foster the "psychological goods" as well as the social, economic, and political goods of clients commonly seen in direct practice (Maschi et al., 2012). The next section outlines the concepts of empowerment theory that have captured the altruistic imaginations of social workers at every level of practice.

CENTRAL CONCEPTS OF EMPOWERMENT THEORY AND RESEARCH

The central ideas of empowerment theory in social work were influenced by the seminal works on Black empowerment by Barbara Solomon (1976), empowerment practice by Judith Lee (1994, 2001), and culture and diversity by Lorraine Gutierrez et al. (1998). These essential empowerment writings are briefly described to form the foundation to better understand empowerment theory, research, and practice with individuals and groups experiencing oppression.

Solomon's (1976) work defined empowerment as "a process whereby the social worker engages in a set of activities with the client or client system that aim to reduce the powerlessness that has been created by negative valuations based on membership in a stigmatized group" (p. 29). Solomon emphasized that in order to overcome powerlessness, individuals must come to a new understanding of power and see themselves as agents of change, able to influence the powerlessness in their lives. Solomon noted that there are **two levels of power, or "power blocks,"** that inhibit empowerment for clients. The first are **indirect power blocks**, which occur during people's developmental process. That is, individuals may be exposed to situations in the context of their families that limit their ability to develop the necessary skills and resources to fulfill their social roles. For example, a child who grows up in a home where violence is a frequent occurrence may not develop the personal resources to handle the demands or stresses of life. The second level of power block, **direct power blocks**, occurs when our social institutions, including those that we as social workers are engaged in, discriminate or block access to services. This same child does not have access to early childhood education or adequate health care, which may then lead to poor educational outcomes in elementary school. In summary, Solomon's work set the stage for understanding that an essential element of the therapeutic intervention must address the powerlessness that clients experience.

Following in the footsteps of Solomon, Judith Lee (1994) identified **three components of empowerment practice** as part of an **empowerment intervention** (Figure 16.1). These components are critical consciousness, self-efficacy, and developing skills and resources. The first component that Lee identified was **critical consciousness** or the ability to recognize and analyze the societal realities (political, social, and economic) that impinge on one's ability to meet one's

FIGURE 16.1 Empowerment theory and practice.

goals and fulfill one's roles. Critical consciousness is a process by which individuals and groups critically examine a historical and current view of oppression, power, and structural inequalities. Lee's conceptualization is consistent with Freire's concept of conscientization or critical consciousness, which he described as an awareness of oppression in our society, and as such, critical consciousness is an essential piece in fostering personal empowerment (Freire, 1973). Freire came to believe that hope was central to empowerment work (as did Jane Addams) since without hope, neither individuals nor communities can begin the struggle to change.

The second component Lee identified was **self-efficacy**, or the belief that one can affect change and reach goals. Bandura (1982) noted that self-efficacy is "a generative ability in which component cognitive, social and behavioral skills must be organized into integrated courses of action to serve innumerable purposes" (p. 122). Promoting self-efficacy is a cornerstone of an empowerment intervention as it allows clients to change their responses to their social environment. The third component of empowerment practice from Lee's work is **developing skills and resources** to meet personal, interpersonal, and community goals.

Gutierrez et al. (1998) delineate four dimensions or problem-solving activities that make up an empowerment-based intervention: (a) the client–worker relationship that addresses immediate needs or presenting problems, (b) education and skills development, (c) resource development and access to programs and systems, and (d) knowledge and skills for social action and macro change. Based on these perspectives, central themes of empowerment theory and practice were identified and will be reviewed next.

Central Themes of Empowerment Theory

Each of these historical works has led to the development and definition of the **central themes** of **empowerment theory**. A synthesis of these three perspectives identify four key themes: (a) client system powerlessness; (b) four levels of empowerment: intrapersonal, interpersonal, collective (community), and political; (c) empowerment as an ongoing developmental process; (d) empowerment practice as a client-driven intervention process based on strengths and competencies, and not power given but power experienced and exercised; and (5) empowerment as contextual and will vary with diverse groups, situations, and contexts.

The first key theme from the literature on empowerment practice is **client system powerlessness**. As Solomon (1976) clearly documented, the roots of powerlessness are complex. Powerlessness may be manifested in a lack of psychological efficacy (Kieffer, 1984) but is also equally experienced in community dimensions. Powerlessness is maintained by the process of oppression in sociopolitical structures, but it is not a fixed state. Overcoming powerlessness is a process that can be learned and enacted.

The second key theme from the literature on empowerment practice is that there are **four levels of empowerment: intrapersonal, interpersonal, collective (community), and political**. The research presents many case examples that address these levels in an empowerment intervention (Cyril et al., 2015; East, 2000; Glenmaye, 1998; Van Dop et al., 2016). Individual or psychological empowerment is described as a developmental process of gaining a psychological sense of self-efficacy or life skill competence (Kieffer, 1984). This process can occur without an actual change in an external structural system (Zimmerman & Rappaport, 1988). The components of individual psychological empowerment vary in different practice contexts. For example, Gutierrez (1995) identifies individual psychological components of empowerment in the context of ethnic identity as group identification, self-efficacy, and collective efficacy, while McWhirter (1994) does so in mental health service as critical awareness and stress-skill development.

In direct practice with individuals, empowerment interventions may primarily help individuals develop psychological self-efficacy or coping skills to adjust to the existing social environment. However, most authors of the empowerment model of social work practice contend that individual empowerment that emphasizes personal self-efficacy alone is not sufficient to overcome powerlessness (Leonardsen, 2006; Miley et al., 2011). Interpersonal empowerment involves developing the capacity of individuals, families, and groups to more effectively interact with the key individuals in their lives, as well as the institutions that are part of their everyday interactions, such as schools, neighbors, or service organizations. Empowerment is relational, and connection is a key component of interpersonal empowerment, creating power in relationships and collective experiences (Christens, 2012; Gutierrez & Lewis, 1999). Feminist social workers developed the concept of the importance of mutuality and connection in relationships to increase personal empowerment (Jordan et al., 1991). Social group work is a key method of empowerment practice, encouraging collectivity through linking people with others and creating social networks (Henry et al., 2011).

Finally, community or political empowerment is a process of the redistribution of power through community participation in order to change communities, organizations, and institutions that affect people's lives (East, 2000; Gutierrez et al., 1998). This means that empowerment practice is not only about an individual's change; changes in community, organizational, and political settings are also emphasized. Community change occurs through community organizing and collaboration, campaigning, legislative lobbying, social planning, and policy development. During the political empowerment process, social workers and their clients are encouraged to critically reflect on the sociopolitical environment to assess problems, so that consciousness can be raised (Breton, 1994; Gutierrez et al., 1998). The purpose or the outcome of consciousness raising is a new set of values, assumptions, and expectations, embodied in a new set of structures, as well as new personal and social relationships (Bricker-Jenkins & Hooyman, 1986).

A third key theme from the literature on empowerment practice is that **empowerment is an ongoing developmental process**. The process does not necessarily occur in a linear series of intrapersonal, interpersonal, and political changes but rather in a circular and interactive process (Gutierrez, 1990). Home (1999) provides an example in the context of working with survivors of sexual abuse of how the three phases (intrapersonal, interpersonal, and sociopolitical empowerment) are interactive. She describes that in a group for survivors of a sexual abuse, members were encouraged to share their experiences, reflect on societal roots of their oppression, and develop coping strategies to increase self-esteem: "Energized by new critical awareness, the group decided to organize a rally to challenge public attitudes toward women [...] success in this social action increased members' self-esteem and participatory competence" (p. 239). It is worth noting that the critical consciousness raising acts are a catalyst, playing an essential role in connecting the two phases of personal and political empowerment (Gutierrez, 1990). It is the interactive relationship between intrapersonal, interpersonal, and political/community empowerment that has been the subject of several research efforts. Kieffer (1984) found through in-depth interviews with grassroots leaders that increased political efficacy through working in a political organization also influenced perceived self-efficacy and self-esteem. Zimmerman and Rappaport (1988) found that participation in community activities resulted in higher scores in measures of psychological empowerment. Building on this research, intrapersonal empowerment is linked to sociopolitical control and participation in empowering community settings (Christens et al., 2011).

A fourth key theme from the literature on empowerment practice is that **empowerment practice is a client-driven intervention process based on strengths and competencies, and not power given, but power experienced and exercised** (Gutierrez et al., 1998). The assumption is made that despite life's problems, all people and environments have strengths and resources that can be used to improve the quality of people's lives. In the empowerment process, power cannot be given or developed among beneficiaries of programs by social workers; rather, it occurs through people's participation in claiming power on their own behalf (GlenMaye, 1998; Simon, 1994). People become involved in all stages of empowerment programs through the identification of problems and solutions, the implementation of the solutions, and the evaluation of their efforts (Presser & Sen, 2000). Through this participation, people have opportunities to gain skills and assert themselves. This promotes a relationship between social workers and their clients that is egalitarian and based on a partnership perspective (East, 2000; Gutierrez et al., 1998).

The fifth and final key theme from the literature on empowerment practice is that **empowerment is contextual and will vary with diverse groups, situations, and contexts** (Zimmerman, 1990). Race/ethnicity, class, and gender have all been examined for how these factors may influence or form the empowerment experience of individuals, groups, and communities (Gutierrez & Lewis, 1999; Itzhaky & York, 2000; Peterson et al., 2002). There is increasing literature documenting empowerment interventions across age groups (Cox & Parsons, 1994; Stanton-Salazar, 2010). Finally, empowerment models are being practiced and modified worldwide. Scholars are recognizing and delineating how empowerment models in different countries, while having commonalities, also have nuances that are country specific (Pardasani, 2005; Petchesky, 2010; Wang et al., 2011). These concepts and themes of empowerment theory and practice form the basis of the helping process—engagement, assessment, intervention, evaluation of outcomes, and termination—assisting clients to move from a state of powerlessness to pure empowerment.

PHASES OF THE HELPING PROCESS

Engagement

Empowerment practice begins with the helping relationship and the way in which the social worker and client system form a partnership. The first consideration is the power dynamic in the relationship, and how this dynamic will be considered, understood, and explored as an agent of change instead of an agent of social control (Kamiński, 2018). Social workers do bring power to the relationship in the form of knowledge and skills that can help facilitate change. It is also important for social workers to recognize the privilege they carry and hold in the context of a helping relationship. That said, in order to foster clients' empowerment and positive change, the working relationship is formed based on "collaboration, trust and shared power" (Gutierrez & Lewis, 1999, p. 7).

Congruent with the history of the social work relationship as a vehicle for change (Perlman, 1979), the helping relationship in an empowerment intervention is a key component of the change process. "Social workers know that the connection between the worker and the client is the most powerful tool available to the social worker" (Marsh, 2005, p. 195). This stance is acknowledged in the common factors model where the relationship is considered a cornerstone of the change process (Norcross, 2011).

The first principle of the engagement process is that dialog and safe space are important elements in this process. Miley et al. (2011) identify three elements or actions of the social worker in the dialog process: (a) forming partnerships, (b) articulating situations, and (c) defining directions. Dialog leads to mutual understanding of the context of the client's concerns or problems and allows for mutuality in the relationship where both client and worker are affected by the story and the process (Jordan, 1991). Based on the dialog process, the following practices are encouraged in an empowerment model of engagement:

- a strong acknowledgment of clients' definitions of the problem, based on the belief that clients are experts, not only in their life experiences but also in their relationships with the systems in their lives;
- "[s]tarting where the client is," especially in meeting concrete needs as it relates to day-to-day survival;
- a focus on eliciting strengths and using the strengths perspective (Saleebey, 2009) to have clients explicitly name their strengths and how they have used them to manage their lives; and
- instilling hope that change is possible and sustaining hope for the future.

Assessment

Assessment in an empowerment model is framed in the meaning of the problem or the situation to the client. At the same time, the social worker contextualizes this meaning in a social, political, and economic context. Understanding causality, while looking forward, is an important element of the assessment process. Key questions of assessment include:

- What manifestations of powerlessness are being experienced at intrapersonal, interpersonal, and community levels?
- How is the client's experience of the problems/concerns manifested in oppression?
- What are the client's transactions with the environment? Where are the connections? Where are the disconnections?
- How can strengths be mobilized, and what is the potential for strengths to counter disadvantages?
- What natural helping networks are available or can be initiated?

Contracting and Intervention

The contract or service agreement between the client and the social worker is a foundation of social work practice (Compton et al., 2005). In the empowerment model of practice, the contract is an agreement based on mutuality and trust and is a tool for accountability for both the social worker and the client. The essence of the contract is what power, in terms of knowledge, skills, and resources, the client will bring to the relationship and what roles the social worker will take in facilitating the change process. The intervention goals are established in a way that the client understands and embraces. Numerous sources identify empowerment roles in the intervention process (Gutierrez et al., 1998; Solomon, 1976). The roles include the following:

- *Listener:* Social workers using an empowerment model start with the basic listening and communication skills that validate experience, demonstrate empathy and mutuality, identify and promote strengths, and pay attention to immediate needs. The practice of "mindfulness" is important in this process.
- *Educator and teacher:* Social workers play a key role in sharing information and teaching their clients knowledge and skills for change. Particularly empowering is when the social worker and client together can gather new information and evaluate the information in light of the client's experience.

- *Resource consultant:* Part of gaining power is having access to the necessary resources for change. Social workers link clients to needed services. This is done in a way that is empowering, meaning that clients learn how to analyze the power dynamics in accessing resources, how to advocate for themselves, and how-to problem-solve difficult situations.
- *Question poser:* Developing and asking questions is not just about seeking information. Questions can form the basis, if done in a non-threatening way, of raising issues that are important to consider in the empowerment relationship and process. For example, clarifying cultural experiences, expectations, and differences form a basis for a direct conversation and model openness. Critical consciousness uses questions to explore experiences and challenge the status quo.
- *Mobilizer/system activist:* In an empowerment model, social workers are constantly looking for ways to mobilize people and promote change in the system. While at times the social worker is the activist, empowerment practice promotes training clients to become leaders and activists in the community.

Evaluation and Termination

The ultimate evaluation of the empowerment intervention is that clients have both perceived and actual evidence of increased power. Evaluation is an ongoing process of celebrating gains and reassessing areas of continued vulnerability. Termination, or a planned ending of a relationship and intervention, is an essential process in any social work relationship. Possibly unique in empowerment practice is that clients can terminate a counseling relationship but continue work in groups and community change efforts.

APPLICATION TO FAMILY AND GROUP WORK

Family Work

Family work in a generalist model is based on understanding families as systems. Interventions to improve family functioning are built on understanding the internal dynamics of families, roles, relationships, and family patterns (Kirst-Ashman & Hull, 2012). An empowerment perspective on work with families moves away from focusing primarily on internal dynamics and examines how vulnerable families are situated in an environment that can negatively affect well-being (Hodges et al., 1998). Family work begins at the interpersonal level and considers that family units have strengths. Capacity building is encouraged through supporting, teaching, and linking families to community systems of support. Models of family work that are congruent with family empowerment include family-based services that partner with families in developing treatment plans (Jager & Carolan, 2010). In addition, programs such as family health advocacy and health promotion are good examples of family empowerment practices (Baffour & Chonody, 2012).

Group Work

Group work is a foundation of empowerment practice and can serve as a link between the individual or family and the community (Breton, 1994). Given that a key principle of the empowerment process is "validation through collective experience" (Gutierrez et al., 1998, p. 4), the opportunity for clients to participate in group experiences becomes essential to empowerment practice. The types of groups can vary, including mutual aid or self-help groups, clinical groups, psychoeducational groups, or social action groups. The group experience provides several important elements to the empowerment process. First, the group experience provides an opportunity for an individual to experience both autonomy and interdependence. The group also acts as a resource for social functioning. Second, the group process allows individuals to practice life skills, such as communication and problem-solving, which occur in natural groups in one's life. Finally, the group provides a means for individuals to engage in addressing common problems, finding collective solutions, and helping others, which in turn can help individual growth and reduce self-blame.

The direct social work practitioner can take on three roles that promote group work as part of the clinical intervention. The first is looking for opportunities to connect clients to group opportunities. For example, when a client is struggling with a problem that is common to many others in the same situation, the role of the social worker is to help find or create opportunities for those with similar concerns to connect. The second role is to connect the client strengths and potential to community activities, naming for the client the possibilities for collective action. This might include noticing that a client is a natural leader in her neighborhood when she takes her neighbors to the local food bank. By naming and acknowledging this strength with the client, the social worker can encourage additional activities that would support the client's positive interaction with the community and environment. Finally, it is the responsibility of an empowerment social worker to understand the sociopolitical environment in which the client is situated and, when appropriate, to share with the client the social action activities in the community that might be an avenue of collective social change work. The link between participation in social action groups and the increase in self-efficacy and psychological empowerment is well documented (Christens et al., 2011).

COMPATIBILITY WITH THE GENERALIST-ECLECTIC FRAMEWORK

Human Rights Framework

A human rights framework is an overarching perspective that can inform social work interventions about the pathways to empowerment for individuals, families, and communities at the local or global level. A human rights framework has underlying values and principles (United Nations [UN], 2015). Fundamental to human rights values are dignity, worth, and respect for all persons, the intrinsic value of each person, and the duty of governments (i.e., duty bearers) to their citizens (rights holders) and duty bearing citizens to other rights-holding citizens (UN, 1948).

The six major principles of a human rights framework are: (a) universality, (b) nondiscrimination, (c) the indivisibility and interdependence of rights (political, civil, social, economic, and cultural), (d) participation, (e) accountability, and (f) transparency, which are described in the following (Ife, 2012; Maschi, 2016; UN, 2015; see Box 16.1). These major principles inform the right to power and empowerment in social work intervention with individuals and groups affected by oppression.

BOX 16.1 Human Rights Framework

Protects civil, political, economic, social, and cultural rights
Promotes personal and collective empowerment

BASIC PRINCIPLES

1. Universality
2. Participation
3. Accountability
4. Transparency
5. Non-discrimination

1. The principle of *universality* states that human rights belong to everyone and there are no exceptions for any individual. The mere fact of being human entitles every human to political, civil, social, economic, and cultural rights.
2. The principle, *nondiscrimination*, ensures access to rights for everyone. In an ideal world, there should be no intended or unintended discrimination of international laws, policies, or practices.
3. The principle, *indivisibility and interdependence*, guides governments to ensure political, civil, social, economic, and cultural rights to everyone. For example, if a government does not recognize a social right, such as the right to health and well-being, it challenges citizens' access to also achieving these other areas of rights, such as the right to education and safety and protection from violence and discrimination.
4. The principle of *participation* refers to everyone's rights, especially those most affected, and conveys that they have the right to participate in decisions that may infringe upon the protection of their rights. In the most ideal situation, governments should engage, support, and provide a platform for the participation of civil society on political, civil, social, economic, and cultural issues.
5. The principle of *accountability* suggests that governments are responsible for creating a mechanism of accountability for the enforcement of equal rights, which includes monitoring and evaluating the implementation of laws and policies that protect rights.
6. The principle of *transparency* means that governments should communicate to civil society about all information and decision-making processes affecting human rights. Society's members should be educated to become informed participants in the decision-making process as it affects their rights. This includes not only at the national and international levels but also at the institutional level, such as public institutions, such as social services and other institutions are structured and managed, which are needed to protect such rights, such as the right to social equality and education (Maschi, 2016; UN, 2015).

The Universal Declaration of Human Rights (UDHR) is a human rights document that also can inform empowerment practice with individuals and groups who experience oppression. It is a non-binding document that informs the compendium of human rights in political, civil, social, economic, and cultural rights that all humans regardless of their backgrounds have (UN, 1948). As shown in Figure 16.2, the human rights map provides a brief overview of the human rights framework and the 30 articles of the UDHR, such as the right to education and an adequate standard of living. After the signing of the UDHR in 1948, additional instruments, such as covenants, conventions, and treaties, were developed to further operationalize and monitor the implementation of these 30 basic human rights that also can be used to inform empowerment-based assessment and interventions in social work (Wronka, 2017).

Oppression Theory

Oppression theory also helps inform prevention, assessment, and intervention with oppressed Individuals and groups. Oppression generally refers to the unjust use of power and authority of one group over another. The levels of oppression framework consists of four levels of oppression: personal, structural, cultural, and internalized. These levels of oppression have relevance to understanding the experiences of diverse oppressed groups (Figure 16.3).

Structural level oppression refers to oppression that is transmitted via institutions (e.g., economic and social institutions), organizations (e.g., mental health, aging, and criminal justice service providers), structures (e.g., local, state, and federal governments), laws, and policies. Structural oppression can be found when the society disproportionately allocates good jobs, healthcare, and housing to the dominant group. In contrast, the subordinate group gets their unfair share of unemployment, poor healthcare, homelessness, poverty, incarceration, and low social status. Social inequalities also are socially sanctioned in the form of physical and psychological violence. This violence may be imposed upon the subordinate groups with little to no consequences socially or legally (Mullaly & West, 2017).

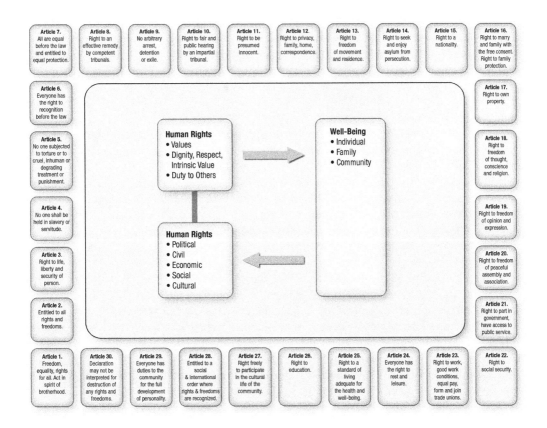

FIGURE 16.2 A human rights map: Therapeutic jurisprudence, empowerment, and well-being.

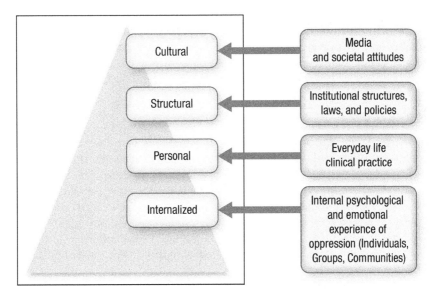

FIGURE 16.3 Levels of oppression prevention, assessment, and intervention model

Cultural-level oppression consists largely of overall societal attitudes and judgments, including the use of media. Although there is no one universal definition, culture has been described as a common set of values and norms, including shared pattern of seeing, thinking, and acting, that a group holds, such as different racial/ethnic groups or professional disciplines. Communication serves as the ways and means of culture, including the use of verbal and non-verbal language and symbolism. Daily, most individuals experience some type of culture, such as music, television, novels, and movies.

Personal-level oppression consists of every experience with individuals in one's immediate micro-level network. This contact can be with family members, neighbors, strangers, and/or professionals. Personal-level oppression consists of the transmission of thoughts, attitudes, and behaviors that depict negative prejudgments of subordinate groups. Personal-level oppression is usually based on stereotypes. It occurs overtly or covertly and may or may not be intentional. It may manifest in the form of conscious acts of microaggressions, overt aggression and/or hatred, including violence. It also may manifest as unconscious acts of aversion and avoidance (Mullaly & West, 2017).

Internalized-level oppression is characterized by the individual's psyche (internal experience) and their experience and interpretation of the reciprocal relationship with the environment made up of social, cultural, political, and economic factors. Oppression emanates from the sociopolitical conditions and environmental factors, which have the potential to influence individuals' psyches or psychological and emotional well-being. Oppressive social conditions include discrimination, powerlessness, subordination, exclusion, exploitation, scapegoating, and low social status. These conditions also block opportunities and may have a negative psychological impact on individuals (Mullaly & West, 2017).

Internalized oppression also referred as internalized control has been considered as the key component to the development and continuation of individuals feeling oppressed and disempowered. The adage, if you believe it, you will see it, is quite fitting here. Internalized oppression not only affects oppressed persons' belief system (e.g., 'I am less than a second-class citizen') but also may influence their behaviors. In other words, they may mistrust their own thinking and intelligence and may subconsciously reenact negative stereotypes of behavior. Then in essence, it becomes almost a self-fulfilling prophecy, which is often self-destructive and even reinforces the dominant culture negative stereotypes of them (Mullaly & West, 2017). Internalized oppression at the psychological level occurs when one's personal identity matches the negative portrait or social identity influence by the external world. However, when there is incongruence with the negative societal portrayal, an oppressed person may resist and seek social change. On the other hand, a person may respond to this incongruence by experiencing adverse thoughts or feelings, such as uncertainty, insecurity, guilt, and anguish (Mullaly & West, 2017).

Feminist Theory

Feminist theory also is consistent with oppression and empowerment theories. Feminism emphasizes the importance of the social, political, and economic structures that shape human societies and stresses that gender must be considered when examining the effects of oppression, domination, power, and powerlessness in our society. In feminist theory, there are four core concepts: (a) mutuality, (b) critical self-awareness, (c) cultural-relational approach, and (d) collaboration. When working directly with clients, feminist and empowerment theories and practice are useful in guiding social workers to help clients claim their power, and build self-confidence and self-esteem as they engage in mutual, non-hierarchical relationships (Crenshaw, 1991; Jordan, 2010).

A Person-in-Environment Perspective That Is Informed by Ecological Systems Theory

Ecological systems theory is also useful toward informing empowerment thought and practices. Empowerment-based interventions consider the relationship between individuals, families, systems of care, and the larger environment to address their rights and mutual needs of health, well-being, and public safety. At the intrapersonal, interpersonal, and community levels, the conceptualization of empowerment practice as an intervention supports the person-in-environment perspective. Additionally, empowerment practice supports the ecological systems principle of mutual causality. In other words, all parties involved experienced some type of change when serving individuals and groups with a history of oppression. For example, community service providers have the opportunity to build their capacity to better serve diverse groups; individuals and their families may experience personal well-being and liberation; and ultimately, communities become healthier and safer for people of all ages.

An Emphasis on the Development of a Good Helping Relationship That Fosters Empowerment

The empowerment helping relationship is built on the principles of collaboration and trust together with the fundamentals of the social work relationship. Empowerment is relational, and relationships are key to the change process. As outlined earlier in this chapter, the dynamic and conscious understanding of the power dynamic in the helping relationship is essential for the empowerment social worker to acknowledge. Empowerment-based social workers respect the knowledge, skills, and values of the client systems and promote the client's strengths to help create opportunities to increase one's sense of power or the ability to act on what matters.

The Flexible Use of a Problem-Solving Model to Provide Structure and Guidelines for Work With Clients

Empowerment practice is based on a problem-solving model that includes the definition of strengths and problem finding/identification; goal setting; role taking on the part of the social worker; interventions at the intrapersonal, interpersonal, and community levels; and collaborative evaluation of accomplishments. Problems are not considered individual deficits, but examples of structural oppression and the effects of powerlessness on individuals, families, and groups. This conceptualization of the problem-solving model is congruent with the flexibility principle of the generalist-eclectic approach.

A Holistic, Multilevel Assessment That Includes a Focus on Issues of Diversity, Oppression, and Strengths

A holistic assessment with focus on diversity, oppression, and strengths is a foundational principle of empowerment theory and practice. As noted throughout this chapter, understanding oppression and its effects on individuals, families, and communities is a key to developing an empowerment intervention. In the assessment process, an empowerment-based social worker considers a client's experience and story as a narrative that is embedded in both personal and political structures.

CRITIQUE OF EMPOWERMENT THEORY

Strengths of Empowerment Theory

One of empowerment theory's greatest strengths is its congruence with social work values and ethics. As noted at the beginning of the chapter, empowerment is embedded in the NASW Code of Ethics' preamble and implied in values such as the dignity and worth of all people and the idea of self-determination. Another strength of empowerment theory is that it deals directly with power as a key dynamic in the change process. Power is acknowledged as not only a component of the social work relationship but also as a means and goal for change. Finally, empowerment theory and practice situate social work interventions at the intersection of micro, mezzo, and macro practice. The empowerment principles can facilitate direct practice with individuals, families, and groups as well as set the stage for community interventions, advocacy, and policy practice.

Weaknesses of Empowerment Theory

Despite the strong inclusion of empowerment as a tenet of social work practice, the criticisms of empowerment theory are clearly articulated (Humphries, 1996; Riger, 1993). First, there is a critique of the application of empowerment to micro or direct practice with individuals and families. Leonardsen (2006) clearly argues that empowerment is a structural intervention and work with individuals or families alone cannot be empowerment practice. However, in contrast to this viewpoint, Bransford (2011) argues that an empowerment approach may discount a client's need for the authority and protection of the worker.

A second critique of empowerment is that it is conceptually "messy" and cannot be well defined or measured. Empowerment research has been criticized by positivistic standards (Robbins et al., 2012). That said, empowerment research has contributed substantially to not only the development of conceptual models of practice but also to the relationship of specific interventions to positive outcomes.

Finally, empowerment is challenged as an idea that has been too easily embraced by social workers, yet not given adequate critique. This challenge includes the notion that we, as social workers, claim to empower others, rather than critically examine the social worker–client relationship in the context of power and the role of social control that social workers play (Pease, 2002; Wendt & Seymour, 2010). In a post-structural analysis, empowerment is a grand truth or narrative that needs to be carefully deconstructed and recognized for its "potential to be dangerous" (Wendt & Seymour, 2010, p. 678). Despite these critiques, empowerment as both an intervention model and an outcome continues to have salience for the social work profession.

Populations Most Suited to Empowerment Practice

Key empowerment principles are applicable to all populations. Gaining a sense of self-efficacy and competence could apply to anyone in a situation where a person may experience or feel powerless. That said, empowerment is most suited to work with populations that have experienced oppression and disadvantage in society. Principles such as sharing power, consciousness raising, and gaining an equal share of valued resources are especially pertinent to groups who have experienced institutional oppression. Empowerment interventions have been designed for women (Travers, 1995), persons with disabilities (Wehmeyer, 2004), mental health consumers (Kelley, 2004), communities of color (Hodges et al., 1998), and LGBTQ youth (Matthews & Salazar, 2012).

CASE STUDY 16.1: INDIVIDUAL

This case example is the story of a woman who worked with an agency that was based in an empowerment model and worked with women who were financially vulnerable.

Rhonda is a 28-year-old mother of four, a son aged 15, a daughter aged 12, and two young boys, aged 3 and 4. Rhonda attended a leadership evening at the agency with her sister, and stated later, "I had never been to an agency where we were treated like that before—there was a positive attitude about change and it was not focused on what I was doing wrong." The leadership evenings were a component of the agency programs, which also included individual counseling, support and educational groups, training and leadership development on issues facing women, and social action in the community. Rhonda immediately engaged in the leadership training and activities of the agency and was articulate about the issues facing women like herself. The critical reflection on issues discussed, like welfare reform or domestic violence, engaged Rhonda's keen intellect and passion.

After about 6 months of involvement at the agency, Rhonda asked if she could see a counselor. In this therapeutic relationship, built on trust and collaboration, Rhonda revealed a personal history that was quite complex. She was sexually abused by her mother's boyfriend, she had married at 18, and was abused by her husband, whom she later divorced. He was the father of her older children. The 15-year-old son was in residential treatment and suffered severe mental problems, and the daughter was already acting out, staying out late, and skipping school. The father of her two young boys was out of state and not involved with the children, but they were still legally married. He was also abusive and would often threaten that if Rhonda divorced him, he would fight for custody of the boys. At this time, Rhonda was working part-time as a retail clerk, and she and her children lived in a home with a man who had befriended her, although they were not involved romantically. Rhonda felt very discouraged about her situation and admitted to often feeling very depressed, with episodes of manic-type behavior, staying up all night to work on a project or going out and partying.

Once these aspects of Rhonda's life were revealed, it was apparent to agency staff that Rhonda could benefit from the empowerment model of working toward intrapersonal, interpersonal, and community change to build on Rhonda's strengths and increase her self-understanding, self-efficacy, and access to resources that may help address the problems she identified. The counseling relationship was key to validating Rhonda's fears and experiences and to reducing the self-blame she experienced about her relationships and about what was going to be the future for her children. Empowerment is a developmental process, with steps forward and steps back. While Rhonda displayed many strengths and increased hope in the leadership activities, in counseling she often portrayed her situation as beyond her control. It took 4 months of encouragement and education before Rhonda was willing to go to the mental health center for an evaluation and decide that medication could help her undiagnosed bipolar disorder. As part of this process, the social worker had Rhonda do her own research on the issue and attend some meetings of a mental health advocacy group for parents. The group helped her gain knowledge and receive support regarding her oldest son.

Slowly, Rhonda began to feel enough control and hope to begin the process of talking about her past relationships with men, as well as her desire to divorce her husband. As this process unfolded, in fact, as she predicted, the husband took on a legal battle for custody. The stress of this event created some relapse incidents for Rhonda. As a result, the agency worked with Rhonda to create a support team of friends, professionals, and her lawyer to work together to support Rhonda through the divorce and custody process and make sure both she and her children were safe and had the resources they needed. It was another year before the divorce was finalized. Rhonda continued to participate in the agency programs, testified at the state legislature on a bill on domestic violence, found employment in a nonprofit agency where she could use her advocacy skills, and moved into a housing program that could help create some needed structure for her life. Rhonda found additional resources for her daughter, which helped her to graduate from high school. Her older son eventually aged out of placements and continued to struggle, but, through support and advocacy groups, Rhonda was able to be supportive to him and link him to community resources.

As Rhonda became more stable, her relationships improved, and her parenting became more consistent. She continued to fear her ex-husband, the father of the two boys, so she maintained a relationship with a domestic violence program and the empowerment-based agency, attending events for both support and community engagement.

CASE STUDY 16.2: COMMUNITY

This case example is of a partnership between community service providers and community members, in which service providers collaborated to create a community empowerment intervention to improve health and well-being of community members of all ages. They coordinated services, intersectoral assessment, and intervention models to increase access to services and justice for individuals and families who had previously experienced barriers to services. This northeastern urban community was very concerned that many marginalized individuals and groups, such as aging undocumented workers with a history of mental health and legal issues, were often denied access to needed health, social, and legal services. As in the case of Carlos (Exhibit 16.1), his undocumented immigration status and legal issues, such as driving while intoxicated, created difficulties for him accessing services. He also experienced being detained in jail and prison on different occasions.

EXHIBIT 16.1 Case Study of Carlos

Carlos is a 55-year-old male from Mexico who identifies as heterosexual. He was seeking community services after being released from jail 2 months ago in New York City. Carlos was diagnosed with generalized anxiety, major depression, and alcohol use disorder. In addition, he also has hypertension, high cholesterol, morbid obesity, and diabetes. Carlos is married and has two children, a 24-year-old daughter and an 18-year-old son. His wife, also undocumented, works as a housekeeper. Both of their children were born in the United States. The daughter is a nurse, and the son goes to college full time. During his childhood, Carlos witnessed domestic violence and alcoholism, and was a victim of physical and verbal abuse from his father. He also has a history of juvenile delinquency (theft) and incarceration (age 12–13). Poverty conditions in his home country prompted Carlos and his father to immigrate to the United States when he was 16 years old. They crossed the U.S. border, leaving the rest of the family in Mexico. Carlos has lived here as an undocumented immigrant since then. At age 25, his father tried to kill Carlos with a knife in his sleep.

Since leaving jail, Carlos was reunited with his wife and children and is looking for a utility worker job in restaurants. Carlos spent 10 months in jail because he was driving under the influence of alcohol. In addition, he was also charged with a misdemeanor for driving without a license. Before being arrested, Carlos used to work in different restaurants as a utility worker and food prep. He also was filing an immigration petition for a work permit. Now, Carlos is concerned that the DUI record will negatively impact on his immigration case and is looking for assistance. As an undocumented immigrant, besides being in constant fear of deportation, Carlos does not have access to Medicaid or private health insurances. He grew up as a Catholic, and even though he does not go to church, he uses prayer as a source of strength.

Care Systems	Services Needed (yes/no)	Assessment & Intervention Plans
Aging		
Mental Health		
Health Care		
Social Services		
Criminal Justice		
Legal Services		
Employment		
Family		
Social Community Supports		
Spiritual/Religious Supports		
Basic Needs/Transportation		
Housing		
Disability Services		
Others		

EXHIBIT 16.2 Care coordination eco-wheel intervention plan.

Client's Name: Carlos		
Care Systems	Services Needed (yes/no)	Assessment & Intervention Plans
Aging	yes	Refer to preventive care
Mental Health	yes	Refer to mental health professional
Health Care	yes	Connect client with community healthcare center for sliding fee program
Social Services	yes	Connect client with different support systems within the community
Criminal Justice	no	
Legal Services	yes	Connect client with immigration lawyer
Employment	yes	Refer client to a job program
Family	no	
Social Community Supports	yes	Refer client to a diabetes and depression support group
Spiritual/Religious Supports	no	
Basic Needs/Transportation	yes	Connect client with transportation assistance program
Housing	no	
Disability Services	no	
Others	yes	Refer client to AA program

EXHIBIT 16.3 Care coordination eco-wheel intervention plan—sample.

The community service providers developed a community empowerment model of practice. They created a coordinating council of all health, social service, legal, and other providers to provide a wraparound model of care. A research team developed an eco-wheel and intervention plan to map the assessment and intervention plan for clients who needed ongoing access to multiple systems. Following is an example of a case vignette and eco-wheel assessment and intervention plan completed by the originating health service provider (see Exhibits 16.2 and 16.3 for the service plan). Due to this coordination, Carlos and his family were able to relate to the multitude of services needed. Carlos and his family were very thankful to their social worker as well as the additional assistance provided by the other community service providers. He told his social worker: *"Soy muy grato por su asistencia, Dios te la bendiga"* ("I am grateful for all of your assistance, may God bless you.").

As illustrated in Figures 16.4 and 16.5, the eco-wheel has a circle in the center that represents the client. Outside of the circle are influences within the client's various systems (aging, mental health, health, housing) and social support systems (family, social, community supports and employment), which are drawn in circles. The service provider can work with the client to notate the nature of each relationship and how those relationships impact the client's life. The relationships are indicated by different types of lines and can be positive, strong, stressful, weak, tenuous/uncertain, and terminated or nonexistent at the chosen point in time represented on the eco-wheel (Kemp et al., 1997). Relationships are both directional and non-directional, represented by arrows on the end of each line. The eco-wheel can be updated as the situation for the client changes over time. Interventions can be designed to strengthen areas in which social or service linkages need to be connected and/or strengthened.

CONCLUSION

Empowerment theory and practice are grounded in the values of the social work profession, with particular attention to social justice and its explicit values perspective on power and collective action. These values promote transformative change, if social workers believe "deeply that people can change and environments can be transformed" (Simon, 1994, p. 3). However, empowerment is more than a values and philosophical perspective. The development of empowerment theory and the related interventions have resulted in concrete strategies and

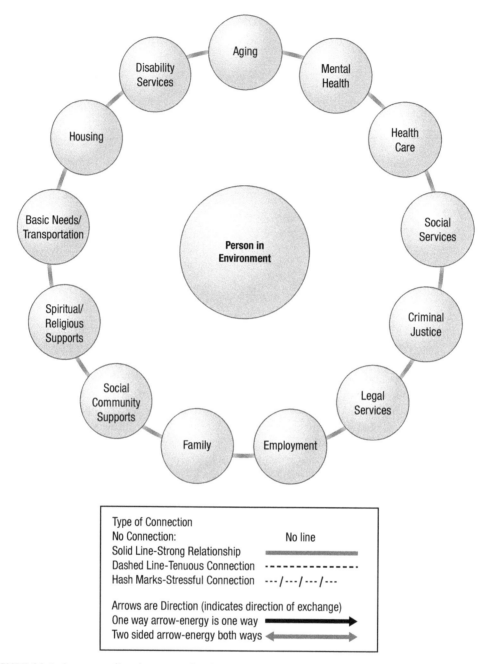

FIGURE 16.4 Care coordination eco-wheel.

Source: Copyright Maschi and Kaye (2019).

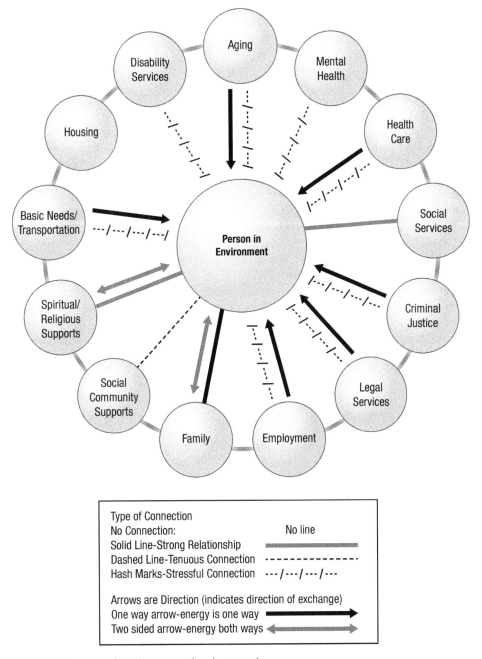

FIGURE 16.5 Care coordination eco-wheel—sample.

processes that social workers can use to create change and increase power at intrapersonal, interpersonal, and political levels. For direct practitioners, empowerment models offer the opportunity to affect client powerlessness with multiple intervention points, thereby increasing the opportunities for growth and well-being.

SUMMARY POINTS

- Empowerment theory and practice are grounded in the values of the social work profession, with attention to advancing human rights and social, economic, and environmental justice,
- empowerment is a values and philosophical perspective and a practice model,
- the explicit values of empowerment theory and practice are the acknowledgment of disempowerment and the attainment of personal and collective power and inspired action,
- the underlying values of empowerment promote human and community well-being and psychological and environmental transformation,
- if social workers adopt a belief that people and environments have the capacity to embrace their wellness and power, the conditions to move empowerment from a process of change to an observable outcome are achievable,
- the evolution of empowerment theory and the related interventions have resulted in concrete strategies and processes that social workers can use to create change and increase power at intrapersonal, interpersonal, and political levels, and
- for direct practitioners, empowerment models offer the opportunity to affect client powerlessness with multiple intervention points, thereby increasing the opportunities for individual and community empowerment and holistic well-being.

ACKNOWLEDGMENT

This chapter is dedicated in loving memory to Jean East who was its original author. We are quite honored to have had the opportunity to update it for her.

KEY REFERENCES

Only key references appear in the print edition. The full reference list appears in the digital product found on http://connect.springerpub.com/content/book/978-0-8261-6556-5/part/sec03/part/sec034/chapter/ch16

Bandura, A. (1982). Self-efficacy mechanism in human agency. *American Psychologist, 37*, 122–147.
Bricker-Jenkins, M., & Hooyman, N. (1986). Not for women only: Social work practice for a feminist future. National Association of Social Workers.
Council on Social Work Education. (2015). *Educational policy and accreditation standards for baccalaureate and master's social work programs*. Author.
Cyril, S., Smith, B., & Renzaho, A. (2015). Systematic review of empowerment measures in health promotion. *Health Promotion International*, dav059.
East. J. (2000). Empowerment through welfare rights organizing: A feminist perspective. *Afflia, 15*, 311–328.
Freire, P. (1973). *Education for critical consciousness*. Seabury.
Gutierrez, L. M. (1990). Working with women of color: An empowerment perspective. *Social Work, 35*, 149–153.
Kieffer, P. C. (1984). Citizen empowerment approach to social work practice (2nd ed.). Columbia University Press.
Lee, J. A. B. (2001). *The empowerment approach to social work practice*. Columbia University Press.
Mullaly, R., & West, J. (2017). *Challenging oppression and confronting privilege* (3rd ed.). Oxford University Press.

National Association of Social Work (NASW). (2017). Code of ethics. NASW Press.

Presser, H. B., & Sen, G. (2000). *Women's empowerment and demographic processes—Moving beyond Cairo.* Oxford University Press.

Reichert, S. (2006.) *Understanding human rights.* Sage.

Saleebey, D. (2009). The strengths perspective in social work practice (5th ed.). Pearson.

Simon, B. L. (1994). The empowerment tradition in American social work. Columbia University Press.

Anti-Oppressive Theory and Practice

Alicia M. Sellon and Heather Lassman

By the end of this chapter, you should be able to

- recognize the role of systemic oppression in the lives of service users,
- understand the stages of practice through the lens of anti-oppressive theory and practice (AOP),
- understand the importance of critical reflection in AOP, and
- apply key concepts of AOP to practice situations.

INTRODUCTION

Challenging social structures and environments that create inequalities or otherwise oppress individuals, families, and communities is at the core of social work's value of social justice and fundamental to practice. The National Association of Social Workers (NASW) charges social workers with pursuing "social change, particularly with and on behalf of vulnerable and oppressed individuals and groups of people. Social workers' social change efforts are focused primarily on issues of poverty, unemployment, discrimination, and other forms of social injustice" (NASW, 2008; ethical principles). Anti-oppressive theory, also referred to as anti-oppressive practice (AOP), is a social justice and emancipatory framework that can help social work practice to better align with the values of the profession. Rooted in the concepts of equality, egalitarianism, inclusivity, and social change, AOP helps social workers to identify instances of oppression—even within our own practice—to increase the service user's understanding of oppressive systems, and to empower and work with them to dismantle oppressive structures (Baines, 2017; Campbell, 2003; Dominelli, 1996, 2002; Hines, 2012; Langley, 2001; Mullaly & West, 2018; Sakamoto & Pitner, 2005; Strier & Binyamin, 2010).

AOP is an orientation to practice rather than a specific approach and draws on ideas from many sources including anti-racism, feminist, Marxist, and postmodern theories; social work's history of social change efforts; and social movements (e.g., Disability Rights Movement). AOP focuses attention and action on identifying and opposing oppressive systems and social environments across the levels of social work practice in order to create a more socially just society (Baines, 2017; Campbell, 2003; Dominelli, 1996, 2002; Mullaly & West, 2018; Sakamoto & Pitner, 2005; Strier & Binyamin, 2010). According to Dominelli (1996), a leader in developing AOP:

> AOP embodies a person-centered philosophy; an egalitarian value system concerned with reducing the deleterious effects of structural inequalities upon people's lives; a methodology focusing on both process and outcome; and a way of

structuring relationships between individuals that aims to empower users by reducing the negative effects of social hierarchies on their interaction and the work they do together. (p. 170)

Anti-oppressive social workers have a dual focus of critically reflecting on power imbalances and inequalities that affect service users and working to identify and remove oppressive systems in society (Baines, 2017; Dominelli, 2002; Mullaly & West, 2018; Sakamoto & Pitner, 2005; Strier & Binyamin, 2010). AOP social workers recognize that structural inequalities and oppression shape the lives of service users and the context in which social workers practice and use this holistic framework to identify and challenge oppression at every level of practice (Baines, 2017; Dominelli, 2002; Mullaly & West, 2018; Sakamoto & Pitner, 2005).

This chapter provides a review of AOP and describes how it can be used in practice. The chapter begins with an overview of the approach, including a discussion of key terms related to AOP, a brief review of the history of the approach, how it views human behavior, and its relevance to social service and clinical settings. Key themes and concepts of the approach are also reviewed. The chapter then focuses on how the approach can be used to guide practice, and an example case study is provided. The chapter concludes with a discussion on the strengths and weaknesses of AOP as an approach for social work practice.

AN OVERVIEW OF ANTI-OPPRESSIVE THEORY AND PRACTICE

Review of Key Terminology

Before beginning a more in-depth discussion of AOP, it is useful to understand three key terms related to AOP: *oppression*, *privilege*, and *intersectionality*. Central to the process of engaging in AOP is the recognition that power imbalances and oppression exist and are often reinforced based on privilege related to the perceived membership of individuals within and across social groups (Baines, 2017; Mullaly & West, 2018). Indeed, Mullaly and West (2018) argue that privilege and oppression are two sides of the same coin and that you cannot have one without the other.

While there are many definitions of oppression (e.g., Baines, 2017; Dominelli, 2002), Mullaly and West (2018) provide a comprehensive definition that ties in well with ideas related to intersectionality (discussed in the following). According to the authors, *oppression* can be described as targeting and denying individuals access to opportunities and resources, based on the perceived membership in social groups. These groups are often socially created and reinforced through the conscious and unconscious actions of dominant groups or those with more social, economic, and political power. Frequently based on stereotypes and carried out in social and institutional contexts, oppression, often referred to as the *isms* (racism, sexism, ableism, etc.), both cast subordinate groups as problematic and needing to be controlled and limit the ability of groups to access needed resources and fully participate in their communities and society (Baines, 2017; Dominelli, 2002; Mullaly & West, 2018). Often, these stereotypes become so entrenched in society that they become part of people's automatic thought process, and many people do not realize that they are making racist, sexist, and so forth assumptions about others (Dominelli, 2002; Fook, 2002; Mattsson, 2014; Mullaly & West, 2018).

The second key term, *privilege*, is seen as the unearned advantages that some groups have that allow them greater access to resources and opportunities. This is not to say that members of these groups do not work hard or have not earned some of their status. Rather, the concept of privilege suggests that perceived membership to some groups (e.g., being White and male) provides individuals with more advantages and opportunities than those who are perceived to be members of other groups (e.g., being Black and male). Mullaly and West (2018) also point out that some people with privilege may experience hardships. However, if these difficulties are not directly connected with structural barriers (e.g., ableism in hiring practices that limit the opportunities of people with disabilities to be gainfully employed), then they should not be considered to be experiencing oppression.

AOP draws on a third key concept, *intersectionality*, to help provide an analytical framework for practice to help social workers understand the complex ways that individuals and groups may experience oppression or privilege (Mattson, 2014; Mullaly & West, 2018). This concept was first introduced by Crenshaw (1989) to highlight how Black women experienced discrimination based on the interconnected and overlapping constructs of race and gender. That is, a single categorization of Black women as either Black or women did not adequately capture their complex and unique experiences with discrimination and oppression. Thus, it is important to understand that privilege and oppression are not cumulative or additive. Rather, we must look at an individual's privilege or oppression in different contexts for each of their identities (Black or Woman) and at the intersection of a person's identities (Black × Woman; Mattsson, 2014; Mullaly & West, 2018).

Since Crenshaw's conceptualization, intersectionality has expanded in academic and popular discourse to include a variety of social identities (e.g., age, disability, sexuality; Mattsson, 2014; Mullaly & West, 2018). Critical to this discussion is the exploration of how different systems of power and discrimination may privilege or oppress these multiple, intersecting identities. Using intersectionality as an analytical tool helps the AOP social worker to consider larger structural inequalities that different groups may experience, while also being sensitive to a person's unique experiences of privilege or oppression within and across different groups (Mattsson, 2014; Mullaly & West, 2018).

AOP social workers recognize that oppression is a complex phenomenon that can have a profound impact on individuals, communities, and society overall. Individuals who experience racism, sexism, ableism, or other forms of oppression may begin to believe the negative stereotypes about their social groups and internalize this stigma. This can have profound impact on a person's sense of self, self-esteem, belief in their abilities, physical and emotional well-being, and desire and ability to participate in their communities (Dominelli, 2002; Hines, 2012; Langley, 2001; Larson, 2008; Mullaly & West, 2018; Strier & Binyamin, 2010).

Historical Development

First introduced in the late 1980s, AOP has become an important part of social work education in many schools in Canada and the United Kingdom, and its value is increasingly being recognized in the United States (Mullaly & West, 2018). In recent years, AOP has gained prominence as questions have been raised about the ability of social workers to respond to the needs of service users in the face of increasing wealth inequalities and dominant and oppressive social discourse that stigmatizes service users and promotes individual instead of collective responsibility for social problems (Baines, 2017; Domenelli, 2002; Strier & Binyamin, 2010). Indeed, AOP has been developed in response to concerns that social work has moved away from its social justice mandate and requires a more holistic framework for understanding and addressing oppression in society (Baines, 2017; Dominelli, 2002; Mullaly & West, 2018; Strier & Binyamin, 2010). AOP scholars have drawn on two main sources to guide the development of the framework: social change movements in social work and the larger society and the blending together of different theoretical perspectives to help explain and address systemic inequalities.

While attention is often given to micro and mezzo levels of practice, social work in the United Kingdom, Canada, and the United States also has a strong tradition of engaging in more macro-level efforts to address political, economic, and social injustices. Social work's roots in the Settlement House movement, the Rank and File movement, and the development of radical social work in the 1960s and 1970s highlight social work's dual focus on not only working with individuals and families but also acting to address systemic structural inequalities (Baines, 2017; McLaughlin, 2005; Mullaly & West, 2018; Reisch & Andrews 2002). In addition, AOP social workers have drawn inspiration from several social movements (Civil Rights, Disability Rights, LGBTQ Liberation, and Feminist), which sought to remove barriers related to social, community, and economic participation and opportunities and to create a more socially just and egalitarian society (Baines, 2017; McLaughlin, 2005; Mullaly & West, 2018).

AOP emerged from anti-racism theory and radical social work, which had been critiqued for focusing almost exclusively on racism and classism and largely ignoring intersectionality and other forms of oppression (Macey & Moxon, 1996; Mullaly & West, 2018). Providing a more holistic approach that encompasses intersectional identities and oppression, AOP has been described as an umbrella framework that includes social justice approaches from many different theories. For example, Baines (2017) notes that AOP draws ideas about power imbalances, structural inequalities, oppressed groups, and resistance strategies from anti-racism, feminist, Marxist, queer, and structural theories. Depending on the group or inequalities targeted, these theories help to guide AOP social workers to use practices that empower and lead to the liberation of these groups (Baines, 2017; Mullaly & West, 2018). Ideas about ways of knowing, the need to understand people's subjective experiences, and how language can be used to reinforce oppression are drawn from Postmodernism. While concerns have been raised about the blending of these frameworks, given their different ontological orientations, Baines (2017) and others have argued that the eclectic approach of AOP is appropriate for dealing with the challenges that arise at the practice level. Indeed, AOP scholars argue that this dynamic approach makes AOP useful for responding to ever-changing social conditions (Baines, 2017; Mullaly & West 2018).

Understanding of Human Problems

AOP situates a social worker's understanding of human problems within the context of social, political, and economic inequalities that are maintained and reinforced by oppressive systems. Indeed, Mullaly and West (2018) noted that:

> Anti-oppressive social workers are well aware that the vast majority of social service users are members of oppressed groups who, not coincidentally, enjoy few privileges and are unable to exercise power to the same extent as those who are not oppressed on the basis of their class, gender, race, ethnicity, religion, age, sexuality, or ability. (p. 362)

Moreover, AOP social workers argue that because oppression permeates so much of our society, we will not adequately address social problems, such as depression, addiction, and suicide, without considering the role played by poverty and experiences with discrimination (e.g., sexism, racism; Baines, 2017; Dominelli, 2002; Hudson et al., 2012; Mullaly & West, 2018).

AOP further challenges the social worker to apply a critical lens to their understanding of person-in-environment transactions, with particular attention given to interactions that may create or reinforce oppression. Taking a person-in-environment approach, scholars have identified three overlapping and reinforcing levels at which oppression occurs (Morgaine & Capous-Desyllas, 2015; Mullaly & West, 2018; Thompson, 2002):

- *Personal/individual level:* Individuals may experience more overt forms of oppression, such as threats of violence, and more subtle forms of oppression, such as stereotypes, negative assumptions, and avoidance, in day-to-day interactions. These interactions can lead to internalization of oppression and isolation.
- *Cultural/social level:* Shared values and norms about appropriate ways to think and act held by the dominant culture may also be a source of oppression. Cultural values and norms are learned through our interactions with others and especially through the news, movies and TV shows, and social media.
- *Institutional/structural level:* Laws, policies, programs, and social processes may structurally sanction oppression for dominant groups. Less privileged groups may be marginalized or excluded from social, economic, and/or political contexts and opportunities.

Broadly speaking, AOP social workers reflect on how oppression informs and influences human behavior. Using this approach, AOP social workers ask questions about the nature of human problems, such as how these problems are defined, who is defining them, and who experiences these problems. This approach also encourages social workers to consider the roles of privilege and oppression in creating and perpetuating human problems.

Social Service Organizations

AOP social workers also recognize that oppressive systems often shape the context in which social workers practice (Baines, 2017; Dominelli, 2002; Langely, 2001; Mattson, 2014; Strier & Binyamin, 2010). Funding or programmatic restrictions often limit the services offered and the scope of practice. This can lead to social work practice wherein the oppressive status quo is maintained, service users are pathologized and blamed for their problems, and interventions are focused on helping individuals to adapt (Dominelli, 2002; Strier & Binyamin, 2010). AOP social workers try to balance this knowledge with a more egalitarian and empowerment approach to practice. They strive to create an open and collaborative relationship with the service user wherein the individual's oppressed identities are validated and their experiences with oppression are explored. AOP social workers critically reflect on how their agencies define service users and whether the agency's guiding values align with an anti-oppressive and social justice approach to practice (Dominelli, 2002; Langley, 2001; Mullaly & West, 2018; Strier & Binyamin, 2010).

Conception of Therapeutic Intervention

As a framework for recognizing and responding to discriminatory and oppressive structures and contexts, AOP can be seen as a lens that can help inform a social worker's practice rather than a set of specific skills or techniques. While AOP originally focused on macro-level changes and does not include specific skills or therapeutic techniques, it does encourage social workers to reflect on and ask critical questions related to their practice and to draw from a variety of therapeutic approaches to build on the strengths of and to best meet the needs of the service user (Baines, 2017; Mullaly & West, 2018). AOP social workers also critically reflect on their own practice and question the assumptions that they are making about a service user, reflect on who is defining the service user's experiences with oppression, and consider why they are making a particular diagnosis and what the short- and long-term consequences of that diagnosis will be for the service user (Larson, 2008; Mullaly & West, 2018).

CENTRAL CONCEPTS OF ANTI-OPPRESSIVE THEORY AND PRACTICE

Drawing on the rich traditions outlined previously, AOP is an integrated framework that seeks to address oppression at the individual, cultural, and structural levels. There are two key themes that underpin AOP: *reject neutrality* and *bridge the micro–macro gap*. In addition, there are five key concepts that have implications for AOP practitioners: *critical self-reflection*, *affirming identities and experiences of oppression*, *participatory approaches*, *explore strengths*, and *promote empowerment*.

Key Themes

At its heart, AOP is an emancipatory approach to social work practice that recognizes that individuals and groups are oppressed by the way in which society is structured and that social workers have a responsibility to address these injustices in our own practice and in the larger society (Baines, 2017; Dominelli, 2002; Mullaly & West, 2018; Sakamoto & Pitner, 2005). An AOP approach encourages social workers to *reject neutrality* or to reject both the idea that the status quo is acceptable and the notion that social work is a politics-free zone (Baines, 2017; Dominelli,

2002). Indeed, Baines (2017) argues that "every action we take is political and ultimately about power, resources, and who has the right and opportunity to feel positive about themselves, their identities, and their future" (p. 7). This is not to say that AOP social workers dismiss the importance of clinical and direct practice and the need to help clients in crisis. Rather, this approach pushes social workers to constantly reflect on the nature of oppression in our society and how it is influencing service users and our own practice. It encourages us to seek out approaches that are participatory and emancipatory and to actively address oppression in our own practice and organizations and in society.

Related to the first theme is the idea that social workers must *bridge the micro–macro* gap, referring to the age-old debate of whether social work should be primarily focused on providing individual treatment and case management or engaged in social reform efforts (Abramovitz, 1993; Baines, 2017; Feit, 2003; Haynes, 1998; McLaughlin, 2002). On the one hand, concerns have been raised that engaging in social reform politicizes social work and is often outside the bounds of social workers who are involved in more clinical settings. On the other hand, AOP social workers and others have raised concerns that social work's emphasis on clinical practice, particularly in today's restrictive welfare climate, leads it to serve as a mechanism of social control and maintenance of the oppressive status quo (Abramovitz, 1993; Baines, 2017; Dominelli, 2002; Haynes, 1998).

However, social work need not be an either/or approach (Abramovitz, 1993; Baines, 2017; Dominelli, 2002; Haynes, 1998), and AOP can be particularly useful for avoiding this dichotomy. Social workers in more clinical practice settings can work to assist individuals to meet their needs but can also engage in more broadly based social reform approaches through critical reflection on how their own practice may be contributing to the oppression or liberation of service users. In this way, they can help service users to identify oppressive contexts within their immediate experiences and to explore how their circumstances are influenced by discrimination and oppression, while at the same time, connecting themselves and service users with groups engaged in social change efforts (Baines, 2017).

Key Concepts

As members of society, social workers are not immune from learning stereotypes or developing preconceived notions about others. Without meaning to, social workers may make negative assumptions about or further contribute to the oppression of service users. The first key concept, *critical self-reflection*, challenges AOP social workers to critically reflect on their practice in two ways. First, social workers examine the values and assumptions that they are making about a client or a situation. This includes reflecting on how we view the service user and their situation, and on how we interpret the information that they provide to us (Fook, 2002; Mattsson, 2014; Sakamoto & Pitner, 2005). It is possible to dismiss someone else's experiences with oppression if we have not experienced it ourselves, and AOP social workers must guard against dismissing the lived experiences of service users (Mullaly & West, 2018).

Second, social workers reflect on their own privilege as a social worker and, based on their own intersecting identities, maintain awareness of unequal power dynamics in the relationship with the service user (Fook, 2007; Sakamoto & Pitner, 2005). Through critical self-reflection, AOP social workers can challenge their own biases, reduce the likelihood that they will force their own values onto service users, and more effectively practice from where the client is at (Fook, 2002; Sakamoto & Pitner, 2005; Mullaly & West, 2018). In addition, critical self-reflection allows the social worker to consider their positionality in relation to the community that they are working with (Baines, 2017; Mullaly & West, 2018; Wehbi, 2017). Indeed, Wehbi (2017) suggests that social workers should ask questions about their relationship to the community, such as whether they are a member of the community and if they have been invited in by the community.

The second concept, *affirming identities and experiences of oppression*, challenges AOP social workers to create safe spaces wherein service users can explore their experiences with oppression (Milner, Myers, & O'Bryan, 2015; Morgaine & Capous-Desyllas, 2015; Mullaly & West, 2018). While it can be uncomfortable, AOP social workers should ask service users about their experiences with oppression and how their different identities (race, sex, disability, sexual orientation, etc.) affect them (Mullaly & West, 2018). Through this dialog, social workers can respectfully create space for individuals to explore how oppression has influenced their lives, their ability to persevere in challenging and oppressive environments, and their perceptions of the strengths or benefits of belonging to particular groups (Milner, Myers, & O'Bryan, 2015; Mullay & West, 2018). This approach is particularly useful for working with members of the LGBTQ+ community and other marginalized populations who often have to hide their identity in different contexts due to fear of harassment and violence (Langley, 2001; Mullaly & West, 2018).

The third concept, *participatory approaches*, challenges AOP social workers to develop collaborative relationships with service users across the levels of practice and in research settings (Danso, 2015; Langley, 2001; Morgaine & Capous-Desyllas, 2015; Mullay & West, 2018; Strier, 2007). AOP social workers recognize that service users are the experts in their own lives and have insights and experiences that they can contribute to the relationship. AOP social workers treat service users as equals and create an open dialog that allows each party to learn from the other. While power differences between the social worker and service user can never be fully addressed, a collaborative approach helps to avoid reproductions of oppressive relationships (Morgaine & Capous-Desyllas, 2015; Mullay & West, 2018). Working from a community organizing approach, AOP scholars also argue that the inclusion of marginalized populations in the research process is essential to developing social work knowledge (Danso, 2015; Langley, 2001; Strier, 2007). Indeed, Strier (2007) argues that AOP researchers should strive to include marginalized populations in the research process and that the overall goal of the research should be the "systemic study of oppression and the development of knowledge that supports people's actions to achieve freedom from oppression" (p. 860).

The fourth concept, *explore strengths*, encourages AOP social workers to avoid pathologizing service users and to look instead at their strengths and abilities (Larson, 2008; Mullaly & West, 2018). Indeed, Larson (2008) suggests that the strengths perspective is a particularly useful approach for working with stigmatized populations, particularly those with whom the medical model is commonly used. This is not to suggest that oppression should be ignored or that the focus should be on helping marginalized individuals and groups to use their strengths to adapt to discrimination and oppressive contexts. Rather, the focus on strengths is included as an approach to help AOP social workers challenge and counter cultural norms that may depict social groups as less capable or inferior (Larson, 2008; Mullaly & West, 2018).

The fifth concept, *promote empowerment*, directs AOP social workers to work with and help marginalized individuals and groups to access the resources and develop the skills that they need to gain greater control over their lives and social environments (Mullaly & West, 2018; Sakamoto & Pitner, 2005). One of the main ways that AOP social workers promote empowerment is through helping marginalized individuals and groups engage in critical consciousness raising (Baines, 2017; Mullaly & West, 2018; Sakamoto & Pitner, 2005). This approach, similar to the feminist idea of "the person is political," focuses on helping individuals and groups understand the different levels of oppression and how structural inequalities affect their lives (Baines, 2017; Freire 2010; Mullaly & West, 2018; Sakamoto & Pitner, 2005). While AOP social workers can work with individuals, Mullaly and West (2018) note that consciousness raising works best when service users are connected with other groups that share similar experiences with oppression. For example, helping a person with a disability connect to a disability advocacy organization can help them to situate their experiences in the larger history of the Disability Rights Movement.

DESCRIPTION OF THE PHASES OF HELPING

While AOP does not include a specific set of skills or therapeutic techniques, it is a useful tool for helping us to practice in a more socially just way. In particular, AOP is a useful lens for

BOX 17.1 Reflective Questions for the Engagement Phase

- What assumptions did I make when the person walked into my office?
- Are my questions based on my own assumptions and/or personal knowledge?
- How does what the person is describing fit or not fit with my own understanding of the world?
- Am I meeting with this person/family to support them? Or am I meeting with them to meet some agency policy regarding the frequency of visits?
- What are the values of my agency and how do they fit (or not with) the person's experiences of oppression?
- Does leadership support shared decision-making processes?

critically reflecting on oppression and privilege within the helping process and how the service user's experiences with discrimination influence them and your work together. Reflective questions are included in this section to help the reader reflect on their own practice and oppression in the larger society.

Engagement

Prior to engaging with and throughout the helping process, AOP social workers reflect on the privilege that their various identities afford them and the assumptions and preconceived notions that they may have about service users (Box 17.1). During this process of reflection, social workers should consider their own values and beliefs and where those values and beliefs came from, as well as how they impact their actions (Fook, 2002; Mattsson, 2014; Mullaly &West, 2018; Sakamoto & Pitner, 2005).

The most important factor in the relationship between the service user and the social worker is the interpersonal relationship. Within the framework of AOP, social workers strive to create a collaborative and safe place environment, within which service users can relate their story in their own words. Drawing on ideas from feminist and empowerment theories, AOP social workers seek to create a more egalitarian and collaborative relationship. AOP social workers seek to demystify the helping process by openly discussing the power dynamics between the social worker and the service user. AOP social workers also recognize the agency of the service user and affirm their experiences. Importantly, in a collaborative approach, the social worker may not have all the answers and must be willing to listen and learn from the service user (Dominelli, 2002; Mullaly & West, 2018).

Creating an open and safe space can be done in many ways, such as having Black Lives Matter signage or signage that confirms that this is an LGBTQ+ safe space and using language that is inclusive (asking a person what pronouns they go by). AOP social workers can also invite service users to share their experiences with oppression. Listening openly to the descriptions of oppression by the service user can result in a better understanding of how these experiences have contributed to the person's current circumstances (Dominelli, 2002; Hines, 2012; Larson, 2008; Mullay & West, 2018).

Assessment

During this phase, the social worker and the service user collaborate to explore the service user's sense of self and to gather information on the person's social experiences. The social worker and the service user also work together to make sense of the information gathered in order to ensure a common understanding of the problems the service user is facing. The goal of the AOP social worker during the assessment phase is not to make judgments about the role of oppression in the service user's life or the desired outcomes from their work together; rather, it is to explore the experiences and needs of the service user and the person's level of awareness of the role of systemic oppression in their life (Dominelli, 2002; Langley, 2001; Morgaine & Capous-Desyllas, 2015; Mullaly & West, 2018).

AOP social workers pay particular attention to both how service users define and discuss their intersecting identities and the role oppression plays in their lives. It is important for the social worker not only to examine whether intersectionality may be complicating the service user's experiences but also to help the service user understand how their own oppression may be influencing their own experiences. This can help the service user begin to develop a critical consciousness about the role of oppression in their lives (Mattsson, 2014; Mullay & West, 2018). For instance, when working with a service user who is Black and uses a wheelchair, the social worker should discuss with the service user how they believe the combination of race and disability may be affecting their experiences of oppression. Additionally, the AOP social worker should discuss with the service user how oppression experienced throughout their entire life may be affecting their perceptions of the role oppression is playing in their current situation. It is possible that, due to being oppressed constantly throughout their lifetime and having lived with being treated differently by the dominant culture, the service user has begun to underestimate the effect oppression has on their life (Dominelli, 2002; Mullaly & West, 2018). See Box 17.2.

Planning and Intervention

During the planning and intervention phase, the social worker and service user collaboratively identify the areas they will focus on, the resources needed to implement the plan of action, and what the individual hopes to get out of their work together (Dominelli, 2002).

Any plan for intervention should recognize that the service user is at the center of the intervention, and the social worker's efforts should involve working *with* that person, not *for* them. The goal of any intervention is to develop new or reconstructed coping strategies. Within the framework of AOP, the aim of these strategies should be determined by the service user and is directed at either reducing oppressive factors affecting the service user's life or increasing coping strategies to manage oppressive systems and mitigate the effects of oppression (Mattson, 2014). A variety of therapeutic approaches are consistent with AOP, such as mindfulness-based therapy, feminist therapy, and music therapy (Baines, 2013; Berila, 2016; Dominelli, 2002).

Depending on the need and readiness of the client, AOP social workers may also work with the service user to increase their critical consciousness. This will likely require both the social worker and the service user to engage in discussions around increasing their knowledge about their own intersecting identities and the traditions and structures that maintain oppression. Helping the service user connect with groups or social movements that share one or more of their social identities may be an important part of the intervention plan (Baines, 2017; Dominelli, 2002; Mattsson, 2014; Mullaly & West, 2018). See Box 17.3.

BOX 17.2 Reflective Questions for the Assessment Phase

- How could my personal values be skewing the information I am gathering?
- Am I helping the person so that they can get a better understanding of their situation? Or am I defining their situation for them because it is easier for me to understand?
- What is the person's understanding of oppression and the role it plays in their life?
- What resources do they believe they need? What resources do they have access to and what additional resources need to be located?
- What strengths does the person possess that they can build on?

BOX 17.3 Reflective Questions for the Planning and Intervention Phase

- Does the person feel as though they were involved in developing the intervention?
- Has the intervention been shown to be effective with marginalized groups?
- Does this intervention help to empower the person?
- What oppressive systems or contexts may make it difficult to carry out the intervention plan?
- Are there groups or social movements that could help to empower the person?

BOX 17.4 Reflective Questions for the Evaluation Phase

- How well did the intervention work for the person?
- Does the intervention perpetuate the inclusion of privileged groups or exclusion of oppressed groups?
- What knowledge and skills did they gain?
- What knowledge and skills did I gain?
- How well did I check my own biases? Where did I struggle?

Evaluation

During this phase, the service user and the social worker should reflect on the work that was accomplished and discuss the effectiveness of the interventions used. From the perspective of AOP, the service user should be invited to discuss how they felt during the process and how effective it was for them. The effectiveness may be judged by the service user's growth, their increased knowledge and awareness of the impact of oppression, a reduction in oppressive systems, or some other criteria the service user has determined to be important (Dominelli, 2002).

This is also a time for the social worker to reflect on their practice (Box 17.4). In line with the AOP framework, the social worker can reflect on and evaluate how well they acknowledged and addressed their own biases (Dominelli, 2002; Mattsson, 2014). In particular, they can reflect on how comfortable they were discussing issues of oppression and how well they engaged in discussions of race, gender, class, ability, or other social constructs. Finally, social workers can reflect on their knowledge about oppression, ways to increase their knowledge, groups and social movements they want to connect with, and opportunities to collaborate with and educate other social workers.

APPLICATION AT THE MESO AND MACRO LEVEL

Using many of the approaches outlined previously, AOP is also a useful framework for practice with families, groups, and communities. While challenging, the use of AOP in meso and macro practice settings can play an important role in helping social workers to recognize and affirm the many social identities of each person and to identify and address the creation or re-creation of oppressive norms at these levels.

Families

While AOP has primarily been applied to groups and communities, it can provide useful insights into family dynamics. In particular, AOP social workers can work with family members individually and as a whole to explore their own social identities. Social workers and families can then collaboratively explore how dominant cultural norms and values in society are being reproduced within the family, based on these identities, and how this may be impacting individual members and the family as a unit (Few-Demo, 2014; Mattsson, 2014). For example, social workers working with LGBTQ+ couples and their children may explore how issues related to heterosexism are affecting one or more family members, such as whether the parents feel included in the community and have social support in the community and whether the children have experienced discrimination or bullying from their peers (Few-Demo et al., 2016).

Groups

An AOP approach can provide social workers with important insights into group dynamics as "The small group is a social microcosm of the wider society in which it is located" (Brown & Mistry, 2006, p. 133). Groups often include a blend of individuals with a variety of identities and life experiences. Members may overtly or subtly reproduce oppressive social and cultural norms within the group. Social workers can draw on AOP to critically reflect on and discuss issues related to privilege and oppression with the group (Brown & Mistry, 2006; Mattsson, 2014). In particular, social workers can work to make sure that the group is a safe space for those with less privilege to share their experiences and ideas.

Organizations and Communities

Focusing on organizations, an AOP approach directs social workers to consider how well the mission, values, and cultural norms of agencies align with social justice approaches to practice. In addition, AOP social workers evaluate service delivery systems in terms of who is allowed to receive services, the guidelines and potential restrictions for providing services, and the regulations and laws that govern the system. Importantly, through their efforts to do their job as trained, social workers could be upholding and reinforcing the social structures of oppression they are striving to fight (Langley, 2001). AOP social workers critically reflect on their own contributions to the paternalism of the organization and consciously choose actions that do not reinforce those oppressive attitudes and practices (Dominelli, 2002; Langley, 2001; Larson, 2008).

Working with communities, AOP social workers recognize that they are often coming in as outsiders and are there to work with and not on behalf of the community. AOP social workers critically reflect on their identity and privilege and how they relate to the individuals that they are working with. This approach also directs social workers to learn more about the community and its history with oppression (Wehbi, 2017). For example, a social worker working with a disability advocacy group could spend time learning about the history of the Disability Rights Movement and laws such as the Americans with Disabilities Act that provide protections for people with disabilities. In addition, AOP social workers recognize the agency of the community and listen openly to the group's discussions of their strengths and their experiences with oppression.

COMPATIBILITY WITH THE GENERALIST-ECLECTIC FRAMEWORK

An AOP approach to social work fits well within a generalist-eclectic framework, as it is a lens that can guide practice and is rooted in a range of other theories. As a framework, AOP is particularly useful for generalist practice, as it helps social workers focus their attention on the role of oppression in influencing human behavior across levels of practice.

Holistic Assessment

AOP was developed in recognition of the need for a social justice–oriented framework that was inclusive of multiple identities (Dominelli, 2002). From the start, AOP has been inclusive of multiple identities and forms of oppression, and in recent years, it has adopted feminist ideas related to intersectionality (Mattsson, 2014; Mullaly & West, 2018). Indeed, Baines (2017) argues that the dynamic and evolving nature of AOP helps to make this framework more responsive to ever-changing social conditions and concerns. The inclusion of intersectionality and a more intentional focus on the influence of oppression on person-in-environment transactions at the personal/individual level, the social/cultural level, and the institution/structural level provide social workers with a more complete way to make sense of and address human problems.

Attention to Diversity and Empowerment

Social justice and emancipatory approaches are at the heart of AOP. Social workers using an AOP approach seek to create inclusive and safe environments in their practice. In addition, this approach calls on social workers to challenge the status quo by supporting and empowering service users to take back control of their lives and make informed decisions regarding their actions for change (Baines, 2017; Dominelli, 2002; Mullaly & West, 2018).

CASE STUDY 17.1

Anthony, a 29-year-old Black man, lived a very active and healthy life. He used to run, go to the gym, worked over 50 hours per week, and still made time to socialize with his friends and family. Last year, he was in a serious car accident and incurred a spinal cord injury (SCI). As a result of the injury, Anthony has full function in his upper body, but has no sensory or motor functioning below the waist and now uses a wheelchair.

After the accident, Anthony was transferred to a rehabilitation center specializing in SCI. His health care insurance covered most of his costs. He worked with an interdisciplinary team to rebuild his existing muscle function, to learn about how to care for himself and prevent complications, and received advice on how to increase his quality of life and independence after he returned home.

While he was given referrals to agencies and programs that support people with disabilities, he has preferred to rely on support from his girlfriend and family. His girlfriend and sister have become worried about him, as he has become increasingly withdrawn and prone to angry outbursts. Although initially reluctant, he agreed to come in for at least one meeting.

He shares with you that it has been very difficult to adjust to his new reality. He has become increasingly frustrated and upset with himself and his current situation. He tells you that he "does not feel like a man anymore" because it has been very difficult to find work and that he has had to rely on his girlfriend to help take care of him. He has avoided going to the gym or out into the community because people stare at him, avoid him, ignore him and talk to whoever he is with, and laugh at him behind his back. He is not sure if it is because he is Black, in a wheelchair, or both. He is not sure how you can help him but figures that anything is better than nothing.

Prior to their first meeting, a social worker using AOP to frame their practice would reflect on their knowledge and comfort level in working with a person with a disability. They would also reflect on what assumptions and biases they might have about people of color and people with disabilities and set these aside so as to be able to take a stance of "not knowing" and to ask clear and unbiased questions (Dominelli, 2010). Finally, the social worker would also work to make the space as physically accessible as possible, such as making sure that there are no chairs or other objects in the lobby, hallways, or office that could impede someone using a wheelchair. It is easy for able-bodied people to overlook seeming small things, such as the placement of chairs or desks, that are easy for them to negotiate but could pose an obstacle for someone using a wheelchair. Without this careful consideration of and removal of potential barriers, the social worker and the agency could unconsciously recreate an environment that is oppressive for people with disabilities.

The social worker would begin work with Anthony by outlining what he can expect from the relationship and the type of work that they could do together. The social worker would inform Anthony that they cannot offer suggestions on what he should do or make a decision for him but can instead be a support and guide for helping him to reflect on his situation. The social worker would invite Anthony to share his experiences and frustrations in order to better understand the context of his story. Recognizing that Anthony has multiple, intersecting identities, they would explore his understanding of his identities. The social worker would ask Anthony about his experiences with racism and discrimination before his accident and after. The social worker would also invite him to talk about his views of people with disability, whether he sees himself as a member of that community, and if he is interested in connecting with any disability groups in the community. As Anthony discussed his feelings about his masculinity, the social worker could also explore the idea of gender norms with him. Together, they could work to unpack his identify and explore how his situation may be unique as a Black man with a disability as compared to a White or Hispanic man with a disability. Throughout this discussion, the social worker would also work with Anthony to draw connections between his experiences and structural cultural oppressive norms in society.

Over the course of their work together, the social worker would help Anthony to recognize his strengths and would encourage him to consider the links between his personal problems to the social/political context. They may also work together to develop an understanding of what Anthony would like his life to look like and the resources that he needs to help him accomplish his goals.

CRITIQUE OF ANTI-OPPRESSIVE PRACTICE

Strengths

As a holistic framework that helps to raise awareness of the impact of structural oppression on the lives of service users, AOP has much to offer social workers. At its heart, AOP is a social justice and emancipatory approach to practice that acknowledges multiple worldviews and embraces service user empowerment and self-determination (Baines, 2017; Dominelli, 1996, 2002; Mullaly & West, 2018). As such, one of its greatest strengths is its congruence with social work values of social justice, recognizing the significance of human relationships, and respecting the dignity and worth of all people (NASW, 2008). Another strength of AOP is its usefulness as a framework for helping social workers to identify and address issues of privilege and oppression within our own practice and across practice settings. Finally, as a framework that draws on multiple theories and perspectives, AOP is a dynamic approach to practice that can be adapted to different and changing social realities.

Limitations

The final strength of AOP is also one of its greatest weaknesses. As a relatively new and broad framework for practice, AOP can be rather unwieldy to use in practice (Sakamoto & Pitner, 2005; Tester, 2003). Indeed, Sakamoto and Pitner (2005) suggest that further work is needed to develop a clearer definition of AOP and to more clearly identify the criteria for what should be included in an AOP approach. In addition, several scholars have noted that it can be challenging for social workers to practice from an AOP approach in many public or government settings as legal, policy, and funding restraints often dictate when and how social workers work with service users (Baines, 2017; McLaughlin, 2005; Rush & Keenan, 2014; Sakamoto & Pitner, 2005). Concerns have also been raised about the lack of inclusion of service users in discussions and development of AOP (Wilson & Beresford, 2000). Despite these critiques, and in light of the recent work being done around the use of AOP as a framework to guide research and increase service user involvement, AOP provides social workers with a useful tool for developing a more socially just and empowering practice.

CONCLUSION

AOP offers a useful framework for helping social workers to practice in a more socially just and emancipatory manner. AOP is grounded in social work values of social justice, importance of human relationships, and respect for the dignity and worth of the person, and directs social workers' attention to identifying and addressing power imbalances and inequalities within our own practice and in society (NASW, 2017; Dominelli, 2002; Mullaly & West, 2018). While broad in scope, AOP provides a dynamic lens for helping social workers address oppression in an ever-changing world.

SUMMARY POINTS

- AOP is a useful framework for helping social workers to identify instances of oppression— even within our own practice—to increase the service user's understanding of oppressive systems, and to empower and work with them to dismantle oppressive structures,
- people have multiple, intersecting identities that may be privileged or oppressed in different contexts,
- critical reflection is a key component of AOP and should be used throughout the helping process,
- social workers can apply the principles of AOP to micro, meso, and macro situations, and
- AOP fits within the generalist framework due to its focus on understanding human problems, empowerment, and person-in-environment interactions.

KEY REFERENCES

Only key references appear in the print edition. The full reference list appears in the digital product found on http://connect.springerpub.com/content/book/978-0-8261-6556-5/part/sec03/part/sec034/chapter/ch17

Baines, S. (2013). Music therapy as an anti-oppressive practice. *The Arts in Psychotherapy*, 40(1), 1–5.
Dominelli, L. (2002). *Anti-oppressive social work theory and practice*. Macmillan.
Hines, J. M. (2012). Using an anti-oppressive framework in social work practice with lesbians. *Journal of Gay & Lesbian Social Services*, 24(1), 23–39.
Larson, G. (2008). Anti-oppressive practice in mental health. *Journal of Progressive Human Services*, 19(1), 39–54.
Mattsson, T. (2014). Intersectionality as a useful tool: Anti-oppressive social work and critical reflection. *Journal of Women and Social Work*, 29(1), 8–17.
Mullaly, B., & West, J. (2018). *Challenging oppression and confronting privilege: A critical approach to anti-oppressive and anti-privilege theory and practice* (3rd ed.). Oxford University Press.
Sakamoto, I., & Pitner, R. O. (2005). Use of critical consciousness in anti-oppressive social work practice: Disentangling power dynamics at personal and structural levels. *British Journal of Social Work*, 35, 435–452.

Narrative Therapy

J. Christopher Hall

LEARNING OBJECTIVES

By the end of this chapter, you should be able to:

- understand the historical development of narrative therapy (NT),
- understand the guiding theory of NT,
- understand the stages of NT,
- understand how NT is used in a case,
- integrate narrative into the generalist-eclectic approach, and
- evaluate the strengths and limitations of NT.

INTRODUCTION

> When people consult therapists they tell stories. People don't come along and say "depression." Rather, they say, "I've been feeling depressed lately and it's something that has been getting worse. If I think back over the last 3 or 4 years I can pinpoint some events which have contributed to this. Let me tell you about them...." People are pretty specific about how these events of their lives are linked to each other in sequence.... Engaging with the narrative metaphor in the development of therapeutic practice invites us to think about how can we encourage people to do what they routinely do—to place the events of their lives into storylines—but in relation to some of the more neglected events of their lives. This opens possibilities for the further development of therapeutic practices that are more de-centring of the therapist and centring of the meaning-making skills of people who consult us. This has been one of the big attractions for me about the narrative metaphor. (White, 2001, p. 11*)

Narrative therapy (NT) was developed by Michael White and David Epston in the mid 1980s as a way to honor the indigenous and innate knowledges of the people with whom they work. White and Epston envisioned a model of practice that did not impose ideas of mental illness or solutions onto people; rather, an approach that was rooted in a practice of cultural ethics in which social power dynamics could be explored to assist people to regain power over their narratives and recapture their preferred ways of being in their worlds (White & Epston, 1990). At its most basic, a narrative is a story that can be defined as a series of events, linked in sequence, through time, according to a specific plot (Bruner, 1991).

---

*Thanks is given to Rudy Buckman and Jonathan Buckman, the authors of the first editions of this chapter.

White and Epston proposed that from a narrative perspective, how we come to understand ourselves is through stories. The past exists as a memory in story form with some events remembered or *privileged,* and some events forgotten or *marginalized.* Identities are built on privileged events in our lives, and these events are put together in sequence to form a plot. This plot is an identity. For example, if a question were asked about how you are as a student or professional, you would think back to past life events that would support your idea and then tell a story of those events around the conclusion that you have drawn about yourself. What can be problematic is when, due to power differentials in culture, family, or social systems of which we are all a part, we are not able to decide which events in our lives are marginalized or privileged, nor the meanings that will be ascribed to these events. In these cases, the result may be the development of a story of self that is *problem saturated.* We may come to see ourselves as problematic, recruited into a problematic narrative in which we may define ourselves as abnormal, failures, or at worst disordered in comparison to an internalized view of a normative self (Hall, 2012).

At its basic, a narrative approach helps to make visible the meanings that have been applied to our clients' lives, explore power dynamics that may have contributed to these meanings, deconstruct power, and create definitional space for clients to restory and redefine who they are. During therapeutic conversations, the problem-saturated story can be challenged and new preferred stories generated and performed by noticing and more fully narrating moments (thickening the story) in which clients have been able to better manage the influence of problematic stories. Clients may also be engaged in externalizing problematic stories, a therapeutic conversation that seeks to separate the person from the problem by objectifying and at times personifying the problem as an external oppressive entity. As clients author stories that support their preferred identities, relationships, and lives, they are invited and encouraged to share their stories with others in their community, which enlists the support of others who may join them in a shared purpose to challenge unfair, harmful, and unjust social discourses (Morgan, 2000). Therefore, "All narrative work is social justice work in that it always has the intent of countering and under-mining the marginalization that can happen in pathology-based approaches to 'mental health'" (Combs & Freedman, 2012, p. 1041).

OVERVIEW OF NARRATIVE THERAPY

The freedom to explore new ideas and practices outside the dominance of established therapy schools led White and Epston (1990) to organize the development of NT on the "text analogy" (p. 9). The text analogy, adopted from social sciences critique of modernism's claim that humans can have objective knowledge of the world, proposes that since stories are always interposed between people and the world "out there," stories select, organize, and construct the meanings of a person's lived experiences. A story is a preexisting interpretive framework or "procrustean bed" formed from the broader sociocultural context into which people are born and live their lives. In Greek mythology, Procrustes, using the size of his iron bed as a "one size fits all" norm, forced people to conform to the size of his iron bed by stretching them if they were too short or chopping off their legs if too tall. Similarly, as stories become reified and harden into preexisting iron-like structures, they also become unquestioned "one-size-fits-all" truths that have the power to constitute or shape people's lives (notice how knowledge and power are inextricably linked in the Procrustes myth and the text analogy). This means that as stories constitute or shape our identities and lives, we actually "become the narratives by which we 'tell about' our lives" (Bruner, 1987, p. 15). However, stories are not individual achievements; they are intertwined with the stories of others and the preexisting narratives of our sociocultural context. Therefore, stories are also a form of social control. This relationship of narratives and social control is further highlighted by White (1987), when he suggests that narratives are a

> particularly effective system of discursive meaning production by which individuals can be taught to live ... an unreal but meaningful relation to the social formations

in which they are indentured to live out their lives and realize their destinies as social subjects. (p. 80)

In constituting or establishing an organized existence, stories are helpful for providing meaning and continuity to life experiences but are unable to completely "encompass the full richness of lived experiences" (White & Epston, 1990, p. 11). These unnoticed and unstoried aspects of lived experiences are obscured and subjugated by the foreground of preexisting dominant stories and relegated to the background of the unstoried and untold, which when awakened by being noticed have the potential to provide "a rich and fertile source for the generation, or re-generation of alternative stories" (White & Epston, 1990, p. 15).

HISTORICAL DEVELOPMENT

Influences on the Ideas and Practices of White and Epston

Before meeting in person at the Second Australian Family Therapy Conference held in Adelaide in 1981 and starting their intellectual partnership, both White and Epston were already utilizing similar ideas and practices in their work. Describing his attendance of Epston's conference workshop in 1981, White stated that he immediately "recognized certain correspondences in our respective ideas and practices" (White & Epston, 1990, p. xv), especially their correspond-ing use of Bateson's "restraint of redundancy" (i.e., a network of beliefs/presuppositions that constitute people's "maps" of the world). White's (1984, 1985, 1986a, 1986b) early work was heavily influenced by Bateson's (1972, 1979) ideas of negative explanation, restraint, and news of difference.

Epston, trained as an anthropologist and social worker and already well known as a creative therapist and writer in New Zealand (Epston, 1983, 1985, 1986, 1989), had also been influenced by Gregory Bateson and Milton Erickson. After meeting at the 1981 conference, White and Epston collaborated extensively and conducted workshops on applying Bateson's ideas to ther-apy (White, 2009). However, during the late 1980s, Epston began to reimagine his work by mov-ing toward a "text/story" metaphor and encouraged White's interest in this metaphor. White (2001) described this transitional time:

> In the later 1980s, I began to relate more significantly to the narrative metaphor. This was partly due to Cheryl White's encouragement of me to privilege this metaphor in my work, which in turn was informed by her engagement with feminist writings. This interest in the narrative metaphor was also something that came out of my col-laboration with David Epston. (p. 134)

White and Epston, influenced by Bateson's interpretive method, which proposed that "all knowing requires an act of interpretation" (White & Epston, 1990, p. 2), and the narrative meta-phor (Geertz, 1983, 1986; Goffman, 1974), concluded that direct knowledge of the world is not possible. In other words, stories or "interpretive frameworks" are always interposed between people and events and determine which events can be selected and what meaning can be made of these events. Therefore, just as the meaning of a "text" emerges as a "reader" interacts with a written "text," the meaning of an event or a person only emerges as a person's story selects, interacts with, and interprets the event or person. By embracing these ideas, along with Foucault's (1979, 1980, 1982; Foucault & Rabinow, 1984) analysis of discourse and power, White and Epston (1990) situated the development of NT among numerous transdisciplinary critiques of modernism that emerged in the mid-20th century (e.g., interpretive anthropology, linguistic philosophy, poststructuralism, postmodernism, literary criticism, and social constructionism). Although originating in different fields of study and differing in important ways, these trans-disciplinary critiques bear a strong family resemblance and are united in challenging the philosophical assumptions and claims of modernism and its kin (structuralism, essentialist self, and correspondence theory of truth). In order to better understand these critiques, especially those associated with poststructuralism, the philosophical assumptions and claims of modernism and its kin will be described and their influence on psychology, social work, and counseling examined.

Philosophical Assumptions and Claims of Modernism

Modernism's philosophical assumptions centered around the claim that "objects" (e.g., reality, nature, universe, and other humans) exist independent of human observation and have an inherent structure composed of specific qualities or properties (structuralism) that are governed by universal laws discoverable through observation, reason, and the scientific method. Separated from nature and community, humans are conceived as discrete beings capable of stepping outside of their sociocultural context and able to analyze "objects" objectively outside the constraints of time and space (Robbins, 2005). Conceived in this way, the human self is constituted as being autonomous, coherent, and universal (i.e., existing independent of historical period, culture, and society) and endowed with reason, consciousness, and the ability to self-reflect. Thus constituted, the essentialist self is equipped to use reason and the positivistic methods of science to objectively arrive at universally true facts about the structure of the universe, nature, people, and society. Once these universal laws governing the structure of the universe, people, and society are discovered, they can be used to unlock nature's secrets and predict/control humans and their social systems, thereby producing human/social progress and possibly even the perfection of humans and their social institutions. The language of the essentialist self is considered to be rational and transparent in that it represents or mirrors reality as it objectively exists (correspondence theory of truth).

The philosophical assumptions and claims of modernism and its kin created a knowledge/power hierarchy that legitimated and privileged objective knowledge and those who possessed it over other types of knowledge (e.g., contextual knowledge, stories based on lived experiences). As those trained in academic disciplines rooted in and founded on modernism's assumptions and claims became enshrined at the apex of the knowledge/power hierarchy, they were anointed as authorities and experts who wielded the power of their objective knowledge over others. Interestingly, this included not only those trained in the natural sciences (e.g., physics, chemistry, biology) but also those trained in the social sciences (e.g., psychology, social work, counseling; Cushman, 1990; Gergen, 1985, 1991, 1992; Hoshmand & Polkinghorne, 1992; Slife, 1993; Toulmin, 1990).

Poststructuralism

Poststructuralism proposes that "objects" (e.g., reality, nature, universe, other humans), rather than having a universal structure existing independent of human observation, exist only to the extent that they are brought forth, interpreted, and storied via pre-existing interpretive frameworks or narratives. In other words, a human observer *cannot* become a disembodied supernatural entity who exists outside time/space and the influences of a sociocultural context, and uses "immaculate perception" to objectively analyze and discover the true essence or structure of "objects." Without a universal inherent structure that can be discovered through observation, reason, and the methods of science, there is no fixed or objective meaning of self, reality, nature, the universe, or even lived experiences. Therefore, meaning is ambiguous as there are only interpretations that arise from the preexisting interpretive frameworks or narratives associated with different sociocultural contexts (Bateson, 1972, 1979; Bruner, 1986, 1991; Foucault, 1979, 1980, 1982; Foucault & Rabinow, 1984; Geertz, 1983). Poststructuralists also propose that since self and the broader sociocultural context are intertwined, a self is culturally and discursively constituted. This means that self is created in symbolic interaction with others within a network of cultural meanings and discursive practices. Since there are multiple contexts and discursive practices available, multiple selves emerge; selves are incomplete and always under construction as they are tailored and performed to fit many different contexts (Gergen, 1985, 1991, 1992). Therefore, poststructuralists

> believe that it is useful to focus on contextualized meaning making, rather than on universal truths or an all-encompassing reality. In this meaning-focused approach, culture, language, and discourse are explored in terms of how they contribute to the experience and identity of people in context. Proponents of poststructuralism seek specific details of particular people's experience. Lives are valued in terms of how they embody exceptions or uniqueness, rather than how they fit general categories. (Combs & Freedman, 2012, p. 1036)

In addition to meaning making, poststructuralists view narratives as "structures of power as well" (Bruner, 1986, p. 144), which means they inherently privilege some views over others (Bruner, 1991) and therefore are never objective. In pursuing this intertwining of narratives and power, White and Epston (1990) drew heavily from Foucault's philosophical/historical approach to power and knowledge. Foucault's (1965, 1973, 1979, 1980, 1982; Foucault & Rabinow, 1984) body of work mainly focuses on how sociocultural "discursive formations" (i.e., a set of fundamental assumptions that are so widely held and embedded in a sociocultural context, they are like water to fish—invisible) form an "epistemological unconscious" or Procrustean bed of "normalizing truths" that operate within specific historical periods or epochs. This means that since sociocultural "discursive formations" constitute "truth" claims about all aspects of life, they have the power to incite people to forge their bodies, identities, and lives to fit the requirements of these mostly unconscious and invisible sociocultural "normalizing truths" (Foucault, 1980; White & Epston, 1990). In describing this discursive process, White and Epston (1990) wrote:

> According to Foucault, a primary effect of this power through "truth" and "truth" through power is the specification of a form of individuality, an individuality that is, in turn, a "vehicle" of power. Rather than proposing that this form of power represses, Foucault argues that it subjugates. It forges persons as "docile bodies" and conscripts them into activities that support the proliferation of "global" and "unitary" knowledges and, as well, the techniques of power. (p. 20)

As Foucault investigated and analyzed the complex relations between power and knowledge, he concluded that power and knowledge are inseparable and illustrated their inseparability by placing the terms together (power/knowledge; Foucault, 1980). In doing so, he drew attention to the power of these "normalizing truths" to not only constitute or shape lives but also conscript persons, as "vehicles" of power, into subjugating and policing themselves. Furthermore, he argues that since persons are born into and participate in historically situated social discourses or webs of invisible/unconscious "normalizing truths," they actively participate in or stand with the power of a "regime of truth" to subjugate and colonize their lives.

Architectural Example of Poststructuralism: Bentham's Panopticon

To illustrate these ideas, White and Epston (1990) used Foucault's (1979) analysis of Jeremy Bentham's Panopticon, an architectural form Bentham created to represent the ideal and most efficient technique for social control. This technique of social control is based on objectifying, isolating, and recruiting persons into measuring and policing themselves against socially constructed and widely held "normalizing truths" that are maintained and advanced by "regimes of truth" (e.g., science, school and political systems, churches, and media). Architecturally simple, the Panopticon is a circular building of several stories with each story subdivided into small rooms that have only a rear window and a large window facing a courtyard that contains a watchtower or "inspection house" at its center. This structure allows the constant observation and scrutiny of persons isolated in each room by a guardian or guardians residing in the watchtower; however, guardians are never visible to persons isolated in each room. Therefore, those isolated have to assume they are constantly observed, scrutinized, and measured against the norms held by the institution as employed and enforced by the "gaze" of its guardians. Assuming they are always subjected to the "gaze" of the guardians, persons inhabiting the rooms would increasingly experience themselves as being subjugated and would become incited to scrutinize, measure, and police themselves against the "normalizing truths" conveyed by the ever present "gaze." Foucault's analysis of the Panopticon led discussions of power away from it being located in and used by specific people, groups, and social structures to coerce others. Instead, power was viewed as being everywhere, meaning it is diffused and embedded in social discourse or stories that have the power of the ever present "gaze" to not only constitute lives but also conscript persons, as "vehicles" of power, into subjugating and policing themselves.

Unwilling to stand with or participate in social discourse or stories claiming universal and objective "normalizing truths" that objectify, isolate, and recruit persons into measuring and policing themselves against socially constructed "normalizing truths," White and Epston (1990) developed many counter ideas and practices, which are presented next.

CENTRAL THEORETICAL CONSTRUCTS AND KEY THERAPEUTIC PRACTICES/CONVERSATIONS

Central Theoretical Constructs

The central component of NT is NT's first and foremost theoretical construct: the narrative metaphor, which proposes that since individual narratives are situated in and intertwined with the preexisting interpretive structures or cultural canonical forms of a broader social context and not constructed from "thin air," they have the power to constitute and control people's lives. Therefore, narratives are a form of social control, in that they provide a preexisting social discourse of culturally and scientifically sanctioned stories that have the power to recruit people into measuring and judging themselves against their normalizing "truths" (e.g., the meaning of lived experiences, what is good/bad, normal/abnormal). However, even in situations where people appear to have become totally dominated by cultural and scientific "truths," narrative therapists assume that there are always lived experiences existing outside of these "truths" that have the potential to provide "a rich and fertile source for the generation, or re-generation of alternative stories" (White & Epston, 1990, p. 15).

Consistent with the narrative metaphor and in contrast to the essentialist self proposed by modernism/structuralism, NT views "identity as relational, distributed, performed, and fluid" (Combs & Freedman, 2012, p. 1042). Identity is relational in that it is brought forth in stories that are performed by persons and intertwined with stories performed by others existing within the sociocultural discourses of "truths" (e.g., family, schools, science, churches). Identity is also fluid, as these stories are in flux. This means that NT, by engaging clients in unmasking and examining the power of stories to constitute and support their problematic identities, relationships, and lives, is "inevitably engaged in a political activity … that challenges the techniques that subjugate persons to a dominant ideology" (White & Epston, 1990, p. 29). Finding many of Foucault's ideas (e.g., power/knowledge, modern power, discursive formations) helpful in unmasking and taking apart (deconstructing) the power of narratives to conscript people into policing themselves against supposedly objective and universal "normalizing truths," White and Epston developed therapeutic practices to destabilize these "taken-for-granted and routinely accepted" social discourses. In doing so, "new avenues of inquiry into the context of many of the problems and predicaments for which people routinely seek therapy" could be rendered "strange and exotic" (White, cited in Combs & Freedman, 2012, pp. 1039–1040).

Key Therapeutic Practices/Conversations

DIFFERENT RELATIONAL STANCES: CLIENTS AND PROBLEMS

In working with clients to develop stories that do not support problems, the preferred relational stance of narrative therapists differs from traditional therapeutic approaches with regard to persons and problems (White, 2007). Narrative therapists prefer a collaborative, respectful, and nonblaming stance that honors clients as the authors of and experts on their own lives (Morgan, 2000). This stance is described by Madsen (2007) as being an "appreciative ally" and by White (2007) as "decentered but influential" (p. 39). The therapist's relational stance is decentered in NT in that clients are the authors of their own lives and it is influential since narrative therapists provide opportunities for clients "to define their own position in relation to their problems and to give voice to what underpins this position" (White, 2007, p. 39). Also in contrast to traditional therapeutic approaches, narrative therapists prefer to objectify, categorize, name, and at times even personify problems as oppressive entities (externalizing the problem; White, 1984; White & Epston, 1990).

NARRATIVE QUESTIONS

Therapeutic inquiries/conversations are developed from a decentered but influential posture of curiosity, in which therapists carefully craft questions that invite and encourage clients to take center stage in using their own language to describe their lived experiences. Since narrative questions are asked to generate experiences and further conversation rather than used merely as a way to gather information (Freedman & Combs, 1996), they are believed to be therapeutic in that they can incite and stimulate clients to deconstruct problematic stories and author alternative stories that support preferred identities, relationships, and lives. The following categories and examples of narrative questions are commonly used in therapeutic inquiries/conversations (Madigan, 2011; Madigan & Goldner, 1998; White, 1988, 2005; White & Epston, 1990).

Mapping the Influences and Effects of the Problem Questions

These questions are designed to help everyone involved in therapy develop a mutual understanding of how the problem-saturated story that brings the client/couple/family to therapy has affected them across several broad domains of life (e.g., home, work, school, view of self/selves, relationships with family/friends/God, dreams, hopes, future possibilities). For example, in mapping the influences and effects of the problem with a couple who is dominated by arguments, the therapist might ask: "What influences in your lives have made it easier for the 'arguments' to get in between the two of you?" and "How have these 'arguments' affected … each of you? …. your relationship with each other? …. your view of yourself and your partner? … your hopes and dreams of a future together?"

Mapping the Tactics and Strategies of the Problem

Questions about the strategies and tactics of the problem invite clients to face and unmask how the problem-saturated story has come to dominate and restrain them from performing stories that would support more preferred ways of being, relating, and living. In facing and unmasking the problem's strategies and tactics, clients are encouraged to explore the "life support" required by problem-saturated stories that allow the problem to continue to dominate their lives. Some strategies and tactics of the problem questions for the couple dominated by arguments might include: "How have the 'arguments' been able to grow and become so destructive to your relationship?" "What keeps the 'arguments' alive and growing more destructive?"

"What thoughts, feelings, and behaviors seem to 'feed' the 'arguments' so that they get stronger and more destructive?" and "What seems to 'feed' the 'arguments' and make them worse?" As clients face and unmask the "life support" required by problem-saturated stories, they gradually become aware of how they and others contribute, many times inadvertently, to the life of the problem. With this awareness, clients may want to change their relationship to the problem by experimenting with ways of reducing or even removing "life support" from problem-saturated stories.

Mapping the Influence and Effects of Clients on the life of the Problem (Unique Accounts and Reauthoring Conversations)

Questions crafted to map the influence of clients on the life of the problem are based on the assumption that the problem-saturated story never totally dominates or speaks the absolute and unquestionable "truth" about the identities, relationships, and lives of clients. Based on this assumption, unique outcome questions are designed to encourage therapists and clients to notice actions and intentions that lead to moments in which clients and/or their relationships are able to influence the problem (Madigan, 2011; Madigan & Goldner, 1998; White & Epston, 1990). Unique account questions "use a grammar of agency and locate any unique outcome in its historical frame … linked in some coherent way to a history of struggle/protest/resistance to oppression by the problem or an altered relationship with the problem" (Madigan, 2011, p. 89). These questions are designed to invite and encourage clients to take unique outcomes or "sparkling moments" that are "out of phase" with their problem-saturated dominant story lines and use them as a "starting point for re-authoring conversations" (White, 2007, p. 61). As reauthoring conversations co-evolve between the client and the therapist, clients are invited "to stretch their minds, to exercise their imagination, and to employ their meaning making resources," which enable them to "develop new initiatives in addressing the problems, predicaments, and dilemmas of their lives" (p. 62).

For the couple dominated by "arguments," the following unique account questions could be asked to invite them to notice and story some of their "sparkling moments" and then use them as a starting point for reauthoring conversations: "Can you describe a time that you were able to reduce the intensity (frequency) of the 'arguments'?" "Can you describe a time that the 'arguments' could have taken over but you refused to go along with it?" "Can you describe a time that you resisted the attempts by the 'arguments' to devalue you (or your relationships)?" "Can you describe a time you were able to talk with your partner in a way that the 'arguments' had a hard time butting in?" and "What does it mean about you and your relationship that you were able to keep the 'arguments' from butting in?"

EXTERNALIZING CONVERSATIONS

White and Epston (1990) originally defined *externalization* as

> an approach that encourages persons to objectify and, at times personify the problem that they experience as oppressive. In this process, the problem becomes a separate entity and thus external to the person or relationship that was ascribed the problem. Those problems that are considered to be inherent, as well as those relatively fixed qualities that are attributed to persons and to relationship, are rendered less fixed and less restricting. (p. 38)

In separating the problem from the person, White and Epston constructed an alternative discursive option; the person or relationship is not the problem, the problem is the problem. This discursive option encourages clients to separate their own identities from the problem (i.e., from being the problem to facing and changing their relationship to the problem). Consequently, as clients face and change their relationship to the problem by performing alternative stories that support their preferred identities, relationships, and lives, they assume and internalize more responsibility for themselves, their relationships, and their lives (Tomm, 1989).

To assist and encourage other therapists engaged in learning how to perform externalizing conversations, White (2007) reviewed and summarized the ideas that informed the development of this practice and proposed a map consisting of four categories of inquiry that describe how to engage and journey with clients in externalizing conversations. To initiate the externalizing journey, White negotiates an "experience near" description of the problem that uses the language of clients (rather than professional language) and is relevant to their sociocultural context of meanings and understandings. Second, he proposes questions to identify and map the influences and effects of the problem across various broad domains of the lives of clients (e.g., home, work, school, and view of self/selves, relationships with family/friends/God, dreams, hopes, and future possibilities). Third, he asks questions, such as "Are these activities okay with you?" "How do you feel about these developments?" and "Where do you stand on these outcomes?" Such questions invite and encourage clients to evaluate the "operations and activities of the problem, as well as its principal effects on their lives" (White, 2007, p. 44). Last, he invites and encourages clients to justify their evaluation of the effects of the problem on their lives by asking questions such as: "How come this is/is not okay for you?" "How come you feel this way about this development?" and "How do you come to take this stand/position on this development?" (adapted from White, 2007, "Why" questions on p. 48).

EXTERNALIZATION AND THE OPPRESSION/LIBERATION METAPHOR

Consistent with Foucault's (1979, 1980) concerns about the power of "normalizing truths" to not only constitute or shape lives but also conscript persons, as "vehicles" of power, into subjugating and policing themselves, early externalizing conversations privileged the oppression/liberation metaphor (Durrant, 1989; White, 1984, 1988; White & Epston, 1990). Typically, this metaphor constructs a discourse in which the problem is personified as an oppressive character who dominates the lives of clients. Therefore, the goal of therapy is for clients to resist being dominated by the problem and to liberate their lives from the problem's oppression. For example, White's (1984) earliest published account of externalizing the problem describes how a child diagnosed with encopresis, and his family named and personified the problem as "Sneaky Poo," a sneaky character who was skilled in dominating the lives of both the child and his family. Eventually, this different way of talking about the problem enabled the child and his family to liberate their lives from the domination of this sneaky, dirty character.

DEFINITIONAL CEREMONIES: DOCUMENTING/CIRCULATING PREFERRED STORIES, OUTSIDER WITNESS GROUPS, AND RE-MEMBERING PRACTICES

White and Epston (1990), drawing on the work of Myerhoff (1982), developed definitional ceremonies in order to counter the power of "expert" professional documents and their associated ceremonies of degradation (Goffman, 1961) that stigmatize and induct people into careers of deviancy and social exclusion. Definitional ceremonies invite and encourage clients to play a central role in developing therapy artifacts and recruiting witnesses as they challenge problem identities by developing preferred stories. By playing a central role in definitional ceremonies, clients have the opportunity to become more aware of how they are able to increase their sense of personal agency by authoring alternative stories that bring forth preferred identities, relationships, and lives. In participating in this process, White and Epston (1990) indicate that definitional ceremonies can "lead to a profound sense of personal responsibility, as well as, a sense of possessing the capacity to intervene in the shaping of one's life and relationships" (p. 191). As NT evolved, artifacts used in definitional ceremonies grew to include certificates, declarations, letters, audio/video recordings, artwork, and/or poetry, and specific types of definitional ceremonies began to emerge, including documenting new stories, outsider witness groups, and re-membering practices.

DOCUMENTING/CIRCULATING PREFERRED STORIES

Documenting and circulating new preferred stories originally included the use of certificates, declarations, and letters (Epston & White, 1992). Certificates and declarations are official documents that proclaim and certify the achievements of clients and may even recognize them as having expertise in coping with specific problems; for example, children certified as fear busters sometimes offered their expertise to other children plagued by fear (White & Epston, 1990). These documents are frequently presented at public gatherings (e.g., parties and ceremonies) in order to spread the news and provide opportunities for clients and participants to "thicken" the development of new preferred stories, abilities, and changes in identities. Letters, typically written and mailed to clients and sometimes others (e.g., parents, family members, friends, and teachers) between sessions, are described by Freeman et al. (1997) as being "Structured to tell the alternative story that is emerging along with the therapy, it documents history, current developments, and future prospects" (p. 112). Of course, different combinations of these therapeutic documents can be used as therapists see fit. For example, Epston (White & Epston, 1990) used letters and a declaration of independence from asthma while working with Daniel, a 14-year-old boy suffering from repeated attacks by life-threatening asthma; his parents; and other medical personnel. These documents played a key role in helping all involved work together toward helping Daniel acquire the knowledge and expertise needed to become an "asthma expert." Using his newly developed expertise, Daniel was able to reduce both the incidence/severity of life-threatening asthma attacks and the frequency of hospital admissions.

OUTSIDER WITNESS GROUPS

Since NT views "identity as relational, distributed, performed, and fluid" (Combs & Freedman, 2012, p. 1042) and considers the development of new and preferred stories to be a "social achievement" (Carey & Russell, 2003, p. 4), the inclusion of others to listen to and acknowledge these developments is an important narrative practice. This practice of inviting others (e.g., friends, family members, community members) to openly and publicly participate as witnesses of therapy conversations arose from Andersen's (1991) challenge to the anonymity of therapists observing clients through a one-way mirror and Myerhoff's (1986) account of how communities and people construct their identities in definitional ceremonies that "provide opportunities for being seen and in one's own terms, garnering witnesses to one's own worth, vitality, and being" (Myerhoff, 1986, p. 267).

RE-MEMBERING PRACTICES

Re-membering, a term coined by anthropologist Barbara Myerhoff (1982) and hyphenated to distinguish it from ordinary recollection, is "the reaggregation of one's members, the figures who properly belong to one's life story" (p. 111). Michael White (1997) used this term to introduce several therapeutic practices into NT based on the "club of life" metaphor, a metaphor situated in the poststructuralist claim that identity is relational and multivoiced, meaning stories constituting self-identity are intertwined with the stories of others who are members in one's club of life. Since certain members are afforded more attention, respect, and higher status than others, those with higher ranks in a club of life are given more credence and, therefore, more influence on how "self" is storied and experienced. The club of life metaphor, by emphasizing membership and rank, allows the reorganization of one's club by upgrading/downgrading the rank of members, which changes their influence on how one stories and experiences "self," or by creating an imagined team of supporters and advisors who offer more supportive stories along life's journey. NT uses these ideas and practices of re-membering to invite and encourage clients to thicken and situate their lives in preferred stories of identity, and create a community or club of life based on choice and not one of simple fortune or life circumstance (Carey & Russell, 2003).

APPLICATION TO FAMILY AND GROUP WORK

NT has successfully been used with individuals, families, groups, and communities. For example, narrative-informed approaches have been developed to address specific populations and/or problems such as eating disorders (Epston et al.,2000; Madigan & Goldner, 1999; Maisel et al., 2004), addiction (Diamond, 2000), children and their families (Buckman, 1997; Buckman & Reese, 1999; Freeman et al., 1997; Smith & Nylund, 1997; White & Morgan, 2006), somatic problems and illness (Griffith & Griffith, 1994; Weingarten, 1997), school problems (Winslade & Monk, 1999), couples (Freedman & Combs, 2002), violent and abusive men (Hall, 2011; Jenkins, 1990), pediatric psychology (Suberri, 2004), and conflict resolution (Winslade & Monk, 2000). Group applications of narrative approaches include the Teaching Empowerment through Active Means program (Redivo & Buckman, 2004), the Anti-Anorexia/Anti-Bulimia League (Madigan & Goldner, 1999), and the use of videos (Wagner, 2004, 2006).

New Developments of the Narrative Approach

It was Michael White's hope that narrative practice not be a static set of ideas and to continue to evolve and expand into other areas and modes of helping (White, 2007). The years since Michael White's untimely death in 2008 have seen this dream come to fruition, as practitioners and scholars have built practices upon narrative ideas across the globe. The epilogue of the book *Narrative Practice: Continuing the Conversations* (White, 2011), published posthumously, offers a range of ways in which NTy has been expanded. These collective narrative practices have been used with people whose communities have experienced natural disasters and/or issues such as violence, abuse, and genocide (Combs & Freedman, 2012; Denborough, 2006, 2008; Denborough et al., 2006; 2008; Mitchell, 2006; Ncube, 2006; Sliep, 2003). One of the most compelling is through the work of David Denborough, Cheryl White, and the team at the Dulwich Center in Adelaide, Australia.

In response to trauma, David and his colleague Necazelo Ncube developed a collective narrative practice called the Tree of Life (Denborough, 2008; Ncube, 2006). This method was originally created to assist vulnerable children in South Africa to meet the needs of children who have been orphaned for various reasons including war and AIDS. A request was made for an approach that would allow the children to be able to discuss trauma without having nightmares, without isolating, and while fostering a sense of community. The Tree of Life has since been used in Canada, Russia, Brazil, Nepal, the Palestinian Territories, and Australia.

The Tree of Life

The Tree lf Life is an approach that has four parts and all parts work together to assist clients to meet their goals of the reduced effects of the problem in their lives. In each part there is a focus on *experience near knowledge* rather than *experience far knowledge* (Denborough, 2008). Experience near knowledge is knowledge that emanates from the client, family, community, and/or culture. Those aspects of life that exist and have originated close to the client such as life skills, ways of understanding and coping. Experience far knowledge is information that is developed away from the client. Examples of this type of knowledge might include research done on White males in the 1950's on how they may process emotions, or data collected on trauma from the experiences of 20 American school children. Experience far knowledge, while of value, is not a focus of teaching skills, or assumed symptomology in narrative practice, rather it is the unique and local knowledge of the clients in their unique contexts that are given focus, and how they have come to place meaning on their own lives.

Part One: Tree of Life

In part one, the client draws a tree and each part of the tree is representative of part of the child's narrative. The roots of the tree are what ground the client. It is a prompt for the children to discuss and draw on their tree where they came from, their history, or village, favorite songs and traditions, and so forth. The roots are a base that holds them tightly in their preferred narratives.

The earth around the roots of the tree are where the children live at present and represent what their daily activities are (what they like to do). These daily activities are essentially their coping skills that are drawn on the tree and discussed without the idea of "coping" being part of the conversation. The notion of coping is an experience far idea while what they naturally enjoy, and those things that help them escape, is an experience near idea.

The trunk of the tree is a space for children to draw and write their skills. Those things they do well. What they are most proud of about themselves and what they feel they can offer their friends and family. During this time, the counselor asks questions about where these skills came from and what it means to have them.

The branches of the tree represent the hopes, dreams, and wishes they have for their lives. Those things to which they want to aspire, become, and achieve. The counselor may also have conversations about how they have been able to hold onto these dreams, and where they originated.

The leaves of the tree represent the people who are important to the child. These can be people currently in their lives or those who are no longer present or are deceased. Questions about what the person was like and the kind of relationship it was can be helpful to provide preferred relational context to the client. Questions can also be asked about what the other person liked about the child.

The fruit of the tree represents what others have given the child. For example, a child may say she is strong and may attribute the gift of strength to her grandmother. Questions can be asked about how these traits were learned or carried on, and what it might be like for her grandmother to know that her grandchild was carrying on this legacy.

Flowers represent those gifts that the child would like to give others. Perhaps, courage is something the child is particularly proud of and would like to teach that quality. Questions about how the child may feel in offering these gifs to others and being of benefit to the family are helpful in creating preferred narratives.

Part Two: The Forest of Life

After each child has drawn and discussed their tree individually, the trees are placed together on a wall. The children are then invited to see all of their trees as a forest and to view themselves not alone in their experiences. Their histories are discussed in common ways, what skills do they have in common? What values do they share? What hopes and dreams are common? Questions are asked about how forests and the other animals in the forest support one another. Discussions are held about what common challenges the forests faces. It faces fires, insects, and storms, among other things.

Part Three: When the Storm Comes

The children are then asked what kinds of challenges children, either here or far away, face and how they overcome these challenges. Animals may run or hide. They may put up spikes or fight. How do children handle the challenges that come to them? In this way, an externalizing conversation is had and children can talk about their experiences either through the animals or by talking about what other children may be experiencing. In talking about other children or animals they are processing what they may have been through or hear others talking and relate to the similar events in their lives. In this way, the children can talk, but they don't feel the pressure to talk about their own experiences. The result of this has been an improvement of traumatic symptoms without nightmares associated with recounting trauma (Denborough, 2008).

Part Four: Certificates and a Song

After the children have talked about common struggles and their ways to handle them, there is a celebration of the forest and life. Those members of the children's' lives who are important, and who were placed on their trees, are invited to come and look at the forest. A gathering of celebration occurs where the children sing a song to celebrate their forest community and their sense of selves. A preferred narrative has been created and is thickened through this definitional ceremony.

COMPATIBILITY WITH THE GENERALIST-ECLECTIC FRAMEWORK

Although there are differences, we believe there is a great deal of compatibility between NT and the generalist-eclectic framework for direct social work practice. The following addresses the compatibility of NT with selected components of the generalist-eclectic framework.

Person-in-Environment Perspective Informed by Ecological Systems Theory

By emphasizing the intertwining and reciprocal influence of an individual's story with the stories of others and the preexisting narratives of their sociocultural context, NT aligns itself with the person-in-environment perspective and ecological systems theory emphasis on the interdependence and reciprocal influence of people and their social environments. Thus, NT emphasizes that "personal is political" and vice versa. Narrative therapists view therapy as a way to promote social justice by challenging, deconstructing, and externalizing the problem-saturated stories of clients, and by joining with clients in shared purposes to challenge unfair and unjust social discourses.

An Emphasis on the Development of a Good Helping Relationship That Fosters Empowerment

From its inception, narrative therapists have developed numerous ideas and practices that promote a good working relationship with and the empowerment of clients. Some of the ideas and practices include: (a) developing NT as a collaborative, respectful, nonpathologizing, and non-blaming approach to counseling and community work that honors people as the authors of and experts on their own lives; (b) viewing problems as separate from people; (c) relating to clients as an "appreciative ally" and listening for and encouraging stories of competence and hope that might bring forth new ways of being and relating that create new and more preferred futures; (d) decentering the knowledge and influence of the therapist so that clients can bring forth their own views and perspectives in regard to problems; (e) engaging clients in deconstructing problematic stories and inviting them to thicken narratives that support their new preferred identities, relationships, and lives; and (f) using definitional ceremonies to develop a community of inclusion that supports preferred stories of clients. Such ideas and practices are consistent with the type of helping relationship promoted by the generalist-eclectic framework.

Focus on Issues of Diversity, Oppression, and Strengths

In terms of focusing on issues of diversity, oppression, and strengths, NT is very much attuned to this aspect of the generalist social work perspective. Narrative therapists are very aware of the power of social discourses to dominate, oppress, silence, isolate, and marginalize people. In fact, narrative therapists, in recognizing how their personal stories are intertwined with stories circulating in the sociocultural context, have developed numerous ideas and practices designed to raise their awareness of their own biases and prejudices and to use this awareness to advocate for social justice. For example, narrative therapists in New Zealand have developed "just therapy" (Waldegrave, 1990; Waldegrave et al., 2003), which uses an "accountability process within their agency in which more powerful and dominant groups are required to be accountable to the less powerful and less dominant groups" (Combs & Freedman, 2012, p. 1054). These ideas and practices promote greater accountability to their clients and colleagues and promote social justice in the sociocultural context.

CRITIQUE OF NARRATIVE THEORY AND PRACTICE

In challenging modernism's hegemony in psychotherapy, NT has had no shortage of critics. Salvador Minuchin (1991) criticizes narrative approaches for emphasizing the social construction of reality. Especially in contexts of poverty and harsh conditions of life, he expressed concern that the focus of narrative therapists on stories would interfere with helping clients cope with the "reality" of social injustices. For example, in describing a woman living in poverty, he made the point that her reality "is not a construct; it is a stubbornly concrete world" (p. 50). He implied that only realists who believe in an objective reality are equipped to help clients cope with "real" problems; however, narrative therapists, well aware of the tendency of narratives to harden into reality, would be just as concerned as Minuchin about helping this woman find and navigate programs that could assist her with food, medical services, housing, and so forth.

Barbara Held (1995) also offered a critique of poststructural/postmodern theory in psychotherapy. While not totally negative about the ascent of poststructural/postmodern therapies, she criticized NT therapists for uncritically accepting poststructuralist/postmodern ideas and practices without evidence of their efficacy. This is a serious critique in the context of widespread efforts to restrict therapy to techniques that have been empirically supported (Norcross, 2001) and manualized to ensure they produce replicable results by other therapists (Bryceland & Stam, 2005). Since poststructural/postmodern therapies do not share the same philosophical assumptions and empirical research methods as modernism, they are in danger of becoming disenfranchised from reimbursement and managed care systems (Busch et al., 2004). Poststructural/postmodern researchers and therapists have countered that the empirically supported treatment movement is too restrictive because it does not allow their preference for methodological pluralism in research, tailoring therapy to the individual rather than diagnostic categories, a focus on contextual factors rather than the individual as site of pathology, and a focus on meanings rather than observable behaviors (Hall, 2017; Wallis et al., 2011; Young & Cooper, 2008; White 2001; Gaddis, 2004; Epston, 2004; Larner, 2004; Smith & Sparkes, 2006).

Additionally, poststructural/postmodern practitioners have been critical of the empirically supported treatment (EST) movement's implication that approaches that are not dominated by modernism and objective/empirical research methods are unethical (Bryceland & Stam, 2005). While practitioners of NT believe a therapist should be knowledgeable of outcome studies and empirical research methods, they are concerned that being an informed, competent, and ethical therapist should not be equated with adherence to a list of empirically supported techniques.

In response to these concerns, narrative therapists have tailored research methods to fit with their philosophical preferences and have conducted research that involves clients as coresearchers and published research studies using both qualitative and quantitative methods. NT, by emphasizing the collaborative nature of therapy and viewing the client as the expert, naturally supports clients' involvement as coresearchers in investigating and documenting how problems dominate their lives, the tactics problems use to recruit them into inadvertently keeping the influence of problems alive, and what types of resistance are effective in supporting them in developing alternative and more preferred stories (Epston, 1999; Epston & White, 1992; Maisel et al., 2004). In addition, an extensive list of published research and current research projects investigating the effectiveness of NT is available online ("Research, evidence, and narrative practice," n.d.). These studies, using a mix of qualitative and quantitative research methods, found NT to be effective with specific problems and demographic groups including schizophrenia (Vaskinn et al.2011), severe mental illness (Yanos et al., 2012), chemical dependency and the elderly (Morgan et al., 2011; Garder & Poole, 2009), depression and the elderly (Poole et al. 2009), developmental disorders such as autism (Johnson, 2012; Cashin et al. 2013) and Asperger's (Cashin, 2008), soldiers and posttraumatic stress disorder (Morie, 2011; Aiello, 2010), gay men and transitional issues (McLean & Marini, 2008), adult anxiety (Gallant, 2013), and childhood sexual abuse (Miller et al., 2007), domestic violence perpetrators (Béres & Nichols, 2010; Hall, 2011), depression (Bello, 2011; Santos et al., 2009; Vromans & Schweitzer, 2011), adjusting to hearing loss (Harvey, 2009), enhancing motivation and resistance to treatment (Gold, 2008), couples therapy (Hibel & Polanco, 2010), child therapy (Butler et al., 2009; Wang & Lin, 2011; Ramey et al. 2009), surgery recovery and hospitalizations (Williams, 2009; Hill, 2011; McCoy et al., 2013), body dysmorphia (Da Costa et al., 2007), adult substance abuse (Bacon, 2007; Chan et al., 2012), learning disabilities (Foster & Banes, 2009; Lambie & Milsom, 2010), trauma and violence survivors (Day, 2009; Witney, 2012), attention deficit hyperactivity disorder (Waters, 2011; Looyeh, et al., 2012), encopresis (White, 1984), family therapy (Lander, 2008), self-cutting (Hannen & Woods, 2012), anorexia, (Robbins & Pehrsson, 2009; Scott, et al., 2013), stuttering (Leahy, et al., 2012), and collaborative evidence and life adjustments (Young & Cooper, 2008).

CASE STUDY 18.1

A case study will now be presented illustrating the components of a narrative approach.

A 67-year-old White female comes to a social worker with complaints of worry and fear. The social worker builds rapport with her as she explains that she has been married for 35 years and was hurt 25 years ago by a chiropractor. She describes experiencing severe back pain during rehab, and since that time, she has gotten better, but in the past four years, she has experienced fears that her back will go out again. The social worker uses narrative to explore these concerns.

Externalizing

First, the social worker seeks to separate the problem from the client. This has the effect of providing space between the client and the problem so that the client can reflect on it as something outside of herself rather than a flaw within herself.

SW: Now that we've gotten to know each other a bit I would like to ask you to play a thought game with me. Is that okay? Just go along with me for a bit. What animal do you dislike the most?

Client: Oh, I despise rats. I hate them so much. I used to live in New York City and I would see them walking down the street at night. They're horrible.

SW: Okay, so if this problem that you have that we are discussing, if this problem were like a rat that comes and visits you what could we call it?

Client: Oh wow, I don't know. I guess maybe worry. It bothers me. I know that isn't that creative a name but the problem is worry. I worry to death.

SW: That is a great name. It is your name to give. So let's call it Worry.

The social worker and client have now externalized the problem and shifted it outside of the client. This allows the client to shift away from seeing herself as flawed and situates her into a reflexive state regarding how she has been affected by the problem.

Personifying and Tracing the Effects

With the problem externalized, the social worker now traces the effects of the problem on the life of the client while also personifying the problem.

SW: Okay, here comes another question that may seem a little strange but I want you to play along with me okay? When this rat named Worry comes around and interrupts your life, how do you feel? What does it do to you?

Client: Well, I am worried, but I think also frustrated. I hate that it bothers me. So it makes me angry. I know it frustrates my husband. He gets upset because I may be in a good mood and we are going to go out and then I get worried and he loses his patience with me.

SW: I want to clarify for a second. Does he lose his patience with you or with the Worry? It seems like both of you have the same reaction to the Worry.

Client: Well, yes, I've never thought of it that way but he gets angry at the Worry. I guess it's not me. It's my reaction to the Worry.

SW: You and your husband sound like you're on the same page, and both of you don't like this rat called Worry. What do you think Worry wants from you? If it was going to ask you to do things what do you think it might be asking. What does Worry want from you?

Client: Well, I am not sure. I know I want to escape it, and what I usually do is not go out, and I will stay in my chair and read or crochet. That really makes my husband mad because he wants me to go out and I wont.

SW: Worry is able to keep you at home when your husband would like you to go out. Does that sound about right?

The social worker has now externalized the problem as Worry and has personified Worry as a rat that bothers both the client and her husband. The client has been given space for her to not see herself as the problem, and additionally, to see her husband as a partner against the problem rather than being upset with an internal flaw in her. The social worker also briefly traced the effects of the problem, and it appears to want her to stay at home rather than go out.

Linking the Problem to a Discourse and Deconstructing

Next, the social worker links the problem to a discourse and deconstructs the problem. This is not always a step in narrative, but in this case, it makes sense to do so because it appears the client may be self-subjugating according to internalized discourses. As a review, a discourse is an idea that the client may have internalized and is now self-subjugating according to those beliefs. The point of deconstructing is to make visible the discourse and break it down to create space for the client to question, and if so chosen, to redefine the idea in a way that is more beneficial.

SW: Thanks for sharing these ideas with me; I appreciate your trust. I would like to explore the motives of Worry just a bit if that's okay? It seems to want you to isolate and stay home. I'm wondering if this is something that you want to do or not? Are there times when you would want to stay home rather than go out?

Client: If I am being honest then yes, there are times when I would rather stay home. I guess in that sense it serves me to worry. Other times I don't want to stay home but it is my favorite place.

SW: Okay, so Worry is not all bad? Sometimes when it wants you to stay home you really want to stay home?

Client: Yes, I think so. I've never really thought of it that way.

SW: So, do you feel like you can stay home when you would like or do you feel pressure to go out when you don't want to go?

Client: Oh my husband really gets upset with me if I sit around the house and do nothing. He has always been a busy person and on his off days he wants me with him.

SW: Are you able to say no to him on those days that you would like to stay home?

Client: I can but he gets upset with me. I will feel guilty about not going with him. But sometimes I do go! Just not always.

SW: I am interested in the idea that you hesitate to say no to your husband about going somewhere when you don't want to go. Where did this idea come from that you are supposed to go with your husband?

The ensuing conversation explores the idea that the client was recruited into about gender and power relations growing up as a girl in the 1950s. The client shared that she was raised with the belief that a good wife "listens to her husband and makes him happy." The benefits of this idea were explored, and the client determined that the idea benefited men but did little to benefit women as they were taught to minimize their own emotional needs. Alternative beliefs were discussed, and ultimately, the client decided that an egalitarian belief benefited both she and her husband and that her needs mattered in the relationship as much as his did. This afforded her the space to consider being able to say no in the relationship without the feeling of guilt and without the help of Worry to support her.

SW: So I am wondering now if Worry has served a purpose in these past four years? You mentioned that Worry came about four years ago.

Client: Yes, that was actually when we retired and moved to Wilmington.

SW: I'm wondering if Worry has served to assist you to say no in the relationship when normally you wouldn't think that you could?

Client: That makes sense.

Reauthoring

Reauthoring is helping the client to revision the past and, in this case, explore times when the client has gone against the belief that her needs come second in the relationship, as well as times that she did not need Worry as a support to assist her in being able to say no to her husband. The social worker uses two types of questioning when reauthoring: *landscape of action* questions, which focus on the details of what and how things happened; and *landscape of meaning* questions, which focus on the feeling and meanings behind the actions.

SW: Have there been times in the past when you were able to say no to going out and you were able to stay home and do what you wanted to do without Worry being involved?

Client: Yes there are times when I have told my husband I'm staying in. Those times are usually on Sundays. I let him know that Sundays I like to relax in my chair and do what I want to do.

SW: During those Sundays what do you say to your husband? How do you explain to him that you're staying home? (*Landscape of action question*)

Client: Well, I am able to say to him that it is Sunday, and Sunday is my day to do the things that I want to do. He will sometimes not like it, but I am able to do it.

SW: What does it mean to you that you are able to claim your time and say this to your husband? How does it feel for you to do this? (*Landscape of meaning question*)

Client: It feels good now that I think about it. I certainly feel like an independent person. I feel a little more powerful.

SW: You mentioned guilt being something that interferes sometimes when you claim your time. How are you able to keep guilt from silencing you in those moments you chose to stand up for your rights? (*Landscape of meaning question*)

Client: I don't know, I don't really think about it. It is like I just know what I want and it's almost like I feel like I deserve it. So when I feel like I deserve it, I don't even think about guilt.

SW: So, a sense of deserving offsets guilt? Okay, I wonder also about times when Worry has been present, when it wants you to stay home but you want to go out. Times when Worry is working against you. Have there been times in the past where you have been able to tell Worry no in the same way that you have said no to your husband?

Client: Wow, let me think about that for a moment. Well, yes, there was a time when I had to travel to help my brother in Kansas because he was dying of cancer. I didn't want to go, I truly hate to fly and to be away that long from the things I like to do, but I went. And I did a good job! I ended up being the executor of his estate when he passed.

SW: How were you able to do that? How were you able to say no to Worry in that situation? *(Landscape of action question)*

Client: Well, I had no other choice. I love my brother.

SW: So love is an enemy of Worry? What does that mean to you that the love you have for your brother is stronger than the Worry? *(Landscape of meaning question)*

The social worker has now assisted the client to recognize exceptions to the problem's influence and to find times when she stood up and asked for what she needed. These events have been marginalized in her life, and through discussion, they are privileged. The next phase is to assist the client to thicken the newly developing story of personal agency. This is done by bringing in the perspectives of others through a form of witnessing.

Thickening the New Story

SW: Who in your life, living or past, would be least surprised to know that you have the power to state your needs in a relationship?

Client: Least surprised? You mean not surprised? Okay, well I think maybe my grandmother Sarah. She always said I was a firecracker and I kind of liked that when I was younger.

SW: You say she called you a firecracker? What did she see in you? What do you think she sees now?

Client: She just knew me as a person who would say things I wanted to say, and no I don't think she would be surprised to know that I stick up for myself now. She would actually be surprised to know I didn't.

SW: Are there others who saw you as a firecracker in your life? Who might agree with your grandmother Sarah?

The social worker and client discuss a range of people in the client's life who see her as a capable person who can stick up for herself. This serves to thicken the new story as the client recognizes others see her in this way and that her story as s strong person is not new at all, it has just existed as a marginalized story in her life.

SW: Now that you more clearly see these things about yourself, and you are no longer caught in an idea that your needs and desires do not matter, how might this affect your future decisions?

Client: I think I won't be as timid, and I think I can stand up to my husband a little more. I also think Worry isn't needed as much. It is interesting that it served a purpose sometimes and also wasn't good for me at other times.

Definitional Ceremony

The last piece of the practice is a ceremony that is of value to the client in defining herself and embracing her preferred story. The client decided to write a short history of how she is a "firecracker" and asked her husband to come to session to listen to her. He attended the session and she explained to him that she had been caught up in a sense of inadequacy and a discourse of gender marginalization. Her husband listened and supported her in her recently discovered historical voice.

CONCLUSION

Although NT challenges many of the philosophical assumptions and practices associated with modernism and its hegemony over the education and training of professionals engaged in human services, we hope your journey through this chapter has enlivened your spirit to continue exploring alternative and possibly more preferred narratives of therapy. NT, pioneered by White and Epston (two social workers), embraces ideas and practices that support working with clients and communities in collaborative, respectful, nonpathologizing, and nonblaming ways, and honoring them as the authors of and experts on their own lives. NT shares many values, perspectives, and practices of the social work profession. Furthermore, NT is compatible with social work's emphasis on: (a) conceptualizing and understanding how clients and their social contexts are intertwined and mutually influence each other; (b) promoting social justice by encouraging therapists to join with clients and other interested parties to challenge unjust social discourse and practices, including those associated with class, race, gender, sexual orientation, and ability; (c) fostering a good client–worker relationship; and (d) developing a collaborative process between clients and workers that empowers clients to recognize, build, and use their strengths to face their problems. Therefore, NT seems well suited for social workers and fits into the finest traditions of the social work profession.

In closing, this chapter is dedicated to Michael White, who died unexpectedly in 2008 doing what he loved, leading a workshop in California; David Epston, who continues to practice, write, lead workshops worldwide, and even found time to encourage and provide guidance to us as we wrote this chapter; and to all of those engaged in narrative approaches to therapy and community work. We feel great respect and gratitude for your contributions, and appreciate your continued commitment to add new pages and even new chapters to the "open book" of NT.

SUMMARY POINTS

This chapter has:

- helped the reader to understand the historical development of NT,
- helped the reader to understand the guiding theory of NT,
- helped the reader to understand the stages of NT,
- helped the reader to understand how NT is used in a case,
- helped the reader to integrate narrative into the generalist-eclectic approach, and
- helped the reader to evaluate the strengths and limitations of narrative therapy.

KEY REFERENCES

Only key references appear in the print edition. The full reference list appears in the digital product found on http://connect.springerpub.com/content/book/978-0-8261-6556-5/part/sec03/part/sec035/chapter/ch18

Epston, D., & White, M. (1992). *Experience, contradiction, narrative & imagination: Selected papers of David Epston & Michael White 1989–1991*. Dulwich Centre Publications.

Foucault, M. (1980). *Power/knowledge: Selected interviews and other writings*. Pantheon Books

Freedman, J., & Combs, G. (1996). *Narrative therapy: The social construction of preferred realities.* W. W. Norton.

Hall, J.C. (2012). Honoring client perspectives through collaborative practice: Shifting from assessment to collaborative exploration. In Witkin, S. (Ed.) *Social constructionist informed practice.* Columbia Press.

Myerhoff, B. (1986). Life not death in Venice: Its second life. In V. Turner & E. Bruner (Eds), *The anthropology of experience* (pp. 261–286). University of Illinois Press.

White, C. (2009). Where did it all begin? Reflecting on the collaborative work of Michael White and David Epston. *Context, 105,* 57–58.

White, M. (1997). *Narratives of therapists' lives.* Dulwich Centre Publications.

White, M. (2007). *Maps of narrative practice.* W. W. Norton.

White, M., & Epston, D. (1990). *Narrative means to therapeutic ends.* W. W. Norton.

Witkin, S. & Hall, J. C. (2020). *Social construction and social work practice.* In S. McNamee, M. Gergen, C. Camargo Borges, & E. Rasera (Eds.), *The Sage handbook of social constructionist practice.* (pp. 89–123). Sage.

19

Collaborative-Dialogic Therapy

Adriana Gil-Wilkerson and Susan B. Levin

LEARNING OBJECTIVES

By the end of this chapter, you should be able to:

- understand the history of collaborative-dialogic therapy,
- understand the central philosophical constructs associated with collaborative-dialogic therapy, and
- understand the application of collaborative-dialogic therapy to families and groups.

INTRODUCTION

The authors of this chapter would like to acknowledge the readers' part in this process, as there are several audiences for this writing: the readers, the editors, and the authors, ourselves. Our objective is to engage the readers with ideas that invite them into dialog and conversation. We hope to create engagement in sense making that births descriptions, stories, and discussions of our work in ways that are meaningful.

We would also like to acknowledge that as we engage in this way of practicing psychotherapy, our practices, ways of speaking, and language evolve. And we would like to focus the reader on the most recent evolution of a way of describing collaborative therapy that Harlene Anderson has introduced: collaborative-dialogic practices, which include collaborative therapy (Anderson, 2007, 2012a, & 2012b). Collaborative-dialogic therapy is a postmodern and philosophical approach to psychotherapy that was developed by Harlene Anderson and her colleagues at the Houston Galveston Institute (HGI). According to Anderson (2012b), the way we work is

> more a philosophy of therapy than a theory (an explanatory map that informs, predicts, and yields standardized procedures, structured steps, categories, etc.). Philosophy seems a better fit because [we] emphasize a *way of being with* versus a system of doing for, to, or about. (Anderson, 2012b, p. 13)

The philosophical underpinnings of collaborative-dialogic therapy include postmodernism, hermeneutics, social constructionism, and poststructuralism. The epistemology of meaning making is at the heart of this way of working and thinking. In this approach, therapists and clients work together as conversational partners engaged to explore new understandings and possibilities that address clients' concerns. Collaboration calls for an attitude of shared inquiry and respect through dialogical and reflective processes. Reflecting teams (Andersen, 1991) are often used to provide the space for clients and therapists to hear multiple perspectives that contribute to the generation of new ideas and possibilities for conversational partners to explore.

HGI is a nonprofit counseling center and training institute that immerses clients and therapists in a community of collaboration. Consultation and research activities are also approached in this way of being with each other and with our clients. Our way of being creates an environment that encourages the successful dissolving of problems, increased competence, and confidence to co-create sustainable outcomes (Anderson, 1997). Designed for use with individuals, families, and mental health systems, this approach has also proven effective with a variety of individuals and groups in various contexts, including daily life, organizations, businesses, higher education, and research (www.harleneanderson.com).

AN OVERVIEW OF COLLABORATIVE THERAPY

Understanding of Human Problems

In daily life, we all accept and name the concrete and the abstract items, concepts, and experiences with which we interact. Language allows us to negotiate the world around us, and using common and consensual language stabilizes our relationships and confirms our identity and existence. When our descriptions and language are out of sync with the reality that others experience, we may become isolated, ostracized, and begin to think we are "crazy." "Craziness" and mental health issues or human problems are therefore socially constructed rather than being a brain-based illness or disease.

Conception of Therapeutic Intervention

The process of therapy is a meaning-making collaborative process that occurs in dialog between client and therapist. It is generative and co-created within the therapeutic relationship and in conversations. We do not refer to the work we do as intervention-based although one could consider the conversation as an intervention that is generated from local knowledge. This kind of conversation creates space for the exploration of many more alternatives and opportunities than are typically made available because of our standard assumptions about "truth" and "fact."

HISTORICAL DEVELOPMENT

Collaborative-dialogic practice has its roots in family therapy and is closely linked to with others, historically, in that field. The founders of HGI were originally in the child psychiatry department at the University of Texas Medical Branch and had been working in teams since they created multiple impact therapy (MIT) in the 1950s (MacGregor et al., 1964). MIT used a team of therapists to work with a family for a period of 1 to 3 days. These families were referred by the juvenile probation system because they were chronic treatment failures, stuck cases, or revolving-door clients. The team approach allowed for much flexibility, with therapists available to meet with family members independently as well as a whole, or in subsystems.

In late 1978, HGI was founded, originally as the Galveston Family Institute (GFI), and Harold Goolishian took on the role as director with Harlene Anderson as the other key leader. Family therapy was beginning to blossom around the country, and GFI became a sought-after training institute by therapists hungry for a new way to understand problems. The family systems approach looked at the problem (or the person who was the identified patient) as a symptom of a problem in the family structure or relationships.

Constructivism

Various schools of family therapy influenced those at GFI, and we tried many of them on for size. Strategic and brief therapies fit fairly well, as did the Milan School (Selvini-Palazzoli et al., 1980).

Hoffman (1985, 1990) became a longtime friend and shared ideas and projects as did Tom Andersen and Anna-Margrete Flam and their colleagues in Norway. After some time of being identified with family therapy, we made a shift. This was quite obvious when we dropped the word "family" from the organization's name. Though having roots in the family therapy field, the definition of a "family institute" doing family therapy became limiting as we worked with individual clients, groups of people who were not "blood" family, and so forth. Our clients defined who should come in to therapy, not us, nor the "model" or therapeutic approach we were using.

The shift was toward constructivism, based on the work of Maturana and Varela (1987). A constructivist views reality as the result of perception, and uses a visual metaphor to talk about how one "sees the world." From this "view," each of us sees the world based on our individual biological and physical attributes, our previous life experiences, and our belief systems.

Social-Constructionism and Problem-Determined Systems

One of the biggest shifts in the way we think happened when we began learning about social constructionism from Gergen (1985, 2009), McNamee and Gergen (1992), and others. Rather than a focus on individuals' perceptions, this theory was about how we use language to socially negotiate our realities. This moved us to think about how we talk about the problem, who we talk with, what stories we tell, and the labels that are used in these descriptions.

This informed our view of systems from being determined by social groupings, such as the family, the couple, and the work group, to systems of people in conversation about a problem (Anderson et al., 1986). For example, if my child, Michael, was failing sixth grade, I may be very involved in talking to his teacher, insisting that there was something wrong in the classroom. At the same time, my husband and his mother might disagree and think that we were not being tough enough on him at home. Additionally, Michael's friends might be comparing notes and telling him that it was no big deal to fail and not to worry about it. These people are participating in languaging the "problem" that we are living. If we were in therapy, each of their ideas, their viewpoints, and their suggestions would be considered and invited. To resolve a problem situation, all members of the problem-determined system must be involved and satisfied with the plan and/or outcome. If, for example, the therapist agreed with my husband and his mother about having more consequences at home and nothing changed at school, I would not feel good about the process; thus, if only part of the system is satisfied with a change in the situation and others are not, the situation would not end.

Language Systems Theory

Closely following the shift to using the label "problem-determined systems" to describe our work, we recognized that term *problem* was limiting. We may have been influenced by our colleagues and "cousins" from the solution-focused approach; however, we also did not want to have our focus limited to the "solution" either. We value and honor the language and way that *the client(s)* talks about what brings them to therapy.

This brought us to use the term *language systems therapy*. This term emphasized that everything we do and feel is only known to us in language. This is a radical notion that many critique. Ironically, one could not critique this idea if there were no language of critique. The ways we talk and think about our "problems" or "issues" are language based, and thus, if one could talk and think differently, the problem situation may no longer exist.

Here we can note that the vehicle for change in therapy evolved to being conversational (language based), dialogic, and collaborative.

Collaborative Therapy/Collaborative Dialogic Practices

In the late 1980s and early 1990s, the word "collaborative" was introduced and became useful to describe the therapeutic relationship that was becoming the focus of our work. Instead of defining the locus of change in a structure, such as the family, individual, or even "problem system," the client(s) and therapist(s) *together* decided who should come in for therapy. The membership of therapy changed and shifted during the process, as different issues, needs, and interests changed. This is the current phase of HGI's therapeutic work and will be described in more detail in the following.

Past and Current Connections to Social Work

The Clinical Social Work Association *Code of Ethics* says its

> core values include a commitment to the dignity, well-being, and self-determination of the individual, a commitment to professional practice characterized by competence and integrity, and a commitment to a society which offers opportunities to all its members in a just and non-discriminatory manner. (www.clinicalsocialworkassociation.org/CSWA-Ethics)

These values align with collaborative-dialogic therapy, as our commitment to the therapeutic relationship is one that is based on respecting the client as competent and worthy and in honoring the client as the expert in their life (Anderson & Goolishian, 1992). Our intentional accessibility demonstrates our interest in reaching all people in need and reducing barriers to service.

One of our most important practices is "meeting clients where they are." This can be interpreted as a physical meeting place (e.g., going to their home or another convenient location) or as a metaphorical place (e.g., respecting their views and belief system). We often work with clients who have different religious, cultural, socioeconomic, and educational backgrounds from us. We find that learning their "local" languages and meanings will support a strong therapeutic relationship.

CENTRAL PHILOSOPHICAL CONSTRUCTS

Social Constructionism

Meaning is created and co-created within the context of relating to others and their ideas. In therapy, the client and therapist engage in conversation together, and from there, each participant makes sense of what happened or makes meaning of the interaction, reflection, and conversation. Gergen (1999) defined social constructionism as a way to situate, in relationships, our sense of what might be true. He also indicated that this definition limits the potential for evolution of the stories that emerge due to the ever-changing meanings and questionings each member of a relationship or community brings with them. As each person developed their own understanding, sometimes the story changed or made sense in a different way.

Collaborative-Dialogic Practices

In collaborative-dialogic therapy, therapists are unique individuals with experiences and values of their own. Therapists have their own stories and ways of looking at the world. The values that most collaborative-dialogic therapists share are that they trust their clients to have resilience and the desire to have good interactions and relationships in their lives (Anderson, 2012b). The approach we use is founded in philosophy and does not rely on a set of interventions or suggestions. What we carry forward from our philosophy is that prescriptive and diagnostic language can be damaging and is based on assumptions rather than the client's life story. We endeavor to provide conversations that help create shifts and possibilities in the participants: a client, therapist, or reflecting team member. Each of the voices included in the therapeutic process has the potential to contribute many possibilities, and we strive to provide an environment where this may happen. In order to co-create this scenario, we rely on our ways of being and the systems that inform us to engage clients in the kinds of conversations we call "generative," where the participants are speaking about and exploring curiosities and questions that the therapist has raised in the moment. Our experiences and values are challenged in each unique conversation (Levin et al., 2018).

Not Knowing and Curiosity

Not knowing and curiosity are hallmarks of collaborative-dialogic therapy. Therapists enter the conversation with the intention of being curious, to learn about the client, their life, the circumstances, and information related to what the client wants to share. Then, without deciding what the problem is or what treatment approach to take, the therapist engages the client in a conversation to explore the topics and themes that they have raised.

As Harlene Anderson (personal communication, December 16, 2014) has said:

> The therapist's questions are informed by the client's story: the desire to learn more about it. This is in contrast to asking questions to steer a client's story in a direction that the therapist has considered best. In sum, the therapist relies upon the client's expertise on his or her life and their defined needs and desired futures.

On an existential level, we can agree that we do not know anything, but we coordinate our lives based on past experience and a co-constructed, shared reality. Order is developed and maintained through social constructs such as laws and rules that set out ways of living together. For example, we assume that if we drive through an intersection on a green light, we will not get hit by another car. In general, we can predict that following driving rules will keep us safe, but we *cannot know* with certainty that someone will not go through a red light and hit us.

We never know if our intentions, helpful ideas, and conversations will work for a particular client. Even though they may have helped our last five clients, the next client may not benefit at all. Therefore, when sharing ideas, thoughts, and suggestions, the collaborative-dialogic therapist uses a tentative tone of voice and frames the suggestion with a comment, such as "I am not sure this will be helpful for you, but I will share it if you like." Some may recognize this way of presenting a suggestion as paradoxical, or strategic, *a la* brief therapy (Fisch, 1994; Watzlawick et al., 1974). The collaborative-dialogic therapist, however, intends to convey uncertainty about the suggestion and to respectfully ask the person if they would even be open to hearing the thought in that moment.

The Client Is the Expert

The client becomes positioned as the "expert" in collaborative-dialogic therapy (Anderson, 2007; Anderson & Goolishian, 1992). The client is the one who "knows" the experience of the problem or problematic situation, and the client can give a narrative of how the problem developed, what has or has not worked thus far, and what outcome is preferred. The client–therapist relationship is different than in most therapeutic approaches. They become a team, working together to find new possibilities and options that change the nature of the problematic situation.

The client is also the expert on the direction and goal of therapy each step of the way. Though the therapist may prioritize problems differently than the client, the client is the decision maker. One way we have begun to reinforce this is the use of the Partner for Change Outcome Management System (PCOMS; Duncan, 2012), which includes two simple but reliable feedback tools measuring client wellness (the Outcome Rating Scale) and the therapeutic alliance (the Session Rating Scale [SRS]). The SRS provides a frequent check-in with clients regarding the degree to which they feel "heard," understood, respected, and are getting to talk about what they want to talk about. PCOMS is listed in the Substance Abuse and Mental Health Services Administration's (SAMHSA) National Registry of Evidence-Based Practices and Programs.

A therapist is only involved in the client's story from what a client is willing to share with them and remains interested in what the client is sharing by asking questions that are framed in curiosity as opposed to trying to confirm a hypothesis (Anderson, 1997). The client brings forth their knowledge and shares theirr experiences in conversation and in responses to questions, adding to what has already been shared. The therapist's role in this process is to listen with the intention of learning more and to be responsible for maintaining a respectful and tentative approach to the conversation. Each therapist's approach will look slightly different because it is a process that occurs naturally, depending on conversational style and the level of comfort the client and therapist have with each other, in the moment. Sometimes, as a therapist, one is in a listening position while a client might share stories that are uncomfortable to listen to or of an unethical nature. Even during these kinds of stories, the therapist maintains an attitude of curiosity with the intention of creating an environment that is safe for the client to share more of their story.

The therapist's role in collaborative-dialogic therapy is very different than in modernist approaches where the therapist is the expert on what is normal and abnormal, and uses this knowledge to assess the client's problem and prescribe a treatment that will rid them of symptoms and abnormalities. Without a belief system that pigeonholes behaviors and personalities into a psychological schema such as the *Diagnostic and Statistical Manual of Mental Disorders, Fifth Edition* (American Psychiatric Association, 2013), collaborative therapists work within clients' expertise on their life—understandings, descriptions, and beliefs—to jointly create clients' desired future. The client and therapist, together, create language that describes the situation that is the focus of therapy. The therapist is no longer the expert on diagnosis and prescription but rather in creating a generative, meaning-making dialog. Practicing from a not-knowing stance emphasizes the tentativeness with which any "information" is shared with the client, including information about protocols and standard practices in our field.

The therapist is an expert in how to share these kinds of ideas, especially during times when we have to make public our professional or personal responsibilities.

The Reflecting Process

The search for new possibilities is enhanced with the addition of reflecting teams to the therapeutic process (Andersen, 1991). Reflecting teams, first developed by Andersen and his colleagues in northern Norway, involve having several people observe the session. Usually these people are therapists; however, we have also had family members and friends of the client join the reflecting team. Teams are used only with the client's permission, and many people are surprised at how many of our clients agree to this process and come to depend on it. Partway through the session, the reflecting team members are invited to become the active participants while the therapist and client listen to their conversation. The reflecting team members engage in conversation with each other about what they have heard, the ideas and questions that were sparked, and any thoughts or comments they want to share with the client or the therapist. The clients and therapist are encouraged to take or leave the reflections offered by the team, and they often will discuss this following the reflecting time.

The original practice of reflecting has evolved and is now used very flexibly by practitioners of collaborative-dialogic therapy. For example, our teams at HGI operate in the same room as the therapist and clients, not behind a one-way mirror. Our intention for having the team together with the client is to expand the therapeutic relationship to include others, and to break down hierarchies and separations that are not necessary.

Intentional Accessibility

Access to mental health services has been limited in many ways, including cost of services, location of services, hours of services, and languages offered. Stigma also limits access, as people are often intimidated and ashamed to ask for help. Once someone decides to go to counseling, they often encounter waiting lists, screenings to determine "eligibility," and other obstacles. Those who need a "sliding scale" may be required to bring proof of their income (a practice that has the underlying message that clients will lie about their financial situation). Therapists, and the organizations they work for, determine the location of services and the hours they are available, putting the therapists in charge of access.

A good example of an unintentional accessibility problem occurred after Hurricane Katrina displaced more than 200,000 people to Houston. Many benevolent therapists offered free services to help those who were suffering. Very quickly, it became clear that despite this generous offer, most of those in need did not have a car or had never driven across such a big city with so much traffic. The bus system in Houston is not the best, and traveling across the city would require much time and effort. Even with transportation, going to therapy was a foreign concept to many who were survivors of Katrina as they could see no use for "mental health services." Also, creating a trusting relationship with people who had just had their government fail them miserably was not easy. Having an office and a website to offer therapy is not all that it takes to be accessible. HGI's therapists were able, and honored, to offer counseling services after Katrina, and did so with the support of Americares and other funders. With backing from these funders, HGI was able to buy a modified, 34-foot recreational vehicle that we could drive to apartment complexes on the outskirts of town and see clients on a walk-in basis or by appointment. We also participated in several community meetings and planning sessions to support relocated families with efforts they made to improve their communities. This Rolling Conversations Project operated for 4 years after Katrina and was one way to go "outside the box" to make therapy and community service accessible. We presented the community of those displaced with an opportunity to have conversations, many of which were meaningful and helpful in creating significant changes in the lives of those involved.

There are many ways to increase accessibility. We do so by offering a sliding scale, Internet and tele-therapy, walk-in counseling, evening and weekend hours, and community and home-based services. Clients of collaborative-dialogic therapists are also offered access to our inner thoughts. Our thoughts are able to be "public" as they are usually tentative (we do not "know" but we may "think") and are rarely about pathology or blame. Collaborative-dialogic therapists are trained to think that clients are doing the best they can, given the circumstances that we are learning about (Anderson, 2012b). We believe it is important to offer to share our ideas so that the client is not left wondering what the therapist is thinking. Clients may be intimidated to ask the therapist to unveil their thoughts, so the therapist initiates this, especially at times when the therapist is aware of thoughts about which the client may be concerned.

PHASES OF HELPING

In our approach, we do not adhere to a linear modality of treatment. As we describe our practice, we hope to convey what the process *might* look like; however, there is no one way that we do things. Rather, it is the uniqueness of each client and each situation that determines how we move through the therapeutic process. Another important note about "phases of helping" is that we embrace the possibility of single-session and very brief therapy.

DISCUSSION ABOUT THE SINGLE-SESSION MINDSET

A number of centers around the world are using single-session therapy (Bobele & Slive, 2011). This approach holds to an idea that there is much opportunity to resolve problems in a single session, a series of single sessions, or occasional single sessions. For some, this is a good fit, while others prefer a longer relationship. When clients do not return after the first session, we usually do not know why. In some cases, it is likely that they have obtained what they needed.

This awareness, that clients may only need one session, leads us to spend each session focusing on what the clients wants to talk about and what they want to achieve in our time together. The first time we meet with a client, they may tell us that they want to spend the session giving us background, getting to know each other, and so forth, and indicate that they will be coming back. Others are ready to begin working on a problem immediately. The therapist may be the one who believes it necessary to get background or sees the presenting problem as a symptom of other underlying issues. Often, it is the therapist's model that drives the length and process of therapy. With clients as the expert on their own needs and choices, the client decides how to use the session and when therapy is over. Phases of helping, in a single session, happen during the session—we find out what brought the client in, together we create a plan of how we can try to help and/or resolve the presenting problem, and we then wrap-up the session.

The language we use to end all sessions is tentative and respectful. We ask clients how they want to handle things going forward; sometimes clients indicate that they would like to come back, and we schedule an appointment at their convenience. Sometimes clients indicate that they think they may be in a good place to go forward without scheduling additional appointments, and we welcome them to contact us in the near or distant future to revisit their work or bring new challenges. Some clients indicate that they would like to be in therapy on a weekly basis, every other week, or to have the option to call on an "as needed" basis. We allow the space for the client to make those choices, and we remain supportive of the decisions the client is making. If we do not agree, or have another opinion, or sense that there could be more sessions, we may contribute that to the conversation. Acknowledging that the therapist and client may have a difference of opinion, or opposing thoughts on the topic at hand, we ask the client if they would like to hear our thoughts or not.

Though we also have clients who come for sustained amounts of therapy, some for a year or more, we try to think of each session with them as a new session. This keeps the therapist "fresh" and attentive to new possibilities as they emerge. The therapist does not assume that the clients will return for another session nor that the issues present for the clients in the previous session are continuing and need to be discussed in future sessions. Clients often adjust their focus from one issue to another, and the therapist travels with them, the clients in the lead. In longer term therapy, we use similar conversational shifts to help clients make decisions about their treatment and whether they need it to continue.

Along with our single-session mindset, HGI also offers walk-in services, meaning a client can come for a session without an appointment. This helps fill the gap for people who want to start therapy but cannot get an appointment without a long waiting list. People who are in crisis can come to see a therapist at our office instead of going to an emergency department, the typical option for communities that do not have walk-in programs. Walk-in clients may decide to use this approach as a way to begin a longer therapeutic relationship with an ongoing therapist, and/or they are welcome to come back to walk-in as often as they like.

Engaging Clients

We believe that the earliest contacts with clients, from their first phone call, set the stage for therapy. This means that our office staff are *only* involved with clients to get basic information so that the assigned therapist can call and talk about who they think should come to the session, when and where the session might occur, what is the initial reason for therapy, who is most concerned about the "problem," and the fee. We consider all of these arrangements to be more than "business" and that the first phone call is our opportunity to begin to position ourselves as therapeutic partners rather than experts on how therapy should and will be conducted. Asking the caller to help us understand their ideas about these questions gives us a general understanding of the client's story and minimizes the need for the client to repeat it multiple times. Clients have told us that they had to meet or talk to an intake person who then refers them to another therapist. By the time they begin therapy, if they decide to stick with it, they have talked to several people.

In addition to the initial engagement process, the dialogical nature of our approach promotes engagement throughout therapy. Dialog is generated through the use of open-ended questions based on curiosity—which are much more engaging than asking yes or no and other closed-ended questions.

Data Collection: Using Feedback (Partner for Change Outcome Management System) to Have a Therapeutic Conversation

In line with making therapy more accessible, HGI has always tried to minimize the amount of paperwork that clients fill out when they start therapy. Despite our intentions, we do ask for some demographic information to use for reporting purposes (age, race, ethnicity, gender) and for information on who lives in the family "home." In response to funders who ask for measures of success, HGI adopted PCOMS in 2014, a feedback "tool" to systematize discussions about clients' progress and the therapeutic alliance. Though HGI already had a "culture of feedback" (Duncan, 2012), we decided that it was important to have records of the feedback we get from clients for our own growth, to share our learning, as well as to provide to our stakeholders, including funders. We were already aware of the PCOMS through our shared practicums with Our Lady of the Lake University (OLLU) in Houston. OLLU has been using PCOMS for many years and began training practicum instructors to use the system, as well.

The system is made up of two feedback forms that are given to clients each session. The Outcome Response Scale (ORS) is given at the beginning of each session and has four areas of client well-being, which they are asked to indicate on a 10-cm line. The four areas are individual, interpersonal, social, and general. Each line is measured with a 10-cm ruler, and the scores are totaled (scores range from 0 to 40). This process takes no more than 3 to 5 minutes. The feedback gives the therapist an idea, which is checked with the client, of where to focus the session. The score is compared to that of the previous session(s), and this provides another topic of conversation—Is the client seeing improvement or not, and what could be changed to see greater effects?

The second form is the SRS, and it measures the therapist–client alliance by asking for feedback about the session. Again, there are four 10-cm lines for the client to mark indicating feeling understood and heard by the therapist, talking about what they wanted to talk about, feeling respected, and general satisfaction. Though this is given at the end of the session, time is left to measure and total the scores, using the ruler, and to discuss any scores that are low.

This system has been studied for many years and used by many providers. They have over 200,000 implementations to base some analytics on (Duncan, 2014). These benchmarks for the ORS and SRS are also used for discussion purposes. A very extensive resource for those who are interested in PCOMS can be found online (www.heartandsoulofchange.com), and many books and articles are listed there.

The Timing of Therapy: Planning and Termination

When the client experiences the feeling of being valued as the expert, many things shift because they participate in decisions about the who, what, when, and duration of therapy. The client decides when to go to therapy, how often, who should participate, when they participate, and the duration of the therapy relationship. As mentioned earlier, we embrace the possibility of any session being a single session instead of longer therapy, which promotes the possibility that many clients can get what they want out of one session. We do not use the concept of termination in our work, as we think in more of a wellness metaphor; we have clients who check in with us from time to time when issues arise.

APPLICATION TO FAMILY AND GROUP WORK

Collaborative-dialogic therapy is a practice that grew out of the family therapy field. Additionally, since the collaborative therapy philosophy and practices are based on social constructionist ideas, there is an assumption that each person co-creates their reality in and through relationships. The therapist offers possibilities in the initial phone conversation and asks about whom the client would like to invite to the therapy process. Collaborative-dialogic therapists are attuned to hearing about significant others in the client's life and may bring them into the session metaphorically, if unable to bring them in "in vivo." Family is broadly defined to take all significant people into account, and sessions may include one-time participants and/or people who are part of therapy from start to finish. The constellations of therapy will change if the focus of therapy changes. It is possible that a client may begin therapy as an individual and then bring in other family members as their focus of therapy evolves.

With conversation and dialog, the process of family and group work may take on the same form. Whether in couple, family, group, or individual work, the therapist engages the participants from a place of curiosity to explore possibilities and the "not known." In most cases, this exploratory stance becomes "contagious" and people begin to question each other to learn more and to understand more, leading to new outcomes. When running groups on particular topics, such as "grief" or "self-esteem," collaborative therapists will likely ask the group to inform the process from the first session. One of the ways we do this is to be prepared with topics the group may be interested in, but also ask the group members to name their expectations of this group and what they hope to gain from it. This approach works well with groups of people of all ages. When we have a list, we compare with the materials we have prepared and then offer additional options to the group, customizing along the way.

COMPATIBILITY WITH THE GENERALIST-ECLECTIC FRAMEWORK

There are a number of similarities between collaborative therapy and the generalist-eclectic framework that make them compatible. One of them is attention to the clients' environment or context. Collaborative therapy embraces the generalist perspective's recognition of "an interrelatedness of human problems, life situations, and social conditions" (Schatz et al., 1990, p. 223). Similar to the generalist perspective, collaborative therapy believes that it is important to see the big picture in terms of the reciprocal influence of people and the various systems (e.g., family, work, community) with which they interact.

The importance of the therapeutic, or helping, relationship is another point of compatibility between collaborative therapy and the generalist-eclectic framework. Both approaches stress the importance of a collaborative, warm, and empathic relationship. Similarly, both approaches stress identifying and building upon clients' strengths.

One point of departure from the generalist-eclectic framework is that collaborative therapy is situated in one theory and philosophy. In addition, despite the similarities to the process of therapy, Anderson et al. (1986) stated that they had tended to steer away from the eclectic framework as they had noticed that in the eclectic model, the work seemed a bit muddled and not always focused. On the other hand, the therapist (depending on their style and way of being) may draw from various techniques and theories when needed to match clients' expectations of the therapeutic process.

CASE STUDY 19.1

INVITING A CLIENT TO WRITE ABOUT THE EXPERIENCE

To offer an example of collaborative-dialogic practices, we would like to share the work we have done with a man named Jeremy, a 41-year-old male (his identity has been changed to anonymize his story and protect his confidentiality). Before writing this case example, we have worked together with Jeremy to make sure that only parts that he would be comfortable sharing are included. We invited Jeremy into conversation about how we were approaching this part of our writing and to have space for him to inform the process. Jeremy came to HGI to seek help after having been released from an inpatient treatment center. The providers at the treatment center recommended he seek help at HGI, so he came to our walk-in counseling program (Levin et al., 2018). He was originally seen by a therapist who was a master's level intern at the time. This therapist agreed to continue seeing Jeremy on an ongoing basis as he reported he was going to need additional support. After attending two more sessions, Jeremy told his therapist that a case manager had told him to seek help from a more experienced therapist because the case manager was concerned that Jeremy's problems were "more serious" and possibly beyond the expertise of an intern. The therapist considered Jeremy's request and invited a more experienced therapist to join her. I, Sue, joined as co-therapist and began seeing Jeremy with her.

Jeremy looked and acted younger than his years when I first met him. He appeared shy and uncomfortable, telling his story in halting sentences. He looked up to smile and make eye contact occasionally, and wanted and asked for confirmation that we were listening and approving of his story. Jeremy told me (as he had told the intern-therapist) about his recent hospitalization but said he did not feel comfortable sharing a lot of details. He said he had psychosis and was doing much better after being in the hospital.

As we continued to work together, I learned more of his story: Jeremy had received approximately 6 years of intensive treatment and had been in residential care, in group homes and halfway houses, as a person with chronic mental illness. Jeremy spoke about how he left that lifestyle after feeling as though he was being taken advantage of in several ways. He told us of some experiences he had with drugs (including meth) and about how he had almost been abducted and barely escaped a potentially exploitative situation. Jeremy told us that at a group home where he was staying a few years ago, he was engaging in an inappropriate relationship with another resident of the house whom he really didn't like. He said he didn't know why he was doing it. This is the way he would talk initially, with confusion and doubt about his behaviors and decisions. At that point, Jeremy's parents were "done" with him and not willing to help him. They reportedly viewed his behavior as manipulative, "crazy," and so forth, and had been guided to disconnect from him during these times when he was in crisis.

Some may wonder how all of this started, since Jeremy was from a stable family with resources and had no obvious trauma in his background. Jeremy wonders about this a lot himself. At the time he came to HGI, he was living independently in an apartment, working a part-time job in a health food store, and living on disability. He explained, somewhat sheepishly, that he has the qualifications to get a more professional job, and hoped that he could do so at some point in the future.

Therapy with Jeremy has continued with some variations. The master's level intern-therapist graduated, and Adriana joined me as a co-therapist. Occasionally, we have included reflecting teams. During this time, Jeremy became more comfortable discussing his experiences, though usually in bits and pieces that are not always told in a linear manner. We began making sense of his hospitalizations as they related to the exploitation, suffered in care homes. We offered Jeremy tentative descriptions (possible understandings) of his response to these events such as anger and aggression when people did not listen to him, escalating to him running out of these situations and ultimately ending up in a hospital under sedation. Jeremy described that his responses also included self-destructive behaviors such ase cutting and overdosing.

Instead of seeing Jeremy as "crazy," we saw him as attempting to find ways to escape the reality of his situation; getting himself admitted to hospitals as his way of finding safety. Bits and pieces of the story continue to be shared, and Jeremy has begun to use language to describe his past experiences as abusive. We met him where he was and addressed the topics he identified as important to him at each session. Jeremy has brought in questions or writings from his journals where he explores past events, sometimes asks to have us reflect on his writing, for us to share our reactions, and to ask him questions as he continues to make meanings out of his past. We invite him into the process of a session by asking what might be on his mind at that time, which comes from our collaborative-dialogic practice of considering our client an expert in his life. Jeremy sometimes includes his realizations about how we are working with him in comparison to how other practitioners in his past have worked with him. He is interested in our reasoning and choice of questions. As the "experts" in conversation and dialog, we address his inquiries about our own thought processes and questions by offering to make our private thoughts and ideas public. In these interactions, we are able to discuss what thoughts are happening in our minds as we talk—making this dialogical process reflexive.

During our time working together, Jeremy has been admitted to the hospital twice. Both times were due to overdosing on medications that he has "reserved" for these purposes. In conversation, Jeremy has discussed how difficult life has been and currently is for him. He has many fears, which we are connecting, together with him, to his past. He is afraid and lonely living alone. He has developed compulsive behaviors related to this fear, including checking that his door is locked and that the oven is off, numerous times. Another fear is that his parents will die soon, leaving him all alone. When overwhelmed with these fears, Jeremy may think about, and attempt, suicide.

Jeremy's last hospitalization was about 3 months ago and lasted only one night. Compared to other hospital stays of 3 to 5 weeks, this was a major change. He has identified a wish to stay out of the hospital—a new goal for him as, in the past, going to the hospital was a way to escape situations that may have been frightening and unmanageable. He has recently decided that it is not a good place for him, as he now makes sense of being in the hospital as something that keeps him from accomplishing goals and interrupts his life, threatening his job and housing security. We have been talking about ways to manage the fear and anxiety that he experiences instead of turning to his medications. Though he is not cutting, or thinking about cutting, at all at this time, he is having some issues with food: controlling, purging, and obsessive thinking are things he is discussing in therapy.

Jeremy has recently applied for a part-time job in his field, though also has considered volunteering for a while to get more familiar with the challenges of working in a more professional environment. Jeremy's parents continue to advise him in ways that increase his doubts about moving forward. For example, they have suggested that volunteering may make it difficult for him to get hired, making it appear that he doesn't really need to work. Jeremy was disappointed that his mom reacted this way, as he had been very excited about the idea. Jeremy has also discussed how difficult it is for him to feel as though his loved ones do not believe in him, but he also has acknowledged that his past has been difficult for his parents.

CRITIQUES OF THE COLLABORATIVE-DIALOGIC APPROACH

There are some critiques of collaborative-dialogic philosophy and practice about which the reader should be aware. You may have already begun thinking about some of these critiques. Some of the common critiques are of the underlying social construction theory. Many people have a hard time with the notion that reality is constructed in language or, to a lesser degree, that "knowledge" is socially constructed. The critics assume that with this belief we would then discount pain, or all events, as not being "real." To counter this concern, one might offer that we consider all descriptions real to the person who is holding them, and rarely, if ever, question the validity of someone's account. This means our bias is to believe our clients rather than diminish their accounts of reality.

Another critique is about the "not-knowing" stance of the therapist, because it does not use standard protocols that people use in certain situations. We have heard it called a "do-nothing" or "know-nothing" approach. Some equate the not-knowing stance with becoming a blank slate or starting without anything concrete: ideas, thoughts, perceptions, or intentions (Anderson, 2000). This is far from the intention of the proponents of collaborative-dialogic practices. To be engaged in a process of listening and talking from a not-knowing stance carries a simpler meaning: A therapist does not assume that they know the client's story or circumstances even when the therapist thinks they may have heard similar stories from others in the past.

Mentioned earlier, this concern or critique comes from those who maintain the hierarchical and privileged position of the therapist as the expert. Many people feel that the years of schooling and experience it takes to become a therapist, and their hard work, are being thrown out (with the bathwater). The way we think about it, what we have learned, is very important and allows us to have different ways to think about things. Learning about the various approaches to therapy exposes us to the multiple descriptions of problems and solutions, and teaches us that there is no "right" way, but many ways may work. We believe our responsibility is in exploring what might fit for each client and providing them opportunities to figure this out. The "client is the expert" approach, which goes along with the "not-knowing" approach, also is critiqued. We believe that in both cases, those who are critical may feel uncomfortable with being in a collaborative relationship.

Another critique is that this approach to therapy is based on language and conversation, making it inappropriate for young children, people with a limited vocabulary, and others with conversational challenges. Sometimes this is a challenge; however, doing therapy with people who are nonconversational (for whatever reason) leads us to explore new ways of communicating. For some, this might be drawing or using props and acting out different situations. Others sometimes bring in music that is meaningful, and the client and therapist can use this to add to, or substitute for, verbal conversation.

Though there are many collaborative-dialogic therapists practicing from this philosophical stance around the world, many still do not know about this approach. Therefore, another concern for the field of collaborative-dialogic therapy is that there is not a sufficient body of literature to capture the intricacies with which the therapy is practiced in different contexts.

Finally, some therapists critique collaborative-dialogic therapy as it appears to be nothing more than an eclectic approach. Collaborative-dialogic therapists approach each session from the same philosophical stance and work with each client in unique ways that are co-designed (with the client) to fit the goals of the client. In some ways, this may seem to be eclectic as the therapist may draw on different ways to understand the situation and offer possible solutions; however, the philosophical and theoretical basis of this approach is singular and stable and always rooted in social constructionism.

General Strengths and Weaknesses

A general weakness of this way of working is how difficult it is to teach and how long it takes to learn, as well as to unlearn, many of our common practices (e.g., being an expert in another person's life, treatment, and future). Though much of the practice appears to be simple, the subtleties of being curious and not knowing are very challenging at first. People who train with us at HGI are invited in to an apprentice-type relationship where they work together with more experienced clinicians and faculties. After several months of working together, the trainees are paired with each other to do co-therapy. They often also participate in (and with) reflecting teams. We believe an intensive training experience is necessary to learn these practices, and thus, we only offer 1-year internships. Interns and trainees are often frustrated that their peers are given caseloads as soon as they start. They also witness our faculty and clinical associates using reflecting teams and participating in others' sessions as reflectors and willingly positioning themselves in a learning position. After a short period of time, the benefits of being in a learning position and working with a team are appreciated by most of our trainees.

Within these weaknesses that are time consuming and tailored to each learner, the strengths of the approach emerge. Each learner is supported through the challenges they encounter as new collaborative-dialogic therapists. They receive their supervision and training in a parallel way to how we work with our clients. Each learner is an expert in their development and growth as well as in their own story. As we work with them in their training as therapists, they become adept at managing conversations and situations that might be challenging. They develop ways of maintaining flexibility in conversations that have space for many voices and perspectives, and they begin to formulate their identities as practitioners offering therapeutic services to those clients who are often referred out as difficult or challenging. Through this process, the strengths of the approach become self-sustaining in that we create potential healing contexts for individuals and families who would otherwise not get help.

Populations Most and Least Suited

There are many populations that are well suited for work in collaborative therapy. As one of our core values is to make therapy accessible to all who want help, we do not screen people out of our services. As previously mentioned, working with people who have limited language for various reasons can mean that therapy occurs in ways that are unusual and/or nonverbal. We believe it is the therapist's responsibility to find ways to connect and converse with any client, from any walk of life, regardless of differences in religion, sexual identity, race, culture and ethnicity, physical ability, age, and so forth.

As we are located in a large geographical, multicultural, and metropolitan area, HGI trains therapists from all walks of life, as well. Our therapists learn how to work with clients who are different from them, to not assume they know the other person based on pre-knowing such as stereotypical descriptions and to be curious to learn about their uniqueness. People from the same culture may have different religious beliefs, just as people from the same family might. Supervision, consultation, and using teams all help HGI therapists connect to clients and provide a place for discussing challenges. Despite our best efforts, not all therapists are comfortable with all clients, and vice versa.

CONCLUSION

The work of collaborative-dialogic therapists has been developing for over 40 years with significant contributions from Harlene Anderson (e.g., Anderson, 1990, 1999, & 2001) and Harry Goolishian (e.g., Anderson & Goolishian, 1992), the founders of this philosophy. Anderson has published many works explaining her ideas, influences, and how she arrived at her own ways of practicing and being as a therapist, supervisor, consultant, and coach. Our hope is that more readers will be exposed to the relational ideas and postmodern practices embodied in collaborative-dialogic therapy so that there can be more possibilities in research, practice, and supervision with this philosophy-based approach.

In times like these when professional licenses are threatened by larger systems, it is important to maintain a focus on the future and how professionals in the mental health fields can work together to support each other in preserving our areas of expertise and practice.

Collaborative-dialogic therapy provides a framework from which many kinds of practitioners can work. We have found value in the way that we work, and we hope the ideas are adopted and used in many possible ways by other professionals. As we have adapted the ideas from this philosophical approach to walk-in and single session work as well as to our training and supervision, we hope that others will find creative approaches that serve in their unique contexts. As we discussed, training in this approach can take a long time, but once a practitioner has been immersed in this way of practicing, the influence is lifelong and the ideas continue to shape our interactions with our clients, other professionals, and larger systems. We also hope that others are inspired to have intentional conversations about training, professional growth, and development.

SUMMARY POINTS

- Explore the history of collaborative-dialogic therapy,
- examine the central philosophical constructs associated with collaborative-dialogic therapy, and
- describe the application of collaborative-dialogic therapy to families and groups.

ACKNOWLEDGMENT

We would like to acknowledge and thank our mentor and colleague, Harlene Anderson, for her continued support and inspiration while we wrote this chapter. Her encouragement and support have provided us both with many opportunities to continue our journey as lifelong learners.

KEY REFERENCES

Only key references appear in the print edition. The full reference list appears in the digital product found on http://connect.springerpub.com/content/book/978-0-8261-6556-5/part/sec03/part/sec035/chapter/ch19

American Psychiatric Association. (2013). *Diagnostic and statistical manual of mental disorders* (5th ed.). Author.

Andersen, T. (1991). *The reflecting team: Dialogues and dialogues about the dialogues.* W.W. Norton.

Anderson, H. (1990). Then and now: A journey from "knowing" to "not knowing." *Contemporary Family Therapy, 12*(2), 193–197.

Anderson, H. (1997). *Conversation, language and possibilities: A postmodern approach to therapy.* Basic Books.

Anderson, H. (1999). Collaborative learning communities. In S. McNamee & K. Gergen (Eds.), *Relational responsibility*
(pp. 65–70). Sage.

Anderson, H. (2000). Becoming a postmodern collaborative therapist: A clinical and theoretical journey. Part I. *Journal of the Texas Association for Marriage and Family Therapy, 3*(1), 5–12.

Anderson, H. (2001). Postmodern collaborative and person-centered therapies: What would Carl Rogers say? *Journal of Family Therapy, 23*(4), 339–360.

Anderson, H. (2007). Dialogue: People creating meaning with each other and finding ways to go on. In H. Anderson &
D. Gehart (Eds.), *Collaborative therapy: Relationships and conversations that make a difference* (pp. 63–79). Routledge/Taylor and Francis.

Anderson, H. (2012a). Collaborative practice: A way of being "with." *Psychotherapy and Politics International, 10*(2), 130–145.

Anderson, H. (2012b). Collaborative relationships and dialogic conversations: Ideas for a relationally responsive practice. *Family Process, 51*(1), 8–24.

Solution-Focused Therapy

Jacqueline Corcoran

LEARNING OBJECTIVES

By the end of this chapter, you should be able to:

- understand the historical development of solution-focused brief therapy,
- understand the central tenets of solution-focused brief therapy, and
- understand the application of solution-focused brief therapy to a case.

INTRODUCTION: OVERVIEW OF SOLUTION-FOCUSED PRACTICE

In solution-focused therapy, clients are viewed as having the necessary strengths and capacities to solve their own problems (De Jong & Berg, 2012; Greene & Lee, 2010). Because individuals have the right to determine what they want, the task of the practitioner is to identify strengths and amplify them so that clients can apply their own "solutions." The solution-focused model orients toward the future when "the problem will no longer be a problem."

Given the lack of emphasis on problems, history taking and detailed discussions of symptoms are not a focus. Neither is there need to figure out how the problem began because this knowledge may offer little in terms of how to solve the problem. In general, the past is deemphasized other than times when exceptions to problems occurred, times when the problem is either not a problem or is lessened in terms of duration, severity, frequency, or intensity (Greene & Lee, 2010; O'Hanlon & Weiner-Davis, 1989).

The construction of solutions from exceptions is considered easier and ultimately more successful than stopping or changing existing problem behavior. When exceptions are identified, the practitioner explores with clients the strengths and resources that were utilized. These resources are enlarged upon through the use of questions presupposing that positive change will occur (e.g., "When you are doing better, what will be happening?"; "When our work here is successful, what will be different?"), since changes in language are assumed to lead to changes in perception. When clients view themselves as resourceful and capable, they are empowered toward future positive behavior. Behavioral, as well as perceptual, change is implicated since the approach is focused on concrete, specific behaviors that are achievable within a brief time period. The view is that change in specific areas can "snowball" into bigger changes due to the systems orientation assumed to be present: Change in one part of the system can lead to change in other parts of the system (Greene & Lee, 2010; O'Hanlon & Weiner-Davis, 1989). The systemic basis of solution-focused therapy also means that the context of a particular behavior is more influential than innate individual characteristics. In this model, the individual is depathologized; instead, the emphasis is on situational aspects—the who, what, where, when, and how of a particular behavior (Durrant, 1995).

HISTORICAL DEVELOPMENT

Although some of the key figures associated with solution-focused therapy are social workers (e.g., Insoo Kim Berg, Michele Weiner-Davis, Wallace Gingerich), the model has arisen out of the field of family therapy. Originators include Insoo Kim Berg and Steve de Shazer (who were married), forming the Brief Family Center in Milwaukee, where they worked with other key figures. The model developed using a consulting team and making systematic observations on the process of therapy to cull down its essential elements to find what really worked. Steve de Shazer was responsible for early publications that theorized about influences and formulations (de Shazer, 1982, 1984; de Shazer & Molnar, 1984), and he continued to be a prolific author as the model developed. The following section draws on Visser's (2013) excellent discussion of the history of solution-focused therapy.

One major influence on solution-focused therapy is the work of the psychiatrist Milton Erickson (O'Hanlon & Weiner-Davis, 1989; Visser, 2013). Erickson believed that individuals have the strengths and resources to solve their own problems and that the practitioner's job is to uncover these resources and assist the client in activating them. For Erickson, many times an activation of these resources involves an amplification of symptomatic behavior through the use of paradoxical directives (e.g., prescribing symptoms).

Erickson was also an influence on the Mental Research Institute (MRI), which was founded in 1958 by Don Jackson, with other key figures taking part: Jay Haley, Paul Watzlawick, John Weakland, Richard Fisch, and Janet Beavin. MRI brief therapy became concerned with the patterns of interactions around a problem, with the idea that the family, in trying to solve a problem, was inadvertently entrenching it in place. In both MRI and solution-focused approaches, the pattern around a problem is altered as opposed to discovering its underlying cause (O'Hanlon & Weiner-Davis, 1989). Where the models depart is that MRI brief therapy focuses on problems, whereas solution-focused therapy emphasizes solutions to problems. Unlike MRI brief therapy, which also employs paradoxical interventions on a routine basis, solution-focused therapy relies on paradox only as a last resort when other more direct or suggestive attempts to elicit change have not worked.

A further theoretical influence on solution-focused therapy is social constructivism, the view that knowledge about reality is constructed from social interactions (Berg & De Jong, 1996). In other words, reality is relative to the social context. Therefore, the concept of the "expert" practitioner, who categorizes, diagnoses, and solves client problems objectively, is viewed with skepticism. Sharing perceptions with others through language and engaging in conversational dialogs is the medium by which reality is shaped (de Shazer, 1994). Thus, the solution-focused practitioner uses language and questioning to influence the way clients view their problems, the potential for solutions, and the expectancy for change (Berg & De Jong, 1996).

PHASES OF HELPING

The phases of helping in solution-focused therapy can be described as (a) engagement, (b) assessment, (c) goal setting, (d) intervention, and (e) termination. However, it must be noted that phases are typically not as discrete as they are in a generalist-eclectic framework. Indeed, engagement occurs concurrent to helping the client formulate treatment goals, with questions such as "What needs to happen so that you won't have to come back to see me?" Discussion of goals leads to exception finding: the identification of times when movement toward treatment goals already happens. Evaluation in the solution-focused model most commonly involves noting progress on solution-focused scales; however, solution-focused scales are also used for goal setting, task construction, and exception finding. In addition, termination is a focus from the beginning of treatment since goal setting and solution finding orient the client toward change in a brief time period (De Jong & Berg, 2012).

Engagement

The practitioner gains cooperation of the client in finding solutions by "joining" with the client as the initial phase of engagement. "Joining" is the clinician's task of establishing a positive, mutually cooperative relationship (Berg, 1994). The worker should convey acceptance of the client's positions and perspectives rather than becoming invested in who is "right" and who is "wrong." These strategies are seen as counterproductive in that defensive clients are less amenable to working with the practitioner and to change (Cade & O'Hanlon, 1993).

Strategies for enhancement of joining involve recognition of idiosyncratic phrasing the client uses and adopting this language (Berg, 1994; O'Hanlon & Weiner-Davis, 1989). For example, a person may describe anxiety as problems with their "nerves." The assumption is that clients feel understood when their language is used by the worker. Additionally, the use of client language means less reliance on clinical terms, which may be viewed as pathologizing.

As well as using language idiosyncratic to the client, the worker should also be vigilant for any strengths and resources to compliment, recognizing that every problem behavior contains within it an inherent strength (O'Hanlon & Weiner-Davis, 1989). For example, a child whom a parent describes as "hyperactive" could be viewed as "energetic" and "high spirited." Through reframing, the client is given credit for positive aspects of their behavior, and the joining process is enhanced.

A related intervention, normalizing, involves depathologizing people's concerns. For example, a parent objecting to their teenager's dress style can be told that a normal process of adolescence involves finding an identity, and this may include experimentation with different styles. The objective is to help people view themselves as struggling with ordinary life difficulties rather than overwhelming problems that cannot be solved. Normalizing thus makes more manageable problems previously viewed as insurmountable. Further, normalizing "de-escalates" the tendency of some problems to exacerbate beyond their original nature. In the previous example, if a parent continually argues with a child about dress style and attempts to control the behavior, conflict might take hold of the relationship and the child may become increasingly rebellious. However, if the parent views experimentation as a normal part of identity development, they may be better able to see this as fairly harmless.

Assessment

Assessment involves determining the client's relationship to the helping process, finding strengths, and inquiring about pretreatment changes. There are three main client relationships in the solution-focused model: the customer, the complainant, and the visitor (De Jong & Berg, 2012). Most traditional treatment models assume the presence of a "customer," a person who comes in voluntarily to make changes in their life. The second type of client is the complainant. Complainants ostensibly come to the helping process voluntarily to change, but it soon becomes apparent that they want someone or something else outside of themselves to change. These clients tend to blame other people, events, and circumstances for their problems. The third type of client, the visitor, is directed or mandated to visit a practitioner by another person or entity invested in the client's change. The visitor, therefore, is an involuntary participant in treatment whose main goal is ending contact with the helping system.

The person presenting with the visitor or the complainant relationship to the helping process is often difficult to engage since these clients are not interested in change for themselves (Berg, 1994). In the solution-focused model, strategies are used with both client types. For example, visitors can be engaged toward the goal of getting the mandating body "off their backs" ("Whose idea was it that you come to see me?"; "What would they say you need to do so you don't need to come here anymore?"), and change can be directed toward that end. Complainants can be engaged through the use of "coping questions," which are designed to elicit the resources people use to cope with difficult circumstances: "This sounds very hard. How do you manage? How do you have the strength to go on?" (Lipchick, 1988). An additional intervention with complainants is to emphasize the context for behavior ("What are you doing when he is behaving?"), which orients individuals to their own personal agency in the situation.

A key part of assessment in solution-focused therapy is for the social worker to be vigilant for strengths clients display outside the problem area, such as in their employment, schooling, hobbies, and relationships (Bertolino & O'Hanlon, 2002). For example, potential strengths to exploit could involve patience, energy, communication skills, organizational ability, the ability to delay gratification, managerial skills, attention to detail, and so forth. Here, the intent is to help clients see themselves as resourceful, as such a person will be presumably more hopeful about the future and their own abilities to confront problems, as well as to build upon existing strengths in order to solve presenting problems.

Another aspect of assessment involves inquiry about pretreatment changes, that is, asking clients what kind of changes they have noticed between the time they first scheduled their appointment and the first session. Drawing clients' attention to pretreatment changes might bolster client motivation to stay in treatment (Allgood et al., 1995; Weiner-Davis et al., 1987). Furthermore, attention to pretreatment change might have a "snowball effect" in that small changes lead to bigger changes. For example, if someone feels more hope for the future as a result of scheduling an appointment, they might be more prone to see people as helpful and react to them in kind.

Goal Setting

In the solution-focused model, emphasis is on well-formulated goals that are achievable within a brief time frame. Although goal setting will be discussed as a discrete phase of helping, it is more accurate to view discussion of goal formulation as starting as soon as the client comes in contact with the practitioner: "What will be different about your life when you don't need to come here anymore?" The presuppositional phrasing of this question is presumed to affect the way clients view their problems and the potential for change (Cade & O'Hanlon, 1993), and underlies all solution-focused questioning. Further, expectancy for change is conveyed by using words such as *when* and *will*. Examples of such questioning include "*When* you are sober, what *will* you be saying/doing?" The use of definitive phrasing to convey an expectancy for change is consistent with the solution-focused orientation toward the future. People who have experienced a negative and stressful past may easily project this past into the future and assume their lives will always be the same. Use of the "miracle question" and "scaling questions" is a way to help clients envision a more hopeful future.

THE MIRACLE QUESTION

In the miracle question, clients are asked to conjure up a detailed view of a future without the problem: "Let's say that while you're sleeping, a miracle occurs, and the problem you came here with is solved. What will let you know the next morning that a miracle happened?" (de Shazer, 1988). Specifics are elicited about this no-problem experience so that clients may develop a vision of a more hopeful and satisfying future. Sometimes asking clients to envision a brighter future may help them be clearer on what they want or to see a path to problem-solving. By discussing the future in a positive light, hope can be generated, and change can be enacted in the present by the recognition of both strengths to cope with obstacles and signs of possibilities for change (Cade & O'Hanlon, 1993; see also Corcoran, 2005, for a list of other future-oriented change techniques).

SCALING QUESTIONS

After the client is encouraged to expand their future and the possibilities, the practitioner helps the client develop concrete, behaviorally specific goals that can be achieved in a brief time frame (De Jong & Berg, 2012). Clients typically begin to discuss their goals in abstract and nonsensory-based language: "I will feel better." The task of the clinician is to encourage and develop observable correlates of these states (Cade & O'Hanlon, 1993). For example, rather than "not feeling depressed," goals might involve "getting to work on time," "calling friends," and "doing volunteer work." As this example illustrates, indicators should involve the presence of desired behaviors rather than the absence of negative behaviors (De Jong & Berg, 2012).

A useful technique for making concrete even the most abstract of goals involves scaling questions, which were first introduced by de Shazer (1986). Scaling questions involve asking clients to rank order themselves on a scale from 1 to 10, with "1" representing "the problem" and "10" representing "when the problem is no longer a problem." The practitioner then develops with the client specific behavioral indicators of the "10" position.

Scales offer a number of advantages (Cade & O'Hanlon, 1993). First, a rank ordering will enable clients to realize they have already made some progress toward their goals ("You're already at a 5? You're halfway! What have you done to get to that point?"). Any progress made can then be the basis for exception finding (this will be covered in more detail in the following section). Scales can also be used to guide task setting ("What will you need to do to move up to a 6?"). Clients identify specific behaviors that will help them move up one rank order on the scale. Finally, scales can be used to track progress over time.

Scales can further be used as a basis for the exploration of "relationship questions" (Berg, 1994). Relationship questions help clients understand the context of situations and the part they themselves play in interactions. Typical questions include "Where do you think your partner would rank you?" or "Where would your teacher put you?" Further questioning can help the client identify the steps necessary to take so that other key people will recognize progress: "What would she say you need to do to move up a number?" When more than one person is present in the session, relationship questions can be used to stimulate interaction, helping family members clarify their expectations of each other. Relationship questions also enable clients to become more adept at taking on the perspective of others. This ability opens up new meanings and possibilities for client change as they reflect on how they might act differently (Berg & De Jong, 1996).

Intervention

The major intervention of solution-focused practice is identifying exceptions—times when the problem is not a problem or when the client solved similar problems in the past (Molnar & de Shazer, 1987). Exceptions provide a blueprint for individuals to solve their problems in their own unique way. Exceptions assist people to access and expand upon the resources and strengths they already own, which is seen as easier than teaching them entirely new behaviors. Exception finding also reduces the way people often view problems as all-encompassing and unchangeable. When people realize there are exceptions, problems are viewed as much more manageable.

Once exceptions are identified, the social worker helps the client deconstruct the contextual details of the exception through the following types of investigative questions: who ("Who was there? What did they do? How was that helpful?"), what ("What did you do differently? What's different about those times?"), where ("Where does the exception occur? How does that contribute to the outcome?"), when ("When is the problem a little better? At what times of the day and what days? Before or after?"), and how ("How did you get that to happen? How are you managing to do this?"); see Bertolino and O'Hanlon (2002). People come to see, through such inquiry, that behaviors are the result of certain situations and personal choices rather than ingrained personality traits.

A further way to find and build on exceptions involves an intervention borrowed from narrative therapy, called "externalizing the problem" (White & Epston, 1990). Externalizing the problem involves making a linguistic distinction between the person and the problem by personifying the problem as an external entity (e.g., "the anger," "the arguing," "the urge to use"). In this way, a problem that is considered inherent or fixed can be viewed as less stable and rigid. Since problems are no longer viewed as innate, pathological qualities, people are more able to generate options.

Externalizing also has the benefit of freeing up people to take a lighter approach to "serious" problems, particularly when problems are named in a humorous vein; for instance, "sneaky poo" for encopresis (White, 1984). A final benefit of externalizing is that it can act as a bridge between talk about problems and talk about solutions (Dyes & Neville, 2000). People are empowered to "fight against" these problems through the use of "relative influence questions" (White & Epston, 1990), which ask clients to determine the extent of their influence over their problems, as well as the influence of the problem over them: "When are you able to stand up to the anger and not let it tell you what to do?" "When can you resist the urge to smoke/shoot up?" "When are you able to overcome the temptation to just stay in bed instead of getting your kids ready for school?" "What percentage of the time do you have control over the craving to see him again?" In this way, clients discover exceptions by identifying times when they are able to exert control over their problems.

A final way to help clients discover exceptions is to prescribe the "first formula task" for homework after the first session. De Shazer (1985) pioneered the following question: "This week, notice all the things that are happening that you want to have continue to happen." The purpose of the task is to have clients focus on what is already working for them. Adams et al. (1991) compared the use of the solution-focused "first formula task" and a task focusing on details of the problem. The authors found that the solution-focused task resulted in greater improvement on presenting problems and clearer formulation of treatment goals. Other solution-focused homework tasks are detailed in Corcoran (2005).

Termination

Since change is oriented toward a brief time frame in the solution-focused model, work is oriented toward termination at the beginning of treatment. Questions include "What needs to happen so you don't need to come back to see me?" "What will be different when our work here has been successful?" (Berg, 1994). Once clients have maintained changes on the small concrete goals they have set, the practitioner and client start to discuss plans for termination, as it is assumed that achievement of these small changes will lead to further positive change in the client's life. Termination is geared toward helping clients identify strategies so that change will be maintained and the momentum developed will cause further change to occur.

Although the practitioner does not want to imply that relapse is inevitable, the client must be prepared with strategies to enact if temptation presents itself or if the client begins to slip into old behaviors. Therefore, it is during termination that possibility rather than definitive phrasing is used. For example, "What *would* be the first thing you'd notice *if* you started to find things slipping back?" "What *could* you do to prevent things from getting any worse?" "*If* you have the urge to drink again, what *could* you do to make sure you didn't use?" might be typical inquiries to elicit strategies to use if there is a return to old behavior.

Termination also involves building on the changes that have occurred, with the hope they will continue into the future. Selekman (1995, 1997) has proposed a number of such questions, including "With all the changes you are making, what will I see if I was a fly on your wall 6 months from now?" or "With all the changes you are making, what will you be telling me if I run into you at the convenience store 6 months from now?" Questions are phrased to set up the expectation that change will continue to happen.

APPLICATION TO FAMILY AND GROUP WORK

Family Work

Because of the emphasis on the context of the relationship for behavior change, solution-focused therapy works well with couples and families, and, in fact, the model emerged from the family therapy field. Solution-focused questions are asked of family members so that they can understand the way their behavior influences others ("What are you doing when he is behaving?"). The solution-focused orientation also redirects the blaming and attacking stance of family members into requests for the presence of positive behaviors ("What would you like her to be doing?"). Then the focus turns to times when the hoped for behavior already occurs and what is different about the context, particularly the responses of other family members, during these nonproblem times. This focus presumably leads to a more positive view of other family members, which, in turn, leads to more positive behaviors.

Solution-focused therapy also poses advantages for family work because it addresses the various types of relationships that present to the change process. There are strategies for complainants, typically parents who bring their children to treatment. Coping questions elicit the resources parents employ to deal with "such difficult circumstances." Parents are asked to consider how their own behavior impacts their children's behavior. Focus on when their children display appropriate behavior cultivates in parents a more positive view of their child and encourages future positive behavior. Solution-focused questioning further engages children, who usually represent the visitor type of relationship, in developing treatment goals and in taking responsibility for the work in the helping process.

Group Work

A solution-focused approach alone or in combination with another model can offer advantages for group therapy. First, the goal-oriented and short-term nature of solution-focused therapy is adaptable to either closed-ended groups of a brief nature (Selekman, 1995) or open-ended groups (Corcoran, 2020). Solution-focused therapy can empower clients who might otherwise find a group too problem focused or complaint driven. A solution-focused model can also build on the strengths of individuals in groups, offering inspiration and solutions to problems.

A couple of studies provide examples of solution-focused therapy group work that have been researched. A recent study, conducted in China, examined posttraumatic growth in mothers whose children were recently diagnosed with an autism spectrum disorder (Zhang et al., 2014). Women were randomized to six sessions of the group or no treatment, compared to women who did not receive treatment. At both posttest and 6-month follow-up, mothers who attended the six-session solution-focused group demonstrated more posttraumatic growth.

A more recent study involved solution-focused therapy for parents whose children were removed and placed into foster care and who had a substance use disorder. Participants were randomized to solution-focused group treatment or what the researchers called "research-supported" treatment. The two conditions performed equally well on addiction severity and trauma. It wasn't clear if modality was controlled (i.e., if the research-supported treatment was also offered as group modality). If so, solution-focused group therapy might be more cost-effective.

In addition, a solution-focused approach can be advantageous for people who have been mandated to attend groups, such as those who have been involved in criminal offending or substance use. As mentioned, involuntary populations can be difficult to engage in traditional treatment models, but solution-focused therapy has many strategies to manage the "visitor" relationship. One example is Lee et al. (2003), who describe a group treatment protocol for those court mandated for intimate partner violence.

COMPATIBILITY WITH THE GENERALIST-ECLECTIC FRAMEWORK

Solution-focused therapy shares many similarities with a generalist-eclectic framework. Although solution-focused therapy is classified as a "therapy" approach, it is actually applicable to the wide range of settings and problems with which direct practice social workers are involved (Greene & Lee, 2010), including crisis intervention (Greene et al., 2005) and child protective services (Berg, 1994; Berg & Kelly, 2000; Corcoran, 1999; Corcoran & Franklin, 1998). Solution-focused and social work practices share a systemic view, acknowledging the importance of context rather than an emphasis on individual pathology. Although both solution-focused therapy and social work address the key influence of the immediate relationship context, social work also emphasizes systems, ecological, and broader environmental levels. In both perspectives, a systemic notion of change is promoted in recognition that a small change in one part of the system can produce change in another part of the system. However, solution-focused therapy departs from a generalist-eclectic framework in eschewing a holistic assessment of the various system levels, along with information gathering about the problem and history taking. Although the generalist-eclectic framework espouses an emphasis on health, normality, and client strengths, in actuality "assessment" implies the diagnosis of a problem. The practitioner has to decide on the client's problem so that it can be solved. Hence, the assumption is that a logical link exists between the problem and the solution (De Jong & Berg, 2012). In contrast, solution-focused therapy does not emphasize the problem; neither does it assume that an understanding of a problem leads to its solution.

Although both solution-focused therapy and a generalist-eclectic framework speak of a collaborative relationship between practitioner and client, the solution-focused approach concretely puts this into practice. First, there are specific techniques to assist in joining, such as normalizing and reframing, and specific interventions depending on the client type involved. The spirit of collaboration is also seen in clients being given respect for their unique worldviews and being allowed to determine their own treatment goals. Respect is further conveyed for people's individual strengths and resources, with the assumption that people are capable of solving their own problems. The task of the practitioner is to help clients identify their resources and then enlarge upon them. This approach is in contrast to a view of an "expert" practitioner who possesses specialized knowledge of a mental health diagnosis, which is applied to client problems. It appears, therefore, that although a collaborative process is touted in a generalist-eclectic framework, "expert" knowledge is still required.

Although eclecticism is not as central a feature in solution-focused therapy as it is in the generalist-eclectic framework, allowance is made for the use of other models and theories if these fit with the client's needs and goals. For example, Bertolino and O'Hanlon (2002) talk about medication as one possible solution for people with mental disorders.

CRITIQUE OF SOLUTION-FOCUSED PRACTICE

Strengths

A main strength of solution-focused practice is its compatibility with social work values, including the importance of context for understanding behavior, a systemic perspective, client self-determination, a focus on strengths and resources of the individual, and applicability to a range of social work settings and problems. The focus on strengths is a particularly unique orientation since many other practice models are pathologizing (De Jong & Berg, 2012). The focus on client resources and what the client is doing right empowers and offers hope to people who are often beleaguered by the time they come to a social worker for assistance. Solution-focused questioning offers a concrete way to implement these values in social work practice.

An additional by-product of working with vulnerable and oppressed clients is that social workers often work in public agencies with people who have been ordered by the courts to attend services or are pressured to attend by partners, spouses, supervisors, or under some threat of future punishment. As discussed, in solution-focused therapy, there are many strategies to engage the person who has a visitor relationship to the change process (De Jong & Berg, 2001). The work of treatment is placed on the client rather than on the practitioner. Clients have to decide on their own goals and clarify what they want in concrete terms. Practitioner collaboration helps clients discover and build on the resources they employ during nonproblem times. Through this process, clients are empowered to help themselves.

The respect for unique worldviews and helping clients formulate relevant goals and solutions means that solution-focused therapy is compatible for work with people from ethnic minority backgrounds (Corcoran, 2000; Kim, 2013; Lee, 2003), which is a definite strength. Solution-focused techniques operationalize social workers' ethical responsibility to clients in terms of understanding, and being sensitive to, clients' diverse social backgrounds: ethnicity, immigration status, gender, sexual orientation, age, marital status, political beliefs, and disability (National Association of Social Workers [NASW] *Code of Ethics*, 1999). When discussing how to work with clients from other cultures, the solution-focused literature frequently mentions "the importance of incorporating a client's worldview, empowering the client, and utilizing a client's strengths in cross-cultural social work practice" (Lee, 2003, p. 387). Lee explores the ways in which solution-focused therapy operationalizes these ideas, including emphasizing collaborative work with clients, eliciting and building upon client strengths, and helping clients find solutions that fit within their worldview. A short-term, goal-focused approach that attends to interactional patterns and context, rather than individual dynamics, also makes solution-focused therapy compatible with the worldview of clients from many ethnic minority backgrounds. Kim (2013) elaborates on solution-focused work with clients from various diverse social groups, and Corcoran (2000) discusses the application of solution-focused therapy with behavior problems in children who are from ethnic minority families.

Limitations

Despite its strengths, there are certain limitations that may be posed for the solution-focused model. One potential limitation of solution-focused therapy involves the assumption that clients have the necessary resources and strengths to solve their own problems. Sometimes clients may have deficits in their knowledge or skills; if the social worker has information that may assist the client with a certain deficit, then it appears that it would be unethical to hold back this knowledge and rely on only what the client brings. It seems that a "balanced" approach, working with skills and deficits and risk and protection, is needed to optimally help clients (McMillen et al., 2004).

Another critique of solution-focused therapy relates to its emphasis on behavior and perception rather than feelings. Lipchick (2002) argues that feelings, behaviors, and cognitions are linked, and feelings cannot be ignored as they are an inextricable facet of human existence. If feelings are ignored, they may cloud people's ability to remember the exceptions to their problems or to imagine a future without the problem. She suggests that the role of feelings can be integrated into solution-focused work. For example, exceptions can center around times individuals felt better and what was different about their behaviors and cognitions when they felt that way.

Solution-focused therapy has also been critiqued from a feminist perspective. Dermer et al. (1998) commended the model for its emphasis on competence and strengths, but decried the lack of sensitivity to gender and power differentials.

Another critique that may be leveled at solution-focused therapy has to do with the limited attention paid to client diversity. Social work professes a commitment to "cultural competence" and "culturally sensitive" interventions. The solution-focused position on diversity is that although practitioners may have knowledge of and experience with a particular popula-tion, they do not know a particular individual with a unique history, traits, strengths, and limi-tations (De Jong & Berg, 2012). To make assumptions about that person due to cultural membership verges on stereotyping. Instead, the client is considered the expert; practitioners should respectfully inquire about clients' worldview and distinctive ways of solving problems. Although social workers will not argue with the idea of treating people as individuals, one of the requirements put forth by NASW (2017) is that social workers have a knowledge base on diverse groups and be able to deliver services that are congruent with these populations.

Research on Solution-Focused Therapy

Studies on solution-focused therapy have increased in the last two decades (see a list of studies that are now being maintained by the European Brief Therapy Association on www.blog.ebta.nu/wp-content/uploads/2017/12/SFTOCT2017.pdf). There is a treatment manual now avail-able (Trepper et al., 2012), as well as an edited book focused solely on solution-focused therapy as evidence-based practice (Franklin et al., 2011).

On the list of studies are several systematic reviews (e.g., Franklin et al., 2009; Kim, 2008), and the international interest and scope of solution-focused therapy has been reflected in reviews on studies with specific populations, including clinical populations in China (Kim et al., 2015) and with Latino populations in the United States and in Latin American countries (Suitt et al., 2016).

Authors of the reviews typically conclude that solution-focused therapy is "promising." However, the inconsistency of populations, problems, and measures used in studies means that firm conclusions cannot be drawn. In an attempt to manage this variability, Zhang Franklin et al. (2018) restricted studies to those examining solution-focused therapy in medical settings but including both youth and adults. The variety of outcomes was categorized into three main domains of interest: psychosocial outcomes (distress, adjustment), health behaviors (e.g., exer-cise), and health status (e.g., body mass index). Pertinent to social work, patients appeared to feel better emotionally after solution-focused therapy, but change was not reflected in health behavior or status. The authors hypothesize that internal change (mood, adjustment) precedes behavioral change.

Taking all the evidence together, improvements have been made in the quantity and quality of research in the last two decades. It appears solution-focused therapy might be at least as effective as treatment as usual or other established treatments, but more methodologically rig-orous designs and reviews that center around particular populations, problems, and outcomes will be more informative.

CASE STUDY 20.1

A 25-year-old woman, Sarah Matthews (fictitious name), presented in treatment because she had never had a serious boyfriend, much less a date, due to her extreme anxiety and discomfort when speaking to men. Sarah coped with this anxiety by avoiding contact with men. When contact was inevitable, her heart would pound, and she would blush, stammer, and mumble. Sarah related she had been sexually abused as a child (a one-time incident when she was 5 years old) by a teenage uncle. Sarah had never told anyone before about the abuse and was adamant about not discussing it any further in therapy. She said she only wanted to tackle the social anxiety.

The first intervention with Sarah was the construction of a *solution-focused scale*. Sarah was asked about specific behaviors that would indicate she was at a "10," *when she didn't need to come to therapy anymore*. She described that she would be able to speak to men in casual social contact and to feel comfortable in social and work situations that might include men. Sarah's description entailed *a* behaviorally specific goal that was achievable within a brief time period. She did not, for instance, state that she wanted to be able to date men or have a boyfriend. These objectives might have been possible only after she had been able to meet her more immediate goal, as a small change can "snowball" into bigger changes.

Sarah was then asked to rank herself on the solution-focused scale. Sarah placed herself at a 2 since she was able to speak to one man at her workplace. Sarah was *complimented*; she had made some progress toward her goal. Inquiry about the *exceptions* that had occurred to get her to this point were explored. Sarah said that the exception involved a delivery man who came out weekly to her work setting. Her job as office manager was to get him to sign for the order he delivered. She said at first she had avoided him, conveniently being "way too busy" when he came by, forcing a coworker to get him to sign. However, her coworker's job duties then changed and Sarah had no choice but to have contact with him. She said she would experience extreme dread at the prospect of him coming to the office. When he would make his weekly visit, she described that she would shake and sweat, avoid eye contact, and mutter enough of a response to get the job done. After 4 months of this, she said she was finally at the point where she no longer dreaded his visits and could respond to him very brusquely with one-word answers, but at least she was no longer submerged with anxiety. When asked about the *resources* she had employed to get to this point, she said that becoming familiar with him and seeing him joke around with her coworkers had helped. She was asked how she could apply the resources she had employed in the past to current situations that were bothering her. She identified that the exception involved exposing herself to contact with a man over time, which allowed her to eventually perceive him as safe. She denied that there were any other men with whom she had contact on a regular, or even an occasional, basis.

When asked how she could make more of that happen in her life, she stated that she had considered joining a church social club. She was *complimented* for coming up with such a creative solution and was asked how she could go about joining such a group. She said she had attended a couple of different churches in the area and had found one with which she felt comfortable, and that this church offered a singles group. It was agreed that the task for the following week, which would get her to a 3, would involve calling about meeting times for the singles group.

Sarah came in to the session the next time, smiling and pleased. She reported that not only had she called about the singles group, she had also attended a meeting on Friday night. She was asked again about the *resources* she had used to do this. How had she been able to face her fears and get herself to this group? She said she was just at the point where she was sick of having her life so curtailed. She said she wanted a husband and children one day, so she needed to get past this problem if she was to achieve this. She reported that the group comprised both young women and men, and that everyone was very welcoming and accepting; she only felt minor anxiety in the presence of so many men. When asked how she had been able to do this, she said that getting the courage up to call and then to attend the meeting had been the hard part. She further stated that she had been able to summon up the courage because she was so motivated to deal with this problem. She said that scheduling a therapy appointment had also meant she was serious about tackling her problem. For Sarah, calling about a therapy appointment seemed to comprise *pretreatment change*. It appeared as if taking such a positive step toward action motivated her to make further changes. As a result of these changes, Sarah ranked herself at a 5 on the solution-focused scale.

As sessions progressed, she ranked herself at a 7, an 8, a 9, and a 10, respectively. She was able to make these changes by attending the singles group meetings on a regular basis, as well as other social events connected with the group. Through hearing people disclose, Sarah learned that even the male members were no different from her in having problems and difficulties with which they struggled. Over time, Sarah became comfortable with relating to men on a social basis with none of her earlier anxiety symptoms.

CONCLUSION

This case example illustrates how the solution-focused model can be used to identify and enlarge upon people's strengths in order to facilitate change. The present chapter has also suggested that solution-focused therapy can be used in combination with other helping models when the practitioner is faced with certain client problems. However, further empirical work is needed to establish how effective solution-focused therapy is both alone and in combination with other models for different populations and in different problem areas.

SUMMARY POINTS

- Explored the historical development of solution-focused brief therapy,
- explained the central tenets of solution-focused brief therapy and
- described the application of solution-focused brief therapy.

KEY REFERENCES

Only key references appear in the print edition. The full reference list appears in the digital product found on http://connect.springerpub.com/content/book/978-0-8261-6556-5/part/sec03/part/sec035/chapter/ch20

Adams, J., Piercy, F., & Jurich, J. (1991). Effects of solution focused therapy's "formula first session task" on compliance and outcome in family therapy. *Journal of Marital and Family Therapy*, 17, 277–290.

Allgood, S., Parham, K., Salts, C., & Smith, T. (1995). The association between pretreatment change and unplanned termination in family therapy. *American Journal of Family Therapy*, 23, 195–202.

Berg, I. K. (1994). *Family-based services: A solution-focused approach*. W.W. Norton.

Berg, I. K., & De Jong, P. (1996). Solution-building conversations: Co-constructing a sense of competence with clients. *Families in Society*, 77, 376–391.

Berg, I. K., & Kelly, S. (2000). *Building solutions in child protection*. W.W. Norton.

Bertolino, B., & O'Hanlon, B. (2002). *Collaborative, competency-based counseling and therapy*. Allyn & Bacon.

Cade, B., & O'Hanlon, W. H. (1993). *A brief guide to brief therapy*. W.W. Norton.

Corcoran, J. (1997). A solution-oriented approach to working with juvenile offenders. *Child and Adolescent Social Work Journal*, 14, 277–288.

Corcoran, J. (1999). Solution-focused interviewing with child protective services clients. *Child Welfare*, 78, 461–479.

Corcoran, J. (2000). Solution-focused family therapy with ethnic minority clients. *Crisis Intervention and Time-Limited Treatment*, 6, 5–12.

Mindfulness-Based Approaches

James Beauchemin

By the end of this chapter, you should be able to:

- provide a general understanding of mindfulness as a construct, as well as historical development and integration into Western treatment paradigms;
- examine mindfulness components, theoretical underpinnings, and underlying change mechanisms including awareness, intention, attitude/nonjudgment, and attention;
- explore research supporting the effectiveness of mindfulness-based interventions across a variety of clinical presentations and contexts;
- provide an overview of common mindfulness-based therapeutic approaches and interventions such as mindfulness-based stress reduction (MBSR), mindfulness-based cognitive therapy (MBCT), dialectical behavior therapy (DBT), and acceptance and commitment therapy (ACT); and
- examine mindfulness within a clinical social work context and provide examples of both formal and informal mindfulness practices that can be utilized by both social workers and individuals served.

INTRODUCTION

Mindfulness is a commonly misunderstood construct that relates to the basic human ability to be fully aware and attentive to present moment experiences. Because of the abstract and subjective nature of mindfulness as a construct, it is sometimes easier to describe what mindfulness is not rather than reciting one of the many definitions presented in the literature. For the sake of simplicity, it may be beneficial to examine some differences between mind*less*ness and mind*ful*ness by asking yourself the following questions: When meeting someone new, do you sometimes forget their name almost immediately after you've been told it? Is it often difficult to maintain focus on what is happening in the present? Have you ever driven to a particular destination and been so lost in thought that you are surprised when you arrive? These are all examples of being "mindless" or functioning on "automatic pilot."

Mindfulness on the other hand is about bringing one's full attention to the present experience in an accepting, nonjudgmental manner. In simplistic terms, mindfulness can be thought of as a state of consciousness, the awareness that comes from systematically paying attention on purpose in the present moment to whatever is being experienced. The numerous potential benefits across multiple domains of wellness including physical, psychological, and emotional, are well documented in the research literature (and will be discussed shortly). Given the associated positive implications of mindfulness, it is no surprise that mindfulness practices have gained in popularity, and efforts to improve accessibility have resulted in numerous therapeutic approaches, models, and techniques. This chapter discusses mindfulness and its application to clinical social work practice, examining specific construct components, supporting research, and evidence-based therapeutic approaches that integrate mindfulness as a core component, as well as basic introductory mindfulness practices.

HISTORICAL DEVELOPMENT

Although mindfulness has been practiced for thousands of years in various contexts, its growth in popularity in the Western world has been relatively recent. Historically, Eastern spiritual traditions have placed significant emphasis on being present and mindful, developing systematic practices to foster these attributes and consciousness states. While mindfulness has been called the "heart of Buddhist meditation" (Kabat-Zinn, 2003), concepts are considered universal and have played an important role in many spiritual traditions including Christianity, Judaism, Taoism, and Hinduism (Stahl & Goldstein, 2019). From an historical perspective, mindfulness is an English translation of the Pali word "sati" meaning awareness, attention, and remembering. It was conceptualized as a means of eliminating suffering through greater understanding of how the mind works, essentially moving toward peaceful acceptance.

Mindfulness in the contemporary Western world conflicts in many ways with traditional medical and psychological paradigms. The evolution of mindfulness in Western society has paralleled the gradual acceptance of complementary and alternative therapies, and the related knowledge base has changed dramatically through its relatively brief history in Western society. Jon Kabat-Zinn has been credited with playing a pivotal role in the secularization of mindfulness practice in the West through the development of mindfulness-based stress reduction (MBSR), which was created in the late 1970s in a medical facility in Massachusetts. Because the MBSR program integrates adaptations of specific Buddhist techniques intended for general stress reduction, implementation necessitated sensitivity to the existing medical paradigm to minimize concerns of ulterior motives such as promoting particular religious beliefs or practices. Despite differences in theoretical underpinnings between mindfulness-based interventions (MBIs) and conventional Western medical models, increased interest in alternative and complementary practices has helped to create a paradigm in which mindfulness can be explored with greater interest and value. This acceptance has led to the implementation of mindfulness practice and research beyond its spiritual foundations into mainstream wellness promotion across contexts including psychology, neuroscience, and medicine. Although mindfulness has evolved as a result of its introduction into Western society and integration with existing paradigms, foundational concepts and practices are consistent with the historical origins in that they continue to focus on reduction of suffering and improving quality of life.

RESEARCH

The acceptance of mindfulness in Western society as a beneficial practice has led to a convergence of evidence-focused inquiry of historically spiritually focused practices not previously researched. Research related to mindfulness has grown exponentially in the past 30 years (Figure 21.1). Initially, mindfulness research focused primarily on outcomes—or what the specific benefits of mindfulness practice are. This interest in therapeutic outcomes led to a multitude of research studies, as evidenced by the significant number of systematic reviews and meta-analyses. These reviews provide evidence for the effectiveness of mindfulness in

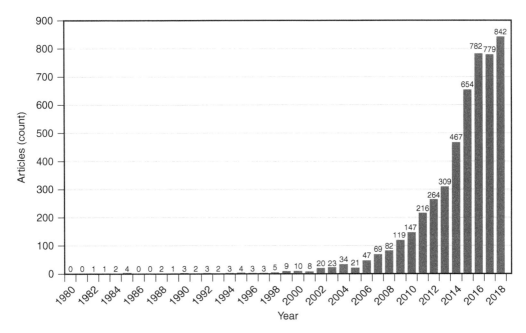

FIGURE 21.1 Mindfulness journal publications by year (1980–2018).

treatment of physical, psychological, and behavioral contexts. Within the physical well-being literature, mindfulness has demonstrated effectiveness in treating individuals with somatization disorders (Lakhan & Schofield, 2013), improving psychological health in breast cancer patients (Cramer et al., 2012) and patients with vascular disease (Abbott et al., 2014), as well as impacting quality of life and mental health of individuals with multiple sclerosis (Simpson et al., 2014) and fibromyalgia (Lauche et al., 2013).

In addition, several systematic reviews and meta-analyses support mindfulness as an effective intervention in treating psychological and behavioral symptoms. Vøllestad et al. (2012) concluded in their review that mindfulness and acceptance-based interventions are associated with reductions in symptoms of anxiety and depression. These conclusions were subsequently supported by Strauss et al. (2014) and build on previous research demonstrating positive effects of mindfulness on depression and anxiety (Hofmann et al., 2010). MBIs are also effective in treating substance use disorders (Chiesa & Serretti, 2014), eating disorders (Wanden-Berghe et al., 2010; Katterman et al., 2014), and severe mental illness (Davis & Kurzban, 2012). Mindfulness has also been found to be an effective intervention across populations including students (Zenner et al., 2014), individuals with developmental disabilities (Hwang & Kearney, 2013), and incarcerated populations (Shonin et al., 2013), as well as in reducing behaviors such as aggression (Fix & Fix, 2013) and adolescent delinquency (Montgomery et al., 2013).

Given the overwhelming positive results of studies focusing on "what" the beneficial outcomes are, recent research has shifted toward "why" these changes occur. This has resulted in research focusing on examination of mechanisms of change within the construct of mindfulness, and what role components such as awareness, attention, or attitude may play in facilitating change. Although the majority of mindfulness research studies rely on self-report measures, the interest in change mechanisms has also led to an increase in study related to neurological aspects of mindfulness practice and identifying brain changes through use of neuroimaging and functional MRI (fMRI). Research has revealed significant findings that indicate that mindfulness may promote positive long-term structural and functional brain changes across several regions, further reinforcing the therapeutic utility of mindfulness practice (Lu et al., 2014).

THEORETICAL UNDERPINNINGS/COMPONENTS OF MINDFULNESS

Despite the wealth of research illustrating the vast benefits of mindfulness practice, there is no consensus understanding of mechanisms of change. The extensive related literature demonstrates considerable variance in descriptions of the nature of mindfulness from both a theory and implementation perspective. In fact, the lack of consensus definition and understanding of mindfulness has resulted in it being conceptualized as both state and trait, as well as a meditation practice and psychological intervention. Unfortunately, this can present challenges for both research and clinical work, as the lack of fidelity may create significant implementation and validity issues. In an effort to create a stable foundation for research and practice, there have been several attempts to conceptualize mindfulness in a cohesive theory.

For example, Shapiro et al. (2006) propose a model of mindfulness that includes three primary axioms: intention, attention, and awareness. They hypothesize that these axioms create change in mindfulness practitioners referred to as *reperceiving*, a shift in perspective that facilitates the ability to objectively observe moment-to-moment experiences. This metamechanism also includes four additional components that influence mindfulness-based change such as self-regulation; values clarification; cognitive, emotional, and behavioral flexibility; and exposure. Similarly, the Monitor and Acceptance Theory (MAT; Lindsay & Creswell, 2017) proposes that attention monitoring and acceptance are the basic mechanisms that underly the positive effects of mindfulness. Specifically, attention monitoring is directly related to recognizing when the mind wanders from the intended focus, as well as improving cognitive outcomes. According to MAT, acceptance encompasses a broad range of related constructs (e.g., nonreactivity, nonjudgment), which rely upon an acceptance orientation toward experiences. In essence, the tenets of MAT state that attention monitoring skills improve present-moment awareness, and acceptance skills modify the way one relates to these present-moment experiences.

In addition, there have been a number of conceptualizations of mindfulness that attempt to identify specific components or mechanisms of mindfulness, and hypothesize how these components may interact and lead to beneficial changes. For example, Brown et al. (2007) propose mechanisms that include clarity of awareness, nondiscriminatory awareness, flexibility of awareness and attention, stability of attention and awareness, and present-oriented consciousness. As a result of the variability in components of mindfulness models, numerous assessment measures have been developed and validated in an effort to provide insight into mindfulness-based change. Among the commonly used measures are the Mindful Attention Awareness Scale (MAAS; Brown & Ryan, 2003), the Five-Facet Mindfulness Questionnaire (FFMQ; Baer et al., 2006), the Toronto Mindfulness Scale (TMS; Davis et al., 2006), and the Philadelphia Mindfulness Scale (PHLMS; Cardaciotto et al., 2008).

Revisiting the basic definition of mindfulness, the awareness that comes from systematically paying attention on purpose in the present moment, without judgment, it is clear that there are several mechanisms including awareness, attention, intention, and nonjudgment that work concurrently. In simplistic terms, these mechanisms work collaboratively to help us bring our focus to whatever is happening in the moment, and it is only in the present moment that we can make changes. For example, moment-to-moment nonjudgmental awareness can help individuals recognize habitual thought patterns and other ingrained behaviors or unconscious tendencies, and make new choices that promote psychological and physical health and wellness. Although the way that components are conceptualized may vary depending upon theory and model, commonly identified mechanisms are discussed in the following.

Intention

Intention can be described as a determination to act in a certain way; something that you want and plan to do. According to J. Kabat Zinn, "[I]ntentions set the stage for what is possible. They remind you from moment to moment of why you are practicing in the first place" (Kabat-Zinn

& Hanh, 2009). As noted previously, acting mindlessly is far more common and certainly less work initially than acting mindfully. Thus, intention is a critical component of mindfulness—as mindfulness states do not typically arise without effort, and without intentionality, they are often fleeting and unobserved. Those who practice mindfulness tend to have varying intentions, shifting from self-regulation to self-exploration and self-liberation (Shapiro, 1992), and it is essential to note that intentions are often not static, rather can change as one practices. Regardless of the specific intention, it is important to note that intention is critical as a mechanism for practicing. Mindfulness practice can be likened to sharpening an axe.

> If one has a limited amount of time to chop an enormous pile of wood, stopping to sharpen your axe may not seem like an efficient use of time. However, continuing to chop without stopping to sharpen the blade often results in an increasingly dull blade, and thus, slower progress. The axe can be likened to one's mind, and the act of sharpening is similar to mindfulness practice. (Kozak, 2009)

Without intention, mindfulness practice may be sporadic, unfocused, inefficient, and unfulfilling. Although the relationship between mindfulness components can be multifaceted and at times undefined, it is clear that intention is also related to awareness and attention, as in order to successfully attend to the present moment experience and shift between awareness and attention, one has to have intention to do so.

Awareness

Awareness can be thought of as a level of consciousness in which one is cognizant of a situation or subject in the present moment. In a mindfulness context, awareness relates the thoughts, emotions, sensations, and environment—both internal and external experiences as they exist at any given moment. Within this context, thoughts may be regarded as objects of awareness, not to be judged, rather acknowledged. Beginning practitioners of mindfulness often struggle with the perception that mindfulness is antithetical to thinking when, in practice, becoming aware of thoughts without engaging and evaluating them fosters a different relationship with thinking. As the Buddha instructs "Develop a mind that is vast like space, where experiences both pleasant and unpleasant can appear and disappear without conflict, struggle, or harm. Rest in a mind like vast sky." It is easy to become consumed with the content of our thoughts, slip into automatic pilot mode, and get entangled with conditioned patterns or lost in the past or future.

The component of awareness that adopts the observational role and conceptualizes thoughts and feelings as separate from the self is referred to as "meta-awareness." From this viewpoint, thoughts such as "I'd like to go out with my friends but I am anxious" can be perceived as "I'd like to go out with my friends and I am having anxious thoughts." In fact, meta-awareness creates the possibility of viewing awareness itself as a focus of attention, allowing one to identify when their attention has shifted and return to a "clean slate" of awareness. The Zen cook metaphor illustrates this return to awareness:

> Usually when we want to begin a new project we're in a hurry. We want to jump right in and do something, anything. But the Zen cook knows that we can't prepare a meal if the kitchen is cluttered with last night's dishes. In order to see the ingredients we already have in our lives, we need to clear a space. "Clean the chopsticks, ladles, and all other utensils, handle them with equal care and awareness, putting everything back where it naturally belongs." So we always begin by cleaning. Even if the kitchen looks clean, we still have to clean it again each time we want to start a new meal.

In this way, mindfulness practice helps to foster a level of consciousness that allows for acknowledging present-moment experiences and returning to open awareness.

Similar to how direct connections can be drawn between intention and awareness, awareness and attention are closely related components. For example, it is necessary to have an awareness of present-moment experiences in order to effectively shift or modify attention as it relates to these experiences, and therefore distinguish oneself from thoughts about the experience. In essence, awareness is required in order for attention to be regulated.

Attention

In addition to intention and awareness, mindfulness is also associated with attentional control. Attention is often described as one's ability to focus awareness on a particular facet of internal or external experience—essentially selecting an element from the field of awareness and directing focus toward it. This ability requires monitoring moment-to-moment experiences (awareness) and consciously managing or directing attention (intention). For example, in mindfulness meditation practice, the breath is often used as the primary focus of attention. By increasing one's ability to recognize when the attention has wandered and redirecting back to the breath, we are in essence training attention. When speaking of mindfulness and attention, a parade metaphor can serve as a helpful reminder for identifying when we get "stuck" on the content of our thoughts or emotions:

> In the parade metaphor, it is helpful to envision all thoughts, emotions and other mental events as being participants or floats in a parade. Each of these parade members is representative of a thought or emotion. Ideally, using a mindful approach, we would view the parade from the point of view of being in the judges seat or other fixed point, so that we could simply witness the parade as it passes. However, given the nature of the human mind, this can sometimes be challenging. Our minds may find a particular parade float or participant that is particularly interesting, and will get consumed as our attention is dragged down the parade route with it. This is similar to how our minds can become "stuck" or fixated on specific thoughts or emotions. However, if we could remain in the judges' seats and keep our attention on the experience as a whole, we could simply watch and enjoy as the parade simply passes by without getting caught up with a particular float (or thought). Once we recognize that we have gotten caught up watching a specific parade float, we can return our attention to the view from the judge's seat.

Non-Judgment/Attitude

Another critical component of mindfulness relates to one's attitude toward practice. Attitudes can be described as evaluative thoughts or feelings that can lead to value-laden opinions, essentially coloring the present moment experience by how we perceive or interpret it. This is certainly not inherently bad; in fact, forming opinions and judgments can be a valuable tool in many circumstances. However, by accepting our experiences without judgment, we are more likely to see things as they are without the influence of emotional reactivity or cognitive narratives. When adopting a mindful perspective, these experiences can be viewed with curiosity rather than with judgment. Nonjudgment is similar to acceptance in that it allows the individual to notice experiences as they truly are. This common human practice of influencing experiences through emotional lenses is illustrated in the Zen story about a fisherman:

> A fisherman is in a boat on a river at dusk. He has had an unsuccessful day fishing, and his mood is reflective of this. Suddenly the fisherman notices that another boat is headed straight for him, coming faster and faster. He gets upset, and starts to yell angrily, "Hey! Watch out! Turn!" trying to warn the other person in the boat, but the boat continues and ultimately crashes into him. By this time the man is furious and shaking his fist, continuing to yell, until he finally notices that the boat is empty.

PRACTICING MINDFULNESS

Although many people use the terms mindfulness and meditation interchangeably, it may be more useful to think of mindfulness as the "what" and meditation as the "how." That being said, meditation is simply one strategy for improving states of mindfulness. There are a multitude of formal and informal ways to be mindful in everyday life. For example, formal practice often is described as identifying specific, structured time to focus on breathing, body sensations, and so forth—akin to traditional meditation practice. Informal practice on the other hand can be as simple as paying attention mindfully to any daily activity, be it eating, exercising, or washing the dishes (Stahl & Goldstein, 2019).

There is no consensus agreement with regard to how much mindfulness practice "is enough." Some suggest just minutes a day is all it takes; however, the vast majority of research investigating mindfulness is based on consistent, daily practice. Confounding the question of "how much?" is the subjective nature of the experience, what constitutes "good" practice, and what the aims of practice are. It may be helpful to remember that mindfulness practice is in fact a practice. While we may notice some changes and benefits through practice, there is no fixed destination or end state that is being strived for. Thus, from this perspective, even a practice session in which it is difficult to feel settled and thoughts continue to race is still beneficial. Following are some brief descriptions of some basic introductory mindfulness practices.

Mindfulness Meditation

While there are many ways to practice mindfulness, historically the traditional means of formal training is through meditation. To practice mindfulness meditation, one would begin by sitting on a meditation cushion or chair (though technically this could be done while lying down or even standing), with back straight so that the head and neck are in line with the spine. It is important to find a seat and posture that provide a stable, comfortable position. Sitting on a cushion, legs are crossed comfortably in front of you, and hands are typically placed on knees or thighs, or resting in the lap facing down.

Many people choose to meditate with eyes closed; however, it is possible to meditate with eyes open if that is preferable. Should you choose to practice with eyes open, simply let your gaze fall gently downward, so that it rests gently on the floor in front of you about 4 to 6 feet away. The gaze is not tightly focused; simply let whatever appears before your eyes be there without focusing on it. Bring your attention to the breathing, noticing the air moving through the nose or mouth, and the rising and falling of the belly and/or chest.

It is likely that attention will drift away from the breath. Notice when your mind wanders from your breath and when you notice your mind wandering gently return your attention to the breath. It may be helpful to silently label your thoughts "thinking" when you notice them as a means of bringing attention to the present before returning to the breath. This labeling is not a judgment; it is a neutral observation. If the practice feels difficult or challenging, remember not to be too hard on yourself—that's why it is called practice.

Mindful Breathing

Mindful breathing can be an effective strategy to access a more mindful state, manage a stressful moment, or simply practice attending to the present moment experience. There are several ways to utilize this technique, all of which integrate mindful awareness and attention. As the name would imply, mindful breathing focuses attention on the breath. Similar to the previously described meditation practice, we can increase our awareness of the mind's tendency to jump from one thing to another. Simply observe each breath without trying to change it, and notice when thoughts or feelings start to pull you away. The discipline of bringing our focus back to the breath can be an effective strategy to develop mindfulness. This practice can be used in virtually any setting and can last for whatever duration is needed or possible at the moment.

To facilitate the practice, sometimes using breath counting can be an effective strategy. For example, after the out-breath counting one, followed by the in-breath and out-breath for two, and so on up to 10, starting over again at one. An alternative counting strategy could incorporate counting the in-breath, hold, and exhalation separately. For example, count four on the in-breath, hold for two, and exhale for a four count. Some people prefer a more visual or kinesthetic approach to mindful breathing. This may involve imagining a balloon in the stomach that inflates as one inhales and deflates as one exhales, creating the rise and fall of the abdomen. Similarly, it may be useful for some to attend to the sensations of the rise and fall of the stomach as the breath moves in and out of the body. Ultimately, mindful breathing can be a simple technique that can have a positive effect on one's entire physical and mental state. By paying attention to the breath, and nonjudgmentally noticing when thoughts or feelings arise, one can simultaneously intentionally "let go" of those thoughts and gently bring attention back to the breath.

Mindful Eating

Mindful eating is a mindfulness practice that involves paying full attention to the experience, both inside and outside the body, of eating and drinking. It focuses on bringing full attention to your experiences, cravings, and physical cues when eating by increasing awareness of the colors, smells, textures, flavors, temperatures, and even the sounds of our food. In practice, mindful eating may include eating slowly and without distraction, appreciating the food that you are consuming; noticing the thoughts and emotions before, during, and after eating; and maintaining a present-focused awareness of the entire process of eating. This is often a very different experience from how we typically eat, which may involve multi-tasking and watching television, reading, talking on the phone, or any number of simultaneous activities that distract from the experience of eating.

Similar to the previously discussed activities, mindful eating can help train our present-centered attention, so that when we become distracted or "lost in thought," we can redirect our attention the experience at hand. There are a number of ways to practice eating mindfully. For example, mindful eating practice could include eating one meal a week mindfully in silence or taking 5 minutes at the beginning of every meal to eat mindfully without distraction, or perhaps focusing on one aspect of the experience such as texture or taste. By attending to the experience intentionally, and noticing and redirecting when our attention wanders, we can experience the process more fully. While eating mindfully can be a simple and accessible way to practice, the same concepts can be generalized to other daily activities or tasks such as going for a walk, washing your hands, or folding clothes, so that your awareness and attention allow for nonjudgmentally observing the full experience as it is.

Mindfulness in Social Work Practice

The research-informed benefits of mindfulness have led to increased integration in therapeutic contexts. In clinical social work, mindfulness can be applied in various ways. For example, social work practitioners using mindfulness can assist in maintaining present-centered awareness while meeting with clients. Attending to one's reactions, thoughts, and feelings in clinical interactions can be beneficial for noticing emotional reactivity or judgment, and managing affect and interaction patterns. For example, the awareness that a client's presenting concerns can have a triggering effect on a social worker can help in emotion identification, nonjudgmentally allowing these feelings to exist without becoming "stuck" and bringing attention back to the present moment. This acknowledgment of thoughts and emotions can allow for social workers to truly be present with clients.

According to the National Association of Social Workers Code of Ethics, social work requires that social workers treat each person in a caring and respectful fashion. Part of being present with clients and interacting in caring and respectful ways involves positive regard and non-judgment. Using mindfulness as a clinician when interacting with clients creates a dynamic where the intention to form connections is facilitated by the awareness of any bias or judgment, and the intention to return to the connection again and again. This focus on being present with clients and the intention to create and maintain connection highlights any countertransference that may arise, and the awareness of accompanying thoughts and emotions. Additionally, being mindful in a clinical context can create an increased focus on the verbal interactions that are taking place, as well as on the silence: being present with and attending to the space between the spoken words.

Mindfulness in clinical social work practice may involve introducing concepts and techniques to clients as appropriate. As the evidence has grown related to the effectiveness of mindfulness as a treatment modality, its application in clinical social work has become more appropriate and beneficial across populations and presenting concerns. Though there are no required credentials to teach mindfulness, it is beneficial if the social worker has experience practicing, and thorough understanding of both the benefits and challenges that may accompany practice. Taking a mindfulness-based approach to clinical work with clients can increase awareness of emotions and thoughts, which is critical for addressing any number of behavioral health concerns. In addition to the research-supported benefits of MBIs discussed previously, encouraging clients to suspend self-judgment can be a beneficial starting point for self-care.

Mindfulness can be useful not only for clients but for practitioners as well. Given that social workers and healthcare professionals have exceedingly high rates of burnout, especially newer professionals, self-care is of particular importance. Maslach and Jackson (1984) defined the construct of burnout as a prolonged response to chronic emotional and interpersonal stressors related to one's occupation. Social workers face many risk factors for burnout including workload/client caseload, compassion fatigue, vicarious traumatization, as well as work content (e.g., percentage of time spent on paperwork, case management). Maintaining a personal mindfulness practice has been shown to be an effective strategy in reducing symptoms of job burnout, stress, depression, and anxiety in a variety of helping professions (Richards et al., 2010). In addition, research supports the positive implications of mindfulness for both senior social workers and trainees (McGarrigle & Walsh, 2011).

To illustrate the ubiquitousness of mindfulness in clinical social work practice, there are a number of theoretical orientations that incorporate mindfulness as a significant component of the approach. Research supports the effectiveness of mindfulness-based programs such as MBSR and mindfulness-based cognitive therapy (MBCT; Fjorback et al., 2011). In addition, therapeutic approaches such as dialectical behavior therapy (DBT) and acceptance and commitment therapy (ACT) have integrated mindfulness as a core modality component, and are supported by several reviews examining clinical effectiveness (Khoury et al., 2013; McCarney et al., 2012).

Mindfulness-Based Stress Reduction

MBSR is a mindfulness program developed and implemented by Jon Kabat-Zinn at the University of Massachusetts in 1979 with the goal of decreasing stress and its detrimental effects on health and well-being. Given the research supporting the impact that stress can have on both physiological and psychological wellness, MBSR was designed to help participants identify how they will respond to stressors and manage stress through mindfulness practice. The stress response in the human body leads to an increased production of hormones such as cortisol, and the release of neurotransmitters such as epinephrine and norepinephrine, resulting in the body moving into "fight-flight-freeze" mode. Chronic sustained periods of this stress response can lead to a variety of symptomologies including headaches, muscle tension, gastrointestinal issues, and sleep problems, as well as exacerbate any existing illnesses.

MBSR was developed based on the hypothesis that a reduction in stress will result in improved quality of life. The program is traditionally structured as an 8-week intervention, with weekly 2 to 3 hour sessions, as well as one full day "practice session" devoted to silent meditation practice between the sixth and seventh sessions. Although there is some variability in the sessions due to group discussion and participant interactions, the protocol calls for specific themes for each session, as well as the introduction of formal and informal mindfulness practice (e.g., meditation, body scan) progressively throughout the 8 weeks. During the program, participants are encouraged to examine life stressors using a mindfulness lens, and increase awareness of how we respond to these experiences on an emotional and cognitive level. This awareness allows for the conceptualization of thoughts as events rather than fact and helps individuals separate thoughts from self.

In addition to participation in the eight-session intervention, the MBSR program has the expectation that participants will maintain an ongoing individual practice outside of the structured sessions, utilizing the techniques learned in class sessions. Research on MBSR has consistently yielded results indicating that the program is beneficial in alleviating symptoms of a variety of conditions and disorders including chronic pain, sleep disorders, depression, anxiety, fibromyalgia, and burnout (Fjorback et al., 2011).

Mindfulness-Based Cognitive Therapy

MBCT is an adaptation of MBSR developed by Segal et al. (2002), and designed specifically for treatment of depressive symptoms. Similar to MBSR, MBCT consists of eight consecutive weekly sessions lasting approximately 2 hours, and includes expectations for completing homework assignments 6 days a week (e.g., listening to audio recordings, practicing mindfulness meditation). However, there are some significant differences between MBSR and MBCT including the introduction of elements of cognitive therapy including psychoeducation about symptomology. MBCT emphasizes changing the relationship with thoughts, feelings, and experiences rather than focusing on the need to change thought content, in essence integrating meta-awareness to assist in examining these experiences as events rather than truth. MBCT follows a progression in which early sessions (e.g., sessions 1–4) consist of guided practice with the goal of training awareness and attention, whereas later sessions focus on the development of independent practice and "leaning into" or exploring difficult or historically avoided thoughts and feelings.

Among the aims of MBCT is to support participants in developing strategies and resources that can be used to reduce symptomology specific to depression and unhappiness. Central to this skill development are formal and informal meditation practices such as sitting and walking meditations, guided body scans, breathing practices, and the application of present-centered awareness in daily life activities. Increasing awareness through mindfulness can assist with becoming familiar with patterns of thinking that can lead to depressed states. Individuals can then begin to conceptualize separation between thoughts, emotions, and the self, and develop a new relationship with them. This awareness and separation can allow people to disrupt the patterns that lead to and perpetuate depressive cycles and interject positive thoughts, thereby altering mood states. These strategies can be beneficial in prevention of the downward spirals consistent with depressive cycles, as well as application when feeling overwhelmed or in crisis. Numerous research studies confirm the psychological benefits of MBCT, leading to reduced depressive symptoms specifically (MacKenzie et al., 2018), while also positively impacting a number of mental health and wellness-related outcomes (Gu et al., 2016).

Acceptance and Commitment Therapy

ACT is a therapeutic approach developed by Steven C. Hayes in 1982 that integrates aspects of both cognitive and behavioral therapies. The goal of ACT is psychological flexibility, which requires clients to stop avoiding or repressing inner emotions but rather develop a willingness to accept and experience thoughts and feelings as they are in the present moment. As a means of undermining the avoidance of unwanted thoughts or emotions, mindfulness is utilized to increase direct awareness and acceptance of experiences. Rather than trying to change the way one thinks, ACT proposes alternatives including use of a mindfulness perspective, attention to personal values, and commitment to action.

ACT theorizes that while attempting to stop unwanted thoughts or emotions is an understandable response, it is not only unproductive but can also increase distress. Thus, learning to accept psychological experiences and committing to making needed value-based behavioral changes can eventually lead to changes in psychological and emotional states. By utilizing MBIs, individuals can simultaneously accept that their current thoughts and feelings are appropriate responses to certain situations, while working to modify or integrate behaviors reflective of personal values. In addition, to facilitate the cognitive decision-making related to whether or not behaviors are values consistent, ACT incorporates the use of metaphors, paradox, and experiential exercises. Collectively, these strategies lead to psychological flexibility and movement toward value-based living. Research has demonstrated that ACT can be an effective therapeutic modality across multiple populations and physical and psychological disorders (A-tjak et al., 2015).

Dialectical Behavioral Therapy

DBT is a multifaceted treatment approach originally developed by Marsha Linehan in the 1980s for the treatment of adult self-harming females with a diagnosis of borderline personality disorder (BPD). Individuals who have a diagnosis of BPD often experience pervasive emotion dysregulation, self-injurious behaviors, and interpersonal challenges, resulting from a biological predisposition toward emotional regulation challenges in conjunction with an invalidating social environment. DBT attempts to support these individuals through a variety of skill-building modules and utilization of a dialectical worldview in which self-acceptance and change are balanced. Though there have been several adaptations of DBT dependent upon the population and context, basic components of DBT typically include individual psychotherapy, group skills training, intersession patient coaching, and clinician team consultation to ensure support for clinicians.

DBT helps clients develop skills in several areas including distress tolerance, emotion regulation, interpersonal effectiveness, and mindfulness. DBT is one of the first psychological treatment approaches to integrate mindfulness as a core component. Mindfulness in DBT is conceptualized as a set of skills independent of a particular form of practice, designed to serve several functions. It is used to encourage individuals to enter into the present moment nonjudgmentally, noticing and accepting thoughts and emotions, thereby improving the ability to tolerate distress and act without impulse. Mindfulness is also beneficial in this context as a means of acceptance of thoughts, emotions, and behaviors that may have previously been judged as unacceptable, leading to an understanding of dialectics such as change and self-acceptance. As nonjudgmental acceptance of the present experience improves, the ability to regulate emotions also improves, paving the way for more effective interactions and relationships with others. DBT introduces three states of mind: reasonable mind, emotion mind, and wise mind. In wise mind, the individual synthesizes both reason and emotion, and is able incorporate a mindful perspective of the present moment experience.

CASE STUDY 21.1

The following is an example of the utilization of mindfulness within a clinical context. It involves a client meeting with a social worker to address presenting concerns related to anxiety. The social worker in this case example utilizes a mindfulness-based approach, while integrating aspects of other therapeutic approaches (e.g., cognitive therapy) as appropriate.

Francesca was a 24-year-old female graduate student in her second semester studying engineering. She was attending college away from home, lived alone, and considered herself very independent. In addition to her graduate school responsibilities, she worked part time as a waitress at a local eatery in an effort to minimize future student loan debt. She described herself as sociable and able to make friends easily. However, without much free time to foster relationships, she spends the majority of her "down time" alone. Francesca's busy schedule has left little time for self-care. Previous activities that she enjoyed, including mountain biking, hiking, going to the gym, and spending time with friends, had decreased significantly due to her rigorous class and work schedule. She had been hesitant to ask for support due to her strong desire to be independent. Francesca was adamantly opposed to medication, had a desire to manage symptoms herself, yet had recognized an inability to successfully address her anxiety on her own.

Francesca began meeting with the social worker after noticing an increase in anxiety symptoms since enrolling in graduate school. Though she had experienced mild anxiety in the past, she described an acute increase in racing thoughts—particularly when trying to fall asleep. She described this experience as "not being able to turn her brain off." She also reported a noticeable change in emotional reactivity including outbursts due to frustration, crying, and being less patient, and stated that friends and family have commented that she seems stressed. Francesca described her emotions as constantly feeling "closer to the surface" and often feels guilt or shame after outbursts. These symptoms had been compounded by her strong desire to be independent and handle things on her own, leading to added pressure to manage things perfectly. In addition to the stress of placing added pressure on herself, when Francesca was not able to meet her expectations regarding responsibilities or tasks, her perfectionistic mindset led to negative self-talk and feeling that she was "failing" or "not good enough." This in turn made her feel bad about herself and perpetuated the cycle of her feeling the need to get everything correct (e.g., more racing thoughts, low mood).

In her work with Francesca, the social worker supported her desire to be independent and address challenges on her own, discussing evidence-based practices for the treatment of anxiety symptoms to collaboratively develop a treatment plan. The social worker introduced the concept of mindfulness and explained that it is an approach requiring Francesca's commitment to practice on her own. Because mindfulness is abstract in nature and sometimes difficult to grasp, the social worker chose to introduce mindfulness using a metaphor to facilitate understanding (watching the parade). Francesca was able to connect to this metaphor, indicating that's how the thoughts felt when she gets "stuck" on thoughts about needing to get things done or when she "beat herself up" after having an emotional outburst.

As is often a common source of hesitancy about the implementation of mindfulness, Francesca discussed feeling concerned that she would not have time in her busy schedule to commit to the practice needed to make meaningful change. The social worker normalized this concern nonjudgmentally, noting that Francesca definitely already has much on her plate. This concern opened up some beneficial dialog related to how multi-tasking actually can paradoxically be a means of becoming less efficient, whereas staying present and giving full attention to the task at hand can in practice save time. From a practical perspective, this approach appealed to Francesca because of her desire to manage multiple responsibilities and accomplish them at a high level.

To introduce what mindfulness practice may look like, the social worker conducted a brief experiment, asking Francesca just to sit quietly with her eyes closed for 60 seconds. After the 60 seconds were up, the social worker asked what Francesca had been thinking about. Francesca was able to list several thoughts and feelings including a list of things that she felt she needed to get accomplished, feeling hungry, as well as questioning the purpose of the exercise. The social worker normalized the thoughts and feelings as part of the human experience, and asked Francesca to repeat the exercise with a couple of minor modifications. She asked her to begin by paying attention to her breathing, and whenever a thought inevitably arose, simply notice and label it "thinking" to herself. As soon as she noticed the thought or feeling, she was instructed to "let go" of it and gently bring her attention back to her breath.

This exercise highlighted the differences between the two experiences, and Francesca's initial inclination to try to stop the thoughts and feelings immediately as they came up. The social worker was able to help Francesca reframe this desire through a discussion about how "stopping" thoughts can ironically often lead to them returning with increased frequency and intensity. Thus, the focus of Francesca's mindfulness practice initially was to increase awareness of thoughts and emotions, and change her relationship with them. There was no effort to eliminate them; the focus was on accepting them as they are nonjudgmentally and simply allowing them to pass. Through practice, Francesca's awareness of the time and emotional and psychological energy that she had been devoting to unproductive internal narratives and judgments gradually increased.

Based on Francesca's desire to understand the process of altering her relationship with thoughts and feelings, the social worker integrated aspects of cognitive therapy to help highlight the ways that negative internal narratives can impact mood and behaviors. Mindfulness, in turn, sheds light on the attention given to this dialog. By continuing to develop her nonjudgmental awareness of her thoughts, feelings, and experiences, Francesca was able to begin differentiating between thoughts and self. This change from internalization to simply observing without judgment or emotional reactivity led to Francesca noticing that she was no longer "giving them as much power over me."

Throughout their work together the social worker was able to support Francesca in maintaining a mindful perspective through integration of exercises and activities pulled from evidence-based approaches including MBSR and MBCT designed to enhance present-centered awareness and nonjudgmental attention. For example, exercises such as the raisin activity (mindful eating), body scan, and meditation practices were introduced as formal practice techniques that were integrated into meetings with the social worker. However, while Francesca agreed to practice outside of their meetings, the issue of finding time to intentionally integrate mindfulness continued to be a challenge. Collaboratively, the social worker and Francesca were able to brainstorm informal mindfulness activities that could provide opportunities to practice at home (e.g., walking at lunch, washing dishes). For instance, the social worker inquired about brief, simple activities that Francesca engaged in multiple times throughout the day. Francesca indicated that she washed her hands whenever she was going to eat, used the restroom, and so forth. Using this as an opportunity to practice, every time Francesca washed her hands during the day, she focused solely on the full experience of the water running over her hands, lathering soap, rinsing, reaching for a paper towel, drying hands, and so forth. Whenever a thought would pull her away from the experience, she simply acknowledged the thought, "let it go," and gently redirected her attention to the experience of washing her hands. In this way she was able to begin integrating mindfulness practice into her daily life using existing activities to augment her formal practice.

As Francesca was able to alter her relationship to her own thoughts and feelings, she was able to expand awareness beyond her internal experience. One of the ways that this manifested was in her ability to be fully present during interactions. This awareness of the present experience was regularly reinforced through modeling by the social worker who consistently brought attention to the present moment with such comments as "As we talk about these stressors try to pay attention what feelings come up for you." One of the benefits of being present in meetings with the social worker was increased connection and development of the therapeutic relationship. The social worker's present-centered, nonjudgmental attention allowed Francesca to feel heard and understood, which in turn allowed for more open and meaningful dialog.

Through their work together, Francesca was able to experience a gradual reduction of anxiety symptoms. She reported an improved ability to "let go" of thoughts and feelings that would have previously left her fixated and upset. By changing her relationship to her thoughts, Francesca was able to reduce the amount of internalizing she experienced, and as a result change some of the critical narratives that had impacted her mood, in essence reducing the power of the self-defeating thoughts by recognizing the difference between thoughts and self. Although she continued to be very busy, she was able to integrate mindfulness practice into her schedule without disrupting the normal flow of her day, resulting in her feeling like she was able to engage in more self-care. Francesca also reported feeling empowered to be able to take ownership and make changes to manage symptoms on her own, which, as someone who values independence, was something that was very important to her.

CONCLUSION

Mindfulness-based approaches and interventions have increased significantly in recent decades. Extensive research supports its effectiveness across a variety of physical and psychological presentations, establishing mindfulness as an evidence-based tool for clinical social work practice. While general acceptance of mindfulness has been established through research and implementation, as the existing paradigm continues to shift toward holistic treatment models, mindfulness as both a perspective and an intervention is being integrated into mainstream practice with increased frequency among helping professions. Consistent with social work guiding principles, mindfulness can be utilized to support and empower individuals in improving well-being across a variety of contexts. By fostering an increased awareness of thoughts and emotions, and by improving the ability to attend to the present moment without judgment, social workers can create opportunities for individuals to modify relationships with their thoughts, emotions, and experiences.

The variability in practice techniques, both formal to informal, allow for accessibility and application in many arenas, without the need for invasive processes or rigid therapeutic protocols. Incorporating mindfulness into daily life can help individuals establish a personal practice that generalizes outcomes useful for both prevention and treatment. The accessible nature of mindfulness also creates opportunities for social workers to integrate not only into their clinical work but also into their own personal practice, improving therapeutic outcomes, self-care, and ultimately the well-being of both practitioners and individuals served.

SUMMARY POINTS

- Explored mindfulness as a construct, as well as historical development and integration into Western treatment paradigms,
- described mindfulness components, theoretical underpinnings, and underlying change mechanisms including awareness, intention, attitude/nonjudgment, and attention,
- explored research supporting the effectiveness of MBIs across a variety of clinical presentations and contexts,
- provided an overview of common mindfulness-based therapeutic approaches and interventions such as MBSR, MBCT, DBT, and ACT, and
- examine mindfulness within a clinical social work context and provided examples of both formal and informal mindfulness practices that can be utilized by both social workers and individuals served.

KEY REFERENCES

Only key references appear in the print edition. The full reference list appears in the digital product found on http://connect.springerpub.com/content/book/978-0-8261-6556-5/part/sec03/part/sec035/chapter/ch21

Abbott, R. A., Whear, R., Rodgers, L. R., Bethel, A., Thompson Coon, J., Kuyken, W., & Dickens, C. (2014). Effectiveness of mindfulness-based stress reduction and mindfulness based cognitive therapy in vascular disease: A systematic review and meta-analysis of randomised controlled trials. *Journal of Psychosomatic Research, 76*(5), 341–351.

A-tjak, J. G., Davis, M. L., Morina, N., Powers, M. B., Smits, J. A., & Emmelkamp, P. M. (2015). A meta-analysis of the efficacy of acceptance and commitment therapy for clinically relevant mental and physical health problems. *Psychotherapy and Psychosomatics, 84*(1), 30–36.

Baer, R. A., Smith, G. T., Hopkins, J., Krietemeyer, J., & Toney, L. (2006). Using self-report assessment methods to explore facets of mindfulness. *Assessment, 13*(1), 27–45.

Brown, K. W., & Ryan, R. M. (2003). The benefits of being present: Mindfulness and its role in psychological well-being. *Journal of Personality and Social Psychology, 84*(4), 822.

Brown, K. W., Ryan, R. M., & Creswell, J. D. (2007). Mindfulness: Theoretical foundations and evidence for its salutary effects. *Psychological Inquiry, 18*(4), 211–237.

Cardaciotto, L., Herbert, J. D., Forman, E. M., Moitra, E., & Farrow, V. (2008). The assessment of present-moment awareness and acceptance: The Philadelphia Mindfulness Scale. *Assessment, 15*(2), 204–223.

Cramer, H., Lauche, R., Paul, A., & Dobos, G. (2012). Mindfulness-based stress reduction for breast cancer—A systematic review and meta-analysis. *Current Oncology, 19*(5), e343.

Eye Movement Desensitization and Reprocessing

Anka Roberto and Ashley Swinson

LEARNING OBJECTIVES

By the end of this chapter, you should be able to:

- understand the origination of eye movement desensitization and reprocessing (EMDR);
- explore theoretical constructs leading to the formation of the eight- phased EMDR protocol;
- understand the context of the use of EMDR and its efficacy in healing posttraumatic stress disorder, anxiety, substance use disorders, and other symptoms associated with trauma-related disorders;
- explore evidence that supports the use of EMDR with clients of all ages; and
- apply tenets of EMDR to clinical cases.

INTRODUCTION

In the vast research regarding traumatic stress, there are several universal themes that stand out due to the exposure to such experiences. The human brain is designed to adapt to experience by perceiving and learning, so as one encounters the world, one's brain will develop core beliefs systems that shape thoughts, feelings, behaviors, and decision-making. These core beliefs are built upon three developmental concepts: personal power, personal safety, and personal responsibility.

Current research supports the claim that unprocessed traumatic memories contribute to psychopathology. The unprocessed portions of traumatic memories that reside in the hippocampus, and are connected to the limbic system, impact the neurophysiology of the brain causing biophysical changes in brain structure and brain function (Shapiro et al., 2007; Wheeler, 2014; Van Der Kolk, 2015). These biophysical changes appear on functional magnetic resonance imagining (fMRI) studies like a traumatic brain injury (Fosha et al., 2009).

It has been estimated that one in four children experience abuse, and 60% of men and 51% of women in the United States have experienced at least one traumatic event (Richardson, 2018). The *Diagnostic and Statistical Manual of Mental Disorders, Fifth Edition* (American Psychiatric Association [APA], 2013) defines traumatic experience as, "exposure to actual or threatened death, serious injury, or sexual violence" (p. 271). It goes on to explain that we can experience trauma in four different ways:

1. directly experiencing a personal trauma;
2. directly witnessing a trauma that occurs to someone else;

3. indirect exposure of a traumatic experience when a close family member, friend, or associate has direct experience (e.g., a loved one is in a severe car accident); or

4. vicarious exposure through the repeated or extreme exposure to aversive details due to professional responsibilities (e.g., child abuse investigators; Pai et al., 2019).

In addition to these life-threatening and violent experiences (referred to as big "T" traumas), research also indicates that the less intense but adverse experiences (referred to as little "t" traumas) can be as equally impactful on the brain (Barbash, 2019). See Table 22.1.

According to global organizations such as the Substance Abuse and Mental Health Services Administration (SAMHSA; 2016), adverse childhood experiences (ACEs) are defined as stressful life or traumatic events that happen to children ages 0 to 18. ACEs include the following experiences for children ages 0 to 18: physical abuse, sexual abuse, emotional abuse, physical neglect, emotional neglect, intimate partner violence, living with a mother who was treated violently, substance misuse within the household, household mental illness, parental separation or divorce, and having a parent who has been incarcerated (Anda et al., 2006). In the 1990s, the Centers for Disease Control and Prevention led an investigation on the epidemic of childhood trauma and its correlation with adulthood disease, what is now known as the Adverse Childhood Experiences Study (Felitti et al., 1998). These adverse experiences consisted of big "T" and little "t" traumatic events. This research drastically shaped our understanding of how traumatic experiences affect overall lifelong wellness. While it is possible for someone to develop posttraumatic stress disorder (PTSD) in response to being exposed to traumatic experiences, there are many more negative consequences. ACEs and their impact on the developing brain and body are multidimensional, with long-lasting effects causing chronic disease into adulthood such as heart disease, diabetes, cancers, autoimmune disease, mental health disorders, higher suicide rates, and earlier mortality by 10 years (Felitti et al., 1998). Nationally, economic hardship and divorce or separation of a parent or guardian are the most common ACEs. Close to half of children in the United States have experienced at least one ACE and one in 10 children experienced three or more ACEs in their lifetime, which puts them at higher risk of long-term negative effects (Murphey & Bartlett, 2019; Redford & Pritzker, 2016).

The symptoms stemming from adverse and/or traumatic experiences span the mental, behavioral, and medical health spectra. Thus, treatment protocols addressing these symptoms should prioritize the relationship between the brain, body, and experience, while considering one's past, present, and future; eye movement desensitization and reprocessing (EMDR) therapy does just that. This leading, innovative approach in resolving symptoms of PTSD as well as anxiety disorders, cognitive disturbances, addictions, and life stressors has been deemed by many clinicians and researchers the gold standard of treatment when used according to its

TABLE 22.1 BIG T AND LITTLE t	
Types of Big "T" traumas	**Types of Little "t" Traumas**
• Exposure to gun violence • Car or plane accidents • Directly experiencing or witnessing physical violence or sexual abuse • Natural disasters • Losing a child • War/combat • Severe neglect as a child • Severe, life-threatening medical events	• Chronic or traumatic grief (loss by suicide) • Family or marital distress including chronic conflict, infidelity, and divorce • Bullying • Postpartum issues • Financial stress • Feeling unloved or unimportant • Providing extensive caregiving • Mental illness or addiction in the family • Chronic medical issues

protocol and treatment regimens (Adler-Tapia & Settele 2009, 2010; Bisson et al., 2007). EMDR has been noted to be more beneficial than cognitive-behavioral therapy in a meta-analysis for patients with prominent intrusion or arousal symptoms (Chen et al., 2015).

HISTORICAL DEVELOPMENT

In 1987, Dr. Francine Shapiro stumbled across the relationship between bilateral stimulation (BLS; left to right lateral eye movement) and the reduction of internal stress. During her infamous "walk in the park," she found that her uncomfortable thoughts about a stressful, disturbing situation had dissipated by the end of her walk. Dr. Shapiro had previously battled cancer for 10 years, so she was particularly intrigued by the mind-body connection, and she quickly noticed that during this walk, her eyes were tracking back-and-forth across the landscape while she ruminated on her stress. So, she repeated this activity: consciously thinking about a bothersome thought while rapidly moving her eyes back and forth, and she concluded that each time she repeated this, the negative feelings she held about her stress improved. She hypothesized that traumatic memories, which are composed of negative thoughts and affect, could be improved with the use of BLS, hence an outpouring of breakthrough research that resulted in a rigorous, evidence-based treatment protocol for PTSD: EMDR therapy (Shapiro, 2012).

Much like other studies on PTSD at that time, the initial subjects for EMDR research consisted of combat veterans. Following the Vietnam War, PTSD had become a substantiated mental health illness in the late 1970s, and as a difficult condition to treat, the most successful treatment modalities remained in question. The emergence of EMDR and its effectiveness in symptom remission, hallmarked by the efficiency of its delivery, set this therapy apart from other therapeutic interventions. And, unlike other treatment modalities that have undergone several revisions throughout the years, the rigid methodology of EMDR has been mostly unchanged since 1990 (Shapiro, 2001).

The early focus of EMDR was on the immediate relief of distressful symptoms: consciously holding adverse thoughts while bilaterally stimulating the body to achieve desensitization of the nervous system. However, for symptom remission to remain successful, long-term research revealed that one's deeply held core belief system needed to be reprocessed as well. In addition to a client being able to remember a traumatic memory without feeling distress, the client could also recall that memory and maintain a positive core belief about oneself, evidence of true adaptive resolution in the brain and body.

It was also determined that multiple methods of BLS were effective in the treatment protocol, like alternating tapping sensations on each hand or alternating sound in each ear, though it has been established that lateral eye movements are the most efficacious (Solomon, 2014).

EMDR research subjects have expanded since then to include the civilian/general population, and consistently, these studies reveal that EMDR is an equivalent or superior intervention to cognitive-behavioral therapies, exposure therapies, and the use of SSRIs to reduce symptoms of PTSD (Bisson et al., 2007). After treatment is completed, EMDR is also more effective at maintaining symptom remission at 6 and 12 months out (Shapiro, 2001). Remarkably, debunking what we have assumed to be true about therapeutic processing, EMDR does not require a trusting relationship between the client and the therapist to be effective, does not require in vivo homework, and does not require a person to divulge the details of their traumatic story in order to heal from it.

Not everyone is an appropriate candidate for EMDR therapy, and the setting in which a client is receiving this intervention can impact the treatment direction. It is the clinician's responsibility to adequately assess a client's readiness and integrative capacity in order to proceed. While some contraindications are cautionary, there are clinical concerns that restrict utilization of this approach entirely. A client's ability to maintain dual awareness by holding focus of the past and remaining safe in the present is key for reprocessing to occur, so if a client has intrusive, dissociative symptoms that hinder stability and safety, or if there are acute symptoms such as life-threatening substance use, active suicidality, self-injury, or homicidal/assaultive behavior, then EMDR therapy would be postponed until the client can demonstrate personal safety. Moreover, medications that inhibit one's ability to learn (e.g., benzodiazepines), high doses of psychotropics, and polypharmacy can hinder the effectiveness of EMDR, as a client needs to be able to access affect while they are reprocessing. Therefore, the clinician should closely coordinate the client's care with primary providers, psychiatrists, or psychiatric mental health nurse practitioners who may be prescribing such medications to allow for treatment planning to safely adjust doses appropriately. Caution should also be given to those clients who have a history of epilepsy or eye problems as these issues can worsen with eye movement sets, and when eye movements cannot be used, the clinician can use alternate forms of BLS. In the event of legal matters that may require client testimony detailing specific events, the clinician should advise the client of the possibility that EMDR treatment may affect the client's ability to access vivid details and emotions that pertain to the event. It should be considered that if a client has received any special kind of assistance, caretaking, or compensation for their emotional disability (e.g., disability check), EMDR may remit the symptoms that warranted this resource, which could pose new challenges for the client (e.g., loss of income; Shapiro, 2001).

Conversely, those clients who are stable and have high integrative capacity are great candidates for EMDR, which is evidenced by the ability to maintain dual awareness/co-consciousness, present a coherent narrative of the experiences, learn and utilize new information, and access positive memory networks. Regardless of the intensity and severity of symptoms, a client's ability to tolerate an emotional disturbance while self-regulating to lower their level of arousal and shift emotional states can be predictive of EMDR success. It is also helpful for clients to have social supports available between EMDR sessions to assist with soothing and comfort along the way (Solomon, 2014).

Ultimately, the goal of EMDR is to eliminate the presenting symptoms of distress in clients in an accelerated manner. Meta-analyses and clinical trials (randomized and non-randomized studies) that compare EMDR to other cognitive-behavioral and exposure therapies, like trauma-focused cognitive behavioral therapy, are consistent that EMDR is a comparable or more effective approach yielding long-lasting results with fewer attrition rates (Wheeler, 2014). It has been noted that fewer EMDR therapy sessions are required to achieve these results, and upon completion of treatment, symptom remission is maintained at 6- and 12-month follow-ups (Solomon, 2014).

Given the success of utilizing EMDR for those with PTSD, the research has further explored this protocol with other mental, behavioral, and medical health challenges. The assumption is that pathological symptoms are the result of maladaptively stored information in the brain's memory networks, so it has been hypothesized that other health-related challenges could benefit from EMDR as well. Specialty EMDR protocols have been developed for populations like those with addiction, grief, pain, phobias, recent traumatic events, and so forth. For instance, the Recent Traumatic Events Protocol (R-TEP) was created by Elan Shapiro to address an acute event that has recently occurred to prevent the development of serious posttraumatic symptoms, which can be uniquely utilized with individuals or groups (Tofani & Wheeler, 2019). In the same way, AJ Popky developed the Desensitizing Triggers and Urge Reprocessing (DeTUR) protocol for addictions , particularly addressing the intensity of an urge that a client experiences when they are exposed to a trigger and have a desire to use substances (Shapiro, 2005).

CENTRAL THEORETICAL CONSTRUCT: ADAPTIVE INFORMATION PROCESSING THEORY

From a developmental perspective, we know that the interplay between predispositions and life experiences shapes the way individuals evolve over time. At the core, people hold belief systems regarding the central themes of personal responsibility, personal power, and personal safety that create conscious and unconscious consequences, greatly impacting the way one experiences oneself and the world around oneself. Therapeutic interventions are designed to address these themes and the coinciding psychopathologies.

Regarding treatment modalities that directly address trauma-based symptoms and disorders, there are two main modes of processing: top-down and bottom-up. In top-down therapeutic processing, one's perception is driven by the internal cognitions that relate to what the brain already knows. Narrative therapies are top-down processes, as the therapy heavily relies on the stored context of thoughts and expectations. On the other hand, in bottom-up processing, one's perception is driven by new sensations that are coming in and becoming known to the brain with no surrounding context or meaning. Interoceptive awareness is a key component of bottom-up processing, particularly with EMDR therapy, as one's experience of somatic sensation in the present moment can positively alter one's internal perception of safety, power, and responsibility.

The adaptive information processing (AIP) model is the central, theoretical construct of EMDR. It is assumed that memory networks are the basis of human functioning in which belief systems, perceptions, emotions, attitudes, behaviors, and symptoms are formed and expressed. As one experiences the world, the brain integrates information by either assimilating or accommodating the information into memory networks, and depending on the nature of the experience, different brain centers are activated.

For those experiences that are characteristically adverse or traumatic, the amygdala of the hind brain, sometimes referred to as the *trauma brain* or *emotional brain*, becomes activated. This limbic brain center is responsible for our survival instincts, emotional perceptions, and the storage of this respective memory into the hippocampus preparing oneself for similar events in the future, particularly those events that trigger fear. Similarly, the hippocampus, also connected to the limbic system of the brain, helps regulate our emotions and is associated with the storage of long-term memory. Both organs work in tandem when integrating life experiences into memory networks, storing information as bodily sensations, cognitions, emotions, and beliefs in order to survive and adapt (Van Der Kolk, 2015).

When these limbic centers of the hind brain become activated by events that heighten negative affect and arousal, the frontal lobe of the brain shuts down, hindering the executive control of our brain and limiting our ability to adapt in a healthy way. The frontal lobe is responsible for the information processing system that exercises judgment, reasoning, and decision-making. When this brain center is inhibited, memory becomes dysfunctionally stored in the brain, and these maladaptively stored memories become the basis of our pathology (Solomon, 2014).

The AIP model is a three-pronged protocol, in which the past, present, and future experiences are attended to. Regarding the diagnosis of PTSD, the past is considered to be the present, and true healing of the illness cannot be achieved with properly addressing the way in which the past experiences are stored in the brain. AIP asserts that in order to achieve an appropriate and ecological resolution of symptoms, you need to access the maladaptively stored memories and simultaneously activate the information processing system in the frontal lobe through BLS in order to move the information into adaptive resolution. BLS keeps the frontal lobe engaged even when the hind brain is turned on, so that the limbic system can become desensitized and memories can be reprocessed differently, resulting in true resolution (Solomon, 2014).

PHASES OF EYE MOVEMENT DESENSITIZATION AND REPROCESSING

Phase 1: History Taking/Treatment Planning Phase

This phase involves a few steps to ensure the emotional safety of the client, which in turn, allows for the practitioner and the client to establish rapport. This is a time of exploration in a neutral, safe environment for the client through assessing history, exploring coping strategies, and treatment planning of future memories to be reprocessed. Focus will be given to the assessment of the client's stability, current life situations, and barriers to reprocessing. Further assessment will include using the Dissociative Experiences Scale (DES; see Exhibit 22.1) to rule out dissociation, screening for safe use of EMDR, and identifying small t's and big T's to use for treatment planning of reprocessing sessions (Shapiro, 2001).

There are two key qualifiers when assessing a client's trauma history: touchstone experiences and worst experiences. The AIP model presumes that traumatic memories are stored based on the level of intensity and impact of the event. Therefore, those traumatic experiences that either occurred earliest in a client's life ("touchstone" experiences) or are considered the worst experience of a client's life should be identified as target memories in the treatment plan. Sometimes, it can be difficult for a client to identify touchstone experiences, so the *floatback* technique is suggested. When a client is preoccupied with a present-day stressor, the provider can direct the client to identify the concurrent cognitions, emotionality, and somatic responses that relate to that stressor. Then, the provider will prompt the client to float back in time to identify an experience earlier in their life that felt the same, "As you notice how this stressor makes you feel in your body and the core Negative Cognition (NC) that corresponds with that discomfort, float back in your mind as far as you can go to see if there is an earlier experience in your life that feels the same." This earlier experience, possibly a touchstone memory, could be an identified target for reprocessing.

EXHIBIT 22.1 Dissociative Experiences Scale—II.

Instructions: This questionnaire asks about experiences that you may have in your daily life. We are interested in how often you have these experiences. It is important, however, that your answers show how often these experiences happen to you when you **are not** under the influence of alcohol or drugs. To answer the questions, please determine to what degree each experience described in the question applies to you, and circle the number to show what percentage of the time you have the experience.

For example: 0% (Never)   10   20   30   40   50   60   70   80   90   100% (Always)

There are 28 questions. These questions have been designed for adults. Adolescents should use a different version.

Disclaimer: This self-assessment tool is not a substitute for clinical diagnosis or advice.

1. Some people have the experience of driving or riding in a car or bus or subway and suddenly realizing that they don't remember what has happened during all or part of the trip. Circle the number to show what percentage of the time this happens to you.

0%   10   20   30   40   50   60   70   80   90   100%

2. Some people find that sometimes they are listening to someone talk and they suddenly realize that they did not hear part or all of what was said. Circle the number to show what percentage of the time this happens to you.

0%   10   20   30   40   50   60   70   80   90   100%

3. Some people have the experience of finding themselves in a place and have no idea how they got there. Circle the number to show what percentage of the time this happens to you.

0%   10   20   30   40   50   60   70   80   90   100%

4. Some people have the experience of finding themselves dressed in clothes that they don't remember putting on. Circle the number to show what percentage of the time this happens to you.

0%   10   20   30   40   50   60   70   80   90   100%

5. Some people have the experience of finding new things among their belongings that they do not remember buying. Circle the number to show what percentage of the time this happens to you.

0%   10   20   30   40   50   60   70   80   90   100%

6. Some people sometimes find that they are approached by people that they do not know, who call them by another name or insist that they have met them before. Circle the number to show what percentage of the time this happens to you.

0%   10   20   30   40   50   60   70   80   90   100%

7. Some people sometimes have the experience of feeling as though they are standing next to themselves or watching themselves do something and they actually see themselves as if they were looking at another person. Circle the number to show what percentage of the time this happens to you.

0%   10   20   30   40   50   60   70   80   90   100%

8. Some people are told that they sometimes do not recognize friends of family members. Circle the number to show what percentage of the time this happens to you.

0%   10   20   30   40   50   60   70   80   90   100%

9. Some people find that they have no memory of some important events in their lives (e.g., a wedding or graduation). Circle the number to show what percentage of the time this happens to you.

0%   10   20   30   40   50   60   70   80   90   100%

10. Some people have the experience of being accused of lying when they do not think that they have lied. Circle the number to show what percentage of the time this happens to you.

0%   10   20   30   40   50   60   70   80   90   100%

11. Some people have the experience of looking in a mirror and not recognizing themselves. Circle the number to show what percentage of the time this happens to you.

0%   10   20   30   40   50   60   70   80   90   100%

12. Some people have the experience of feeling that other people, objects, and the world around them are not real. Circle the number to show what percentage of the time this happens to you.

0%   10   20   30   40   50   60   70   80   90   100%

13. Some people have the experience of feeling that their body does not seem to belong to them. Circle the number to show what percentage of the time this happens to you.

0%   10   20   30   40   50   60   70   80   90   100%

14. Some people have the experience of sometimes remembering a past event so vividly that they feel as if they were reliving that event. Circle the number to show what percentage of the time this happens to you.

0%   10   20   30   40   50   60   70   80   90   100%

15. Some people have the experience of not being sure whether things that they remember happening really did happen or whether they just dreamed them. Circle the number to show what percentage of the time this happens to you.

0%   10   20   30   40   50   60   70   80   90   100%

16. Some people have the experience of being in a familiar place but finding it strange and unfamiliar. Circle the number to show what percentage of the time this happens to you.

0%   10   20   30   40   50   60   70   80   90   100%

17. Some people find that when they are watching television or a movie they become so absorbed in the story that they are unaware of other events happening around them. Circle the number to show what percentage of the time this happens to you.

0%   10   20   30   40   50   60   70   80   90   100%

18. Some people find that they become so involved in a fantasy or daydream that it feels as though it were really happening to them. Circle the number to show what percentage of the time this happens to you.

0%   10   20   30   40   50   60   70   80   90   100%

19. Some people find that they sometimes are able to ignore pain. Circle the number to show what percentage of the time this happens to you.

0%   10   20   30   40   50   60   70   80   90   100%

20. Some people find that they sometimes sit staring off into space, thinking of nothing, and are not aware of the passage of time. Circle the number to show what percentage of the time this happens to you.

0%   10   20   30   40   50   60   70   80   90   100%

21. Some people sometimes find that when they are alone they talk out loud to themselves. Circle the number to show what percentage of the time this happens to you.

0%   10   20   30   40   50   60   70   80   90   100%

22. Some people find that in one situation they may act so differently compared with another situation that they feel almost as if they were two different people. Circle the number to show what percentage of the time this happens to you.

0%   10   20   30   40   50   60   70   80   90   100%

23. Some people sometimes find that in certain situations they are able to do things with amazing ease and spontaneity that would usually be difficult for them (e.g., sports, work, social situations). Circle the number to show what percentage of the time this happens to you.

0%   10   20   30   40   50   60   70   80   90   100%

24. Some people sometimes find that they cannot remember whether they have done something or have just thought about doing that thing (e.g., not knowing whether they have just mailed a letter or have just thought about mailing it). Circle the number to show what percentage of the time this happens to you.

0%   10   20   30   40   50   60   70   80   90   100%

25. Some people find evidence that they have done things that they do not remember doing. Circle the number to show what percentage of the time this happens to you.

0%   10   20   30   40   50   60   70   80   90   100%

26. Some people sometimes find writings, drawings, or notes among their belongings that they must have done but cannot remember doing. Circle the number to show what percentage of the time this happens to you.

0%   10   20   30   40   50   60   70   80   90   100%

27. Some people sometimes find that they hear voices inside their head that tell them to do things or that comment on things that they are doing. Circle the number to show what percentage of the time this happens to you.

0%   10   20   30   40   50   60   70   80   90   100%

28. Some people sometimes feel as if they are looking at the world through a fog, so that people and objects appear far away or unclear. Circle the number to show what percentage of the time this happens to you.

0%   10   20   30   40   50   60   70   80   90   100%

Total:DES Score:

Total divided by 28)

Scoring the Dissociative Experiences Scale—II

The average of all the answers is the DES score, giving a maximum of 100. The questions are scored by dropping the zero on the percentage of each answer, for example, 30% = 3 and 80% = 8; these numbers are then added up to give a total. The total is multiplied by 10 and then divided by 28 (the number of questions) to calculate the average score.

Dissociative Experiences Scale Scores

High and low DES scores and high levels of dissociation are indicated by scores of 30 or more; scores under 30 indicate low levels (Carlson & Putnam, 1993, p. 22). Successful treatment of a dissociative disorder should reduce the DES score when compared to the result before treatment began (Carlson & Putnam, 1993, p. 23). Very high scores do not necessarily mean a more severe dissociative disorder is present; this is because the scale measures both normal and pathological dissociation (Carlson & Putnam, 1993, p. 18).

Dissociative Identity Disorder and the Dissociative Experiences Scale

Only 1% of people with dissociative identity disorder have been found to have a DES score below 30. A very high number of people who score above 30 have been shown to have posttraumatic stress disorder or a dissociative disorder other than dissociative identity disorder (Carlson & Putnam, 1993).

Clinical Uses of the Dissociative Experiences Scale

If a person scores in the high range (above 30), then the DES questions can be used as the basis for a clinical interview, with the clinician asking the client to describe examples of the experiences they have had for any questions about experiences that occur 20% of the time or more. Alternatively, the *Dissociative Disorders Interview Schedule* or *Structured Clinical Interview for Dissociative Disorders-Revised* can be used to reach a diagnosis (Carlson & Putnam, 1993).

Average DES Scores in research

General adult population	5.4
Anxiety disorders	7.0
Affective disorders	9.35
Eating disorders	15.8
Late adolescence	16.6
Schizophrenia	15.4
Borderline personality disorder	19.2
Posttraumatic stress disorder	31
Dissociative disorder not otherwise specified (OSDD)	36
Dissociative identity disorder (MPD)	48

Note: The Dissociative Experiences Scale-II is included in Appendix.

MPD, multiple personality disorder; OSDD, other specified dissociative disorder.

Source: Carlson, E. B. & Putnam, F. W. (1993). *An update on the Dissociative Experience Scale. Dissociation 6*(1), 16-27.

EXHIBIT 22.2 Subjective Unit of Disturbance (SUD) Scale.

SUD: Provider asks: "On a scale of 0 to 10, where 0 is no disturbance or neutral and 10 is the highest disturbance you can imagine, how disturbing does it feel now?"										
No disturbance/neutral										Worst possible
0	1	2	3	4	5	6	7	8	9	10

EXHIBIT 22.3 Validity of Cognition (VOC) Scale.

VOC: Provider asks: "When you think of the incident, how true do those words (*repeat the positive cognition*) feel to you now on a scale of 1 to 7, where 1 feels completely false and 7 feels totally true?"						
Not true at all						Completely true
1	2	3	4	5	6	7

Phase 2: Preparation Phase

During this phase, the practitioner gathers informed consent from the client and family (if applicable) and educates the client and/or family on the use of EMDR. Considerable attention is given toward resource identification, in which the practitioner and the client explore coping resources that will optimize the client's stabilization throughout treatment. Examples include teaching meditation techniques, breathing exercises, relaxation exercises, establishing a Safe Place or Calm Place resource, and creating a Container that holds negative, intrusive thoughts and feelings about oneself. Specific EMDR resources, such as the Safe Place, Calm Place, and Container, involve the use of slow BLS, and these particular internal resources can be used during the additional phases of treatment to elicit self-soothing.

    Facilitating the Resource of a Calm/Happy Place: The provider facilitates a mindfulness exercise in which the client is asked to close their eyes and create a real or imagined picture in their mind that allows them to feel the most happy, relaxed, or calm. If the client is not comfortable closing their eyes, they are asked to simply focus on the floor to help decrease outside distractions or stimuli. With a focus on the five senses, the provider asks the client to verbalize aloud what they notice as they visualize their happy/calm place in sight, smell, touch, sound, taste, and finally, the emotional somatic relationship of how they feel this place in their body. Lastly, the client is encouraged to establish a cue word that captures the experience in its entirety, essentially giving the happy/calm place a name that gets paired with the pleasurable cognitive, emotional, and somatic experience. The use of resourcing is two-fold: (a) the provider can encourage the client to access this calm/happy place at the end of each EMDR reprocessing session to successfully close down the session by connecting their somatic sense of self to a feeling or emotion of calm/happy, and (b) the client can independently self-direct use of this resource outside of therapy sessions to cope and soothe when distressed.

    Facilitation of the Resource of a Container: The provider guides the client in a mindfulness exercise to create an imaginary container that can be made up of any substance, can be any color, and can be as large or as small as it needs to be. This container should be able to hold any negative beliefs, images, or memories that may intrude during sessions. The container must have a lid or a top and must be able to be locked. The provider then guides the client to explain verbally what the container looks like and the approximate size of the container. The client then is instructed to open the lid and place all memories, beliefs, and thoughts into the container.

When all is in the container, the client is asked to close it and lock it, and then place the container somewhere safe where they can access if need be, but far enough away so that it doesn't bother them. The provider asks the client where the container is stored. The container resource can be utilized at the end of each EMDR reprocessing session, and before use of the calm/happy place resource. This ensures that the client safely contains all that has been spoken about or reprocessed in session so that the session content is outside of one's thoughts. If working with a child or an adolescent, a physical container may be useful to create and can be made from plastic blocks, cardboard, a metal can, or any other material to allow for the child to engage developmentally while using concrete thinking.

Phase 3: Assessment Phase of Eye Movement Desensitization and Reprocessing

As the provider begins the treatment planning process, this phase consists of the identification of target memories or experiences in present and past life events that cause emotional disturbance to the client. Identification of negative cognitions (NCs) and desired positive cognitions (PCs) is also established. NCs represent a negative, critical, or judgmental thought or feeling of oneself associated with a target memory, whereas a PC represents how the client would like to think and feel about themselves. When thinking of the target, the client is asked to measure their NC by indicating the level of disturbance it brings to them on a scale of 0 to 10; this is called the Subjective Unit of Disturbance (SUD; see Exhibit 22.2). The client may report that they have a SUD level of 0 if the target causes no distress to them when thinking about the target, or they may report a SUD level of 10 if the target causes them a very high level of disturbance, like panic symptoms or a hypervigilant reaction. When a client has successfully desensitized a target, the goal is to have a reported SUD of 0. The PC is measured by a Validity of Cognition (VOC) score on a scale of 1 to 7, 1 being not true at all and 7 being the most or very true (Exhibit 22.3). The VOC represents how true the PC feels to the person in the current place and time or in the here and now. When a client has successfully reprocessed a target and installed a PC, the goal is to have a reported VOC of 7.

Phase 4: Desensitization Phase

The goal of the desensitization phase is to reprocess memories that have been stored maladaptively so that they become adaptively resolved memories. This allows the client to be freed of symptoms associated with a trauma response such as anxiety, dissociation, and the triggering of the fight, flight, or freeze reactions. An example of this would be a client who smells smoke and is automatically triggered into symptoms of panic or emotional paralysis, in which the prefrontal cortex inhibits their ability to reason and make decisions to establish a safety plan to respond to the smoke in an adaptive way. This client may have been in a house fire and has not processed the event adaptively. EMDR reprocessing allows the amygdala to let go of the association of the core NC and feeling held in the body when the smell of fire takes place. Due to AIP, resolution of this event would then allow the client to not have a panic response to the smell of smoke in the future.

Interestingly, this similarly occurs during dream cycles. The brain naturally reprocesses life events during rapid eye movement (REM) sleep. EMDR replicates this methodology at an accelerated rate during the reprocessing phase via BLS. Bilateral stimulation is accessed by allowing the client to follow the providers fingers from left to right, watching a light on a light bar from left to right, using tappers that vibrate in ones left and right hand alternatively, or listening to tones via a headset from left to right. Some clients have a hard time tracking with eye movement due to visual disturbances, migraines, or head trauma and prefer to reprocess via BLS with eyes closed and using tactile and auditory BLS via tappers or tones. As the client is asked to focus on the negative thought and belief of oneself (NC), the memory is targeted, BLS is applied, and reprocessing occurs continuously to allow the SUD to decrease.

The time period of desensitization varies from client to client as compounded traumas and complex cases can be more complicated to resolve. Many times, memory networks that are associated with a traumatic or disturbing event stem from early childhood with many roads that lead back to the original negative thought, belief, and body sensation.

Studies have shown an increase in hippocampal volume as a result of reprocessing and the successful reintegration of positive emotions associated with new memories that can be stored after the negative memories are resolved (Cozolino, 2010). The provider will recognize that when a target has resulted in a SUD of 0, the target is then considered to be reprocessed, and desensitization of that target is complete. Clients who have successfully reprocessed adverse events that cause disturbances in function and emotionality report having healthier relationships, a release of negative thoughts of oneself, and overall PCs with an absence of anxiety related symptoms (Adler-Tapia & Settle, 2009, 2010; Shapiro, 2012).

Phase 5: Installation Phase

The goal in this phase is to successfully install the client's desired PC while it is being paired with the identified target. First, the provider will assess the original PC to see if it is still valid and fitting for the target that was desensitized in Phase 4. The PC is measured by assessing the VOC, with a goal of reaching a 7 on a scale of 1 to 7. The truer the PC, the closer the client is to a VOC of 7. The provider in this phase installs the PC with the use of BLS at the same rate and rhythm used during the desensitization phase. In many instances, this pacing of BLS will also allow for unresolved data to emerge. As previously mentioned, there are lots of intricacies when reprocessing memory networks, especially when working with complex cases, so even installing a core PC can trigger unresolved material. Ultimately, this phase is considered complete when the original PC associated with a target has a VOC of 7.

Phase 6: Body Scan

This phase consists of scanning the body to identify any residual somatic responses or feelings a client may have lingering that are associated with a target, a NC, or a memory. If the client notices any negative bodily sensations, the provider conducts BLS similar to Phase 4 to facilitate continued reprocessing to further "clean up" the disturbance. This ensures that NCs and affect associated with targets have been fully resolved and ensures that the body is not holding onto any negative reactions toward a target. If necessary, BLS is also used after desensitization to install PCs to maintain a VOC of 7 as mentioned in Phase 5.

Phase 7: Closure Phase

This phase occurs at the end of each EMDR session, whether the client has completed all phases or is working from phase to phase. It is essential that the provider allows for the client to leave each session feeling grounded and safe. This is where the Container resource and Happy/Calm Place are used, in that order, for the client to safely reintegrate into their world outside of the EMDR session. Additionally, it is important in this phase to teach the client how to mitigate flooding and to use positive coping strategies in between sessions. The provider may ask the client to journal in between sessions, practice self-directed cueing of their EMDR resources, and even use slow integration of BLS, such as the Butterfly Hug, as they venture into the world.

Providers often use a combination of mindfulness strategies to allow the client to feel the most grounded as they continue to contain negative thoughts, beliefs, and emotions associated with what was discussed in session. Many times, there will be sessions that need to close in the middle of reprocessing, and these moments in particular require that providers understand how to safely and adequately close down the session. It should be noted that the brain continues reprocessing for up to 72 hours after an EMDR session, so a safety and coping plan should be clearly established if the client's distress worsens, and the client needs immediate support (Shapiro, 2001).

Phase 8: Re-evaluation

Re-evaluation happens at the start of each new EMDR session (see Exhibit 22.4). At the beginning of every EMDR session, the provider assesses the SUD associated with the identified target and NC, as well as the VOC of the desired PC, allowing for the provider to evaluate the progress between sessions. Because the brain continues reprocessing after an EMDR session, resolution of symptoms may occur outside of the office space (Shapiro, 2001). Conversely, if the client reports any distress, either with a SUD score greater than 0 or a VOC score less than 7, the provider will proceed with Phases 4 through 6 to achieve successful resolution. This phase continues throughout the entire EMDR process in-between sessions to allow all targets to be completely addressed. Resolution of symptoms may occur outside of the office space (Shapiro, 2001). Conversely, if the client reports any distress, either with a SUD score greater than 0 or a VOC score less than 7, the provider will proceed with Phases 4 through 6 to achieve This phase continues throughout the EMDR process in-between session, which allows all targets to be addressed; resolution of symptoms may occur outside of the office space (Shapiro, 2001).

EYE MOVEMENT DESENSITIZATION AND REPROCESSING PHASES

EXHIBIT 22.4 Eye Movement Desensitization and Reprocessing Treatment Plan.

Presenting issues (symptoms, relationship stressors, etc.)

Treatment goals:

1.

2.

3.

4.

Pick on presenting issues to start with here:

When did this problem begin? (triggering event)

What are your symptoms related to this event?

Have there been any changes in symptoms (frequency, intensity, duration, or new triggers)?

What is your negative belief about yourself when you think of this problem? (Negative Cognition or NC)

*If unable to determine a NC, any other symptom cluster, a dominant emotion or bodily sensation?

What you would like to believe about yourself? (Positive Cognition or PC)

First time you felt this way/thought this way about yourself?

Float back/affect scan to any other earlier times you felt this way?

Most intense:

Touch stone memory (first time)

Most recent:

Other minor incidents:

Source: Adapted from Leeds, A. M. (2013). Basic training in EMDR. Sonoma Psychotherapy Training Institute.

APPLICATION FOR SPECIAL POPULATIONS

Children

The use of EMDR with children has been deemed as a successful approach to help children overcome trauma symptoms from a variety of causes, including medical conditions and adverse childhood events (Diehle et al., 2015; Rodenburg et al., 2009). The basic tenets of implementing the use of EMDR with children is to provide a sense of safety and parental/caregiver involvement, if they are in fact a resource to the child. If the parent/caregiver is part of the trauma, it is important to establish therapeutic rapport with the child by allowing for Phase 2 of the EMDR protocol to be optimized. EMDR with children requires specialized training for providers who have received levels 1 and 2 training with specialized consultation hours. While the Phases 1 to 8 are still the same, the VOC, SUD, NC, and PC are obtained using developmentally appropriate language and using various contexts to identifying targets. Typically, children do well as Phase 2 is developed and children's environments are made more stable and predictable. Play therapy and sand tray therapy are mediums for reprocessing of targets and can allow for accessing of memories, feelings, and thoughts for children. In addition, children have been known to reprocess faster and with more ease than adults given that their environment is stable, and they have at least one stable caregiver of support (Adler-Tapia & Settle, 2012). The case study that follows shows just how the eight phases of EMDR were used with a child with great success.

CASE STUDIES

Case Study 22.1: A CHILD

The following is an example of utilizing EMDR therapy with a 9-year-old boy who presented with anxiety and paranoia in the aftermath of a school shooting in which he was a survivor located in a neighboring classroom:

B was a nine-year-old at the time of treatment residing with a two-parent family and two younger siblings. B was in the first grade at the time of the school shooting where many of his friends and classmates did not survive. B presented with aggression, frustration, and an overwhelming feeling of sadness and avoidance of talking about the events that occurred. He presented to the office with both parents being concerned that he was not sleeping well, as well as having a hard time at home, was easily aggravated fighting with younger siblings, having a hard time focusing at school on school work, and having a hard time at Boy Scouts and baseball with his peers. He was known to run off the ball field throwing the bat when he missed a pitch and hide in his room when home with his family after an argument over a toy with younger siblings or when arguing over typical things with parents. His emotions as mom and dad reported, "were over the top," and "he easily goes from 0 to 100 over little things." He came for EMDR therapy after dropping out of trauma-focused cognitive-behavioral therapy (tf-CBT) as he couldn't handle the journaling or story telling of the sessions. B was also not sleeping well and was having nightmares.

The clinician used sand tray and play therapy as a medium to assess, plan, and treat the events of the school shooting and other events that occurred in the home after the events of the shooting. The clinician met one-on-one with each parent, both parents together, the child alone, and then the child and one of the parents during Phases 3 to 8 at each subsequent session.

Phase 1 consisted of verbal story telling by each parent from their perspective individually and as a couple and individually with the child via play/sand tray therapy. Both parents jointly shared that their son was exposed to the sounds of the shooting in the school and was overexposed to media, conversations, and the politics of the community he resided in during the immediate aftermath of the shooting. B's father was very involved in the community through his volunteer work and was very involved in the recovery efforts as well. B reportedly attended five funerals of victims that caused more symptomatology to present itself as per both mom and dad. In retrospect, both parents admitted his overexposure of the events caused more harm than the actual event itself. The provider educated the child and family on EMDR and how it works and used language that would allow for the child to understand how it works in the brain. An analogy that is used often is as follows:

> If you hold your hand out, your thumb is your emotional brain and your other four fingers are the thinking part of the brain. When you fold your hand into a ball with the thumb as the center of your hand and the other fingers over the thumb closing your fist, your brain is in calm mode. When something makes you afraid or reminds your brain of the bad thing that happened, your thumb/emotional brain acts out and reacts by running or fighting and then freezing making all your other fingers/your thinking brain go offline. This is what happens when your brain becomes activated and your mixed-up thoughts take over your brain. Many kids say they get confused or become afraid and feel like it's happening again. That's because the negative thing that happened which caused your brain to react in an unhealthy way may feel like it's happening again because we need to allow for the memory of that event not have so much power over the brain. EMDR helps the emotional brain or your thumb not have that reaction anymore. It helps to calm your brain by changing the power of the memory. Almost like when super-heroes use their superpower to fight the bad guy. EMDR is a super-power that you can use to fight the bad memories.

Phase 2 consisted of building a physical container with B in the office made of plastic building blocks. He built a huge fortress that had a hatch on the top of it that could only be opened using a secret code that the provider and client had the code to. B reinforced this fortress using a double layer of blocks at the foundation and at the roof of the fortress. B asked if he could pick a spot on the top shelf in the provider's locked closet to store the fortress. During this phase, B also created his happy/calm place in the sand tray. His calm place was at the lake in his dad's boat with his family. He created a lake surrounded by trees, a family, and used a toy boat to signify the family boat. During this phase, the provider installed his happy/calm place with slow BLS via tappers. B tolerated this phase well each session. During this phase, the provider also had whichever parent was present for the session partake in the happy/calm place exercise to allow for a positive resource to be identified for the parent as well. This phase was also spent on conversations with the client and parents on stop signals, allowing him to know he could have control over when he wanted to stop once we brought up the bad thing that happened.

    Phase 3 consisted of showing the provider in the sand tray about the bad thing that happened. B did not want to use his words or talk about his feelings but was able to use plush emoji toys to clarify emotions associated with the bad thing that happened. B was able to show the provider that he was sad, confused, and angry at what happened that day. He was also able to show the provider with his hand how disturbing the event was to him. A SUD of 10 = arms opened all the way and 0 = hands together, and a VOC of 7 being arms opened all the way and hands closed together as 1. The targeted event was the day of the shooting and going to the funerals with an SUD of 10 for both with an NC of "I'm not safe" and a VOC of 2 for "I am safe." The provider used NC and PC playing cards to identify NC and PC with B.

    Phase 4 consisted of play/sand tray therapy that started with B building two sides to his sand tray, both sides with building block structures at each end with monsters on the left side and people on the right side. The people were surrounded by army soldiers and warriors with shield and swords. B was given a set of tappers that he put into the sides of his sneakers as he created the bad thing that happened. He was asked to notice what he felt in his body as the tappers tapped during the play session; he moved the figures into an attack mode where the good and bad guys fought each other with the bad guys killing the good guys after the first session. The provider stopped B after 30 sets of BLS, cueing him to pause, breathe, and continue. B continued the desensitization phase for four sessions as he continued to reprocess the events of the day by burying babies in the sand, figures that were chaotic all around the sand tray, monsters attacking the people, army men fighting the monsters with a final resolution in the last session of reprocessing when B took a dollhouse and placed it in the middle of the sand tray, put people in the house, placed a tractor outside with a father in it and two dogs. He stated, "it's over" and placed a happy emoji and placed it in the middle of the house. B put both his hands together when the provider asked how hard the mixed-up thoughts were now (signifying a SUD of 0) and a 7 on the VOC scale when asked how true the statement of feeling safe was.

Phase 5 was initiated after the completion of the reprocessing event for B by using BLS to install the PC of feeling safe; during this session, the parents were holding B on their lap as they tapped B on his legs from left to right and rocking back and forth.

Phase 6 was initiated after the installation phase as the child was given a play magnifying glass to scan his body to detect any spots that were bugging him or felt funny when he thought of the bad thing that happened. B stated that his belly felt funny during his first pass through. The provider then allowed B to recreate the event in the sand tray again; this time there was a boy with a baby and some coins that were surrounding the baby. The tappers were given to him; he put them in his shoes and he continued to bury the baby, find the baby, bury the baby, find the baby, and then bury the money and placed the baby in the boy's lap in the sand tray. He then stated that they were both in heaven and safe. BLS stopped here, and B was asked to rescan his body. He stated, "It went away and the funny feeling is better." Phase 6 repeated itself for three more sessions as B continued to scan his body on his heart and in his head, and needing to reprocess for three more sessions. The first session was his dad yelling in the house about money, the second was sadness and missing his friends, and the third about his mom being in bed all day demonstrated with a dollhouse and play dolls with him taking care of his mom. This phase returned to Phase 4 of desensitization ending with a SUD of 0 at completion.

Phase 7 was utilized at the end of each session by allowing B to place all his thoughts, memories, and emoji feelings into his fortress. B physically leaned his head over into his fortress each session and asked the provider to help him lock it up with the code. B recreated his happy/calm place visualizing it many times and then actually going out on the lake with his family in-between sessions, which was very helpful.

Phase 8 was utilized at the beginning of each session as the provider assessed SUD and VOC using hand measurements as playing cards were displayed. B also simply picked up where his brain left off at the start of his sessions, knowing exactly what he needed to reprocess in the sand tray and asking for the tappers when he knew he needed to start using them. It became an unspoken language in the office allowing for B to have power over his mixed-up thoughts and the emotions that they had on his body and brain.

B successfully completed EMDR with the provider and was able to play baseball with his team, performed better at school, and was able to restore relationships with peers and siblings. He was sleeping through the night and his nightmares went away. B came back a few times after EMDR for a few tweaks here and there but overall did very well. See Table 22.2.

Case study 22.2: a MIDDLE-AGED ADULT

The following is an example of utilizing EMDR therapy with a middle-aged adult who presented with a single-incident trauma and reported no prior trauma history.

K is a 62-year-old Caucasian female who lives at home with her husband. They have been married for 30 years and have two adult children who live out of state. K is the youngest of five siblings, and her parents are deceased. She reports no significant mental health histories on either side of her family. K's parents divorced when she was a young child, and her father remarried a "great woman." K works full-time as an engineer, has a positive relationship with her colleagues, and enjoys her career.

TABLE 22.2 EYE MOVEMENT DESENSITIZATION AND REPROCESSING PHASES		
Phase 1	Client history and treatment planning	- Assess trauma history - Interviews - Play therapy/sand tray therapy
Phase 2	Preparation phase	- Informed consent - Resource development - Evaluation of trauma and dissociation - Establishing Safe/Calm Place and Container exercise
Phase 3	Assessment phase	- Identification of target (T) - Selecting image (I) - Negative cognition/positive cognition (NC/PC) - Emotion triggered by the memory (E) - Subjective Unit of Disturbance (SUD), 10-point scale where 0 = not disturbing at all and 10 = very disturbing - Validity of Cognition (VOC) assessment, 7-point scale where 1 is completely false and 7 is completely true - Identification of body sensations and location of disturbance in the body
Phase 4	Desensitization phase	- Holding image/creating image, identifying the negative cognition (NC) and body sensation - Initiation of bilateral stimulation (BLS) - Continue BLS until SUD = 0
Phase 5	Installation phase	- PC identification or new one - Assessing validity of cognition (VOC) 7-point scale where 1 is completely false and 7 is completely true - Continues until PC is installed via BLS with positive outcome
Phase 6	Body scan	- Original target (T) and PC, assess for discomfort in body - BLS, if necessary, to get rid of disturbance or discomfort
Phase 7	Closure	- Safe Place, Happy/Calm Place - Container Exercise - Teach Butterfly Hug
Phase 8	Reevaluation	- Reevaluation between sessions - Overview of all phases to evaluate progress - Goal is SUD of 0 and VOC of 7 for all targets and PCs

Source: Adapted from Adler-Tapia, R., & Settle, C. (2009). Evidence of the efficacy of EMDR with children and adolescents in individual psychotherapy: A review of the research published in peer-reviewed journals. *Journal of EMDR Practice and Research, 3*(4), 232–247; Greenwald, R. (1999). *Eye Movement Desensitization and Reprocessing (EMDR) in Child and Adolescent Psychotherapy.* Book-mart Press, Inc.

K sought EMDR therapy to address her symptoms of PTSD following a traumatic car accident 2 months prior when she was on her way to work on a dark, rainy morning. The at-fault driver hit K's driver-side door at a speed of 45 mph. K reports that she had been in a minor car accident several years before this event, but she did not experience heightened symptoms following that accident. She was currently challenged with frequent tearfulness, mood lability (mostly feeling depressed), general hyperarousal, preoccupation with the accident, hypervigilance and flashbacks while driving, frequent thoughts of mortality, difficulty concentrating, social withdrawal, and insomnia. She was medically evaluated by her general practitioner who referred her for physical therapy. No medications were administered.

The clinician utilized the standard EMDR protocol for an acute, single incident trauma and met with the client for weekly psychotherapy sessions at 60 minutes in duration. Sessions 1 to 3 entailed history-taking and preparation phases. K presented with a general understanding of this trauma-based approach and endorsed minimal symptoms prior to this event; therefore, she did not require significant preparation for the therapy. K was favorably responsive to BLS via eye movements in long, rapid sets, and she successfully completed two EMDR resources followed by self-directed cueing—Calm Place and Protective Figure. This indicated a high integrative capacity and readiness for reprocessing.

Sessions 3 to 8 consisted of memory reprocessing in which Phases 3 to 8 were implemented, with the exception of Phase 5, installation phase. The identified target for reprocessing was this recent car accident with a central NC: I am going to die, and a desired PC: I am alive. By Session 6 and in subsequent sessions, K was achieving a SUD score of 0 during Phase 4 (desensitization) in relation to the target memory and working through Phase 5 (installation of the PC). Phases 5 (installation) and 6 (body scan) were successfully completed in Session 8 in which K could think of her car accident without experiencing any cognitive, emotional, or somatic distress while simultaneously feeling the truth of her PC, "I am alive."

During these 2 months of EMDR therapy, K's endorsement of PTSD symptoms fully remitted in that she felt safe again while driving and in those uncomfortable moments, like being stuck in congested traffic, K's distress was momentary and quick to subside. K continued therapy with this clinician at a monthly frequency to work through other psychosocial needs, and at months 4 and 7 (Sessions 10 and 13), Reevaluation of the initial target memory indicated some distress related to presently driving under similar circumstances to the car accident (foggy or rainy conditions at dawn). Similarly, at month 9 (Session 15), K was distressed by the possibility of having another car accident.

As previously discussed in this chapter, the AIP model is a three-pronged protocol in which past, present, and future experiences are addressed (Solomon, 2014). Phases 3 to 8 were also applied in these sessions to "clean up" the lingering and maladaptively stored information, desensitizing the distressing experience of current and future triggers and successfully installing the PC: I am alive. By Session 15, K's PC evolved to also include the statements, "It will all work out, I can only do what I can do, I am doing the best I can."

At 18 months since the onset of EMDR therapy, K reports no pathological symptoms related to the car accident or to driving. Any respective distress appears normative given the circumstances. K graduated from EMDR therapy, and it was agreed that she could return at any time for booster support.

Case Study 22.3: A GERIATRIC/OLDER ADULT

The following is an example of utilizing EMDR therapy with a geriatric adult who presented with health-related anxiety and an underlying trauma history:

L is a 79-year-old Caucasian female who cohabitates with her partner of 4 years. She was in a previous marriage and has two adult children from that marriage with whom she is close. L is the oldest of three and raised in a Roman Catholic home, attending private Catholic school for many years. As a teenager, she lost her father suddenly, which greatly impacted her family's affluent status in the community as he was reputable physician. L is a retired psychotherapist and has spent many years in therapy herself addressing psychosocial needs.

At the suggestion of a friend, L sought therapy from this clinician to address pressing anxiety struggles. Her partner had been recently diagnosed with cancer, which was greatly affecting her personal sense of security and power. She was afraid most of the time, particularly of death, and often felt like a child. L disclosed a long history of traumatic loss, chronic resentment, and spiritual angst. Of her many years of therapy, she had never been introduced to EMDR. In the history-taking and preparation phases, L gained new awareness that her present anxieties were directly related to her central belief systems that stemmed from childhood:

It's my fault, I am going to die, God has betrayed me. She was willing and amenable to proceeding with EMDR.

Due to the chronicity of L's symptoms, her present struggle to self-regulate, and her frequent experience of feeling childlike, this clinician spent the first five sessions over the course of a month in Phase 2 (Preparation) implementing a blend of EMDR resourcing and ego states therapy to mitigate L's dissociative tendencies when distressed by fear. It was determined that L responded more favorably to BLS via tapping in slow, brief sets. L was able to successfully establish an internal meeting place for her Parts, so that she could practice and maintain full adult consciousness when distressed (Seubert, 2017).

In Session 6 during Phase 3 (Assessment), L and clinician utilized the *floatback technique* to identify an EMDR *target* memory. In the present, L was mostly challenged by her health-related fears and preoccupations and felt tremendous anxiety in her body, mostly in her gut. Her central *NC* related to this experience was "I am trapped and miserable and I can't handle it," and she was able to connect this present awareness to her early childhood experience of feeling trapped and anxiety ridden in Catholic school.

Phase 4 (desensitization) occurred through Sessions 6 to 8, and it was noted that L's Catholic experience *chained* to an earlier traumatic childhood memory at age 3 in which L felt trapped in her crib that she had soiled, and when she called to her father for help, he did nothing to help her. This past *target* memory was successfully desensitized in Session 8, and as the clinician facilitated movement into Phase 5 (Installation) with a desired PC, "I am free and able to handle it," L struggled to fully accept this a true belief. Her current health anxieties and her realistic fear of aging and mortality were hindering Phase 5. Phase 4 (desensitization) was then implemented again for three more sessions with an identified *target* of this present triggering experience as well as a *future template* of her worst-case scenario: her partner becoming incredibly ill and disabled resulting in L having to provide care for him through his death. Both the present trigger and future scenario were successfully desensitized in Session 11, and installation of "I am free and able to handle it" became a true PC throughout this entire *target* experience by Session 12 (spanning early childhood through future adulthood).

At 12 months since the onset of EMDR therapy, L's partner was diagnosed with a fatal and disabling illness, "my worst-case trigger," she claimed. L had a brief emergence of anxiety symptoms for a week that remitted after she reached out for social support. She and her partner were also engaged in couple's therapy to work on life adjustments together. L and the clinician agreed that they would continue to utilize EMDR as needed.

CRITIQUES OF EYE MOVEMENT DESENSITIZATION AND REPROCESSING

Strengths

The original and standardized EMDR protocol has remained relatively the same since the 1990s, and substantial research affirms its efficacy, particularly regarding the remission of PTSD. The duration of symptom remission achieved through EMDR sets this modality apart from other treatment interventions, and unlike what is needed for narrative-processing therapies, EMDR does not require therapeutic rapport or trust to be effective.

EMDR has become a versatile intervention in that it can be applied across all ages and many clinical populations. It can stand alone as a primary modality and can also be administered as an adjunct intervention. For example, a client who is receiving cognitive-behavioral therapy for an eating disorder may disclose that they experienced an early childhood trauma that perpetuates the eating disorder symptomology. If the primary therapist does not specialize in trauma therapy, it could be beneficial for this client to be referred to an EMDR provider to specifically address the comorbid trauma symptoms as a separate, concurrent service.

Limitations

The original EMDR protocol is very manualized. Trainers even recommend that new EMDR practitioners utilize their workbook scripts in session with clients when they begin to facilitate this approach. This can be aversive to providers and even awkward for clients, but the goal in utilizing a scripted text is so that new practitioners will honor the integrity of the approach as this yields the most favorable outcomes.

It has been found that EMDR is more effective for adults who have developed PTSD as an adult, instead of for adults with PTSD who also report a history of chronic childhood abuse (73% cured at 8 months versus 25% cured at 8 months; Van Der Kolk, 2015).

Additionally, the research is consistent that eye movements are the most efficient modality for BLS, and this particular technique can require a provider to sit closely to the client so that the client's eyes can track the provider's fingers that are being waved in front of the client's face. Clients with a history of sexual trauma may be particularly sensitive to someone being so physically close to them, so administering eye movements in this manner may not be ideal for the client. There are EMDR devices, such as light bars, that facilitate the same eye movement for the client, but these devices can be cost prohibitive.

Optimal reprocessing sessions require a duration of 90 or more minutes to successfully execute Phases 3 through 7, and typical outpatient psychotherapy settings hold sessions for up to 60 minutes. Moreover, reprocessing sessions can be cognitively and physically taxing on a client, so a client may need some time to rest after an intense session, which may not be conducive to their schedule.

In the 30 years of EMDR development, many training organizations have delineated from Shapiro's training institute. Some of these trainers have used their creative liberties to expand on and revise the original protocol, which has created variability in the approach. When these organizations do not promote respective research to determine the effectiveness of their EMDR methodology, it can adversely impact client outcomes.

CONCLUSION

EMDR is an effective therapy with an emerging evidence base to support the use of this therapy with diverse populations. The intervention protocol consists of eight phases, which include a blend of coping resources and memory reprocessing until dysfunctionally stored memories move into adaptive resolution, ultimately freeing clients from distressful symptoms and pathology. The history of trauma has bearing on the number of EMDR processing sessions that are required. For example, adult clients with complex and/or early childhood traumatic experiences require more EMDR reprocessing sessions than those with single incident traumatic experiences. Clinical social workers trained in EMDR are able to apply this therapeutic model in diverse settings.

SUMMARY POINTS

- There are eight phases of treatment in the EMDR protocol, which include a blend of coping resources and memory reprocessing until dysfunctionally stored memories move into adaptive resolution, ultimately freeing clients from distressful symptoms and pathology,
- EMDR therapy is effective for individuals of all ages,
- the central construct of EMDR is the AIP theory in which past, present, and future experiences are attended to for true healing of the brain to occur,
- both the amygdala and hippocampus are directly and positively altered in the brain with the implementation of EMDR therapy,

- adult clients with complex and/or early childhood traumatic experiences require more EMDR reprocessing sessions than those with single incident traumatic experiences, and
- research supports that EMDR therapy is a comparable or superior protocol to cognitive therapies, exposure therapies, and psychopharmacological interventions for the treatment of PTSD.

KEY REFERENCES

Only key references appear in the print edition. The full reference list appears in the digital product found on http://connect.springerpub.com/content/book/978-0-8261-6556-5/part/sec03/part/sec035/chapter/ch22

Adler-Tapia, R., & Settle, C. (2012). Specialty topics on using EMDR with children. *Journal of EMDR Practice and Research*, 6(3), 145–153.

Shapiro, F. (2001). Eye movement desensitization and reprocessing: Basic principles, protocols, and procedures. Guilford Press.

Solomon, R. (2014). EMDR Institute Basic Training Course 1. EMDR Institute.

Van Der Kolk, B. (2015). The body keeps the score: Brain, mind, and body in the healing of trauma. Penguin Books.

Summary and Conclusion

Revisiting the Generalist-Eclectic Approach

Kristin W. Bolton and Kim Stansbury

By the end of this chapter, you should be able to:

- understand the conceptualizations of levels of theory,
- understand the relationship between the direct practice theories and the generalist-eclectic approach, and
- understand the application of the problem-solving model and the generalist-eclectic approach.

INTRODUCTION

The first two chapters (Part I) of this book dealt with the major elements and basic principles of the generalist-eclectic approach to direct social work practice. Given that the last chapters have focused on various theoretical perspectives for direct practice, for purposes of review and integration it is important to revisit the generalist-eclectic approach in this final chapter.

In the first part of this chapter, we review conceptualizations of levels of theory and broad classes of mid-level practice theory (psychodynamic, cognitive behavioral, humanistic, critical, and postmodern) that were discussed in Chapter 1 and revisit how these conceptualizations can facilitate an eclectic use of theory in practice. Second, the compatibility between the various mid-level practice theories reviewed in Part III (Chapters 7–22) of the book and the generalist-eclectic approach are considered. The third part of the chapter revisits how the problem-solving model is a useful framework for integrating the eclectic use of theory with the artistic, reflective, and intuitive-inductive elements of practice. Finally, some of the challenges to generalist-eclectic practice are identified and strategies for dealing with these challenges are suggested.

THE USEFULNESS OF CONCEPTUALIZING LEVELS AND CLASSES OF THEORY TO FACILITATE ECLECTICISM

Reflecting on the variety of theoretical perspectives that are represented by chapters in this book raises the potential for feeling confused and overwhelmed by the wide variety of views about the causes of human problems and ways of helping. This potential for *theoretical overload* becomes heightened when one considers that in the 1980s, estimates of the overall number of theories for direct practice ranged from 200 (Henrick cited in Lambert, 2013a) to 400 (Kazdin cited in Lambert, 2013a) and that this number is likely much higher presently.

Given this confusing and overwhelming array of theories, many of which feature rather esoteric and mystifying language, one can understand why some practitioners eschew eclecticism because they prefer the simplicity, structure, and certainty that can be provided by a narrow allegiance to a single theoretical framework. As understandable as this may be, we are convinced of the arguments for eclecticism that were reviewed in the first chapter. In order to make eclecticism feasible, however, strategies for simplifying and demystifying the vast array of theoretical perspectives are necessary. It is our hope that the organization of this book reflects two helpful strategies in this regard: (a) differentiating among high-, mid-, and low-level theoretical perspectives, and (b) classifying the vast array of mid-level practice theories into like categories and providing general descriptions of the commonalities within each broad category.

Differentiating Among the Levels of Theory

A consideration of the differential function and usefulness of the various levels of theory can be a helpful first step in dealing with theoretical overload. Most theories for direct practice exist at or are linked closely to the mid-level of abstraction denoted in Figure 2.1, and most of this book is devoted to reviewing mid-level theories. Although there has been a recent trend toward the development of many low-level models and therapies for specific problems and populations, many of these have a primary allegiance to one of the mid-level practice theories (e.g., cognitive-behavioral therapy for anorexia nervosa).

In the 1980s, estimates of the overall number of theories for direct practice ranged from 200 (Henrick cited in Lambert, 2013a) to 400 (Kazdin cited in Lambert, 2013a). It is likely that this number is now higher. Because of the overwhelming and confusing array of direct practice theories from which to choose, another useful strategy for conceptualizing and understanding these theories is to organize the mid-level practice theories in like groupings. We believe that mid-level direct practice theories can be divided into five major classifications: (a) psychodynamic theories, (b) cognitive-behavioral theories, (c) humanistic theories, (d) critical theories, and (e) postmodern theories. Table 23.1 provides a broad characterization of these five major classifications of direct practice theories. After a brief discussion of the usefulness of this broad characterization of the major classifications of theory, each of the five classifications will be discussed in more detail.

The broad characterization of the major classifications of direct practice theory found in Table 23.1 allows for identifying the commonalities among theories in each of the five groups, as well as for pointing out differences across groups. This description helps to bring order and clarity to the overwhelming number of theories within the field and allows for the identification of the strengths and weaknesses of the various classes of theory, both of which facilitate the eclectic use of theory.

The concepts in the left-hand column of the table represent some of the important dimensions by which theoretical perspectives can be compared. It should be emphasized that the characterizations of the classes of theory with regard to these dimensions are very general and should be construed as descriptions of central tendencies. For example, although the primary focus in most cognitive-behavioral and humanistic therapies is on the present, this is not to say that such therapies do not focus on the past at all. The same caution applies to the characterization of the classes of theory with regard to focus on affect, cognition, and behavior; focus on symptoms or general growth/development; and degree of structure and directiveness. The dangers of such broad characterizations include the potential to minimize differences within groups of theory and to overlook similarities across groups.

An example of the danger of minimizing differences within groups of theory is found in some of the major differences between solution-focused therapy and the other types of postmodern theory. As pointed out in the discussion of postmodern theories (see later in this chapter), solution-focused therapy concentrates more on specific symptoms and behaviors and is

TABLE 23.1 CHARACTERIZATION OF CLASSES OF DIRECT PRACTICE THEORIES

	Psychodynamic	Cognitive Behavioral	Humanistic	Critical	Postmodern
View of causation of human problems	Traumatic experiences or inadequate nurturance in childhood leads to unconscious internalization of conflict or developmental deficits	Maladaptive behaviors and/or cognitions are learned through conditioning, reinforcement, and/or modeling	Defenses against painful aspects of experience lead to losing touch with authentic experiencing in the present	Oppressive social structures and personal relationships result in exploitation and marginalization; powerlessness results in not meeting needs or achieving aspirations	Negative interpretation of self and of life experience, and/or internalization of toxic cultural narratives that oppress marginalized groups
Goal of intervention	Develop emotional/cognitive understanding of connection between early and current problems	Learn more adaptive thoughts and behaviors	Develop new awareness of and meaning about experiences in the present	Raise consciousness of oppression and effects of powerlessness, connect personal and social issues, empower for personal and social change	Develop more positive views of self and of life experience, and/or develop freedom from oppressive cultural assumptions
Primary focus on past or present	Past and present	Present	Present	Present and past	Present and past
Primary focus on affect, cognition, or behavior	Affect and cognition	Cognition and behavior	Affect	Affect, cognition, and behavior	Cognition
Primary focus on specific symptoms or general growth/development	General growth/development	Specific symptoms	General growth/development	General growth/development (and social change)	General growth/development
Degree of structure and directiveness (low, medium, high)	Low–medium	Medium–high	Low–medium	Medium	Low–medium

Note: The characterizations in this table are broad generalizations that do not hold for all of the more specific approaches within these classes (see discussion in this chapter).

more directive compared with narrative and collaborative therapies. With regard to the danger of exaggerating differences across groups of theory, integrative theorists have demonstrated how seemingly antithetical theories are not as different and incompatible as one might suppose (e.g., see discussion in Wachtel et al. (2005) for integrative relational therapy that combines psychodynamic and behavioral theories).

With these limitations in mind, a general consideration of how the concepts in the left-hand column of Table 23.1 are construed by or manifested in each class of theory can help the practitioner to consider which class of theory might best suit particular clients at particular points in the counseling process, as well as to consider which classes of theory might be used simultaneously to address clients' concerns more holistically. For instance, a client who wants to focus on specific symptoms in current day-to-day functioning, to avoid exploration of painful feelings, and to have a high degree of structure and direction in counseling, may be best served, at least initially, by a cognitive-behavioral approach. Once this client learns to cope more effectively with presenting symptoms, however, they and the worker may decide that a focus on feelings (i.e., affect) may be helpful to consolidate and further gains. If client issues seem to be connected to early problematic relationships with caregivers, a psychodynamic approach might then be used to explore the link between affective difficulties in the present and the past and to work through such feelings. If a connection to earlier intimate relationships is not apparent or if the client is averse to exploring such connections, a humanistic approach may be more appropriate for dealing with affective issues. If the client's presenting issues seem to be connected to oppression and marginalization, it would be important to integrate a critical approach (e.g., empowerment and/ or feminist) with any of these other approaches. Also, a postmodern approach could be integrated with any of the other theoretical approaches or used as a follow-up to other approaches in order to integrate changes into more empowering views of one's self and one's life story.

These theories represent foundational knowledge for generalist-eclectic practice, and their main value is in providing broad, normative lenses for data collection and assessment. Although these high-level theories can also provide general ideas for intervention, they do not provide the guidelines or prescriptions for interventions that lower level theories do.

The conceptualization of levels of theory is one way of bringing order to the overwhelming number of theoretical perspectives for practice. The three levels of theory can be viewed as complementing rather than competing with each other. High- and low-level theories can be construed as providing support to the use of mid-level theories. High-level theories provide a broad lens for viewing human behavior and ensure that a broad range of factors (e.g., biological, personal, interpersonal, environmental, and sociocultural factors) are considered in the effort to understand clients' problem situations. These theories ensure that the big, person-in-environment picture is considered in data collection and assessment, and they guard against the danger of tunnel vision or myopia that exists with mid- and low-level theories. On the other end of the spectrum, the type of in-depth knowledge that low-level theories provide about specific client problems can be seen as a valuable resource to support the use of more general, mid-level theory. For example, even if one is drawing eclectically from a range of mid-level theories in working with a client, if a specific clinical issue (e.g., grief) surfaces, it would be helpful to refer to low-level models (e.g., interactive trauma/grief-focused therapy) for more specific ideas for understanding and treating such issues.

THE COMPATIBILITY OF THE DIRECT PRACTICE THEORIES WITH THE GENERALIST-ECLECTIC APPROACH

Compatibility With Elements of the Generalist Perspective for Social Work

All of the chapters in Part III of this book included a brief discussion of the compatibility between the particular practice theory under consideration and at least some of the five elements of the generalist social work perspective that are central to our generalist-eclectic approach (as outlined in Table 1.1 in Chapter 1). Although there were differences in emphasis noted by some authors, overall there was a strong endorsement of the importance of (a) a person-in-environment perspective that is informed by ecological systems theory, (b) the development of a good helping relationship that fosters empowerment, (c) the flexible use of a problem-solving process to provide structure and guidelines for practice, (d) a holistic assessment that includes a focus on issues of diversity and oppression and on strengths, and (e) an eclectic use of other theories and techniques.

A cynic might wonder if authors felt compelled to endorse such principles, either to conform to the wishes of the editors or to the social work profession's commitment to the generalist perspective; however, we do not think that this was the case. Instead, it seems to us that this convergence in thinking reflects the relatively recent trend in the clinical field toward valuing these elements of the generalist social work perspective. We think that this is a major and healthy shift in thinking because the historical legacy of the clinical field has been marked, to a large extent, by rigid adherence to single models of therapy that tended to have narrow, mostly psychological, views of human problems and noncollaborative, expert orientations.

It is particularly noteworthy that the older, more traditional theoretical perspectives (i.e., psychodynamic and cognitive-behavioral theories) have undergone significant changes in emphasis over the years. In general, psychodynamic theories have broadened their intrapsychic focus to include much greater consideration of environmental factors; have moved away from a rather distant, expert-oriented therapeutic stance toward a much more collaborative and empathic approach; and have become more open to the value and usefulness of other theories and their techniques. It should be noted, however, that we chose to include in this book the psychodynamic theories that had moved furthest in these directions. There are still psychodynamic theories that do not embrace these trends.

Similarly, cognitive-behavioral theories, particularly the more behaviorally oriented ones, have not always embraced generalist principles. Over time, these theories have broadened their focus of assessment beyond stimulus–response patterns to include cognitive and social factors; have embraced the importance of a good therapeutic relationship, at least as a facilitating factor for change; and have become more open to eclecticism. Again, for the cognitive-behavioral section of the book, we selected theories that were most compatible with the generalist approach. In particular, readers should be reminded that the task-centered and crisis intervention models have a strong connection to social work and are perhaps better conceptualized as theoretical and eclectic models, respectively. There are still traditional behavioral theories that are not consistent with generalist principles.

Despite the overall compatibility between the variety of practice theories presented in this book and the elements of the generalist social work perspective that are central to our generalist-eclectic approach, it would be remiss to not make a closer examination of differences. The strongest contrast that we noted between an element of the generalist social work perspective and a theoretical perspective is solution-focused therapy's dismissal of the value of holistic assessment. In Chapter 20, Corcoran states that "solution-focused therapy departs from a generalist-eclectic framework in eschewing a holistic assessment of the various system levels, along with information gathering about the problem and history taking" (p. 286). This and other conflicts between solution-focused therapy and mainstream social work principles have been noted by others (Stalker et al., 1999). This suggests that social workers should be particularly mindful of following generalist social work principles when using solution-focused therapy as part of their eclectic approach.

Another difference that emerged between some theoretical perspectives and an element of the generalist perspective related to the use of a problem-solving process. Again, the strongest difference was with solution-focused therapy. Corcoran challenged any focus on problems or problem-solving as antithetical to a focus on strengths. We expressed our disagreement with this view in Chapter 2 when we cited the argument by McMillen et al. (2004) that those who

406 IV. SUMMARY AND CONCLUSION

advocate for a strength versus a problem focus set up a false dichotomy. We agree with McMillen et al.'s contention that "the best social work practice has always maintained a dual focus on both problems and capacity building" (p. 317). Similarly, Walsh (2009) has stated that "problem-focused and strengths-oriented social work are not dichotomous, but complementary" (p. 32).

There were more moderate challenges to the use of a problem-solving process expressed by other authors. Authors of the chapters on existential, narrative, and collaborative theories noted that the open, process-oriented nature of their approaches did not fit well with a structured, pragmatic, problem-solving focus. We understand this concern, but we think it is based on a misconception of our use of a problem-solving process. We believe that problems can be defined in many different ways. Although identification of a specific, tangible problem may be the pre-ferred approach of a cognitive behaviorist or a task-centered practitioner, our generalist-eclectic approach allows for a much broader conception of problems, including problem conceptions of an existential or postmodern nature. Also, we believe that the problem-solving process needs to be used flexibly and that, while it can offer guidelines for practice, these should not be con-strued as prescriptions or followed rigidly. Our valuing of artistic, reflective, intuitive-inductive practice processes attests to this and reflects openness to the less structured, more process-ori-ented theories. As Perlman (1957) argued many years ago about the problem-solving model: "In no sense is such a structure a stamped out routine. It is rather an underlying guide, a pattern for action which gives general form to the caseworker's inventiveness or creativity" (p. vi).

We agree that a good helping relationship is often not sufficient to cause change, but we maintain that it can contribute directly to change and that it is sometimes sufficient. A good helping relationship contributes directly to change by combating demoralization, instilling hope, and bolstering self-esteem. For some clients, particularly for those who have not been subjected to severe, longstanding stressors and who have supportive networks, this may be sufficient. We would also contend that our understanding of the impact of relationship factors is consistent with the research. As a recent review of research concluded, "research supports the potential causal role that a positive therapeutic alliance plays in leading to relatively better treatment outcomes" (Crits-Christoph et al., 2013, p. 308; see Chapter 1 for a brief review of research on the importance of relationship and other common factors).

More generally, we should also note that, despite endorsement of the elements of the gener-alist perspective that are central to our generalist-eclectic approach, there are certainly differ-ences in the degree to which various theories emphasize these elements. First, despite a commitment to a person-in-environment perspective and holistic assessment by all but one practice theory represented in the book (i.e., solution-focused therapy), specific practice theo-ries, by definition, have more preconceptions and are less comprehensive than a generalist per-spective. Every practice theory has preconceived ideas about the cause of human problems. For example, psychodynamic theories may give consideration to environmental and sociocultural factors in assessment, but focus is directed primarily to intrapsychic and interpersonal issues. Thus, despite a commitment to broad-based assessment, the preconceptions that exist for all practice theories can function as blinders.

Second, most practice theories pay much less attention to issues of diversity and oppression than a generalist social work perspective. Of the practice theories reviewed in this book, only task-centered, feminist, and empowerment theories devote considerable attention to broad social issues (e.g., poverty). These same three theories, along with narrative therapy, are the only theories that focus considerably on issues of diversity and oppression.

Finally, despite an openness to eclecticism, by virtue of their primary theoretical orientation, all practice theories are less theoretically and technically "open" than the generalist-eclectic approach. Thus, despite the general compatibility between many theoretical perspectives and the generalist-eclectic approach, we believe that, when drawing on theories, clinical social workers need to consciously integrate the central principles and values of the generalist per-spective of social work into their practice.

REVISITING THE IMPORTANCE OF THE PROBLEM-SOLVING MODEL AS A FRAMEWORK FOR INTEGRATING THE ARTISTIC AND SCIENTIFIC APPROACHES TO PRACTICE

As discussed in Chapter 2, the downside to both the reflective, intuitive-inductive approach to practice and the deductive, eclectic use of theory in practice is a lack of structure and guidelines for practice. Without some dependable structure and guidelines, both the artistic and the theoretically eclectic approaches to practice can lack focus and direction and become haphazard—which is the common criticism from those who advocate following a single model of therapy. We have argued that the problem-solving model provides such structure and guidelines for practice and thus facilitates the integration of the artistic and scientific approaches to practice.

The broad guidelines that are contained in the problem-solving model for each phase of practice provide sufficient structure for the eclectic use of various theories, but because they are not rigidly prescriptive they also afford enough flexibility to allow for reflection, intuition, and inductive reasoning. For instance, with regard to data collection and assessment, the general structure and guidelines of the problem-solving model remind practitioners to use a person-in-environment perspective and direct them to give consideration to a broad range of factors (micro and macro, stressors and strengths) in order to understand clients' life situations. The problem-solving guidelines in this phase of practice also direct practitioners to consider a broad range of theoretical perspectives to help make sense of clients' situations, including mid- and low-level practice theories, as well as high-level or metatheories. Furthermore, the general nature and the flexibility of these problem-solving guidelines allow for practitioners to use reflection, intuition, and inductive reasoning to develop together with their clients an in-depth understanding of unique problem situations. Thus, as with other phases of the problem-solving process, the general guidelines of the data collection and assessment phase allow for a synthesis of an eclectic use of theory and intuitive-inductive processes.

CHALLENGES FOR GENERALIST-ECLECTIC DIRECT SOCIAL WORK PRACTICE

Given the fact that we have tried to extol the virtues of, and argue persuasively for, a generalist-eclectic approach to direct social work practice, we would be remiss if we did not consider some of the challenges that exist for this approach. In the following, we discuss important challenges for research and for practice, as well as strategies for dealing with these challenges.

Challenges for Research

Although cumulative research on psychotherapy has found no significant differences in the effectiveness of the various theoretical approaches (the "equal outcomes" phenomenon), the research indicates clearly that psychotherapy is effective compared with nonintervention (Lambert, 2013b). Because single-theory approaches have predominated historically in the helping professions, the cumulative research that has established the effectiveness of psychotherapy has been based primarily on single-theory approaches. Due to the newness of the movement toward eclecticism in psychotherapy and to the preoccupation with theory development in this movement, until recently, research on eclectic models has been neglected. In 1997, Norcross noted, "the commitment to psychotherapy integration is largely philosophical rather than empirical in nature. The adequacy of various integrative and eclectic approaches remains to be proven" (p. 87).

Even before much research on eclectic therapies had been conducted, however, proponents of eclecticism argued for the probable effectiveness of such approaches. In 1992, Lambert argued:

> To the extent that eclectic therapies provide treatment that includes substantial overlap with traditional methods that have been developed and tested, they rest on a firm empirical base, and they should prove to be at least as effective as traditional school-based therapies. (p. 71)

In recent years, research on eclectic/integrative therapies has increased significantly. As reported in Chapter 1, a recent review of such research (Schottenbauer et al., 2005) found empirical support from randomized controlled studies for 20 such therapies. This accumulating body of research on eclectic/integrative therapies provides support for Lambert's (1992) prediction that eclectic therapies will prove to be at least as effective as single-theory approaches. Still, research on eclectic approaches is in its early stages. Prochaska and Norcross (2014) have noted that "perhaps the only conclusions that can be reliably drawn are that coherent 'eclectic' and 'mixed' psychotherapies outperform no treatment and that these treatments are insufficiently compared to other systems of psychotherapy" (p. 446).

In Chapter 1, we considered how the cumulative research findings of the equal outcomes of various types of therapy and the importance of factors that are common across therapies (particularly the therapeutic relationship) provide indirect empirical support for the movement toward eclecticism. We also reviewed how, despite these research findings and the emerging direct empirical support for eclectic therapies, the empirically supported treatment (EST) movement in psychology has continued to push a research focus of establishing the effectiveness of single-theory approaches with specific disorders. Furthermore, because EST research protocols that require the use of treatment manuals (in order to standardize treatment) and a focus on specific disorders with outcome measurements related to the disorder are best suited to cognitive behavioral treatments, the vast majority of treatments that have achieved "empirically supported" status are cognitive-behavioral therapies (Messer, 2001; Wachtel, 2010; Wampold & Imel, 2015).

Although some eclectic approaches have been supported by EST research, most eclectic approaches are ill-suited to the protocol requirements of this research. In particular, the EST requirement for the development of standardized, manualized treatments for specific disorders does not fit well with the flexible, creative nature of most eclectic therapies. Because most eclectic therapies cannot and would not want to specify what therapists should do during therapy sessions, treatment manuals are not used, results of studies on eclectic therapy cannot be replicated (i.e., because what therapists do during treatment is not clearly defined or standardized), and eclectic therapies cannot achieve the status of an empirically supported therapy. For similar reasons, the same is true for most psychodynamic, humanistic, critical, and postmodern therapies. This becomes especially problematic because ESTs have been made mandatory by some managed care and insurance companies and thus practitioners feel pressured to use ESTs (Wampold, 2001).

We will not repeat here our critique of the EST movement in Chapter 1; however, among many other authors, we believe that the focus of EST research is misplaced and the interpretations of the results are misleading. As Lambert (2013a) has concluded from reviewing the research:

> Although many practitioners and the public may be comforted by the notion that they are offering or receiving an empirically supported psychotherapy that works best, the fact is that success of treatment appears to be largely dependent on the client and the therapist, not on the use of "proven" empirically based treatments. (p. 8)

Nevertheless, the EST movement presents a serious challenge to establishing the credibility of eclectic therapies. The solution is not, however, to make eclectic therapies more standardized in order to fit EST research protocol requirements. This could compromise the effectiveness of eclectic therapy, which we think depends in large part on the artistry of relationship development and reflection and on the flexible, creative use of theory.

On an individual level, one response to counter the negative effects of the EST movement is to become familiar with the conceptual and empirical arguments against ESTs and to enter into the debate on the issues (e.g., in classroom, agency, or professional training settings). We refer readers to Chapter 1 for a summary discussion of the issues and for references to more detailed arguments provided by authors such as Henry (1998), Lambert (2013a, 2013b), Messer (2001), Norcross (2001), Wachtel (2010), and Wampold and Imel (2015).

On the level of a program of research, Wampold and Imel (2015) have called for a move away from the current dominant paradigm of clinical trials that compare the effectiveness of different treatments for specific disorders. They cite a review of eight such studies conducted between 1992 and 2009 (Laska et al. cited in Wampold & Imel, 2015) that had cumulative funding in excess of $11 million from the National Institute of Mental Health. The review of the results of these eight studies determined that little useful knowledge was generated from them, other than to further reinforce the equal outcomes conclusion. Wampold and Imel (2015) have argued that such research money could be used more productively:

> Money should be spent investigating what makes various treatments work. Consider what we might learn if we had a well-funded research agenda to investigate the characteristics and actions of effective therapists. Such an agenda would lead to results that would likely improve the quality of care and focus training efforts. (p. 268)

Challenges in Practice

A generalist-eclectic approach to practice does not provide the comfort and certainty for practitioners that following a single model of therapy can provide. Practitioners who adhere to one theoretical approach, particularly if it has a narrow focus and prescriptive guidelines, can gain comfort in "knowing" at the outset of counseling what the problem is and/or what they need to do to help ameliorate it. In generalist-eclectic practice, the emphasis on theoretical openness and broad-based assessment precludes this type of certainty. Furthermore, the emphasis on the artistic, reflective, intuitive-inductive elements of practice, as well as on collaboration and partnership with the client, involves giving up control and certainty in the helping process.

Although the guidelines of the problem-solving model and understanding and/or techniques gleaned from a variety of theories provide helpful guidance for practice, a generalist-eclectic approach requires the practitioner to be creative and to find courage "in the face of the uncertain" (Papell & Skolnik, 1992, p. 22). This can be difficult, particularly for beginning practitioners who frequently yearn for "a 'secret handbook' of practical 'how-to-do-it' knowledge" (Mahoney, 1986, p. 169); however, it is our contention that clients respond better to this humble, open, and humane approach to practice than to theoretical certainty and prescriptive formulas. As Cameron (2014) has argued in promoting a common factors approach to social work practice: "We are at our best when we are being who we really are ... (helpers) empowered by the sharing of their imperfect and compassionate humanity, not their 'expertise'" (p. 155). Wampold and Imel (2015) have noted empirical support for this argument: "Interestingly, therapists who report having professional self-doubt have better outcomes, which suggests that a reflective attitude toward one's practice is helpful" (p. 275).

Another obvious challenge in this approach to practice is that of becoming familiar with the wide variety of theories for direct practice. Although we have offered strategies for simplifying and demystifying the confusing array of clinical theories (i.e., conceptualizing levels and broad classes of theory, and identifying the general characteristics of classes of theory), there is no denying that developing in-depth knowledge and skill in a variety of theoretical approaches is a formidable task. This is particularly difficult given the unfortunate but continuing use of "idiosyncratic jargon" by many theoretical orientations (Goldfried & Castonguay, 1992). This not only makes learning different theories more difficult and intimidating but also hinders the development of understanding about similarities across theories.

With regard to the latter issue, we support the long-range goal of translating theories into ordinary English in order to further demystify and facilitate cross-theory dialog (Goldfried & Castonguay, 1992). With regard to the more general difficulty of becoming a "master of all trades" (i.e., of all theories and techniques), we think that practitioners should construe this as a career-long goal, in the context of understanding that theoretical knowledge and technical expertise can never be complete and that artistic elements of practice such as interpersonal sensitivity and relationship skills are of prime importance to counseling effectiveness.

A third general challenge to practicing from a generalist-eclectic orientation concerns the necessity of integrating a consideration of broader social issues, particularly issues of diversity and oppression, into both assessment and intervention. As noted earlier in this chapter, very few counseling theories pay much attention to these issues. Thus, from a generalist social work perspective, there is a need to utilize other sources of knowledge about working with issues of diversity and oppression. In addition to the generalist social work literature, practitioners can draw from critical theories, such as feminist theory (Chapter 14) and empowerment theory (Chapter 15), as well as the strengths perspective (Chapter 6), all of which pay special attention to these issues.

Managed Care

The major transformation in counseling services that has been brought about over the past 20-plus years by the managed care industry deserves special attention as a potential challenge to a generalist-eclectic approach to practice. We surmise that the managed care industry, which frequently limits the number of counseling sessions they will reimburse to about eight sessions (Lambert, 2013a), might be skeptical of an approach to practice that values holistic assessment, the development of in-depth understanding within the context of a good therapeutic relationship, and the intervention that draws on a range of theories and techniques. In fact, in advising practitioners how to present themselves to case managers within the managed care industry, Nichols and Schwartz (2004) suggest that "calling yourself 'eclectic' is more likely to sound fuzzy than flexible" (p. 87). We do not doubt that this type of pejorative thinking about eclecticism continues to exist, particularly with regard to brief treatment, and we see this as a challenge that needs to be addressed.

Although we do have concerns about the rigid enforcement of short-term counseling limits, particularly for clients who have multiple, severe, and/or longstanding stressors, we believe that a generalist-eclectic approach to practice can be used effectively in the context of brief treatment and managed care. Holistic assessment does not usually involve a long, drawn-out process of data collection. Practitioners can learn to focus a broad lens rather quickly and some holistic assessments (which are always tentative and subject to change) can be completed in single sessions. Similarly, the development of a strong therapeutic relationship does not usually require long periods of time; research has shown that alliances predictive of outcome are usually formed within the first few sessions (Horvath & Greenberg, 1994).

With regard to intervention, a generalist-eclectic approach to practice can be as focused and brief as necessary. Within a managed care context, practitioners and clients should plan and contract to focus on the most pressing problem that can be dealt with within the allotted time frame. From a generalist-eclectic perspective, however, practitioners working within the managed care industry would be obligated to attempt to secure longer term help for those clients who want and require it. This could involve lobbying a case manager for extending the counseling limits, contracting with the client to continue work together after the managed care session limits have been reached (and working out payment issues), or referring the client to other services.

There are two myths that can limit the managed care industry's openness to eclectic and other process-oriented therapeutic approaches and that therefore need to be challenged. First, as previously discussed, is the myth that designated ESTs are, by virtue of the designation, more effective than other therapeutic approaches. Psychotherapy researchers who challenge the empirical basis of this contention need to continue to debate proponents of ESTs in professional arenas (e.g., in refereed publications and in professional associations) and to educate the managed care industry about this issue.

The second myth is that only therapeutic approaches that are self-labeled as "brief" are suitable for the parameters set by the managed care industry for treatment duration. In particular, brief solution-focused therapy's "promise of quick solutions has endeared it to the managed care industry. Indeed … many applicants for provider status call themselves 'solution-focused' regardless of whether or not they have any training in this approach" (Nichols & Schwartz, 2004, p. 312). There are, however, good reasons to believe that most models of therapy (whether single theory or eclectic) are adaptable to the treatment duration parameters of managed care. Reviews of studies that have examined length of treatment across settings and theoretical orientations have established that the median or mean number of sessions was between five and eight (Garfield, 1994; Hansen et al. cited in Lambert, 2013a). Thus, traditional counseling approaches are often as brief as the so-called brief therapies. Even the psychodynamic school, which is traditionally the longest term approach to counseling, has developed brief treatment models that can fit the constraints of managed care (Barber et al., 2013; Koss & Shiang, 1994; Messer, 2001). Thus, the managed care industry needs to be educated to the fact that all theoretical orientations, including an eclectic orientation to the use of theory, are adaptable for brief treatment.

SUMMARY

In addition to providing a survey of contemporary theories for direct social work practice, this book represents an attempt to integrate a number of important and compatible ideas in the field of counseling into a broad framework for practice. To summarize, there are three important aspects to what we have called the generalist-eclectic approach to direct practice.

The first aspect is commitment to social work principles and values reflected by elements of the generalist perspective of social work practice. These elements include a person-in-environment perspective informed by ecological systems theory, an emphasis on a good helping relationship that fosters empowerment, the flexible use of a problem-solving process to guide practice, holistic assessment that includes a focus on issues of diversity and oppression and on strengths, and the flexible and eclectic use of a wide range of theories. The latter element is informed by theory and research in the broader movement toward eclecticism in the fields of counseling and psychotherapy. A second important aspect of our approach to practice is the valuing of the artistic elements of practice, or what we have called reflective, intuitive-inductive practice. This includes the recognition that much of the time practice does not involve the conscious application of theory and technique and that reflection, intuition, inductive reasoning, and creativity play important roles in practice. The third key aspect of our approach is the use of the problem-solving model of generalist practice to provide a flexible structure and general guidelines for practice in order to support the integration of the eclectic use of theory with the artistic elements of practice.

In conclusion, we wish to stress that the generalist-eclectic approach is not meant to represent yet another competing approach to or framework for direct social work practice. It is a way of conceptualizing practice that encourages flexibility in the use of multiple theories, perspectives, and ideas, while placing the principles and values central to the profession of social work at the forefront.

KEY REFERENCES

Only key references appear in the print edition. The full reference list appears in the digital product found on http://connect.springerpub.com/content/book/978-0-8261-6556-5/part/sec04/chapter/ch23

Barber, J. P., Muran, J. C., McCarthy, K. S., & Keefe, J. R. (2013). Research on dynamic therapies. In M. J. Lambert (Ed.), *Bergin and Garfield's handbook of psychotherapy and behavior change* (6th ed., pp. 443–494). Wiley.

Cameron, M. (2014). This is common factors. *Clinical Social Work Journal, 42*, 151–160.

Crits-Christoph, P., Gibbons, M. B. C., & Mukherjee, D. (2013). Psychotherapy process-outcome research. In M. J. Lambert (Ed.), *Bergin and Garfield's handbook of psychotherapy and behavior change* (6th ed., pp. 298–340). Wiley.

Garfield, S. L. (1994). Research on client variables in psychotherapy. In A. E. Bergin & S. L. Garfield (Eds.), *Handbook of psychotherapy and behavior change* (4th ed., pp. 190–228). Wiley.

Goldfried, M. R., & Castonguay, L. G. (1992). The future of psychotherapy integration. *Psychotherapy, 29*, 4–10.

Henry, W. P. (1998). Science, politics, and the politics of science: The use and misuse of empirically validated treatment research. *Psychotherapy Research, 8*, 126–140.

Horvath, A. O., & Greenberg, L. S. (1994). Introduction. In A. O. Horvath & L. S. Greenberg (Eds.), *The working alliance: Theory, research, and practice* (pp. 1–9). Wiley.

Koss, M. P., & Shiang, J. (1994). Research on brief psychotherapy. In A. E. Bergin & S. L. Garfield (Eds.), *Handbook of psychotherapy and behavior change* (4th ed., pp. 664–700). Wiley.

Lambert, M. J. (1992). Psychotherapy outcome research: Implications for integrative and eclectic therapists. In J. C. Norcross & M. R. Goldfried (Eds.), *Handbook of psychotherapy integration*. Basic Books.

Lambert, M. J. (2013a). Introduction and historical overview. In M. J. Lambert (Ed.), *Bergin and Garfield's handbook of psychotherapy and behavior change* (6th ed., pp. 3–20). Wiley.

Wachtel, P. L., Kruk, J., & McKinney, M. (2005). Cyclical psychodynam-ics and integrative relational psychotherapy. In J. Norcross & M. Gold-fried (Eds.), *Handbook of psychotherapy integration* (2nd ed., pp. 172–195). New York, NY: Oxford University Press.

Index

Printed in the USA
CPSIA information can be obtained
at www.ICGtesting.com
CBHW061625261223
2963CB00006B/84